The Singapore International Arbitration Act

The Singapore International Arbitration Act

A Commentary

PAUL TAN
NELSON GOH
JONATHAN LIM

OXFORD
UNIVERSITY PRESS

Great Clarendon Street, Oxford, OX2 6DP,
United Kingdom

Oxford University Press is a department of the University of Oxford.
It furthers the University's objective of excellence in research, scholarship,
and education by publishing worldwide. Oxford is a registered trade mark of
Oxford University Press in the UK and in certain other countries

© Nelson Goh, Jonathan Lim, and Paul Tan 2023

The moral rights of the authors have been asserted

First Edition published in 2023

All rights reserved. No part of this publication may be reproduced, stored in
a retrieval system, or transmitted, in any form or by any means, without the
prior permission in writing of Oxford University Press, or as expressly permitted
by law, by licence or under terms agreed with the appropriate reprographics
rights organization. Enquiries concerning reproduction outside the scope of the
above should be sent to the Rights Department, Oxford University Press, at the
address above

You must not circulate this work in any other form
and you must impose this same condition on any acquirer

Public sector information reproduced under Open Government Licence v3.0
(http://www.nationalarchives.gov.uk/doc/open-government-licence/open-government-licence.htm)

Published in the United States of America by Oxford University Press
198 Madison Avenue, New York, NY 10016, United States of America

British Library Cataloguing in Publication Data

Data available

Library of Congress Control Number: 2023932536

ISBN 978–0–19–882869–3

DOI: 10.1093/law/9780198828693.001.0001

Printed and bound by
CPI Group (UK) Ltd, Croydon, CR0 4YY

Links to third party websites are provided by Oxford in good faith and
for information only. Oxford disclaims any responsibility for the materials
contained in any third party website referenced in this work.

Foreword

At the core of Singapore's extraordinary success in establishing itself as one of the world's leading centres for dispute resolution was the decision taken in 1994 to enact legislation specifically for international arbitration. By largely adopting the 1985 UNCITRAL Model Law on International Commercial Arbitration and incorporating the 1958 New York Convention, Singapore's 1994 International Arbitration Act (IAA) signalled to the world a commitment to apply internationally accepted norms and standards to international arbitrations conducted in Singapore. This commitment was not just on paper. In the three decades since, Singapore has actively implemented, and indeed developed, these norms and standards, such as to become one of the most trusted and preferred seats for international arbitration. Alongside its state-of-the-art legislation, this achievement has been in large part due to the collective efforts of Singapore's judiciary (which now includes a distinguished panel of international jurists in the Singapore International Commercial Court); the Government (which has demonstrated notable agility in updating the IAA and related legislation whenever needed); first-class arbitration professionals practising at the highest levels; and world-respected academic faculty.

Given the vital importance of the IAA as the backbone of international arbitration activity in Singapore, *The Singapore International Arbitration Act: A Commentary* is a timely and extremely welcome addition to the existing literature on international arbitration in Singapore. In particular, it is a pioneering work that focuses on the legislation itself, provision by provision, setting it against its historical background, and providing a meticulous analysis of its consideration and elaboration in commentaries and cases. There has been an exponential growth in Singapore arbitration case law and academic commentary over the years, and there is now a formidable volume of material available in this field. This work provides a masterful distillation of this material, with an explanation of its impact on each section of the Act, all brought together with expert and readily accessible commentary. The result is both authoritative and easy to navigate. This is the quintessential "White Book" companion to the IAA.

But the importance of this work extends far beyond Singapore's borders: Singapore case law and commentary is now routinely cited before courts and in commentaries across numerous jurisdictions worldwide – both Model Law and non-Model Law. Further, the IAA itself is increasingly a point of reference for countries seeking to upgrade their own arbitration legislation. This will be an invaluable resource for anyone seeking to understand how Singapore's statutory provisions have been developed, and how key concepts that run through the heart of the Model Law and the New York Convention have been interpreted and applied. And as such, it will no doubt contribute materially to what are now lively international judicial conversations in this field.

The authors, each an outstanding practitioner in leading global arbitration practices, have marshalled not only Singapore jurisprudence but comparative authorities wherever relevant. There is considerable depth in articulating the current state of play, and in sketching the future in areas that remain untested. The authors draw on their deep understanding of arbitration theory and extensive practical experience to offer clear and insightful perspectives on the myriad of issues that arise in arbitration-related litigation.

I congratulate Paul Tan, Nelson Goh, and Jonathan Lim on this significant work.

And I wish the IAA a well-deserved 30th birthday.

Toby Landau KC
Duxton Hill Chambers (Singapore Group Practice)
Singapore
August 2023

Preface

Singapore is one of the world's leading arbitration seats. Whereas this statement would have been open to debate when we started practice, it is no longer so. Singapore has, through constant evolution, engagement with arbitration best practices, and the embrace of international talent, established its position as a leading jurisdiction for arbitration. Singapore is home to well-known arbitrators and leading arbitration practices. It has a world-class arbitration institution as well as first-rate facilities for private dispute resolution. Overall, it would not be unfair to say that Singapore's ascent in the world of arbitration has been remarkable and that, today, it has a matured and world-class arbitration eco-system.

The judiciary's role in establishing Singapore's place on the arbitration world map cannot be gainsaid. The Singapore courts are assiduously pro-arbitration and have taken every opportunity to clarify and develop Singapore's arbitration jurisprudence. This has resulted in an impressive corpus of arbitral case law that also serves as useful precedent for other Model Law countries or more generally as a persuasive source of law.

Alongside the judiciary, the Singapore Government also deserves immense credit for ensuring that Singapore's arbitration laws and regulations keep pace with developments elsewhere. Indeed, at the heart of Singapore's state-of-the-art architecture for international arbitration is the International Arbitration Act 1994 – a modern piece of legislation that is constantly-updated and at the forefront of international developments, while staying fundamentally rooted in the Model Law. The Act is the centrepiece and symbol of Singapore's success as an arbitral seat and hub.

When this project was mooted by Nelson some five years ago, we decided that we wanted to create a reference text to the Act which would provide precise answers for the busy practitioner as well as in-depth analysis on contentious issues requiring further treatment. Although this balance proved challenging to strike in practice, we felt that a provision-by-provision commentary with in-depth exposition might become a genuine contribution to the existing literature, and hoped it might have some part to play in conversations about the further development of Singapore law.

As students of the law first and foremost, this book is our homage to the law of arbitration in Singapore. To the extent possible, we hope it will be "all things to all people"—a reference point for Judges, practitioners, professors and lecturers, and students – not just in Singapore but possibly to readers in other Model Law jurisdictions and arbitral seats. It was a challenging task to produce a work catering to such a wide audience – particularly with the Singapore Courts' prolificacy on arbitration issues – but we hope we have acquitted ourselves adequately.

viii PREFACE

Given our other commitments and personal foibles, completing this commentary would not have been possible without the support and help of many others.

Paul wishes to thank the Judges of the Supreme Court for whom he clerked and with whom he had his first taste of arbitration-related litigation; the Honourable the Chief Justice Sundaresh Menon who was his mentor in the formative years of practice; his present colleagues at Gibson Dunn & Crutcher LLP; former colleagues at Rajah & Tann, Clifford Chance and Cavenagh Law; Toby Landau KC, Salim Moollan KC, Joe Smouha KC, Sam Wordsworth KC, Dan Sarooshi KC, Jern-Fei Ng KC; his friends at Lalive with whom he spent a wonderful autumn in 2012; Chong Ren Jie for assisting in the drafts; and of course his family and loved ones who have tolerated his divided attention.

Nelson wishes to dedicate this book to his family: Dad, for being a rock and wellspring of wisdom; Mum, for embodying grit; Jasmine, for your constant support; Adele and Isabel, for your laughter and friendship – may you continue to shine like bright and colourful lights when the path around may appear dim (Matt 5:16; Phil 2:15, 4:18). In no particular order, he wishes to thank Donald Donovan, Catherine Amirfar, Natasha Harrison, Wendy Miles KC, Andre Yeap SC, Danny Ong, Adrian Wong, William Hooker, Dominic Chan and Jansen Chow who have acted as mentors and guiding lights. He owes a debt of gratitude to the following colleagues who have helped with various parts of his chapters: Seraphina Chew, Rachel Ong, Arundathi Venkataraman, Sue Ng, Shaurya Upadhyay, Darius Ng, Noel Low, Ng Sze Hian, and Soh Yun Wen. Finally, he wishes to thank Professor Michael Waibel, Professor Richard Fentiman, Professor Alex Loke, Professor Dora Neo, Professor Tang Hang Wu, Professor Wee Meng Seng and Professor Burton Ong, who, in their individual ways, have inspired him to love the law.

Jonny wishes to record the immense debt of gratitude owed to family, mentors, colleagues, and friends who made this book possible. He is deeply grateful to present and former colleagues that have shaped his thinking and encouraged his professional and academic endeavours, particularly: Gary B. Born, Cavinder Bull SC, Charlie Caher, Steven P. Finizio, Rachael D. Kent, Sabrina Lee, Danielle Morris, John V.H. Pierce, Maxi Scherer, Franz T. Schwarz, Duncan Speller, and John A. Trenor. He also wishes to thank his former teachers for their unstinting encouragement and inspiration over the years, not least: Professors Gary F. Bell, Dan W. Puchniak, Margaret E. Tahyar, and Eleanor Wong. He also wishes to acknowledge the talented young lawyers who provided exceptional assistance with his chapters: Amer Abu-Sham, Bay Jia Wei, Cai Xiaohan, Farshad Rahimi Dizgovin, Benson Fan, Samuel Koh, Umang Bhat Nair, Ng Sze Hian, Rachel Ong, Ibukunoluwa Owa, Tan Jun Hong, Charles Tay, and Samuel Wittberger. Finally, this book would not have been completed but for the forbearance and sacrifices of Jonny's greatest champions – his parents, his partner Michelle, and his son Noah – to whom this book is dedicated in large part.

We also owe a debt of gratitude to Toby Landau KC, a giant in the field, for agreeing to pen the foreword to this work, as well as to Rebecca Lewis, Fay Gibbons and the team at Oxford University Press for their patience and guidance throughout the writing process.

The law is constantly evolving. Changes in commerce will doubtless lead to a shift in current perspectives on dispute resolution. This book is not intended to provide an answer to every possible question that may or will arise in the field of arbitration in Singapore. However, we hope that the systemic treatment of the relevant legal principles in this commentary will serve as a useful starting point for readers of all descriptions that are seeking to tackle the deceptively simple topic of international arbitration in Singapore and access the wealth of judicial wisdom interpreting and applying the Act.

The law is stated as at January 2023.

P. T.

N. G.

J. L.

Contents

Table of Cases	xv
Table of Legislation	xxix
List of Abbreviations	xxxix

1. Arbitration in Singapore — 1
- A. Introduction — 1
- B. Overview of International Arbitration — 2
- C. Advantages and Disadvantages of Commercial Arbitration — 4
- D. The Legislative Framework for International Arbitration in Singapore — 5
- E. Singapore's Pro-Arbitration Approach — 13
- F. The Future of International Arbitration in Singapore — 15

2. Regulation of Procedural Aspects of Arbitration — 17
- A. Introduction — 17
- B. International Arbitration Rules — 17
- C. Regulation of Counsel in International Arbitration — 23
- D. Third-Party Funding — 29
- E. Confidentiality — 37

3. Interface with Other Dispute Resolution Forums — 42
- A. Mediation and Negotiation — 42
- B. Singapore International Commercial Court (SICC) — 44
- C. Expert Determination — 45

4. Interpretation of Part II of the Act — 46
- A. Section 2(1)—'arbitral tribunal' — 47
- B. Section 2(1)—'appointing authority' — 48
- C. Section 2(1)—'arbitration agreement' — 48
- D. Section 2(1)—'award' — 48
- E. Section 2(1)—'Model Law' — 49
- F. Section 2(1)—'party' — 49
- G. Section 2(2)—The Meaning of Terms Used in Both the Model Law and the IAA — 50

5. Arbitration Agreements — 51
- A. An Overview of Arbitration Agreements — 52
- B. Validity and Construction of Arbitration Agreements — 56
- C. Section 2A(1)—'an agreement by the parties to submit to arbitration all or certain disputes which have arisen or which may arise ... in respect of a defined legal relationship, whether contractual or not' — 58
- D. Section 2A(2)—In the Form of an Arbitration Clause or in the Form of a Separate Agreement — 61
- E. Section 2A(3)–(5)—In Writing — 61

xii CONTENTS

F. Section 2A(6)— 'Where … a party asserts the existence of an arbitration
agreement … and the assertion is not denied'   62
G. Section 2A(7)—Incorporation by Reference   64
H. Section 2A(8)—Bills of Lading   67

6. The Effect, Interpretation, and Applicability of the Model Law   68
A. Section 3—Model Law to Have Force of Law   68
B. Section 4—Interpretation of Model Law by Use of Extrinsic Material   69
C. Section 5—Application of Part II of the IAA   71

7. Stay of Court Proceedings in Favour of Arbitration   75
A. Introduction   76
B. Mandatory Nature of Stay   78
C. Burden of Proof   78
D. *Prima Facie* Standard of Review   79
E. Other Remedies for Breach of Arbitration Agreement   82
F. Section 6(1)—'an arbitration agreement to which the Act applies'   84
G. Section 6(1)—'party to the arbitration agreement'   88
H. Section 6(1)—'at any time after filing and serving a notice of intention to
contest or not contest and before delivering any pleading … or taking any
other step in the proceedings'   89
I. Section 6(1)—Subject Matter Falls within the Scope of the Arbitration
Agreement   93
J. Sections 6(2) and 6(3)—Possible Orders under Section 6   96
K. Section 6(2)—Arbitration Agreement Null and Void, Inoperative, or
Incapable of Being Performed   97
L Case Management Powers   99

8. Number and Appointment of Arbitrators   104
A. Section 9—Number of Arbitrators   104
B. Section 9A—Appointment of Arbitrators   105
C. Section 9B IAA—Appointment of Arbitrators in Multi-Party Arbitrations   106

9. Appeals from Jurisdictional Rulings and Order 48   109
A. Section 10—Introduction   110
B. Section 10(1)—Relationship and Key Differences between Section 10 of
the IAA and Article 16(3) of the Model Law   111
C. Section 10(2)—Negative Jurisdictional Rulings   113
D. Section 10(3)—Nature of Court's Power to Rule on Arbitral Tribunal's
Jurisdiction   114
E. Section 10(3)—Ambit of Court's Power to Rule on Arbitral Tribunal's
Jurisdiction   117
F. Section 10(3)—Standard of Review   118
G. Implications on the Court's Power to Make an Award or Order of Costs
(Sections 10(7) and 10(8) of the IAA)   121
H. Stay of Arbitration under Section 10(9)(a) of the IAA   122
I. Order 48 Rules of Court   124

10. Arbitrability   134
A. The Applicable Test   135
B. Choice of Law on Arbitrability   136

C.	Non-arbitrable Matters	137
D.	Insolvency and Arbitration	138
E.	Claims Involving Section 216 of the Companies Act	139
F.	Where Relief from Court is Required	140

11. Powers of the Arbitral Tribunal — 143

A.	Legislative History of Section 12	145
B.	Section 12(1)—Powers of an Arbitral Tribunal	145
C.	Section 12(1)(a)—Security for Costs	146
D.	Section 12(1)(b) and (c)—Discovery of Documents and Interrogatories	147
E.	Sections 12(1)(d)—Preservation, Interim Custody, or Sale of Property	148
F.	Section 12(1)(g)—Security for Claim	148
G.	Section 12(3)—Power to Adopt an Inquisitorial Process	150
H.	Section 12(4)—Limitation on the Power to Award Security for Costs	151
I.	Section 12(5)—Scope of Relief and Governing Law	152
J.	Section 12(5)(a)—Any Remedy or Relief in Civil Proceedings	153
K.	Section 12(5)(b)—Interest	154
L.	Section 12(6)—Enforceability of Orders and Directions with Leave of Court	155

12. Court Powers in Aid of Arbitration — 157

A.	Section 12A—Court-ordered Interim Measures	158
B.	Legislative Background to Section 12A	159
C.	Section 12A(1)	160
D.	Section 12A(2)—Scope of the Powers of a Court to Grant Interim Relief	161
E.	Section 12A(2)—Anti-suit Injunctions	161
F.	Section 12A(3)	167
G.	Section 12A(4)—Urgency	168
H.	Section 12A(4)—Rights and Assets	169
I.	Section 12A(5)	171
J.	Section 12A(6)	172
K.	Section 12A(7)	175
L.	Section 13—Summoning of Witnesses by Subpoena	175
M.	Subpoenas and Civil Procedure	176
N.	Principles Governing Subpoena Applications	176
O.	Subpoenas in Aid of Foreign-seated Arbitrations	178

13. Disapplication of the Model Law and the IAA, the Application of Rules of Arbitration, and Conciliation — 181

A.	Section 15—Law of Arbitration Other than Model Law	181
B.	Section 15A—Application of Rules of Arbitration	183
C.	Sections 16 and 17—Conciliation	184

14. Awards and Interest on Awards — 190

A.	Section 18 of the IAA and Article 30 of the Model Law—Award by Consent	190
B.	Section 19 of the IAA—Enforcement of Awards	194
C.	Section 19A of the IAA—Awards Made on Different Issues	195
D.	Section 19B—Award is 'Final and Binding'	199
E.	Section 19B—Finality Does Not Preclude Challenge	200
F.	Section 19C—Authentication of Awards and Arbitration Agreements	201
G.	Section 20—Interest on Awards	203

xiv CONTENTS

15. Assessment of Costs and Proceedings Otherwise Than in Open Court 206
    A. Section 21—Assessment of Costs 206
    B. Section 22—Proceedings to Be Heard in Private 207
    C. Section 23—Restrictions on Reporting of Proceedings Otherwise than in
       Open Court 208

16. Setting Aside an Award 210
    A. Introduction and Overview 211
    B. Scope of Setting Aside Action and other Cross-Cutting Issues 214
    C. Grounds for Setting Aside 237

17. Immunities of Arbitrators, Appointing Authorities and Arbitral
    Institutions 310
    A. Section 25—Immunity of Arbitrators 310
    B. Section 25A—Immunity of Appointing Authorities and Arbitral Institutions 312

18. Recognition and Enforcement of Foreign Awards 315
    A. Introduction 315
    B. Sections 27 and 28—Scope and Interpretation of Part III 316
    C. Sections 29 and 30—Procedure for Enforcement of Foreign Awards 318
    D. Section 31—Refusal of Enforcement 320
    E. Enforcement of Awards under Other Provisions of Law 328

Index 331

Table of Cases

A v B (Arbitration: Security) [2010] EWHC 3302 (Comm),
  [2011] 2 All ER (Comm) 935 . . . . .14.31.n68
A v B (Rev 1) [2020] EWHC 2790 (Comm); [2021] 1 Lloyd's Rep. 281 . . . . 14.05.n9, 14.09.n19
A and B v C, D and E [2020] EWCA Civ 409. . . . . .12.45.n89
A Best Floor Sanding Pty Ltd v Skyer Australia Pty Ltd [1999] VSC 170
  (Supreme Court of Victoria). 10.06.n15
AAY v AAZ [2011] 1 SLR 1093 (Singapore High Court). 2.57.n115, 2.58, 2.59.n120,
                                                                                2.59.nn122–123, 2.62.n133,
                                                                                2.64.n139, 2.65.n142
ABC v XYZ Co Ltd [2003] 3 SLR(R) 546; [2003] SGHC 107. . . . . 9.43.n101, 9.45.n104, 16.43.n85,
                                                                                16.48.n97
ADG and another v ADI and another matter [2014] 3 SLR 481; [2014]
  SGHC 73 . . . . 1.09.n18, 16.132.n296, 16.135.n302, 16.138.n307, 16.141.n315,
                                          16.146.n330, 16.147.n333, 16.170.n379, 16.257.n573
AES Ust-Kamenogorsk Hydropower Plant LLP v Ust-Kamenogorsk Hydropower Plant JSC
  [2013] UKSC 35; [2013] 1 WLR 1889 . . . . 7.25.n51, 7.26, 12.15.n31, 12.25.n49
AJT v AJU [2010] 4 SLR 649 . . . . .16.290.n641
AJU v AJT [2011] SGCA 41; [2011] 4 SLR 739 . . . . 1.37.nn91–92,
                            16.05.n11, 16.276.n611, 16.279.n620, 16.280.n622, 16.290.n642,
                            16.291.n644, 16.294.n.655, 16.295.n657, 16.299.n.667,
                            16.300–16.301, 16.303, 16.304.n675,
                            16.310.n680, 18.17.n23
AKN v ALC [2015] 3 SLR 488; [2015] SGCA 18. . . . . 9.25.nn54–55, 16.24.n47, 16.83, 16.88.n194,
                            16.138.n305, 16.139.n308, 16.139.n311, 16.152.n338,
                            16.188.n422, 16.191.n431, 16.194.n.438, 16.195.nn439–441,
                            16.211.n478, 16.211.n482, 16.215.n490
AKN and another v ALC and others and other appeals [2016] 1 SLR 966. . . . . . .14.08.n16, 16.11.n20,
                            16.51.n106, 16.52.n109, 16.53.n110,
                            16.54.n115, 16.58.n123
ALC v ALF [2010] SGHC 231 . . . . 12.66.n122, 12.67, 12.70
Ali Shipping Corporation v Shipyard Trogir [1999] 1 WLR 314 . . . . .2.63.n138
Aughton Ltd (formerly Aughton Group Ltd) v MF Kent Services Ltd (1991) 31
  Con LR 60 . . . . 5.39.n86, 5.43.n100
Aloe Vera of America Inc v Asianic Food (S) Pte Ltd [2006] 3 SLR(R) 174; [2006]
  SGHC 78 (Singapore High Court) 7.40.n94, 9.19.n41, 9.58.n128, 10.11.n21, 16.111.n253,
                                          16.113.n257, 16.272.n603
Amar Hoseen Mohammed Revai v Singapore Airlines [1994] 3 SLR(R) 290 . . . . .11.25.n55
Amoe Pte Ltd v Otto Marine Ltd, [2014] 1 SLR 724 . . . . .7.50.n117
AMZ v AXX [2016] 1 SLR 549 (Singapore High Court) 16.205.n467, 16.215.n491, 16.238.n525,
                                          16.242.n541, 16.267.n591, 16.334.n730
AnAn Group (Singapore) Pte Ltd v VTB Bank (Public Joint Stock Co)[2020] 1 SLR 1158;
  [2020] SGCA 33 . . . . .7.22.n40, 10.15.n29, 10.16.n34
AnAn Group (Singapore) Pte Ltd v VTB Bank (Public Joint Stock Co) [2022]
  1 SLR 771; [2021] SGCA 112. . . . . .10.16.n31
Anupam Mittal v Westbridge Ventures II Investment Holdings
  [2023] SGCA 1 . . . . .5.06.n13, 5.12.nn29–31, 10.03.n9

xvi TABLE OF CASES

Anzen v Hermes One Limited (British Virgin Islands) [2016] UKPC 1;
  [2016] 1 WLR 4098 . . . . .5.22.n57
Apis AS v Fantazia Kereskedelmi KFT [2001] 1 All E.R. (Comm) 348 Com Ct 1999/1252. . . . . . .16.69
AQZ v ARA [2015] 2 SLR 972. . . . . .2.14.n16, 2.16.n21,
  5.20.n50, 5.27.n67, 9.23.n46, 9.25.n54, 9.27.n65,
  9.46.n106, 9.48.n110, 16.13.n26, 16.95.n211, 16.96,
  16.97.n215, 16.97.n217, 16.101.n224, 16.114.n261,
  16.115.n262, 16.122.n281, 16.229.n511, 16.250.n559
Re An Arbitration Between Hainan Machinery Import and Export Corp and
  Donald & McArthy Pte Ltd, Re [1995] 3 SLR(R) 354
  (Singapore High Court). 16.259.n575, 16.262.n581
Arenson v Casson Beckman Rutley Co [1977] 1 AC 405 (HL) (UK House of Lords) 17.02.n2
Asiana Airlines, Inc v Gate Gourmet Korea Co, Ltd [2022] 4 SLR 158 . . . . . .16.85.n182, 16.177.n399,
  16.200.n457
Associated Electric and Gas Insurance Services Ltd v European Reinsurance Co of Zurich
  [2003] 1 WLR 1041 (PC). 2.58.n117, 2.59.n123
Astro Nusantra International BV v PT Ayunda Prima Mitra [2013] 1 SLR 636;
  [2012] SGHC 212. . . . . .9.60.n135, 16.43.n85, 18.09.n9
Astro Nusantara International BV and others v PT Ayunda Prima Mitra and others
  [2016] 2 SLR 737. . . . . .16.46.n93
AUF v AUG and other matters [2016] 1 SLR 859 . . . . .16.155.n346, 16.175.n394, 16.179.n403
Austrian franchisor v South African franchisee, Final Award, ICC Case No. 5460,
  1987 in A.J. van den Berg (ed), Yearbook Commercial Arbitration 1988, Vol. XIII
  (Kluwer Law International 1988). 11.30.n59
AYY v AYZ [2015] SGHCR 22 . . . . .9.38.n86

Bar Council of India v. A.K. Balaji and Others, (2018) 5 SCC 379 . . . . .2.21.n30
BAZ v BBA [2020] 5 SLR 266 . . . . .16.12.n24, 16.93.n208, 16.278.n616, 16.286.n634, 16.288.n639
BBA v BAZ [2020] SGCA 53. . . . . .3.04.n4
BBA and others v BAZ and another appeal [2020] 2 SLR 453. . . . . . .16.105.n237, 16.107, 16.279.n621,
  16.286.n634
BC Andaman Co limited & Ors v Xie Ning Yun and Ors [2017] SGHC 64. . . . . .7.25.n50
BCY v BCZ [2017] 3 SLR 357; [2016] SGHC 249 . . . . 5.03.n5, 5.04.n10,
  5.06.nn13–14, 5.07.n15, 5.08.n19, 5.11.n25,
  5.12, 5.19.n47, 9.31.n71, 9.32
Beijing Sinozonto Mining Investment Co Ltd v Goldenray Consortium (Singapore)
  Pte Ltd [2014] 1 SLR 814 (Singapore High Court). 9.50.n114, 16.86.nn186, 16.87.n189,
  16.310.n681, 16.312.n684, 16.312.n687, 16.325.n713
Berkeley Burke SIPP Administration LLP v Wayne Charlton and Financial Ombudsman
  Service Ltd [2017] EWHC 2396 (Comm), [2018] 1 Lloyd's Rep. 337 . . . . .14.32.n69
Betamax Ltd v State Trading Corporation (Mauritius) [2021] UKPC 14 . . .16.294.n656, 16.300.n669,
  16.302–16.303
Bevan Ashford v Geoff Yeandle (Contractors) Ltd [1999] Ch 239 . . . . .2.36.n61
Black & Veatch Singapore Pte Ltd v Jurong Engineering Ltd [2004] 4 SLR(R) 19
  (Singapore Court of Appeal). 2.15.n17, 2.15.n19, 2.16.n21, 2.17.n24
BLB and another v BLC and others [2013] 4 SLR 1169 . . . . . . 16.186.n419, 16.208.n473, 16.211.n479,
  16.212.n484, 16.213
BLC and others v BLB and another [2014] 4 SLR 79 . . . . 16.03.n5, 16.23.n.46, 16.24, 16.53.n112,
  16.54, 16.78.n163, 16.139.n310, 16.171.n384,
  16.211.n481, 16.213.n486
Bloomberry Resorts and Hotels Inc and another v Global Gaming Philippines LLC and
  another [2020] SGHC 113. . . . . .16.05.n11, 16.286.n635, 18.17.n23
Bloomberry Resorts and Hotels Inc and another v Global Gaming Philippines LLC
  and another [2021] 1 SLR 1045. . . . . .16.45.n88, 16.46.n94, 16.314.n690

TABLE OF CASES xvii

Bloomberry Resorts and Hotels Inc v Global Gaming Philippines LLC [2021]
2 SLR 1279 . . . . .16.279.*n620*, 16.286.*n637*, 16.291.*n643*

Bloomberry Resorts and Hotels Inc and another v Global Gaming Philippines LLC
and another [2021] 3 SLR 725 . . . . .16.46.*n93*, 16.312.*n688*, 16.313*n689*, 16.314.*n691*,
16.315.*n694*, 16.321.*n706*

Blue Flame Mechanical Services Limited v David Lord Engineering Limited (1992) 8
Const LJ 266 . . . . .7.48

BLY v BLZ [2017] 4 SLR 410; [2017] SGHC 59 . . .9.37.*n82*, 938.*n87*, 9.40.*nn92–93*, 9.41.*n95*, 9.41.*n97*

BMO v BMP [2017] SGHC 127 . . . . 7.51.*n125*, 7.54.*n130*

BNA v BNB [2019] SGHC 142 . . . . 5.12.*n27*, 9.32.*nn72–73*

BNA v BNB and another [2020] 1 SLR 456; [2019] SGCA 84 . . . . .5.03.*n5*, 9.26.*n62*, 9.28.*n68*,
9.32.*n72*, 9.34.*n80*, 16.110.*n252*, 16.251.*n562*

BNX v BOE [2017] SGHC 289 . . . . 16.276.*n613*, 16.277.*n614*, 16.283.*n627*, 16.299.*n668*

BOI v BOJ [2018] 2 SLR 1156 . . . . 16.332

BQP v BQQ [2018] SGHC 55 . . . . 9.09.*n15*, 9.26.*n60*, 9.26.*n63*, 9.28.*n67*, 9.29.*n69*, 9.34.*n80*

Bremer Vulkan Schiffbau und Maschinenfabrik v South India Shipping Corp
[1981] AC 909 . . . . .5.03.*n7*

BRQ v BRS [2019] SGHC 260 . . . . .14.38.*n78*

BRS v BRQ and another and another appeal [2021] 1 SLR 390 . . . . 16.49.*n99*, 16.74.*n154*

Re BSL [2018] SGHC 207 . . . . .2.25.*n40*

BSM v BSN and another matter [2019] SGHC 185 . . . . .16.53.*n110*

BTN and another v BTP and another [2020] 5 SLR 1250 . . . . .9.07.*n11*, 9.23.*n49*, 16.285.*n632*

BTN and another v BTP and another and other matters [2021] SGHC 271 . . . . 9.07.*n11*, 16.215.*n493*

BTN and another v BTP and another [2021] 1 SLR 276 . . . . .16.285.*n633*

BTN and another v BTP and another [2021] 4 SLR 603 . . . . .16.85.*n181*

BTY v BUA and other matters [2018] SGHC 213 . . . . .11.34.*n63*

Buckeye Check Cashing Inc v Cardegna 546 US 440 (2006) 5.03.*n7*

Bunge SA v Kruse [1979] 1 Lloyd's Rep 279 . . . . .2.15.*n18*

BVU v BVX [2019] SGHC 69 . . . . 12.65.*n120*, 16.88.*n195*, 16.312.*nn687–688*, 16.318.*n699*,
16.320.*nn702–703*

BXH v BXI [2019] SGHC 141;[2020] 3 SLR 1368 . . . . 5.03.*n5*, 5.21.*n54*, 16.115.*n263*, 16.117.*n266*,
16.119, 16.123

BXH v BXI [2020] 1 SLR 1043; [2020]
SGCA 28 . . . . 5.16.n44, 5.16.*n45*, 7.35.*n79*, 16.119.*n274*,
16.123, 16.123.*n282*

BXS v BXT [2019] SGHC(I) 10; [2019] 4 SLR 390 . . . . .1.41.*n106*, 3.11.*n13*, 6.06.*n9*, 9.44.*n103*

BXS v BXT [2019] 5 SLR 48 . . . . .16.229.*n511*

BXY and anor v BXX and anor [2019] SGHC(I) 11; [2019] 4 SLR 413 . . . . .1.41.*n106*, 3.11.*n14*,
9.10.*n17*

BYL and anor v BYN [2020] SGHC(I) 6; [2020] 4 SLR 1 . . . . 1.41.*n106*, 3.11.*n14*, 16.133.*n298*, 16.287

BZV v BZW and another [2021] SGHC 60 . . . . .16.64.*n133*

BZW and another v BZV [2022] SGCA 1 . . . .16.47.*n95*, 16.66.*n140*, 16.67, 16.176.*n397*, 16.178.*n400*

C v D [2022] HKCA 729 . . . . .3.04.*n5*

CAJ and another v CAI and another appeal [2021] SGCA 102 . . . . .16.63.*n131*, 16.153.*n341*,
16.198.*n450*, 16.199.*n454*, 16.265.*n587*

Cameron Lindsay Duncan v Diablo Fortune Inc. [2018] 4 SLR 240;
[2017] SGHC 172 . . . . 7.53.*n128*, 10.13.*n27*

Car & Cars Pte Ltd v Volkswagen AG [2010] 1 SLR 625 (Singapore High Court) . . . 2.17.*n22*, 2.17.*n24*

Carlsberg Breweries A/S v CSAPL (Singapore) Holdings Pte Ltd [2020] SGHC(I) 5;
[2020] 4 SLR 35 . . . . 1.41.*n106*, 3.11.*n14*

Carona Holdings Pte Ltd and others v Go Go Delicacy Pte Ltd [2008] 4 SLR(R) 460 . . . . . . 7.46.*n108*,
7.51.*n122*

Cassa di Risparmio di Parma e Piacenza SpA v Rals International Pte Ltd [2015] SGHC 264 . . . . .4.10.*n18*

xviii TABLE OF CASES

CBP v CBS [2020] SGHC 23 . . . . .16.143.n319
CBS v CBP [2021] 1 SLR 935. . . . . .16.55.n116
CBX and anor v CBZ and ors [2020] 5 SLR 184, [2020] SGHC(I) 17 . . . . .11.39.n75, 11.39.n78,
14.41.n82, 16.280.n623, 16.297.n661
CBX and anor v CBZ and ors [2022] 1 SLR 47; [2021] SGCA(I). 9.35.n81, 11.39.n78, 16.82.n166,
16.83, 16.187.n421, 16.201.n458,
16.202, 16.217.n496, 16.219.n498
CDI v CDJ [2020] 5 SLR 484 . . . . .14.15.n29, 16.87.n189, 16.88.n192, 16.277.n614, 16.310.n682
CDM and another v CDP [2021] 2 SLR 235 . . . . . 16.84.n179, 16.187.n421, 16.188.n423, 16.189.n425
CEB v CEC [2020] SGHC(I) 11; [2020] 4 SLR 183 . . . . .1.41.n106, 3.11.n14, 16.64.n135, 16.213.n487,
16.275.n610
CEF v CEH [2022] SGCA 54. . . . . .16.240.n535
CEF and another v CEH [2021] SGHC 114. . . . . 16.175.n394, 16.179.n403, 16.188.n424,
16.190.n427, 16.238.n526, 16.240.n530
Central Trading & Exports Limited v Fioralba Shipping Co [2014]
EWHC 2397 (Comm) 16.101.n226, 16.102.n228
Centrotrade Minerals and Metals Inc v Hindustan Copper Ltd. (2017) 2 SCC 228 . . . . .14.31.n68
Cetelem SA v Roust Holdings Ltd [2005] 1 WLR 3555 . . . . 12.39.n69, 12.40.n71, 12.41, 12.43.n84
CFJ v CFL [2023] SGHC(I) 1. . . . . .16.332.n727
CGS v CGT [2020] SGHC 183 . . . . .2.20.n27
Chapelgate Credit Opportunity Master Fund Ltd v Money & Others [2020]
EWCA Civ 246 . . . . .2.56.n110
Charles M Willie & Co (Shipping) Ltd v Ocean Laser Shipping Ltd ('The Smaro')
[1999] CLC 301. . . . . .14.29.n65
The Chartered Institute of Arbitrators v B & Ors [2019] EWHC 460 (Comm). 2.65.n145
CHH v CHI [2021] 4 SLR 295 . . . . .2.60.n126
China Machine New Energy Corp v Jaguar Energy Guatemala LLC and another [2018]
SGHC 101 . . . . 16.142.n317, 16.157.n348, 16.166.n369, 16.239.nn527–528, 16.254.n567
China Machine New Energy Corp v Jaguar Energy Guatemala LLC and another [2020]
1 SLR 695, [2020] SGCA 12. . . . . 6.06.n10, 16.88.n193, 16.136.n304, 16.141, 16.157.n350,
16.168.n376, 16.183.n414, 16.239.nn527–528,
16.264.n585, 16.265, 16.327.n715
CHY and another v CIA [2022] SGHC(I) 3. . . . . 16.298.n666, 16.302.n674
CIM v CIN [2021] 4 SLR 1176. . . . . 16.180.n404, 16.190.n430
CIZ v CJA [2021] SGHC 178. . . . . .16.197.n445
CJA v CIZ [2022] 2 SLR 557 . . . . .16.197.n447
CJY v CJZ and others [2021] 5 SLR 569 . . . . 2.62.n133, 2.63.n136
CJY v CJZ and others [2021] SGHC 69 . . . . .7.86.n203
CKG v CKH 5 SLR 84; [2021] SGHC(I) 5 . . . . .16.62.n129, 16.200.nn455–457, 16.208.n473,
16.211.n483
CKH v CKG and another matter [2022] 2 SLR 1. . . . . .16.53.n110
CKR v CKT [2021] SGHCR 4 . . . . 9.59.n132, 18.10.n11
CLX v CLY and another and another matter [2022] SGHC 17 . . . . .16.314.n691, 16.315.n693,
16.318.n699
CMJ and another v CML and another [2022] 3 SLR 319 . . . . .16.159.n353
CNA v CNB and another and another matter [2021] SGHC 192 . . . . .16.49.n101, 16.73.n152,
16.74.nn154–155, 16.75, 16.77.n162
Coal & Oil Co LLC v GHCL Ltd [2015] 3 SLR 154 . . . . 16.41.n82, 16.138.n306, 16.170.n381,
16.241.n536, 16.246.n552, 16.248,
16.281.n624, 16.284.n629, 16.327.n715
Commerzbank Aktiengesellschaft v Liquimar Tankers Management Inc [2017]
EWHC 161 (Comm); [2017] 2 All ER 829 . . . . .5.23.n61
Compañia De Navegación Palomar v Ernest Ferdinand Perez De La Sala [2017] SGHC 14 . . . . . .2.30.n47
Company 1 v Company 2 [2017] EWHC 2319 (QB) 12.06.n13

TABLE OF CASES   xix

Coop International Pte Ltd v Ebel SA [1998] SGHC 425; [1998] 1 SLR(R) 615 . . . . 1.22, 1.23.n52
CPU and others v CPX [2022] SGHC(I) 11. . . . . 16.06.n13, 16.93.n206
Credit Suisse Fides Trust SA v Cuoghi [1998] QB 818. . . . . .12.32.n62
Credit Suisse First Boston (Europe) Ltd v MLC (Bermuda) Ltd [1999] CLC 579. . . . . . . 7.29.n62, 7.31
Credit Suisse First Boston (Europe) Ltd v MLC (Bermuda) Ltd [1999] 1 Lloyd's Rep 767 . . . .7.29.n62
CRW Joint Operation v PT Perusahaan Gas Negara (Persero) TBK [2011] 4 SLR 305; [2011]
    SGCA 33 . . . . 1.40.n99, 16.03.n7, 16.40.n77, 16.146.n331,
                                         16.151.n336, 16.184.n416, 16.185.n418, 16.187.n421,
                                         16.195n.439, 16.208.n472, 16.209.n474,
                                         16.210, 16.215.n489, 16.217
CVG v CVH [2022] SGHC 249. . . . . 16.153.n343, 18.08.n6
In re Cybernaut Growth Fund LP, Cause No FSD 73 of 2013 (23 July 2013)
    (Grand Court of the Cayman Islands). 10.11.n20
The Czech Republic v European Media Ventures SA [2007] EWHC 2851 (Comm) 9.24.n51

Daimler South East Asia Pte Ltd v Front Row Investment Holdings (Singapore)
    Pte Ltd [2012] 4 SLR 837 . . . . .16.39.n75
Dalian Deepwater Developer Ltd v Dybdahl [2015] NZHC 151 .12.76.n136
Dalian Hualiang Enterprise Group Co Ltd and anor v Louis Dreyfus Asia
    Pte Ltd [2005] 4 SLR(R) 646 . . . . 7.08.n10, 7.11.n13, 7.58.n134
Dalian Huarui Heavy Industry International Co Ltd v Clyde & Co Australia (a firm)
    [2020] WASC 132. . . . . 11.18.n34, 11.19.n37
Dallah Real Estate and Tourism Holding Co v Ministry of Religious Affairs of the
    Government of Pakistan [2010] UKSC 46,[2011] 1 AC 763 . . . . 9.11.n20, 16.95.n210, 16.120,
                                         16.188.n422
DDT Trucks of North America Ltd and ors v DDT Holdings Ltd [2007]
    EWHC 1542 (Comm), [2007] 2 Lloyd's Rep 213 . . . . .16.314.n692
Denmark Skibstekniske Konsulenter A/ S I Likvidation (formerly known
    as Knud E Hansen A/ S) v Ultrapolis 3000 Investments Ltd
    (formerly known as Ultrapolis 3000 Theme Park Investments Ltd)
    [2010] 3 SLR 661. . . . . .16.113.n259, 16.226.n509, 16.258.n574
Denmark Skibstekniske Konsulenter A/S I Likvidation (formerly known as Knud E Hansen
    A/S) v Ultrapolis 3000 Investments Ltd (formerly known as Ultrapolis 3000 Theme Park
    Investments Ltd) [2011] SGHC 207. . . . . .4.08.n14
Dermajaya Properties Sdn Bhd v Premium Properties Sdn Bhd [2002] SGHC 53;
    [2002] 1 SLR(R) 492. . . . . 1.25.n61, 1.26.n66, 6.08.n15
Dolling-Baker v Merrett [1990] 1 WLR 1205. . . . . .2.59.n121
Dongwoo Mann & Hummel Co Ltd v Mann & Hummel GmbH [2008]
    3 SLR (R) 871 . . . . 16.87.n187, 16.88.n196, 16.140.n314,
                                         16.164.n362, 16.312.n686,
                                         16.318.n699, 16.319
Dowans Holding SA v Tanzania Elec. Supply Co. Ltd [2011] EWHC 1957. . . . . .18.27.n42
The 'Duden' [2008] 4 SLR(R) 984 . . . . 7.10.n11, 7.65.n155, 7.66.n158
Dukkar SA v Thailand Integrated Services Pte Ltd [2015] SGHC 234. . . . . .12.03.n6
Dyna-Jet Pte Ltd v Wilson Taylor Asia Pacific Pte Ltd [2016] SGHC 238 . . . . .5.22.n60

Eagle Star Insurance Co Ltd v Yuval Insurance Co Ltd [1978] 1 Lloyd's Rep 357 . . . . .7.52.n127
Econ Piling Pte Ltd v Shanghai Tunnel Engineering Co Ltd [2011]
    1 SLR 246. . . . . 16.73.n152, 16.74.n153
Econet Wireless Ltd v Vee Networks Ltd [2006] 2 Lloyd's Rep 428. . . . . .12.30.n56
Electrosteel Castings Ltd v Scan-Trans Shipping & Chartering Sdn Bhd [2002]
    EWHC 1993 (Comm); [2003] 1 Lloyd's Rep 190 . . . . .16.96.n214
Emerald Grain Australia Pty Ltd v Agrocorp International Pte Ltd [2014] FCA 414 . . . . .16.179.n402
Enka Insaat Ve Sanayi AS v OOO Insurance Co Chubb [2020] UKSC 38. . . . . 5.09.n20, 5.12

XX TABLE OF CASES

Equatorial Marine Fuel Management Services Pte Ltd v The 'Bunga Melati 5'
[2010] SGHC 193 . . . . .14.33.*n*70
Equinox Offshore Accommodation Ltd v Richshore Marine Supplies Pte Ltd
[2010] SGHC 122 . . . . .12.06.*n*16
Essar Oilfields Services Ltd v Norscot Rig Management Pvt Ltd [2016] EWHC 2361
(Comm) (England and Wales High Court). 2.55.*n*108
ETI Euro Telecom International NV v Republic of Bolivia [2008] EWCA Civ 880;
[2008] 2 Lloyd's Rep. 421 . . . . 12.06.*n* 17, 12.32.*n*59
Etihad Airways PJSC v Prof Dr Lucas Flother [2019] EWHC 3107 (Comm);
[2020] QB 793. . . . . .5.23.*n*61
EuroGas Inc and Belmont Resources Inc v Slovak Republic, ICSID Case
No ARB/ 14/ 14, Transcript of the First Session and Hearing on Provisional
Measures dated 17 March 2015. . . . . .2.46.*n*86
Evergreat Construction Co Pte Ltd v Presscrete Engineering Pte Ltd [2006] 1 SLR(R) 634 . . .3.13.*n*15
Excalibur Ventures v Texas Keystone and others [2016] EWCA Civ 1144 . . . . .2.56.*n*110
Excess Insurance Co Ltd v Mander [1995] CLC 838 . . . . 5.39.*n*86, 5.43.*n*100

Fiona Trust & Holding Corp v Privalov [2007] UKHL 40, [2008]
1 Lloyd's Rep 254 . . . . .5.03.*n*7, 10.24.*n*56, 16.117
Five Ocean Corp v Cingler Ship Pte Ltd [2015] SGHC 311. . . . . 11.15.*n*27, 12.01.*n*2, 12.34.*n*63,
12.35.*n*66, 12.42.*n*75
Front Carriers Ltd v Atlantic & Orient Shipping Corp [2006] 3 SLR(R) 854;
[2006] SGHC 127. . . . . .9.52.*n*118, 11.17.*n*33, 12.04.*n*8
Front Row Investment Holdings (Singapore) Pte Ltd v Daimler South East
Asia Pte Ltd [2010] SGHC 80 . . . . .16.54.*n*114
Fulham Football Club (1987) Ltd v Richards and another [2012] Ch 333
(England and Wales Court of Appeal). 7.77.*n*182

Galsworthy Ltd of the Republic of Liberia v Glory Wealth Shipping Pte Ltd
[2011] 1 SLR 727. . . . . .9.62.*n*138
GD Midea Air Conditioning Equipment Co Ltd v Tornado Consumer Goods Ltd and
another matter [2018] 4 SLR 271 . . . . 16.186.*n*420, 16.193.*n*434, 16.194, 16.216.*n*494, 16.217
Re Gearing, Matthew Peter QC [2020] 3 SLR 1106 . . . . .2.25.*n*40
Gelatissimo Ventures (S) Pte Ltd & Ors v Singapore Flyer Pte Ltd [2010] 1 SLR 833. . . . . .2.50.*n*97
Gerald Metals SA v Trustees of the Timis Trust & others [2016] EWHC 2327 . . . . . . 12.46.*n*90, 12.53
Getwick Engineers Limited v Pilecon Engineering Limited [2002] 1020 HKCU 1 . . . . .7.59.*n*137
Gokul Patnaik v Nine Rivers Capital Ltd [2021] 3 SLR 22. . . . . .16.298.*n*664
Government of the Lao People's Democratic Republic v Sanum Investments Ltd [2015]
2 SLR 322; [2015] SGHC 15 . . . . .9.24.*n*52, 9.25.*n*54, 9.47.*n*109,
2.64.*n*114, 16.100.*n*222
Government of the Republic of the Philippines v Philippine International
Air Terminals Co, Inc [2007] 1 SLR(R) 278. . . . . .16.162.*n*359
GPF GP Sàrl v The Republic of Poland [2018] EWHC 409 (Comm) 9.08.*n*12
Grand Pacific Holdings Ltd v Pacific China Holdings Ltd (in liq) (No 1) [2012] 4 HKLRD 1 . . . .16.41
Gulf Hibiscus Limited v Rex International Holding Limited and anor [2017]
SGHC 210 . . . . .7.79.*n*184, 7.80.*n*186, 7.83.*n*191

Habas Sinai Ve Tibbi Gazlar Isthisal Endustri AS v Sometal SAL [2010] EWHC 29
(Comm); [2010] Bus LR 880. . . . . .5.39.*n*87
Habas Sinai Ve Tibbi Gazlar Istihsal Endustrisi AS v VSC Steel Co Ltd [2013] EWHC 4071
(Comm) (England and Wales High Court). 5.08.*n*17
H&C S Holdings Pte Ltd v Mount Eastern Holdings Resources Co [2015] SGHC 323 . . . . . 11.17.*n*33,
12.44.*n*87
Halvanon Insurance Co Ltd v Companhia de Seguros do Estado de Sao Paulo
[1995] LRLR 303. . . . . .7.74.*n*175

TABLE OF CASES xxi

Hancock Prospecting Pty Ltd v Rinehart [2017] FCAFC 170 . . . . .7.19.*n*25
Harbour Assurance Co (UK) Ltd v Kansa General International Insurance Co Ltd
    [1993] 1 Lloyd's Rep 455 . . . . .5.03.*n*7
Re Harish Salve [2018] 1 SLR 345 . . . . .2.25.*n*40
Hilton International Manage (Maldives) Pvt Ltd v Sun Travels & Tours Pvt Ltd
    [2018] SGHC 56 . . . . 7.26.*n*54, 9.55.*n*127, 12.16.*n*35, 12.17
HKL Group Co Ltd v Rizq International Holdings Pte Ltd [2013] SGHCR 5 . . . . 5.15.*n*42, 7.68.*n*164
Ho Yew Kong v Sakae Holdings Ltd [2018] SGCA 33 . . . . .10.18.*n*37
Hrvatska Elektropirvreda v Slovenia (ICSID Case No. ARB/05/24) .2.32.*n*53
HSBC Trustee (Singapore) Ltd v Lucky Realty Co Pte Ltd [2015] 3 SLR 855 . . . . .9.27.*n*66

I-Admin (Singapore) Pte Ltd v Hong Ying Ting and others [2020] 1 SLR 1130 . . . . .12.28.*n*53
Ikon International (HK) Holdings Public Co Limited v Ikon Finance Limited and ors.
    [2015] EWHC 3088 (Comm) 12.51.*n*98
Insigma Technology Co Ltd v Alstom Technology Ltd [2008] SGHC 134; [2009]
    1 SLR(R) 23 . . . . .5.13.*n*35, 9.12.*n*21, 16.227.*n*510
Insigma Technology Co Ltd v Alstom Technology Ltd [2009] SGCA 24; [2009]
    3 SLR(R) 936 . . . . 5.13.*n*32, 5.14.*n*36, 5.14, 13.09.*n*8, 16.227.*n*510
International Coal Pte Ltd v Kristle Trading Ltd and Another and Another Suit
    [2008] SGHC 182 . . . . .2.58.*n*119
International Research Corp PLC v Lufthansa Systems Asia Pacific Pte Ltd and another
    [2013] SGCA 55 . . . . 5.37.*n*84, 5.40.*n*88, 5.41.*n*91, 5.43.*n*100, 12.75.*n*134
International Research Corp plc v Lufthansa Systems Asia Pacific Pte Ltd
    [2013] 1 SLR(R) 973 . . . . .9.13.*n*22
International Research Corp Plc v Lufthansa Systems Asia Pacific Pte Ltd [2014]
    1 SLR 130 . . . . .3.04.*n*2, 9.14.*n*25, 9.15.*n*27, 9.21.*n*42
IPCO (Nigeria) Ltd v Nigerian National Petroleum Corporation [2005]
    EWHC 726 (Comm) 18.27.*n*42, 18.31.*n*50

Jane Rebecca Ong v Lim Lie Hao [1996] SGHC 140 . . . . .2.36.*n*56
Jiangsu Overseas Group Co Ltd v Concord Energy Pte Ltd
    [2016] 4 SLR 1336; [2016] SGHC 153 . . . . 9.47.*n*108, 9.48.*n*112, 16.05.*n*11,
                                                            16.92.*n*203, 16.98.*n*218, 16.99, 16.110.*n*251,
                                                                        16.121.*n*277, 18.17.*n*23
John Forster Emmott v Michael Wilson & Partners Ltd [2008] 2 All ER (Comm) 193
    (England and Wales Court of Appeal) 2.58.*n*117, 2.59.*n*120, 2.62.*n*133, 2.63.*n*137
John Holland Pty v Toyo Engineering Corp (Japan) [2001] SGHC 48;
    [2001] 1 SLR(R) 443 . . . . 1.22, 1.23.*n*55, 16.31.*n*58, 16.145.*n*329
Re Joseph David QC [2012] 1 SLR 791 . . . . .2.25.*n*40
Josias Van Zyl v Kingdom of Lesotho [2017] 4 SLR 849; [2017] SGHC 104 . . . . . 9.60.*n*134, 9.63.*n*140
Judgment of 7 January 1992, Sociétés BKMI et Siemens v Société Dutco,
    119 JDI. (Clunet) 707 (1992) (French Cour de Cassation Civ. 1e) 8.11.*nn*21–22, 8.12
Judgment of 12 February 1993, Unichips Finanziara v Gesnouin, 1993
    Rev. Arb. 276 (Paris Cour d'Appel) 18.22.*n*29
Judgment of 23 March 1994, Omnium de Traitement et de Valorisation, 1994
    Rev. Arb. 327 (French Cour de Cassation Civ. 1) 18.22.*n*28
Judgment of 14 January 1997, 1997 Rev. Arb. 395 (Paris Cour d'Appel) 18.*n*29
Judgment of 10 June 1997, Omnium de Traitement et de Valorisation v Hilmarton,
    1997 Rev. Arb. 376 (French Cour de Cassation Civ. 1) 18.22.*n*28
Judgment of 29 June 2007, PT Putrabali Adyamulia v Rena Holding, 2007
    Rev. Arb. 507 (French Cour de Cassation Civ. 1) 18.22.*n*28
Judgment of 28 April 2009, Yukos Capital Sarl v OAO Rosneft,
    XXXIV Y.B. Comm. Arb. 703 (Amsterdam Gerechtshof) (2009) 18.23.*nn*30–32
Judgment of 24 November 2011, Egyptian Gen. Petroleum Corp. v Nat'l Gas Co.,
    2012 Rev. Arb. 134 (Paris Cour d'Appel) 18.22.*n*29

xxii   TABLE OF CASES

Judgment of 19 February 2013, République Démocratique Populaire du Lao v
Thai Lao Lignite Co., Case No. 12/09983 (Paris Cour d'Appel) 18.22.*n*29
Judgment of 27 September 2016, XLII Y.B. Comm. Arb. 461
(Amsterdam Gerechtshof) (2017) 18.23.*n*30
Judgment of 17 November 2017, Maximov v OJSC 'Novolipetsky Metallurgichesky
Kombinat', XXXVII Y.B. Comm. Arb. 274 (Amsterdam Gerechtshof) (2012). 18.23.*n*30
Judgment of 23 June 2020, Case No.17/22943 (Paris Cour d'Appel) 5.07.*n*16
Jurong Engineering Ltd v Black & Veatch Singapore Pte Ltd [2003] SGHC 292;
[2004] 1 SLR 333. . . . . 1.20.*n*49, 6.08.*n*14
Jurong Town Corp v Wishing Star Ltd [2004] 2 SLR(R) 427 . . . . 11.25.*n*54
JVL Agro Industries v Agritrade International Pte Ltd [2016] 4 SLR 768 . . . . .11.22.*n*45, 11.23,
11.37.*n*73, 16.61.*n*126, 16.135.*n*302, 16.178.*n*400,
16.180.*n*404, 16.205.*n*465, 16.257.*n*573

Kabab-Ji SAL (Lebanon) v Kout Food Group [2020] EWCA Civ 6 . . . . 5.07.*n*16
Kabab-Ji SAL (Lebanon) v Kout Food Group (Kuwait) [2021] UKSC 48 . . . . 5.07.*n*16, 5.09.*n*23
Kempinski Hotels SA v PT Prima International Development [2011]
4 SLR 633 . . . . 16.52.*n*109, 16.64.*n*133–16.65, 16.162, 16.181.*n*428, 16.190,
16.328.*n*719, 16.331.*n*725
Kılıç İnşaat İthalat İhracat Sanayi ve Ticaret Anonim Şirketi v Turkmenistan
(ICSID Case No. ARB/10/1) 2.47.*n*91
Kingdom of Lesotho v Swissborough Diamond Mines [2017] SGHC 195;
[2019] 3 SLR 12. . . . . 1.43.*n*112, 9.23.*n*49, 14.08.*n*16, 16.104.*n*235
Kingdom of Spain v Infrastructure Services Luxembourg S.A.R.L. and anor
[2021] FCAFC 3 . . . . 18.09.*n*9
Koh Bros Building and Civil Engineering Contractor Pte Ltd v Scotts Development
(Saraca) Pte Ltd [2002] 2 SLR(R) 1063. . . . . .16.237.*n*521
KVC Rice Intertrade Co Ltd v Asian Mineral Resources Pte Ltd
[2017] 4 SLR 182. . . . . 5.14.*n*38, 7.19.*n*24, 7.65.*n*156, 7.67.*nn*160–162, 8.02.*n*3

L Capital Jones Ltd v Maniach Pte Ltd [2017] 1 SLR 312; [2017] SGCA 3 . . . . 7.51.*n*121, 10.19.*n*43
Ladd v Marshall [1954] 1 WLR 1489 . . . . 9.47.*n*109, 16.100.*n*222, 16.101.*n*225
Re Landau, Toby Thomas QC [2016] SGHC 258 . . . . .2.25.*n*40
Lao Holdings NV v Government of the Lao People's Democratic Republic
and another matter [2021] 5 SLR 228; [2021] SGHC(I) 10 . . . . .16.267.*n*594
Larsen Oil and Gas Pte Ltd v Petroprod Ltd (in official liquidation in the Cayman
Islands and in compulsory liquidation in Singapore) [2011] 3 SLR 414; [2011]
SGCA 21 . . . . 7.61.*n*144, 10.01.*n*2, 10.05.*n*11,
10.06.*n*14, 10.12.*n*22,
10.14.*n*28, 12.75.*n*134
Lassiter Ann Masters v To Keng Lam [2004] 2 SLR(R) 392. . . . . .9.47.*n*109
Lawrence and another v Fen Tigers Ltd and others [2014] AC 822 . . . . .12.29.*n*55
LC v ALF [2010] SGHC 231 . . . . 2.*n*136
Lee Kuan Yew v Tang Liang Hong [1997] 2 SLR(R) 862. . . . . .9.09.*n*15
The Londonderry Port and Harbour Commissioners v W S Atkins Consultants Limited and
Charles Brand Limited [2011] NIQB 74 . . . . .7.50.*n*120
Lorand Shipping Limited v Davof Trading (Africa) B.V., MV 'Ocean Glory' [2014]
EWHC 3521 (Comm), [2015] 2 All ER (Comm) 940 . . . . .14.17.*n*36
Lucky-Goldstar International (HK) Ltd v Ng Moo Kee Engineering Ltd
[1993] HKCFI 14 . . . . .5.15.*n*43
Luzon Hydro Corp v Transfield Philippines Inc [2004] 4 SLR(R) 705 . . . . .16.242.*n*538
LW Infrastructure Pte Ltd v Lim Chin San Contractors Pte Ltd and another [2013] 1 SLR 125;
[2012] SGCA 57 . . . . 1.40.*n*98, 12.21.*n*46, 14.42.*n*85, 16.79.*n*164,
16.80, 16.136.*n*304, 16.258.*n*574

TABLE OF CASES   xxiii

Maldives Airports Co Ltd and another v GMR Malé International Airport Pte Ltd
  [2013] 2 SLR 449 (Singapore Court of Appeal)............ 12.35.*n*65, 12.38.*n*67, 12.41.*n*73, 12.42
Malhotra v Malhotra [2012] EWHC 3020 (Comm).................................12.32.*n*60
Malicorp Ltd v Government of Arab Republic of Egypt [2015] EWHC 361 (Comm).......18.24.*n*34
Malini Ventura v Knight Capital Pte Ltd [2015] 5 SLR 707 .... 7.20.*n*30, 7.89.*n*222
Man Diesel Turbo SE v IM Skaugen Marine Services Pte Ltd [2019] 4 SLR 537;
  [2018] SGHC 132........................... 9.62.*nn*137–139, 18.32.*n*51, 18.33.*n*52, 18.36.*n*61
Maniach Pte Ltd v L. Capital Jones Ltd and Jones the Grocer Group Holding
  Pte Ltd [2016] SGHC 65 .... 7.51.*n*124, 11.36.*n*68
Manuchar Steel Hong Kong Ltd v Star Pacific Line Pte Ltd [2014] 4 SLR 832...............7.40.*n*95
Mauritius Commercial Bank Ltd v Hestia Holdings Ltd and another [2013]
  EWHC 1328 (Comm); [2013] 2 All ER 898 ....5.23.*n*61
Maybank Kim Eng Securities Pte Ltd v Lim Keng Yong [2016] 3 SLR 431 ....7.85.*n*200
Methanex Motunui Ltd v Spellman [2004] NZCA 418; [2004] 3 NZLR 454..............16.35.*n*68
Ministry of Defense & Support for the Armed Forces of Iran v Cubic
  Defense Sys., Inc., 665 F.3d 1091, 1100 (9th Cir. 2011) 18.26.*n*41
Mitsui Engineering and Shipbuilding Co Ltd v Easton Graham Rush and another
  [2004] SGHC 26; [2004] 2 SLR 14 .... 1.20.*nn*46–47
Mobil Cerro Negro Ltd v Petroleos de Venezuela SA [2008] 1 Lloyd's Rep 684 ....12.32.*n*61
Motorola Credit Corporation v Uzan [2003] EWCA Civ 752...........................12.32.*n*62
Motorola Solutions Credit Co LLC v Kemal Uzan [2015] 5 SLR 752......................2.51.*n*99
Myanma Yaung Chi Oo Co Ltd v Win Nu [2003] SGHC 124 .... 2.59.*n*121, 2.62.*n*134

National Oilwell Varco Norway AS (formerly known as Hydralift AS) v Keppel FELS
  Ltd (formerly known as Far East Levingston Shipbuilding Ltd) [2022] 2 SLR 115........18.13.*n*15
Navigator Investment Services Ltd v Acclaim Insurance Brokers Pte Ltd [2009]
  SGCA 45; [2010] 1 SLR 25...................................2.15.*n*17, 6.08.*n*16, 7.45.*n*105
NCC International AB v Alliance Concrete Singapore Pte Ltd [2008]
  2 SLR(R) 565 .... 6.08.*n*16, 12.52.*n*100
Ngee Ann Development Pte Ltd v Takashimaya Singapore Ltd [2017] 2 SLR 627 ....3.13.*n*15
Nigel Peter Albon v Naza Motor Trading Sdn Bhn [2007] 2 All ER 1075; [2007]
  2 Lloyd's Rep 1..7.20.*n*32
Noble China Inc v Lei Kat Cheong, (1998) 42 OR (3d) 69...........................16.35.*n*67
Noble Resources International Pte Ltd v Shanghai Xintai International
  Trade Co Ltd (2016) Hu 01 Xie Wai Ren No. 1 ....16.230.*n*512
Northern Elevator Manufacturing Sdn Bhd v United Engineers (Singapore)
  Pte Ltd [2004] 2 SLR(R) 494 ....16.22.*n*42
Nova (Jersey) Knit Ltd v Kammgarn Spinnerei GmbH [1977] 1 WLR 713...............7.64.*n*152
NWA & FSA v NVF & others [2021] EWHC 2666 (Comm)............................3.04.*n*5

Oei Hong Leong v Goldman Sachs International [2014] 3 SLR 1217................. 7.32.*n*71, 7.34
Oil & Natural Gas Corp Ltd v SAW Pipes Ltd AIR 2003 SC 2629
  (Supreme Court of India) 16.22.*n*44
The Oriental Insurance Co Ltd v Reliance National Asia Re Pte Ltd. [2008] SGHC 236.....11.38.*n*74
Otech Pakistan Pvt Ltd v Clough Engineering Ltd [2007] 1 SLR 989 ....2.36.*n*60

Pacific Crown Engineering Ltd v Hyundai Engineering and Construction Co Ltd
  [2003] 3 HKC 659...7.19.*n*27
Pacific Maritime (Asia) Ltd v Holystone Overseas Ltd [2007] EWHC 2319 (Comm).......12.49.*n*93
Pacific Recreation Pte Ltd v S Y Technology Inc and another appeal [2008]
  2 SLR(R) 491 ....16.111.*n*254
Paul Smith Ltd v H & S International Holding Inc [1991]
  2 Lloyd's Rep 127 ....7.36.*n*83, 7.39, 16.119
PCCW Global Ltd v Interactive Communications Service Ltd [2007] 1 HKLRD 309........7.19.*n*27

xxiv   TABLE OF CASES

PEC Limited v Asia Golden Rice Co Ltd [2012] EWHC 846 (Comm), [2013]
  1 Lloyd's Rep. 82 . . . . .14.31.*n*68
Permasteelisa Japan KK v Bouyguesstroi [2007] EWHC 3508 . . . . .12.46.*n*90
Petrochemical Logistics Ltd & Axel Krueger v PSB Alpha AG & Konstantinos
  Ghertsos [2020] EWHC 975 (Comm). 12.06.*n*13
Phoenixfin Pte Ltd and others v Convexity Ltd [2022] SGCA 17 .16.182.*n*407
Piallo GmbH v Yafriro International Pte Ltd [2014] 1 SLR 1028 . . . . 7.62.*n*145, 7.64
Popack v Lipszyc 2015 ONSC 3460 (Ontario Superior Court of Justice). 16.35.*n*67
Prestige Marine Services Pte Ltd v Marubeni International Petroleum (S)
  Pte Ltd [2012] 1 SLR 917 . . . . .16.75.*n*157
Prima Paint Corp. v Flood & Conklin Mfg. Co. (1967) 388 US 395 . . . . .5.03.*n*7
Prometheus Marine Pte Ltd v King, Ann Rita and another [2017] SGCA 61;
  [2018] 1 SLR 1 . . . . 1.38.*n*94, 16.22.*n*45, 16.188.*n*424
Prometheus Marine Pte Ltd v Ann Rita King and other matters [2017] SGHC 36. . . . . . . .16.282.*n*625
PT Asuransi Jasa Indonesia (Persero) v Dexia Bank SA [2006] 1 SLR(R) 197 . . . . 16.161.*n*356,
                                                                      16.183.*n*416
PT Asuransi Jasa Indonesia (Persero) v Dexia Bank SA [2007]
  1 SLR(R) 597 .9.04.*n*2, 9.13.*n*24, 9.16.*n*32, 9.22.*n*44, 14.16.*n*33, 16.20.*n*40,
                              16.22.*n*43, 16.184.*n*416, 16.187.*n*421, 16.273.*n*605,
                                          16.274.*n*607, 16.275, 16.279.*n*618
PT Central Investindo v Franciscus Wongso and others and another matter [2014]
  4 SLR 978. . . . . .16.17.*n*35, 16.133.*n*299, 16.235.*n*518, 16.310.*n*681,
                                                          16.328.*n*716, 16.329
PT First Media TBK v Astro Nusantara International BV [2013] SCGA 57, [2014] 1
  SLR 372 . . . . 1.18.*n*42, 1.40.*n*100, 6.01.*n*2, 6.02.*n*4,
                          6.06.*n*11, 9.11.*n*20, 9.18.*n*40, 9.22.*n*43, 9.25.*n*56, 14.08.*n*17,
                          14.12.*n*24, 14.14.*n*28, 14.26.*nn*54–55, 14.28.*n*58,
                          14.30.*n*66, 16.10.*n*17, 16.12.*n*23, 16.15.*n*31,
                          16.16.*n*34, 16.20.*n*39, 16.32.*n*62, 16.94.*n*209, 16.95,
                          16.120, 16.126.*n*287, 18.16.*n*20, 18.20.*n*24
PT Garuda Indonesia v Birgen Air [2002] 1 SLR(R) 401 . . . . 6.04.*n*7, 9.53.*n*123, 9.54.*n*126
PT Perusasahaan Gas Negara (Persero) TBK v CRW Joint Operation
  [2010] 4 SLR 672 . . . . .16.238.*n*526
PT Perusahaan Gas Negara (Persero) TBK v CRW Joint Operation [2015] 4 SLR 364;
  [2015] SGCA 30 . . . . 4.07.*n*13, 11.06.*n*11, 14.19.*n*39–40, 14.20–14.21, 14.22.*n*48,
                                          14.24–14.25, 14.27.*n*56, 16.87.*n*187
PT Prima International Development v Kempinski Hotels SA and other appeals [2012]
  4 SLR 98. . . . . 2.*n*232, 16.32.*n*61, 16.52.*n*109, 16.64.*n*133, 16.65.*n*136,
                                          16.162.*n*361, 16.181.*n*405, 16.190.*n*428,
                                          16.219.*n*499, 16.328.*n*719
PT Pukuafu Indah and others v Newmont Indonesia Ltd and another [2012]
  SGHC 187 . . . . .4.07.*n*11, 11.40.*n*79, 11.41.*n*86, 12.01.*n*1
PT Pukuafu Indah v Newmont Ltd [2012] 4 SLR 1157 (Singapore High Court) 16.43.*n*85
PT Thiess Contractors Indonesia v PT Kaltim Prima Coal and another [2011]
  EWHC 1842 (Comm) 7.33.*n*75
PT Tugu Pratama Indonesia v Magma Nusantara Ltd [2003] SGHC 204; [2003]
  4 SLR(R) 257. . . . . 5.15.*n*41, 10.*n*10
PUBG Corp v Garena International I Pte Ltd and others [2020] 2 SLR 379 . . . . .7.88.*n*212

Quanzhou Sanhong Trading Limited Liability Co Ltd v ADM Asia-Pacific
  Trading Pte Ltd [2017] SGHC 199 . . . . 16.195.*n*439, 16.196.*n*444
Quarella SpA v Scelta Marble Australia Pty Ltd [2012] 4 SLR 1057 . . . . .16.245.*n*548
Quasar de Valores SICAV S.A. et al. v The Russian Federation
  (SCC Arbitration No. 24/2007) 2.55.*n*106

TABLE OF CASES   XXV

R v Deputy Industrial Injuries Commissioner, ex parte Moore [1965] 1 QB 456 . . . . 16.179.*n*402
R (Factortame) v Secretary of State for Transport (No. 8) [2003] QB 381 . . . . .2.35.*n*58
Rakna Arakshaka Lanka Ltd v Avant Garde Maritime Services (Pte) Ltd [2019]
      2 SLR 131 . . . . 16.173.*n*390, 16.206.*n*469, 16.263.*n*582, 16.296.*n*660,
                                                                                               16.308.*n*677, 16.311.*n*683
Rakna Arakshaka Lanka Ltd v Avant Garde Maritime Services (Private) Limited
      [2019] 4 SLR 995 . . . . 16.15.*n*33, 16.173.*n*387, 16.296.*n*658, 16.308.*n*676
Rals International Pte Ltd v Cassa di Risparmio di Parma e Paicenze SpA
      [2016] SGCA 53 . . . . 4.10.*n*21, 7.42.*n*102
Rals International Pte Ltd v Cassa di Risparmio di Parma e Piacenza SpA
      [2016] 5 SLR 455 . . . . .7.41.*n*96, 7.63, 7.64.*n*149
RBRG Trading (UK) Ltd v Sinocore International Co Ltd [2018] EWCA Civ 838 . . . . .16.294.*n*656
Recydia Atik Yonetimi Yenilenebilir Enerji Uretimi Nakliye Ve Lojisk Ik
      Hizmetleri San Ve Ticaret AZ v Collins-Thomas [2018] EWHC 2506 (Comm) 12.32.*n*61
Republic of Ecuador v Occidental Exploration and Production Co [2006] QB 432 . . . . .9.24.*n*50
Republic of Haiti v Duvalier [1989] 2 WLR 261 . . . . .12.32.*n*62
Republic of India v Vedanta Resources plc [2020] SGHC 208 . . . . 2.61.*n*129, 14.29.*n*64
Republic of India v Vedanta Resources plc [2021] 2 SLR 354; [2021] SGCA 50 . . . . 1.43.*n*112,
                                                                                                     2.61.*n*132, 16.25.*n*48
Republic of Sierra Leone v SL Mining Ltd [2021] EWHC 286 (Comm) 3.04.*n*5, 3.05.*nn*7–8
Rex International Holding Ltd and Rex International Investments Pte Ltd v
      Gulf Hibiscus Limited [2019] 2 SLR 682 . . . . 7.84.*n*195, 7.87
Rhone Mediterranee Compagnia Francese di Assicurazioni e Riassicurazioni v
      Achille Lauro 712 F2d 50 (3d Cir 1983) 7.71.*n*169
Robotunits Pty Ltd v Mennel [2015] VSC 268 . . . . .5.15.*n*43
The Rompetrol Group NV v Romania (ICSID Case No. ARB/06/3) 2.32.*n*53
R1 International Pte Ltd v Lonstroff AG [2014] SGHC 69; [2014] 3 SLR 166 . . . . . 5.42.*n*96, 12.10.*n*19,
                                                                                                     12.12.*n*25, 12.15.*n*33,
                                                                                                               12.19, 12.27
R1 International Pte Ltd v Lonstroff AG [2015] 1 SLR 521 . . . . .12.12.*n*24
Russian Federation v Everest Estate LLC et al., Gerechtshof, The Hague,
      Case No. 2019200.250.714-01, 11 June 2019 . . . . .16.70.*n*148

Sabmiller Africa BV v Tanzania Breweries Ltd [2009] EWHC 2140 . . . . .12.46.*n*90
Sai Wan Shipping Ltd v Landmark Line Co, Ltd [2022] SGHC 8 . . . . .16.154.*n*344
Sanum Investments Ltd v Government of the Lao People's Democratic Republic
      [2016] SGCA 57; [2016] 5 SLR 536 . . . . .1.43.*n*112, 9.11.*n*20, 9.25.*n*59, 16.100.*n*222
Sanum Investments Ltd v ST Group Co. Ltd, and ors [2020] 2 SLR 225;
      [2018] SGHC 141 . . . . 7.30.*n*63, 16.05.*n*11, 16.252.*n*563, 18.17.*n*23
Sanum Investments Ltd and another v Government of Lao People's Democratic
      Republic and others and another matter [2022] SGHC(I) 9 . . . . .16.150.*n*335
Sebastian Holdings Inc v Deutsche Bank AG [2010] 2 EWCA Civ 998 . . . . .7.29.*n*62
The Secretary of State for the Home Department v Raytheon Systems Ltd [2015]
      EWHC 311 (TCC) 16.67.*n*142
Seele Middle East Fze v Drake & Scull Int Sa Co [2013] EWHC 4350 (TCC) 12.46.*n*90
Seele Middle East Fze v Drake & Scull Int Sa Co [2014] EWHC 435 (TCC) 12.50.*n*96
Sembawang Engineering Pte Ltd v Priser Asia Engineering Pte Ltd [1992]
      2 SLR(R) 358 . . . . .11.25.*n*55
Sembawang Engineers and Constructors Pte Ltd v Covec (Singapore) Pte Ltd
      [2008] SGHC 229 . . . . 6.08.*n*16, 7.72.*n*170
Re Shankar Alan s/o Anant Kulkarni [2007] 1 SLR(R) 85 . . . . .16.328.*n*719
Siag and Vecchi v The Arab Republic of Egypt (ICSID Case No. ARB/05/15) 2.55.*n*106
Silica Investors v Tomolugen Holding Ltd and ors [2014] 3 SLR 815 . . . . .11.35.*n*64
Silverlink Resorts Ltd v MS First Capital Insurance Ltd [2020] SGHC 251 . . . . 5.16.*n*45, 7.37.*n*87

xxvi TABLE OF CASES

Sim Chay Koon v NTUC Income Insurance Co-operative Ltd [2016]
2 SLR 871 . . . . 7.20.*n*34, 7.89.*n*222

Sinclair Roche & Temperley, Jeff Morgan, Stuart Beadnall, Michael Stockwood,
Struan Robertson v Siân Heard, Siân Fellows [2004] 7 WLUK 669 . . . . .16.67.*n*144

Sinolanka Hotels & Spa (Private) Limited v Interna Contract SpA
[2018] SGHC 157 . . . . .9.23.*n*49

Skandinaviska Enskilda Banken AB (Publ), Singapore Branch v Asia Pacific Breweries
(Singapore) Pte Ltd and Other Appeals [2007] 2 SLR (R) 367 . . . . .2.50.*n*97

Sobati General Trading LLC v PT Multistrada Arahsarana [2010] 1 SLR 1065 . . . . .16.196.*n*443

Soh Beng Tee & Co Pte Ltd v Fairmount Development Pte Ltd [2007] SGCA 28;
[2007] 3 SLR(R) 86 . . . . 14.08.*n*16, 16.20.*n*40, 16.136.*n*304,
16.145.*n*329, 16.147.*n*332, 16.180.*n*404

Soleh Boneh International Ltd and anor v Government of Republic of Uganda and
National Housing Corporation [1993] 2 Lloyd's Rep 208 . . . . .18.35.*n*57

Soleimany v Soleimany [1999] QB 785 . . . . 16.293.*n*650, 16.295, 16.300

Solvadis Commodity Chemicals GmbH v Affert Resources Pte Ltd [2013] SGHC 217 . . . . . .12.03.*n*6

South American Silver Limited v Plurinational State of Bolivia
(PCA Case No. 2013-15) 2.46.*n*86, 2.47.*n*91

Splosna Plovba International Shipping and Chartering d o v Adria Orient Line
Pte Ltd [1998] SGHC 289 . . . . 7.10.*n*11, 7.65.*n*155

ST Group v Sanum Investments Limited [2020] 1 SLR 1 . . . . 16.11.*n*21, 16.231.*n*513, 16.232.*n*515,
16.241.*n*537, 16.251.*n*561, 16.252.*n*564,
16.263.*n*583, 16.268.*n*595

Starlight Shipping Co & Anor v Tai Ping Insurance Co Ltd, Hubei Branch & Anor
[2007] EWHC 1893 (Comm) 12.47.*n*91

Star-Trans Far East Pte Ltd v Norske-Tech Ltd [1996] SGCA 35; [1996] 2 SLR (R) 196. . . . . . .5.39.*n*85

The Stelios B, and Emilia Shipping Inc v State Enterprise for Pulp and Paper
Industries [1991] 1 SLR(R) 411 . . . . .12.43.*n*86

Strandore Invest A/ S v Soh Kim Wat [2010] SGHC 151 . . . . .9.58.*n*130

Sui Southern Gas Co Ltd v Habibullah Coastal Power Co (Pte) Ltd [2010] 3 SLR 1. . . . . . 16.195.*n*439,
16.196.*n*442, 16.277.*n*615

SulAmérica Cia Nacional de Seguros SA & others v Enesa Engenharia SA
[2012] EWCA Civ 638; [2013] 1 WLR 102; [2012] Lloyd's Rep 671
(England and Wales Court of Appeal) 5.06.*n*13, 5.07, 5.11, 9.31.*n*70, 12.66, 12.68, 12.72

Sun Travels & Tours Pvt Ltd v Hilton International Manage (Maldives) Pvt Ltd
[2019] 1 SLR 732. . . . . .12.20.*n*41

Sutcliffe v Thackrah [1974] AC 727 . . . . .17.02.*n*2

Swift-Fortune Ltd v Magnifica Marine SA [2006] 2 SLR(R) 323; [2006] SGHC 36 . . . . .9.53.*n*122

Swift-Fortune Ltd v Magnifica Marine SA [2006] SGCA 42; [2007] 1
SLR(R) 629 . . . . .1.28.*n*69, 9.53.*n*122, 11.04.*n*9, 12.04.*n*7, 12.16.*n*34,
12.19, 12.77, 12.79–12.80

Swiss Singapore Overseas Enterprises Pte Ltd v Exim Rajathi India Pvt Ltd [2010]
1 SLR 573. . . . . .16.87.*n*191, 16.88, 16.273.*n*605, 16.312.*n*685, 16.314, 16.317

Swissbourgh Diamond Mines (Pty) Ltd and others v Kingdom of Lesotho
[2019] 1 SLR 263; [2018] SGCA 81 . . . . 6.07.*n*12, 9.19.*n*41, 16.124.*n*285, 16.203

Tan Poh Leng Stanley v Tang Boon Jek Jeffrey [2000] 3 SLR(R) 847; [2000]
SGHC 260 . . . . 11.37.*n*72, 16.59.*n*124, 16.60, 16.74.*n*154

Tang Boon Jek Jeffrey v Tan Poh Leng Stanley [2001] 2 SLR(R) 273 . . . . .14.16

Tay Eng Chuan v United Overseas Insurance Ltd [2009] 4 SLR(R) 1043. . . . . .16.74.*n*154

TCL Air Conditioner (Zhongshan) Co Ltd v Castel Electronics Pty Ltd [2014]
FCAFC 83 . . . . .16.179.*n*402

Teck Guan Sdn Bhd v Beow guan Enterprises Pte Ltd [2003] SGHC 203;
[2003] 4 SLR(R) 276. . . . . .5.17.*n*46

The 'Titan Unity' [2014] SGHCR 4; [2013] SGHCR 28 ......5.43.n101, 6.06, 7.20.n34, 8.12, 9.11.n18
Thune v London Properties Ltd [1990] 1 All ER 972 ....11.25.n56
Tjong Very Sumito and others v Antig Investments Pte Ltd [2009]
    4 SLR(R) 732...1.01.n2, 7.02.n2, 7.14–7.16, 7.20, 7.57.n134,
                                            7.59–7.61, 7.74, 12.75.n134
TMM Division Maritima SA de CV v Pacific Richfield Marine Pte Ltd [2013]
    4 SLR 972........................16.175.n394, 16.192.n433, 16.193, 16.210, 16.215.n492,
                                                  16.328.n719, 16.330
TMT Co Ltd v The Royal Bank of Scotland plc (trading as RBS Greenwich Futures)
    and others [2018] 3 SLR 70; [2017] SGHC 21 ....5.15.n42, 7.74
Tomolugen Holdings Ltd v Silica Investors Ltd [2016] 1 SLR 373; [2015]
    SGCA 57 ....5.04.n9, 5.04.n11, 7.08.n10,
                     7.11.n12, 7.14–7.15, 7.18.n23, 7.19.n29, 7.21.n35, 7.34, 7.55.n131,
                     7.56, 7.61.n141, 7.77.n182, 7.78.n183, 7.81.n187, 7.89.n222,
                     10.01.n2, 10.03.n8, 10. 04.n10, 10.06.n14, 10.06.n16,
                     10.11.n20, 10.12.n23, 10.13.n26, 10.18.n36, 10.18.n38,
                     10.18.n40, 10.20.n44, 10.21, 10.23,
Torkington v Magee [1902] 2 KB 427......................................12.39.n70
Transfield Philippines, Inc. v Luzon Hydro Corporation [2002] VSC 215 ....12.76.n136
Transocean Offshore International Ventures Ltd v Burgundy Global
    Exploration Corp [2010] 2 SLR 821 .... 5.16.n45, 7.30–7.31, 7.33, 7.38
Travelport Global Distribution Systems BV v Bellview Airlines Ltd, 2012 WL 3925856......5.15.n43
Triulzi Cesare SRL v Xinyi Group (Glass) Co Ltd [2015] 1 SLR 114; [2014]
    SGHC 220 ....16.41.n80, 16.132.n296,
            16.135.n301, 16.140.n312, 16.145.n329, 16.158, 16.174.n391,
            16.220.n500, 16.221.n502, 16.222.n504, 16.241.n536,
            16.243.n542, 16.244, 16.253.n565, 16.256,
            16.261.n578, 16.267
Turf Club Auto Emporium Pte Ltd v Yeo Boong Hua [2018] 2 SLR 655 ....12.28.n52
Turner (East Asia) Pte Ltd v Builders Federal (HK) Ltd [1988] 1 SLR(R) 281...............2.24.n33
Turner (East Asia) Pte Ltd v Builders Federal (Hong Kong) Ltd & Anor (No 2) [1988]
    1 SLR(R) 483..16.237.n523
TW Thomas & Co., Limited v Portsea Steamship Co, Limited [1912] AC 1 (HL).....5.39.n86, 5.43.n100
Twarit Consultancy Services Pte Ltd and another v GPE (India) Ltd and others
    [2022] 3 SLR 211...16.272.n601

U&M Mining Zambia Ltd v Konkola Copper Mines plc [2013] 2 Lloyd's Rep 218 ....12.32.n61
UBS AG v HSH Nordbank AG [2009] 2 Lloyd's Rep 272.......................7.29.n62, 7.31.n68
Union des consommateurs v Dell Computer Corp [2007] 2 SCR 801 ....7.19.n26
Ursem v Chung [2014] NZHC 436...7.19.n28

Re Vanguard Energy Pte Ltd [2015] SGHC 156 ....2.37.n62
The 'Vasiliy Golovnin' [2007] 4 SLR 277 ....14.33.n70
Vitol Asia Pte Ltd v Machlogic Singapore Pte Ltd [2020] SGHC 209................ 5.31, 18.17.n23
Vitol Asia Pte Ltd v Machlogic Singapore Pte Ltd [2021] 4 SLR 464 ....16.05.n11, 16.101.n225,
                     16.116.n265, 16.127, 16.309.n678
VTB Commodities Trading DAC v JSC Antipinsky Refinery [2020] EWHC 72 (Comm) ...12.45.n88
VV and another v VW [2008] 2 SLR(R) 929 ....16.277.n614, 16.284.n631

W v P [2016] HKCFI 316...14.17.n 37
Wall v The Royal Bank of Scotland Plc [2016] EWHC 2460 (Comm) 2.50.n98
West Tankers [2007] 1 Lloyd's Rep 391 ....12.25.n50
Westacre Investments Inc v Jugoimport-SPDR Holding Co Ltd and others
    [1999] QB 740...16.292, 16.304.n675

xxviii TABLE OF CASES

Westacre Investments Inc. v Jugoimport-SPDR Holding Co. Ltd. and Others
[2000] QB 288 . . . . 16.292.*n*647, 16.292.*nn*648–649, 16.294, 16.304.*n*675
Westbridge Ventures II Investment Holdings v Anupam Mittal [2021] SGHC 244 . . . . 10.03.*n*9,
16.86.*n*183
Westwood Shipping Lines Inc and another v Universal Schiffahrtsgesellschaft
MBH and another [2012] EWHC 3837 (Comm) 2.64.*n*141
Wilson Taylor Asia Pacific Pte Ltd v Dyna-Jet Pte Ltd [2017] 3 SLR 267; [2016]
SGHC 238 . . . . .5.23.*n*62, 7.15.*n*17, 7.70.*n*166, 7.72.*n*171, 7.73.*n*173, 7.76.*n*180
Wilson Taylor Asia Pacific Pte Ltd v Dyna-Jet Pte Ltd [2017] 2 SLR 362 . . . . 7.15.*n*19, 7.19
Winterthur Swiss Insurance Co & Anor v AG (Manchester) Ltd & Ors [2006]
EWHC 839 . . . . .2.51.*n*100
Wishing Star Ltd v Jurong Town Corp [2004] 1 SLR(R) 1 . . . . .11.10.*n*14
Re Wordsworth, Samuel Sherratt QC [2016] 5 SLR 179 . . . . .2.25.*n*40
WSG Nimbus Pte Ltd v Board of Control for Cricket in Sri Lanka [2002] SGHC 104;
[2002] 1 SLR(R) 1088. . . . . 5.22.*n*58, 9.51.*n*115

The Xanadu [1997] 3 SLR(R) 360 . . . . .7.66.*n*157
Xiamen Xinjingdi Group Co Ltd v Eton Properties Limited and Others [2020]
HKCFA 32. . . . . 14.05.*n*9, 18.12.*n*12

York International Pte Ltd v Voltas Ltd [2022] SGHC 153. . . . . 14.28.*nn*60–62
Yukos Capital v OJSC Rosneft Oil Co. [2012] EWCA Civ 855 . . . . .18.24.*n*33

ZCCM Investment Holdings Plc v Kansanshi Holdings Plc and another
[2019] EWHC 1285 (Comm) 14.28.*n*61
Zhong Da Chemical Development Co Ltd v Lanco Industries Pte Ltd
[2009] 3 SLR(R) 1017. . . . . 11.08.*n*13, 11.10.*n*15, 11.27.*n*58
Zurich Insurance (Singapore) Pte Ltd v B-Gold Interior Design & Construction
Pte Ltd [2008] SGCA 27. . . . . .5.41.*n*90

Table of Legislation

SINGAPORE

Statutes

Arbitration Act 1953 . . . . .1.12, 1.13
  s 20 . . . . 14.12
Arbitration Act 1987
  s 14 . . . . 15.59
Arbitration Act 1994 . . . . .1.12
Arbitration Act 2001 . . . . 6.15, 12.07, 12.59
  s 2
    (1). 2.27, 2.44.n81
  s 3 . . . . .1.19.n44
  s 30 . . . . 15.59, 12.60, 12.66
  s 48 . . . . 16.21
  s 49 . . . . . 1.20.n50, 16.02.n2, 16.22.n42, 16.39
    (2). 16.39.n75
Arbitration (Foreign Awards) Act 1986
       (No. 24 of 1986). 1.14, 1.18,
                                18.03.n3
Arbitration (International Investment
       Disputes) Act 1968 . . . . . .9.63n.141
Arbitration Ordinance 1809 . . . . .1.12
Bills of Exchange Act (Cap. 23,
       2004 Rev. Ed.)
  s 47 . . . . .7.64.n150
  s 57 . . . . .7.64.n150
  s 92 . . . . .7.64.n150
  s 97 . . . . .7.64.n150
Civil Law Act 1909 . . . . .2.39
  s 4(10) 12.04, 12.05.n11, 12.14–12.16,
           12.19, 12.23, 12.26–12.27, 12.79
Civil Law (Amendment) Act 2017 . . . 1.34, 2.38,
                                  2.47
  s 5A
    (1). 2.38.n65
    (2). 2.38.n66
  s 5B. 2.39–2.40
    (2). 2.38.n67
    (10) 2.39.n70, 2.40.n27
Civil Law Ordinance 1878 . . . . 12.26
Companies Act (Cap 50, 2006 Rev. Ed.)
  s 131 . . . . .7.53
    (1). 10.13
  s 216 . . . . 10.17–10.19, 10.22
    (1). 10.17.n35
    (2)
      (a) 10.19

    (d) 11.36
    (f). 11.36
  s 272(2)(c) 2.37
Courts (Civil and Criminal Justice) Reform
       Act No. 24 of 2021. . . . . . . .15.02.n1
Courts (Civil and Criminal Justice)
       Reform Amendment
       Act No. 25 of 2021. . . . . . . .15.05.n4
Evidence Act (Cap. 97)
  Pt II. 9.27
  ss 93–102 . . . . .9.26.n61
Intellectual Property (Dispute Resolution)
       Act 2019 .1.33
Interpretation Act 1965 (Cap 1)
  s 5 . . . . .6.05.n8
  s 9A. 6.05
  Sch 1 . . . . .6.05.n8
International Arbitration Act 1994
       (Cap 143A) 1.16, 1.20, 2.01,
                          3.01, 3.11, 6.15
  Preamble 13.11
  Pt II (ss 2–26) . . . . 1.18–1.19, 1.23–1.25, 1.26.
        n66, 4.01, 4.04, 4.11, 6.08, 12.02,
               12.07, 12.74, 12.80,
           13.02–13.02, 13.04–13.05,
         13.07–13.08, 14.11, 16.253, 18.07
  s 2 . . . . .4.01, 5.01, 8.01, 18.08
    (1). 2.27, 2.44.n81, 4.02, 4.05–4.07,
                   4.09–4.10, 5.22,
               8.03.n4, 9.13, 16.08
    (2). 4.11, 6.03.n5, 14.18
  s 2A. 4.09.n16, 5.01–5.02, 5.22, 7.28.n61,
                   16.115, 18.03
    (1). 5.18, 5.24, 18.03.n4
    (2). 5.25
    (3). 5.26–5.28
    (4)–(7) 5.26
    (4). 5.27
    (5). 5.28–5.29
    (6). 5.30–5.35, 5.40, 16.127
    (7). 5.36–5.37
    (8). 5.43
    (9). 5.01, 6.03.n5
    (10) 5.29
  s 2B. 13.18.n23
    (1). 13.18.n24
  s 3 . . . . .1.18, 10.07

XXX   TABLE OF LEGISLATION

(1)....6.03–6.04
(2)....6.04, 16.269.n597, 16.273.n604
s 4....6.05–6.06
s 5....1.19.n44, 12.02, 12.07, 12.74, 14.11
(1)....1.19, 6.08, 12.74
(2)....6.03.n5, 6.09, 6.16, 12.74
(a)....6.10–6.11, fig 6.1
(b)
(i)....6.12, fig 6.1
(ii)....6.13, fig 6.1
(c)....6.14, fig 6.1
(3)....6.13
(4)....6.15
s 6....4.10, 5.05, 5.15.n5.24, 7.01–7.03,
7.12, 7.15, 7.20, 7.23, 7.31–7.32,
7.34, 7.43, 7.45, 7.81–7.82, 10.10
(1)....6.03.n6, 7.03, 7.08–7.09, 7.28–7.29,
7.35, 7.40–7.42, 7.44–7.45, 7.49
(2)....5.04.n10, 7.03, 7.05,
7.07–7.08, 7.10–7.11, 7.13–7.16,
7.21, 7.56–7.57, 7.65–7.66,
7.69–7.70, 7.74, 10.03
(3)–(5)....7.03
(3)....7.65
(5)....4.10, 7.04, 7.41–7.42
s 7....4.10
s 8
(2)....2.05, 8.03.n4
(3)....4.05
s 9....8.01–8.02, 13.08
s 9A....8.01–8.03, 13.08
(1)....8.03–8.05
(2)....8.03
s 9B....1.30, 8.06–8.07, 8.10–8.13
(1)
(a)....8.07.n11
(b)....8.07.n12
(c)....8.07.n13
(2)....8.08.n14
(3)....8.08.n15, 8.09.n17
(4)....8.08.n16
s 10....9.01–9.04, 9.07, 9.13–9.15, 9.19–9.21,
9.24, 9.26, 9.33, 9.47.n109, 16.13, 16.94
(1)....9.01.n1, 9.03, 9.21
(2)....9.07.n10, 9.11
(3)....9.07.nn10–11, 9.10–9.12, 9.14–9.15,
9.23, 9.25, 9.31–9.32, 9.38
(a)....9.19
(b)....9.07.n11, 9.19
(4)....9.08–9.09
(6)....9.08
(7)....9.33, 9.35
(9)....9.40.n93
(a)....9.36

s 11....10.01
(1)....10.01, 10.10
(2)....10.01
s 11A....4.10
s 12....4.04, 4.07–4.08, 11.01–11.02, 11.04,
11.06, 11.08, 11.15, 11.37–11.38,
11.43, 12.01, 12.77, 12.80,
14.18, 14.21
(1)....11.05, 11.06.n11
(a)....11.07, 11.24, 11.26
(b)....11.13
(c)–(i)....12.13, 12.37
(c)–(j)....12.08, 18.07
(c)....11.13, 12.02, 12.77
(d)....11.15, 12.02, 12.42.n76
(e)....9.56, 11.43.n94, 12.02
(f)....9.56, 11.43.n94, 12.02
(g)....11.17–11.18, 11.20, 12.02
(h)....12.02
(i)....4.07.n12, 11.06, 11.40, 12.02, 12.14
(3)....11.22
(4)....11.07, 11.11–11.12, 11.24, 11.26
(5)....11.28, 11.35–11.36
(a)....11.33–11.37, 15.01
(b)....11.38
(6)....4.04, 4.08, 11.40, 11.42–11.43
(a)....11.26n.57
(b)....11.26n.57
(7)....11.04, 12.04, 12.52, 12.77
s 12A....11.04, 11.15, 11.42, 12.01,
12.03–12.04, 12.34, 12.40,
12.52, 12.55, 12.61, 12.75,
12.77, 12.79, 15.06
(1)....12.02, 12.07, 12.30
(2)....12.02, 12.04, 12.08–12.09,
12.13–12.14
(3)....12.02, 12.06, 12.30–12.32
(4)–(6)....12.02, 12.33, 12.55
(4)....11.15, 12.13, 12.33–12.35, 12.37,
12.39, 12.41–12.42, 12.44
(5)....12.44–12.45
(6)....12.36, 12.46
(7)....12.02, 12.57
s 13....12.58–12.62, 12.66, 12.73–12.78
(1)....12.63, 12.72
(2)....12.63, 12.72
(3)....12.71–12.72
(4)....12.72
s 15....1.19, 1.22–1.26, 13.01–13.03
(2)....13.04, 16.31
s 15A....1.26, 13.05, 13.07, 13.09
(1)....13.07, 16.220.n501
(3)....13.018
(4)....13.08

TABLE OF LEGISLATION xxxi

(5). 13.08
(6). 13.08
(7). 13.06
s 16 . . . . 1.18, 13.10, 13.12
(1). 13.14
(2). 13.14
(3). 13.12, 16.227
(a) 13.15, 13.18.n25
(b) 13.16
(4). 13.17
(5). 13.10
s 17 . . . . . 1.18, 3.01, 13.10, 13.12, 13.18, 13.21
(1). 13.18
(2). 13.19
(3). 13.20
(4). 13.21
s 18 . . . . 9.51, 13.10.n10, 14.01, 14.04
(a). 14.06
s 19 . . . . .6.01, 6.06.n11, 9.51, 14.11–14.15,
14.33, 16.02, 16.09, 16.116.n265,
16.126, 18.01, 18.09–18.10, 18.13
s 19A 13.08, 14.08.n17, 14.16–14.19
s 19B. 14.16, 14.26–14.27, 14.30, 14.32
(2). 14.28
(4). 14.30
s 19C. .14.34–14.35
(4)(a) 14.35
s 20 . . . . .11.38, 13.08, 14.36–14.38, 14.41
(1). 11.38, 14.38
(a) 14.37
(3). 14.43
s 21 . . . . .15.02, 15.04
(2). 15.03.n2
(3). 15.04.n3
s 22 . . . . 1.18, 2.57.n113, 1505
s 23 . . . . 1.18, 2.57.n113, 15.06
(1). 15.07.n5
(2). 15.07.n5
(3). 15.07.n6
(4). 15.08.n7
s 24 . . . . . 1.20.nn47–48, 1.41.n106, 9.13, 9.15,
11.09, 16.01–16.02, 16.04–16.07,
16.13, 16.20–16.21, 16.30–16.31,
16.33, 16.43–16.45, 16.86–16.87,
16.146, 18.17–18.18
(a). 16.06, 16.36, 16.273, 16.307,
16.315.n693, 16.316, 16.325
(b) 11.22, 16.05.n11, 16.06.n13,
16.23, 16.36, 16.132–16.133, 16.136,
16.143, 16.145, 16.208, 16.218, 16.257,
16.273, 16.310–16.311, 16.314,
16.326–16.327, 18.17.n23
s 25 . . . . .1.18, 17.01, 17.04–17.05, 17.08
(a). 17.02, 17.04

(b) 17.03–17.04
s 25A 17.08, 17.10
(1). 17.09
(2). 17.09
(3). 17.09
Pt IIA (ss 26A–26G). 10.12.n22
s 26A 10.12.n22
s 26B(3) 10.12.n22
Pt III (ss 27–33) 1.18, 4.01, 6.01, 14.11,
18.01, 18.03–18.06,
18.20, 18.37
s 27 . . . . 14.11, 18.04, 18.08
(1). 18.03, 18.05, 18.07, 18.08
s 28 . . . . 18.04
(1). 18.06
(2). 18.06
s 29 . . . . 9.51, 16.09, 18.09
(1). 18.09, 18.11
(2). 18.09
s 30(1) 18.10
s 31 . . . . .1.20.n48, 16.02, 18.14, 18.32
(1). 18.14
(2). 18.10, 18.14, 18.17
(b) 16.113
(c) 18.30
(e) 16.262
(f). 16.68, 16.70, 18.18–18.19,
18.26, 18.28
(3). 18.14, 18.18, 18.29
(4). 18.10, 18.14, 18.17
(a) 10.03.n7, 10.07
(5). 16.68.n146, 18.14, 18.18, 18.31,
18.33, 18.35–18.36
(a) 18.32
s 33
(1). 18.37
(2). 18.38, 18.40
(3). 18.39
Pt IV (ss 34–35) 1.18
Sch 1. . . . . 1.18, 6.01.n1
Sch 2. . . . . 16.68
International Arbitration (Amendment) Act
2001 (No. 38 of 2001) 4.06.n.8,
11.04.n7, 14.16
s 13 . . . . .13.11.n15
International Arbitration
(Amendment) Act 2002
(No. 28 of 2002)
s 3 . . . . 13.05
International Arbitration
(Amendment) Act 2009
(No. 26 of 2009). . . . . .4.06.
n8, 5.01, 11.04.n10,
12.01, 12.06–12.07

xxxii TABLE OF LEGISLATION

International Arbitration
(Amendment) Act 2012
(No. 12 of 2012)........5.01, 14.36
s 2
(a)................... 4.02.n2, 4.04.n4
(b) 4.07.n11
s 2A..........................1.29, 4.06
s 6 ....12.60n.111
International Arbitration (Amendment)
Act 2020 (No. 32 of 2020).....1.30,
12.08.n18
s 7
(1)...........................8.06.n9
(3)...........................8.06.n9
s 12A 2.57.n114
(2)............... 1.31.n79, 2.57.n114
s 2B............................1.29
s 12(1)(j) 1.31, 2.57.n114
Legal Profession Act 1966
(2020 Rev. Ed.) 2.21–2.22, 2.24,
2.42, 2.44, 2.47
s 15 .... 2.22–2.23, 2.25, 2.27, 16.112.n255
s 32 ....2.21.n30
s 33 ....2.21.n30
s 35 ....2.21, 2.28
(1).............................2.21
(2).............................2.21
s 36P............................2.25
s 36O 2.25.n38
s 107(1) 2.42.n77
ss 115A–115F....................2.42.n76
Legal Profession (Amendment) Act 1992
s 2 ....2.24.n35
Legal Profession (Amendment) Act 2004
s 35 ....2.24.n36
Prisons Act (Cap. 247)
s 38 .... 12.71
Reciprocal Enforcement of Commonwealth
Judgments Act 1921
(the RECJA)............... 18.38
s 2(1) 18.39
s 3 .... 18.38
Sch 18.40
Reciprocal Enforcement of
Commonwealth Judgments
(Repeal) Act 2019 .... 18.40
Reciprocal Enforcement of Foreign
Judgments (Amendment)
Act 2019..............18.40.n66
State Immunity Act 1979
s 14..............................9.63
Statutes (Miscellaneous Amendments)
(No. 2) Act 2005
Sch 5........................12.60.n111

Rules/ Regulations

Civil Law (Third Party Funding)
Regulations 2017........1.34, 2.40
reg 3 ....2.39
reg 4(1)(a) 2.40.n73
(b) 2.40.n74
Civil Law (Third-Party Funding)
(Amendment)
Regulations 2021.............2.39
Legal Profession (Professional Conduct)
Rules 2015 ....2.27–2.30
r 2 .... 2.27, 2.44.n81
r 3 ....2.27.n41
r 9 ....2.27
r 10 ....2.27
r 11 ....2.27
r 12.............................2.27
Legal Profession (Professional Conduct)
Rules 2017 ....2.44
r 18..........................2.42.n77
r 49A 2.44
(2)..........................2.44.n79
r 49B.........................2.41.n75
Legal Profession (Representation in
Singapore International
Commercial Court)
Rules 2014 ....2.44
r 2 ....2.25.n38
Sch 1, paras 4A and 4B............2.44.n82
Singapore International commercial
Court Rules 2021
(SICC Rules)
Ord 3
r 1..........................16.112.n1
(1)(d)..................16.112.n256
Supreme Court's Rules of Court 1970
RSC Ord 29
r 4.........................12.43.n86
Supreme Court's Rules of Court 2014 .... 11.25
RSC Ord 11 (now Ord 8)..............9.55
r 1.............................9.54
r 2.............................9.54
RSC Ord 69
r 3.........................16.04.n3
RSC Ord 69A (now Ord 48) 9.45
r 2.......................... 16.97
(1) 16.45, 16.48
(4) 16.44
(4A)(c) 16.96
r 4.............................9.55
r 5(2) 11.43
r 6.............................9.58
RSC Ord 28
r 4(3) (now Ord 15 r 7(6)) 9.48

Supreme Court's Rules of Court
2021 .... 3.11, 9.54, 11.25
RSC Ord 8 .... 9.55
  r 1 .... 9.55
  r 2 .... 9.63
  r 3 .... 9.63
  r 7 .... 9.63
  r 8 .... 9.63
RSC Ord 15
  r 4 .... 12.62
  (10)–(12) 12.71
RSC Ord 23 .... 11.09–11.10
  r 1(a) 11.25.n52
RSC Ord 40A
  r 2 .... 16.111
  r 3 .... 16.111
RSC Ord 48 .... 9.58, 12.62
  r 2 .... 16.97
  (1) 9.44–9.45
  (d) 9.45–9.46
  (3) 9.44, 16.43, 16.45, 16.48
  (4) 9.44–9.46
  (c) 16.96
  r 3 .... 9.50
  (1) 9.49
  (2) 9.50
  (3) 9.51
  r 4 .... 9.52
  (2) 9.52
  r 5 .... 9.56
  (2) 11.43
  r 6 .... 9.56, 14.13, 18.10
  (1) 9.57, 9.60
  (2) 9.57
  (3) 9.60
  (4) 9.63
  (5) 9.60
  r 7 .... 12.62
RSC Ord 110
  r 1(1) 2.25
  r 25(1) 16.112

Orders

International Arbitration (Appointed
        Persons under Section 19C)
        Order 2009 (Cap. 143A,
        S 651/2009) 1.33, 14.34.n72
International Arbitration (Appointed
        Persons under Section 19C)
        Order 2010 (GN No
        S 738/ 2010) 1.33, 14.35.n72
International Arbitration (New York
        Convention Countries)
        Order (Cap. 143A, OR 1) 1.33

OTHER
NATIONAL LEGISLATION

Australia

International Arbitration Act 1974 (Cth)
  s 19 .... 16.06.n13
  s 23C 2.57.n112

Austria

Code of Civil Procedure (ZPO)
  s 594(3) 2.20.n26

Belgium

Judicial Code
  Art 1694(4) 2.20.n26
  Art 1718 .... 16.34.n64

Canada

Uniform Arbitration Act in 2016 ..... 16.35.n67
Ontario International Commercial
        Arbitration Act 2017 .... 16.35.n67

China

Arbitration Law of the People's Republic
        of China
  Art 16 .... 2.06n.1
  Art 19 .... 5.03.n6

Egypt

Arbitration Law
  Art 54(1) 16.34.n64

FIJI

International Arbitration Act 2017
  s 55(1) 16.06.n13

FRANCE

Civil Code (2011 revision)
  Art 144 .... 5.03.n6
Civil Procedure Code
  Art 1501 .... 18.28.n46
  Art 1502 .... 18.22, 18.28.n46
  Art 1504 .... 18.28.n46
  Art 1506 .... 18.28.n46
  Art 1522 .... 16.34.n65
  Art 1526 .... 18.28.n46

Hong Kong

Arbitration Ordinance 2013 .... 14.37, 17.05

xxxiv TABLE OF LEGISLATION

s 18 ....2.57.n112
s 33(4)(b)......................13.20.n32
s 34 ....5.03
s 66
  (1)............................14.07.n15
  (2)............................ 14.07
s 67(1) 14.07.n15
s 71 .... 14.17
s 79 ....14.37.n75
  (3)............................14.37.n76
s 80 ....14.37.n75
s 99 ....16.26.n52
s 104 ....17.05.n14
  (2)............................17.05.n15
s 105(1) 17.10
Sch 2, s 5.......................16.26.n52

India

Advocates Act 1961
  s 1961..........................2.21.n30

Italy

Code of Civil Procedure
  Art 829(1) 16.34.n64

Japan

Arbitration Law
  Art 13(6) 5.03.n6

Netherlands

Arbitration Act
  Art 1065(6) 16.214.n488

New Zealand

Arbitration Act 1996
  s 12............................ 11.35
  s 13........................17.01.n1, 17.02
  s 34(6) 16.06.n13
  Sch 2, s 5.......................16.26.n52
Draft Arbitration Act
  Cl 11............................ 17.02
  s 36(3) 16.06

Portugal

Law on Voluntary Arbitration 2011
  Art 46(5) 16.34.n64

Sweden

Arbitration Act
  s 51 ....16.34.n64

Switzerland

Private International Law Act
  Art 180......................16.334n.733
  Art 192(1) 16.34.n64

United Kingdom

Access to Justice Act 1999 ....2.42.n78
Arbitration Act 1950 .... 16.04
  s 41 ....7.43
  s 26............................. 14.12
Arbitration Act 1996 ....5.10, 6.07, 8.13,
             11.06.n11, 14.37, 17.05
  s 2(3) 12.32
  s 7.............................5.03.n6
  s 9(3) 7.43
  s 24(1)(a) 16.334n.733
  s 29
    (1)............................17.05.n12
    (2)............................17.05.n13
  s 32 ....9.08
    (1)............................9.40.n93
    (4)............................9.40.n93
  s 36 ....2.20.n26
  s 44 .... 12.01, 12.15, 12.32, 12.50–12.51,
                12.53, 12.55
    (3)............................12.39, 12.50
    (4)............................ 12.45
    (5)............12.46, 12.48, 12.50, 12.53
    (6)............................ 12.57
  s 47 .... 14.17
  s 49 ....14.37.n75
    (5)............................14.37.n76
  s 51
    (2)............................ 14.07
    (3)............................ 14.07
  s 58 .... 14.32
  s 59(1)(c) 2.55
  s 63.............................2.53
  s 67 .... 9.08, 16.56.n121, 16.101–16.102
  s 68
    (2)............................ 16.56
    (3)............................16.56–16.67
  s 69 .... 16.26
    (2)............................16.26.n51
    (3)............................16.26.n51
  s 70(2)(b)....................16.214.n488
  s 74 .... 17.08
  s 103.2(f) 16.69–16.70
  s 103.5 .... 18.35
Civil Judgments and Jurisdictions
      Act 1892
  s 25...................... 12.06.n17, 12.32
    (2)............................12.32.n59

Civil Procedure Rules
r 32 .... 16.103
Criminal Law Act 1967 ....2.35
  s 13(1) 2.35.n57
  s 14(1) 2.35.n57
Damages- Based Agreements
        Regulations 2013.........2.42.n78
Legal Aid, Sentencing and Punishment of
        Offenders Act 2012
  s 45 ....2.42.n78
Senior Courts Act 1981 .... 12.15
  s 37 .... 12.15
  (1).........................12.23, 12.25
  s 50 .... 12.29
Supreme Court of Judicature Act 1873
        (SCJA) 3.11
  s 18 ....12.21, 12.29
  (2)............. 12.16, 12.19, 12.28–12.29
  s 23 ....12.24.n48
  s 25(8) 12.23, 12.26–12.27
  Sch 1, para 14 12.16, 12.19, 12.21, 12.28–12.29

INTERNATIONAL TREATIES, CONVENTIONS AND OTHER INSTRUMENTS

Chartered Institute of Arbitrators (CIArb)
        Protocol for the Use of Party-
        Appointed Expert Witnesses in
        International Arbitration.... 13.06
China- Laos Bilateral Investment Treaty
        (BIT) to Macau 1.43
Convention on the Recognition and
        Enforcement of Foreign
        Arbitral Awards New York, 10
        June 1958 .... 1.04, 1.05, 1.10, 1.14,
        1.16, 1.18, 1.36, 2.48, 3.03, 6.02,
        7.70–7.71, 10.01, 14.11–14.12,
        16.05, 16.304–16.305,
        18.01, 18.06, 18.27
  Art I
    (2)............................ 18.03
    (3)............................ 18.05
  Art II 5.04.n10, 16.90, 17.06
    (1)............ 1.04.n10, 2.19, 5.26, 18.03
    (2)............................ 18.03
    (3).................... 2.19, 7.16, 7.69
  Art V ....1.04.n10, 16.19, 16.69, 18.02, 18.22.
        n27, 18.25, 18.30
    (1)............................ 16.86
    (a) 16.89–16.90, 16.108
    (b) 2.19, 16.128, 16.221
    (c) 16.208.n 472, 18.30
    (d) 8.12.n24

  (e) 16.02.n1, 16.12, 16.68,
        18.19–18.20, 18.26, 18.28
  (2)............................ 16.86
    (a) 10.07
  Art VI............................ 18.31
  Art VII.......................... 18.22
Convention on the Use of Electronic
        Communications in
        International Contracts 2005
  Art 4............................5.29
  Art 9(2) 5.28
Geneva Convention 1927 .... 1.04.n8, 18.27
Geneva Protocol 1923 ....1.04.n8
Hague Convention for the Pacific Settlement
        of Disputes 1899 ..... 1.04.n8, 2.10
Hague Convention for the Pacific
        Settlement of International
        Disputes 1907 ....1.04.n8
International Centre for Settlement of
        Investment Disputes by
        Convention 1.42
Montevideo Convention 1889 ....1.04.n8
UN Convention on Contracts for the
        International Sale of Goods....6.10
UNCITRAL Model Law on International
        Commercial Arbitration
        1985 .... 1.05, 1.13, 1.15–1.20,
        1.23, 1.27, 1.36, 4.09, 4.11,
        6.01, 6.07, 7.70, 8.01,
        13.12, 17.01
  Ch III 1.18
  Ch VIII 6.01–6.02
  Art 1
    (1)..........................6.03.n6
    (2)................. 6.04, 12.78, 16.02
    (3)................6.03.n5, 6.09, 6.11
    (a) 6.11
  Art 4................. 16.33, 16.260, 16.263
  Art 5................ 12.21, 16.02.n4, 16.17
  Art 7............ 4.06, 5.01, 5.22.n58, 5.25,
        6.03.n5, 16.115
    (2)............................5.40
  Art 8.......5.04.n10, 6.03.n5, 6.04, 7.02, 7.09
    (1)............................7.69
  Art 9............................6.04
  Art 11............................8.10
    (2)............................8.04
    (3)............................8.02
    (5)........................... 16.224
  Art 12......................16.334.n733
    (2).....................16.224, 16.235
  Art 13................. 16.16–16.17, 16.266
    (1)........................... 16.236
    (2)........................... 16.236

TABLE OF LEGISLATION

(3)................16.16–16.17, 16.236
Art 16...7.17, 9.04–9.05, 9.16, 9.18, 9.20–9.21
(1)...................5.03, 16.116.n264
(2)..............................5.35
(3)..............9.01, 9.03–9.04, 9.09,
9.14–9.15, 9.17–9.18,
9.23, 9.36, 16.13, 16.15,
16.94, 16.174
Art 17.............. 11.01.n1, 11.03, 11.41
Art 18........ 6.06, 11.14, 11.22, 16.05.n11,
16.35, 16.134–16.136, 16.183,
16.221–16.222, 16.254–16.255,
16.257, 18.17.n23
Art 19........... 2.03, 16.220.n501, 16.253
(2)............................. 16.222
Art 24(1) 16.162
Art 27........................... 12.78
Art 28.....................11.28–11.29
(2)............................. 11.30
(3)............................. 11.32
(4)............................. 11.32
Art 30........14.01–14.03, 14.06.n12, 14.07
(1)............................. 14.06
(2).....................14.04, 14.06
Art 31............. 14.06–14.07, 18.01.n1
(2)....................14.06, 16.175
Art 32(3) 16.53
Art 33...... 14.08, 14.16, 14.26, 16.42, 16.49,
16.71, 16.74
(1).............. 16.71.n149, 16.72.n150
(a) 16.70.n147, 16.75
(b) 16.70.n147, 16.76.n159, 16.77
(2)............................. 16.71
(3)..............16.71.n149, 16.72.n150,
16.79–16.80, 16.212–16.214, 18.29
(4).......................16.72.n151
Art 34.......1.41.n106, 9.15, 9.18–9.19, 9.34,
16.01–16.02, 16.04–16.07, 16.13,
16.15–16.16, 16.18–16.19, 16.21–16.22,
16.30–16.31, 16.33, 16.35, 16.43, 16.48,
16.60, 16.86, 16.207, 18.17–18.18
(1)................. 16.02, 16.19, 16.21
(2)................ 16.40, 16.45, 16.219
(a) 16.35–16.36, 16.86–16.87
(i)................16.05.n11, 16.60,
16.89–16.90, 16.92, 16.94,
16.108–16.110, 16.114,
16.116.n265, 16.120–16.121,
16.123–16.124, 16.126–16.127,
16.203, 18.17.n23
(ii) ... 16.05.n11, 16.41, 16.128–16.129,
16.131–16.134, 16.136,
16.145–16.146, 16.208, 16.218,
16.257, 16.310, 16.326–16.327,
18.17.n23

(iii) 1.41.n106, 16.60, 16.120,
16.123–16.24, 16.184,
16.186–16.187, 16.193,
16.195, 16.203–16.204,
16.207–16.208, 16.215–16.216
(iv).........16.05.n11, 16.17, 16.41,
16.132–16.133, 16.220–16.224,
16.227–16.228, 16.235, 16.238,
16.240, 16.244–16.246,
16.253–16.254, 16.258, 16.261,
16.267–16.268, 16.327, 18.17.n23
(b) 16.35–16.36, 16.86–16.87
(i)..................10.03.n7, 10.07,
16.269–16.271, 16.273
(ii) 16.45, 16.273.n604, 16.291,
16.273, 16.300–16.301,
16.307, 16.310
(3)........9.44, 16.42–16.45, 16.47, 16.49
(4)....14.08, 14.16, 14.26, 16.50–16.60, 16.67
Art 35.................... 1.18, 6.01, 6.04
Art 36.......... 1.18, 6.01, 6.04, 9.18–9.19,
16.70.n147
(1)............................. 14.15
(a)
(i)............. 16.05.n11, 18.17.n23
(ii) 16.05.n11, 18.17.n23
(iv)........... 16.05.n11, 18.17.n23
(v) 16.68.n146
UNCITRAL Model Law on International
Commercial Arbitration
2006 .... 4.09, 11.01.n1
Art 7, Option 1 4.06, 4.09.n16, 5.01, 5.26, 5.30
Art 17J 12.01, 12.55.n108
United Nations Convention on
International Settlement
Agreements Resulting
from Mediation.........1.35, 3.03
UNGA Resolution 31/ 98, UNCITRAL
Arbitration Rules 2.09
Vienna Convention on the Law of Treaties
Art 31(3) 1.43

ARBITRATION RULES

Arbitration Foundation of Southern
Africa (AFSA)
r 30 ....2.46
IBA Guidelines on Conflicts of Interest in
International Arbitration (2014)
General Standard 3(a), 3(d) 13.20.n31
IBA Rules on the Taking of Evidence in
International Arbitration
2010 ....11.14, 12.67, 12.70,
13.02, 13.06
r 9.2(b) 2.48.n94

TABLE OF LEGISLATION xxxvii

ICC Arbitration Rules 2021.....1.23, 2.60, 5.14,
7.68, 8.04–8.05, 13.06,
16.31, 16.225, 16.244
Art 3.........................16.130.n295
Art 6(8) 16.172.n386
Art 10...........................1.11.n25
Art 12...........................8.01.n2
  (5)..................... 8.04.n6, 8.05.n7
  (6)........................8.12.n23
Art 13(5) 16.225.n507
Art 22.......................16.244n.547
  (3)..........................2.60.n125
Art 31...........................2.55
Art 35(6) 16.39.n74
Art 36.......................16.77.n160
Art 40.......................16.260.n577
Art 41....................17.07, 17.11
Appendix V.......... 1.11.n25, 12.54.n105
ICC Rules 1998
Art 20(2) 16.162
  (7)........................... 16.167
Art 23(4) 16.198.n453
Art 28(6) 16.39
ICC Rules 2004
Art 17........................ 16.245
ICC Rules 2012
Art 39........................ 16.261
ICSID Rules of Procedure for Arbitration
  Proceedings (amended 10
  April 2006)
r 1(4) 13.20.n28
r 41(5) 2.13
HKIAC Administered Arbitration
  Rules 2018
Art 3.........................16.130.n295
Art 26..................... 16.1752.n386
Art 39.......................16.76.n160
HKIAC Rules 2018 .... 13.06
Art 8(2) 8.12.n23
Art 28.........................1.11.n25
Art 45..........................2.60.n124
LCIA Arbitration Rules 2020 .... 13.06, 16.76.n160
Article 4.3 ....16.130.n295
Art 8(1) 8.12.n23
Art 9A–9C......................1.11.n25
Art 9B........................12.54.n105
Art 15.8 ....16.172.n386
Art 30........................2.60.n124
Rules on the Efficient Conduct of
  Proceedings in
  International Arbitration
  2019 (Prague Rules).... 11.14, 11.263
Art 2.........................11.23.n51
Art 3............... 11.15.n25, 11.23.n51

SCC Rules 2017
Art 15.........................1.11.n25
Appendix II.....................1.11.n25
SCMA Rules
r 33.1(c) 16.143
UNCITRAL Rules of Arbitration
  1976
Art 21(2) 5.03.n8
Art 33........................11.31.n61
UNCITRAL Arbitration Rules 1976 ....2.09
Art 15......................... 16.255
UNCITRAL Arbitration
  Rules 2013 ....1.26, 1.42, 2.09–2.11
r 6(2) 2.10.n5

SINGAPORE INTERNATIONAL ARBITRATION CENTRE (SIAC)

SIAC Arbitration Rules 2007.......2.17, 16.126
r 24(b) 16.126
r 27.1 .... 16.248
SIAC Arbitration Rules 2013.... 16.230–16.231
r 6.1....................... 16.231–16.233
SIAC Arbitration Rules 2016....1.40, 2.12, 3.06,
7.35, 8.05, 13.06,
16.39, 16.244
r 2.1.........................16.130.n295
r 5.3......................... 16.230
r 7 ....2.13.n13
r 7.4.........................2.12.n11
r 8 ....2.13.n13
r 8.4.........................2.12.n11
r 9 ....8.01.n2
r 9.1.........................16.232.n514
r 11.2 ....8.05.n7
r 11.3 ....8.04.n5
r 12......................... 8.12 n.23
r 16.1 ....2.12.n11
r 19.........................16.244.n547
r 21.........................2.12.n14
r 24.3 ....16.272.n386
r 24.4 ....2.60.n124
r 28.1 ....2.12.n11
r 29.........................2.12.n12
r 32.2 ....2.12.n10
r 32.11 ....16.39.n74
r 33.........................16.77.n160
r 37.........................2.54
r 38.1 ....17.07, 17.11
r 38.2 .... 17.07
r 39.........................2.12.n9

xxxviii TABLE OF LEGISLATION

r 41.1 . . . . .16.260.n577
Sch 2.12.n8
Sch 1. . . . . 1.11.n25, 12.54.n105
SIAC Domestic Arbitration Rules. 2.17
SIAC Investment Arbitration Rules 2.54
r 24. . . . . .2.46
r 33.1 . . . . .2.54.n105

r 5 . . . . .2.54.n105
SIAC Rules 1991 . . . . 16.248
SIAC Rules 1997 . . . . 16.248
SIAC Rules 2007 . . . . 16.250
SIAC Rules 2010 . . . . 16.248
r 5 . . . . 16.250
SIAC Rules 2013 . . . . 16.248

List of Abbreviations

AA	Arbitration Act
AAA-ICDR	American Arbitration Association International Centre for Dispute Resolution
ADR	Alternative Dispute Resolution
AEO	Attorneys' eyes only
AFSA	Arbitration Foundation of Southern Africa
BIT	Bilateral Investment Treaty
CIArb	Singapore International Arbitration Centre
CLA	Civil Law Act
CPR	Civil Procedure Rule
DAB	Dispute Adjudication Board
DOJ	Department of Justice (United States)
EDI	Electronic data interchange
HKIAC	Hong Kong International Arbitration Centre
HKLRC	Hong Kong Law Reform Commission
IAA	International Arbitration Act
IBA	International Bar Association
ICC	International Chamber of Commerce
ICCA	International Council for Commercial Arbitration
ICSID	International Centre for Settlement of Investment Disputes
IP	Intellectual property
LCIA	London Court of International Arbitration
LMAA	London Maritime Arbitrators Association
PCA	Permanent Court of Arbitration
QMUL	Queen Mary University of London
RECJA	Reciprocal Enforcement of Commonwealth Judgments Act 1921
REFJA	Reciprocal Enforcement of Foreign Judgments Act 1959
SCJA	Supreme Court of Judicature Act
SCMA	Singapore Chamber of Maritime Arbitration
SEC	Securities and Exchange Commission (United States)
SIAC	Singapore International Arbitration Centre
SIArb	Singapore Institute of Arbitrators
SICC	Singapore International Commercial Court
SICOM	Singapore Commodity Exchange
SIMC	Singapore International Mediation Centre
TCC	Technology and Construction Court
UNCITRAL	United Nations Commission on International Trade Law
WIPO AMC	World Intellectual Property Organisation Arbitration and Mediation Centre

1

Arbitration in Singapore

A.	Introduction	1.01	4. Amendments to the IAA and Subsidiary Legislation	1.21
B.	Overview of International Arbitration	1.03	5. Legal Developments Outside the IAA Affecting Arbitration	1.33
C.	Advantages and Disadvantages of Commercial Arbitration	1.08	E. Singapore's Pro-Arbitration Approach	1.36
D.	The Legislative Framework for International Arbitration in Singapore	1.12	F. The Future of International Arbitration in Singapore	1.41
	1. Brief Overview of the History of Arbitration in Singapore	1.12	1. The Singapore International Commercial Court	1.41
	2. History of the International Arbitration Act	1.15	2. Investment Arbitration Disputes before the Singapore Courts	1.42
	3. Two Separate Regimes: The IAA and the Arbitration Act	1.19		

A. Introduction

Scholars and practitioners have long explored the emergence and growth of arbitration **1.01** as a form of alternative dispute resolution.[1] Over time, arbitration has evolved from perceived outlier to dispute resolution mechanism of choice. In Singapore, the role of a supportive judiciary as a driver behind this transformation is perhaps best captured by the following passage from the Singapore Court of Appeal in *Tjong Very Sumito v Antig Investments*:

> There was a time when arbitration was viewed disdainfully as an inferior process of justice. Those days are now well behind us. An unequivocal judicial policy of facilitating and promoting arbitration has firmly taken root in Singapore ... the need to respect party autonomy (manifested by their contractual bargain) in deciding both the method of dispute resolution (and the procedural rules to be applied) as well as the substantive law to govern the contract, has been accepted as the cornerstone underlying judicial non-intervention in arbitration. In essence, a court ought to give effect to the parties' contractual choice as to the manner of dispute resolution unless it offends the law.[2]

This chapter introduces international arbitration in Singapore. It begins with an over- **1.02** view of international arbitration and its salient characteristics and then explores the

---

[1] See e.g. M.J. Mustill, 'Arbitration: History and Background' (1989) 6 Journal of International Arbitration 43.
[2] *Tjong Very Sumito and Others v Antig Investments Pte Ltd* [2009] 4 SLR(R) 732 [28].

2 ARBITRATION IN SINGAPORE

history of arbitration in Singapore and the establishment of the current legal regime. The remainder of the chapter provides an overview of the legislative framework for international arbitration in Singapore and the judicial support for arbitration, before concluding with some observations on trends for the future.

B. Overview of International Arbitration

1.03 Arbitration is a dispute resolution mechanism with origins traceable to 'antiquity'[3] that has, in modern times, evolved into a preferred method of dispute resolution for international commercial disputes.[4] There is little room for doubt now that arbitration has gained widespread acceptance as a mechanism for dispute resolution. This is in part due to the procedural flexibility and respect for party autonomy that are inherent to arbitration. One recent industry survey found that as many as 90% of respondents recommended its use for the settlement of disputes, either as a standalone method or in conjunction with Alternative Dispute Resolution (ADR).[5] Indeed, arbitration is frequently used in specialised sectors of the international economy such as shipping[6] and construction,[7] where the inherent procedural flexibility of arbitration marries well with the need for specialised expertise.

1.04 Arbitration's status as the preferred means of resolving cross-border disputes is due in no small part to the enforceability of arbitral awards pursuant to the New York Convention on the Recognition and Enforcement of Arbitral Awards (the New York Convention). Further to a number of earlier multilateral treaties,[8] in 1958, several States signed the New York Convention, which set out a global framework for the

---

[3] See G. Born, *International Commercial Arbitration* (3rd edn, Kluwer Law International 2021) 8: 'The origins of international arbitration are sometimes traced, if uncertainly, to ancient mythology' (hereafter Born, *International Commercial Arbitration*).

[4] Ibid, 92 et seq: '[A]rbitration has for centuries been perceived as the most effective—if by no means flawless—means for resolving international commercial disputes' and 'it is an oversimplification to say that international arbitration is the "dominant" form of dispute resolution in international matters. The number of disputes that are settled by negotiation dwarfs those that are litigated or arbitrated.... Parties frequently consider the relative advantages and disadvantages of international arbitration and forum selection agreements, not infrequently opting for the latter if their negotiating power permits.'

[5] Queen Mary University of London and White & Case, '2021 International Arbitration Survey: Adapting arbitration to a changing world' (QMUL and White & Case, 2021) <https://arbitration.qmul.ac.uk/media/arbitration/docs/LON0320037-QMUL-International-Arbitration-Survey-2021_19_WEB.pdf>, accessed 1 March 2022.

[6] Shipping and maritime arbitrations are on the rise: for example, in 2020 the London Maritime Arbitrators Association (LMAA) saw a total of 3,010 arbitrator appointments (LMAA, 'Statistics of Appointments & Awards' (LMAA) <https://lmaa.london/statistics-of-appointments-awards/>, accessed 1 March 2022). In the context of Singapore, the Singapore Chamber of Maritime Arbitration (SCMA) was established to serve the commercial needs of maritime disputants. See the SCMA official website, available at <https://www.scma.org.sg/>.

[7] Singapore remains one of the most preferred seats for international construction arbitration. See QMUL and Pinsent Masons, 'International Arbitration Survey—Driving Efficiency in International Construction Disputes' (*Pinsent Masons*, 2019), which notes that 22% of the international construction arbitration cases had Singapore as their seat, <https://www.pinsentmasons.com/-/media/pdfs/en-gb/special-reports/international-arbitration-survey-november-2019.pdf?la=en-gb&hash=2BF84CD21097CCBAD3C1A9DCD9263EBB>, accessed 17 February 2021, 11.

[8] Prior to the enactment of the New York Convention, the first international commercial arbitration treaty in the modern era was the Montevideo Convention, signed in 1889 by multiple Latin States. After its adoption, the 1899 Hague Convention for the Pacific Settlement of International Disputes and the 1907 Hague Convention for

B. OVERVIEW OF INTERNATIONAL ARBITRATION   3

enforcement of arbitration awards. There were 24 signatories at the date of signing,[9] and the Convention subsequently entered into force on 7 June 1959. At this time of writing, the New York Convention has been ratified by 169 Contracting States, which means an overwhelming majority of States apply the Convention rules in determining whether and how to enforce or recognise an award. In general terms, the Convention requires Contracting States to give full effect to arbitration agreements,[10] and provides for a limited set of narrow grounds for refusing enforcement of arbitral awards.[11]

The New York Convention's influence on international arbitration cannot be under-estimated. With it, parties have the assurance that an arbitral award will be enforced consistently across States and subject only to narrow grounds for refusing enforcement. It is arguably one of the most important legal instruments in the history of international commercial law.[12] The 1985 United Nations Commission on International Trade Law (UNCITRAL) Model Law on International Commercial Arbitration (the Model Law), which has been used as the foundation for numerous local arbitration laws,[13] is modelled after the New York Convention.   **1.05**

The application of the New York Convention in national courts has led to a corpus of arbitration case law across common law and civil law jurisdictions. Even though there is no formal system of precedent or coordination, there has been some degree of convergence and the amount of arbitration-related court decisions provides some certainty that allows users to navigate the legal and commercial risks associated with arbitration as a form of dispute resolution.   **1.06**

The development of international arbitration has been further bolstered by the proliferation of arbitral institutions. Whereas between the 1970s and the 2000s there only were a small number of arbitral institutions—for example, the International Chamber of Commerce, the London Court of International Arbitration, the Hong Kong International Arbitration Centre, the Singapore International Arbitration Centre, the Stockholm Chamber of Commerce, and the International Centre for Dispute Resolution—there are now many arbitration institutions in many places.[14] Examples closer to Singapore include the Asian International Arbitration Centre (formerly the Kuala Lumpur Regional Centre), the BANI Arbitration Centre, Korean Commercial Arbitration Board International), the Mongolian International and National   **1.07**

---

the Pacific Settlement of International Disputes were signed. Afterwards, the Geneva Protocol of 1923 was signed, followed by the Geneva Convention of 1927. All of these treaties attempted to promote the use of international arbitration. See Born, *International Commercial Arbitration* (n 3) 61–7.

[9] United Nations Treaty Collection, 'Commercial Arbitration and Mediation—Convention on the Recognition and Enforcement of Foreign Arbitral Awards, New York, 10 June 1958' <https://treaties.un.org/Pages/ViewDetails.aspx?src=TREATY&mtdsg_no=XXII-1&chapter=22&clang=_en> accessed 28 April 2020.

[10] Article II(1), New York Convention.

[11] Article V, New York Convention.

[12] See e.g. M. Paulsson, *The 1958 New York Convention in Action* (Kluwer Law International 2016) 1–3.

[13] D. De Meulemeester and P. Lefebvre, 'The New York Convention: An Autopsy of its Structure and Modus Operandi' (2018) 35(4) Journal of International Arbitration 413, 415–16.

[14] M. Abdel Raouf, 'The Evolution and Future of International Arbitration' (Kluwer International 2016) 1.

4 ARBITRATION IN SINGAPORE

Arbitration Centre, the Philippine Dispute Resolution Centre, the Thai Arbitration Institute, and the Vietnam International Arbitration Centre.

C. Advantages and Disadvantages of Commercial Arbitration

1.08 International arbitration has seen widespread acceptance due to certain benefits it offers over litigation before national courts. Traditionally, arbitration has been prized as a neutral and flexible form of dispute resolution.[15] By comparison, for contracting parties from different jurisdictions, the notion of litigating in the other party's courts may be perceived as ceding 'home ground' advantage. Arbitration is also confidential, a trait valued by its users especially where confidential commercial information or trade secrets may be involved.[16]

1.09 Confidentiality aside, another attendant benefit is the flexibility of process coupled with the broad scope of powers of the tribunal. The procedural latitude enables arbitration to be tailored to the needs of the parties.[17] As noted by the Court in *ADG v ADI*, the 'party-mandated flexibility to adapt the procedure to the dispute is one of the hallmarks and main attractions of arbitration [and] represents one of its key advantages over traditional litigation'.[18] Indeed, flexibility is central to an 'effective system of commercial arbitration for international cases because in such cases there is a special need to be free of unfamiliar local standards ... it expresses a profound confidence in the ability of parties and arbitrators to conduct the arbitration in a fair and orderly manner so as to arrive at a just resolution of a dispute'.[19]

1.10 Another advantage of arbitration is that the New York Convention undergirds the finality of awards[20] and promotes the universality of enforcement.[21] Typically, short of a treaty on the reciprocal enforcement of judgments, commercial parties may face difficulties in enforcing a court judgment from one jurisdiction in another.

1.11 Although these advantages have bolstered the ever-increasing popularity of arbitration to resolve international commercial disputes, arbitration has not been spared criticism. Presciently, in an early extrajudicial piece, Lord Mustill highlighted some

---

[15] Born, *International Commercial Arbitration* (n 3) 81–7.

[16] Confidentiality is implied under Singapore law for arbitrations seated in Singapore, subject to a number of exceptions. See Chapter 2 section E of this book.

[17] N. Blackaby et al. (eds), *Redfern and Hunter on International Commercial Arbitration* (7th edn, OUP 2022) 13, 284–294 (hereafter Blackaby et al. (eds), *Redfern and Hunter on International Commercial Arbitration*).

[18] *ADG and another v ADI and another matter* [2014] 3 SLR 481; [2014] SGHC 73 [111].

[19] H.M. Holtzmann and J.E. Neuhaus, *A Guide to the UNCITRAL Model Law on International Commercial Arbitration: Legislative History and Commentary* (Kluwer Law 1989) 564.

[20] See e.g. A. Mourre and L. Radicati di Brozolo, 'Towards Finality of Arbitral Awards: Two Steps Forward and One Step Back' (2006) 23(2) Journal of International Arbitration 171.

[21] Born, *International Commercial Arbitration* (n 3) 75–8. See also Blackaby et al. (eds), *Redfern and Hunter on International Commercial Arbitration* (n 17) 15–16.

of the potential pitfalls of the arbitral process, including that of excessive time and cost.[22] Indeed, in a recent user survey, 67% of participants cited cost as arbitration's worst characteristic.[23] Additional perceived disadvantages include potential difficulties relating to multiparty proceedings, joinders and consolidations, jurisdictional issues with non-signatories, and the possibility of conflicting awards. There is also the complaint of the increasing judicialisation of the process—with extensive document production and witness testimony—which makes arbitration less of an alternative to litigation.[24] It may be argued, however, that many of these issues are being addressed by innovative changes to arbitral institutional rules[25] or are features which will be corrected as the system matures.

D. The Legislative Framework for International Arbitration in Singapore

1. Brief Overview of the History of Arbitration in Singapore

Arbitration in Singapore can be traced back to the Arbitration Ordinance (the Ordinance) of 1809, which existed when the British Empire controlled the Straits Settlements (comprising Singapore, Penang, and Malacca). This Ordinance stayed in force until it was replaced by the 1953 Arbitration Act.[26] The 1953 Arbitration Act did not distinguish between domestic and international arbitration, and it was not until the 1994 Arbitration Act that this distinction was introduced. **1.12**

In the late 1980s and early 1990s, the Singapore Government conceived plans to develop Singapore into an international arbitration hub.[27] Against this backdrop, there was concern about the usability of the 1953 Arbitration Act, because of foreign parties' lack of familiarity with it, and separately, the perceived interventionist approach of the Singapore courts.[28] By contrast, competing international arbitration seats in the Asia Pacific, such as Hong Kong and Australia, had already adopted the Model Law.[29] **1.13**

---

[22] M.J. Mustill, 'Arbitration: History and Background' (1989) 6 Journal of International Arbitration 43, 56.

[23] QMUL, '2018 International Arbitration Survey: The Evolution of International Arbitration (*QMUL*, 2018) 8 <http://www.arbitration.qmul.ac.uk/media/arbitration/docs/2018-International-Arbitration-Survey---The-Evolution-of-International-Arbitration-(2).PDF> accessed 28 April 2020; The Honourable Chief Justice S. Menon, 'Chartered Institute of Arbitrators London Centenary Conference' (*Supreme Court of Singapore*, 2 July 2015) <https://www.supremecourt.gov.sg/docs/default-source/default-document-library/media-room/ciarb-centenary-conference-patron-address.pdf> accessed 23 April 2020.

[24] Blackaby et al. (eds), *Redfern and Hunter on International Commercial Arbitration* (n 17) 35–37.

[25] Many institutional rules now have clauses addressing the issue of consolidation: Article 10 of the 2021 ICC Rules, Article 28 of the 2018 of the HKIAC Rules and Article 15 of the 2017 SCC Rules (on consolidation). For emergency arbitrators, see also Appendix V of the ICC Rules (Emergency Arbitrator), Article 9A to 9C of the 2020 LCIA Rules, Appendix II SCC Rules, Schedule 1 SIAC Rules. The ICC, for instance, has also introduced an expedited procedure in its rules, which is intended to apply to less complex cases.

[26] M. Pillay, 'The Singapore Arbitration Regime and the UNCITRAL Model Law' (2004) 20(4) Arbitration International 355 (hereafter Pillay, 'The Singapore Arbitration Regime').

[27] Ibid, 360.

[28] Ibid, 358.

[29] Ibid.

6 ARBITRATION IN SINGAPORE

1.14 For a start, Singapore acceded to the New York Convention in 1986 and shortly thereafter enacted the Arbitration (Foreign Awards) Act of 1986.[30] This was a short piece of legislation, providing for the basic framework of the New York Convention to be incorporated into the laws of Singapore. This did not, however, provide a comprehensive legal regime which could address more complex legal issues capable of arising in international arbitration proceedings.

2. History of the International Arbitration Act

1.15 In 1991, following the establishment of Singapore's first international arbitration institution, the Singapore International Arbitration Centre (SIAC), a Sub-Committee of the Law Reform Committee of Singapore (the Committee) was appointed to reform the existing arbitration laws. It considered reports of law reform commissions set up in Hong Kong, Australia, New Zealand, and the United Kingdom, which were set up for the purpose of considering whether or not the Model Law should be adopted.[31] Following its review, the Committee made its recommendations, which included: (i) adopting the Model Law;[32] (ii) maintaining two regimes for arbitration in Singapore—international and domestic—thereby permitting parties in international arbitrations the freedom to agree to arbitration with less curial intervention;[33] and (iii) ensuring that the Singapore courts are empowered to grant interim measures for the interim preservation of property pending the making of an award in an international arbitration.[34] In October 1994, the Committee's recommendations were accepted.

1.16 In 1994, the International Arbitration Bill was introduced in Parliament by the then Minister of Home Affairs Mr Wong Kan Seng to 'make provision for the conduct of international commercial arbitrations based on the Model Law on International Commercial Arbitration adopted by the United Nations Commission on International Trade Law and conciliation proceedings and to give effect to the New York Convention on the Recognition and Enforcement of Foreign Arbitral Awards and for matters connected therewith'.[35] The International Arbitration Act (IAA) came into force on 27 January 1995. The IAA broadly adopted the Model

---

[30] Singapore acceded to the New York Convention by depositing its instrument of accession on 21 August 1986. It entered into force for Singapore on 19 November 1986, with the enactment of the Arbitration (Foreign Awards) Act 1986, Act No. 24 of 1986.

[31] Singapore Academy of Law, 'Report on Review of Arbitration Laws' (*Law Reform Committee*, 1993) <https://www.sal.org.sg/sites/default/files/PDF%20Files/Law%20Reform/1993-08%20-%20Review%20of%20 Arbitration%20Laws.pdf> accessed 23 April 2020 (hereafter Singapore Academy of Law, 'Report on Review of Arbitration Law').

[32] Ibid, 8.

[33] Ibid, 14.

[34] Ibid, 47.

[35] Parliament Sitting 2 on 25 July 1994, first reading of the International Arbitration Bill, Mr Wong Kan Seng's statement, col 122.

D. THE LEGISLATIVE FRAMEWORK 7

Law and represented a departure from the English approach to international arbitration.[36]

As part of its review, the Committee considered the Mustill Report,[37] which discussed the implementation of the Model Law in England and Wales. The Mustill Report concluded that the Model Law should not be adopted in England and Wales for a number of reasons, including because it did not cover matters such as the interpretation of arbitration agreements, as well as the powers, duties, and liabilities of arbitrators.[38] Notwithstanding these and other criticisms, the Committee leaned in favour of adopting the Model Law, concluding that '[if] Singapore aim[ed] to be an international arbitration centre, it [had to] adopt a world view of international arbitration'.[39]

1.17

Although Singapore broadly adopted the Model Law, it did not do so *in toto*[40] and some key modifications were made. These are easily identifiable, as the IAA is conveniently split into different parts. Relevantly, Part II introduces additional provisions which supplement the Model Law, and are aimed at facilitating arbitration. For example, Sections 22 and 23 discuss the confidentiality of court proceedings arising from arbitration; Sections 16 and 17 provide for conciliation proceedings prior to arbitration; and Section 25 provides for immunity of arbitrators from negligence and mistakes.[41] Part III consolidates other pre-existing statutory provisions on arbitration in Singapore. It re-enacts the Arbitration (Foreign Awards) Act 1986, under the heading 'Foreign Awards', which gave effect to the New York Convention. Finally, Part IV contains general provisions, and the First Schedule incorporates the Model Law. Note however, that Section 3 of the IAA excludes Chapter VIII of the Model Law—which concerns the recognition and enforcement of awards—from having force of law. In *PT First Media TBK v Astro Nusantara International BV and others and anor appeal*,[42] the Court of Appeal explained that the exclusion of Chapter VIII (i.e. Articles 35 and 36 of the Model Law) was to enable the enforcement of foreign awards to be governed by the New York Convention exclusively.[43]

1.18

---

[36] L. Boo and C. Lim, 'Overview of the International Arbitration Act and Subsidiary Legislation in Singapore' (1995) 12 Journal of International Arbitration 75 (hereafter Boo and Lim, 'Overview of the International Arbitration Act and Subsidiary Legislation in Singapore').

[37] Lord Justice Mustill, 'A New Arbitration Act for the United Kingdom? The Response of the Departmental Advisory Committee to the UNCITRAL Model Law' (1990) 6(1) Arbitration International 3.

[38] According to the Singapore Academy of Law, 'Report on Review of Arbitration Laws' (1993), the Mustill Report also listed the following as issues not addressed by the Model Law: costs, interest, *res judicata*, capacity, arbitrability, multi-party proceedings, and nullity or avoidance of the contract to arbitrate. The Mustill Report also noted that 'the Model Law is expressed in language which differs from that of a typical UK statute ... existing English law on arbitration is still attracting arbitrations (and must thus be perceived as effective)'.

[39] Ibid, 8.

[40] Pillay, 'The Singapore Arbitration Regime' (n 26) 360.

[41] Boo and Lim, 'Overview of the International Arbitration Act' (n 36) 77.

[42] *PT First Media TBK v Astro Nusantara International BV and others and anor appeal* [2013] SGCA [57]; [2014] 1 SLR 372 (hereafter *PT First Media TBK*).

[43] Ibid, [86].

8 ARBITRATION IN SINGAPORE

3. Two Separate Regimes: The IAA and the Arbitration Act

1.19 The enactment of the IAA led to the creation of two separate statutory regimes for arbitration in Singapore. Arbitrations involving international agreements or foreign companies, and non-international agreements specially providing for the application of Part II of the IAA and the Model Law to apply, are governed by the IAA; by exclusion, all other arbitrations where the place of arbitration is Singapore and where the IAA does not apply are governed by the Arbitration Act (AA).[44] Under this two-Act regime, party autonomy is still respected and ultimately parties may choose one regime over the other. For example, under Section 15 of the IAA parties may 'opt out' of the Model Law regime, and select the AA as the applicable arbitration law.[45] Conversely, parties to a domestic arbitration can 'opt in' to the IAA by virtue of Section 5(1) of the IAA.

1.20 The main distinguishing feature between the international and domestic regimes is the degree of court intervention. Under the IAA, this is intended to be minimal[46] and is restricted to circumstances expressly provided in the Model Law and the IAA.[47] For example, the IAA provides very limited recourse against an arbitral award.[48] Conversely, the AA allows for appeals on questions of law arising out of the award,[49] both by agreement of parties or by obtaining leave of the Singapore courts.[50]

4. Amendments to the IAA and Subsidiary Legislation

1.21 The IAA has subsequently undergone several amendments since it was first enacted in 1994, as a result of legal, social, and economic developments. As it stands, the IAA is the product of amendments in 2001, 2002, 2006, 2009, 2012, 2016, 2019, and 2020. The most significant amendments are those introduced in 2001, 2002, 2009, and 2012. Each will be discussed briefly in turn.

---

[44] See Sections 5 IAA and 3 AA. See also M. Hwang et al., 'National Report for Singapore (2018)' in L. Bosman (ed), *ICCA International Handbook on Commercial Arbitration* (ICCA & Kluwer 2019, Supplement No. 99, June 2018) 1–2; see also C. Leng Sun SC, *Singapore Law on Arbitral Awards* (Academy Publishing 2011) 1–8.

[45] Pillay, 'The Singapore Arbitration Regime' (n 26) 363.

[46] *Mitsui Engineering and Shipbuilding Co Ltd v Easton Graham Rush and Another* [2004] SGHC 26; [2004] 2 SLR 14 [14].

[47] Section 24 of the IAA. See e.g. *Mitsui Engineering and Shipbuilding Co Ltd v. Easton Graham Rush and Another* [2004] SGHC 26; [2004] 2 SLR 14.

[48] Sections 24 and 31 IAA allow for setting aside and refusal of enforcement, on limited grounds. See Chapters 16 and 18.

[49] See *Jurong Engineering Ltd v. Black & Veatch Singapore Pte Ltd* [2003] SGHC 292; [2004] 1 SLR 333 [29] ('The principle of party autonomy is also reflected in the fact that parties are free to choose the arbitral regime to govern their arbitration. More commonly, parties to a domestic arbitration, who, for example, wish their arbitral award to carry a higher degree of finality may agree in writing for the IAA to apply').

[50] Section 49 of the AA allows for appeal against award on a question of law, which may be excluded by agreement of parties.

D. THE LEGISLATIVE FRAMEWORK 9

In 2001, Singapore made notable amendments to its 'opt in' regime to address some un-   **1.22**
certainty surrounding Section 15 (in its pre-2001 form).[51] This issue was highlighted in
two High Court decisions, *Coop International v Ebel SA* and subsequently *John Holland
Pty Ltd v Toyo Engineering Group (Japan)*.

In *Coop International v Ebel SA*,[52] the High Court had to consider whether a Singapore-   **1.23**
seated arbitration, subject to the rules of arbitration of the Chamber of Commerce and
Industry in Geneva was considered 'opting out' of Part II of the IAA. Chan Seng Onn JC
(as he then was) held that Section 15 did not require express exclusion, and that it was
unnecessary to have an explicit agreement doing so.[53] He further held that by choosing
procedures which were 'alien and contrary' to the mandatory provisions in the Model
Law or Part II of the IAA, parties would have implicitly opted out of the IAA.[54] By
contrast, in *John Holland Pty v Toyo Engineering Corp (Japan)*,[55] the High Court had
to consider whether the Model Law could be excluded from Section 15 on its own.
This was because the parties had expressly consented to arbitrate under the ICC Rules,
which were different to the Model Law.[56] Choo Han Teck JC (as he then was) held that
Section 15 of the IAA indeed required parties to expressly state if they wanted to 'opt
out' of the Model Law.[57] He further held that the express wording of Section 15 allowed
parties to exclude either the Model Law or the IAA, but not both. This diverged from
Coop International, where Chan JC suggested that both the Model Law and Part II of
the IAA ceased to apply if parties opted out of either.[58]

Parliament amended the IAA to clarify this confusion. In the second reading of the   **1.24**
International Arbitration (Amendment) Bill 2001, the then Minister of State for Law,
Associate Professor Ho Peng Kee, explained that 'section 15 was intended to allow parties who desire[d] a greater degree of judicial intervention to opt out of the Model Law
regime into the domestic Arbitration Act'.[59] The effect of this amendment was twofold.
First, it clarified that an express agreement is needed by parties to opt out of Part II IAA
or the Model Law; this cannot be implied as a result of the mere adoption of a different
set of rules. Second, if parties excluded either the Model Law or Part II IAA, the AA
would instead apply.[60]

Despite the legislative intervention in 2001, the amended Section 15 continued to pro-   **1.25**
vide lingering uncertainty on the applicability of institutional rules adopted by the

---

[51] The original Section 15 read: '15. If the parties to an arbitration agreement have (whether in the arbitration agreement or in any other document in writing) agreed that any dispute that has arisen or may arise between them is to be settled or resolved otherwise than in accordance with this Part or the Model Law, this Part and the Model Law shall not apply in relation to the settlement or resolution of that dispute'.

[52] *Coop International Pte Ltd v Ebel SA* [1998] SGHC 425; [1998] 1 SLR(R) 615 (hereafter *Coop International*).

[53] Ibid, [144].

[54] Ibid, [146].

[55] *John Holland Pty Ltd v Toyo Engineering Corp (Japan)* [2001] SGHC 48; [2001] 1 SLR(R) 443.

[56] Ibid, [3].

[57] Ibid, [14].

[58] *Coop International* (n 52). See also Pillay, 'The Singapore Arbitration Regime' (n 26) 377.

[59] Second Reading of the International Arbitration Act (Bill) 2002, Professor H. Peng Kee, col 2222.

[60] Pillay, 'The Singapore Arbitration Regime' (n 26) 379.

10   ARBITRATION IN SINGAPORE

parties, when parties did not expressly exclude either the Model Law or the IAA. These issues were raised in *Dermajaya Properties v Premium Properties*.[61] Woo JC (as he then was) held that the mere adoption of the UNCITRAL Rules, did not constitute express opting out of Part II IAA or the Model Law.[62] Therefore, Woo JC considered whether an incompatible set of rules selected by the parties should be excluded in full, or only insofar as they were inconsistent with the Model Law. He concluded that an incompatible set of rules would be excluded in full.[63] In response to the apparent confusion created by these findings,[64] Parliament made further amendments to Section 15 of the IAA.[65]

1.26   The Amendment Bill 2002 introduced a new Section 15, which clarified the application and effect of arbitration rules agreed by the parties. Under the new Section 15A, arbitration rules agreed by the parties would be given effect, insofar as they are not inconsistent with the IAA's 'mandatory provisions'. Further, the Ministry of Law, specifically referring to *Dermajaya*, noted that the UNCITRAL Rules and the IAA were not incompatible, and should be read together.[66]

1.27   Separate to this, in 2006, the Model Law was amended to reflect 'current practices in international trade and modern means of contracting with regard to the form of the arbitration and the granting of interim measures'.[67] This led to Singapore's Ministry of Law proposing the International Arbitration (Amendment) Bill 2009, in a bid to ensure that Singapore's laws remained consistent with the international standards. Some of the changes arising out of the 2009 Amendments include modernising the definition of 'arbitration agreement[s]' to include 'electronic communications' and allowing the Minister to appoint an entity to authenticate awards 'made in Singapore'.[68]

1.28   In addition to the 2006 amendments to the Model Law, the Court of Appeal's decision in *Swift-Fortune*[69] played a major part in a round of amendments in 2009. In that case, Swift-Fortune appealed against Prakash J's (as she then was) decision to set aside an injunction which was ordered pending the conclusion of ongoing arbitration proceedings seated in London. On appeal, the Court of Appeal was faced with the question of the powers of the Singapore courts to grant interim relief in aid of foreign-seated

---

[61] *Dermajaya Properties v Premium Properties* [2002] SGHC 53; [2002] 1 SLR(R) 492 (hereafter *Dermajaya*).

[62] Ibid, [68].

[63] Ibid, [68].

[64] See Parliament Sitting 8 on 1 October 2001, Second Reading of the International Arbitration (Amendment) Bill 2002, 2. ('Nevertheless, my Ministry has received feedback that lawyers in some international law firms have advised their clients that, as a result of the Dermajaya case, the legal position in Singapore is now uncertain . . .'). See also Pillay, 'The Singapore Arbitration Regime' (n 26) 382.

[65] Pillay, 'The Singapore Arbitration Regime' (n 26) 382.

[66] See Parliament Sitting 8 on 1 October 2001, Second Reading of the International Arbitration (Amendment) Bill 2002, 2. *Dermajaya* (n 61) [87] ('the inclusion of the UNCITRAL rules in the Agreement does not oust their application. The UNCITRAL rules do not apply but it is open to the parties to now agree that such rules will apply to fill any vacuum in the Model Law and Part II or to apply such rules on an ad hoc basis.').

[67] Resolutions adopted by the General Assembly, 40/72. Model Law on International Commercial Arbitration of the United Nations Commission on International Trade Law.

[68] Parliament Sitting 12 on 19 October 2009, Second Reading of the International Arbitration (Amendment) Bill, Minister for Law, 3.

[69] *Swift-Fortune Ltd v Magnifica Marine SA* [2006] SGCA 42; [2007] 1 SLR(R) 629 [1] (hereafter *Swift-Fortune*).

arbitrations.[70] After careful review of the IAA, the Court of Appeal concluded that the Singapore courts were not empowered to do so.[71] The 2009 Amendment Act addressed this issue by permitting court-ordered interim measures in support of foreign arbitrations, although these powers were not intended to extend to procedural matters or evidential matters dealing with the actual conduct of the arbitration itself, such as discovery, interrogatories, or security for costs.[72]

The IAA was further amended in 2012. One of the most significant changes brought about by this round of amendments was the expansion of the definition of 'arbitration agreement[s]'.[73] Prior to the implementation of the 2012 Amendment, an arbitration agreement was defined as an agreement in writing. The introduction of the new Section 2A IAA extended the scope of the definition of 'arbitration agreement' to include agreements conducted orally or by other means. Other notable amendments made in 2012, include allowing the Singapore courts to review negative jurisdictional rulings, affording emergency arbitrators the same legal status and powers as any arbitrators, and defining the scope of a tribunal's ability to award post-award interest.[74] **1.29**

In 2020, the International Arbitration (Amendment) Act 2020 implemented two of the proposed amendments which were the subject of public consultations beginning in 2019. The first was new Section 9B of the IAA, which provides a default procedure for appointment of arbitrators in multi-party arbitrations where the parties' agreement does not specify the procedure that would apply for such appointments.[75] Under this default procedure, all claimants are to appoint an arbitrator jointly and all respondents are to do the same, and the two party-appointed arbitrators are to appoint the third, presiding arbitrator jointly.[76] If any of the relevant appointments cannot be agreed within the specified timeframe, the appointing authority (i.e. the President of the Court of Arbitration of the SIAC) is to appoint the relevant arbitrator(s).[77] This amendment filled a lacuna in the IAA, which previously only addressed the process for default appointment of a three-member arbitration tribunal in the typical non-multi-party situation.[78] The aim of the default procedure was to reduce uncertainty and delays in complex multi-party arbitration proceedings, which had become increasingly common in recent years. **1.30**

---

[70] Ibid, [2].

[71] Ibid, [59]. See also R. Wong, 'Interim Relief in Aid of International Commercial Arbitration: A Critique on the International Arbitration Act' (2012) 24 Singapore Academy of Law Journal 499, 522.

[72] Parliament Sitting 12 on 19 October 2009, Second Reading of the International Arbitration (Amendment) Bill, Minister for Law, 3.

[73] Ibid.

[74] International Arbitration Amendment Act 2012.

[75] Section 9B, IAA. International Arbitration (Amendment) Act 2020, New Section 9B.

[76] Ibid.

[77] Ibid.

[78] Ministry of Law Singapore, Enhancing the Regime for International Arbitration through the International Arbitration Amendment Bill (*Ministry of Law*, 1 September 2020) <https://www.mlaw.gov.sg/news/press-releases/international-arbitration-amendment-bill> accessed 22 July 2021.

12   ARBITRATION IN SINGAPORE

1.31   Section 12(1)(j) was also introduced in 2020 to provide explicit recognition of the powers of the arbitral tribunal and the High Court[79] to enforce obligations of confidentiality, by making orders or giving of directions, where such obligations exist.[80] This amendment does not codify parties' obligations of confidentiality but merely makes clear that any such obligations can be enforced.[81]

1.32   These recent amendments, as well as the ones prior, demonstrate Singapore's efforts to keep up with the ever-evolving world of arbitration and to ensure Singapore remains a preferred seat for international arbitration. Singapore's efforts in this regard have paid off: based on a well-regarded survey, Singapore recently tied with London as the most preferred place for arbitration in the world.[82]

5. Legal Developments Outside the IAA Affecting Arbitration

1.33   In addition to the above, Parliament has enacted several laws (apart from the IAA) which impact arbitral law and practice. These include, for example: (i) the Intellectual Property (Dispute Resolution) Act of 2019, which sought to clarify the arbitrability of intellectual property (IP) disputes;[83] (ii) the International Arbitration (New York Convention Countries) Order,[84] specifying the list of Convention Countries for the purpose of the Act; (iii) the International Arbitration (Appointed Persons under Section 19C) Order 2009,[85] appointing the Registrars of the SIAC, and Chief Executives of Maxwell Chambers as persons appointed to authenticate awards for enforcement in any Convention country; and (iv) the International Arbitration (Appointed Persons under Section 19C) Order 2010, appointing the Registrar and the Chairman of the Singapore Chamber of Maritime Arbitration for the same purpose.

1.34   Singapore's legislative developments relating to third-party funding also directly impact international arbitration. In 2017, the Civil Law (Amendment) Act of 2017 on Third Party Funding along with the Civil Law (Third Party Funding) Regulations 2017 were enacted to undo outdated champerty and maintenance laws, and to establish a

---

[79] Section 12A(2).

[80] Ibid. See also Chapter 2 section E of this book, where this is discussed in more detail.

[81] Ministry of Law Singapore, Enhancing the Regime for International Arbitration through the International Arbitration Amendment Bill (n 78). See also, J. Chaisse and A. Solanki, Singapore's Amendment to Its International Arbitration Act Pledges Its Leadership in the Asia-Pacific Region (*Kluwer Arbitration Blog*, 18 October 2020) <http://arbitrationblog.kluwerarbitration.com/2020/10/18/singapores-amendment-to-its-international-arbitration-act-pledges-its-leadership-in-the-asia-pacific-region/> accessed 22 July 2021.

[82] Queen Mary University of London and White & Case, '2021 International Arbitration Survey: Adapting arbitration to a changing world' (QMUL and White & Case, 2021) <https://arbitration.qmul.ac.uk/media/arbitration/docs/LON0320037-QMUL-International-Arbitration-Survey-2021_19_WEB.pdf>, accessed 1 March 2022.

[83] See e.g. Allen & Gledhill, Intellectual Property (Dispute Resolution) Bill passed in Parliament: Enhancing Singapore's IP dispute resolution system (*Allen & Gledhill*, 29 August 2019) <https://www.allenandgledhill.com/sg/publication> accessed 3 March 2021.

[84] International Arbitration (New York Convention Countries) Order, Cap. 143A, OR 1.

[85] International Arbitration (Appointed Persons under Section 19C) Order 2009, Cap. 143A, S 651/2009.

framework for the use of third-party funding in Singapore-based international arbitration and related court and mediation proceedings.[86] Subsequently, in June 2021, the Ministry of Law announced that it would extend the third-party funding framework to cover domestic arbitration proceedings, court proceedings arising from domestic arbitration proceedings, and proceedings commenced in the Singapore International Commercial Court.[87]

The United Nations Convention on International Settlement Agreements Resulting **1.35** from Mediation (the Singapore Convention on Mediation) also signalled a strong commitment by the Singapore Government to advance Singapore's position as a multi-faceted dispute resolution hub for alternative dispute resolution. This is discussed further in Chapter 3.

E. Singapore's Pro-Arbitration Approach

Singapore is generally perceived as a pro-arbitration jurisdiction. Indeed, Chief Justice **1.36** Sundaresh Menon once noted that a party may face a 'near-Herculean task' when attempting to set aside or resist enforcement of an award,[88] because of the Singapore Courts' robust application of the Model Law and the New York Convention.[89] Singapore's judiciary has a reputation for being efficient, and its work in promoting and developing its international arbitration regime continues to be internationally acknowledged.[90]

The Singapore Courts' pro-arbitration approach is evident from many of the cases dis-**1.37** cussed in this commentary. For present purposes, we highlight a few. In *AJU v AJT*,[91] the Singapore High Court set aside an arbitration award on public policy grounds, finding that the contract in question was illegal. The Court of Appeal later reversed the High Court's decision. The judgment engaged the question of the extent to which a court should intervene with a tribunal's finding on the validity of an arbitration agreement. The Court of Appeal held that the High Court had 'erred in reopening the Tribunal's

---

[86] See Chapter 2 section D of this book.

[87] Ministry of Law Singapore, 'Third-Party Funding to be Permitted for More Categories of Legal Proceedings in Singapore' (Ministry of Law, 21 June 2021) <https://www.mlaw.gov.sg/news/press-releases/2021-06-21-third-party-funding-framework-permitted-for-more-categories-of-legal-preceedings-in-singapore> accessed 1 March 2022.

[88] The Honourable Chief Justice S. Menon, 'Judicial Attitudes toward Arbitration and Mediation in Singapore' (*Supreme Court of Singapore*, 25 October 2013) 29 <https://www.supremecourt.gov.sg/docs/default-source/default-document-library/media-room/judicial-attitudes-to-arbitration-and-mediation-in-singapore.pdf> accessed 23 April 2020 (hereafter CJ Menon, 'Judicial Attitudes toward Arbitration and Mediation in Singapore'). See also the Keynote Address by the Honourable Chief Justice S. Menon, the Chartered Institute of Arbitrators International Arbitration Conference (*Supreme Court of Singapore*, 22 August 2013) <https://www.supremecourt.gov.sg/docs/default-source/default-document-> accessed 23 April 2020.

[89] CJ Menon, 'Judicial Attitudes toward Arbitration and Mediation in Singapore' (n 88) 29.

[90] See e.g. Straits Times, 'Chief Justice Sundaresh Menon recognised for promoting access to justice by Geneva-based NGO' (*Straits Times*, 18 November 2019) <https://www.straitstimes.com/singapore/chief-justice-sundaresh-menon-recognised-for-promoting-access-to-justice-by-geneva-based> accessed 3 March 2021.

[91] *AJU v AJT* [2011] SGCA 41; [2011] 4 SLR 739 [69] (hereafter *AJU*).

14 ARBITRATION IN SINGAPORE

finding on fact',[92] and highlighted that the aim of the IAA was to give 'primacy to the autonomy of arbitral awards'.[93]

1.38   Similarly, in *Prometheus Marine Pte Ltd v King, Ann Rita and another*,[94] the Court of Appeal reiterated its pro-arbitration stance and the high threshold needed to annul an award. Here, the Singapore Court of Appeal dismissed two applications to set aside an SIAC arbitration award on grounds of fraud, corruption, and illegality. It considered that any errors of law or fact made by an arbitrator were not grounds for setting aside an arbitration award.[95] It explained that a 'critical foundational principle' of arbitration was to allow parties to choose their adjudicators, and that just as parties 'enjoy many of the benefits of party autonomy, they must also accept the consequences of their choices, which is reflected in the policy of minimal curial intervention'.[96]

1.39   As a general matter, the Singapore Courts have also given deference to arbitrators and have allowed them wide latitude on issues of procedure, preferring on balance to avoid findings of due process breaches unless it is clear that was a breach of material prejudice to one party which was not self-induced.[97]

1.40   However, minimal intervention by the Singapore courts does not mean an unquestioning deference to the decisions of arbitrators. In a number of cases, the Singapore courts have exercised their discretion to set aside arbitral awards where tribunals have acted in breach of natural justice. For example, in *L W Infrastructure v Lim Chin San*,[98] the plaintiff applied to set aside an award for grant of pre-award interest, on the ground that the arbitrator breached the rules of natural justice. The Court of Appeal found that the tribunal rendered the award without affording the plaintiff the opportunity to be heard on its submissions concerning the jurisdiction of the tribunal to make such an award.[99] In *PT First Media TBK v Astro Nusantara International BV*,[100] the Court of Appeal refused the enforcement of an award on the basis that the tribunal did not have the power under the SIAC Rules to bind parties that were not party to the arbitration agreement and thus, the award suffered from a 'deficit in jurisdiction'.[101]

---

[92] The Tribunal had found that nothing in the agreement suggested that the agreement was for an illegal purpose or that illegal acts would be performed by the party, see *AJU* (n 91) [75].

[93] Ibid, [60].

[94] *Prometheus Marine Pte Ltd v King, Ann Rita and another* [2017] SGCA 61; [2018] 1 SLR 1.

[95] Ibid, [57].

[96] Ibid, [57]. On the facts, the Court also awarded personal costs against the lawyer for alleging bias against the tribunal, a move which may be perceived as consistent with the Court's pro-arbitration stance.

[97] See the cases cited in K. Beale and N. Goh, 'Due Process Challenges in Asia: An Emerging High Bar' (2017) 13 Asian International Arbitration Journal 1. This is consistent with the approach in England and Wales and Hong Kong.

[98] *L W Infrastructure v Lim Chin San* [2012] SGCA 57; [2013] 1 SLR 125 (hereafter *L W Infrastructure v Lim Chin San*).

[99] Ibid, [75]–[76]. See also *CRW Joint Operation v PT Perusahaan Gas Negara* [2011] 4 SLR 305; [2011] SGCA 33.

[100] *PT First Media TBK* (n 42).

[101] Ibid, [230].

F. The Future of International Arbitration in Singapore

1. The Singapore International Commercial Court

While arbitration-related applications are ordinarily heard by the Singapore High **1.41** Court and Court of Appeal, Singapore set up the Singapore International Commercial Court (SICC) in 2015,[102] and the SICC may hear such cases as well. The SICC has two distinct features: first, it is empanelled by 12 international judges and 22 Singaporean judges, making it both international and diverse;[103] second, in order for the SICC to have jurisdiction over the claim, the claim must be 'of an international and commercial nature', and the parties must have submitted to the SICC's jurisdiction. Alternatively, it may also hear a case transferred to it from the High Court.[104] The establishment of the SICC is premised on Singapore wanting to enhance its status as a leader in international dispute resolution.[105] The Supreme Court of Judicature (Amendment) Bill, passed on 9 January 2018, makes several amendments to the operation of the SICC, including clarifying that its jurisdiction extends to international commercial arbitration matters. The SICC has already heard a number of important arbitration matters and is likely that this caseload will increase in years to come.[106]

2. Investment Arbitration Disputes before the Singapore Courts

In addition to the growth of commercial arbitration, investor–State disputes have also **1.42** increased. The reader is directed elsewhere[107] for a more detailed account on investment arbitration, but for present purposes, these are disputes typically involving a foreign investor suing a sovereign State for breach of certain protections provided under a bilateral or multilateral investment treaty. These treaties often provide for arbitration as the

---

[102] Singapore International Commercial Court, 'Establishment of the SICC' <https://www.sicc.gov.sg/about-the-sicc/establishment-of-the-sicc> accessed 5 May 2020.

[103] A. Godwin et al., 'International Commercial Courts: The Singapore Experience' (2017) 18(2) Melbourne Journal of International Law 3–5.

[104] Ibid, 8–9.

[105] Ibid, 3.

[106] A number of decisions concerning international arbitration matters have already been issued by the SICC, for example: *CEB v CEC* [2020] SGHC(I) 11; [2020] 4 SLR 183 (award was challenged under Section 24 IAA and Article 34 UNCITRAL Model Law on the basis that arbitrator had failed to consider one party's claim and that the award also contravened public policy); *BXY and anor v BXX and anor* [2019] SGHC(I) 11; [2019] 4 SLR 413 (appeal was made against a tribunal's preliminary decision *inter alia* that it had jurisdiction over an non-party); *BXS v BXT* [2019] SGHC(I) 10; [2019] 4 SLR 390 (award challenged under Article 34(2)(a)(iii) UNCITRAL Model Law on the basis that it exceeded the scope of one party's submission); *Carlsberg Breweries A/S v CSAPL (Singapore) Holdings Pte Ltd* [2020] SGHC(I) 5; [2020] 4 SLR 35 (application to stay court proceedings); *BYL and anor v BYN* [2020] SGHC(I) 6; [2020] 4 SLR 1 (arbitrator was challenged for apparent bias).

[107] See e.g. R. Dolzer and C. Schreuer, *Principles of International Investment Law* (2nd edn, Oxford University Press 2012); Z. Douglas, *The International Law of Investment Claims* (1st edn, Cambridge University Press 2009); W.M. Reisman et al. (eds), *Foreign Investment Disputes: Cases, Materials and Commentary* (2nd edn, Kluwer Law International 2014); C. McLachlan et al., *International Investment Arbitration, Substantive Principles* (2nd edn, Oxford University Press 2017).

16   ARBITRATION IN SINGAPORE

method of dispute resolution.[108] The World Bank established the International Centre for Settlement of Investment Disputes (ICSID) by the Convention on the Settlement of Investment Disputes between States and Nationals of other States (ICSID Convention), which entered into force in 1966.[109] The ICSID's objectives were to facilitate the settlement of disputes between Contracting States. As at 1972, ICSID had registered one case.[110] As at December 2021, ICSID had registered a total of 869 cases, with 538 of them in the last decade.[111] While the majority of investor–State arbitration cases are administered by ICSID, there are some which apply other rules such as the UNCITRAL Rules and are seated in national court jurisdictions, with the effect being that the arbitral process subject to the supervision of seat courts in the same way as a commercial arbitration.

1.43   To date, the Singapore courts have heard three significant Singapore-seated investor–State arbitration related matters: *Sanum Investments Ltd v Government of the Lao People's Democratic Republic*; *Kingdom of Lesotho v Swissborough Diamond Mines*; and *Republic of India v Vedanta Resources plc*.[112] The appearance of investment arbitration in the Singapore Courts has provided Singapore judges the opportunity to address complex issues of international law and international investment law. For instance, *Sanum Investments* concerned the applicability of the China-Laos Bilateral Investment Treaty (BIT) to Macau. The Court of Appeal examined the territorial scope of the BIT, the use of subsequent practice and subsequent agreement under Article 31(3) of the Vienna Convention on the Law of Treaties, issues of state succession, and the interpretation of fork-in-the-road clauses. *Kingdom of Lesotho v Swissborough Diamond Mines* concerned an application to set aside an investment treaty award seated in Singapore. In that case, the Singapore Court of Appeal dealt with issues of international investment law such as jurisdiction *ratione temporis*, the meaning of 'investment' under the treaty, and the principle of exhaustion of local remedies. *Vedanta Resources* concerned two related investment treaty arbitrations, wherein the appellant had sought to implement a regime to permit cross-disclosure of documents between the two arbitrations. The application before the Court of Appeal was for declarations to the effect that documents disclosed in one of the arbitrations were not confidential or private, and that the disclosure thereof would not breach any obligation of confidentiality or privacy. The Court had to examine *inter alia* issues of confidentiality in the context of Singapore-seated investment treaty arbitrations.

---

[108]   As on 3 March 2021, The Investment Policy Hub of the UN UNCTAD currently lists a total of 2,896 (2,336 in force) Bilateral Investment Treaties and 416 (323 in force) Treaties with Investment Provisions <https://investmen tpolicy.unctad.org/international-investment-agreements> accessed 3 March 2021.

[109]   Introduction, ICSID Convention, Regulations and Rules (ICSID, 2006).

[110]   ICSID Caseload Statistics <https://icsid.worldbank.org/resources/publications/icsid-caseload-statistics> accessed 19 June 2022.

[111]   ICSID, Caseload Statistics 2022 (Issue 1) <https://icsid.worldbank.org/sites/default/files/documents/The_ICSID_Caseload_Statistics.1_Edition_ENG.pdf> accessed 3 March 2022. (This includes cases registered under the Additional Facility Rules provided by the ICSID).

[112]   *Sanum Investments Ltd v Government of the Lao People's Democratic Republic* [2016] SGCA 57; [2016] 5 SLR 536 (hereafter *Sanum Investments*); *Kingdom of Lesotho v Swissborough Diamond Mines* [2017] SGHC 195; [2019] 3 SLR 12 (hereafter *Kingdom of Lesotho*); *Republic of India v Vedanta Resources plc* [2021] 2 SLR 354; [2021] SGCA 50 (hereafter *Vedanta Resources*). It is noted that each of these proceedings have generated a number of decisions in lower courts and on ancillary issues, and only selected decisions are discussed here.

2
Regulation of Procedural Aspects of Arbitration

A. **Introduction**	2.01	2. Rules on Professional Conduct in Arbitrations in Singapore	2.26
B. **International Arbitration Rules**	2.03	D. **Third-Party Funding**	2.33
1. Institutional and *Ad Hoc* International Arbitration	2.05	1. The Historical Position: Champerty and Maintenance	2.34
2. Institutional Arbitration Rules	2.07	2. The Amendments to the Civil Law Act in 2017	2.38
3. *Ad Hoc* International Arbitration Rules	2.09	3. Disclosure of Third-Party Funding Arrangements	2.43
4. The SIAC Arbitration Rules	2.12	4. Effect of Third-Party Funding on Privilege	2.48
5. Incorporation of International Arbitration Rules	2.14	5. Cost Consequences in Cases Involving Third-Party Funding	2.52
C. **Regulation of Counsel in International Arbitration**	2.19	E. **Confidentiality**	2.57
1. Requirements for Party Representation under Singapore Law	2.21		

A. Introduction

This chapter addresses certain procedural aspects of the international arbitra- **2.01** tion process that are not specifically regulated by the International Arbitration Act (IAA). Although the IAA sets out a framework for international arbitrations seated in Singapore, it does not purport to deal with all the procedural issues that could potentially arise in an international arbitration. Other statutes or sources of law may also be relevant to the procedure of an international arbitration seated in Singapore.

This chapter covers a number of topics. First, it addresses international arbitration rules **2.02** that may be selected by the parties to apply in a Singapore-seated arbitration. Second, it examines ethical rules that may apply to the regulation of arbitration practitioners and arbitrators in Singapore. Third, it discusses recent developments on the prac- tice of third-party funding and how they impact international arbitrations seated in Singapore. Finally, it discusses confidentiality in arbitration.

B. International Arbitration Rules

Many sets of rules may apply to an international arbitration and some confusion may **2.03** arise when one uses the phrase 'international arbitration rules'. In the present context,

18 REGULATION OF PROCEDURAL ASPECTS OF ARBITRATION

this Chapter refers to international arbitration rules as the principal means by which parties to arbitration agreements exercise their autonomy to determine the arbitral procedures that apply to their disputes. Article 19 of the United Nations Commission on International Trade Law Model Law on International Commercial Arbitration (the Model Law) expressly recognises the parties' freedom to agree on the procedure to be followed by the arbitral tribunal in conducting proceedings. This freedom includes the parties' freedom to select international arbitration rules to apply to their disputes.

2.04 International arbitration rules provide a framework covering multiple facets of procedure over the life cycle of an arbitration. These include the commencement of arbitration proceedings, default form and timing requirements for written submissions, the number of arbitrators and the processes for their appointment, the powers of the arbitral tribunal, and requirements for hearings and awards. They may also contain obligations that are not merely procedural, such as provisions on *kompetenz-kompetenz* or confidentiality, or provisions that guarantee a basic level of procedural fairness and equality. In general, international arbitration rules are framed in a way that accord the parties substantial freedom to tailor, by agreement, the process according to their needs, subject to the discretion of the arbitral tribunal to manage and control the arbitral procedure.

1. Institutional and *Ad Hoc* International Arbitration

2.05 International arbitration can be either institutional, meaning that an arbitral institution, such as the Singapore International Arbitration Centre (SIAC), acts as an administrative authority with certain powers and supervisory functions over the arbitral process, or *ad hoc*, meaning that there is no such administrative authority involved. This distinction can be more nuanced in practice. *Ad hoc* arbitration may often involve an arbitral institution or some other body acting in a limited capacity as an appointing authority, which will select the arbitrator or arbitrators if parties are unable to reach agreement, or which will decide challenges to arbitrators. For arbitrations seated in Singapore, where there is no appointing authority chosen by the parties, the President of the Court of Arbitration of the SIAC is designated under Section 8(2) of the IAA as the default appointing authority.

2.06 Arbitration being a voluntary consensual process, the parties are free to choose either institutional arbitration or *ad hoc* arbitration seated in Singapore. This choice is usually made *ex ante* in the parties' arbitration agreement, although parties may reach such an agreement subsequent to their dispute arising. The parties' freedom to choose their form of arbitration is consistent with the approach of most Model Law jurisdictions that make no distinction between institutional or *ad hoc* arbitration. There are, however, a minority of other jurisdictions that do not recognise the

B. INTERNATIONAL ARBITRATION RULES 19

validity of parties' choice of *ad hoc* arbitration.[1] In general, the involvement of an arbitral institution will mean some additional costs for the parties. But it also comes with certain benefits: parties will avoid the need to negotiate fees with their arbitrators, and benefit from active case management by the arbitral institution, which reduces the risks of procedural deadlocks or delays (for example, in the appointment of arbitrators) and the risks of technical defects that may impair the overall enforceability of the arbitral award.

2. Institutional Arbitration Rules

Institutional arbitration is often conducted pursuant to institutional arbitration rules promulgated by arbitral institutions. If parties choose institutional arbitration, they can agree, usually in their arbitration clause, on a particular arbitral institution or its arbitration rules. Parties can even subsequently agree to institutional arbitration after a dispute has arisen.   **2.07**

Parties are not limited in their choice of arbitral institutions (or institutional arbitration rules) to those arbitral institutions that are situated at the seat of arbitration. Thus, parties may choose to have an arbitration seated in Singapore but administered, for example, by the London Court of International Arbitration (LCIA). In practice, however, parties do associate particular seats with particular institutions. Thus, for arbitrations seated in Singapore, the SIAC is a frequent choice for parties. It bears noting, however, that the SIAC is not the only institution based in Singapore. The International Chamber of Commerce (ICC), the Permanent Court of Arbitration (PCA), the World Intellectual Property Organisation Arbitration and Mediation Centre (WIPO AMC), and the American Arbitration Association International Centre for Dispute Resolution (AAA-ICDR) all have offices in Singapore and administer arbitration cases in Singapore and around the region.   **2.08**

3. *Ad Hoc* International Arbitration Rules

Where parties choose *ad hoc* arbitration, they can also agree on a set of arbitration rules to govern the procedure in their arbitration. The United Nations Commission on International Trade Law (UNCITRAL) Arbitration Rules, first published by UNCITRAL in 1976, and most recently updated in 2010, 2013, and 2021 are the most frequently used set of arbitration rules for *ad hoc* arbitration.[2] As noted by the United   **2.09**

---

[1] See e.g. Arbitration Law of the People's Republic of China, Article 16. However, at the time of publication, China is considering proposals for law reform on this issue.

[2] In a 2018 survey of arbitration users and practitioners, 84% of respondents who had experience with *ad hoc* arbitration had chosen the UNCITRAL Arbitration Rules. See Queen Mary University of London and White & Case LLP, '2018 International Arbitration Survey: The Evolution of International Arbitration' (QMUL and White & Case, 2021) 15 <http://www.arbitration.qmul.ac.uk/media/arbitration/docs/2018-International-Arbitration-Survey-report.pdf> accessed 2 December 2020.

20 REGULATION OF PROCEDURAL ASPECTS OF ARBITRATION

Nations General Assembly when it first adopted the UNCITRAL Arbitration Rules in 1976, these Rules were developed after extensive consultation with arbitral institutions and centres of international commercial arbitration and were intended as rules for *ad hoc* arbitration that could be used in countries with different legal, social, and economic systems.[3] This breadth of ambition is reflected in the widespread adoption of the UNCITRAL Arbitration Rules around the world in not only commercial arbitration disputes, but also in public international law disputes involving States, including both investor–State arbitration and State-to-State arbitration.[4]

2.10 The UNCITRAL Arbitration Rules address the procedural aspects of an arbitration from start to finish and include provisions on: the process of commencing an arbitration, the number and appointment of arbitrators, the challenge and replacement of arbitrators, the conduct of arbitral proceedings and hearings, and the rendering of an arbitral award. Under the UNCITRAL Arbitration Rules, the PCA, an intergovernmental organisation established by the 1899 Hague Convention for the Pacific Settlement of International Disputes, has an important role to play. In the absence of any agreement by the parties, the Secretary-General of the PCA designates the appointing authority, a body to select the arbitrator or arbitrators if parties are unable to reach an agreement or decide challenges to the arbitrators.[5]

2.11 In general, the UNCITRAL Arbitration Rules are intended to be a self-contained set of rules that can be applied by parties and arbitrators without an arbitral institution playing an overall supervisory or administrative role. At the same time, due to the popularity of the UNCITRAL Arbitration Rules and the success of arbitral institutions, in practice, parties sometimes choose to apply them along with the choice of an arbitral institution to administer the arbitration proceedings. Thus, the UNCITRAL Arbitration Rules are not only used in *ad hoc* arbitrations; many arbitral institutions, including the SIAC and the PCA, regularly administer arbitrations under the UNCITRAL Arbitration Rules.

4. The SIAC Arbitration Rules

2.12 It is not possible to provide an overview of international arbitration in Singapore without some mention of the SIAC, which was first established in March 1990 and has since enjoyed a well-documented rise to prominence as one of the world's premier arbitral institutions.[6] Recent surveys indicate that SIAC is the most preferred arbitral

---

[3] Resolution 31/98 adopted by the General Assembly of the United Nations, 'Report of the UNCITRAL on the Work of Its Ninth Session' (15 December 1976) UN Doc. A/31/17, 20–7, 66–82.

[4] See e.g. D. Caron and L. Caplan, *The UNCITRAL Arbitration Rules: A Commentary* (2nd edn, Oxford University Press 2013) 7–8; G. Born, *International Commercial Arbitration* (3rd edn, Kluwer Law International 2021) 192–4 (hereafter Born, *International Commercial Arbitration*).

[5] UNCITRAL Arbitration Rules 2021, Article 6.

[6] Queen Mary University of London and White & Case, '2021 International Arbitration Survey: Adapting Arbitration to a Changing World' (QMUL and White & Case, 2021), 10, 33 <https://arbitration.qmul.ac.uk/media/arbitration/docs/LON0320037-QMUL-International-Arbitration-Survey-2021_19_WEB.pdf>, accessed

institution in Asia and second most preferred arbitral institution in the world.[7] Some of the key features of SIAC arbitration include its *ad valorem* fee structure, which fixes arbitration costs and arbitrator fees based on the value of the claim according to specified scales;[8] an express duty of confidentiality on the parties, the tribunal, any person appointed by the tribunal;[9] and scrutiny of the arbitral award by the SIAC Registrar, assisted by the SIAC Secretariat.[10] Under the SIAC's arbitration rules, the SIAC Court of Arbitration makes a number of important procedural determinations, including the appointments of arbitrators, applications for joinder and consolidation, *prima facie* jurisdiction or the competence of the SIAC to administer an arbitration, and challenges to arbitrators.[11]

The Arbitration Rules of the SIAC (SIAC Rules) were most recently revised in 2016. **2.13** The 2016 SIAC Rules were the sixth iteration of the SIAC Rules and entered into force on 1 August 2016. The 2016 SIAC Rules introduced a number of innovations, including, among other things, a new provision on the early dismissal of claims and defences modelled after ICSID Rule 41(5) (as well as summary judgment procedures in common law civil litigation proceedings),[12] and provisions on joinder and consolidation both before and after the constitution of the arbitral tribunal.[13] The 2016 SIAC Rules also saw the delocalisation of SIAC arbitrations with the removal of Singapore as the default seat of SIAC arbitrations.[14] This was intended to signal a more global ambition for SIAC and it is consistent with the approach taken by other leading global arbitral institutions such as the ICC. On 30 December 2016, the SIAC also promulgated the first edition of its Investment Arbitration Rules, which are rules specially designed for use in investment disputes involving States, State-controlled entities, or intergovernmental organisations. SIAC is currently in the process of considering further revisions to the SIAC Rules.[15]

---

1 March 2022, 10, 33: 'Our 2015 and 2018 surveys highlighted a noticeable growth in the percentage of respondents selecting SIAC ... SIAC was chosen by 21% of respondents in 2015, 36% in 2018 and 49% in this survey (2015 International Arbitration Survey, p. 17 (Chart 13); 2018 International Arbitration Survey, p. 13 (Chart 12)).' The SIAC's Annual Report also shows the significant year-on-year growth in the caseload of the SIAC: see SIAC, 'Where the World Arbitrates: Annual Report 2020' (31 March 2021) 16 <https://siac.org.sg/images/stories/artic les/annual_report/SIAC_Annual_Report_2020.pdf>, accessed 1 March 2022.

  [7] Queen Mary University of London and White & Case, '2021 International Arbitration Survey' (n 6) 9, 10 <https://arbitration.qmul.ac.uk/media/arbitration/docs/LON0320037-QMUL-International-Arbitration-Sur vey-2021_19_WEB.pdf>, accessed 1 March 2022: 'Of all the nominations, the ICC stands out as the most preferred institution (57%), followed by SIAC (49%), HKIAC (44%) and the LCIA (39%)... The ICC ranks first in all regions except for Asia-Pacific, where it is outranked by the SIAC.'

  [8] See SIAC Rules 2016, Schedule of Fees.
  [9] See Ibid, Rule 39.
  [10] See Ibid, Rule 32.3.
  [11] See Ibid, Rules 7.4, 8.4, 16.1, 28.1.
  [12] See Ibid, Rule 29.
  [13] See Ibid, Rules 7, 8.
  [14] See Ibid, Rule 21.
  [15] On 7 July 2020, the SIAC announced commencement of revisions for the SIAC Rules. SIAC, 'SIAC Announces Commencement of Revisions for SIAC Arbitration Rules' (7 July 2020) <https://siac.org.sg/ysiac/about-us/69-siac-news/669-siac-announces-commencement-of-revisions-for-siac-arbitration-rules> accessed 1 March 2022.

22 REGULATION OF PROCEDURAL ASPECTS OF ARBITRATION

5. Incorporation of International Arbitration Rules

2.14 Under Singapore law, the reference to international arbitration rules in the parties' arbitration agreement is sufficient to incorporate them as part of the parties' arbitration agreement.[16] Because international arbitration rules are often updated to take into account recent developments or feedback by arbitration users, one issue that arises is whether the arbitration rules that are incorporated are the arbitration rules applicable and in existence at the date of contracting, or the arbitration rules that are applicable at the date of commencement of the arbitration. This may be significant because one party may seek to rely on provisions in a newer set of rules that are not found in an older set of rules.

2.15 Singapore courts have adopted the presumption, first applied by English courts, that a reference to rules in an arbitration clause refers to rules that are applicable at the date of commencement of arbitration, provided that the rules contain mainly procedural provisions.[17] Practical considerations underlie this presumption. As explained by Brandon J in *Bunge SA v Kruse*,[18] procedural provisions can easily become out of date and amendment is necessary to make them workable, and thus 'if a clause incorporating such rules were not construed as incorporating them in their subsequently amended form, the operation of the clause might well be frustrated'. The Singapore Court of Appeal has expressly adopted this reasoning.[19]

2.16 The developing jurisprudence on this issue has not yet conclusively defined the circumstances under which the presumption might be displaced. The Singapore courts have, however, rejected arguments that different sets of rules promulgated by the same arbitral institution were not different versions of rules, but different sets of rules altogether.[20] The Singapore courts have also rejected arguments based on the parties' failure to designate a specific and more recent version of the rules by spelling out its full title, holding that the presumption would apply and was not displaced in such a case, and that it would only be displaced if there was a specific reference to the full title and date of the older version of the rules.[21] Therefore, as a practical matter, the version of the arbitration rules in force at the time of commencement of the arbitration will generally apply, unless the parties clearly indicate otherwise.

2.17 Singapore courts have also not determined the exact contours of the distinction between 'procedural' and 'substantive' provisions. As a starting point, Singapore courts have made clear that provisions that are procedural in nature include provisions on the appointment of arbitrators, the conduct of proceedings and admissibility of

---

[16] See e.g. *AQZ v ARA* [2015] 2 SLR 972 [125].
[17] See Ibid; *Navigator Investment Services Ltd v Acclaim Insurance Brokers Pte Ltd* [2010] 1 SLR 25 [34]; *Black & Veatch Singapore Pte Ltd v Jurong Engineering Ltd* [2004] 4 SLR(R) 19 [15], [19]–[20].
[18] *Bunge SA v Kruse* [1979] 1 Lloyd's Rep 279, 286.
[19] *Black & Veatch Singapore Pte Ltd v Jurong Engineering Ltd* [2004] 4 SLR(R) 19 [19]–[20].
[20] Ibid, [23].
[21] *AQZ v ARA* [2015] 2 SLR 972 [17]; *Black & Veatch Singapore Pte Ltd v Jurong Engineering Ltd* [2004] 4 SLR(R) 19 [24]–[25].

evidence by experts and other witnesses.[22] Thus, the Singapore courts have held that a reference to arbitration rules that contain 'mainly' such procedural provisions is presumed to be a reference to the version of the rules in force at the time of commencement of the arbitration. The Singapore courts have also observed that rules that are procedural in *nature* can have substantive *impact*, holding that what is relevant is the procedural nature of the rules.[23] Thus, in several cases where the issue was whether the parties had chosen the repealed SIAC Domestic Arbitration Rules, which would have meant that the Arbitration Act applied, or the more recent SIAC Rules 2007, which expressly designated that the IAA would apply, the Singapore courts have held that the more recent version of the rules applied because the rules were procedural in nature, even though it was argued that the outcome would have substantive implications.[24]

However, the Singapore courts have not addressed the question of whether it would **2.18** adopt the same position with respect to provisions that are not purely procedural in nature, and which may arguably constitute an agreement on the parties' substantive obligations and rights, for example, provisions on confidentiality or provisions designating the seat of the arbitration. Where such provisions are addressed in one version of the arbitration rules and not the other, there may be a stronger argument that the parties' agreement on the extent of their substantive obligations *inter se* at the time of contracting should apply, and those substantive obligations should not be modified by the decisions made by an arbitral institution or other third parties to the parties' contract. Even if such substantive provisions are contained in rules that contain 'mainly procedural' provisions, there should be no reason in principle why the arbitration rules should be treated as an indivisible whole. The better construction in such cases may be that the parties' agreement to incorporate the rules in force at the time of commencement of the arbitration, save where such rules impose obligations that are substantive in nature that the parties have not consented to.

C. Regulation of Counsel in International Arbitration

The IAA does not address the qualifications required for a person, whether a lawyer or **2.19** otherwise, to represent a party in an arbitration or to provide arbitration-related legal advice in Singapore. This is similar to the approach under the Model Law, which does not address this subject. The New York Convention also does not address the applicable qualification requirements for party representatives. However, commentators have taken the view that Articles II(1) and II(3) of the New York Convention guarantee the parties' freedom to legal representation of their choice, and that this is also inherent

---

[22] *Car & Cars Pte Ltd v Volkswagen AG and another* [2010] 1 SLR 625 [31].
[23] Ibid.
[24] *Black & Veatch Singapore Pte Ltd v Jurong Engineering Ltd* [2004] 4 SLR(R) 19 [22]; *Car & Cars Pte Ltd v Volkswagen AG and another* [2010] 1 SLR 625 [31].

24   REGULATION OF PROCEDURAL ASPECTS OF ARBITRATION

in the parties' right to be heard that is recognised in Article V(1)(b) of the New York Convention.[25]

2.20   The approach under the IAA may be contrasted with the approach taken in other juris-dictions, including in England, Austria, and Belgium, which is to provide for an explicit guarantee in arbitration legislation—sometimes expressed as a right—that parties may be represented in arbitral proceedings by persons or representatives of their choice.[26] These laws do not include any requirement that such persons or representatives have to be lawyers qualified in any jurisdiction. Any authorised person, including internal staff of a company, can represent a party in arbitral proceedings.[27] This is not mutually ex-clusive with having external counsel.[28]

1. Requirements for Party Representation under Singapore Law

2.21   In Singapore, the requirements for party representatives in arbitration proceedings are regulated by the Legal Profession Act.[29] Section 35 of the Legal Profession Act pro-vides that arbitrators and party representatives are exempted from the qualification re-quirements for practising Singapore law in Singapore (and the offences for practising without such qualification requirements).[30] Specifically, Section 35(1) provides that those requirements do not apply in the case of 'any person representing any party in ar-bitration proceedings' or 'the giving of advice, preparation of documents and any other assistance in relation to or arising out of arbitration proceedings except for the right of audience in court proceedings'.[31] Section 35(2) provides a very expansive definition of 'arbitration proceedings' for the purposes of the Section 35(1) exemption, meaning any proceedings governed by the Arbitration Act or the IAA, as well as any other arbi-tration proceedings that 'would have been governed' by the Arbitration Act or the IAA had they been seated in Singapore.

---

[25] Born, *International Commercial Arbitration* 3063–7 (n 4).

[26] See English Arbitration Act 1996, Section 36 ('Unless otherwise agreed by the parties, a party to arbitral pro-ceedings may be represented in the proceedings by a lawyer or other person chosen by him.'); Austrian Code of Civil Procedure (ZPO), Section 594(3) ('The parties may be represented or counselled by persons of their choice. This right cannot be excluded or limited.'); Article 1694(4) Belgian Judicial Code ('Each party shall have the right to be represented by a lawyer or by a representative, in possession of a special power of attorney in writing, ap-proved by the arbitral tribunal. Each party may be assisted by a lawyer or any person of his choice, approved by the arbitral tribunal. Parties may not be represented or assisted by an agent d'affaires.'). See also UK Departmental Advisory Committee on Arbitration Law, *Report on the Arbitration Bill* (1996), para 183 ('It seems to us that this reflects a basic right, though of course the parties are free to dispense with it if they wish.').

[27] *CGS v CGT* [2020] SGHC 183 [13].

[28] Ibid, [15].

[29] Legal Profession Act 1966 (2020 Rev. Ed.) (hereafter Legal Profession Act).

[30] The qualification requirements for practising Singapore law in Singapore, and the offences for practising without such qualification requirements, are set out in Sections 32 and 33 of the Legal Profession Act. C.f. Indian Advocates Act 1961, Section 1961 (foreign lawyers cannot practice law in India). Unlike the Singapore Legal Profession Act, there is no statutory exception to this rule for arbitration. However, a judgment of the Supreme Court has created an exception for international arbitrations conducted on a 'casual' visit or on a 'fly-in fly-out' basis, provided that such visits are not so frequent such that they amount to practising Indian law. See *Bar Council of India v AK Balaji and others* (2018) 5 SCC 379, Civil Appeal Nos 7875–7879 of 2015.

[31] Legal Profession Act, Section 35(1).

C. REGULATION OF COUNSEL IN INTERNATIONAL ARBITRATION 25

Thus, the exemption from the requirements of the Legal Profession Act applies to all **2.22** persons representing parties in (or advising parties in relation to) all arbitration proceedings, whether they are domestic or international arbitration proceedings, or whether they are arbitration proceedings seated in Singapore or elsewhere. However, the exemption does not apply for anything that involves 'the right of audience on court proceedings'. In practical terms this means that parties may be represented in arbitration proceedings by any person of their choice, whether such persons are qualified Singapore lawyers or not, and this may include non-lawyers, although they will need qualified Singapore lawyers to represent them in any arbitration-related court proceedings (with the exception of foreign lawyers that are admitted on an *ad hoc* basis under Section 15 of the Legal Profession Act).[32]

The approach of Section 35 of the Legal Profession Act is consistent with Singapore's **2.23** reputation as a leading seat of arbitration with a supportive legal framework. Section 35 was introduced by a legislative amendment in 2004, with the position preceding the amendment being the subject of serious criticism by international commentators.

In *Turner (East Asia) Pte Ltd v Builders Federal (HK) Ltd*, Chan Sek Keong JC (as he **2.24** then was) held that a leading New York firm could not represent its clients in an arbitration in Singapore where Singapore law was the governing law of the contract because that contravened certain provisions of the Legal Profession Act which prohibited practising without a Singapore practising certificate.[33] Unsurprisingly, commentators observed at the time that this decision would have negative repercussions for Singapore's reputation as a seat of international arbitration.[34] Thereafter, in 1992, the Legal Profession Act was amended to permit foreign lawyers to represent parties in international arbitrations in Singapore, but only where the applicable law was not Singapore law.[35] In 2004, the Legal Profession Act was amended again, this time to add a new Section 35 that fully recognises the parties' freedom to select their party representatives in arbitration proceedings seated in Singapore and elsewhere, regardless of the applicable law to the dispute.[36]

For completeness, in order to represent parties in proceedings before the SICC, foreign **2.25** lawyers would have to be registered under Section 36P of the Legal Profession Act, either as a foreign lawyer who is granted full registration under Section 36P of the Legal Profession Act ('full registration foreign lawyer') or a foreign lawyer who is granted restricted registration under Section 36P of the Legal Profession Act ('restricted

---

[32] Section 15 of the Legal Profession Act allows for the *ad hoc* admission of a person who holds 'Her Majesty's Patent as Queen's Counsel' or any 'appointment of equivalent distinction of any jurisdiction' or who does not ordinarily reside in Singapore of Malaysia and 'has special qualifications or experience for the purposes of the case'.

[33] *Turner (East Asia) Pte Ltd v Builders Federal (HK) Ltd* [1988] 1 SLR(R) 281 [21], [34].

[34] See e.g. D. Rivkin, 'Restrictions on Foreign Counsel in International Arbitrations' in A.J. van den Berg (ed), *Yearbook Commercia Arbitration 1991—Volume XVI* (Kluwer Law International 1991) 404 ('As long as ... foreign counsel cannot represent their clients in arbitration proceedings there, ... Singapore is ... less likely to be chosen as the situs of arbitration by parties contemplating arbitration.').

[35] See Legal Profession (Amendment) Act 1992, Section 2.

[36] See Legal Profession (Amendment) Act 2004, Section 35.

26   REGULATION OF PROCEDURAL ASPECTS OF ARBITRATION

registration foreign lawyer'). The latter may only represent parties for the purposes of making submissions on matters of foreign law, and the former may represent parties in 'offshore cases', that is, a case with international elements.[37] However, although full registration foreign lawyers may have rights of audience in an 'offshore case'[38] before the Singapore International Commercial Court (SICC)—that is, a case with international elements—this excludes any applications made under the IAA. Order 110 Rule 1(1) of the Rules of Court[39] expressly provides that an 'offshore case' for purposes of the SICC exclude proceedings under the IAA. Therefore, for a foreign lawyer to argue an application before the SICC under the IAA, he or she would need to seek *ad hoc* admission under Section 15 of the Legal Profession Act.[40]

2. Rules on Professional Conduct in Arbitrations in Singapore

2.26 The IAA also does not address the ethical rules that apply to arbitration practitioners in international arbitrations seated in Singapore. The IAA neither contains substantive rules on the subject nor prescribes a choice-of-law rule for determining the ethical rules that apply.

2.27 The applicable ethical rules in a Singapore-seated arbitration are addressed— but only partially—by the Legal Profession (Professional Conduct) Rules 2015, which prescribe a set of ethical rules and sanctions that apply to lawyers that hold a Singapore practising certificate, lawyers that are admitted on an *ad hoc* basis under Section 15 of the Legal Profession Act, and foreign lawyers regulated under the Legal Profession Act.[41] A number of these Rules, including Rule 9 (conduct of proceedings), Rule 10 (responsibility for client's conduct), Rule 11 (conflicts of interest) and Rule 12 (communications and dealings with witnesses), apply to proceedings before 'a court or tribunal'. Rule 2 in turn defines 'tribunal' to include 'any arbitral tribunal as defined in section 2(1) of the Arbitration Act (Cap. 10) or section 2(1) of the International Arbitration Act (Cap. 143A)'.[42] Thus, the Rules that

---

[37] See SICC, 'SICC User Guides Note 3: Foreign Representation', in 'Singapore International Commercial Court User Guides' (31 December 2021) <https://www.sicc.gov.sg/docs/default-source/guide-to-the-sicc/2021-12-21-sicc-user-guides-(as-at-31-dec-2021)(clean).pdf>, accessed 1 March 2022.

[38] See LPA, Section 36O and 36P; Legal Profession (Representation in Singapore International Commercial Court) Rules 2014, Section 2.

[39] Rules of Court, R 5, 2014 Rev. Ed.

[40] There are two stages to an application for *ad hoc* admission. An applicant must first meet the threshold requirements and show that: (i) he or she is a King's Counsel or equivalent; (ii) does not ordinarily reside in Singapore; and (iii) has special qualifications or experience for purpose of the case. Once these threshold requirements are met, the Court will consider certain discretionary factors in deciding whether to grant *ad hoc* admission, namely: (i) the nature of the factual and legal issues involved; (ii) the necessity for the services of a foreign senior counsel; (iii) the availability of local Senior Counsel; (ii) having regard to all the circumstances, whether it is reasonable to admit foreign senior counsel. See e.g. *Re Joseph David QC* [2012] 1 SLR 791 (Admitted); *Re Wordsworth, Samuel Sherratt QC* [2016] 5 SLR 179 (Admitted); *Re Harish Salve* [2018] 1 SLR 345 (Admitted); *Re Landau, Toby Thomas QC* [2016] SGHC 258 (Application dismissed); *Re BSL* [2018] SGHC 207 (Application dismissed); *Re Gearing, Matthew Peter QC* [2020] 3 SLR 1106 (Application Dismissed).

[41] Legal Profession (Professional Conduct) Rules 2015, Rule 3.

[42] Ibid, Rule 2.

C. REGULATION OF COUNSEL IN INTERNATIONAL ARBITRATION 27

apply to proceedings before a 'tribunal' apply to all arbitration proceedings seated in Singapore, and this applies to any lawyer admitted or qualified to practise in Singapore under the Legal Profession Act. This makes sense in principle, since the Legal Profession (Professional Conduct) Rules 2015, being a subsidiary legislation to implement the Legal Profession Act, cannot purport to regulate persons that are not subject to the Legal Profession Act.

However, any persons that are not admitted or qualified to practise in Singapore under **2.28** the Legal Profession Act are not subject to the Legal Profession (Professional Conduct) Rules 2015. As explained above, Section 35 of the Legal Profession Act permits parties to be represented in arbitration proceedings in Singapore by any person of their choice, without being restricted to persons admitted or qualified to practise in Singapore under the Legal Profession Act. For example, lawyers qualified only in New York or England and Wales are permitted to represent parties in arbitration proceedings in Singapore, even if they are not ordinarily based in Singapore and are not foreign lawyers regulated under the Legal Profession Act, as they will not be subject to the Legal Profession (Professional Conduct) Rules 2015.

Where the Legal Profession (Professional Conduct) Rules 2015 do not apply, the **2.29** position is less straightforward. In general, in the absence of express provision, it is unsettled whether counsel in an international arbitration are subject to the rules of professional conduct in the arbitral seat or the rules of professional conduct of their home jurisdiction,[43] and this is compounded by the fact that there are no uniform rules at an international level or any supra-national body to enforce such rules.[44] Commentators have noted that this lack of clarity may contribute to the impression that no rules apply, leading to predatory or Machiavellian behaviour by counsel in arbitration proceedings, which has the potential to undermine the legitimacy of the international arbitration system as a whole.[45]

---

[43] See Preamble to the IBA Guidelines on Party Representation in International Arbitration (15 March 2013) 1 ('high degree of uncertainty ... regarding what rules govern party representation in international arbitration'). IBA Task Force on Conduct of Counsel in Arbitration, '2010 Survey: Counsel in International Arbitration' (63% of practitioners surveyed believed they were subject to their home jurisdictions' rules, while 27% were uncertain and 10% had no opinion or did not believe they were subject to home jurisdiction rules); C. Benson, 'Can Professional Ethics Wait? The Need for Transparency in International Arbitration' (2009) 3 Dispute Resolution International 78, 79, 81 ('in any given arbitration, "even counsel from the same jurisdictions may have diverging views on the extent to which their national ethical codes apply to international arbitration"'); Born, *International Commercial Arbitration* (n 4), 3116 ('counsel in international arbitrations are frequently uncertain what rules of professional responsibility apply to their conduct'). We note that certain professional conduct rules, such as the New York Rules of Professional Conduct, may apply to the conduct of New York-qualified lawyers outside of the jurisdiction.

[44] V.V. Veeder, 'The Lawyer's Duty to Arbitrate in Good Faith' (2002) 18(4) Arbitration International 431, 431–3; S. Menon, 'Some Cautionary Notes for An Age of Opportunity' (Keynote Address at Chartered Institute of Arbitrators International Arbitration Conference, Penang, 22 August 2013) 16.

[45] C. Benson, 'Can Professional Ethics Wait? The Need for Transparency in International Arbitration' (2009) 3 Dispute Resolution International 78, 79 ('[the lack of clarity on what national professional rules apply in the arbitration process] might permit arbitration counsel to entertain the following conclusion: national professional rules do not apply and there are no international rules; hence, conduct of counsel and their clients is not regulated by any minimal ethical standards but rather by a Machiavellian cost-benefit analysis of what conduct can be "gotten away with without undue risk of discovery or sanction by the tribunal"').

28   REGULATION OF PROCEDURAL ASPECTS OF ARBITRATION

2.30 Others have noted that this normative uncertainty creates the risk of an uneven playing field.[46] This may be the case, for example, where one party is represented by Singapore counsel, who are subject to the Legal Profession (Professional Conduct) Rules 2015, and may be subject to certain prohibitions on the 'coaching' of witnesses,[47] whereas the opposing party may be represented by New York lawyers that are not ethically barred from preparing witnesses from testimony, including through 'mock cross-examination' exercises (and for whom failing to do so, conversely, could be a breach of their ethical duties).[48] Party representatives may also be subject to differing rules on document disclosure—for example, counsel from civil law jurisdictions that do not have extensive document production regimes may lack express ethical obligations relating to document preservation or the disclosure of documents harmful to a client's case.[49]

2.31 These issues can be delicate, and where they arise in practice, party representatives and arbitrators are likely to take a pragmatic approach. In the absence of clear guidance from legislation and professional conduct regulation, soft law instruments can provide relevant guidance. The International Bar Association (IBA) Guidelines on Party Representation in International Arbitration (the 'IBA Guidelines on Party Representation'), published in May 2013, set out 27 guidelines on the ethical conduct of party representatives in international arbitration. Although the IBA Guidelines are a well-intentioned attempt to consolidate consensus on ethical standards amongst international arbitration practitioners from different common law and civil law jurisdictions, they have also been subject to criticism by commentators who argue that they are, at best, ineffectual because they do not override mandatory rules that may already apply and at worst, more harmful than helpful by encouraging tactical challenges.[50] In Singapore, the Singapore Institute of Arbitrators has also issued a set of Guidelines on Party-Representative Ethics (the SIArb Guidelines), which are intended to be a distillation of principles and practices common across Asia-Pacific jurisdictions.[51] Although both the IBA Guidelines and the SIArb Guidelines are non-binding, they may be adopted by the agreement of the parties. They may also be adopted by tribunals as a reference point, in order to establish common ground and facilitate dialogue with party representatives on the ethical standards that would apply in particular arbitrations.

---

[46] V.V. Veeder, 'The Lawyer's Duty to Arbitrate in Good Faith' (2002) 18(4) Arbitration International 431, 453 ('diversity can unbalance the arbitral process'); C. Rogers, 'The Ethics of Advocacy in International Arbitration' in D. Bishop and E.G. Kehoe (eds), *The Art of Advocacy in International Arbitration* (2nd edn, JurisNet 2010) 49, 55 ('when attorneys who are bound by different ethical rules participate in a single international proceeding, the proceedings may be structurally unfair').

[47] See e.g. *Compania De Navegacion Palomar v Ernest Ferdinand Perez De La Sala* [2017] SGHC 14 [273].

[48] See e.g. Born, *International Commercial Arbitration*, 3091–3 (n 4); V.K. Rajah, 'The Case for Singapore to Take the Lead in International Arbitration Ethics' (2018) 14(1) Asian International Arbitration Journal 37, 48.

[49] C. Benson, 'Can Professional Ethics Wait? The Need for Transparency in International Arbitration' (2009) 3 Dispute Resolution International 78, 84.

[50] See e.g. Born, *International Commercial Arbitration*, 3087–9 (n 4); M. Schneider, 'Yet Another Opportunity to Waste Time and Money on Procedural Skirmishes: The IBA Guidelines on Party Representation' (2013) 31 ASA Bulletin 497, 499; T. Landau QC and J. Weeramantry, 'A Pause for Thought' in A.J. van den Berg (ed), *International Arbitration: The Coming of a New Age?* (Kluwer Law International 2013) 496, 503, 508.

[51] Singapore Institute of Arbitrators Guidelines on Party-Representative Ethics.

There is also considerable debate about whether tribunals may, or should, exercise **2.32** their inherent powers to address violations of ethical rules. The argument against such exercise of powers is that the mandate of the arbitrators is to resolve the parties' disputes, not issues to do with the compliance of their representatives with rules of ethical conduct that may have nothing to do with the parties' disputes.[52] While this is generally correct, arbitral tribunals have in some well-known, but rare cases that ordered sanctions against party representatives based on their inherent powers, even excluding them from arbitration proceedings where doing so was necessary to 'preserve the integrity of the proceedings'.[53] Commentators have suggested that such inherent powers may be more broadly available to arbitral tribunals and may be exercised whenever a potential ethical breach threatens the integrity of the arbitration or the fairness and efficiency of the arbitral process.[54]

D. Third-Party Funding

Third-party funding is an arrangement whereby a third party with no direct interest in **2.33** a dispute agrees to pay for the legal fees of a party to the dispute based on terms to be reflected in a funding agreement, which usually provide for the third-party funder to receive a multiple of the amount funded or a share of the party's successful recovery. The IAA does not regulate third-party funding. It is addressed by other sources of law. Historically, third party-funding was prohibited in Singapore. However, in early 2017, Singapore introduced legislative changes to permit third-party funding in certain dispute resolution proceedings, including international arbitrations seated in Singapore and related court and mediation proceedings. Subsequently, in June 2021, the Ministry of Law announced that it would extend the third-party funding framework to cover domestic arbitration proceedings, court proceedings arising from domestic arbitration proceedings, and proceedings commenced in the Singapore International Commercial Court.[55]

1. The Historical Position: Champerty and Maintenance

Third-party funding was originally barred in Singapore by the doctrines of mainten- **2.34** ance and champerty, which Singapore inherited as part of the English common law.

---

[52] See e.g. J. Paulsson, 'Standards of Conduct for Counsel' (1992) American Review of International Arbitration 214, 215 ('[a]rbitrators are named to resolve disputes between parties, not to police the conduct of their representatives, and therefore do not rule on complaints of violations of codes of conduct').

[53] See *Hrvatska Elektroprivreda v Slovenia* (ICSID Case No. ARB/05/24) [33]. C.f. *The Rompetrol Group NV v Romania* (ICSID Case No. ARB/06/3) [22].

[54] Landau and Weeramantry, 'A Pause for Thought' (n 50) 525–6.

[55] Ministry of Law Singapore, 'Third-Party Funding to be Permitted for More Categories of Legal Proceedings in Singapore' (Ministry of Law, 21 June 2021) <https://www.mlaw.gov.sg/news/press-releases/2021-06-21-third-party-funding-framework-permitted-for-more-categories-of-legal-preceedings-in-singapore> accessed 1 March 2022.

30   REGULATION OF PROCEDURAL ASPECTS OF ARBITRATION

Maintenance means intermeddling in a litigation by a third party with no genuine commercial interest in the dispute, and champerty refers to agreeing to assist another in bringing a claim in order to receive a share of the recovery. Historically, under the common law, maintenance and champerty were both criminal offences and torts under English law, and any agreements to provide maintenance or champerty were contrary to public policy and therefore void.[56]

2.35   In the United Kingdom, the Criminal Law Act 1967 abolished both maintenance and champerty as crimes and torts.[57] However, this left intact the rule that agreements involving unlawful maintenance or champerty would be contrary to public policy and voided. In subsequent years, the English courts made clear that only funding arrangements that 'undermine … the ends of justice' would be regarded as contrary to public policy, and this would include circumstances where a funder exerts undue control over a funded case or where a funder fails to make provision for its fair share of adverse cuts.[58]

2.36   In Singapore, prior to the legislative amendments in 2017, the standing of the doctrines of maintenance and champerty was considered, but not definitively resolved, in *Jane Rebecca Ong v Lim Lie Hao*. In the High Court, Chao Hick Tin J (as he then was) noted *obiter* that champerty and maintenance had been abolished in England and held that this reflected the position then in Singapore.[59] However, the Court of Appeal did not address this issue on appeal and instead determined the case on the basis that the arrangements in question did not constitute champerty. Subsequently, in *Otech Pakistan Pvt. Ltd. v Clough Engineering Ltd*,[60] the Court of Appeal confirmed that the doctrine of champerty applied to the third-party funding of arbitration proceedings. This followed the view of the English High Court in *Bevan Ashford v Geoff Yeandle (Contractors) Ltd* that it would be artificial to differentiate between litigation and arbitration proceedings.[61]

2.37   The status of the doctrines of maintenance and champerty in Singapore continued to be unclear, particularly in the context of the funding of arbitration proceedings. In 2015, in *Re Vanguard Energy Pte Ltd*,[62] the High Court expressed *obiter* in an insolvency case that contractually assigning a bare cause of action and the fruits of such action might be acceptable under some circumstances, taking into account case laws in England, Hong Kong, and Australia. Although the *ratio* of the case was based on the then-existing Section 272(2)(c) of the Singapore Companies Act, which provided for a statutory power of sale and permitted the sale of a cause of action in the event of liquidation, Chua Lee Ming JC reasoned *obiter* that certain funding arrangements might be permissible

---

[56] C. Bao, 'Third Party Funding in Singapore and Hong Kong: The Next Chapter' (2017) 34 Journal of International Arbitration 387, 392–3. See *Jane Rebecca Ong v Lim Lie Hao* [1996] SGHC 140 [22].

[57] Criminal Law Act 1967, Sections 13(1) and 14(1).

[58] *R (Factortame) v Secretary of State for Transport (No. 8)* [2003] QB 381 [40].

[59] [1996] SGHC 140.

[60] *Otech Pakistan Pvt. Ltd. v Clough Engineering Ltd* [2007] 1 SLR 989.

[61] *Bevan Ashford v Geoff Yeandle (Contractors) Ltd* [1999] Ch 239.

[62] *Re Vanguard Energy Pte Ltd* [2015] SGHC 156.

if they were incidental to the transfer of a property right or interest, if the funder had a legitimate interest in the outcome of proceedings, or where there was 'no realistic possibility that the administration of justice may suffer'.[63] Many commentators viewed this decision as signalling a change in judicial attitudes towards litigation funding.[64]

2. The Amendments to the Civil Law Act in 2017

The landscape for third-party funding transformed in March 2017, when Singapore abolished the torts of maintenance and champerty through amendments to the Civil Law Act.[65] These legislative amendments preserved the general position at common law that contracts for champerty or maintenance were contrary to public policy and therefore void.[66] However, the amendments also expressly permitted arrangements whereby a 'qualifying Third-Party Funder' agrees to fund all or part of the costs in certain 'prescribed dispute resolution proceedings', and that such arrangements would not be contrary to public policy or otherwise illegal on the grounds of maintenance or champerty.[67] These changes were made to strengthen Singapore's position as a dispute resolution hub and arbitral seat, and to allow businesses a legitimate 'financing and risk management tool'.[68] **2.38**

The prescribed dispute resolution proceedings for which funding arrangements would be permitted are defined in Section 5B of the Civil Law Act[69] and Regulation 3 of the Civil Law (Third-Party Funding) Regulations 2017, as amended by the Civil Law (Third-Party Funding) (Amendment) Regulations 2021.[70] When the regulations were first promulgated in 2017, third-party funding arrangements were only permitted for international arbitration proceedings, court or mediation proceedings arising from or connected with international arbitration proceedings, and proceedings in connection with the enforcement of an arbitration agreement or arbitral award under the IAA. From 28 June 2021, the third-party funding framework was then expanded to include domestic arbitration proceedings, court proceedings arising from or connected with domestic arbitration proceedings, proceedings commenced in the SICC (for as long as those proceedings remain in the SICC), appeal proceedings arising from any decision made in the SICC, and mediation proceedings relating to domestic arbitration or SICC proceedings.[71] **2.39**

Under the new regime for third-party funding arrangements in Singapore, funding arrangements would only be exempted from the public policy restrictions if the funder meets **2.40**

---

[63] Ibid, [43].
[64] See e.g. Bao, 'Third Party Funding in Singapore and Hong Kong' (n 56) 395.
[65] Civil Law Act, Section 5A(1).
[66] Ibid, Section 5A(2).
[67] Ibid, Section 5B(2).
[68] Singapore Parliamentary Debates, Official Report (10 Jan. 2017) vol 94 (Indranee Rajah, Senior Minister of State for Law).
[69] Civil Law Act 1909 (2020 Rev. Ed).
[70] Ibid, Section 5B(10); Civil Law (Third-Party Funding) Regulations 2017, Reg 3.
[71] Ibid, Reg 3, read with the Civil Law (Third-Party Funding) (Amendment) Regulations 2021.

32   REGULATION OF PROCEDURAL ASPECTS OF ARBITRATION

certain requirements as a 'qualifying Third-Party Funder'.[72] These requirements are set forth in Section 5B of the Civil Law Act and the Civil Law (Third-Party Funding) Regulations 2017. The first requirement is that the funder must be a person who 'carries on the business of funding all or part of the costs of dispute resolution proceedings to which the person is not a party'.[73] The second requirement is that the funder must have a paid-up share capital of not less than SG\$5 million or managed assets of not less than SG\$5 million.[74]

2.41 Therefore, under the current legislative framework, third-party funding is only permitted for professional third-party funders who meet the minimum capitalisation requirements under the relevant regulations. Notably, this would not extend to persons or businesses that are not professional funders but who agree to fund an arbitration on an *ad hoc* basis, or *pro bono* funders. Lawyers and law firms are also prohibited from having any financial interests in qualifying third-party funders, or from receiving commissions, fees, or shares of proceeds from such funders.[75]

2.42 The 2017 amendments did not extend to conditional fee arrangements, which are agreements by lawyers to forego some or all of their legal fees in exchange for receiving payments, including any uplift on account of success, only if the claim is successful. They also did not extend to contingency fee arrangements, which involve agreements to pay lawyers based on an agreed percentage of the sums recovered by the client, with no direct correlation between the work done and the amounts paid. However, in 2022, Singapore enacted amendments to the Legal Profession Act that would allow conditional fee arrangements in the same categories of proceedings for which third-party funding is available, namely international and domestic arbitration proceedings, certain legal proceedings in the SICC, and related court and mediation proceedings.[76] Contingency fee arrangements are not covered by the amendments and are still arguably prohibited under Singapore law as agreements involving maintenance and champerty.[77] The 2022 amendments bring Singapore closer in line with many other leading arbitral seats, including England and Wales, which has permitted conditional fee arrangements since 1990 and contingency fee arrangements since 2013.[78]

3. Disclosure of Third-Party Funding Arrangements

2.43 When a third-party funding arrangement is in place, questions of disclosure frequently arise in practice. Parties and arbitral tribunals will have to confront questions about

---

[72] Civil Law Act, Section 5B(10).
[73] Ibid; Civil Law (Third-Party Funding) Regulations 2017, Reg 4(1)(a).
[74] Ibid, Reg 4(1)(b).
[75] Legal Profession (Professional Conduct) Rules 2017, Rule 49B.
[76] See Legal Profession Act, Sections 115A to 115F.
[77] Legal Profession Act, Section 107(1); Legal Profession (Professional Conduct) Rules 2017, Rule 18.
[78] See e.g. Ministry of Law, *Public Consultation on Conditional Fee Agreements in Singapore* (27 August 2019) [5]; Access to Justice Act 1999; Legal Aid, Sentencing and Punishment of Offenders Act 2012, Section 45; Damages-Based Agreements Regulations 2013; Lord Justice Jackson, *Review of Civil Litigation Costs: Final Report*, 21 December 2009.

whether the existence and identity of a third-party funder should be disclosed, or whether the details of the third-party funding arrangement should be disclosed.

For lawyers admitted or qualified to practise in Singapore under the Legal Profession **2.44** Act in Singapore, there is an express, mandatory obligation of disclosure under the Legal Profession (Professional Conduct) Rules 2017. In particular, Rule 49A requires disclosure to the court or tribunal and to every other party of the proceedings the existence of any third-party funding contract and the identity and address of the funder. Rule 49A requires disclosure to be made either at the date the proceedings are commenced or, if there are no third-party funding arrangements in place at such date, as soon as practicable after funding is in place.[79] These rules do not apply to foreign lawyers that are not regulated or registered under the Legal Profession Act, which might create an unequal playing field in certain Singapore-seated arbitrations.[80] As explained above, the Legal Profession (Professional Conduct) Rules 2017 only apply to all arbitration proceedings seated in Singapore,[81] so lawyers regulated under the Legal Profession Act are not subject to such mandatory disclosure requirements in arbitrations seated outside Singapore. For completeness, for proceedings before the SICC, the Legal Profession (Representation in Singapore International Commercial Court) Rules 2014 provides that foreign lawyers registered under the Legal Profession Act also have a mandatory obligation to disclose the existence of any third-party funding contract, and the identity of any third-party funder.[82]

Apart from the professional conduct rules in Singapore that may require disclosure, **2.45** there is an emerging consensus in the arbitration community that disclosure of the existence and identify of third-party funders is necessary so that parties and arbitrators can make informed decisions regarding circumstances that may lead to potential conflicts of interest between third-party funders and the arbitrators.[83] Examples of such circumstances include the appointment of certain arbitrators as consultants reviewing potential funding decisions on a professional funder's investment committee, or particularly close working relationships between particular law firms and certain professional funders.[84] The IBA Guidelines on Conflicts of Interest reflects this, and provides that a party with 'a direct economic interest in, or a duty to indemnify a party for, the award to be rendered in the arbitration' is to be treated as the same as a party for the purposes of determining whether there is a conflict of interest with an arbitrator.[85]

---

[79] Legal Profession (Professional Conduct) Rules 2017, Rule 49A(2).

[80] D. Chan, 'Three "pitfalls" for the unwary: Third-party funding in Asia, 2018' (Law Gazette, November 2018).

[81] Legal Profession (Professional Conduct) Rules 2015, Rule 2 defines 'tribunal' as referring to 'any judicial, quasi-judicial, administrative or regulatory body or authority *in Singapore*, or any tribunal *in Singapore* that is established by law, and includes ... any arbitral tribunal as defined in section 2(1) of the Arbitration Act (Cap. 10) or section 2(1) of the International Arbitration Act (Cap. 143A)'. The references to 'Singapore' in the definition of 'tribunal' in the Rules strongly suggest that the Rules were only intended to regulate counsel in arbitrations seated in Singapore and not elsewhere.

[82] Legal Profession (Representation in Singapore International Commercial Court) Rules 2014, First Schedule (Code of Ethics), paras 4A and 4B.

[83] International Council for Commercial Arbitration, *Report of the ICCA–Queen Mary Task Force on Third-Party Funding in International Arbitration* (The ICCA Reports No. 4, April 2018) 83.

[84] Ibid.

[85] IBA Guidelines on Conflicts of Interest, General Standard 6(B).

34 REGULATION OF PROCEDURAL ASPECTS OF ARBITRATION

2.46 For this reason and in order to address any such potential conflicts, a number of arbitral tribunals in investment treaty arbitrations have ordered funded parties to disclose the existence and identity of a third-party funder,[86] and this can be rationalised as part of the tribunal's inherent power to preserve the integrity of the arbitral process.[87] A number of arbitration rules provide for an express power to order such disclosure, including the SIAC's Investment Arbitration Rules and the Arbitration Rules of the Arbitration Foundation of Southern Africa (AFSA).[88] The SIAC has also published a practice note stating that arbitral tribunals have the power, under the SIAC Rules, to order the disclosure of the existence of a funding arrangement and the identify of a third-party funder.[89]

2.47 Different regimes for disclosure are triggered by different thresholds and require disclosure to varying extents. For example, the definitions of 'third-party funder' under the SIAC practice note and the IBA Guidelines are not limited to professional funders and are therefore broader than the definition of a 'qualifying Third-Party Funder' under the Civil Law Act, which would trigger the obligation of disclosure for lawyers regulated under the Legal Profession Act in Singapore. As another example, the SIAC practice note states that the arbitral tribunal has the power to order the disclosure of the existence of any funding relationship, the identity of the funder and, 'where appropriate, details of the [funder's] interest in the outcome of the proceedings, and/or whether or not the [funder] has committed to undertake adverse costs liability'.[90] This is a potentially broader scope of disclosure than the obligation of disclosure for lawyers regulated under the Legal Profession Act in Singapore. As a matter of arbitral practice, there is not yet any settled consensus on whether a tribunal may order disclosure of the terms of the third-party funding arrangement.[91] However, commentators have noted that tribunals should exercise caution in requiring disclosure of confidential financing agreements that are irrelevant to the substance of the dispute, which are commercially sensitive and may confer an undeserved tactical advantage on an opposing party.[92]

4. Effect of Third-Party Funding on Privilege

2.48 Another pertinent issue in practice is whether privileged information that is disclosed to a third-party funder would retain privilege. As a starting point, the determination of

---

[86] *South American Silver Limited v Plurinational State of Bolivia* (PCA Case No. 2013-15) [79]–[84]; *EuroGas Inc and Belmont Resources Inc v Slovak Republic* (ICSID Case No. ARB/14/14), Transcript of the First Session and Hearing on Provisional Measures (17 March 2015) 145.

[87] See e.g. International Council for Commercial Arbitration (n 83), 82.

[88] SIAC Investment Arbitration Rules, Rule 24. Arbitration Foundation of Southern Africa (AFSA), Rule 30.

[89] SIAC, *Practice Note on Arbitrator Conduct in Cases Involving External Funding* (31 March 2017) [5].

[90] Ibid.

[91] See *South American Silver Limited v Plurinational State of Bolivia* (n 86) [79]–[84]; C.f. *Kılıç İnşaat İthalat İhracat Sanayi ve Ticaret Anonim Şirketi v Turkmenistan* (ICSID Case No. ARB/10/1) [9]–[12].

[92] International Council for Commercial Arbitration (n 83) 108; O. Gayner and S. Khouri, 'Singapore and Hong Kong: International Arbitration Meets Third Party Funding' (2017) 40 Fordham International Law Journal 1033, 1043–4.

the law governing such privilege issues is a complex matter. The New York Convention, arbitration laws and arbitration rules are generally silent on the issue.[93] The IBA Rules on the Taking of Evidence address privilege issues but provide no more guidance on the issue of the law governing privilege than stating that the arbitral tribunal will determine the rules of privilege it considers to be applicable.[94]

In general, commentators have observed that the determination of the applicable law or **2.49** rules on privilege will depend on a multitude of factors, including: (i) the jurisdiction where communications took place or the relevant document was created; (ii) the jurisdiction where the document is physically located or held; (iii) the jurisdiction where the counsel of each party is licensed and/or practises; (iv) the jurisdiction where each party resides; (v) the jurisdiction in which disclosure is sought; (vi) the law of the seat of the arbitration; (vii) the law governing the substance of the dispute; (viii) the law governing the arbitration agreement and/or (ix) the law of the country with the 'closest connection' to the events.[95] One practical approach may be to adopt a 'most-favoured-nation' approach, which applies the strongest protection that could have been expected in the potentially applicable domestic regimes.[96]

With respect to communications with third-party funders, it is at least arguable that **2.50** such communications would be covered by litigation privilege under Singapore law, which applies under Singapore law to protect documents that are prepared for the dominant purpose of litigation that is pending or in reasonable contemplation.[97] Although there is no precedent applying such privilege in Singapore in the context of discussions with third-party funders, such discussions can arguably come within the scope of litigation privilege if the matter could not be pursued without the investment by the third-party funder and the provision of information to the funder is crucial for the proceedings to continue.[98]

Communications with third-party funders also arguably come within the scope of **2.51** common interest privilege, which applies when privileged documents are disclosed to a third-party who has a common interest with the party entitled to the privilege. Common interest privilege is a recognised head of privilege under Singapore law,[99] but

---

[93] Born, *International Commercial Arbitration* 2250 (n 4).

[94] IBA Rules on the Taking of Evidence, Rule 9.2(b).

[95] International Council for Commercial Arbitration (n 83) 126; M.N. Alrashid et al., 'The Impact of Third Party Funding on Privilege in Litigation and International Arbitration' (2012) 6 Dispute Resolution International 109, 126; F. von Schlabrendorff and A. Sheppard, 'Conflict of Legal Privileges in International Arbitration: An Attempt to Find a Holistic Solution' in G. Aksen et al. (eds), *Global Reflections on International Law, Commerce and Dispute Resolution: Liber Amicorum in Honour of Robert Briner* (International Chamber of Commerce 2005) 743; A. Möckesch, *Attorney-Client Privilege in International Arbitration* (Oxford University Press 2017).

[96] Alrashid et al., 'The Impact of Third Party Funding on Privilege in Litigation and International Arbitration' (n 95) 109, 127.

[97] *Gelatissimo Ventures (S) Pte Ltd & Ors v Singapore Flyer Pte Ltd* [2010] 1 SLR 833; *Skandinaviska Enskilda Banken AB (Publ), Singapore Branch v Asia Pacific Breweries (Singapore) Pte Ltd and Other Appeals* [2007] 2 SLR (R) 367.

[98] International Council for Commercial Arbitration (n 83) 129–30; Alrashid et al. 'The Impact of Third Party Funding on Privilege in Litigation and International Arbitration' (n 95) 129. See e.g. *Wall v The Royal Bank of Scotland Plc* [2016] EWHC 2460 (Comm).

[99] See *Motorola Solutions Credit Co LLC v Kemal Uzan* [2015] 5 SLR 752.

36 REGULATION OF PROCEDURAL ASPECTS OF ARBITRATION

it has not been applied in the context of third-party funders. English courts have accepted that common interest litigation privilege applies to insurers for documents created after the inception of the insurance policy,[100] and this may potentially be extended to third-party funders who share a common interest in pursuing litigation in the same way as an insurer.[101] However, doubt remains about whether common interest privilege would be extended to information that was shared during the pre-investment phase prior to the funding arrangement being concluded.[102] As a practical matter, it will be prudent for parties and counsel to ensure that any such pre-investment information that is shared with third-party funders is kept confidential by express agreement.

5. Cost Consequences in Cases Involving Third-Party Funding

2.52 The involvement of a third-party funder can have cost implications. A third-party funder is usually paid a multiple of its investment (or a share of the recovery proceeds) based on the success of the funded party. Therefore, the question of whether a successful funded party can recover all of the payments made to the third-party funder as part of its legal costs can be practically significant. An unsuccessful party could also argue that the funded party has not had to incur any costs, since these costs were paid by the third-party funder. Conversely, in the event that a funded party loses a case, the question then arises as to whether the successful party may seek to recover its costs from the third-party funder directly.

2.53 As discussed in Chapter 15, although the IAA does not expressly deal with the effect of third-party funding on awards relating to the parties' legal costs, a wide margin of discretion is usually accorded to arbitral tribunals on cost determinations. In contrast, Section 63 of the English Arbitration Act 1996 provides that the award may be determined by the tribunal or court 'on such basis as it thinks fit', and 'on the basis that there shall be allowed a reasonable amount in respect of all costs reasonably incurred'.

2.54 For arbitrations seated in Singapore, the arbitral tribunal's power to allocate the parties' legal costs is usually addressed by arbitration rules. Rule 37 of the SIAC Rules, for example, provides that an arbitral tribunal shall have the authority to order a party to pay all or part of the legal or other costs of another party.[103] In its practice note, the SIAC also clarified that the tribunal 'may take into account' the involvement of a third-party funder in apportioning the costs of the arbitration or ordering legal costs. [104] The SIAC's Investment Arbitration Rules also provides that '[t]he Tribunal may take into account any third-party funding arrangements in apportioning the costs of the arbitration' and that '[t]he Tribunal may take into account any third-party funding arrangements in

---

[100] *Winterthur Swiss Insurance Company & Anor v AG (Manchester) Ltd & Ors* [2006] EWHC 839.
[101] Alrashid et al. (n 95) 108.
[102] International Council for Commercial Arbitration (n 83) 134.
[103] SIAC Rules, Rule 37.
[104] SIAC, *Practice Note on Arbitrator Conduct in Cases Involving External Funding* (31 March 2017) [10]–[11].

ordering in its Award that all or part of the legal or other costs of a Party be paid by another Party'.[105]

Singapore courts have not yet considered whether a funded party can recover the costs **2.55** that were paid for by the third-party funder or the full extent of the payments made to the third-party funder as part of its legal costs. As matter of practice, arbitral tribunals have not reached uniform outcomes,[106] and this is still an unsettled issue.[107] In *Essar Oilfields Services Limited v Norscot Rig Management PVT Limited*, the English High Court upheld an ICC tribunal award ordering a party to pay costs on an indemnity basis on account of egregious conduct by the unsuccessful party, which included substantial amounts paid under the terms of a third-party funding arrangement providing for a 300% uplift on the funding advanced or 35% of the recovery, whichever was greater.[108] The English High Court held that the award of such costs fell within the arbitrator's discretion in Section 59(1)(c) of the English Arbitration Act 1996 and Article 31 of the ICC rules.[109] A similar approach is likely to be taken by Singapore courts where arbitration rules accord the arbitrators a broad discretion to allocate costs.

As for whether an arbitral tribunal may order costs against a third-party funder in the **2.56** event the funded party is unsuccessful, it is likely to be difficult for an arbitral tribunal to establish jurisdiction over a third-party funder, who is not generally a party to an arbitration agreement. There may, however, be exceptional circumstances in which a third-party funder can be taken to have submitted to the jurisdiction of the arbitral tribunal. The issue may also arise with respect to the funding of arbitration-related court proceedings under the IAA. Singapore courts have not yet had to consider such issues, but English court decisions imposing adverse cost orders on third-party funders may be of persuasive value.[110]

E. Confidentiality

Users of international arbitration often identify confidentiality as an important aspect **2.57** of the arbitration process.[111] In contrast to jurisdictions such as Australia and Hong

---

[105] SIAC Investment Arbitration Rules, Rules 33.1 and 35.

[106] *Siag and Vecchi v The Arab Republic of Egypt* (ICSID Case No. ARB/05/15) (majority of arbitral tribunal awarded costs based on a specified amount of hourly fees despite the third-party funding arrangement); *Quasar de Valores SICAV S.A. et al. v The Russian Federation* (SCC Arbitration No. 24/2007)) [223] (tribunal denied recovery of costs on the basis that the third-party funder had funded the entirety of the costs of the proceedings).

[107] International Council for Commercial Arbitration (n 83) 155–63.

[108] *Essar Oilfields Services Ltd v Norscot Rig Management Pvt Ltd* [2016] EWHC 2361 (Comm).

[109] Ibid, [56], [68]–[69].

[110] *Excalibur Ventures v Texas Keystone and others* [2016] EWCA Civ 1144; *Chapelgate Credit Opportunity Master Fund Ltd v Money & Others* [2020] EWCA Civ 246.

[111] According to a leading survey conducted in 2018, 87% of respondents considered confidentiality to be of importance, and more than 57% of in-house counsel surveyed considered confidentiality to be 'very important'. Seventy-four per cent of respondents also considered that proceedings should be confidential unless the parties choose otherwise. See Queen Mary University of London and White & Case LLP, '2018 International Arbitration Survey' (n 2) 28 <http://www.arbitration.qmul.ac.uk/media/arbitration/docs/2018-International-Arbitration-Survey-report.pdf> accessed 8 March 2021. See also T.J. Stipanowich and J.R. Lamare, 'Living with ADR: Evolving

38 REGULATION OF PROCEDURAL ASPECTS OF ARBITRATION

Kong,[112] the IAA does not have specific provisions providing for the existence or scope of confidentiality obligations in Singapore-seated arbitrations,[113] although it does provide for the power of tribunals and courts to grant interim orders to enforce any obligation of confidentiality.[114] Nonetheless, Singapore courts have consistently held that Singapore-seated arbitrations are confidential by default, absent agreement otherwise by the parties.[115]

2.58 The nature of the duty of confidentiality under Singapore law has been the subject of some debate, and there was previously some uncertainty in particular whether it is an implied term based on custom or the officious bystander test, or an implied term in law.[116] This was clarified in *AAY v AAZ*, where Chan Seng Onn J (as he then was) held, adopting the reasoning of Lawrence Collins LJ (as he then was) in *Emmott v Michael Wilson & Partners*,[117] that the duty of confidentiality is better characterised as a general principle of arbitration law developed through the common law (as opposed to arbitration statutes).[118] Consistent with this, Singapore courts have rejected arguments that there would be no room for imposing a general or implied duty of confidentiality where the parties have expressly agreed on confidentiality provisions.[119]

2.59 Consequently, as a general principle arising from the private nature of arbitration, parties to an arbitration have the obligation 'not to disclose or use for any other purpose any documents prepared for and used in the arbitration, or disclosed or produced in the course of arbitration, or transcripts or notes of the evidence in the arbitration or award'.[120] This extends to any witness or expert evidence adduced in the arbitration.[121] Beyond this, the Singapore courts have declined to formulate any blanket rule on confidentiality, and have instead held that the scope, nature, and application of any duty of confidentiality depends on the context in which it arises and the nature of the

---

Perceptions and Use of Mediation, Arbitration, and Conflict Management in Fortune 1000 Corporations' (2014) 19 Harvard Negotiation Law Review 1, 21, 61; B. Hanotiau, 'International Arbitration in a Global Economy: The Challenges of the Future' (2011) 28 Journal of International Arbitration 89, 90.

[112] See Australia International Arbitration Act, Section 23C; Hong Kong Arbitration Ordinance, Section 18.

[113] Sections 22 and 23 of the IAA presume, but do not provide for, the confidentiality of arbitrations, by for a party's right to apply to have hearings otherwise than in open court and to apply for measures to preserve the confidentiality of the proceedings, award, and related decisions by the Singapore courts. See Chapter 15.

[114] Section 12(1)(j) was recently introduced to the IAA in 2021 and provides that a tribunal has powers to make orders or give directions to any party for the enforcement of any obligation of confidentiality. Read with Section 12A(2) of the IAA, this power is also extended to the courts provided that the requirements in Section 12A are made out. See Chapter 11.

[115] *AAY v AAZ* [2011] 1 SLR 1093 [55] (hereafter *AAY v AAZ*).

[116] Ibid, [50]–[54]. See also M. Hwang and N. Thio, 'A Contextual Approach to the Obligation of Confidentiality in Arbitration in Singapore: An Analysis of the Decision of the Singapore High Court in AAY and Others v. AAZ' (2012) 28(2) Arbitration International 225.

[117] See *Associated Electric and Gas Insurance Services Ltd v European Reinsurance Co of Zurich* [2003] 1 WLR 1041; *John Forster Emmott v Michael Wilson & Partners Ltd* [2008] 2 All ER (Comm) 193 (hereafter *Emmott*) [105]–[107].

[118] Ibid, [54].

[119] *International Coal Pte Ltd v Kristle Trading Ltd and Another and Another Suit* [2008] SGHC 182, [82].

[120] *AAY v AAZ* (n 115) [33], citing *Emmott v Michael Wilson & Partners Ltd* [2008] 2 All ER (Comm) 193 at [81].

[121] See e.g. *Myanma Yaung Chi Oo Co Ltd v Win Nu* [2003] SGHC 124 [14] (hereafter *Myanma Yaung*); *Dolling-Baker v Merrett* [1990] 1 WLR 1205, 1213.

information or documents at issue.[122] For example, in *AAY v AAZ*, Chan J observed that an award may be subject, in principle, to different confidentiality obligations from documents produced in the course of arbitration, although it was not necessary to decide the point in that case.[123]

While many of the leading arbitration rules expressly provide for a general obligation of confidentiality,[124] the ICC Rules instead provide that the tribunal 'may make orders concerning the confidentiality of the arbitration proceedings'.[125] In *CHH v CHI*,[126] it was contended by the claimant that the ICC Rules do not contain any obligation of confidentiality, and that until and unless the tribunal makes an order regarding the confidentiality of the proceedings, the arbitration was not confidential.[127] Andre Maniam JC (as he then was) disagreed, holding that the ICC Rules were neutral and a 'blank slate' as to confidentiality. Therefore, in a Singapore-seated arbitration, the parties' agreement to the ICC Rules does not displace the general obligation of confidentiality in Singapore curial law.[128]

2.60

Singapore courts have not yet settled whether the general obligation of confidentiality extends to investment treaty arbitrations. In *Republic of India v Vedanta Resources plc*, Vinodh Coomaraswamy J had to consider an application to the Singapore High Court for a declaration, among other things, that the general obligation of confidentiality under Singapore law did not extend to investment treaty arbitrations. Coomaraswamy J refused to make the declaration on the grounds that the circumstances did not justify the exercise of the court's discretion to grant declaratory relief, but also noted that the arbitral tribunal had made an order for cross-disclosure in the arbitration on the premise that parties to investment treaty arbitrations were subject to the general obligation of confidentiality under Singapore law.[129] Acknowledging that this was a novel issue of law yet to be resolved by Singapore courts,[130] Coomaraswamy J noted that the Singapore authorities on confidentiality did not distinguish between commercial arbitration and investment treaty arbitration, although the important issues of public interest and public policy implicated in an investment treaty arbitration may warrant a different approach.[131] This issue was not resolved on appeal.[132]

2.61

---

[122] Ibid, [9]; *AAY v AAZ* (n 115) [54]; *International Coal Pte Ltd v Kristle Trading Ltd and Another and Another Suit* (n 119) [82].

[123] *AAY v AAZ* (n 115) [39]. C.f. *Associated Electric and Gas Insurance Services Ltd v European Reinsurance Co of Zurich* [2003] 1 WLR 1041 at [20].

[124] See e.g. Article 30 of the LCIA Arbitration Rules 2020; Rule 24.4 of the SIAC Rules 2016; Article 45 of the Hong Kong International Arbitration Centre (HKIAC) Rules.

[125] See Article 22(3) of the ICC Rules 2021.

[126] *CHH v CHI* [2021] 4 SLR 295.

[127] Ibid, [74]–[75].

[128] Ibid, [76]–[77].

[129] *Republic of India v Vedanta Resources plc* [2020] SGHC 208 [22]–[23].

[130] Ibid, [111]–[116].

[131] Ibid, [117].

[132] The Singapore Court of Appeal dismissed the appeal on the basis that the application for declaratory relief was a backdoor appeal and therefore an abuse of process. See *Republic of India v Vedanta Resources plc* [2021] SGCA 50 [56]–[57].

40 REGULATION OF PROCEDURAL ASPECTS OF ARBITRATION

2.62 The general obligation of confidentiality is subject to several exceptions. Singapore courts have, following English authority, affirmed the following exceptions to confidentiality, namely where: (i) there is express or implied consent; (ii) disclosure is permitted by the tribunal or with the leave of court; (iii) disclosure is reasonably necessary for the protection of the legitimate interests of a party to the arbitration; or (iv) disclosure is required by the interests of justice or the public interest.[133] The Singapore courts have held that leave of court is not necessary for a party seeking to rely on an exception to disclosure, although the Singapore courts may subsequently have to determine whether disclosure fell within an exception, if that is disputed.[134]

2.63 The Singapore courts have applied the third category of exceptions—that is, disclosure where reasonably necessary for the protection of a party's legitimate interests—to permit disclosure of documents in the arbitration necessary to establish a contention that a Singapore litigation action was vexatious and an abuse of court process.[135] The exception has also been found to apply in situations where non-parties to an arbitration disclosed documents arising from the arbitration in the course of seeking a case management stay of related court proceedings.[136] This is consistent with English authority, which has held that the third category applies to disclosures necessary to found a cause of action against a third party, or to defend a claim or counterclaim brought by a third party. Thus, for example, in *Emmott v Wilson*, the English Court of Appeal found that a party's need to disclose documents to its insurers from which it was seeking reimbursement fell within this exception.[137] However, this exception does not apply where disclosure may have a purely commercial impact on a third party and is not required in order to protect a party's legal rights.[138]

2.64 With respect to the fourth category of exceptions, in *AAY v AAZ*, the Singapore High Court held that disclosure to the proper authorities on reasonable suspicion of criminal conduct is an exception to confidentiality where disclosure is required in the public interest.[139] On that basis, the High Court permitted disclosure of a partial award, which made findings on dishonest and fraudulent acts as well as fabrication of evidence, to the Commercial Affairs Department of the Singapore Police Force.[140] It is worth noting that English authorities have not set a high bar for disclosure, requiring only an 'arguable case of unlawful actions' for disclosure to be excepted from confidentiality.[141]

---

[133] *AAY v AAZ* (n 115) [64]; *Emmott* (n 117) [103]–[107]. This was affirmed in the recent case of *CJY v CJZ and others* [2021] 5 SLR 569 [58] (hereafter *CJY v CJZ*).

[134] *Myanma Yaung* (n 121) [19].

[135] Ibid, [23].

[136] *CJY v CJZ* (n 133) [56]–[73].

[137] *John Forster Emmott v Michael Wilson & Partners Ltd* [2008] EWCA Civ 184 [101].

[138] *Ali Shipping Corporation v Shipyard Trogir* [1999] 1 WLR 314, 327.

[139] *AAY v AAZ* (n 115) [70]–[71].

[140] Ibid, [81]–[821].

[141] See e.g. *Westwood Shipping Lines Inc and another v Universal Schiffahrtsgesellschaft MBH and another* [2012] EWHC 3837 (Comm) (disclosure appropriate 'where there is, at least on the face of the material before the court, an arguable case of unlawful actions, unlawful conduct, having taken place, that the court should not allow confidentiality of arbitration materials in any sense to stifle the ability to bring to light wrongdoing of one kind or another').

Singapore courts have also left open the question of whether there should be a fifth **2.65** category of exceptions for disclosure based on 'wider considerations of public interest', although in *AAY v AAZ* Chan J suggested *obiter* that, where disclosure to the public at large is sought to be justified on the grounds of public interest, this should operate as a defence rather than an exception.[142] This means that the burden is on the disclosing party to show that any such disclosure is necessary in the public interest to the extent that it should be excused from any breach of confidentiality.[143] Chan J further observed that, because disclosure to the public at large would 'completely destroy confidentiality', the disclosing defendant ought to show 'a compelling public interest' to justify disclosure.[144] The English courts have also not settled this question, although some recent authorities have tentatively recognised a broader exception for disclosure in the wider public interest. In *The Chartered Institute of Arbitrators v B & Ors*, the English High Court permitted the Chartered Institute of Arbitrators to seek and obtain documents generated in both an arbitration and in an arbitrator removal application before the English courts for use in disciplinary proceedings, on the basis that this was justified by 'general public interest in maintaining the quality of and standards of arbitrators'.[145]

---

[142] *AAY v AAZ* (n 115) [72].
[143] Ibid.
[144] Ibid.
[145] *The Chartered Institute of Arbitrators v B & Ors* [2019] EWHC 460 (Comm).

3

Interface with Other Dispute Resolution Forums

A. Mediation and Negotiation	3.02	C. Expert Determination	3.12
B. Singapore International Commercial Court (SICC)	3.09		

3.01 The arbitral process is not isolated and may at times be a part of a wider dispute resolution process agreed by the parties. Indeed, as we will see in relation to Section 17 of the International Arbitration Act (IAA),[1] there is express statutory recognition of the power of an arbitrator to act as conciliator as well. Anecdotally, however, it is not common practice for arbitrators in Singapore-seated arbitrations to act additionally as a conciliator or mediator even if they could. This is unlike jurisdictions such as China where a hybrid approach is perhaps more prevalent.

A. Mediation and Negotiation

3.02 The above example aside, it may be helpful to discuss the processes of mediation and negotiation, which are two forms of alternative dispute resolution relevant to users of arbitration in Singapore.

3.03 Mediation has long operated alongside arbitration, as it does with the litigation process. 2019 also saw the opening of signatures for the United Nations Convention on International Settlement Agreements Resulting from Mediation, also known as the Singapore Convention on Mediation. The Convention, which came into force in September 2020, allows for the cross-border enforcement of mediated settlement agreements. It aims to have an effect on the enforceability of mediated settlement agreements similar to the effect the New York Convention has had on the enforceability of arbitral awards. This is likely to increase the willingness of commercial parties to consider mediation as part of any anticipated legal process to enforce their rights. Indeed, it is not uncommon for some tribunals to seek the parties' views as to whether the possibility of mediation needs to be considered for the purposes of timetabling.

3.04 Mediation has become an integral, and in some cases mandatory, step that parties stipulate in their dispute resolution clauses. Under Singapore law, any preconditions to arbitrations that are expressed in mandatory terms are in principle enforceable so long as

---

[1] Oddly, an equivalent provision is not found in the domestic regime. See Chapter 13.

they are sufficiently certain. That includes agreements to mediate prior to commencing arbitration proceedings.[2] The failure to satisfy any preconditions to arbitration is arguably seen as a jurisdictional defect[3] rather than a procedural issue that can be cured. If preconditions are treated as jurisdictional, a party that fails to comply with the preconditions will have to re-start proceedings, and the tribunal cannot—at least without the consent of the other party—hold the arbitral proceedings in abeyance pending a further attempt to comply with the preconditions.[4] This stands in contrast to more recent English authority, which holds that non-compliance with preconditions to arbitration in a multi-tiered dispute resolution clause are not jurisdictional questions but questions of the admissibility of the claim before an arbitral tribunal.[5]

Therefore, where mediation or some other form of alternative dispute resolution mechanism is specified,[6] then parties must be careful to adhere strictly to any procedures that have been set out, including the personnel that have to be involved, or else it may be held that the preconditions to arbitration have not been satisfied.[7] It is sometimes the case that parties may segregate disputes relating to certain contractual issues, as opposed to arbitration, or only a sub-set of issues intended for arbitration are subject to the precondition requiring mediation.[8] Attention should be paid to these nuances in a contract in order to avoid a situation where arbitration is triggered prematurely without having satisfied the various preconditions. **3.05**

Second, it is not uncommon for parties to engage in negotiations or even mediation after arbitration proceedings have commenced. Under the SIAC Rules currently in force, there is a formal process by which parties can incorporate an 'arb-med-arb' clause (or agree to it post dispute) that enables parties to put their dispute on the mediation track for a period of time, and if successful, have their mediated settlement recorded as a consent award.[9] The process, in brief, requires the Registrar of the SIAC to inform the Singapore International Mediation Centre (SIMC) that the arbitration commenced pursuant to an 'arb-med-arb' clause. Meanwhile, the arbitral tribunal is constituted, but it will stay proceedings after the exchange of the Notice of Arbitration and the Response to the Notice of Arbitration. These documents will be transmitted to the SIMC, which will then set the mediation process in motion. The mediation is intended to be completed within eight weeks unless the time is extended by the Registrar of the SIAC in consultation with the **3.06**

---

[2] *International Research Corp PLC v Lufthansa Systems Asia Pacific Pte Ltd* [2014] 1 SLR 130.

[3] Ibid [63]; although the Court of Appeal simply stated that 'the Tribunal did not have jurisdiction' as a result of the non-compliance with the preconditions for arbitration, and there was no detailed discussion on the point.

[4] *BBA v BAZ* [2020] SGCA 53 [74]–[79]. See also, *Maxx Engineering Works Pte Ltd v PQ Builders Pte Ltd* [2023] SGHC 71, in which the High Court granted an injunction to enforce a pre-arbitration mediation clause.

[5] *NWA & FSA v NVF & others* [2021] EWHC 2666 (Comm); *Republic of Sierra Leone v SL Mining Ltd* [2021] EWHC 286 (Comm) (hereafter *Sierra Leone v SL Mining*). The position appears to be similar in Hong Kong. See *C v D* [2022] HKCA 729.

[6] For example, escalation of the dispute through various levels of management, or a joint committee of the two parties, or neutral evaluation.

[7] *Sierra Leone v SL Mining* (n 5) [57]; the Court of Appeal undertook a very detailed analysis of the facts in this regard.

[8] *Sierra Leone v SL Mining* (n 5) [58].

[9] Singapore International Mediation Centre, 'SIAC-SIMC ARB-MED-ARB PROTOCOL' (*SIMC*) <http://simc.com.sg/v2/wp-content/uploads/2019/03/SIAC-SIMC-AMA-Protocol.pdf> accessed 8 April 2022.

44 INTERFACE WITH OTHER DISPUTE RESOLUTION FORUMS

SIMC. After the eight weeks, or the time extended, the arbitral process will resume if the matter has not been settled. If there is a mediated settlement, the parties may request the tribunal to record their settlement in the form of a consent award.

3.07 The process, while seemingly straightforward, gives rise to a number of questions. In particular, the protocol does not address the situation where a respondent intends to raise jurisdictional objections. It is not clear if such a party will nevertheless be compelled to mediate since the protocol appears to mandate an automatic stay once the Response to the Notice of Arbitration is filed and exchanged. It seems however that the intention is that the arbitration will be suspended in any event. Therefore, the respondent will not lose anything by simply attempting to settle the dispute through mediation even if it is challenging the arbitral tribunal's jurisdiction. Consenting to the mediation does not equate to consenting to the arbitration, and if the mediation is successful, the respondent will be expressly consenting to the agreement or the award, and no jurisdictional issue can arise from this.

3.08 Another potential issue that arises is that the protocol does not address the situation where interim relief may need to be urgently applied for and cannot wait the eight-week mediation process.[10] If the arbitration is suspended or stayed, then it would seem that one's recourse is to go to court, which may not be the ideal solution in the circumstances.

B. Singapore International Commercial Court (SICC)

3.09 The arbitral process may at times require judicial intervention. As a general matter, applications arising in relation to the IAA may be brought to the High Court. In certain instances, such cases may be transferred to the SICC.

3.10 By way of background, the SICC is a division of the Singapore High Court and comprises all the High Court judges as well as a panel of International Judges. Appeals from first-instance SICC judgments are heard by the Court of Appeal, which coram may include International Judges as well. The *raison d'être* for the SICC and its processes are well documented elsewhere.[11] In brief, the Court was set up to adjudicate over disputes of an international nature.

3.11 Where arbitration-related matters would have been heard by the High Court previously, the Supreme Court Judicature Act has been amended so that the jurisdiction of

---

[10] See P. Tan and K. Tan, 'Links in the SIAC-SIMC Arb-Med-Arb Protocol' (*Singapore Law Gazette*, January 2018) <https://lawgazette.com.sg/feature/kinks-in-the-siac-simc-arb-med-arb-protocol/> accessed 8 April 2022; C. Ford, 'Purpose over Process—Empowering the SIAC-SIMC Arb-Med-Arb Protocol' (*Singapore Law Gazette*, June 2018) <https://lawgazette.com.sg/feature/purpose-over-process-empowering-the-siac-simc-arb-med-arb-protocol/> accessed 8 April 2022.

[11] Singapore International Commercial Court, 'Establishment of SICC' (*SICC*, 14 March 2022) <https://www.sicc.gov.sg/who-we-are/establishment-of-the-sicc> accessed 8 April 2022 and Singapore International Commercial Court, 'SICC Proceedings in General' (*SICC*, 31 March 2022) <https://www.sicc.gov.sg/guide-to-the-sicc/sicc-proceedings-in-general> accessed 8 April 2022.

C. EXPERT DETERMINATION   45

the SICC includes the ability to hear any proceedings relating to international commercial arbitration[12] that the High Court may hear and that satisfy such conditions as the Rules of Court may prescribe. The first of these cases, relating to an application to set aside an award and a simultaneous application for it to be struck out on the basis that it was brought out of time, was heard and decided in June 2019.[13] Since that time, the SICC has heard and decided a meaningful number of international arbitration applications.[14]

C. Expert Determination

It is common for parties to also agree in their dispute resolution clauses for certain issues or claims—usually of a technical nature—to be heard and determined by an expert in the first instance. Such dispute resolution clauses may also provide for the qualifications of such experts, the method for appointing such an expert (either between the parties or appointed by an institution), the procedure before the said expert, how the costs of the expert determination are to be apportioned, and the terms of reference of the dispute to be submitted to the expert. The clause may also provide that the determination of the expert is final and binding on the parties, or that the determination of the expert is subject to review by an arbitral tribunal which may be constituted.   **3.12**

Expert determinations do not enjoy the same degree of international enforceability as arbitral awards or foreign judgments as there is presently no international instrument concerning the enforcement of expert determinations. However, as a matter of Singapore law, expert determinations are enforceable in Singapore.[15] Where parties have so agreed, an expert's determination must be enforced as a contractual bargain, and a court would not substitute its own view on the merits when the parties have already agreed to rely on the expertise of an expert for a final and irrevocable determination.[16] An expert determination, however, may be set aside, on grounds including fraud or corrupt colouring of the expert's determination or breach of an expert's terms of appointment.[17] An error of fact or law would not vitiate an award by an expert if he or she acted within the scope of his or her contractual mandate.[18]   **3.13**

---

[12] Although it is unclear if this includes court proceedings relating to investor–state arbitrations, applications in relation to such disputes are likely to still be brought under the International Arbitration Act, and therefore under the SICC's remit.

[13] *BXS v BXT* [2019] SGHC(I) 10.

[14] See e.g. *CEB v CEC* [2020] 4 SLR 183; *BXY and anor v BXX and anor* [2019] 4 SLR 413; *BXS v BXT* [2019] 4 SLR 390; *Carlsberg Breweries A/S v CSAPL (Singapore) Holdings Pte Ltd* [2020] 4 SLR 35; *BYL and anor v BYN* [2020] 4 SLR 1. Indeed, the SICC has clarified the ability of parties to choose the SICC as their supervisory court for IAA-related matters and has promulgated a model clause to this effect.

[15] *Evergreat Construction Co Pte Ltd v Presscrete Engineering Pte Ltd* [2006] 1 SLR(R) 634 (hereafter *Evergreat Construction v Presscrete Engineering*); *Ngee Ann Development Pte Ltd v Takashimaya Singapore Ltd* [2017] 2 SLR 627 (affirming *Evergreat*).

[16] *Evergreat Construction v Presscrete Engineering* (n 15) [29], [33].

[17] Ibid, [29], [34].

[18] Ibid, [34], [41].

4

Interpretation of Part II of the Act

A.	Section 2(1)—'arbitral tribunal'	4.02	E.	Section 2(1)—'Model Law'	4.09
B.	Section 2(1)—'appointing authority'	4.05	F.	Section 2(1)—'party'	4.10
C.	Section 2(1)—'arbitration agreement'	4.06	G.	Section 2(2)—The Meaning of Terms Used in Both the Model Law and the IAA	4.11
D.	Section 2(1)—'award'	4.07			

<u>IAA, Section 2</u>

(1) In this Part, unless the context otherwise requires—

'arbitral tribunal' means a sole arbitrator or a panel of arbitrators or a permanent arbitral institution, and includes an emergency arbitrator appointed pursuant to the rules of arbitration agreed to or adopted by the parties including the rules of arbitration of an institution or organisation;

'appointing authority' means the authority designated under section 8(2) or (3);

'arbitration agreement' means an arbitration agreement referred to in section 2A;

'award' means a decision of the arbitral tribunal on the substance of the dispute and includes any interim, interlocutory or partial award but excludes any orders or directions made under section 12;

'Model Law' means the UNCITRAL Model Law on International Commercial Arbitration adopted by the United Nations Commission on International Trade Law on 21st June 1985, the text in English of which is set out in the First Schedule;

'party' means a party to an arbitration agreement or, in any case where an arbitration does not involve all of the parties to the arbitration agreement, means a party to the arbitration.

(2) Except so far as the contrary intention appears, a word or expression that is used both in this Part and in the Model Law (whether or not a particular meaning is given to it by the Model Law) has, in the Model Law, the same meaning as it has in this Part.

4.01 Section 2 marks the start of Part II of the International Arbitration Act (IAA),[1] which deals with international commercial arbitrations in Singapore. Section 2 contains a

---

[1] International Arbitration Act (Cap. 143 A, Rev. Ed. 2002) (hereafter IAA).

A. Section 2(1)—'arbitral tribunal'

Section 2(1) of the IAA, as adopted in 1994, defined an 'arbitral tribunal' as either a sole **4.02** arbitrator, panel of arbitrators, or a permanent arbitral institution. To address a lacuna in the law at the time, the IAA was amended in 2012 to include emergency arbitrators as part of the definition of 'arbitral tribunal'.[2]

Emergency arbitrator procedures allow a specially appointed arbitrator to adjudicate **4.03** solely on the issue of urgent relief needed prior to the constitution of an arbitral tribunal, with his or her decision subject to the adjudicatory powers of the later-constituted tribunal. In recent years, many arbitral institutions have introduced such procedures.[3] This was intended to plug a gap whereby users of arbitration were previously unable to seek urgent relief within the arbitration until a tribunal had been constituted. Where such relief could not await the constitution of the tribunal, users had no option but to seek such relief from a municipal court. Doing so, however, meant that obtaining urgent interim relief prior to the constitution of an arbitral tribunal would depend on the efficiency and processes of a municipal court, which a party might have wished to avoid by choosing arbitration. There was also some risk that the municipal court might decline to grant relief due to a misappreciation of the arbitral process or its role in the arbitral process.

There was, however, uncertainty about whether an emergency arbitrator's decision **4.04** could be enforced the same way as an order or award issued by an arbitral tribunal. To address this issue in Singapore, the definition of 'arbitral tribunal' in Part 2 of the IAA was amended in 2012 to include 'an emergency arbitrator'.[4] As explained in Parliament at the Second Reading of the amendment bill, the amended definition would allow emergency arbitrators to 'exercise the full range of powers available to [a] tribunal under the Act [with their] awards ... enforceable in our courts in the same way as awards by any other tribunal'.[5] Where an emergency arbitrator's decision is in the form of orders or directions under Section 12, it can be enforceable with leave of court under Section 12(6).

---

[2] International Arbitration (Amendment) Act 2012 (No. 12 of 2012), Section 2(a) (hereafter IAA (Amendment), 2012).

[3] Emergency arbitrator provisions were introduced by various arbitral institutions from 2012. See e.g. C. Tung and A.M. Utasy, 'The Framework of Emergency Arbitrator Procedures: A Comparative Discussion of Institutional Provisions—Part I' (2013) 15(1) Asian Dispute Review 7, C. Tung and A.M. Utasy, 'The Framework of Emergency Arbitrator Procedures: A Comparative Discussion of Institutional Provisions—Part 2' (2013) 15(2) Asian Dispute Review 42

[4] IAA (Amendment), 2012 (n 2), Section 2(a).

[5] International Arbitration (Amendment) Bill, Parliament No. 12, Session No. 1, Vol. No. 89, Sitting No. 1 (9 April 2012), Second Reading, page 66.

48   INTERPRETATION OF PART II OF THE ACT

B. Section 2(1)—'appointing authority'

4.05   Section 2(1) of the IAA defines the 'appointing authority' as the authority designated under Section 8(2) or (3). Section 8(2) and (3) in turn specify the designated authority as respectively the President of the Court of Arbitration of the SIAC and any person appointed by the Chief Justice as notified in the Gazette. The powers of the appointing authority under the IAA are addressed in greater detail in Chapter 8.[6]

C. Section 2(1)—'arbitration agreement'

4.06   Section 2(1) of the IAA defines an arbitration agreement as one referred to in Section 2A of the IAA, which is discussed in greater detail below.[7] Section 2(1) has been amended several times.[8] Previous definitions simply cross-referred to Article 7 of the 1985 version of the United Nations Commission on International Trade Law (UNCITRAL) Model Law on International Commercial Arbitration (the Model Law).[9] After the definition of an 'arbitration agreement' was updated in the 2006 version of the Model Law, the IAA was modified to include a new Section 2A, which comprehensively sets out updated definition and form requirements for an arbitration agreement and incorporate Option 1 of Article 7 of the 2006 version of the Model Law.[10]

D. Section 2(1)—'award'

4.07   Section 2(1) of the IAA provides that an award is a decision of an arbitral tribunal on the substance of the dispute and 'includes any interim, interlocutory or partial award'. The definition expressly excludes 'any orders or directions made under section 12',[11] which sets out the non-exhaustive powers of an arbitral tribunal to make orders and directions on matters such as evidence and procedure,[12] and vary from relatively simple directions concerning the giving of evidence to more substantive forms of injunctive relief. The definition in Section 2(1) also excludes any other interlocutory orders that

---

[6]   See Chapter 8.

[7]   See Chapter 5.

[8]   International Arbitration (Amendment) Act 2001 (No. 38 of 2001) (hereafter IAA (Amendment), 2001), International Arbitration (Amendment) Act 2009 (No. 26 of 2009).

[9]   IAA (n 1), Section 2(1).

[10]   See Chapter 5.

[11]   The exclusion of orders and directions made under section 12 of the IAA (n 1) is a result of Section 2(b). See IAA (Amendment), 2001 (n 8); *PT Pukuafu Indah and others v Newmont Indonesia Ltd and another* [2012] SGHC 187, [19] (hereafter *PT Pukuafu v Newmont Indonesia (SGHC)*); *PT Perusahaan Gas Negara (Persero) TBK v CRW Joint Operation* [2015] SGCA 30 [50] (hereafter *PT Perusahaan Gas v CRW Joint Operation (SGCA)*).

[12]   Orders and directions under Section 12 vary from relatively simple directions concerning the giving of evidence to more substantive forms of injunctive relief. Section 12(1)(i) completes the list by saying an arbitral tribunal can give directions 'for an interim injunction or any other interim measure'. See Chapter 11.

do not decide the substance of the dispute.[13] The definition of an award and an effect of an award under the IAA is further addressed in Chapter 14.

Although interlocutory orders and directions issued by a tribunal are not 'awards' under the IAA, this does not mean that parties to an arbitration can disregard such directions and orders at will. The exclusion simply means that the specific powers granted to the Singapore courts under the Act and Model Law with respect to awards do not apply to such interlocutory orders and directions. Where necessary, Section 12(6) allows a party, with leave of the High Court, to seek to make a tribunal's orders or directions under Section 12 enforceable 'as if they were orders made by a court'.[14] Particular issues concerning provisional awards or jurisdictional rulings are discussed in Chapters 11 and 14. **4.08**

E. Section 2(1)—'Model Law'

Section 2(1) makes clear that the 'Model Law' is the United Nations Commission on International Trade Law Model Law on International Commercial Arbitration adopted by the UNCITRAL on 21 June 1985, which is found at the First Schedule of the Act. Singapore incorporated the 1985 version of the Model Law on 31 October 1994.[15] When the Model Law was updated in 2006, Singapore did not incorporate the 2006 version of the Model Law. However, specific provisions in the 2006 version of the Model Law have been separately incorporated through amendments to the IAA.[16] Where provisions of the IAA have been impacted by the 2006 Model Law, these are indicated in the relevant parts of this commentary. **4.09**

F. Section 2(1)—'party'

Section 2(1) defines a 'party' as a party to an arbitration agreement. Section 6(5) further adds that for purposes of Sections 6 and 7 (stays), and 11A (interpleader proceedings), a reference to a party includes 'any person claim through or under such a party'.[17] In *Cassa di Risparmio di Parma e Piacenza SpA v Rals International Pte Ltd*,[18] the High Court found that an assignee of a contract containing an arbitration agreement was **4.10**

---

[13] *PT Pukuafu v Newmont Indonesia (SGHC)* (n 11) [20].

[14] C.f. *Denmark Skibstekniske Konsulenter A/S I Likvidation (formerly known as Knud E Hansen A/S) v Ultrapolis 3000 Investments Ltd (formerly known as Ultrapolis 3000 Theme Park Investments Ltd)* [2011] SGHC 207 [40]; see the commentary to Section 12 in Chapter 11.

[15] International Arbitration Bill, Bill No. 14/94, enacted 31 October 1994.

[16] For example, Section 2A of the IAA (n 1) incorporates Option 1 of Article 7 of the 2006 amended Model Law. See the commentary on Section 2A in Chapter 5.

[17] See also Chapter 7.

[18] *Cassa di Risparmio di Parma e Piacenza SpA v Rals International Pte Ltd* [2015] SGHC 264 [50]–[54], [90]; See also, N. Goh, 'An Assignee's Obligation to Arbitrate and the Principle of Conditional Benefit' (2016) 28 Singapore Academy of Law Journal 262.

50   INTERPRETATION OF PART II OF THE ACT

bound to arbitrate a dispute arising therefrom as a result of the 'conditional benefit' principle. There, the assignee who commenced litigation proceedings was found to be a 'party' and would be *prima facie* subject to a stay.[19] The so-called conditional benefit principle holds that an assignee to a contract takes the substantive rights under the contract subject to the obligation to enforce those rights through the agreed dispute resolution mechanism.[20] On appeal, the Court of Appeal noted that the principle merited further consideration.[21] There was no need to decide on the point as the Court of Appeal, agreeing with the High Court, found that the subject matter of the dispute—rights under promissory notes—though connected to the main contract, fell outside the scope of the arbitration agreement.[22]

G. Section 2(2)—The Meaning of Terms Used in Both the Model Law and the IAA

4.11   Section 2(2) makes clear that, where a contrary intention appears, words or expressions appearing in both Part II of the Act and the Model Law should take the meaning that the word or expression has in Part II.

---

[19] The Court however, found that the dispute fell outside the scope of the arbitration agreement.

[20] This is in contrast to a transferee under a novation, which takes both the benefits and obligations under the original contract. In an assignment, only the benefits are assigned.

[21] *Rals International Pte Ltd v Cassa di Risparmio di Parma e Paicenze SpA* [2016] SGCA 53 [54]–[55].

[22] Ibid, [49].

5

Arbitration Agreements

A.	An Overview of Arbitration Agreements	5.02	D. Section 2A(2)—In the Form of an Arbitration Clause or in the Form of a Separate Agreement — 5.25
B.	Validity and Construction of Arbitration Agreements	5.13	E. Section 2A(3)–(5)—In Writing — 5.26
C.	Section 2A(1)—'an agreement by the parties to submit to arbitration all or certain disputes which have arisen or which may arise … in respect of a defined legal relationship, whether contractual or not'	5.18	F. Section 2A(6)—'Where … a party asserts the existence of an arbitration agreement … and the assertion is not denied' — 5.30
			G. Section 2A(7)—Incorporation by Reference — 5.36
	1. Existence of an Agreement	5.19	H. Section 2A(8)—Bills of Lading — 5.43
	2. Optional or Asymmetric Clauses	5.22	

IAA, Section 2A

(1) In this Act, 'arbitration agreement' means an agreement by the parties to submit to arbitration all or certain disputes which have arisen or which may arise between them in respect of a defined legal relationship, whether contractual or not.

(2) An arbitration agreement may be in the form of an arbitration clause in a contract or in the form of a separate agreement.

(3) An arbitration agreement shall be in writing.

(4) An arbitration agreement is in writing if its content is recorded in any form, whether or not the arbitration agreement or contract has been concluded orally, by conduct or by other means.

(5) The requirement that an arbitration agreement must be in writing is satisfied by an electronic communication if the information contained in the electronic communication is accessible so as to be useable for subsequent reference.

(6) Where in any arbitral or legal proceedings, a party asserts the existence of an arbitration agreement in a pleading, statement of case or any other document in circumstances in which the assertion calls for a reply and the assertion is not denied, there is deemed to be an effective arbitration agreement as between the parties to the proceedings.

(7) A reference in a contract to any document containing an arbitration clause is to constitute an arbitration agreement in writing if the reference is such as to make that clause part of the contract.

52 ARBITRATION AGREEMENTS

(8) A reference in a bill of lading to a charterparty or other document containing an arbitration clause is to constitute an arbitration agreement in writing if the reference is such as to make that clause part of the bill of lading.

(9) Article 7 of the Model Law shall not apply to this section.

(10) In this section—

'data message' means information generated, sent, received or stored by electronic, magnetic, optical or similar means, including, but not limited to, electronic data interchange (EDI), electronic mail, telegram, telex or telecopy;

'electronic communication' means any communication that the parties make by means of data messages.

5.01 Section 2A of the IAA is based on Option 1 of Article 7 of the 2006 version of the United Nations Commission on International Trade Law (UNCITRAL) Model Law on International Commercial Arbitration (the Model Law) and contains an updated definition of an 'arbitration agreement'. Section 2A was introduced with amendments made to the International Arbitration Act (IAA) in 2012.[1] Prior to those amendments, the definition of an 'arbitration agreement' was set out in Section 2, along with other defined terms, and was based on Article 7 of the 1985 version of the Model Law, which contains the Model Law's definition of an 'arbitration agreement'. Section 2A(9) expressly disapplies Article 7 of the 1985 version of the Model Law.[2]

A. An Overview of Arbitration Agreements

5.02 The simplicity of Section 2A belies the significant jurisprudence and scholarly thinking on arbitration agreements. Arbitration agreements play an important role in determining issues such as the scope of dispute which may be submitted to arbitration, the proper parties to the arbitration, and where there are multi-tiered arbitration clauses, whether the pre-conditions have been fulfilled.[3] A few key principles that apply to the formation and interpretation of international arbitration agreements are outlined below.

5.03 First, under Singapore law, an arbitration clause is deemed to be a separable agreement from the underlying contract that concerns the parties' substantive rights and obligations. This is known as the separability principle, which holds that an arbitration

---

[1] International Arbitration (Amendment) Act 2012 (No. 12 of 2012). This round of amendments supersedes those made to Section 2 via International Arbitration (Amendment) Act 2009 (No. 26 of 2009).

[2] See International Arbitration (Amendment) Act 2009 (No. 26 of 2009).

[3] Readers are directed to other specialist texts which discuss the nature and impact an arbitration agreement has on the arbitral process. See e.g. D. Joseph QC, *Jurisdiction and Arbitration Agreements and their Enforcement* (3rd edn, Sweet & Maxwell 2015) (hereafter Joseph, *Jurisdiction and Arbitration Agreements and their Enforcement*); G. Born, *International Commercial Arbitration* (3rd edn, Kluwer Law International 2021) §3.01 (hereafter Born, *International Commercial Arbitration*); Lord Collins of Mapesbury and J. Harris (eds), *Dicey, Morris & Collins on the Conflict of Laws* (15th edn, Sweet & Maxwell 2018) 16–011.

A. AN OVERVIEW OF ARBITRATION AGREEMENTS   53

agreement is not necessarily impeached or rendered void if the substantive contract is found to be discharged, rescinded, or invalid.[4] The IAA does not expressly refer to the separability principle. However, it is reflected in Article 16(1) of the Model Law, which provides that an arbitration clause 'shall be treated as an agreement independent of the other terms of the contract', and is a generally accepted principle of Singapore law.[5] The separability principle is also widely reflected in other arbitration statutes,[6] the case law of other established arbitration jurisdictions,[7] and all major arbitral rules.[8]

The separability principle is closely related to the principle of competence-competence,   **5.04**
which, literally refers to an arbitral tribunal's competence to decide issues of its competence.[9] Together, the two principles allow an arbitral tribunal to determine whether the underlying agreement is invalid or unenforceable, without a challenge to the validity of the main contract itself affecting the validity of the arbitration agreement[10] or the tribunal's ability to determine such validity.[11]

Second, it may be possible for an arbitration agreement to be governed by a system of   **5.05**
law that is different from the law that governs the main contract. The former system of law, or the law governing the arbitration agreement, determines whether the arbitration agreement exists and has been validly formed; it is also the law that determines if the agreement is 'null and void, inoperative or incapable of being performed' for the purposes of a stay application under Section 6 of the IAA. The law governing the arbitration agreement is the subject of much scholarly debate.[12]

---

[4] Joseph, *Jurisdiction and Arbitration Agreements and their Enforcement* (n 3) [4.36].

[5] *BCY v BCZ* [2017] 3 SLR 357; [2016] SGHC 249 (hereafter *BCY v BCZ*); *BNA v BNB and another* [2020] 1 SLR 456, [27]–[28]; *BXH v BXI* [2020] 3 SLR 1368, at [82]–[84].

[6] See e.g. Arbitration Act 1996 (UK), Section 7; Hong Kong Arbitration Ordinance 2013, Section 34; Chinese Arbitration Law, Article 19; Japanese Arbitration Law, Article 13(6); French Civil Code (2011 revision), Article 144.

[7] *Harbour Assurance Co (UK) Ltd v Kansa General International Insurance Co Ltd* [1993] 1 Lloyd's Rep 455; *Bremer Vulkan Schiffbau und Maschinenfabrik v South India Shipping Corp* [1981] AC 909; *Fiona Trust & Holding Corp v Privalov* [2007] UKHL 40, [2008] 1 Lloyd's Rep 254; *Buckeye Check Cashing Inc v Cardegna* (2006) 546 US 440; *Prima Paint Corp. v Flood & Conklin Mfg. Co.* (1967) 388 US 395.

[8] See e.g. United Nations Commission on International Trade Law (UNCITRAL) Rules 1976, Article 21(2) ('[A]n arbitration clause which forms part of a contract and which provides for arbitration ... shall be treated as an agreement independent of the other terms of the contract.').

[9] See also *Tomolugen Holdings Ltd v Silica Investors Ltd* [2015] SGCA 57; [2016] 1 SLR 373 [25] (hereafter *Tomolugen v Silica (SGCA)*).

[10] *BCY v BCZ* (n 5) [61]. Note however, the IAA provides that an arbitration award can be denied enforcement if an arbitration agreement is 'null and void, inoperative or incapable of being performed'. See International Arbitration Act, Section 6(2). This language is similarly used in Article 8 Model Law and Article 2 of the New York Convention.

[11] The power to do so is not based on the parties' consent, but precedes and exists independently of such consent. See *Tomolugen v Silica (SGCA)* (n 9) [25].

[12] See e.g. Born, *International Commercial Arbitration* (n 3) 472–635; N. Blackaby et al., *Redfern and Hunter on International Arbitration* (7th edn, Oxford University Press 2022) 131–143 (hereafter Blackaby et al., *Redfern and Hunter*); V. Leong Hoi Seng and H. Tan Jun, 'The Law Governing Arbitration Agreements: BCY v BCZ and Beyond' (2018) 30 Singapore Academy of Law Journal 70; P.A. Karrer, 'The Law Applicable to the Arbitration Agreement' (2014) Singapore Academy of Law Journal 849; R. Nazzini, 'The Law Applicable to the Arbitration Agreement: Towards Transnational Principles' (2016) 65 International & Comparative Law Quarterly 681; D. Chan and T.J. Yang, 'Ascertaining the Proper Law of an Arbitration Agreement: The Artificiality of Inferring Intention When There is None' (2020) 37(5) Journal of International Arbitration 635; W. Miles QC and N. Goh, 'A Principled Approach Towards the Law Governing Arbitration Agreements' in N. Kaplan and M. Moser (eds), *Jurisdiction, Admissibility and Choice of Law in International Arbitration: Festschrift for Michael Pryles* (Kluwer Law International 2018).

54 ARBITRATION AGREEMENTS

5.06   Courts in Singapore have applied a presumptive rule in favour of applying the governing law of the contract as the implied law governing the arbitration agreement, following the approach of the English Court of Appeal in *Sulamérica Cia Nacional de Seguros SA v Enesa Engenharia SA (Sulamérica)*.[13] This presumed implied choice assumes that contracting parties reasonably intended their entire relationship to be governed by the same system of law.[14]

5.07   It should be noted that this is only a presumed implied choice. A generic choice-of-law clause, without more, would not constitute an express choice of law for the arbitration agreement. In *BCY v BCZ*, Clause 9.13.1 of the relevant contract provided: 'This Agreement and any non-contractual obligations arising out of or in connection with it are governed by and shall be construed in accordance with the Laws of the State of New York of the United States of America.'[15] *Sulamérica* concerned a choice-of-law clause in an insurance policy that provided: 'It is agreed that this Policy will be governed exclusively by the laws of Brazil.' Neither of these choice-of-law clauses were held to constitute an express choice of law for the arbitration agreement. As commentators have noted, it is rare for parties to expressly choose a law for the arbitration agreement.[16]

5.08   Where there is no choice-of-law clause in the main contract, there will be no express or implied choice of law for the arbitration agreement, with the consequence that Singapore law, as the law of the seat, is likely to apply to the arbitration agreement. This is the approach the English courts have taken. For example, in *Habas Sinai Ve Tibbi Gazlar Istihsal Endustrisi AS v VSC Steel Coy Ltd*,[17] Hamblen J noted that where the main contract did not contain a governing law clause, the law of the seat applies because it is the system of law with the closest and most real connection to the arbitration agreement. However, Hamblen J also noted that the law of the seat may apply in these circumstances based on an implied choice analysis.[18] In *BCY v BCZ*, Chong J appeared to endorse this view *obiter dicta*.[19]

5.09   Courts in the UK adopt a similar approach, as confirmed by the UK Supreme Court in *Enka Insaat Ve Sanayi AS v OOO Insurance Company Chubb (Enka v Chubb)*.[20] The

---

[13] *BCY v BCZ* (n 5) [49], [55]; see also *Sulamérica Cia Nacional de Seguros SA v Enesa Engenharia SA* [2012] EWCA Civ 638; [2013] 1 WLR 102 (hereafter *Sulamérica*); *Anupam Mittal v Westbridge Ventures II Investment Holdings* [2023] SGCA 1 (hereafter *Westbridge Ventures v Anupam Mittal (CA)*).

[14] *BCY v BCZ* (n 5), [43], [59]; *Sulamérica* (n 13) [11].

[15] *BCY v BCZ* (n 5) [14].

[16] Born, *International Commercial Arbitration* (n 3) 572–3. In *Kabab-Ji SAL (Lebanon) v Kout Food Group* [2020] EWCA Civ 6, the English Court of Appeal held that the parties' boilerplate definition of Agreement (to include all of the clauses in the Agreement) extended the choice-of-law provision to the arbitration agreement by way of express choice. The UK Supreme Court affirmed this reasoning on appeal: see *Kabab-Ji SAL (Lebanon) v Kout Food Group (Kuwait)* [2021] UKSC 48 at [39]. This decision has been criticised by commentators, given that the likelihood that the parties intended to expressly select the law governing the arbitration agreement in this manner 'is infinitesimal'. See e.g. Born, *International Commercial Arbitration* (n 3) 572–3. Subsequently, the Paris Court of Appeal disagreed with the English Court of Appeal and applied the law of the seat, French law, refusing to set aside the award. See Judgment of 23 June 2020, Case No. 17/22943 (Paris Cour d'Appel).

[17] *Habas Sinai Ve Tibbi Gazlar Istihsal Endustrisi AS v VSC Steel Coy Ltd* [2013] EWHC 4071 [101(3)], [103] (hereafter *Habas Sinai v VSC Steel*).

[18] *Habas Sinai v VSC Steel* (n 17) [102].

[19] *BCY v BCZ* (n 5) [67].

[20] *Enka Insaat Ve Sanayi AS v OOO Insurance Company Chubb* [2020] UKSC 38 (hereafter *Enka v Chubb*).

UK Supreme Court held that the law chosen by the parties to govern the main contract would, absent a 'good reason to the contrary', also apply to the arbitration agreement.[21] The majority (comprising Lords Hamblen, Leggatt, and Kerr) identified two factors that may displace this general presumption: first, pursuant to a 'validation principle', the presumption would not apply where there is a 'serious risk' that if governed by the same law as that of the main contract, the arbitration agreement would be ineffective; and second, the presumption would not apply if any provision of the law of the seat provides otherwise.[22] In the UK Supreme Court's subsequent decision in *Kabab-Ji SAL v Kout Food Group*, the UK Supreme Court confirmed the principles in *Enka v Chubb* and held that those principles apply both before an arbitration award is issued and at the stage of award enforcement.[23]

The UK Supreme Court's views in *Enka v Chubb* will have persuasive effects in Singapore. However, it should not be neglected that there is active discussion in England, in the context of revisions to the 1996 Act, about statutorily reversing the default rule in the Supreme Court decisions on the basis that it dilutes the application of the curial law of the seat, which is a major advantage of selecting a 'safe' seat that favours arbitration.[24] This is particularly the case with respect to the Supreme Court's clarification regarding the circumstances in which the parties' presumed choice (in a generic choice-of-law clause for the main contract) would be displaced, given that Singapore courts have not had occasion to clearly delineate these circumstances.

5.10

Singapore courts have appeared to take a slightly different approach to the UK on the circumstances in which the parties' presumed choice of law for the arbitration agreement would be displaced. In *BCY v BCZ*, Chong J observed *obiter* that the parties' presumed choice would be displaced if the consequences of choosing the law of the main contract would '*negate* the arbitration agreement even though the parties have themselves evinced a clear intention to be bound to arbitrate their disputes', or if it would 'fundamentally undercut' the arbitration agreement altogether'.[25] It is not clear whether this language suggests a higher threshold of proof than the 'serious risk' test set forth by the *Enka v Chubb* majority. In the authors' submission, it should not. The better reading of *BCY v BCZ* is that it is consistent with the English approach, particularly given that Chong J's views were based on *Sulamérica*, whereby Moore-Bick LJ had held that commercial parties are unlikely to have intended a choice of governing law for the contract to apply to an arbitration agreement if there is 'at least a serious risk' that such a choice would 'significantly undermine' that agreement.[26]

5.11

---

[21] *Enka v Chubb* (n 20) [43]–[44].
[22] *Enka v Chubb* (n 20) [70]–[72], [90]–[109], [170(b)].
[23] *Kabab-Ji SAL (Lebanon) v Kout Food Group (Kuwait)* [2021] UKSC 48 at [35].
[24] See, for example, 'Lord Hoffman criticises *Enka* in Gaillard Lecture,' *Global Arbitration Review*, available at https://globalarbitrationreview.com/article/lord-hoffmann-criticises-enka-in-gaillard-lecture; and the response by members of Brick Court Chambers, available at: https://www.brickcourt.co.uk/images/uploads/documents/BCC_LC_Consultation_Response_15_Dec_2022.pdf
[25] *BCY v BCZ* (n 5) [74] (emphasis in original).
[26] *Sulamérica* (n 13) [31].

56 ARBITRATION AGREEMENTS

5.12   The status under Singapore law of the validation principle endorsed by the *Enka v Chubb* majority remains unclear. In *BNA v BNB*, Vinodh Coomaraswamy J held that the validation principle was 'nakedly instrumental' and did not form a part of Singapore law, preferring instead to apply the *ut res magis* principle to find that Singapore law, the law of the seat, was the parties' implied choice of law.[27] On appeal, the Court of Appeal declined to make any findings on the status of the validation principle under Singapore law.[28] More recently, in *Westbridge Ventures v Anupam Mittal (CA)*, the Court of Appeal held that the presumptive application of Indian law was displaced because, had the presumption applied, Indian law would have applied with the effect that the subject-matter of the dispute would not have been arbitrable.[29] Although the Court of Appeal did not endorse the validation principle in terms, it quoted the same passage from *Sulamérica* that Chong J had referred to in *BCY v BCZ*, and stated elsewhere that arbitration agreements should generally be upheld unless there was good reason not to.[30] It should be noted that the displacement of the presumed implied choice was not automatic but depended on the Court's appreciation of the evidence regarding the parties' intention to settle disputes by arbitration, which in the case of *Westbridge Ventures v Anupam Mittal (CA)* was based on circumstantial, rather than direct, evidence.[31]

B. Validity and Construction of Arbitration Agreements

5.13   Singapore courts have set forth guidance on the generous pro-validity approach towards arbitration agreements under Singapore law. First, ordinary principles of construction apply to arbitration agreements, which should be construed to give effect to the expressed intentions of the parties.[32] Second, Singapore courts apply something akin to the 'principle of effective interpretation', meaning that where parties have evinced a clear intention to settle the dispute by arbitration, the courts will give effect to that intention, so long as doing so does not prejudice the rights of either party or result in an arbitration that is not within the contemplation of the parties.[33] Third, an arbitration agreement should not be interpreted restrictively or strictly and, as far as possible, a commercially logical and sensible construction should be preferred.[34] Fourth, inefficiency alone cannot render a clause invalid so long as the

---

[27] *BNA v BNB* [2019] SGHC 142 [48], [52], [63]–[64], [117] (hereafter *BNA (SGHC)*). This decision was eventually reversed by the Singapore Court of Appeal on different grounds (on the basis that Shanghai was the seat of arbitration, not Singapore), which meant that the choice of law issue as no dispositive in that case.

[28] Ibid, [95].

[29] *Westbridge Ventures v Anupam Mittal (CA)* (n 13) [70]–[72].

[30] *Westbridge Ventures v Anupam Mittal (CA)* (n 13) [69], [74].

[31] *Westbridge Ventures v Anupam Mittal (CA)* (n 13) [72].

[32] *Insigma Technology Co Ltd v Alstom Technology Ltd* [2009] SGCA 24; [2009] 3 SLR(R) 936 [30] (hereafter *Insigma v Alstom (SGCA)*).

[33] Ibid, [31].

[34] Ibid, [32]–[33].

B. VALIDITY AND CONSTRUCTION OF ARBITRATION AGREEMENTS   57

parties have agreed and intended for the arbitration to be conducted in a particular manner.[35]

Applying these principles, the Singapore Court of Appeal in *Insigma v Alstom* affirmed the validity of a hybrid arbitration clause that provided for disputes to be finally resolved by arbitration before the Singapore International Arbitration Centre (SIAC) but applying the International Chamber of Commerce (ICC) Rules.[36] The Court of Appeal further observed that the agreement was rendered certain and workable by the SIAC's agreement to administer the arbitration in accordance with the ICC Rules, and to nominate appropriate functional bodies that correspond to the bodies required under the ICC Rules to supervise the arbitration.[37] Along similar lines, the Singapore High Court held in *KVC Rice Intertrade Co. Ltd v Asian Mineral Resources Pte Ltd* that a bare arbitration clause, which merely provides for the submission of disputes to arbitration without specifying the seat, the number of arbitrators, or the method for establishing the arbitral tribunal, is a valid and binding arbitration agreement so long as parties have evinced a clear intention to settle the dispute by arbitration.[38]   **5.14**

It follows from the generous approach taken by the Singapore courts that a defect in an arbitration clause does not necessarily negate the existence of an arbitration agreement.[39] In other words, 'pathological' arbitration clauses are not automatically invalidated or void *ab initio*; instead, it depends in each case on the nature or the substance of the defect, or whether the defect is curable.[40] For example, Singapore courts have held that a clause referring disputes to an 'appraiser' instead of an 'arbitrator' does not, of itself, mean that the proceedings conducted by an 'appraiser' will not be arbitration proceedings. Where the clause, read in its entirety along with the context of the business between the parties, indicates that an 'appraiser' is called upon to perform an arbitral function (among other functions), it constitutes a valid arbitration agreement.[41] Likewise, Singapore courts have found that a reference to a non-existent organisation, the 'Arbitration Committee at Singapore', does not render an arbitration agreement unworkable or invalid, so long as there is clear evidence of the parties' intention to arbitrate and a mandatory reference to arbitration.[42] This is consistent with the pro-validation approach in the jurisprudence of other leading jurisdictions for arbitration,   **5.15**

---

[35] *Insigma Technology Co Ltd v Alstom Technology Ltd* [2008] SGHC 134; [2009] 1 SLR(R) 23 [35], quoted with approval in appeal in *Insigma v Alstom (SGCA)* (n 32) [35].

[36] *Insigma v Alstom (SGCA)* (n 32) [29]–[38].

[37] Ibid, [40].

[38] *KVC Rice Intertrade Co Ltd v Asian Mineral Resources Pte Ltd* [2017] 4 SLR 182 [29].

[39] *Insigma v Alstom (SGCA)* (n 32) [38].

[40] Ibid, [38]–[39].

[41] *PT Tugu Pratama Indonesia v Magma Nusantara Ltd* [2003] SGHC 204 [20]–[24].

[42] *HKL Group Co Ltd v Rizq International Holdings Pte Ltd* [2013] SGHCR 5. Note that the Singapore High Court appeared to take a different approach in *TMT Co. Ltd v The Royal Bank of Scotland*, observing that an arbitration clause referring to a dispute to arbitration under the rules of a non-existent 'exchange' was not enforceable under Section 6 of the IAA, although this was arguably *obiter dicta* given that the Court had already concluded that the relevant dispute did not fall within the scope of the arbitration agreement. See *TMT Co. Ltd v The Royal Bank of Scotland* [2017] SGHC 21 [64]–[65].

58   ARBITRATION AGREEMENTS

where courts have excised pathological references to non-arbitral institutions or arbitration rules in order to give effect to an expressed intention to arbitrate.[43]

5.16   As yet another example of this pro-validation approach, Singapore courts have found that where the parties' agreement contains both an arbitration clause and a jurisdiction clause selecting Singapore courts, the court should give effect to the parties' intention to arbitrate and take a 'generous and harmonious interpretation' with respect to the allegedly conflicting clauses, interpreting the jurisdictional clause as conferring only supervisory jurisdiction over the arbitration.[44] The workability and construction of such agreements containing both arbitration clauses and jurisdiction clauses are discussed further in Chapter 7.[45]

5.17   The generous approach of the Singapore courts does not mean that a valid arbitration agreement will inevitably be found. For example, the courts have held that extremely vague and badly drafted contracts that merely provide for disputes to be governed by the 'rules of the Cocoa Merchants' Association of America', with no reference to arbitration or any arbitration rules, do not constitute an arbitration agreement.[46] In such cases, there is insufficient evidence of the parties' intention to arbitrate their disputes, whatever presumptions the courts might apply.

C. Section 2A(1)—'an agreement by the parties to submit to arbitration all or certain disputes which have arisen or which may arise … in respect of a defined legal relationship, whether contractual or not'

5.18   Section 2A(1) defines an arbitration agreement expansively to include all agreements 'to submit to arbitration all or certain disputes' that are in respect of a 'defined legal relationship', and provides that non-contractual disputes can also be included in the scope of the parties' agreement to arbitration.

1. Existence of an Agreement

5.19   Issues may arise as to whether or not an arbitration clause is 'agreed' where parties do not conclude an underlying commercial contract but nonetheless agree on the wording of the arbitration clause, for example in an exchange of draft contracts. In such circumstances, as the Singapore High Court held in *BCY v BCZ*, mere agreement on the

---

[43]   See e.g. *Lucky-Goldstar International (HK) Ltd v Ng Moo Kee Engineering Ltd* [1993] HKCFI 14 [6], [17]; *Robotunits Pty Ltd v Mennel* [2015] VSC 268 [9]; *Travelport Global Distribution Systems BV v Bellview Airlines Ltd*, 2012 WL 3925856, at *5.

[44]   *BXH v BXI* [2020] 1 SLR 1043; [2020] SGCA 28 [60]–[62].

[45]   See Ibid; *Silverlink Resorts Ltd v MS First Capital Insurance Ltd* [2020] SGHC 251; *Transocean Offshore International Ventures Ltd v Burgundy Global Exploration Corp* [2010] 2 SLR 821.

[46]   *Teck Guan Sdn Bhd v Beow guan Enterprises Pte Ltd* [2003] SGHC 203; [2003] 4 SLR(R) 276, [10]–[11].

wording of an arbitration clause does not amount to an intention to be contractually bound to arbitrate.[47] In that case, the parties negotiated but did not ultimately sign a sale and purchase agreement. They had exchanged seven drafts and negotiating materials that were specifically stated to be 'subject to contract'. The defendant commenced arbitration proceedings on the basis that the arbitration clause in the sixth draft agreement was agreed, notwithstanding that the overall agreement was not executed.[48] Steven Chong J (as he then was) found that there was no objective manifestation of any mutual intention by the parties to be bound by the arbitration agreement because the parties' correspondence indicated that both the arbitration agreement and the underlying commercial terms were 'subject to contract', and there was also evidence that the plaintiff had indicated that any consensus on the agreement was still subject to review and approval by the management.[49]

Where communications between parties do not expressly state that negotiations are **5.20** 'subject to contract', it is a question of construction whether the parties intended a contract to be formed prior to the execution of formal documents.[50] Thus, in *AQZ v ARA*, Prakash J (as she then was) found that both the arbitration agreement and the underlying commercial contract in that case had been concluded verbally on 8 December 2009, when the parties reached agreement on all the main terms and indicated their intention to be bound by such terms.[51] Prakash J rejected arguments that the contractual negotiations were to be 'subject to contract' and held that the parties had understood that a binding contract could be formed prior to the signing of a formal document and accepted that a contract could be concluded by email alone.[52]

By virtue of the separability principle,[53] the termination of a contract does not *ipso facto* **5.21** terminate the arbitration agreement contained within it. However, this does not mean that the arbitration agreement can never cease to have effect together with the underlying contract of which it is a part; whether the arbitration agreement is also terminated in such circumstances depends on the intention of the parties.[54] Although the intention of the parties is to be ascertained objectively, there is a presumption that the parties intend a dispute resolution clause to survive the substantive contract.[55] Thus, in *BXH v BXI*, the Singapore High Court held that an arbitration agreement contained in a distributorship agreement continued to have contractual force after the expiry of the distribution agreement, absent any evidence of contrary intention.[56]

---

[47] *BCY v BCZ* (n 5) [90].

[48] Ibid, [4].

[49] Ibid, [91]–[93]. Although Chong J applied New York law as the governing law of the arbitration agreement, he also observed that it was common ground that Singapore law was not materially different on the issues of agreement formation.

[50] *AQZ v ARA* [2015] SGHC 49; [2015] 2 SLR 972 [98] (hereafter *AQZ v ARA (SGHC)*).

[51] Ibid, [92], [104].

[52] Ibid, [101]–[103].

[53] See above at [5.03].

[54] *BXH v BXI* [2019] SGHC 141; [2020] 3 SLR 1368 (hereafter *BXH v BXI (SGHC)*) [82]–83].

[55] Ibid, [84].

[56] Ibid, [85]–[87].

60 ARBITRATION AGREEMENTS

2. Optional or Asymmetric Clauses

5.22 Optional and asymmetric clauses can give rise to complexities with respect to the existence of a valid arbitration agreement. An optional clause permits but does not require a party or the parties to arbitrate.[57] This may raise questions as to whether there is a binding 'agreement' to arbitrate. In this context, Singapore courts have found that on a proper construction, language stating that parties 'may elect to submit such matter to arbitration' confers an option on either party to elect for arbitration, but upon such an election, arbitration then becomes mandatory.[58] Such agreements constitute arbitration agreements for the purposes of the IAA.[59] Singapore courts have reached similar conclusions with respect to language referring to arbitration 'at the election' of a party or the parties.[60]

5.23 Asymmetric clauses permit one party, but not the other, to elect how it wishes to sue—via litigation or arbitration. The lack of mutuality in such clauses has given rise to controversy in other jurisdictions.[61] In *Wilson Taylor Asia Pacific Pte Ltd v Dyna-Jet Pte Ltd*,[62] the Singapore Court of Appeal considered and upheld the validity of such an asymmetric arbitration clause, which read:

> Any claim or dispute or breach of terms of the Contract shall be settled amicably between the parties by mutual consultation. If no amicable settlement is reached through discussions, at the election of Dyna-Jet, the dispute may be referred to and personally settled by means of arbitration proceedings, which will be conducted under English law; and held in Singapore.

5.24 Following unsuccessful negotiations, the respondent Dyna-Jet sued before the Singapore courts, thereby electing not to submit the dispute to arbitration, leading the appellant Wilson Taylor to apply for a stay under Section 6 of the IAA. Before the Singapore High Court, Coomaraswamy J dismissed the argument that the respondent's unilateral option to arbitrate meant that there was no valid arbitration agreement 'by the parties' under Section 2A(1) of the IAA because of a lack of mutuality, and affirmed that an arbitration agreement that operates only asymmetrically is nevertheless still an arbitration agreement, relying on the 'overwhelming weight of modern Commonwealth

---

[57] See e.g. *Anzen v Hermes One Limited (British Virgin Islands)* [2016] UKPC 1; [2016] 1 WLR 4098.

[58] *WSG Nimbus Pte Ltd v Board of Control for Cricket in Sri Lanka* [2002] SGHC 104; [2002] 1 SLR(R) 1088 [21], [23]. This decision was rendered prior to the insertion of Section 2A, and specifically drew attention to Article VII of the Model Law as required in the erstwhile Section 2(1).

[59] *WSG Nimbus Pte Ltd v Board of Control for Cricket in Sri Lanka* [2002] SGHC 104; [2002] 1 SLR(R) 1088 [30].

[60] *Dyna-Jet Pte Ltd v Wilson Taylor Asia Pacific Pte Ltd* [2016] SGHC 238 [61] (hereafter *Dyna-Jet v Wilson*).

[61] Asymmetric jurisdiction clauses have given rise to controversy under the Brussels Recast system in the United Kingdom and Europe. English courts have upheld the use of such clauses—effectively giving a nod to the freedom to contract—while European courts have frowned upon the use of such clauses, particularly in cases involving banks and their customers. See e.g. *Etihad Airways PJSC v Prof Dr Lucas Flother* [2019] EWHC 3107 (Comm); [2020] QB 793, *Commerzbank Aktiengesellschaft v Liquimar Tankers Management Inc* [2017] EWHC 161 (Comm); [2017] 2 All ER 829, *Mauritius Commercial Bank Ltd v Hestia Holdings Ltd and another* [2013] EWHC 1328 (Comm); [2013] 2 All ER 898. See also Louise Merrett (2018) 67(1) ICLQ 37.

[62] *Wilson Taylor Asia Pacific Pte Ltd v Dyna-Jet Pte Ltd* [2017] 3 SLR 267; [2016] SGHC 238 (hereafter *Wilson v Dyna-Jet 3 SLR*).

authority' and the principle of party autonomy.[63] This analysis was subsequently endorsed by the Court of Appeal.[64]

D. Section 2A(2)—In the Form of an Arbitration Clause or in the Form of a Separate Agreement

Section 2A(2) is permissive and provides that an arbitration agreement may be in the form of an arbitration clause or in the form of a separate agreement. This language is from Article 7 of the 1985 version of the Model Law (and remains unchanged in the 2006 version). The intention is to ensure that the definition of an arbitration agreement encompasses both arbitration clauses that are contained in a broader contract and cover disputes that may arise in the future, as well as separate agreements to submit disputes that have already arisen to arbitration.[65] In general, although this is not always the case, arbitration clauses are often more concise than submission agreements.[66] **5.25**

E. Sections 2A(3)–(5)—In Writing

Section 2A(3) of the IAA mandates that an arbitration agreement shall be in writing. This is consistent with, and is modelled after, the 'in writing' requirement for arbitration agreements under Article II(1) of the New York Convention. Sections 2A(4) to 2A(7) elaborate upon this writing requirement and are based on Option 1 of Article 7 of the 2006 amendments to the Model Law. **5.26**

Section 2A(4) clarifies that an arbitration agreement will satisfy the writing requirement if its content is recorded in any form, whether or not the arbitration agreement or contract has been concluded orally or by other means. Thus, oral agreements will satisfy the writing requirement in Section 2A(3) so long as there is a record of the agreement 'in any form'. In *AQZ v ARA*, the Singapore High Court confirmed that a record by one party to an oral arbitration agreement is sufficient, even 'without confirmation from the other party', relying on the views expressed in the second reading speech by the Minister for Law for the International Arbitration (Amendment) Bill (Bill 10 of 2012) and the Explanatory Note by the UNCITRAL Secretariat.[67] **5.27**

---

[63] Ibid, [61]–[130].

[64] The appeal centred on whether the dispute fell within the scope of the arbitration agreement. The High Court ([2017] 3 SLR 267) found that there was a valid arbitration agreement, and also found that the dispute fell within the scope of the clause. The Court of Appeal disagreed, holding that by referring the decision to litigation, the dispute no longer fell within the scope of the clause.

[65] One of the aims of the 1985 version of the Model Law is to ensure the validity of both types of arbitration agreements. See 'UNCITRAL Model Law, Chapter II, Article 7 [Definition and Form of Arbitration Agreement]' in H.M. Holtzmann and J.E. Neuhaus, *A Guide to the 2006 Amendments to the UNCITRAL Model Law on International Commercial Arbitration: Legislative History and Commentary* (Kluwer Law International 2015) 29–157, 30. (hereafter Holtzmann and Neuhaus, *A Guide to UNCITRAL Model Law on International Commercial Arbitration*).

[66] Blackaby et al., *Redfern and Hunter* (n 12) [2.02]–[2.07]

[67] *AQZ v ARA (SGHC)* (n 50) [116]–[120].

62 ARBITRATION AGREEMENTS

5.28 Section 2A(5) addresses electronic communications and provides that the writing requirement in Section 2A(3) is fulfilled if there is an electronic communication that is 'accessible so as to be useable for subsequent reference'. This formulation is modelled after Article 9(2) of the Convention on the Use of Electronic Communications in International Contracts and intended to ensure consistency with that Convention.[68]

5.29 Section 2A(10) is also relevant to interpretation of Section 2A(5). Subsection (10) explains that an 'electronic communication' means any form of communication by means of 'data messages'. The same subsection defines 'data message' as including information generated, sent, received, or stored by electronic, magnetic, optical, or similar means, including electronic mail, telegram, telex, and telecopy. The definitions in Section 2A(10) are modelled after the definitions of 'electronic communication' and 'data messages' in Article 4 of the Convention on the Use of Electronic Communications in International Contracts.[69]

F. Section 2A(6)—'Where ... a party asserts the existence of an arbitration agreement ... and the assertion is not denied'

5.30 Section 2A(6) of the IAA provides that if a party asserts the existence of an arbitration agreement, without denial from the other parties concerned, an effective arbitration agreement is deemed to exist between the parties. The assertion regarding the existence of an arbitration agreement must be in 'a pleading, statement of case, or any other document in circumstances in which the assertion calls for a reply'. This language is based on, but also broader than, Article 7(5) of the 2006 Model Law (Option 1), which provides for a deemed arbitration agreement only where an arbitration is 'contained in an exchange of statements of claim and defence in which the existence of an agreement is alleged by one party and not denied by the other'.

5.31 In *Vitol Asia Pte Ltd v Machlogic Singapore Pte Ltd*,[70] Vinodh Coomaraswamy J clarified that a general denial of the contract does not constitute a denial of an arbitration agreement between the parties.[71] Instead, to avoid the deeming mechanism of Section 2A(6), a respondent must *specifically* deny a claimant's assertion that an arbitration agreement exists between the parties.[72]

5.32 Coomaraswamy J gave the following reasons for this conclusion. First, the language of Section 2A(6) expressly requires the respondent to deny the claimant's assertion that an arbitration agreement exists between the parties and thus, denying that a contract exists

---

[68] Holtzmann and Neuhaus, *A Guide to UNCITRAL Model Law on International Commercial Arbitration* (n 65).

[69] Ibid.

[70] *Vitol Asia Pte Ltd v Machlogic Singapore Pte Ltd* [2020] SGHC 209 (hereafter *Vitol Asia v Machlogic (SGHC)*).

[71] Ibid, [55].

[72] Ibid, [55].

between the parties does not engage Section 2A(6).[73] Second, only a specific denial of a claimant's assertion that an arbitration agreement exists advances the twin purposes of Section 2A(6), which are (i) to promote efficiency in the allocation of dispute resolution resources, and (ii) to avoid defeating the reasonable expectations of stakeholders in dispute resolution proceedings.[74] Coomaraswamy J stressed that, where a claimant asserts expressly in dispute resolution proceedings that an arbitration agreement exists, a respondent's general denial of a contract between the parties is ambiguous and indistinguishable from a defence on the merits of the contract, and this may cause the claimant, its legal representatives, the court, or other adjudicating institutions to reasonably assume that the respondent has accepted the existence of the asserted arbitration agreement when it has not.[75] Such ambiguity may consequently lead to a waste of resources in preparing for the dispute to be resolved via arbitration.[76]

Coomaraswamy J further noted that Section 2A(6) must require the same specificity whether the underlying claim arises from a contract and, where there is a contract, whether such contract contains a defective arbitration clause.[77] In other words, the same level of specificity should be required (i) where a claim does not arise out of a contract but which the parties have apparently agreed ad hoc to refer to arbitration; (ii) where a claim arising out of a contract which contains no arbitration clause at all; and (iii) where a claim arising out of a contract which contains a defective arbitration clause.[78]   **5.33**

There is also a temporal aspect to the specificity required by Section 2A(6). As Coomaraswamy J observed, it is the claimant's *present* assertion of an arbitration agreement which must be denied, not any historical conduct or the existence of a putative arbitration agreement in the *past*, and the effect of that failure to deny is an arbitration agreement deemed to be formed by the parties' present conduct.[79] A corollary to this is that fraud or corruption in the formation of the parties' contract is incapable of having any effect on the arbitration agreement which is deemed effective by Section 2A(6) of the Act.[80] Although Section 2A(6) does not cure or validate any defects in the parties' arbitration agreement, Section 2A(6) operates in the present and deems an arbitration to exist by virtue of the parties' present conduct, and this operates whether or not there has been a historical contract between the parties, let alone whether there is a defective arbitration agreement within that contract.[81]   **5.34**

Conceptually, Section 2A(6) may be viewed as giving deeming effect to a form of waiver or estoppel: a party that fails to deny the assertion of an arbitration agreement may be   **5.35**

---

[73] Ibid, [57].
[74] Ibid, [58].
[75] Ibid, [60]–[61].
[76] Ibid, [61].
[77] Ibid, [63].
[78] Ibid, [64]–[65].
[79] Ibid, [66].
[80] Ibid, [86].
[81] Ibid, [86].

64 ARBITRATION AGREEMENTS

bound by an arbitration agreement because that party is estopped from denying the effect of the agreement on it, or waived the objections to application of the arbitration agreement to it.[82] This is broadly consistent with the general principle of waiver underlying Article 16(2) of the Model Law, which provides that a party that does not make jurisdictional objections regarding the existence or validity of an arbitration agreement by the time the statement of defence is filed is precluded from subsequently raising that objection.[83]

G. Section 2A(7)—Incorporation by Reference

5.36 Section 2A(7) makes clear that, when an arbitration agreement is contained not in the contract itself but in a separate document referred to by the provisions of the contract, this may be sufficient for an arbitration 'in writing' to be formed. This may be the case, for example, where the arbitration agreement is contained in a separate set of standard terms or general conditions of contract. As the proviso to Section 2A(7) reflects, the question in each case is whether 'the reference makes the [arbitration] clause part of the contract'.

5.37 In *International Research Corp Plc v Lufthansa Systems Asia Pacific Pte Ltd*,[84] the Singapore Court of Appeal clarified the approach regarding the incorporation by reference of arbitration agreements under Section 2A(7) of the IAA. There the first respondent, Lufthansa, and second respondent, Datamat, entered into a cooperation agreement under which Lufthansa would supply and maintain an electronic data protection system that Datamat had agreed to provide to a third party, Thai Airways. Datamat subsequently ran into financial difficulties. To keep the cooperation agreement going, Datamat, Lufthansa, and the appellant, International Research Corp, entered into a supplemental agreement, which was expressly stated to be 'annexed to and made a part of' of the cooperation agreement. Under the supplemental agreement, Datamat would transfer any money received from Thai Airways to International Research Corp, and International Research Corp would in turn transfer this to Lufthansa for its services. International Research Corp was also required to provide a letter of credit to Lufthansa, which the latter could draw on in the event of non-payment. The same parties also entered into a second supplemental agreement on the settlement of sums due to Lufthansa from Datamat.

5.38 A dispute arose in relation to outstanding payments allegedly due to Lufthansa. Lufthansa subsequently notified the parties it was terminating the cooperation agreement and supplementary agreements and launched arbitration proceedings. The

---

[82] Born, *International Commercial Arbitration* (n 3) §10.02[K].
[83] Ibid, §25.04[A][10], §26.05[B][j].
[84] *International Research Corp PLC v Lufthansa Systems Asia Pacific Pte Ltd and another* [2013] SGCA 55 (hereafter *International Research Corp v Lufthansa (SGCA)*).

G. SECTION 2A(7)—INCORPORATION BY REFERENCE 65

arbitral tribunal held that it had jurisdiction over disputes between the parties under the supplemental agreements on the basis of the arbitration agreement in the cooperation agreement. On an application for a declaration that the arbitral tribunal did not have jurisdiction, the question before the Court of Appeal was whether the arbitration clause in the cooperation agreement had been incorporated by reference into the supplemental agreements.

The Court of Appeal rejected the use of a restrictive approach advocated by the appellant, which had been applied in an older line of English cases and previously followed by the Singapore High Court in *Star-Trans Far East Pte Ltd v Norske-Tech Ltd*.[85] Under the restrictive approach, 'clear and express reference' was required before an arbitration clause in one agreement could be incorporated into another in a 'two contract' case.[86] This was based on a classification set forth by Sir Christopher Clarke J in *Habas Sinai Ve Tibbi Gazlar Isthisal Endustri AS v Sometal SAL*, who distinguished the following categories of incorporation cases, the latter two categories being 'two contract' cases: [87]

5.39

(1) A and B make a contract in which they incorporate standard terms.
(2) A and B make a contract incorporating terms previously agreed between A and B in another contract or contracts to which they were both parties.
(3) A and B make a contract incorporating terms agreed between A (or B) and C. Common examples are a bill of lading incorporating the terms of a charter to which A is a party; reinsurance contracts incorporating the terms of an underlying insurance; excess insurance contracts incorporating the terms of the primary layer of insurance; and building or engineering sub-contracts incorporating the terms of a main contract or sub-sub-contracts incorporating the terms of a subcontract.
(4) A and B make a contract incorporating terms agreed between C and D. Bills of lading, reinsurance and insurance contracts and building contracts may fall into this category.

The Court of Appeal rejected the application of the restrictive approach, considering that such a strict rule was overextended from its original application in the context of bills of lading and charterparties and should not be applied more generally in other commercial contexts.[88] Moreover, relying on the *travaux préparatoires* of the Model Law as well as jurisprudence from other Model Law jurisdictions, the Court of Appeal also held that Article 7(2) of the 1985 Model Law, on which Section 2A(6) is based, permitted incorporation by reference of an arbitration clause where there is only reference to the document containing the arbitration clause and no specific mention

5.40

---

[85] *Star-Trans Far East Pte Ltd v Norske-Tech Ltd* [1996] SGCA 35; [1996] 2 SLR (R) 196 [33]–[35] (hereafter *Star-Trans v Norske (SGCA)*).
[86] *TW Thomas & Co., Limited v Portsea Steamship Company, Limited* [1912] AC 1 (HL); *Aughton Ltd (formerly Aughton Group Ltd) v MF Kent Services Ltd* (1991) 31 Con LR 60; *Excess Insurance Co Ltd v Mander* [1995] CLC 838.
[87] *Habas Sinai Ve Tibbi Gazlar Isthisal Endustri AS v Sometal SAL* [2010] EWHC 29 (Comm); [2010] Bus LR 880 [13] (hereafter *Habas v Sometal (EWHC)*).
[88] *International Research Corp v Lufthansa (SGCA)* (n 84) [34].

66 ARBITRATION AGREEMENTS

of the arbitration clause, unlike the more restrictive approach taken by the English authorities.[89]

5.41 More importantly, the Court of Appeal held that the approach to incorporation of arbitration agreements was ultimately one of construction, based on the principles laid down in *Zurich Insurance (Singapore) Pte Ltd v B-Gold Interior Design & Construction Pte Ltd*,[90] which focuses on 'the *context* and the objective circumstances attending the entry into the contract'.[91] Applying this approach, the Court of Appeal found that the arbitration agreement in the cooperation agreement was not incorporated in the supplemental agreements. The supplemental agreements did not envisage International Research Corp stepping into the shoes of Datamat nor guaranteeing any of its obligations; instead, International Research Corp was only intended to act as a payment agent.[92] Thus, International Research Corp undertook no obligations under the cooperation agreement, and Datamat was still primarily liable for its own obligations under the cooperation agreement.[93] The Court of Appeal rejected the argument that the parties should be presumed to have intended one-stop adjudication under all the agreements, because the parties to the cooperation agreement and the supplemental agreements were not identical.[94] The Court of Appeal further held that its construction was supported by the language and form of the dispute resolution clause at clauses 37.2 and 37.3 of the cooperation agreement, whose terms would not be workable if they were incorporated into the supplemental agreements.[95]

5.42 Besides incorporation by reference, arbitration agreements may also be incorporated by trade custom or course of dealing. These issues were considered in in *R1 International Pte Ltd v Lonstroff AG*,[96] which concerned a dispute arising out of the sale of natural rubber by the plaintiff R1 to the defendant Lonstroff. Although R1 had sent pre-signed contracts containing arbitration clauses to Lonstroff in respect of each of its five orders, none of these contracts were signed by Lonstroff. A dispute arose out of the rubber supplied under the second order, which had been delivered and accepted by Lonstroff, and Lonstroff commenced proceedings in the Swiss courts. In support of its application for an anti-suit injunction from the Singapore courts, R1 alleged that the dispute fell within an arbitration agreement, arguing that the arbitration clauses had been incorporated by trade custom or, in the alternative, that they had been incorporated by the parties' course of dealing.[97] Judith Prakash J (as she then was) rejected both arguments. Prakash J held that evidence by two of the plaintiff's witnesses were insufficient

---

[89] Ibid, [32]–[34].
[90] *Zurich Insurance (Singapore) Pte Ltd v B-Gold Interior Design & Construction Pte Ltd* [2008] SGCA 27.
[91] *International Research Corp v Lufthansa (SGCA)* (n 84), [34].
[92] Ibid, [38]–[41].
[93] Ibid, [42]–[43].
[94] Ibid, [44].
[95] Ibid, [51]–[52].
[96] *R1 International Pte Ltd v Lonstroff AG* [2014] SGHC 69; [2014] 3 SLR 166 (hereafter *R1 International v Lonstroff (SGHC)*).
[97] Ibid, [19].

to establish the existence of a trade custom in the rubber industry.[98] Prakash J also held that one prior transaction between the parties was not enough to establish a course of dealing between them and that the facts did not show a continuity in the transactions, which indicated that there was 'no settled course of dealing between the parties'.[99]

H. Section 2A(8)—Bills of Lading

Section 2A(8) of the IAA deals specifically with incorporation by reference in the context of bills of lading and charterparties. In the light of the Singapore Court of Appeal's decision in *International Research Corp Plc v Lufthansa Systems Asia Pacific Pte Ltd*, which sought to confine the application of the restrictive approach in the English authorities to cases involving bills of lading and charterparties, it is likely that the 'clear and express reference' standard must be met for incorporation of an arbitration clause in one agreement into another in a 'two contract' case involving bills of lading and charterparties.[100] Thus, in *The Titan Unity*,[101] the Assistant Registrar held that the relevant arbitration agreement was incorporated by reference because there was a clear and express reference in the bill of lading to the charterparty which contained the arbitration agreement.[102]

5.43

---

[98] Ibid, [24]–[25].
[99] Ibid, [32].
[100] *International Research Corp v Lufthansa (SGCA)* (n 84) [34]. See also *TW Thomas & Co., Limited v Portsea Steamship Company, Limited* [1912] AC 1 (HL); *Aughton Ltd (formerly Aughton Group Ltd) v MF Kent Services Ltd* (1991) 31 Con LR 60; *Excess Insurance Co Ltd v Mander* [1995] CLC 838.
[101] *The 'Titan Unity'* [2013] SGHCR 28 .
[102] Ibid, [35]–[40].

6

The Effect, Interpretation, and Applicability
of the Model Law

A. Section 3—Model Law to Have Force of Law	6.01	C. Section 5—Application of Part II of the IAA	6.08
B. Section 4—Interpretation of Model Law by Use of Extrinsic Material	6.05		

A. Section 3—Model Law to Have Force of Law

IAA, Section 3

(1) Subject to this Act, the Model Law, with the exception of Chapter VIII of the Model Law, has the force of law in Singapore.

(2) In the Model Law—

'State' means Singapore and any country other than Singapore;

'this State' means Singapore.

6.01   Section 3(1) incorporates the United Nations Commission on International Trade Law (UNCITRAL) Model Law on International Commercial Arbitration (the Model Law) into Singapore law. However, Section 3(1) expressly excludes Chapter VIII of the Model Law, which deals with the recognition and enforcement of arbitral awards (Article 35) and the grounds on which recognition or enforcement may be refused (Article 36).[1] Instead, the recognition and enforcement of foreign awards is dealt with under Part III of the International Arbitration Act (IAA) (Sections 27–33), while the recognition and enforcement of Singapore-seated awards made under the IAA (or 'domestic international awards')[2] is dealt with under Section 19 of the IAA.

6.02   The Model Law was incorporated as part of the IAA in 1995, based on a recommendation by a sub-committee of the Law Reform Committee of the Singapore Academy of Law following its review of the arbitration law in Singapore.[3] The sub-committee recommended the exclusion of Chapter VIII to avoid any conflict between the

---

[1] See Articles 35 and 36 of the Model Law, at the First Schedule of the IAA.

[2] *PT First Media TBK v Astro Nusantara International BV and others* [2013] SGCA 57; [2014] 1 SLR 372 [16].

[3] Sub-Committee on Review of Arbitration Laws, *Report on Review of Arbitration Laws* (Singapore Academy of Law, 1993) 39–40.

enforcement provisions of the Model Law and the equivalent provisions of the New York Convention, which apply in Singapore only to foreign awards from other contracting States to the New York Convention.[4]

Where there are inconsistencies or variances between the Model Law and the IAA, as well as with other instruments of law (such as other laws, or treaties), how should these be resolved? Section 3(1) of the IAA provides the answer: the provisions of the Model Law are always 'subject to this Act', that is, any inconsistencies ought to be resolved in favour of the IAA. In addition, in multiple instances, where there are possible conflicts between provisions of the IAA and the Model Law, the IAA has stated how such a conflict may be resolved.[5] Apart from being subject to the IAA, the text of the Model Law itself also makes clear that it is subject to any agreement in force between Singapore and other States.[6] **6.03**

Section 3(2) defines the terms 'State' and 'this State' in the Model Law. This is relevant to the interpretation of the Model Law. In particular, read with Article 1(2) of the Model Law, Section 3(2) makes clear that all the provisions of the Model Law, with the exception of Articles 8, 9, 35, and 36, only apply if the place of arbitration is Singapore.[7] **6.04**

B. Section 4—Interpretation of Model Law by Use of Extrinsic Material

Section 4

(1) For the purposes of interpreting the Model Law, reference may be made to the documents of—
  (a) the United Nations Commission on International Trade Law; and
  (b) its working group for the preparation of the Model Law,
    relating to the Model Law.
(2) Subsection (1) does not affect the application of section 9A of the Interpretation Act 1965 for the purposes of interpreting this Act.

Section 4 provides that, subject to the overriding purposive approach to statutory interpretation provided for in Section 9A of the Interpretation Act,[8] reference may be made to any UNCITRAL documents or any documents by the UNCITRAL working **6.05**

---

[4] Sub-Committee on Review of Arbitration Laws, *Report on Review of Arbitration Laws* (Singapore Academy of Law, 1993) 39–40. See also *PT First Media TBK v Astro Nusantara International BV* [2013] SGCA 57, [2014] 1 SLR 372 (CA) at [86].

[5] See e.g. Section 2(2) of the IAA (provision for possible conflicts in defined terms); Section 2A(9) of the IAA (exclusion of Article 7 of the Model Law); Section 5(2) of the IAA ('Despite Article 1(3) of the Model Law'); Section 6(1) of the IAA ('Despite Article 8 of the Model Law'); etc.

[6] Article 1(1) of the UNCITRAL Model Law.

[7] See also *PT Garuda Indonesia v Birgen Air* [2002] 1 SLR(R) 401 [21] (hereafter *PT Garuda (SGCA)*).

[8] See Section 9A of the Interpretation Act (Cap. 1). See also Section 5 of the Interpretation Act, which provides that a schedule to an Act is to be construed and have effect as part of that Act. Therefore, Section 4 of the IAA plainly provides that the purposive approach applies to interpretation of the Model Law.

70 THE EFFECT, INTERPRETATION, AND APPLICABILITY OF THE MODEL LAW

group for the preparation of the Model Law for the purposes of interpreting the Model Law. These include any United Nations (UN) General Assembly resolutions, *travaux préparatoires*, and explanatory notes that relate to the Model Law. Such documents explain in detail the considerations underlying the drafting of specific provisions in the Model Law, and they should be consulted when interpreting the Model Law.

6.06 Consistent with Section 4 of the IAA, Singapore courts have made frequent reference to UNCITRAL preparatory documents and drafting history in interpreting provisions of the Model Law. For example, in *The 'Titan Unity'* [2013] SGHCR 28, it was held that in order to ascertain the manner in which a doctrine under the Model Law ought to be applied, attention must be paid to the Model Law's *travaux préparatoires* and related drafting decisions, thereby determining the intention of the drafters of the Model Law.[9] In fact, the starting point of the Court of Appeal's recent analysis of a party's right to have a 'full' opportunity to be heard under Article 18 of the Model Law was its drafting history.[10] Moreover, although Section 4 refers only to the interpretation of provisions of the Model Law, the Singapore courts have also relied on such preparatory documents to interpret provisions of the IAA, reasoning that 'the adoption of the Model Law was a game changer' that necessarily affected the scope and meaning of other provisions of the IAA.[11]

6.07 The principal aim of the Model Law was to harmonise arbitration legislation in different jurisdictions. In interpreting provisions of the Model Law and the IAA, the Singapore courts have regularly referred to court decisions from many jurisdictions, including both common law and civil law jurisdictions.[12] Of particular note, however, is the fact that, while English case law is often referred to by the Singapore courts, English arbitration law and practice must be tested against the principles of the Model Law, and not simply be assumed to be consistent with it. This is because the drafters of the English Arbitration Act expressly chose not to adopt the Model Law, even though the Model Law has played an important part in shaping provisions of the English Arbitration Act.[13]

---

[9] See *The 'Titan Unity'* [2013] SGHCR 28, [14]–[18]. See also at *BXS v BXT* [2019] 4 SLR 390, [2019] SGHC(I) 10, [35] for another example of the High Court's reference to documents of the United Nations Commission on International Trade Law.

[10] *China Machine New Energy Corp v Jaguar Energy Guatemala LLC and another* [2020] 1 SLR 695, [2020] SGCA 12.

[11] *PT First Media TBK v Astro Nusantara International BV* [2013] SGCA 57, [2014] 1 SLR 372 (CA), [55]–[74]. In that case, the Court of Appeal was considering the scope of the power to refuse enforcement in Section 19 of the IAA, and held that a party had a choice of remedies between setting-aside and resisting enforcement after considering the underlying philosophy and architecture of the Model Law. See Chapter 16.

[12] D. Chan and P. Tan, 'International Arbitration: Internationalist Outlook Leading the Development of Local Jurisprudence' in G. Yihan and P. Tan (gen eds), *Singapore Law: 50 Years in the Making* (Academy Publishing 2015) See e.g. *PT First Media TBK v Astro Nusantara International BV* [2014] 1 SLR 372 at [78]–[83], where the Court of Appeal discussed German and Quebec arbitration law but ultimately rejected it as the proper approach under the Model Law. In the context of investor–State arbitrations and treaty interpretation, Singapore courts will also have regard to published awards: see *Swissbourgh Diamond Mines (Pty) Ltd and others v Kingdom of Lesotho* [2018] SGCA 81.

[13] See e.g. The Departmental Advisory Committee on Arbitration (DAC) Report on Arbitration Bill 1996, at [1] and [4]. See also Lord Justice Mustill, 'A New Arbitration Act for the United Kingdom?: The Response of the Departmental Advisory Committee to the UNCITRAL Model Law' (1990) 6(1) Arbitration International 3; J. Steyn, 'England's Response to the UNCITRAL Model Law of Arbitration' (1994) 10(1) Arbitration International 1.

C. Section 5—Application of Part II of the IAA

<u>IAA, Section 5</u>

(1) This Part and the Model Law do not apply to an arbitration which is not an international arbitration unless the parties agree in writing that this Part or the Model Law shall apply to that arbitration.

(2) Despite Article 1(3) of the Model Law, an arbitration is international if—

    (a) at least one of the parties to an arbitration agreement, at the time of the conclusion of the agreement, has its place of business in any State other than Singapore;

    (b) one of the following places is situated outside the State in which the parties have their places of business:

        (i) the place of arbitration if determined in, or pursuant to, the arbitration agreement;

        (ii) any place where a substantial part of the obligations of the commercial relationship is to be performed or the place with which the subject matter of the dispute is most closely connected; or

    (c) the parties have expressly agreed that the subject matter of the arbitration agreement relates to more than one country.

(3) For the purposes of subsection (2)—

    (a) if a party has more than one place of business, the place of business is that which has the closest relationship to the arbitration agreement;

    (b) if a party does not have a place of business, a reference to the party's place of business is to be construed as a reference to the party's habitual residence.

(4) Despite any provision to the contrary in the Arbitration Act 2001 that Act does not apply to any arbitration to which this Part applies.

6.08 Section 5(1) provides that the Model Law and Part II of the IAA do not apply to arbitrations that are not international and only apply to non-international arbitrations if the parties agree in writing that such legislation shall apply. Section 5(1) gives effect to party autonomy: parties may elect to adopt Part II and the Model Law rather than the Arbitration Act for an arbitration to which the Arbitration Act would otherwise apply.[14] There has been some disagreement over what constitutes a proper agreement in this context,[15] but it is likely that an agreement that either the IAA or the Model Law or both shall apply is sufficient to engage Section 5(1). Arguably, the agreement need not directly relate to the IAA and/or Model Law if the necessary effect of the agreement is that at least one of these shall apply to the arbitration.[16]

---

[14] See *Jurong Engineering Ltd v Black & Veatch Singapore Pte Ltd* [2003] SGHC 292, [2004] 1 SLR(R) 333 [29].

[15] See *Dermajaya Properties SDN BHD v Premium Properties SDN BHD* [2002] SGHC 53, [2002] 1 SLR(R) 492 at [84].

[16] See *Sembawang Engineers and Constructors Pte Ltd v Covec (Singapore) Pte Ltd* [2008] SGHC 229 [20]–[34]. See also *NCC International AB v Alliance Concrete Pte Ltd* [2008] 2 SLR(R) 565; *Navigator Investment Services Ltd v Acclaim Insurance Brokers Pte Ltd* [2009] SGCA 45, [2010] 1 SLR 25.

72 THE EFFECT, INTERPRETATION, AND APPLICABILITY OF THE MODEL LAW

6.09 Section 5(2) defines an 'international' arbitration and provides that such definition prevails in the event of any inconsistency with Article 1(3) of the Model Law. An arbitration is 'international' if it fits one of the four following situations.

6.10 First, Section 5(2)(a) provides that an arbitration is international if at least one of the parties to the arbitration agreement has its place of business outside Singapore at the time of the conclusion of the agreement. This is the basic criterion of internationality, adopted from the UN Convention on Contracts for the International Sale of Goods.[17]

6.11 Section 5(2)(a) of the IAA differs slightly in wording from the equivalent provision in Article 1(3)(a) of the Model Law. Under Article 1(3)(a) of the Model Law, it is arguable that if parties have the *same place of business* outside Singapore, then such a situation would not fall within Article 1(3)(a) of the Model Law and would not be considered an 'international' arbitration if the other limbs of Article 1(3) are not met. The broader definition in Section 5(2)(a) applies in preference to the definition in Article 1(3)(a) of the Model Law.

6.12 Second, Section 5(2)(b)(i) provides that an arbitration is 'international' if the place of arbitration is not where the parties have their places of business. No problem arises if the place of arbitration is expressly stated in the arbitration agreement. But Section 5(2)(b)(i) includes situations where the place of arbitration is not only 'determined in' but also 'determined ... pursuant to ... the arbitration agreement'. This suggests that, for the purposes of Section 5(2)(b)(i), the place of arbitration need not have been express, but it would be sufficient if a tribunal or arbitral institution determined that there was an *implied* choice of the place of arbitration. If the agreement simply authorised the tribunal to determine the place of arbitration, without any implied or express agreement on the place of arbitration, that may be a different matter altogether.[18]

6.13 Third, Section 5(2)(b)(ii) provides that an arbitration is 'international' if the place where a substantial part of the obligations of the commercial relationship is to be performed, or the place with which the subject matter of the dispute is most closely connected is situated outside the State in which the parties have their place of business. Section 5(3) then sets out certain rules that apply where a party has more than one place of business or where a party does not have a place of business.

6.14 Fourth, Section 5(2)(c) provides that an arbitration is 'international' where parties expressly agree that the subject matter of the arbitration agreement relates to more than one country. This is drafted somewhat infelicitously, but it must refer to the subject matter of the underlying dispute or disputes that may fall within the arbitration agreement, and not the arbitration itself.[19]

---

[17] H.M. Holtzmann and J.E. Neuhaus, *A Guide to the UNCITRAL Model Law on International Commercial Arbitration: Legislative History and Commentary* (Kluwer Law International 1989) 72 (hereafter Holtzmann and Neuhaus, *A Guide to UNCITRAL Model Law on International Commercial Arbitration*).

[18] Ibid, 73.

[19] Ibid, 74.

C. SECTION 5—APPLICATION OF PART II OF THE IAA

Finally, section 5(4) excludes the application of the Arbitration Act 2001 (AA) where Part II of the IAA applies. In other words, it clarifies that the arbitration regimes in the IAA and AA are mutually exclusive.

6.15

The discussion above is illustrated by Figure 6.1 which demonstrates visually how one determines whether or not an arbitration is international under Section 5(2).

6.16

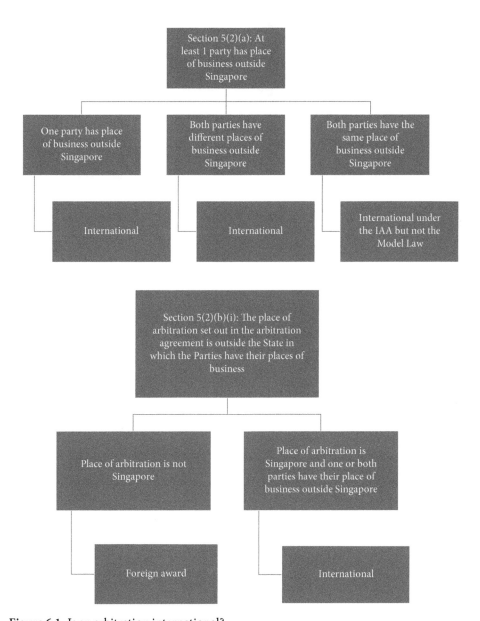

Figure 6.1 Is an arbitration international?

74 THE EFFECT, INTERPRETATION, AND APPLICABILITY OF THE MODEL LAW

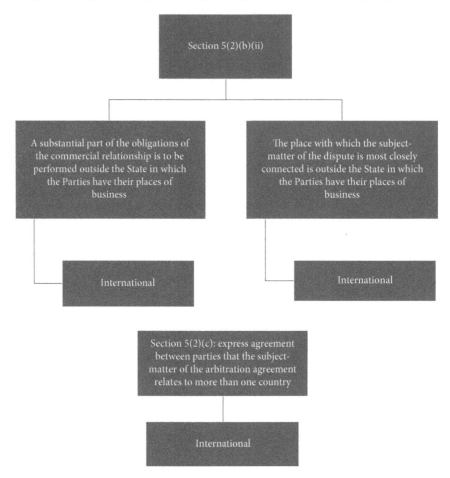

Figure 6.1 (Continued)

7

Stay of Court Proceedings in Favour of Arbitration

A.	Introduction	7.01	1.	General Approach	7.43
B.	Mandatory Nature of Stay	7.11	2.	Particular Procedural Acts	7.49
C.	Burden of Proof	7.13	I.	Section 6(1)—Subject Matter Falls within the Scope of the Arbitration Agreement	7.55
D.	*Prima Facie* Standard of Review	7.17			
E.	Other Remedies for Breach of Arbitration Agreement	7.25	J.	Sections 6(2) and 6(3)—Possible Orders under Section 6	7.65
F.	Section 6(1)—'an arbitration agreement to which the Act applies'	7.28	K.	Section 6(2)—Arbitration Agreement Null and Void, Inoperative, or Incapable of Being Performed	7.69
G.	Section 6(1)—'party to the arbitration agreement'	7.40			
H.	Section 6(1)—'at any time after filing and serving a notice of intention to contest or not contest and before delivering any pleading . . . or taking any other step in the proceedings'	7.43	1.	'Null and Void'	7.71
			2.	'Inoperative'	7.73
			3.	'Incapable of Being Performed'	7.75
			L.	Case Management Powers	7.78

IAA, Section 6

(1) Despite Article 8 of the Model Law, where any party to an arbitration agreement to which this Act applies institutes any proceedings in any court against any other party to the agreement in respect of any matter which is the subject of the agreement, any party to the agreement may, at any time after filing and serving a notice of intention to contest or not contest and before delivering any pleading (other than a pleading asserting that the court does not have jurisdiction in the proceedings) or taking any other step in the proceedings, apply to that court to stay the proceedings so far as the proceedings relate to that matter.

(2) The court to which an application has been made in accordance with subsection (1) is to make an order, upon such terms or conditions as the court thinks fit, staying the proceedings so far as the proceedings relate to the matter, unless it is satisfied that the arbitration agreement is null and void, inoperative or incapable of being performed.

(3) Where a court makes an order under subsection (2), the court may, for the purpose of preserving the rights of parties, make any interim or supplementary order that the court thinks fit in relation to any property which is the subject of the dispute to which the order under that subsection relates.

76 STAY OF COURT PROCEEDINGS IN FAVOUR OF ARBITRATION

(4) Where no party to the proceedings has taken any further step in the proceedings for a period of at least 2 years after an order staying the proceedings has been made, the court may, on its own motion, make an order discontinuing the proceedings without prejudice to the right of any of the parties to apply for the discontinued proceedings to be reinstated.

(5) For the purposes of this section and sections 7 and 11A—

(a) a reference to a party shall include a reference to any person claiming through or under such party;

(b) 'court' means the General Division of the High Court, District Court, Magistrate's Court or any other court in which proceedings are instituted.

A. Introduction

7.01 It is not uncommon for a party to an arbitration agreement to commence litigation in court. Such a party may consider the relevant arbitration agreement to be invalid, inapplicable, or inoperative, or it may simply choose to do so for tactical reasons. Where litigation is commenced in Singapore courts, Section 6 of the International Arbitration Act (IAA) allows any other party to the arbitration agreement to seek a stay of the court proceedings on the basis that the dispute falls within the scope of an arbitration agreement. As the title of Section 6 suggests, this is the primary mechanism for enforcement of international arbitration agreements under the IAA.[1]

7.02 Section 6 takes primacy over Article 8 of the United Nations Commission on International Trade Law (UNCITRAL) Model Law on International Commercial Arbitration (the Model Law).[2] There are some differences in language between the two provisions, notably with respect to the timing requirement for any stay application.[3] Also, while Article 8 requires the court to 'refer the parties to arbitration' if certain specified conditions are met, Section 6 only prevents the continuation of court proceedings and does not require the plaintiff in court proceedings to commence arbitration.[4] Where relevant below, we discuss the interaction and differences between these provisions.

7.03 In terms of the structure of Section 6: Sections 6(1) and 6(2) are the main provisions and set out the key procedural and substantive elements for an applicant to obtain a stay

---

[1] There are other remedies available to parties to enforce international arbitration agreement, including anti-suit injunctions, although these do not fall strictly within the scope of Section 6 of the IAA. See section E of this chapter.

[2] See *Tjong Very Sumito and others v Antig Investments Pte Ltd* [2009] 4 SLR(R) 732 [21] (hereafter *Tjong Very Sumito v Antig Investments*). According to some commentators, this means that a party could not make an application under Article 8 if it had failed to satisfy the Section 6 requirements for a stay. See D. Foxton QC and J.-F. Ng, 'Breach of the Arbitration Agreement: Stay of Judicial Proceedings and Injunctive Relief' in D. Joseph QC and D. Foxton QC (eds), *Singapore International Arbitration: Law & Practice* (2nd edn, LexisNexis 2018) 61.

[3] Note the difference in language and see section H of this chapter.

[4] See Foxton and Ng, 'Breach of the Arbitration Agreement' (n 2) 112.

A. INTRODUCTION 77

of court proceedings, while Sections 6(3) to 6(5)[5] provide further detail on the court's powers in respect of a stay, discontinuance of stay proceeding, and definitions relevant to Section 6. While the case law on these provisions is discussed in further detail below, some general observations may be appropriate here.

The first substantive element is that the stay applicant and the party resisting the stay **7.04** must be a party to 'an arbitration agreement to which this Act applies'. While this may appear uncontroversial at first glance, more complicated issues may arise in cases involving non-signatories to the arbitration agreement, such as assignees.[6] Section 6(5) also provides an extended definition of a 'party' for the purposes of a stay and states that it 'includes a reference to any person claiming through or under such party'.

The second substantive element relates to the validity and workability of the arbitration **7.05** agreement. Section 6(2) provides that a stay will be ordered if the arbitration agreement is not 'null and void, inoperative or incapable of being performed'.

The third substantive element relates to scope. For a stay to be granted, the dispute be- **7.06** fore the Singapore courts must be 'in respect of any matter which is the subject of' the arbitration agreement. The scope of an arbitration agreement is a question that has raised some potentially difficult issues, including what constitutes a dispute, and whether the arbitration agreement can and should cover bills of exchange.[7]

The burden of proof for the first and third elements lies with the applicant for a stay. **7.07** However, it is an open question whether the burden of proving the second element (the proviso under Section 6(2)) is on the applicant or the party resisting the stay. There appears to be conflicting authority under Singapore law on the point, which has not been resolved by the Singapore Court of Appeal, although the better view is that the burden should be placed on the party resisting the stay.[8]

Where all three elements are present, the granting of a stay is mandatory.[9] While it may **7.08** not be apparent from the plain wording of Section 6(1) and 6(2), the Singapore Court of Appeal in *Tomolugen* has clarified that these three substantive elements need only be established on a *prima facie* standard of review.[10] This standard of review, along with its rationale, is discussed further below.

Apart from the three substantive elements discussed above, there is an additional **7.09** element that relates to timing. Section 6(1) requires that a stay application be made

---

[5] Section 6(4) and (5) were first introduced in the 2011 Singapore International Arbitration (Amendment) Bill and were intended to clarify the Court's power to discontinue proceedings as well as to further define the terms 'party' and 'court'. See International Arbitration (Amendment) Bill No. 38/2001, First Reading on 25 September 2001.

[6] See section G of this chapter.

[7] See sections F and I of this chapter.

[8] See section C of this chapter.

[9] See section B of this chapter.

[10] *Tomolugen Holdings Ltd and another v Silica Investors Ltd and other appeals* [2015] SGCA 57 [74] (hereafter *Tomolugen*); *Dalian Hualiang Enterprise Group Co Ltd and anor v Louis Dreyfus Asia Pte Ltd* [2005] 4 SLR(R) 646 (hereafter *Dalian Hualiang Enterprise v Louis Dreyfus Asia*) [74].

78   STAY OF COURT PROCEEDINGS IN FAVOUR OF ARBITRATION

before 'delivering any pleading … or taking any other step in the proceedings'. In this regard, Section 6(1) of the IAA differs slightly from, and modifies, Article 8 of the Model Law, which requires that a stay application be made before the applicant's 'first statement on the substance of the dispute'.

7.10   Finally, Section 6(2) gives the Court the discretion to make any orders it considers fit. This has been said to be an 'unfettered discretion'.[11]

B. Mandatory Nature of Stay

7.11   Where a stay applicant can establish that court proceedings relate to any matter falling within an arbitration agreement, a stay in respect of those proceedings is mandatory unless the court finds that the arbitration agreement is 'null and void, inoperative or incapable of being performed'.[12] Section 6(2) of the IAA expressly provides that the court 'is to' make such an order granting a stay in such circumstances. In contrast, Section 6(2) of the Arbitration Act, which applies to domestic arbitrations, provides that the court 'may' make an order granting a stay, meaning that the court has the discretion to order a stay in the case of domestic arbitrations under the Arbitration Act.[13]

7.12   The mandatory stay pursuant to Section 6 of the IAA may also be distinguished from case management stays that a court has the discretion to order in respect of court proceedings pending the resolution of a related arbitration, at the request of parties who are not subject to the arbitration agreement in question. Such case management stays are discussed further below at section L.

C. Burden of Proof

7.13   It is uncontroversial that a stay applicant bears the burden of proving both that there is a valid arbitration agreement between the parties to the court proceedings and that the dispute in the court proceedings falls within the scope of the arbitration agreement.[14] However, it is not settled in Singapore whether the applicant or the party resisting the stay bears the burden of satisfying the court that the arbitration agreement is not 'null and void, inoperative or incapable of being performed' for the purposes of Section 6(2).

7.14   In *Tomolugen*, the Singapore Court of Appeal appeared to suggest that the burden fell on a stay applicant to establish that the arbitration agreement is '*not* null and void, inoperative or incapable of being performed'.[15] However, in its earlier decision in *Tjong*

---

[11] *The 'Duden'* [2008] 4 SLR(R) 984 [11]–[14] (hereafter *The 'Duden'*). Applying the dicta of Lai SC J in *Splosna Plovba International Shipping and Chartering d o v Adria Orient Line Pte Ltd* [1998] SGHC 289.
[12] *Tomolugen* (n 10) [27].
[13] Ibid, [74]; *Dalian Hualiang Enterprise v Louis Dreyfus Asia* (n 10) [35].
[14] Ibid, [63].
[15] Ibid, [63].

Very Sumito, the Court of Appeal had held that it is for the party resisting the stay to show that one of the statutory grounds in the proviso to Section 6(2) for resisting a stay exists, that is, that the arbitration agreement is 'null and void, inoperative or incapable of being performed'.[16]

These seemingly conflicting positions were explored in *Wilson Taylor Asia Pacific Pte Ltd v Dyna-Jet Pte Ltd* by Vinodh Coomaraswamy J, who observed that the latter approach in *Tjong Very Sumito* accorded with the approach in England, whereby the burden rests on the party resisting the stay to establish that it falls within the proviso in the equivalent of Section 6(2) of the IAA.[17] Coomaraswamy J preferred that approach, reasoning that it is consistent both with the courts' ordinary approach to allocating the burden of proof and also with the ordinary approach to applications under Section 6 of the IAA.[18] On appeal, the Court of Appeal acknowledged Coomaraswamy J's observations but refrained from offering any authoritative view on the issue, given that it did not arise on appeal.[19] It is noteworthy that, when the Court restated the position it took in *Tomolugen*, the Court chose not to adopt the formulation it previously adopted in *Tomolugen*; instead, the Court merely stated that Section 6 of the IAA 'required the court to be satisfied' that the agreement was not null and void, inoperative, or incapable of being performed.[20]

7.15

In the authors' view, the approach taken by Coomaraswamy J and *Tjong Very Sumito* may be preferable. It appears to be consistent with the ordinary meaning of Section 6(2), which requires a court to be persuaded that the arbitration agreement is 'null and void, inoperative or incapable of being performed', rather than the converse, that the arbitration agreement is not 'null and void, inoperative or incapable of being performed'. It is also consonant with Article II(3) of the New York Convention, which obliges courts of Contracting Parties to refer a dispute to arbitration unless the court 'finds that the [arbitration agreement] is null and void, inoperable, or incapable of being performed'.

7.16

D. *Prima Facie* Standard of Review

The generally accepted principle of competence-competence holds that an arbitral tribunal is competent to determine its own jurisdiction.[21] The principle is reflected in

7.17

---

[16] *Tjong Very Sumito v Antig Investments* (n 2) [22] (emphasis added).

[17] *Wilson Taylor Asia Pacific Pte Ltd v Dyna-Jet Pte Ltd* [2017] 3 SLR 267; [2016] SGHC 238 [26]–[27] (hereafter *Wilson Taylor v Dyna- Jet* (3 SLR). Coomaraswamy J also noted that, to meet this burden, the party resisting the stay must establish that no other conclusion on the issue is arguable.

[18] Ibid, [27].

[19] *Wilson Taylor Asia Pacific Pte Ltd v Dyna-Jet Pte Ltd* [2017] 2 SLR 362 [25] (hereafter *Wilson Taylor v Dyna-Jet* (2 SLR)).

[20] Ibid, [11].

[21] There is a wealth of material on the principle. See e.g. N. Blackaby and C. Partasides, *Redfern and Hunter on International Arbitration* (7th edn, Oxford University Press 2022)[5.110]–[5.114] 314–316; P. Landolt, 'The Inconvenience of Principle: Separability and Kompetenz-Kompetenz' (2013) 30 Journal of International Arbitration 511; A. Demolista, 'Separability and Kompetenz-Kompetenz' ICCA Congress Series, no. 9 (Kluwer International Law 1999) 217.

80 STAY OF COURT PROCEEDINGS IN FAVOUR OF ARBITRATION

Article 16 of the Model Law, which states that an arbitral tribunal 'may rule on its own jurisdiction, including any objections with respect to the existence or validity of the arbitration agreement'. The practical benefit of this principle is that it allows a tribunal to proceed with its work without having to wait for judicial intervention.[22]

7.18 However, the competence-competence principle itself is directed at the power of the arbitral tribunal and does not prescribe what approach a court should take in terms of the standard of review of the existence, validity, or scope of an arbitration agreement, and neither do the IAA or the Model Law. In this respect, there may be some tension between the level of review by a court and the autonomy of a tribunal to determine its own competence: the more detailed a review the court undertakes with respect to the existence, validity, or scope of an arbitration agreement, the more this tends to encroach upon the arbitral tribunal's autonomy and competence to determine those jurisdictional questions.[23]

7.19 In reconciling these tensions, Singapore courts have adopted a *prima facie* standard of review in determining the existence and scope of the arbitration agreement in question.[24] Other common law jurisdictions which have adopted the Model Law, such as Australia,[25] Canada,[26] Hong Kong,[27] and New Zealand,[28] have likewise adopted the *prima facie* approach. Different approaches are taken by courts in other jurisdictions, including the English Courts, some of which undertake a 'full merits' determination of the existence and scope of the arbitration agreement.[29]

7.20 The issue of what standard of review to apply came before the Singapore High Court in *Malini Venture v Knight Capital Pte Ltd and ors*,[30] where the party opposing a stay asserted that the contract in question was a forgery. That party argued, relying on English law authorities, that the Singapore courts should conduct a full merits review with respect to the issue of whether the parties had concluded an arbitration agreement.[31] Prakash J (as she then was) declined to follow the English approach and adopted the *prima facie* standard of review on the basis that it cohered better with the 'primacy' given by the IAA regime to the arbitral tribunal.[32] Even prior to the *Malini Venture*

---

[22] Landolt, 'The Inconvenience of Principle: Separability and Kompetenz-Kompetenz' (n 21) 514.

[23] *Tomolugen* (n 10) [28] ('friction … may arise because any determination made by the court on the existence and scope of the arbitration agreement may well intrude into the remit of the arbitral tribunal's *kompetenz-kompetenz*').

[24] See also *Wilson Taylor v Dyna-Jet* (2 SLR) (n 19) [12]; *KVC Rice Intertrade Co Ltd v Asian Mineral Resources Pte Ltd and anor* [2017] 4 SLR 182, [42]. See, however, the discussion below concerning the situation where there are competing dispute resolution clauses.

[25] See e.g. *Hancock Prospecting Pty Ltd v Rinehart* [2017] FCAFC 170.

[26] See e.g. *Union des consommateurs v Dell Computer Corp* [2007] 2 SCR 801.

[27] See e.g. *PCCW Global Ltd v Interactive Communications Service Ltd* [2007] 1 HKLRD 309, [60]; *Pacific Crown Engineering Ltd v Hyundai Engineering and Construction Co Ltd* [2003] 3 HKC 659.

[28] See e.g. *Ursem v Chung* [2014] NZHC 436.

[29] See *Tomolugen* (n 10) [24]–[70] for an extensive discussion of the principles and positions in various jurisdictions.

[30] *Malini Ventura v Knight Capital Pte Ltd and ors* [2015] 5 SLR 707.

[31] Ibid, [21]–[35].

[32] Ibid, [36]–[37]. Prakash J declined to follow the English decision *Nigel Peter Albon v Naza Motor Trading Sdn Bhd* [2007] 2 All ER 1075.

D. *PRIMA FACIE* STANDARD OF REVIEW   81

decision, the Singapore Court of Appeal had held in *Tjong Very Sumito* that a stay should be ordered under Section 6 of the IAA if it was 'at least arguable' that the matter is the subject of the arbitration agreement, and that 'it is only in the clearest of cases that the court ought to make a ruling on the inapplicability of an arbitration agreement'.[33] The *prima facie* standard was subsequently followed in several other decisions of the Singapore High Court.[34]

The *prima facie* standard of review received authoritative endorsement by the   **7.21** Singapore Court of Appeal in *Tomolugen*, which provided several reasons for adopting it. First, the *prima facie* standard accords better with the intention of the drafters of the IAA.[35] The Court of Appeal drew upon the 1993 Report on Review of Arbitration Laws by a sub-committee of the Singapore Academy of Law's Law Reform Committee (whose recommendations were adopted in the drafting of the IAA), which suggested that the overall scheme under the IAA was intended to allow arbitral tribunals to be the 'first arbiter[s]' of their own jurisdiction without needing to wait for judicial determination.[36] Second, in the Court of Appeal's view, a full merits review would 'significantly hollow' the competence-competence principle of its practical effect by reducing an arbitral tribunal's ability to determine its jurisdiction to a 'contingency dependent on the strategic choices of the claimant in a putative arbitration' and whether it chooses to pursue its claim in court proceedings or in arbitration.[37] Third, the Court of Appeal considered that concerns about resource duplication, said to arise from adopting a *prima facie* approach, were not warranted, given that a well-reasoned decision by a tribunal is likely to clarify the issues and avoid re-litigation of those issues.[38] Finally, departing from English jurisprudence, the Court of Appeal held that the word 'satisfied' in Section 6(2) of the IAA does not suggest a full merits review, and noted that the drafters of the Model Law and the English Arbitration Act 1996 did not indicate this intention as well.[39]

The *prima facie* standard of review was more recently applied in the context of a   **7.22** winding-up application in *AnAn Group (Singapore) Pte Ltd v VTB Bank (Public Joint Stock Co)*.[40] In that case, the debtor company, AnAn Group, failed to repay a debt of US\$170 million upon a statutory demand by the creditor, VTB Bank,[41] leading

---

[33] *Tjong Very Sumito v Antig Investments* (n 2) [12].

[34] *Sim Chay Koon v NTUC Income Insurance Co-operative Ltd* [2016] 2 SLR 871; *The Titan Unity* [2013] SGHCR 28; *Malini Ventures v Knight Capital Pte Ltd* (n 30).

[35] *Tomolugen* (n 10) [65].

[36] Ibid, [66]. The Court of Appeal also carefully considered the *travaux préparatoire* to the Model Law but concluded that it was ambivalent on whether a *prima facie* approach should be adopted. See Ibid, [31]–[44].

[37] Ibid, [67]. It should be noted that a respondent in an arbitration may also commence court proceedings in relation to the same dispute and, in that scenario, a full merits review may also hollow the *kompetenz-kompetenz* principle of its practical effect.

[38] Ibid, [68].

[39] Ibid, [69].

[40] *AnAn Group (Singapore) Pte Ltd v VTB Bank (Public Joint Stock Co)* [2020] SGCA 33 (hereafter *AnAn Group v VTB Bank*).

[41] Ibid, [11].

82   STAY OF COURT PROCEEDINGS IN FAVOUR OF ARBITRATION

the creditor to initiate winding-up proceedings.[42] The Singapore High Court rejected the debtor's arguments and ordered the creditor to be wound up.[43] The debtor appealed.

7.23   The key issue before the Singapore Court of Appeal was the standard of review in the context of a winding-up application: when a debtor raises a disputed debt or a cross-claim which is potentially the subject of an arbitration agreement to resist a winding-up application, does the 'triable issue' standard (normally applicable in a challenge to a winding-up petition) or the *'prima facie'* standard apply?[44] The Court of Appeal held that the *prima facie* standard of review applied, reasoning that this would promote coherence in the law concerning stay applications under Section 6 of the IAA and discourage abuse of the Singapore courts' winding-up jurisdiction.[45] The Court of Appeal also reasoned that applying the *prima facie* standard was more consistent with party autonomy because, under the 'triable issue' standard, the court would have to consider the merits of the debtor's defences, in spite of the parties' agreement that such disputes ought to be determined by an arbitrator.[46] Furthermore, the 'triable issue' standard would also create uncertainty, entailing significant costs and delay in the form of protracted interlocutory court proceedings, even though the underlying substantive dispute could have been resolved expeditiously by arbitration.[47]

7.24   Consequently, if a creditor claims for a debt simpliciter before the court, the debtor would have to demonstrate on a *prima facie* basis that there is an arbitration clause and that the dispute is caught by that clause.[48] Once that burden is discharged by the debtor, the court should grant a stay of the claim and defer the actual determination of the dispute to an arbitral tribunal.[49]

E. Other Remedies for Breach of Arbitration Agreement

7.25   Where a party to an arbitration agreement seeks to litigate disputes that fall within the scope of the arbitration agreement, the other parties to that agreement may have remedies other than seeking a stay of court proceedings. Where the arbitration is seated in Singapore and litigation is commenced in courts outside Singapore, such parties may seek an anti-suit injunction enjoining a party from such litigation. Singapore courts will grant an anti-suit injunction on the basis of an arbitration agreement, which will be enforced like other jurisdiction clauses, unless there are 'strong reasons'

---

[42] Ibid, [13]–[17].
[43] Ibid, [18].
[44] Ibid, [25].
[45] Ibid, [56]–[86].
[46] Ibid, [75]–[78].
[47] Ibid, [84]–[86].
[48] Ibid, [91], [97].
[49] Ibid, [63].

E. OTHER REMEDIES FOR BREACH OF ARBITRATION AGREEMENT   83

not to do so.[50] This is consistent with the approach under English law, and has been explained on the basis of the positive and negative aspects of an agreement to arbitrate.[51] As explained by the UK Supreme Court in the *AES Ust-Kamenogorsk* case, an arbitration agreement contains a positive aspect, namely an undertaking to seek relief for disputes in accordance with the arbitration agreement, as well as a negative aspect, meaning the obligation not to seek relief in any other forum.[52] An anti-suit injunction is issued to protect the negative aspect of the arbitration agreement, which is a right enforceable independently of whether any arbitral proceedings exist or are imminent.[53]

The concept of a negative right was affirmed and further developed by Belinda Ang   **7.26** J in *Hilton v Sun Travels*. In Ang J's view, there are two implied negative obligations arising from an agreement to arbitrate.[54] First, similar to that identified in the *AES Ust-Kamenogorsk* case, there is a negative undertaking by the parties that certain disputes between them are to be resolved by arbitration and not to be pursued in another forum.[55] Second, the parties also undertake not to set aside or otherwise attack an award in jurisdictions other than the seat of arbitration (apart from proceedings to resist enforcement).[56] In order to enforce the second negative obligation, Ang J granted an anti-suit injunction against Maldivian court proceedings that were commenced to relitigate a dispute after an award was rendered in a Singapore-seated arbitration.[57]

Remedies apart from injunctive relief may also be available to parties to enforce an   **7.27** international arbitration agreement. For example, under English law, it is generally accepted that a breach of a jurisdictional clause, as with all other contractual breaches, may give rise to a claim in damages.[58] This analysis arguably extends to breaches of arbitration agreements.[59] Although Singapore courts have not yet pronounced on this issue, in principle, a breach of arbitration agreement can give rise to a claim in damages under Singapore law, just like the breach of any other contractual provision.[60]

---

[50] *BC Andaman Co limited & Ors v Xie Ning Yun and Ors* [2017] SGHC 64 [53], [65].
[51] *AES Ust-Kamenogorsk Hydropower Plant LLP v Ust-Kamenogorsk Hydropower Plant JSC* [2013] UKSC 35 (hereafter *AES Ust-Kamenogorsk Hydropower Plant LLP v Ust-Kamenogorsk Hydropower Plant JSC*).
[52] Ibid, [1], [21].
[53] Ibid, [21]–[28].
[54] *Hilton International Manage (Maldives) Pvt Ltd v Sun Travels & Tours Pvt Ltd* [2018] SGHC 56 (hereafter *Hilton International Manage (Maldives) v Sun Travels & Tours*).
[55] Ibid, [53]. The Court also agreed that such an obligation exists even where arbitration proceedings have not been commenced or proposed.
[56] Ibid, [54].
[57] Ibid, [65].
[58] L. Collins et al. (eds), *Dicey, Morris & Collins on the Conflict of Laws* (15th edn, Sweet & Maxwell 2018) [12-164]–[12-165].
[59] G. Born, *International Commercial Arbitration* (3rd edn, Kluwer Law International 2021) 1408. Commentators have noted, however, that calculating the quantum of damages may be difficult.
[60] For a fuller analysis, see also E. Krishna and Y.-J. Kang, 'Damages for Breach of an Arbitration Agreement' (2021) 33 Singapore Academy of Law Journal 786.

84 STAY OF COURT PROCEEDINGS IN FAVOUR OF ARBITRATION

F. Section 6(1)—'an arbitration agreement to which the Act applies'

7.28 The exercise of the power to stay court proceedings under Section 6(1) is contingent on the existence of a valid arbitration agreement, determined on a *prima facie* basis. The jurisprudence on the existence and validity of arbitration agreements is discussed in greater detail in Chapter 5. Generally, Singapore courts have taken a pro-validity approach to the validity and construction of arbitration agreements, giving effect, where possible, to the parties' evinced intention to settle their dispute by arbitration.[61]

7.29 Determining whether an arbitration agreement 'applies' for the purposes of Section 6(1) of the IAA can pose particular difficulties where the parties to the arbitration agreement are also parties to one or more other agreements with different dispute resolution clauses.[62]

7.30 In *Transocean Offshore International Ventures Ltd v Burgundy Global Exploration Corp*,[63] the Singapore High Court had to determine whether a dispute arose under a London Court of International Arbitration (LCIA) arbitration clause in an offshore drilling contract or an escrow agreement governed by a non-exclusive jurisdiction clause in favour of Singapore courts. The entry into the escrow agreement was a condition precedent to the commencement of the drilling contract. Upon failure by the defendant to deposit the escrow amount due under the escrow agreement, the plaintiff began suit in Singapore courts, claiming damages for the defendant's breach and repudiation of the escrow agreement.[64] At first instance, the Assistant Registrar granted a stay in favour of arbitration, on the basis that the escrow agreement was not separate and distinct from the drilling contract and that the true dispute lies under the drilling contract which was subject to LCIA arbitration.[65]

7.31 Andrew Ang J disagreed and allowed the appeal, dismissing the stay. Ang J began by observing that the parties had intended for the two contracts to be subject to different dispute resolution clauses, with disputes under the escrow agreement carved out from the drilling contract, and that there was no provision incorporating the LCIA arbitration clause into the escrow agreement.[66] On a proper construction of the contracts, the plaintiff's claim arose out of the escrow agreement and the dispute resolution clause in

---

[61] See Chapter 5. A significant number of reported cases on Section 6 that involve the existence and validity of an 'arbitration agreement' also involve Section 2A.

[62] Such a situation is not particularly novel, as it has arisen in the context of jurisdictional clauses: see e.g. *Credit Suisse First Boston (Europe) Ltd v MLC (Bermuda) Ltd* [1999] 1 Lloyd's Rep 767; *UBS AG v HSH Nordbank AG* [2009] 2 Lloyd's Rep 272 See also *Sebastian Holdings Inc v Deutsche Bank AG* [2010] 2 EWCA Civ 998; *Credit Suisse First Boston (Europe) Ltd v MLC (Bermuda) Ltd* [1999] CLC 579.

[63] *Transocean Offshore International Ventures Ltd v Burgundy Global Exploration Corp* [2010] 2 SLR 821 (hereafter *Transocean*). See also *Sanum Investments Ltd v ST Group Co. Ltd, and ors* [2020] 3 SLR 225; [2018] SGHC 141 where the Court had to decide between an arbitration agreement in a master agreement and a multi-tiered dispute resolution clause in a participating agreement.

[64] *Transocean* (n 63) [8].

[65] Ibid, [9].

[66] Ibid, [21].

F. SECTION 6(1)—ARBITRATION AGREEMENT UNDER THE ACT 85

the drilling contract did not extend to that claim.[67] Even if the claim were to be treated as arising out of both contracts, in the case of overlapping and inconsistent dispute resolution clauses in different contracts, the dispute resolution regime that applies is that of the contract that a claim arose out of or was more closely connected with.[68] In Ang J's view, the plaintiff's claim was more closely connected with the escrow agreement.[69] Thus, Ang J concluded that Section 6 of the IAA was not applicable as the claim did not fall within the scope of an arbitration agreement.[70]

Subsequently, in *Oei Hong Leong v Goldman Sachs International*,[71] the Singapore High **7.32** Court clarified that in cases involving multiple contracts with competing dispute resolution clauses, Singapore courts will look to the parties' 'objective intentions' with respect to the applicable dispute resolution mechanism rather than apply the *prima facie* (or 'at least arguable') standard to determine the existence of an arbitration agreement. In that case, the plaintiff and defendant were parties to an International Swap Dealers Association Inc. Master Agreement (hereafter ISDA Master Agreement) and a Goldman Sachs Private Wealth Management Client Agreement Pack (hereafter Account Agreement Pack). The ISDA Master Agreement contained a non-exclusive jurisdiction clause in favour of English courts and the Account Agreement Pack contained arbitration clauses providing for LCIA arbitration. The plaintiff commenced suit for alleged fraudulent misrepresentation in the Singapore courts and the defendant applied to stay proceedings under Section 6 of the IAA. The Assistant Registrar granted a stay on the basis of the arbitration clauses.

On appeal, Lee Seiu Kin J agreed that the LCIA arbitration clauses applied and affirmed **7.33** the stay. However, Lee J dismissed the argument by the defendant that the Court need only be persuaded that it is 'at least arguable' that the claims were subject to a binding arbitration agreement. Lee J held that the 'at least arguable' test, which was developed in cases involving a single contract with an arbitration clause, did not apply where there are competing arbitration clauses and non-exclusive jurisdiction clauses in two contracts.[72] In the latter case, the relevant question is which clause the parties objectively intend to apply,[73] and the use of the *prima facie* test would not be appropriate as it would effectively result in arbitration clauses presumptively carrying more weight than other dispute resolution clauses.[74] Referring to both *Transocean Offshore International Ventures Ltd v Burgundy Global Exploration Corp* and the English High Court decision

---

[67] Ibid, [22–24].

[68] Ibid, [26]. Ang J referred to English authority for this proposition. See *Credit Suisse First Boston (Europe) Ltd v MLC (Bermuda) Ltd* [1999] CLC 579 and *UBS AG v HSH Nordbank AG* [2009] 2 Lloyd's Rep 272.

[69] *Transocean* (n 63) [26].

[70] Ibid, [28]. Ang J also reasoned in the alternative that, even if the claims did fall within the scope of the arbitration clause in the drilling contract, that provision had been rendered inoperative by the parties' agreement to a jurisdiction clause in the subsequent escrow agreement, which amounted to a waiver of the agreement to arbitrate. See Ibid, [29].

[71] *Oei Hong Leong v Goldman Sachs International* [2014] 3 SLR 1217 (hereafter *OHL v Goldman Sachs*).

[72] Ibid, [20]–[25].

[73] Ibid, [25].

[74] Ibid, [29].

86 STAY OF COURT PROCEEDINGS IN FAVOUR OF ARBITRATION

in *PT Thiess Contractors Indonesia v PT Kaltim Prima Coal*,[75] Lee J held that the correct approach in a multiple contracts case would be to ascertain the parties' objective intentions as to which dispute resolution mechanism should be applied without any presumption in favour of the arbitration clause.[76] On the facts, Lee J held that the 'pith and substance' of the dispute, which concerned alleged fraudulent misrepresentations, was more closely connected to the Account Agreement Pack, which governed the relationship and communications between the parties.[77]

7.34   Notably, *Oei Hong Leong v Goldman Sachs International* relied upon English authorities, which do not apply a *prima facie* standard of review in deciding on stays in favour of arbitration, in dismissing the 'at least arguable' standard. The case was decided before the Singapore Court of Appeal in *Tomolugen* departed from English law jurisprudence and conclusively affirmed the *prima facie* standard of review for stay applications under Section 6 of the IAA.[78] It may therefore be open to Singapore courts to extend the *prima facie* standard of review in *Tomolugen* to cases involving multiple contracts with inconsistent dispute resolution clauses. However, in the authors' view, the approach in *Oei Hong Leong v Goldman Sachs International* is correct in principle and should be affirmed notwithstanding the decision in *Tomolugen*, because the question of whether Section 6 of the IAA applies at all is separate from, and logically anterior to, the question of whether the requirements of Section 6 are satisfied. The considerations for applying a *prima facie* standard of review to the latter question do not necessarily extend to the former question. Indeed, such an extension may amount to bootstrapping of arbitral jurisdiction, particularly in circumstances where Singapore courts may determine that the dispute is more closely connected to a contract with a jurisdiction clause rather than a contract with an arbitration clause.

7.35   Another circumstance where it can be difficult to determine whether an arbitration agreement 'applies' for the purposes of Section 6(1) of the IAA is where a contract contains both a jurisdiction clause and an arbitration clause that may appear to conflict. In *BXH v BXI*,[79] the relevant arbitration clause stated that 'disputes arising out of or in connection with this Agreement shall be finally settled by arbitration which will be held in Singapore in accordance with the Arbitration Rules of the Singapore International Arbitration Centre'.[80] The same contract also contained a jurisdiction clause which stated that the 'Agreement shall be governed by and interpreted in accordance with the laws of Singapore' and '[t]he jurisdiction and venue for any legal action between the parties arising out of or connected with this Agreement ... shall be in a court located in Singapore'.[81]

---

[75] *PT Thiess Contractors Indonesia v PT Kaltim Prima Coal and another* [2011] EWHC 1842 (Comm).
[76] *OHL v Goldman Sachs* (n 71) [29].
[77] Ibid, [36]–[39].
[78] See section D of this chapter.
[79] *BXH v BXI* [2020] 1 SLR 1043; [2020] SGCA 28 (hereafter *BXH v BXI*).
[80] Ibid, [50].
[81] Ibid, [51].

F. SECTION 6(1)—ARBITRATION AGREEMENT UNDER THE ACT   87

7.36 The Singapore Court of Appeal held that, where parties evince a real intention to have matters resolved by arbitration, the courts ought to give effect to that intention and take a 'generous and harmonious interpretation' of the purportedly conflicting clause,[82] adopting the approach of the English court in *Paul Smith Ltd v H&S International Holding Inc* (the '*Paul Smith* approach').[83] Thus, the Court of Appeal affirmed Vinodh Coomaraswamy J's finding that the parties intended to resolve their substantive disputes in arbitration under the arbitration clause and to resolve any disputes arising out of any such arbitration in the Singapore courts, in exercise of the courts' supervisory jurisdiction.[84] The Court of Appeal was fortified in its conclusion by the amount of detail provided by the parties in the arbitration clause, including the binding effect of the award, the manner in which the award was to be made, and the manner in which arbitrators were to be appointed.[85] In contrast, the jurisdiction clause simply provided for the applicability of Singapore law and the jurisdictions of courts located in Singapore.[86]

7.37 However, in a different case, the Singapore High Court declined to adopt the *Paul Smith* approach. In *Silverlink Resorts Ltd v MS First Capital Insurance Ltd*[87] the plaintiff was one of the insured parties under an Industrial All Risks Policy issued by the defendant, and the COVID-19 pandemic led the plaintiff to make a claim under the policy,[88] which contained both an arbitration clause for '[a]ny dispute arising out of or in connection with [the policy …] not settled [by mediation]' and a non-exclusive jurisdiction clause in favour of Singapore courts for 'any dispute … regarding the interpretation of the application of [the policy]'.[89]

7.38 The defendant sought a stay in favour of arbitration, arguing that the *Paul Smith* approach should be applied such that the jurisdiction clause should be interpreted as giving the Singapore courts only supervisory jurisdiction over any arbitration between the parties.[90] The plaintiff argued that the *Paul Smith* approach was not relevant because the jurisdiction clause carved out disputes regarding the interpretation or application of the policy from the scope of the arbitration clause, similar to the approach taken in multiple contracts case by the Singapore High Court in *Transocean Offshore International Ventures Ltd v Burgundy Global Exploration Corp*.[91] Chua Lee Ming J agreed with the plaintiff, reasoning that the jurisdiction clause did not apply to all disputes and had a narrower scope than the arbitration clause, which pointed to the parties' intention to carve out specific disputes, and that reserving disputes relating to the interpretation or application of the policy for the courts made commercial sense.[92]

---

[82] Ibid, [60].
[83] Ibid, [56] –[61].
[84] Ibid, [59]–[60].
[85] Ibid, [61].
[86] Ibid, [61].
[87] *Silverlink Resorts Ltd v MS First Capital Insurance Ltd* [2020] SGHC 251 (hereafter *Silverlink Resorts*).
[88] Ibid, [2].
[89] Ibid, [16].
[90] Ibid, [49].
[91] Ibid, [34]–[37], [49].
[92] Ibid, [56], [58].

88 STAY OF COURT PROCEEDINGS IN FAVOUR OF ARBITRATION

Chua J also held that applying the *Paul Smith* approach in the case of a narrower juris-diction clause would lead to problems that the parties could not have intended, in par-ticular the conferral of supervisory jurisdiction only on a specific narrower category of disputes but not all disputes falling within the scope of the arbitration clause.[93]

7.39   Although each case turns on the construction of the relevant contractual provisions, the implication from these cases appears to be that the more broadly couched and vaguely drafted the jurisdiction clause, the more likely the Singapore courts will apply the *Paul Smith* approach to narrowly construe the jurisdiction clause as conferring only super-visory jurisdiction over the disputes submitted to arbitration. Conversely, the more spe-cific and detailed the jurisdiction clause, the more likely the Singapore courts will try to give effect to it notwithstanding the existence of an overlapping arbitration clause.

G. Section 6(1)—'party to the arbitration agreement'

7.40   Section 6(1) requires that the stay application must be brought by a 'party to an arbi-tration agreement' against another 'party to the arbitration agreement'. In most cases, this element will be uncontroversial. However, complexities may arise where non-signatories to the arbitration agreement are involved. This can then raise questions such as whether the non-signatory is an alter ego of a party to the arbitration agreement[94] as well as the applicability of other legal doctrines that may bind a non-signatory to an ar-bitration agreement.[95]

7.41   In the case of assignees to arbitration agreements, the Singapore High Court has held that they do not strictly satisfy the core definition of 'a party to an arbitration agreement' in Section 6(1), although they would qualify within the extended definition of a 'party' in Section 6(5), which states that a 'party' includes 'any person claiming through or under such a party'.[96] In *Cassa di Risparmio di Parma e Piacenza SpA v Rals International Pte Ltd,*[97] the plaintiff assignee brought a claim, over unpaid promissory notes, which were the payment mechanism in an underlying supply contract for equipment.[98] The

---

[93] Ibid, [47]–[48], [59].

[94] In the context of a setting aside application, the Singapore High Court upheld an arbitral tribunal's determin-ation that a non-signatory was bound by an arbitration agreement as he was the alter ego of the company that was a party to the arbitration agreement. See *Aloe Vera of America, Inc v Asianic Food (S) Pte Ltd and another* [2006] 3 SLR(R) 174. See Chapter 16.

[95] The Singapore High Court has held that the 'group of companies' or 'single economic doctrine' doctrine is not recognised under Singapore law. See *Manuchar Steel Hong Kong Ltd v Star Pacific Line Pte Ltd* [2014] 4 SLR 832.

[96] *Cassa di Risparmio di Parama e Piacenza SpA v Rals International Pte Ltd* [2016] 1 SLR 79 (hereafter *Cassa di Risparmio v Rals (HC)*). This decision went on appeal: *Rals International Pte Ltd v Cassa di Risparmio di Parma e Piacenza SpA* [2016] 5 SLR 455 (hereafter *Rals v Cassa di Risparmio (CA)*). See also N Goh, 'An Assignee's Obligation to Arbitrate and the Principle of Conditional Benefit: Cassa di Risparmio di Parma e Piacenza SpA v Rals International Pte Ltd [2016] 1 SLR 79' (2016) 28 Singapore Academy of Law Journal 262.

[97] Ibid. This decision went on appeal: *Rals v Cassa di Risparmio (CA)* (n 96). See also Goh, 'An Assignee's Obligation to Arbitrate and the Principle of Conditional Benefit' (n 96) 262.

[98] Ibid, [14]. There was a related services agreement between Oltremare and Rals for the former to assemble and commission the relevant equipment. Payment for these services was included in the purchase price stipulated in the Supply Agreement and nothing turns on this separate but related contract.

defendant applied for a stay on the basis of an International Chamber of Commerce (ICC) arbitration clause in the supply agreement.[99]

Vinodh Coomaraswamy J held that an assignee does not strictly fall within the meaning of a 'party' to the arbitration agreement under Section 6(1) of the IAA, because an assignee does not become a party to the assignor's contract merely by virtue of an assignment.[100] Coomaraswamy J nonetheless held that the assignee was a party 'claiming through or under' a party to the arbitration agreement and therefore qualified as a 'party' by virtue of Section 6(5) of the IAA.[101] On appeal, the Court of Appeal declined to express a view on these issues, noting that the appeal could be disposed of on the basis that the disputes arising out of the promissory notes did not fall within the scope of the arbitration agreement.[102]

7.42

H. Section 6(1)—'at any time after filing and serving a notice of intention to contest or not contest and before delivering any pleading ... or taking any other step in the proceedings'

1. General Approach

Section 6 of the IAA provides that a stay is only available to an applicant 'at any time after filing and serving a notice of intention to contest or not contest and before delivering any pleading ... or taking any other step in the proceedings'. This language is based on Section 4(1) of the English Arbitration Act 1950 and Section 9(3) of the English Arbitration Act 1996, with some minor differences.[103]

7.43

Thus, Singapore courts have considered English authority in interpreting the meaning of the proviso in Section 6(1), which essentially provides that an applicant can waive its rights to obtain a stay by failing to insist on arbitration in a timely fashion. As one commentator has observed, the language in Section 6(1) focuses on the conduct of the stay applicant, rather than fixed 'long stop' dates as imposed by Article 8 of the Model Law.[104]

7.44

Under Section 6(1), the window of time during which a stay applicant may seek a stay begins upon 'filing and serving a notice of intention to contest or not contest'. Prior to amendments in 2021, Section 6(1) provided that the window of time for a stay began 'after appearance'. In *Navigator Investment Services*, the Singapore Court of Appeal interpreted this language to mean that the earliest point in time at which a stay application could be made under Section 6 of the IAA is when a substantive claim has already

7.45

---

[99] Ibid, [18].
[100] Ibid, [52]–[54].
[101] *Cassa di Risparmio v Rals (HC)* [124]–[126].
[102] *Rals v Cassa di Risparmio (CA)* (n 96) [53]–[56].
[103] See S.Y. Tay, 'A Step or Misstep in Court' (2017) 29 Singapore Academy of Law Journal 454.
[104] Ibid, [6]–[7].

90 STAY OF COURT PROCEEDINGS IN FAVOUR OF ARBITRATION

crystallised, because it is only then that an applicant can apply to stay a clear claim that has been brought against it.[105] Thus, the Court held that applications for pre-action discovery or pre-action interrogatories would not fall within the scope of Section 6 of the IAA, meaning that a party resisting such applications could not seek a statutory stay.[106] Notwithstanding that, the Court also held that any application for pre-action discovery or pre-action interrogatories will be carefully scrutinised to ensure that the arbitration process is not being circumvented, and therefore a court would not grant pre-action discovery or pre-action interrogatories absent exceptional circumstances.[107]

7.46 The meaning of a 'step in the proceedings' was authoritatively decided by the Singapore Court of Appeal in *Carona Holdings Pte Ltd and others v Go Go Delicacy Pte Ltd*.[108] In that case, the Court had to consider whether an application to seek an extension of time to file a defence constituted a 'step in the proceedings'. Referring to English authorities, the Court held that a 'step' is to be understood in a practical and common-sensical way, meaning any step that 'manifests a willingness to submit to the jurisdiction of the court instead of evincing an intention to rely on arbitration'.[109] Thus, a 'step' is deemed to have been taken if a stay applicant employs court procedures to enable him to defeat or defend court proceedings on their merits, or if the applicant proceeds beyond a mere acknowledgment of service of process by evincing an unequivocal intention to participate in the court proceedings instead of arbitration.[110] The Court also noted two practical considerations that English courts take into account in assessing whether a 'step' has been taken, namely whether the conduct of the applicant is such as to demonstrate an election to abandon his right to stay and whether the act in question must have the effect of invoking the jurisdiction of the court.[111]

7.47 Following a survey of the approaches taken in jurisdictions such as Hong Kong, Malaysia, and Canada, the Court concluded that it was common practice to take into consideration the following circumstances enveloping an act in deciding whether it constitutes a step in the proceedings. First, where a party performs or carries out a significant act signifying that it is submitting to the court's jurisdiction rather than to arbitration to resolve the disputed issues, that party will be deemed to have taken a step in the proceedings. Second, an act will be regarded as a step if it is in furtherance of the action by advancing the hearing of the matter in court as opposed to one that serves to smother the action. Third, where a party does an act with the consent of the other

---

[105] *Navigator Investment Services Ltd v Acclaim Insurance Brokers Pte Ltd* [2010] 1 SLR 25 [53]–[54] (hereafter *Navigator Investment Services v Acclaim Insurance Brokers*).

[106] Ibid, [53]–[54].

[107] Ibid, [56]–[57]. The Court noted that there may be circumstances where there are valid reasons why an application for pre-action discovery and/or pre-action interrogatories may be sought notwithstanding the *prima facie* applicability of an arbitration agreement. For example, such applications may be made with a view to making a claim, not only against a party to the arbitration agreement, but also against third parties that are not bound by an arbitration agreement.

[108] *Carona Holdings Pte Ltd and others v Go Go Delicacy Pte Ltd* [2008] 4 SLR(R) 460 (hereafter *Carona Holdings*).

[109] Ibid, [52].

[110] Ibid, [55].

[111] Ibid, [59].

H. SECTION 6(1) 91

party, this will not amount to taking a step in the proceedings. Finally, disingenuous reservations will be disregarded, because parties should be decisive about whether they are insisting on arbitration in preference to litigation, meaning that a party that wishes to proceed to arbitration should be ready and willing to do all things necessary for the proper conduct of the arbitration.[112]

Applying these principles, the Court held that an application for the extension of time **7.48** was not a 'step in the proceedings' because it was not tantamount to an unequivocal submission to the court's jurisdiction.[113] An application for extension of time to file a defence is merely an acknowledgement by a defendant that the court has transient jurisdiction over the parties, and makes it abundantly clear to the opposing party and the court that the defendant does not intend to defend the action in court pending the outcome of its application for a stay.[114] The Court stressed that, in ascertaining whether a step has been taken in the proceedings, the context in which the extension of time is sought will be key, endorsing Potter J's statement in *Blue Flame Mechanical Services Limited v David Lord Engineering Limited* that any act that is 'done manifestly without prejudice to an intention to invoke arbitration and *merely to preserve the status quo until a summons to stay is promptly issued*' cannot amount to a step in the proceedings.[115] However, in circumstances where the application for an extension of time is not *bona fide* or for the purposes of staying proceedings pending arbitration, the courts would still have discretion to either refuse the extension of time or dismiss the stay application.[116]

2. Particular Procedural Acts

Several decisions have applied the general approach discussed above to other factual **7.49** scenarios in considering whether a particular procedural step would amount to a step in the proceedings for purposes of Section 6(1).

In *Amoe Pte Ltd v Otto Marine Ltd*, Lee Seiu Kin J found that, on the particular facts of **7.50** the case, a Notice to Produce concerning the inspection of documents referenced in pleadings was not a step in the proceedings.[117] Lee J held that the Notice to Produce was not the same as an application for discovery of documents, and in the circumstances of this case he was satisfied that the application was made in order to ascertain the nature of the claim to see if arbitration was an option.[118] He took particular note of the applicant's evidence that it did not have the underlying contract because its documents had been filed in an offsite warehouse and could not be accessed within a reasonable

---

[112] Ibid, [93].
[113] Ibid, [95].
[114] Ibid, [100].
[115] Ibid, [101].
[116] Ibid, [95].
[117] *Amoe Pte Ltd v Otto Marine Ltd*, [2014] 1 SLR 724 (hereafter *Amoe v Otto*).
[118] Ibid, [19]–[20].

92 STAY OF COURT PROCEEDINGS IN FAVOUR OF ARBITRATION

period of time,[119] and this indicated that the applicant was not capable yet of making an unequivocal election to pursue either litigation or arbitration.[120]

7.51 In *L Capital Jones Ltd v Maniach Pte Ltd*, the Court of Appeal held that an application to strike out litigation proceedings on the merits was a step in the proceedings, but the opposition of an interim injunction application against transferring shares to a third party was not.[121] The striking out application evinced an equivocal intention to participate in court proceedings in preference to arbitration, because it signified a submission to the court's jurisdiction to resolve the dispute on the merits.[122] It did not matter that the striking out application was not pursued at the very last moment at the hearing; the fact that it was filed was sufficient to constitute an irrevocable step in the proceedings.[123] In contrast, the opposition to the injunction was involuntary and a matter of necessity, so the applicant could not be deemed to have taken a step 'having regard to the urgency of the matter and the circumstances in which the application had been made'.[124] The Singapore High Court has also held that an application to discharge an interim injunction is also not a step in the proceedings, because it is merely aimed at undoing the fetters imposed by the interim injunction and not to advance court proceedings.[125]

7.52 However, not every striking out application necessarily constitutes a step in the proceedings. It depends on the grounds relied upon by the applicant.[126] Thus, for example, in the English case of *Eagle Star Insurance Co Ltd v Yuval Insurance Co Ltd*, Lord Denning MR held that an application to strike out a defective statement of claim that was lacking in material particulars did not constitute a step in the proceedings because the application was a 'disaffirmation', rather than affirmation, of court proceedings.[127]

7.53 The question of whether an application to extend time will constitute a step in the proceedings is similarly context-dependent. In *Cameron Lindsay Duncan v Diablo Fortune Inc.*, although not strictly necessary to its decision, the Singapore High Court opined that an application by way of an Originating Summons to extend time to register a lien over a vessel was a step in the proceedings.[128] That was because such an application was not made merely to preserve the status quo; instead, it was a substantive application which could negate the effect of a charge under Section 131 of the Companies Act.[129]

---

[119] Ibid, [12]–[19].

[120] Ibid, [8], [14], [20], quoting from *The Londonderry Port and Harbour Commissioners v W S Atkins Consultants Limited and Charles Brand Limited* [2011] NIQB 74, [25].

[121] *L Capital Jones Ltd v Maniach Pte Ltd* [2017] 1 SLR 312 (hereafter *L Capital (CA)*), [13(c)], [76]–[78],

[122] Ibid, [78], quoting from *Carona Holdings* (n 108) [55].

[123] Ibid, [83].

[124] See the High Court's decision *Maniach Pte Ltd v L. Capital Jones Ltd and Jones the Grocer Group Holding Pte Ltd* [2016] SGHC 65, [53]–[55], [118]–[121]; *L Capital (CA)* (n 121) [76].

[125] *BMO v BMP* [2017] SGHC 127 [116] (hereafter *BMO v BMP*).

[126] Tay, 'A Step or Misstep in Court' (n 103) [42]–[44].

[127] *Eagle Star Insurance Co Ltd v Yuval Insurance Co Ltd* [1978] 1 Lloyd's Rep 357 at 361.

[128] *Cameron Lindsay Duncan v Diablo Fortune Inc.* [2017] SGHC 172 [22]–[24] (hereafter *Cameron Lindsay Duncan v Diablo Fortune*).

[129] Ibid, [24].

The mere acknowledgement of service of process is unlikely to constitute a step in the **7.54** proceedings. In *BMO v BMP*, the Singapore High Court held that ticking the answer 'YES' to the question 'Do you intend to defend the claim?' in an acknowledgement of service form cannot be regarded as a step in the proceeding, because it does not indicate that the applicant would be making a substantive defence.[130]

I. Section 6(1)—Subject Matter Falls within the Scope of the Arbitration Agreement

A stay will only be granted if the subject matter of the dispute *prima facie* falls within **7.55** the scope of the arbitration agreement. To determine whether this is the case, Singapore courts apply a two-prong test as set out by the Court of Appeal in *Tomolugen*, namely that the Court will: first (i) determine what matter or matters are subject to court proceedings; and then (ii) ascertain whether the matter(s) fall within the scope of the arbitration clause.[131]

In applying the first prong, the level of granularity used to characterise the matter or **7.56** matters in question can be determinative. As to this, the Court of Appeal in *Tomolugen* cautioned against characterising the matter(s) in either 'an overly broad or an unduly narrow and pedantic manner', endorsing instead 'a practical and common-sense inquiry in relation to any reasonably substantial issue that is not merely peripherally or tangentially connected to the dispute in the court proceedings'.[132] The Court of Appeal further noted that Section 6(2) of the IAA contemplated that a court is to stay proceedings 'so far as [they] relate to [the] matter', and this militates against taking an overly broad view of a 'matter' or treating it as referring to court proceedings as a whole.[133]

With respect to the second prong, there may be a threshold question in some cases as to **7.57** whether there even exists any 'dispute', 'difference', or 'controversy' within the meaning of a given arbitration clause. In determining this threshold question, Singapore courts have made clear that the merits of the dispute are irrelevant and that they will not consider whether there is 'a genuine dispute', particularly given the deliberate omission in Section 6(2) of the phrase 'or that there is not in fact any dispute between the parties' (previously found in the preceding domestic arbitration legislation).[134]

The question has arisen whether an admission may be regarded as negating the ex- **7.58** istence of a dispute. In *Dalian Hualiang Enterprise Group Co Ltd v Louis Dreyfus Asia Pte Ltd*, Woo Bih Li J observed that the case where 'a defendant may refuse to pay or to

---

[130] *BMO v BMP* (n 125) [115].
[131] *Tomolugen* (n 10) [108].
[132] Ibid, [113].
[133] Ibid.
[134] *Tjong Very Sumito v Antig Investments* (n 2) [39], citing *Dalian Hualiang Enterprise v Louis Dreyfus Asia* (n 10) [75]–[79].

94 STAY OF COURT PROCEEDINGS IN FAVOUR OF ARBITRATION

admit a debt or remain silent because he has no money to pay or simply because he is intransigent' is an example of a case where no dispute exists.[135]

7.59 This was endorsed by the Court of Appeal in *Tjong Very Sumito and ors v Antig Investments Pte Ltd*, which held that a stay would be denied for the non-existence of a dispute only where 'there has been a clear and unequivocal admission' both as to liability and quantum, because this is an exception to the 'scrupulous enforcement of arbitration agreements'.[136] As an example of a case involving such a clear and unequivocal admission, the Court of Appeal cited with approval the Hong Kong decision *Getwick Engineers Limited v Pilecon Engineering Limited*, whereby Geoffrey Ma J declined to order a stay in respect of a dishonoured cheque because it was a 'clear and unequivocal admission on the defendant's part of its liability and quantum'.[137]

7.60 Applying these principles, the Court of Appeal rejected the argument that a mere asserted denial of a claim did not amount to a dispute and upheld the stay that had been granted in favour of the applicant.[138] In its judgment, the Court of Appeal also noted that silence, on its own, 'even in the face of repeated claims', would be insufficient to constitute the clear and unequivocal admission needed to deny the existence of a dispute.[139] Moreover, there may be good reasons to remain silent, including because there are unresolved issues or where certain claims are thought to be preposterous, or perhaps even cultural reasons for silence in certain societies where non-confrontational approaches are preferred.[140]

7.61 Assuming a dispute exists, the main question that arises under the second prong is whether such dispute falls within the scope of the arbitration agreement. As noted by the Court of Appeal in *Tomolugen*, Singapore courts will not adopt an overly technical approach in construing an arbitration clause, and it will instead construe such a clause based on the presumed intentions of rational commercial parties.[141] Singapore courts will identify the 'substance of the controversy', without relying solely on the way the claims are pleaded.[142] In this vein, Singapore courts have also observed that the words 'dispute', 'difference', and 'controversy' used in arbitration agreements are to be generally regarded as conferring the widest possible jurisdiction on any disagreements that are related to the container contract.[143] In *Larsen Oil and Gas Pte Ltd v Petroprod Ltd*, the Court of Appeal held that all arbitration clauses should be generously construed such that all manner of claims, whether common law or statutory, should be regarded as falling within their scope unless there was good reason to conclude otherwise.[144]

---

[135] *Dalian Hualiang Enterprise v Louis Dreyfus Asia* (n 10) [75].
[136] *Tjong Very Sumito v Antig Investments* (n 2) [59].
[137] *Getwick Engineers Limited v Pilecon Engineering Limited* [2002] 1020 HKCU 1.
[138] *Tjong Very Sumito v Antig Investments* (n 2) [47]–[49], [69].
[139] Ibid, [61].
[140] Ibid.
[141] *Tomolugen* (n 10) [124]. See Chapter 6.
[142] Ibid, [124]–[126].
[143] *Tjong Very Sumito v Antig Investments* (n 2) [33]–[50].
[144] See also *Larsen Oil and Gas Pte Ltd v Petroprod Ltd* [2011] 3 SLR 414 [19].

I. SECTION 6(1)—SUBJECT MATTER FALLS WITHIN THE SCOPE   95

Cases concerning claims under bills of exchange can pose particular issues, given the   **7.62**
accepted principle that bills of exchange are separate from the underlying contract.
In *Piallo GmbH v Yafriro International Pte Ltd*, the Singapore High Court declined to
follow Hong Kong authority regarding a 'presumption against taking bills of exchange
into arbitration', rejecting the argument that a claim on a dishonoured cheque falls outside the scope of an arbitration clause in a related distributorship agreement unless specifically referred to.[145] In the Court's view, the claim on the dishonoured cheque and the
cross-claim for damages out of the relevant distributorship agreement arose out of the
'same incident' and therefore it was the intention of the parties that those claims be resolved by the same arbitration process, particularly given that claims on cheques must
have been contemplated by the parties given the provisions of the agreement.[146] The
Court further held that a claim under a bill of exchange would only be excluded if that
were expressly stated.[147]

The High Court and Court of Appeal took a different approach from *Piallo* in a sub-   **7.63**
sequent case, *Rals International Pte Ltd v Cassa de Risparmio*. The High Court Judge
distinguished the facts of this case, which involved a narrowly confined claim for the
face value of eight promissory notes by an endorsee that was not party to the underlying
contract, from *Piallo*, and held that this was a claim arising out of a statutory contract
that was separate and independent from the underlying contract.[148]

The Court of Appeal agreed with the first instance decision, but did not agree with the   **7.64**
reasons the High Court Judge gave for distinguishing *Piallo*.[149] Instead, the Court of
Appeal reached a broader holding based on the principle of cash equivalence—namely,
that bills of exchange are to be treated as cash, to be enforced by the immediate right of
a holder against the drawer and endorsers of a dishonoured bill for the amount claimed
in liquidated damages.[150] Departing from the approach taken in *Piallo*, the Court of
Appeal found that an arbitration clause in an underlying contract 'will generally not
be treated as covering disputes arising under an accompanying bill of exchange in the
absence of express language or express incorporation'.[151] In this regard, the Court of
Appeal adopted the views of the House of Lords in *Nova (Jersey) Knit Ltd v Kammgarn
Spinnerei GmbH*,[152] in particular, the speech of Lord Wilberforce adopting a general
presumption that 'businessmen neither wish nor expect bills of exchange to be taken
into arbitration', in light of the function of bills of exchange to be treated as uncon-
ditionally payable instruments.[153] The court agreed that 'as a matter of commercial

---

[145] *Piallo GmbH v Yafriro International Pte Ltd* [2014] 1 SLR 1028 (hereafter *Piallo v Yafriro*) [26]–[36].
[146]. Ibid, [37]–[38].
[147] Ibid, [39].
[148] *Cassa di Risparmio v Rals (HC)* (n 96) [192]–[204].
[149] *Rals v Cassa di Risparmio (CA)* (n 96) [51].
[150] Ibid, [27]–[29]. See also Sections 47, 57, 92, and 97 of the Bills of Exchange Act (Cap. 23, 2004 Rev. Ed.).
[151] Ibid, [42], [45].
[152] *Nova (Jersey) Knit Ltd v Kammgarn Spinnerei GmbH* [1977] 1 WLR 713.
[153] *Rals v Cassa di Risparmio (CA)* (n 96) [44], quoting from *Nova*, 721–2, 731

96 STAY OF COURT PROCEEDINGS IN FAVOUR OF ARBITRATION

common sense, it is difficult to see why any right-thinking merchant would choose to give up his rights in respect of bills of exchange'.[154]

J. Sections 6(2) and 6(3)—Possible Orders under Section 6

7.65 In ordering a stay, Section 6(2) of the IAA provides that the court may impose 'such terms and conditions as the court thinks fit'. In this respect, the Singapore courts are said to have 'an unfettered discretion' to impose reasonable conditions or such conditions required by justice, although that discretion is to be exercised judiciously and subject to the main guiding principle that the courts should generally be slow to interfere in the arbitration process.[155] Any conditions imposed should seek to support and give effect to the parties' intention and avoid rewriting the parties' arbitration agreement.[156] This part of Section 6(2) is complemented by Section 6(3) which allows a court to make 'interim or supplementary' orders in relation to any property that is subject of the dispute.

7.66 As an example of the flexible use of the court's Section 6(2) powers, in two cases Singapore courts imposed a condition that the stay applicants waive the defence of timebar in the arbitration proceedings. In *The Xanadu*, Lai Kew Chai J held that the stay respondent would suffer undue and disproportionate hardship if the condition was not imposed, because it was reasonable for the respondent to have commenced admiralty proceedings given the ambiguity in the relevant bill of lading, and the applicants had waited until the claim was time-barred to file the stay application.[157] Similarly, in *The 'Duden'*, Andrew Ang J (as he then was) imposed the same condition because there was 'egregious' ambiguity surrounding the identity of the charterparty referred to in the bill of lading, and he therefore held that it was unreasonable to expect the holder of the bill of lading to comply with an arbitration agreement in a charterparty that the carrier was not certain of.[158] Ang J further justified the condition with the observation that the stay applicants appeared clearly to be trying all means to avoid an adjudication of the matter.[159]

7.67 In *KVC Rice Intertrade Co Ltd v Asian Mineral Resources Pte Ltd*,[160] in ordering a stay in favour of arbitration under a 'bare' arbitration clause,[161] Pang Khang Chau JC (as he then was) imposed a condition that the stay applicant would not raise any objections to

---

[154] Ibid, [45].

[155] *The 'Duden'* (n 11) [11]–[15]. Applying the dicta of Lai SC J in *Splosna Plovba International Shipping and Chartering d o o v Adria Orient Line Pte Ltd* [1998] SGHC 289. It has been suggested that there was no such discretion in the United Kingdom. See D. Joseph, *Jurisdiction and Arbitration Agreements and their Enforcement* (Sweet & Maxwell 2005) [11.02].

[156] *KVC Rice Intertrade Co Ltd v Asian Mineral Resources Pte Ltd* [2017] 4 SLR 182 [79] (hereafter *KVC Rice Intertrade v Asian Mineral Resources*).

[157] *The Xanadu* [1997] 3 SLR(R) 360 [6].

[158] *The 'Duden'* (n 11) [22]–[23].

[159] Ibid, [24].

[160] *KVC Rice Intertrade v Asian Mineral Resources* (n 156).

[161] The court's analysis of the validity and workability of such clauses is addressed in greater detail in Chapter 6.

the Singapore International Arbitration Centre (SIAC) President's jurisdiction to appoint an arbitrator in the event the parties could not agree on a nominee.[162] Pang JC reasoned that this was because of the firm position the stay applicant had taken with respect to the workability of the arbitration clause, specifically that there were no obstacles to the SIAC President making an appointment, which meant that it would be unfair and unjust if the applicant could take a different stance in the SIAC arbitration.[163]

In *HKL Group Co Ltd v Rizq International Holdings Pte Ltd*, the Assistant Registrar was **7.68** concerned with a pathological clause that provided that the 'Arbitration Committee at Singapore' was to administer the arbitration in accordance with the ICC Rules.[164] The Assistant Registrar imposed the condition that parties obtain the agreement of the SIAC or any other arbitral institution in Singapore to conduct a hybrid arbitration applying the ICC Rules.[165]

K. Section 6(2)—Arbitration Agreement Null and Void, Inoperative, or Incapable of Being Performed

The second part of Section 6(2) qualifies the powers of the Court. A stay of court pro- **7.69** ceedings must be made unless the Court finds that an arbitration agreement is 'null and void, inoperative or incapable of being performed'. The second part of Section 6(2) is adopted verbatim from Article 8(1) of the Model Law, which is, in turn, based on Article II(3) of the New York Convention.

As a general matter, the Singapore High Court has observed that, given the prevailing **7.70** pro-enforcement approach pursuant to the New York Convention, the Model Law, and the IAA, the terms 'null and void', 'inoperative', and 'incapable of being performed' should be construed narrowly, meaning that these terms would only apply in 'manifest' cases.[166] It has also been observed that the grounds under Section 6(2) are typically contractual in nature.[167] The interpretation of the terms 'null and void', 'inoperative', and 'incapable of being performed' are discussed in the subsections below.

1. 'Null and Void'

An arbitration agreement is null and void only if it is 'devoid of legal effect'.[168] On one **7.71** view, in light of the policy in favour of enforceability under the New York Convention,

---

[162] *KVC Rice Intertrade v Asian Mineral Resources* (n 156) [80].
[163] Ibid.
[164] *HKL Group Co Ltd v Rizq International Holdings Pte Ltd* [2013] SGHCR 5.
[165] Ibid, [37].
[166] *Wilson Taylor v Dyna- Jet* (3 SLR) (n 17) [143]–[144].
[167] Ibid, [145].
[168] Ibid, [176], citing *Albon v Naza Motor Trading Sdn Bhd (No 3)* [2007] 2 Lloyd's Rep 1 [18].

98 STAY OF COURT PROCEEDINGS IN FAVOUR OF ARBITRATION

an arbitration agreement is 'null and void' only if it is subject to an internationally recognised defence such as duress, mistake, fraud, or waiver, or if it contravenes fundamental policies of the forum.[169]

7.72 In *Sembawang Engineers and Constructors Pte Ltd v Covec (Singapore) Pte Ltd*, the Assistant Registrar held that the term 'null and void' would be applicable 'where the arbitration agreement was never entered or is subsequently found to be void *ab initio*'.[170] However, in *Dyna-Jet Pte Ltd v Wilson Taylor Asia Pacific Pte Ltd*, the High Court noted that it is unsettled whether 'null and void' encompasses a putative arbitration agreement which never in fact came into existence as a result of defects in formation or consent, as opposed to an actual arbitration agreement which did come into existence but for some other reason is vitiated or vulnerable to vitiation, but did not consider it necessary to decide the point in that case.[171] Commentators have noted that the former situation should be characterised as a question of whether the claim was even subject to an arbitration agreement, whereas 'null and void' is meant to cater to the validity or efficacy of an arbitration agreement.[172]

2. 'Inoperative'

7.73 An arbitration agreement is 'inoperative' when it ceases to have contractual effect under the general law of contract, including discharge by repudiatory breach, by agreement, or by reason of waiver, estoppel, election, abandonment, or frustration.[173] An arbitration agreement is also inoperative if it contains such an inherent contradiction that it cannot be given effect.[174]

7.74 In *Tjong Very Sumito*, the Court of Appeal held that, where a party has waived its right to arbitrate or is estopped from insisting on arbitration, the arbitration agreement would be 'inoperative' for the purposes of Section 6(2).[175] As the High Court noted in *TMT Co Ltd v The Royal Bank of Scotland plc*,[176] although the relevant dispute fell outside the scope of the arbitration clause, the case could also be decided on the basis that the agreement was 'inoperative' or 'incapable of being performed' since the parties stipulated that any putative arbitration would be governed by stock exchange rules, but there was no relevant exchange to speak of.[177]

---

[169] Ibid, [176], citing *Rhone Mediterranee Compagnia Francese di Assicurazioni e Riassicurazioni v Achille Lauro* 712 F2d 50 (3d Cir 1983). In *Dyna-Jet*, it was conceded that the parties' arbitration was not 'null and void' so the Court did not have to apply its interpretation of the words 'null and void' to the facts of the case.

[170] *Sembawang Engineers and Constructors Pte Ltd v Covec (Singapore) Pte Ltd* [2008] SGHC 229 [39].

[171] *Wilson Taylor v Dyna-Jet* (3 SLR) (n 17) [177].

[172] Foxton and Ng, 'Breach of the Arbitration Agreement' (n 2) 103.

[173] *Wilson Taylor v Dyna-Jet* (3 SLR) (n 17) [162].

[174] Ibid, [163], citing D. St John Sutton, J. Gill, and M. Gearing, *Russell on Arbitration* (23rd edn, Sweet & Maxwell 2007) 7–046.

[175] *Tjong Very Sumito v Antig Investments* (n 2) [53]. See also *Halvanon Insurance Co Ltd v Companhia de Seguros do Estado de Sao Paulo* [1995] LRLR 303.

[176] *TMT Co Ltd v The Royal Bank of Scotland plc* [2018] 3 SLR 70 (hereafter *TMT v The Royal Bank of Scotland*).

[177] Ibid, [64].

3. 'Incapable of Being Performed'

An arbitration agreement is 'incapable of being performed' when there is an insurmountable obstacle which prevents the arbitration from being set in motion, and the list of such circumstances is not a closed one.[178] It has been suggested that examples include where there was contradictory language in the main contract indicating that the parties intended to litigate, or if the parties had chosen a specific arbitrator in the arbitration agreement who was deceased or unavailable at the time of appointment, if the place of arbitration is no longer available, or if the arbitration agreement was so vague, confusing, or contradictory as to prevent the arbitration from taking place.[179]

7.75

As the High Court held in *Dyna-Jet Pte Ltd v Wilson Taylor Asia Pacific Pte Ltd*, the test is 'whether the arbitration proceedings can be effectively set into motion even without the cooperation of the other party'.[180] Whether an arbitration agreement is 'incapable of being performed' comprises, but is not synonymous with, the doctrine of frustration.[181] The High Court held that, because the arbitration agreement was subject to a contingency that could never be satisfied, the parties' arbitration agreement was 'incapable of being performed'.

7.76

Where a non-arbitrable subject matter is the subject of the arbitration agreement, that agreement would be considered either 'inoperative' or 'incapable of being performed'.[182] Arbitrability issues are discussed in greater detail in Chapter 10.

7.77

L. Case Management Powers

The mandatory stay pursuant to Section 6 of the IAA can be distinguished from a case management stay granted in the Court's discretion. As explained above, an application for a mandatory stay under Section 6 can only be made by a party to an arbitration agreement in respect of matters that are subject to an arbitration agreement. However, an application for a discretionary case management stay can be made in respect of matters that are not subject to the arbitration agreement or by non-parties to the arbitration agreement. The power to grant a case management stay derives from 'the wider need to control and manage proceedings between the parties for a fair and efficient administration of justice', and any orders made are those necessary to 'serve the ends of justice'.[183]

7.78

---

[178] *Wilson Taylor v Dyna- Jet* (3 SLR) (n 17) [152]–[154].

[179] Ibid, [154], citing M.L. Moses, *The Principles and Practice of International Commercial Arbitration* (2nd edn, Cambridge University Press 2012) 34.

[180] *Wilson Taylor v Dyna- Jet* (3 SLR) (n 17) [155], citing E. Gaillard et al. (eds), *Enforcement of Arbitration Agreements and International Arbitral Awards: The New York Convention in Practice* (Cameron May 2008).

[181] Ibid, [157].

[182] *Tomolugen* (n 10) [74], citing *Fulham Football Club (1987) Ltd v Richards* [2012] Ch 333 at [35]–[36].

[183] Citing *Tomolugen* (n 10) [188].

100   STAY OF COURT PROCEEDINGS IN FAVOUR OF ARBITRATION

7.79   In deciding whether to grant a stay on case management grounds, Singapore courts aim to strike a balance amongst the following concerns: (i) the plaintiff's right to choose whom he wants to sue and where; (ii) the court's desire to prevent a plaintiff from circumventing the operation of an arbitration clause; and (iii) the court's inherent power to manage its processes to prevent an abuse of process and ensure the efficient and fair resolution of disputes.[184] In this way, Singapore courts have declined to follow the approach of English and New Zealand courts, which only grant case management stays in 'rare and compelling' circumstances.[185]

7.80   Criteria indicating that such a stay should be ordered include: (i) whether the claims in the court proceedings were derived from the claims subject to arbitration; (ii) whether there was overlap between these two sets of claims; (iii) whether there was anything that would bar claims in the court proceedings from being pursued in arbitration; (iv) whether findings made in the arbitration would bind the parties to the court proceedings; (v) the risk of inconsistent findings between the arbitral tribunal and the court; and (vi) duplication of witness and evidence.[186]

7.81   In *Tomolugen*, the Singapore Court of Appeal granted a mandatory stay under Section 6 in respect of certain management participation allegations that fell within the scope of the arbitration agreement.[187] However, there were remaining claims that were not the subject of the mandatory stay, and those claims were not automatically stayed as a matter of course; instead, the Court of Appeal had to consider whether to exercise its inherent case management powers to stay those remaining claims.[188]

7.82   With respect to the remaining claims, the Court of Appeal considered there to be three options: (i) stay all the court proceedings pending the resolution of the arbitration; (ii) stay the court proceedings only to the extent required under Section 6 of the IAA, but on condition that the arbitration is commenced only after the resolution of the remaining court proceedings; or (iii) stay the court proceedings only to the extent that is required under Section 6, and allow the arbitration and the remaining court proceedings to run in parallel.[189] Adopting a pragmatic approach, the Court of Appeal decided to give the plaintiff two weeks to decide whether to pursue the management participation allegations that fell within the scope of the arbitration clause. If it chose not to pursue those claims in arbitration, the court proceedings would not be stayed, but the plaintiff would also not be allowed to rely on those allegations against the remaining defendants. If the plaintiff did choose to pursue those allegations in arbitration, then (subject to having an expedited arbitration) the court proceedings against all the defendants would be stayed.[190]

---

[184]   Ibid, [188]; *Gulf Hibiscus Limited v Rex International Holding Limited and anor* [2017] SGHC 210 [62] (hereafter *Gulf Hibiscus v Rex International*).
[185]   Ibid, [187].
[186]   *Gulf Hibiscus v Rex International* (n 184) [63].
[187]   *Tomolugen* (n 10) [137].
[188]   Ibid, [138]–[139].
[189]   Ibid, [139].
[190]   Ibid, [190].

In *Gulf Hibiscus Ltd v Rex International Holding Ltd & another*, a third party to the arbitration agreements sought a case management stay and argued that certain claims for conspiracy, wrongful interference, and unjust enrichment effectively arose from a shareholders agreement with an arbitration clause, and should therefore be brought in arbitration.[191] At first instance, Aedit Abdullah JC (as he then was) reasoned that, although the plaintiff had not expressly pleaded its claims under the shareholders agreement, the claims were in the nature of shareholders disputes concerning improper actions relating to Lime PLC, and these acts were intended to be regulated by the shareholders agreement. Abdullah JC also noted that there was a sufficient risk of inconsistent findings between the court proceedings and any prospective arbitration, with possible duplication of evidence. In the circumstances, he granted a stay subject to the following conditions: (i) if arbitration proceedings are not commenced within five months from the date of the court's judgment, the parties would be at liberty to apply for the stay to be lifted by the court; and (ii) the defendants would be bound by the findings of fact made by the arbitral tribunal.[192] Subsequently, Abdullah JC granted an application to lift the stay on the basis that no arbitration was commenced within the five-month period.[193] This was because the overall resolution of the parties' dispute would be 'stymied by the continuation of the stay'.[194]

7.83

The Court of Appeal agreed with the High Court's decision, but on different grounds. In its view, the original stay should not have been granted in the first place, in light of the right of a claimant to sue wherever it wants.[195] The right of the claimant to sue the two Rex entities, but not RME which was a party to the arbitration agreement, made this more compelling.[196] In substance, because RME was not the party sued, there was no overlap in the parties or issues, and the situation did not call for a case management stay.[197] For these other reasons, the Court of Appeal agreed that continuing the stay would 'stymie ... the resolution of an already protracted dispute'.[198] The Court noted that a court was not *functus officio* upon granting a stay as it could exercise its inherent powers to manage its own internal processes.[199]

7.84

In *Maybank Kim Eng Securities Pte Ltd v Lim Keng Yong*, the High Court likewise exercised its case management powers to stay court proceedings. This was decided under the domestic arbitration act, which as noted earlier, gives the Court discretionary powers on whether to order a stay. Nonetheless, the Court's approach is instructive. The main contract was between Maybank and the first defendant, and this contained an arbitration clause. The second contract, an indemnity provided by the first defendant's

7.85

---

[191] *Gulf Hibiscus v Rex International* (n 184).
[192] Ibid, [6].
[193] Ibid.
[194] Ibid, [32].
[195] *Rex International Holding Ltd and Rex International Investments Pte Ltd v Gulf Hibiscus Limited* [2019] 2 SLR 682 (hereafter *Rex v Gulf Hibiscus (CA)*), [9].
[196] Ibid, [10].
[197] Ibid, [11].
[198] Ibid, [15].
[199] Ibid, [16].

102 STAY OF COURT PROCEEDINGS IN FAVOUR OF ARBITRATION

husband, contained a non-exclusive Singapore jurisdiction clause. The bank alleged that it had closed out the first defendant's positions due to her express instructions. The Court reasoned that a finding against the first respondent would have an impact on the case against the second respondent,[200] as would a finding on the quantum of damages.[201] The Court found that the issues in the proceedings were 'practically identical'[202] and accordingly exercised its discretion to order a stay.

7.86 The High Court took a similar approach in *CJY v CJZ and others*.[203] In this case, the plaintiff, a construction company, was engaged for certain construction works. In connection with the project, the plaintiff provided two performance bonds and its subcontractor provided one.[204] In April 2017, the project architects released a schedule of defects[205] leading to the employer calling on the performance bonds.[206]

7.87 In July 2018, the plaintiff brought a claim against the employer's head of finance, the project architect and the quantity surveyors in arbitration,[207] alleging that the call on the bonds was wrongful and that it was not responsible for the defects in the schedule.[208] In October 2020, the plaintiff then commenced court proceedings against the defendants, raising various claims that tackled similar issues to that brought in arbitration.[209] A stay of the plaintiff's court proceedings was granted in the High Court on the basis that there was an overlap in parties, issues, and remedies that were being sought in both the arbitration and court proceedings.[210] Citing *Rex International Holding Ltd and Rex International Investments Pte Ltd v Gulf Hibiscus Limited*, the judge emphasised that the basis of granting the stay did not stem from the mere existence of common issues but from the fact that proper ventilation of the issues in the court proceedings was dependent on the resolution of the related arbitration.[211]

7.88 In *PUBG Corp v Garena International I Pte Ltd and others*,[212] the court also discussed its discretionary powers in granting a case management stay. Here, the appellant, PUBG Corporation, commenced an action in the High Court against five respondents regarding the alleged infringement of intellectual property rights.[213] The parties subsequently entered into negotiations in an attempt to reach a settlement.[214] The respondents contended that those negotiations resulted in a concluded settlement agreement

---

[200] *Maybank Kim Eng Securities Pte Ltd v Lim Keng Yong* [2016] 3 SLR 431 (hereafter *Maybank v Lim Keng Yong*), [28]–[29].
[201] Ibid, [36].
[202] Ibid, [38]
[203] *CJY v CJZ and others* [2021] SGHC 69 (hereafter *CJY v CJZ*) [4].
[204] Ibid, [5].
[205] Ibid, [7].
[206] Ibid, [8].
[207] Ibid, [11].
[208] Ibid, [11], [15].
[209] Ibid, [16]–[19].
[210] Ibid, [22]–[40].
[211] Ibid, [44].
[212] *PUBG Corp v Garena International I Pte Ltd and others* [2020] 2 SLR 379 (hereafter *PUBG v Garena*).
[213] Ibid, [1].
[214] Ibid.

with an arbitration clause[215] while the appellant disputed that a valid settlement had ever been reached. The respondents thus commenced arbitration[216] and also applied for a case management stay of the High Court proceedings regarding the intellectual property dispute pending the resolution of the arbitration. In the High Court, the judge granted a stay subject to a time limit of six months. The appellant appealed against the stay, but this was ultimately dismissed by the Court of Appeal.[217]

In arguing against the stay, the appellant pointed out that, as between the court proceedings and the arbitration, there was no overlap in factual and legal issues.[218] It argued that the court proceedings concerned the infringement claims while the arbitration dealt with the alleged settlement.[219] However, the Court explained that the real issue was whether there was a valid settlement between the parties.[220] If so, that would have the effect of compromising current claims, and the court proceedings could not proceed.[221] However, if there was no valid settlement, the court proceedings should proceed. As it concluded that on its face there may have been a settlement with a valid arbitration agreement,[222] the court upheld the stay and deferred to the arbitral tribunal to first determine the validity of the settlement agreement.[223]

7.89

---

[215] Ibid.

[216] Ibid.

[217] Ibid, [18].

[218] Ibid, [14].

[219] Ibid.

[220] Ibid.

[221] Ibid.

[222] Ibid, [16] citing *Tomolugen* (n 10) [63], *Malini Ventura v Knight Capital Pte Ltd* [2015] 5 SLR 707 (n 30) [36] and *Sim Chay Koon and others v NTUC Income Insurance Co-operative Ltd* [2016] 2 SLR 871, [4]–[6].

[223] Ibid, [18].

8

Number and Appointment of Arbitrators

A. Section 9—Number of Arbitrators	8.01	C. Section 9B IAA—Appointment of Arbitrators in Multi-Party	
B. Section 9A—Appointment of Arbitrators	8.03	Arbitrations	8.06

A. Section 9—Number of Arbitrators

<u>IAA, Section 9</u>

Despite Article 10(2) of the Model Law, if the number of arbitrators is not determined by the parties, there is to be a single arbitrator.

8.01 Sections 9 and 9A of the International Arbitration Act (IAA)[1] deal with the appointment of arbitrators, and could be read with Section 2 of the IAA which provides the definition of 'arbitral tribunal'. Both provisions change the default under the United Nations Commission on International Trade Law (UNCITRAL) Model Law on International Commercial Arbitration (the Model Law). In particular, Section 9 of the IAA departs from the Model Law's default position of having three arbitrators. Section 9 provides that 'if the number of arbitrators is not determined by the parties, there shall be a single arbitrator'. The impact of this provision is likely to be minimal, given that many arbitration agreements will incorporate arbitration rules which themselves stipulate how to determine the number of arbitrators in the absence of party agreement.[2]

8.02 It has been assumed (or at least never challenged) that the determination of the number of arbitrators in accordance with arbitration rules would take one outside Sections 9 and 9A as they are an 'agreement' between the parties as to the number of arbitrators. The parties have simply chosen a different mechanism for determining the number of arbitrators, and there is no reason in principle why that chosen mechanism should not prevail. Accordingly, it is not surprising that there are no cases on this point.[3]

---

[1] International Arbitration Act 1994 (hereafter IAA 1994).

[2] See e.g. Singapore International Arbitration Centre Rules 2016, Rule 9 (hereafter SIAC Rules 2016) and International Chamber of Commerce Rules 2021, Article 12 (hereafter ICC Rules 2021).

[3] Possibly the closest suggestion that these sections might have influenced any decision is *K.V.C. Rice Intertrade Co Ltd v Asian Mineral Resources Pte Ltd* [2017] 4 SLR 182. In that case, the court was confronted with a bare arbitration clause that did not stipulate the seat or rules or the number of arbitrators. In enforcing the clause, the court determined that there shall be only one arbitrator. It is not clear if this was inspired by Section 9, though strictly speaking Section 9 would not apply as the seat had not yet been determined to be Singapore.

B. Section 9A—Appointment of Arbitrators

<u>IAA, Section 9A</u>

(1) Despite Article 11(3) of the Model Law, in an arbitration with 2 parties and 3 arbitrators, each party must appoint one arbitrator, and the parties must by agreement appoint the third arbitrator.

(2) Where the parties fail to agree on the appointment of the third arbitrator within 30 days after the receipt of the first request by either party to do so, the appointment must be made, upon the request of a party, by the appointing authority.

8.03 Section 9A also changes the default in the process of appointing the presiding arbitrator in a three-person tribunal. Under Article 11(3) of the Model Law, each party appoints one arbitrator and these two arbitrators will in turn appoint a third arbitrator. In contrast, Section 9A(1) provides that the *parties* (and not their *arbitrators*) have the autonomy to appoint the third arbitrator by agreement. Pursuant to Section 9A(2), if parties fail to do so within 30 days of the receipt of the first request by either party to do so, the appointment shall be made, upon the request of a party, by the appointing authority. The appointing authority referred to is the President of the Court of Arbitration of the Singapore International Arbitration Centre (SIAC).[4] Two quick observations are relevant here.

8.04 First, although Section 9A(1) appears to introduce some confusion into the process for the appointment of the third arbitrator, in practice, this is unlikely to be problematic. Section 9A(1) does not affect the default position under Article 11(2) of the Model Law, which allows parties to 'agree on a procedure of appointing the arbitrator or arbitrators'. In practice, many contracts stipulating arbitration as the choice of dispute resolution would include a provision concerning the process for the appointment of arbitrators. However, even if the contract does not expressly address this issue, there would likely be a choice of the arbitration rules which are incorporated by reference. Often, arbitration rules themselves provide a process for the appointment of arbitrators. For example, the SIAC Rules provide that the President of the SIAC Court will appoint the presiding arbitrator unless another procedure is agreed upon or where the agreed procedure fails to produce a nomination.[5] The International Chamber of Commerce (ICC) Rules (2021) are similar, save that there is a default 30 days for any agreed procedure to produce a nomination for the presiding arbitrator.[6] In most cases therefore, Section 9A(1) is unlikely to apply.

8.05 Second, the optimism of Section 9A(1) does not appear to be shared by the arbitration rules; that is to say, the likelihood of disputing parties agreeing on the appointment of

---

[4] IAA 1994 (n 1), Section 2(1) read with Section 8(2).
[5] See SIAC Rules 2016 (n 2), Rule 11.3.
[6] See ICC Rules 2021 (n 2), Article 12(5).

106 NUMBER AND APPOINTMENT OF ARBITRATORS

a third arbitrator is not high. As mentioned, arbitration rules such as the SIAC Rules (2016) and the ICC Rules (2021), for example, provide a procedure for determining the presiding arbitrator on the assumption that the parties will not agree.[7]

C. Section 9B IAA—Appointment of Arbitrators in Multi-Party Arbitrations

IAA, Section 9B

(1) Despite Article 11(3) of the Model Law, in an arbitration with 3 or more parties and 3 arbitrators—

    (a) the claimant, or all the claimants by agreement if there is more than one claimant, must appoint an arbitrator on or before the date of sending of the request for the dispute to be referred to arbitration and inform the respondent or respondents of the appointment on the date when the request for the dispute to be referred to arbitration is sent to the respondent or respondents;

    (b) the respondent, or all the respondents by agreement if there is more than one respondent, must appoint an arbitrator and inform the claimant or claimants of the appointment within 30 days after the date of receipt of the request for the dispute to be referred to arbitration by the respondent, or by the last respondent to receive the request if there is more than one respondent; and

    (c) the 2 arbitrators appointed under paragraphs (a) and (b) must by agreement appoint the third arbitrator, who is to be the presiding arbitrator, within 60 days after the date of receipt of the request for the dispute to be referred to arbitration by the respondent, or by the last respondent to receive the request if there is more than one respondent.

(2) Despite subsection (1), the appointing authority must, upon the request of any party, appoint all 3 arbitrators and designate any one of the arbitrators as the presiding arbitrator if—

    (a) the claimant or claimants fail to appoint an arbitrator, or fail to inform the respondent or respondents of such appointment, by the date specified in subsection (1)(a); or

    (b) the respondent or respondents fail to appoint an arbitrator, or fail to inform the claimant or claimants of such appointment, within the time specified in subsection (1)(b).

(3) In making the appointments under subsection (2), the appointing authority may, having regard to all relevant circumstances, re-appoint or revoke the appointment of an arbitrator appointed under subsection (1)(a) or (b).

(4) Despite subsection (1)(c), the appointing authority must, upon the request of any party and having regard to all relevant circumstances, appoint the third arbitrator if

---

[7] See SIAC Rules 2016 (n 2), Rule 11.2; ICC Rules 2021 (n 2), Article 12(5).

C. SECTION 9B IAA—APPOINTMENTS IN MULTI-PARTY ARBITRATIONS 107

the 2 arbitrators appointed by the parties fail to agree on the appointment of the third arbitrator within the time specified in subsection (1)(c).

Section 9B was introduced following a broad public consultation by the Ministry of Law[8] and came into force on 1 December 2020. It applies only to arbitral proceedings commenced on or after 1 December 2020,[9] although parties may agree in writing that Section 9B also applies to arbitral proceedings commenced prior to 1 December 2020 if none of the arbitrators for such arbitral proceedings have been appointed by that date.[10] **8.06**

Section 9B provides a default mechanism which applies in multi-party arbitrations. Where there are three or more parties and three arbitrators, the claimant or claimants must appoint an arbitrator by the time of the filing the request for arbitration;[11] the respondent or respondents must thereafter appoint an arbitrator within 30 days of the claimants' request for arbitration;[12] and the two appointed arbitrators must by agreement appoint the third arbitrator, who is to be the presiding arbitrator, within 60 days after the claimants' request for arbitration.[13] **8.07**

In the event that either of the parties fails to appoint an arbitrator within the allotted time, the appointing authority must, upon the request of any party, appoint *all three* arbitrators and designate any one of the arbitrators as the presiding arbitrator.[14] In so doing, the appointing authority has the discretion to either re-appoint or revoke the appointment of an arbitrator already appointed.[15] In the event that the two appointed arbitrators fail to appoint a presiding arbitrator within the allotted time, the appointing authority must, upon the request of any party, appoint the presiding arbitrator.[16] **8.08**

The appointing authority is to consider all relevant circumstances.[17] At the second reading of the amending bill, this was taken to mean that the appointing authority has broad discretion to 'consider all the facts, all the matters which arise in the context of that appointment exercise'.[18] This includes facts such as whether the parties on one side have reached an agreement collectively, or whether a party is attempting to frustrate the process or delay the proceedings.[19] **8.09**

Section 9B modifies the Model Law, which has no provisions specifically addressing the appointment of arbitrators in a multi-party scenario. Arbitrator appointments in such **8.10**

---

[8] Second Reading of the International Arbitration (Amendment) Bill.
[9] International Arbitration (Amendment) Act 2020 (No. 32 of 2020) (hereafter IAA (Amendment) 2020), Section 7(1).
[10] Ibid, Section 7(3).
[11] IAA 1994 (n 1) Section 9B(1)(a).
[12] Ibid, Section 9B(1)(b).
[13] Ibid, Section 9B(1)(c).
[14] Ibid, Section 9B(2).
[15] Ibid, Section 9B(3).
[16] Ibid, Section 9B(4).
[17] Ibid, Section 9B(3).
[18] Second Reading of the International Arbitration (Amendment) Bill.
[19] Ibid.

108 NUMBER AND APPOINTMENT OF ARBITRATORS

scenarios were not discussed during the drafting of Article 11 of the United Nations Commission on International Trade Law (UNCITRAL) Model Law.[20]

8.11 The introduction of Section 9B is eminently sensible and is intended to avoid a situation similar to that which arose in the well-known French Cour de Cassation decision in *Siemens AG and BKMI Industrieanlagen GmbH v Dutco Construction Co (Dutco)*.[21] *Dutco* concerned a three-party arbitration in which the two respondents each claimed the right to appoint a separate arbitrator. The respondents had made a joint appointment, but only under protest because the ICC warned the respondents of its intention to appoint an arbitrator by default. In annulling the resulting award as being contrary to public policy, the Cour de Cassation held that the appointment procedure violated the respondents' right to equal treatment because the claimant was able to appoint its nominated arbitrator and neither of the respondents were able to do so.[22]

8.12 Following *Dutco*, virtually all leading arbitral institutions have since introduced provisions similar to that in Section 9B of the IAA to address the multi-party appointment of arbitrators,[23] and the application of such mechanisms will avoid arguments that there has been inequality in treatment of parties in the appointment of the tribunal, or that the agreed procedure for the appointment of the tribunal was not complied with. While there are few reported decisions in Singapore considering the appointment of arbitrators in a multi-party context, it was suggested in *The 'Titan Unity'* that the Singapore courts are likely to give effect to such provisions.[24]

8.13 In enacting Section 9B, Singapore's curial law has gone further than that of other jurisdictions, which generally do not address multi-party appointment of arbitrators. For example, the English Arbitration Act does not expressly address the appointment of arbitrators in a multi-party scenario.

---

[20] UNCITRAL, *312th Meeting of the United Nations Commission on International Trade Law*, UN Doc. A/CN.9/246 (United Nations 1985).

[21] Judgment of 7 January 1992, *Sociétés BKMI et Siemens v Société Dutco*, 119 JDI. (Clunet) 707 (1992) (French Cour de Cassation Civ. 1e) (hereafter *Sociétés BKMI v Société Dutco*). See also G.B. Born, *International Commercial Arbitration: Law and Practice* (3rd edn, Kluwer Law International 2021) (hereafter Born, *International Commercial Arbitration*) 276.

[22] *Sociétés BKMI v Société Dutco* (n 21). See also Born, *International Commercial Arbitration* (n 21) 297.

[23] See e.g. SIAC Rules 2016 (n 2), Rule 12; ICC Rule 2021 (n 2), Article 12(6); London Court of International Arbitration Rules 2020, Article 8(1); Hong Kong International Arbitration Centre Rules 2018, Article 8(2).

[24] *The 'Titan Unity'* [2014] SGHCR 4 [40]–[41], in the context of discussing a party's right where such a party had been joined as a party *after* the tribunal had been constituted: 'It should ultimately be borne in mind that Art V(1)(d) of the New York Convention does not prescribe that the tribunal must be appointed by parties to an arbitration agreement, but only that the composition of the arbitral tribunal be made in accordance with the agreement of the parties; and as modernised arbitral rules have more than capably shown, a party to an arbitration agreement may agree to a tribunal's composition without having appointed it.'

9

Appeals from Jurisdictional Rulings and Order 48

A.	Section 10—Introduction	9.01	F. Section 10(3)—Standard of Review	9.25
B.	Section 10(1)—Relationship and Key Differences between Section 10 of the IAA and Article 16(3) of the Model Law	9.03	G. Implications on the Court's Power to Make an Award or Order of Costs (Sections 10(7) and 10(8) of the IAA)	9.33
C.	Section 10(2)—Negative Jurisdictional Rulings	9.11	H. Stay of Arbitration under Section 10(9)(a) of the IAA	9.36
D.	Section 10(3)—Nature of Court's Power to Rule on Arbitral Tribunal's Jurisdiction	9.12	I. Order 48 Rules of Court 1. Rule 2 2. Rule 3	9.43 9.44 9.49
E.	Section 10(3)—Ambit of Court's Power to Rule on Arbitral Tribunal's Jurisdiction	9.23	3. Rule 4 4. Rule 5 and 6	9.52 9.56

<u>IAA, Section 10</u>

(1) This section has effect despite Article 16(3) of the Model Law.

(2) An arbitral tribunal may rule on a plea that it has no jurisdiction at any stage of the arbitral proceedings.

(3) If the arbitral tribunal rules—

(a) on a plea as a preliminary question that it has jurisdiction; or

(b) on a plea at any stage of the arbitral proceedings that it has no jurisdiction, any party may, within 30 days after having received notice of that ruling, apply to the General Division of the High Court to decide the matter.

(4) An appeal from the decision of the General Division of the High Court made under Article 16(3) of the Model Law or this section may be brought only with the permission of the appellate court.

(5) There is no appeal against a refusal for grant of permission of the appellate court.

(6) Where the General Division of the High Court, or the appellate court on appeal, decides that the arbitral tribunal has jurisdiction—

(a) the arbitral tribunal must continue the arbitral proceedings and make an award; and

(b) where any arbitrator is unable or unwilling to continue the arbitral proceedings, the mandate of that arbitrator terminates and a substitute arbitrator must be appointed in accordance with Article 15 of the Model Law.

(7) In making a ruling or decision under this section that the arbitral tribunal has no jurisdiction, the arbitral tribunal, the General Division of the High Court or the appellate court (as the case may be) may make an award or order of costs of the proceedings, including the arbitral proceedings (as the case may be), against any party.

(8) Where an award of costs is made by the arbitral tribunal under subsection (7), section 21 applies with the necessary modifications.

(9) Where an application is made pursuant to Article 16(3) of the Model Law or this section—

(a) such application does not operate as a stay of the arbitral proceedings or of enforcement of any award or order made in the arbitral proceedings unless the General Division of the High Court orders otherwise; and

(b) no intermediate act or proceeding is invalidated except so far as the General Division of the High Court may direct.

(10) Where there is an appeal from the decision of the General Division of the High Court pursuant to subsection (4)—

(a) such appeal does not operate as a stay of the arbitral proceedings or of enforcement of any award or order made in the arbitral proceedings unless the General Division of the High Court or the appellate court orders otherwise; and

(b) no intermediate act or proceeding is invalidated except so far as the appellate court may direct.

(11) In this section, "appellate court" means the court to which an appeal under Article 16(3) of the Model Law or this section is to be made under section 29C of the Supreme Court of Judicature Act 1969.

A. Section 10—Introduction

9.01 Section 10 is one of the key provisions of the International Arbitration Act (IAA). It governs appeals from an arbitral tribunal's ruling on its own jurisdiction, which can occur at any stage of the arbitral proceedings. It is critical to note that Section 10 underwent significant amendments in 2012. Prior to the 2012 amendments to the IAA, Section 10 of the IAA almost wholly incorporated Article 16(3) of the Model Law, with the exception of an additional provision that an appeal from a decision of the High Court made under Article 16(3) of the Model Law shall lie to the Court of Appeal only with the leave of the High Court. Both Article 16(3) of the Model Law and the provision on leave remain effective save that Section 10 takes precedence and has effect 'notwithstanding Article 16(3) of the Model Law'.[1]

9.02 As with several other provisions of the IAA, it is imperative to appreciate the nuances involved in reading Section 10 alongside the corresponding part of the Model Law. The

---

[1] International Arbitration Act 1994, Section 10(1) (hereafter IAA).

ex facie differences and the unique nature of Section 10, as elucidated by case law, are noted below.

B. Section 10(1)—Relationship and Key Differences between Section 10 of the IAA and Article 16(3) of the Model Law

9.03 Section 10(1) states that '[t]his section shall have effect notwithstanding Article 16(3) of the Model Law'. Therefore, both the express provisions of Section 10 and Article 16(3) remain effective.

9.04 Essentially, the differences between Section 10 of the IAA and Article 16(3) of the Model Law lie in their ambit and procedure—and Section 10 of the IAA appears to be wider. While Section 10 and Article 16 both permit a tribunal to rule on its own jurisdiction, only Section 10 permits a Singapore court to review a tribunal's negative ruling. In other words, while Article 16(3) of the Model Law empowers the High Court to review an arbitral tribunal's ruling *in favour of* jurisdiction, Article 16 does not permit a court to review a ruling that *denies* jurisdiction. Prior to the 2012 Amendments, under the Model Law, an arbitral tribunal's negative determination on jurisdiction is final and binding, that is, not subject to judicial review under Article 16(3) of the Model Law, and this was confirmed in the case of *PT Asuransi Jasa Indonesia (Persero) v Dexia Bank SA*.[2] With the 2012 amendments, the High Court is now empowered by Section 10 to decide that the arbitral tribunal has jurisdiction even in cases where the latter has come to a negative determination.

9.05 By way of background, although the present-day Article 16 of the Model Law only provides for recourse to court following a *positive* jurisdictional ruling, the Working Group had initially considered providing for similar recourse following *negative* jurisdictional rulings. Prior to the first draft of the articles, it was suggested that a provision 'empowering the court to compel the continuance of arbitral proceedings, where the arbitral tribunal had ruled that it had no jurisdiction' be included.[3] This made its way into the first draft of the Model Law, as Article XXIII(3), the last sentence of which provided that '[a] ruling by the arbitral tribunal that it has no jurisdiction may be contested by any party within 30 days before the Court specified in Article V'.[4] This was ultimately not retained by the Working Group for various reasons. Chief amongst these were the views that a negative jurisdictional ruling by a tribunal 'was final and binding as regards these arbitral proceedings', and that the

---

[2] [2007] 1 SLR(R) 597 (SGCA).

[3] United Nations Commission on International Trade Law (UNCITRAL), *Report of the Working Group on International Contract Practices on the Work of its Third Session*, UN Doc. A/CN. 9/216 (UN, 1982), para 82; UNCITRAL, *Report of the Working Group on International Contract Practices on the Work of its Fourth Session*, UN Doc. A/CN. 9/232 (United Nations 1982) para 157 (hereafter *Report of the Working Group of its Fourth Session*).

[4] UNCITRAL, *Working Paper Submitted to the Working Group on International Contract Practices at its Fifth Session*, UN Doc A/CN.9/WG.Il/WP.40, (United Nations 1983) 81.

112   APPEALS FROM JURISDICTIONAL RULINGS AND ORDER 48

underlying substantive claim could nonetheless be subsequently submitted to a court for determination.[5]

9.06   This point was briefly resurrected in the Commission meetings, where it was suggested that recourse should be had to the courts in situations involving negative jurisdictional rulings as well.[6] However, following the Chairman's explanation that arbitrators 'could not be forced to continue their arbitration if they believed they had no jurisdiction' and that 'the arbitration proceedings were clearly terminated' once a negative jurisdictional ruling was issued, the matter was not addressed further.[7]

9.07   The amendments to Section 10 of the IAA were proposed in response to feedback by practitioners and academics.[8] In particular, a relevant Law Reform Committee Report noted that 'there [was] overwhelming support in the industry for the proposals [to permit review of negative jurisdictional rulings]'.[9] This led to the amendment that now permits an appeal where the tribunal has ruled it has no jurisdiction.[10] Thus far, there are no reported cases of a Singapore court reversing a negative jurisdictional ruling by a tribunal, although there have been attempts by parties to characterise rulings by tribunal as 'negative jurisdictional rulings' and to bring such rulings within the ambit of Section 10 so that the court may review it *de novo*.[11]

9.08   The English High Court in *GPF GP Sàrl v The Republic of Poland*[12] has, however, reversed a negative jurisdictional ruling pursuant to Section 67 of the English Arbitration Act 1996.[13] The case is also relevant to Section 32 of the English Arbitration Act 1996 (which concerns a tribunal's determination of a *preliminary objection* jurisdiction) and thus, instructive for future Section 10(4) applications under the IAA. In that case, after reversing the negative jurisdictional ruling, the English High Court remitted the claims

---

[5] UNCITRAL, *Report of the Working Group on International Contract Practices on the Work of its Sixth Session*, UN Doc. A/CN. 9/245 (United Nations 1984) para 64.

[6] UNCITRAL, *316th Meeting of the United Nations Commission on International Trade Law*, UN Doc. A/CN.9/246 (United Nations 1985) para 16 (hereafter *316th Meeting of UNCITRAL*).

[7] Ibid, paras 17–19.

[8] See e.g. Singapore Academy of Law—Law Reform Committee, *Report of the Law Reform Committee on Right to Judicial Review of Negative Jurisdictional Rulings* (January 2011) (hereafter Singapore Academy of Law, *Right to Judicial Review of Negative Judicial Rulings*). Examples of the views proffered include those found in the following commentary: P. Fohlin, 'A Case for a Right of Appeal from Negative Jurisdictional Rulings in International Arbitrations governed by the UNCITRAL Model Law' [2008] Asian Dispute Review 113, 114; S. Greenberg, C. Kee, and J.R. Weeramantry, *International Commercial Arbitration—An Asia-Pacific Perspective* (Cambridge University Press 2011) 240.

[9] Singapore Academy of Law, *Right to Judicial Review of Negative Judicial Rulings* (n 8) para 14.

[10] IAA (n 1), Section 10(2) and (3).

[11] See e.g. *BTN v BTP* [2020] 5 SLR 1250, where the tribunal had determined in a partial award that the claims submitted to it were *res judicata* and barred by issue estoppel. The applicant sought a declaration under Section 10(3)(b) of the IAA that the tribunal had jurisdiction on the said issue, contending that the partial award was a 'negative jurisdiction' ruling that fell within the ambit of Section 10(3). In deciding the application, Belinda Ang J held that the partial award was not a ruling on jurisdiction, but rather a ruling on the merits, and did not come within the ambit of Section 10: see [45]. Similar arguments were raised in a separate application taken out by the same parties, in relation to further awards rendered by the tribunal: see *BTN v BTP* [2021] SGHC 271. Mohan J similarly decided that the challenged awards were *not* 'negative jurisdiction' rulings and therefore did not fall within Section 10: see [118].

[12] *GPF GP Sàrl v The Republic of Poland* [2018] EWHC 409 (Comm).

[13] Ibid, [144].

to the tribunal for determination,[14] and it is likely that a similar outcome will prevail in Singapore by virtue of Section 10(6) of the IAA, which provides that the arbitral tribunal 'must continue the arbitral proceedings and make an award' if the court finds that the tribunal has jurisdiction.

A further distinction between the IAA and the Model Law is that while the decision by the High Court under Article 16(3) will be final, Section 10(4) of the IAA allows for a further appeal to the Court of Appeal if the High Court grants such permission. In this regard, the High Court will consider whether there is a *prima facie* case of error, a question of general principle decided for the first time, or a question of importance upon which further argument and a decision of a higher tribunal would be to the public advantage.[15] In *BQP v BQQ*,[16] the High Court declined leave to appeal on the question of whether the common law rule excluding pre-contractual negotiations should apply to an arbitral tribunal's ruling on jurisdiction. **9.09**

Section 10(3) provides that any party 'may, within 30 days after having received notice of that ruling, apply to the General Division of the High Court to decide the matter'. Despite the wording of that section, it should be cautioned that the 30-day period to appeal a jurisdictional ruling is mandatory and may not be extended under any circumstances. The only exception is if the tribunal's ruling did not reach the affected party, but strong evidence for this will be required.[17] **9.10**

C. Section 10(2)—Negative Jurisdictional Rulings

Section 10(2) of the IAA expressly states that the arbitral tribunal may rule on a plea that it has no jurisdiction at any stage of the arbitral proceedings. In *The 'Titan Unity'*, [18] the court stated that Section 10(2) and 10(3) provided deference to the arbitral tribunal on the issue of its jurisdiction, but not to the extent where it is the sole arbiter.[19] Instead, the arbitral tribunal is the first arbiter, and its decision may be reviewed *de novo* by the courts. The comment that the courts may accord deference to a tribunal's ruling on jurisdiction is liable to cause confusion as it is now established law that there should be no such deference, regardless how distinguished the tribunal may be. This is no different to when a party challenges a tribunal's jurisdiction in set-aside proceedings.[20] There is no **9.11**

---

[14] Ibid, [144].
[15] *BQP v BQQ* [2018] SGHC 55 [108] (hereafter *BQP v BQQ*), citing *Lee Kuan Yew v Tang Liang Hong* [1997] 2 SLR(R) 862 [16].
[16] Ibid, [109].
[17] *BXY v BXX* [2019] 4 SLR 413.
[18] *The 'Titan Unity'* [2013] SGHCR 28.
[19] Ibid, [31].
[20] *Sanum Investments Ltd v Government of the Lao People's Democratic Republic* [2016] 5 SLR 536; [2016] SGCA 57 [42] (hereafter *Sanum Investments v Government of Laos*), citing *PT First Media TBK v Astro Nusantara International BV* [2014] 1 SLR 372 [163] and *Dallah Real Estate and Tourism Holding Co v Ministry of Religious Affairs of the Government of Pakistan* [2011] 1 AC 763 with approval.

114 APPEALS FROM JURISDICTIONAL RULINGS AND ORDER 48

reason why a negative jurisdictional ruling should be subject to any different standard of review than a positive jurisdictional ruling.

D. Section 10(3)—Nature of Court's Power to Rule on Arbitral Tribunal's Jurisdiction

9.12 Section 10(3) permits the Court to review a tribunal's decision on jurisdiction, positive or negative. The court's jurisdiction to decide on the jurisdiction of an arbitral tribunal is an *original* and not an appellate one.[21]

9.13 It is sometimes thought that there is a lacuna in Section 10 of the IAA. In *International Research Corp PLC v Lufthansa Systems Asia Pacific Pte Ltd*,[22] the High Court observed that a Singapore court could not 'set aside' an arbitral tribunal's preliminary ruling on jurisdiction.[23] This observation was predicated on the decision in *PT Asuransi Jasa Indonesia (Persero) v Dexia Bank SA*,[24] where the court held that an 'award' under Section 2(1) could only refer to a decision which dealt with the 'substance of the dispute'. Since an arbitral tribunal's preliminary ruling on jurisdiction did *not* concern the substance of the dispute referred to it, such a ruling cannot be an 'award' for the purposes of the IAA and thus cannot be set aside pursuant to Section 24. Since only 'awards' could be set aside under Section 24, the High Court suggested that the court cannot set aside an arbitral tribunal's preliminary ruling on jurisdiction pursuant an application under Section 10.

9.14 On appeal, it was held that there was no such lacuna. In *International Research Corp PLC v Lufthansa Systems Asia Pacific Pte Ltd*,[25] the Court of Appeal disapproved of the High Court's observation and stated that 'an application to the court to decide on the jurisdiction of an arbitral tribunal pursuant to Section 10 of the IAA read with Article 16(3) of the Model Law 1985 is a perfectly legitimate means of challenging an arbitral tribunal's preliminary ruling on jurisdiction'.[26] To this extent, it is immaterial if the relief is expressed, as a matter of form, in terms of setting aside the arbitral tribunal's decision on jurisdiction; courts are empowered to 'decide the matter', a phrase used in both Article 16(3) of the Model Law and Section 10(3) of the IAA.

9.15 It has been argued that, while the Court of Appeal's ruling in *Lufthansa Systems*[27] is correct, the better view is that preliminary rulings are capable of being set aside *qua*

---

[21] It is able to re-hear or consider the jurisdictional challenge afresh. See *Insigma Technology Co. Ltd v Alstom Technology Ltd* [2009] 1 SLR(R) 23; [2008] SGHC 134 [21]–[22].

[22] *International Research Corp PLC v Lufthansa Systems Asia Pacific Pte Ltd* [2013] 1 SLR 973.

[23] Ibid, [111]–[114].

[24] *PT Asuransi Jasa Indonesia (Persero) v Dexia Bank SA* [2007] 1 SLR(R) 597 (hereafter *PT Asuransi v Dexia Bank*).

[25] *International Research Corp PLC v Lufthansa Systems Asia Pacific Pte Ltd* [2014] 1 SLR 130 (hereafter *International Research Corp v Lufthansa*).

[26] Ibid, [69].

[27] Ibid.

D. SECTION 10(3)—NATURE OF COURT'S POWER TO RULE   115

awards, by reading Section 10(3) with Section 24 and Article 34.[28] One commentator has argued that tracing the evolution of Article 16(3), on which Section 10(3) is based, there was a preponderance of views towards tying immediate court control to the characterisation of the preliminary ruling as an award, and there was no indication that the court of the seat before which challenges to preliminary rulings would be brought had the discretion to decide the relief which could be granted.[29] On this view, therefore, the intention behind Article 16(3) and the phrase 'decide the matter' in Section 10 is that preliminary rulings are capable of being set aside *qua* awards, as long as it is clear that the tribunal has *finally determined* the question of jurisdiction in its preliminary ruling in a manner that engages Article 16(3).[30]

In our respectful view, the decisions of the Court of Appeal in both *Lufthansa*[31] and **9.16** *PT Asuransi*[32] accord better with the intent and purpose of Article 16 of the Model Law. That provision was hotly debated. Based on existing conventions at the time (such as Article 18(3) of the Strasbourg Uniform Law), it was initially thought that parties' rights to seek judicial review should be restricted so as to avoid impeding the tribunal's ability to determine its own jurisdiction.[33] The Working Group's position on this then underwent fundamental changes, from initially requiring a court to stay its own ruling on the jurisdiction of an arbitral tribunal until after an arbitral award had been made[34] to the development of a provision for 'concurrent court control'.[35] Ultimately, the Working Group removed the provision for concurrent court control (then Article 17 of the Draft Articles) due to concerns that it would open the door to dilatory tactics.[36]

The version of the draft articles submitted by the Working Group to the Commission   **9.17** for consideration in March 1985 thus included an Article 16(3) which only provided for judicial control 'after an award on the merits is rendered, namely in setting aside proceedings'.[37] This was however rejected by the Commission; with a majority of delegates favouring 'allowing the question of the jurisdiction of the arbitral tribunal to be decided by a court at an earlier stage than the award'.[38]

---

[28] N. Poon, 'Setting Aside Preliminary Rulings on Jurisdiction' (2014) 26 Singapore Academy of Law Journal 269 [4] (hereafter Poon, 'Setting Aside Preliminary Rulings on Jurisdiction').

[29] Ibid, paras 8–11; UNCITRAL, *Report of the United Nations Commission on International Trade Law on the Work of Its Eighteenth Session*, UN Doc A/40/17 (United Nations 1985) paras 161–163.

[30] Poon, 'Setting Aside Preliminary Rulings on Jurisdiction' (n 28) para 11.

[31] *International Research Corp v Lufthansa* (n 25) [66].

[32] *PT Asuransi v Dexia Bank* (n 24) [68].

[33] UNCITRAL, *Report of the Secretary-General: Possible Features of a Model Law on International Commercial Arbitration*, UN Doc. A/CN.9/207(United Nations 1981), para 89.

[34] *Report of the Working Group of its Fourth Session* (n 3), para 146.

[35] UNCITRAL, *Report of the Working Group on International Contract Practices on the Work of its Seventh Session*, UN Doc. A/CN. 9/246 (United Nations 1984) paras 54–55 (hereafter *Report of the Working Group of its Seventh Session*).

[36] Ibid, para 55.

[37] UNCITRAL, *Analytical Commentary on Draft Text of a Model Law on International Commercial Arbitration—Report of the Secretary General*, UN Doc. A/CN.9/264 (United Nations 1985), paras 11–12.

[38] *316th Meeting of UNCITRAL* (n 6) para 29.

9.18 On this basis, the present-day version of Article 16(3) was adopted, with the intention of providing for 'instant court control'.[39] This was without prejudice to a further right subsequently to set aside an award or resist enforcement.[40] Whether Article 16 was available depended on whether the tribunal decided to issue a preliminary ruling. If it did not, a party would have no choice but to await an award and seek to set it aside or resist enforcement under Articles 34 or 36. In this context, it made sense for the Working Group not to adopt the language of an 'award' in respect of challenges to preliminary rulings on jurisdiction; this was to avoid confusion with the alternative route the tribunal could take—that is, to render an award.

9.19 Drawing a distinction between 'preliminary rulings' and 'awards' will also entail a clearer understanding of when Section 10, and not Article 34 of the Model Law, operates:

- Section 10(3)(a) will apply in respect of *preliminary rulings* on positive jurisdictional rulings, that is, the arbitration is still ongoing.
- Articles 34 and 36 will apply in respect of *awards* on positive jurisdictional rulings, that is, when the arbitration has come to an end.[41]
- Section 10(3)(b) will apply in respect of a ruling on a plea *at any stage* of the arbitral proceedings that the arbitral tribunal has *no* jurisdiction.

9.20 There is nothing confusing about the legal effect, in an Article 16 application, of a court's decision that the tribunal lacked jurisdiction. The court 'decides the matter'—quite simply, the court's ruling is substituted for the tribunal's. An Article 16 challenge is akin to an appeal; indeed, that is the description given to Section 10 of the IAA by Parliament. There is no need for the ruling to be 'set aside' in the same way as an award because while an award has *erga omnes* effect, a preliminary ruling is simply a 'gateway' ruling that permits the tribunal to carry on its mandate to decide the merits of the dispute.

9.21 Some of this clarity now needs to be reconciled with the amended Section 10 of the IAA. Whereas prior to 2012, Section 10 merely provided for possible appeals to the Court of Appeal (with leave), thus leaving the design of Article 16 intact, this changed with the introduction of a possible challenge to negative rulings on jurisdictions. That being

---

[39] UNCITRAL, *320th Meeting of the United Nations Commission on International Trade Law*, UN Doc. A/CN.9/246 (United Nations 1985) para 47; UNCITRAL, *Report of the Working Group on International Contract Practices on the work of its seventh session*, UN Doc. A/CN.9/246 (United Nations 1997) para 19.

[40] *PT First Media TBK (formerly known as PT Broadband Multimedia TBK) v Astro Nusantara International BV and others and anor* [2014] 1 SLR 372 (hereafter *PT First Media v Astro Nusantara*).

[41] The precise limb will depend on whether it is asserted that a party is not bound by an arbitration agreement at all or whether a party is merely saying that a particular dispute does not fall within the arbitration agreement. In the former case, the first limb is more apposite, and the third limb if it is the latter situation (see the discussions in *Aloe Vera of America, Inc v Asianic Food (S) Pte Ltd* [2006] 3 SLR(R) 174 [69]; *PT First Media v Astro Nusantara* (n 40) [153] and definitively in *Swissbourgh Diamond Mines (Pty) Ltd and ors v Kingdom of Lesotho* [2019] 1 SLR 263; [2018] SGCA 81 [71]–[80], which was in the context of an investor–state award).

said, Section 10(1) simply reproduces the language of Article 16 so far as the court's role is merely to 'decide the matter'. The Court of Appeal in *Lufthansa* quite rightly said it was unnecessary to be distracted by the form of the relief, although it seemed to endorse the view that what the court was doing was 'setting aside the arbitral tribunal's decision on jurisdiction'.[42] As argued above, the court is not 'setting aside' a preliminary ruling on jurisdiction—whether positive or negative. It is simply deciding the tribunal's jurisdiction, which then determines whether the tribunal continues on to an award.

9.22 As the Court of Appeal has itself said in *PT First Media TBK v Astro Nusantara International BV*, certain types of recourse only apply to awards properly so-called.[43] Adopting the approach above would also mean that one need not step into the question as to whether the Court of Appeal in *PT Asuransi*[44] was correct to have drawn an equivalence between the 'substance' and the 'merits' of a dispute.[45] It is probably unhelpful to introduce such fine distinctions into the lexicon of the Model Law.

E. Section 10(3)—Ambit of Court's Power to Rule on Arbitral Tribunal's Jurisdiction

9.23 The types of jurisdictional rulings which can be reviewed under Section 10(3) of the IAA have been clarified by case law. In *AQZ v ARA*, the High Court carefully considered the drafting history of Article 16(3) of the Model Law, which is closely tied to Section 10(3) of the IAA, and concluded that Section 10(3) is not intended to apply to an award that deals with the merits of the dispute, however marginally the merits are dealt with.[46] Further, the tribunal's capacity to rule on its own jurisdiction 'at any stage of the arbitral proceedings' does not weigh against this point.[47] This is because this phrase concerns *when* such a determination can be made, instead of *what* form the determination is to take.[48] *AQZ v ARA* was affirmed in a number of subsequent High Court decisions, but at the time of publication has not yet been considered by the Court of Appeal.[49]

9.24 In the case of a bilateral investment treaty (BIT), the question arises as to the whether the court has the jurisdiction to interpret such an international instrument pursuant to an application under Section 10 of the IAA. It is sometimes argued that the provisions of such instruments are usually not justiciable in the domestic courts. In *Republic of*

---

[42] *International Research Corp v Lufthansa* (n 25) [69].

[43] *PT First Media v Astro Nusantara* (n 40) [229]; Poon, 'Setting Aside Preliminary Rulings on Jurisdiction' (n 28) para 12.

[44] *PT Asuransi v Dexia Bank* (n 24) [62].

[45] Poon, 'Setting Aside Preliminary Rulings on Jurisdiction' (n 28) para 13.

[46] *AQZ v ARA* [2015] 2 SLR 972; [2015] SGHC 49 [65]–[70] (hereafter *AQZ v ARA*).

[47] Ibid, [70].

[48] Ibid.

[49] *Kingdom of Lesotho v Swissbourgh Diamond Mines (Pty) Ltd* [2019] 3 SLR 12; [2017] SGHC 195 at [68]–[69]; *Sinolanka Hotels & Spa (Private) Limited v Interna Contract SpA* [2018] SGHC 157 [79]; *BTN v BTP* [2020] 5 SLR 1250 [85]–[87].

118 APPEALS FROM JURISDICTIONAL RULINGS AND ORDER 48

Ecuador v Occidental Exploration and Production Co,[50] the court held that it had the jurisdiction to interpret an international instrument where it was necessary to do so in order to determine a State's rights and duties under domestic law, including whether they are bound by the arbitration clause in a BIT.[51] The courts should have such jurisdiction because national courts should aspire to give effect to the rights and obligations of the relevant parties arising from a BIT in light of the fact that such agreements have been agreed between states at an international level. This reasoning was applied by the Singapore High Court in *Government of the Lao People's Democratic Republic v Sanum Investments Ltd*.[52] Accordingly, where the application concerns the rights of parties seeking to invoke the court's jurisdiction under Section 10 of the IAA to review the Tribunal's ruling on jurisdiction, issues of international law which arise as part of the application are justiciable.[53] This point was not contested on appeal.

F. Section 10(3)—Standard of Review

9.25 The standard of review for an application under Section 10(3) is *de novo*.[54] This constitutes an exception to the general rule that courts should not, in general, engage with the merits of the dispute when dealing with applications to set aside arbitral awards.[55] In *PT First Media TBK v Astro Nusantara International BV*,[56] the Court of Appeal held that the *de novo* standard of review required a fresh examination of the arbitral tribunal's decision on the issue of joinder and jurisdiction in its award on preliminary issues.[57] In this regard, the tribunal's own view of its jurisdiction has no legal or evidential value before a court that has to determine that question.[58] This standard of review applies even in investor–State arbitrations which concern the interpretation of international treaties.[59]

9.26 If the standard of review is *de novo*, does that mean that the court should apply its own rules of evidence in determining the validity or applicability of the arbitration clause? In *BQP v BQQ*,[60] the applicant appealed a preliminary ruling on jurisdiction

---

[50] [2006] QB 432.

[51] This remains the position in England; see e.g. *The Czech Republic v European Media Ventures SA* [2007] EWHC 2851 (Comm).

[52] *Government of the Lao People's Democratic Republic v Sanum Investments Ltd* [2015] 2 SLR 322; [2015] SGHC 15 (hereafter *Government of Lao v Sanum Investments*).

[53] In the High Court, Edmund Leow JC seem to find it relevant that Singapore was not a party to the treaty in question (see Ibid, [30]). It is unclear why this is relevant.

[54] *AKN v ALC* [2015] 3 SLR 488; [2015] SGCA 18 [112], following *PT First Media TBK v Astro Nusantara International BV* [2014] 1 SLR 372; [2013] SGCA 57 [163] (hereafter *PT First Media v Astro Nusantara*) and affirming *AQZ v ARA* (n 46) [49]. See also *Government of the Lao v Sanum Investments* (n 52) [32].

[55] *AKN v ALC* [2015] SGCA 18 [112].

[56] *PT First Media v Astro Nusantara* (n 54).

[57] Ibid, [162].

[58] Ibid.

[59] *Sanum Investments v Government of Laos* (n 20) [40]–[44].

[60] *BQP v BQQ* (n 15); see, D. Foxton QC, 'Arbitration without Parol? *BQP v BQQ*' [2018] Lloyd's Maritime and Commercial Law Quarterly 309 (hereafter Foxton, 'Arbitration without Parol?').

F. SECTION 10(3)—STANDARD OF REVIEW 119

under Section 10 of the IAA. The applicant argued that the tribunal should not have taken into account evidence of pre-contractual negotiations in determining whether a contract providing for arbitration between the parties had been super-seded by a subsequent contract between different parties. In dismissing the appeal, the Singapore High Court held that the parol evidence rule (whether as enshrined through the Evidence Act[61] or as part of the substantive law of contract)[62] did not apply to arbitral proceedings and therefore the tribunal as well as the court were permitted to take into account such evidence pursuant to the rules of arbitration that permitted a tribunal to admit, consider, and weigh any evidence, regardless of whether they were otherwise admissible by the applicable law. This conclusion was justified on the basis that it would allow parties to achieve a speedy, commercial, and practical outcome to their dispute, and preclude the application of laws and procedures which may be alien to them.[63] The upshot however is that there may be a mismatch between the approach which a court would follow when interpreting a contract to determine if the arbitrators had jurisdiction, and that which the arbitra-tion tribunal would be entitled to follow.[64]

Accordingly, a contrary view argues that, since this case concerned a challenge in court to the jurisdiction of the tribunal, the tribunal's own view of its jurisdiction has no legal or evidential value. It ought to follow that the arbitral rules on the admissibility of evi-dence should not be relevant either since the very question was whether the parties were compelled to arbitrate in the first place.[65] That question had to be determined by the law applicable to the dispute. This was the conclusion reached by another High Court judge, though arguably in *obiter*: **9.27**

> a dispute over how a contract is to be construed must yield the same final judicial de-termination whether the contract is construed at trial in an action (to which Pt II of the Evidence Act does apply) or whether it is construed on a summary judgment ap-plication ... or even in arbitration (to all of which Pt II of the Evidence Act does not apply).[66]

Leave to appeal was not granted in *BQP v BPP*.[67] In a subsequent appeal on a different matter, the Court of Appeal missed an opportunity to address this difficult question. It did—perhaps—suggest some discomfort with that decision, observing that: **9.28**

> The respondents are therefore wrong to contend that *BQP* is authority for the propos-ition that the parol evidence rule does not apply at all in cases that arise out of an arbi-tration. *BQP* is, if anything, *only authority for the far more limited proposition that the*

---

[61] See generally, Evidence Act (Cap. 97), Sections 93–102.
[62] It remains an open question if evidence of pre-contractual negotiations should be admissible: see, most re-cently, *BNA v BNB* [2020] 1 SLR 456 [81]; [2019] SGCA 84 (hereafter *BNA v BNB (SGCA)*).
[63] *BQP v BQQ* (n 15) [125]–[126].
[64] Foxton, 'Arbitration without Parol?' (n 60) 309, 314.
[65] Ibid, 309, 313; see also *AQZ v ARA* (n 46) [163].
[66] *HSBC Trustee (Singapore) Ltd v Lucky Realty Co Pte Ltd* [2015] 3 SLR 855 [57].
[67] *BQP v BQQ* (n 15) [130].

120   APPEALS FROM JURISDICTIONAL RULINGS AND ORDER 48

High Court can consider evidence of pre-contractual negotiations that have already been admitted by the arbitral tribunal.[68]

9.29 Unfortunately, this does not resolve the conundrum because the doctrine of competence-competence means that most, if not all, jurisdictional disputes will first be determined by arbitral tribunals. Moreover, the Court of Appeal seemed to have thought that the parties in *BQP v BPP* did not object to the admission of the pre-contractual evidence, which was not the case or else there would not have been an issue before the High Court. In any event, even this narrower reading of *BQP v BPP*[69] gives tribunals the licence to admit and consider any evidence it finds relevant to interpret or determine the validity of the alleged arbitration agreement, even if the law applicable to the putative agreement would have excluded certain evidence.

9.30 It is submitted that if a jurisdictional ruling by a tribunal is ultimately reviewable by the court, the same approach to contractual interpretation as is taken by the courts should apply to the tribunal. Moreover, until the tribunal's jurisdiction is established, the arbitral rules cannot be determinative since they apply on the assumption that the case is properly before the tribunal. If jurisdiction is not established (whether by the tribunal or the courts), the case would be pursued in court and the arbitral rules would not apply. It is therefore circular to deploy the arbitral rules to decide the evidence admissible for purposes of interpreting the validity and applicability of the alleged arbitration agreement. The interpretative exercise is properly seen as a substantive question to which the law governing the contract applies, not the procedural rules of the institution chosen.

9.31 The *de novo* standard applies to both the determination of the law governing the arbitration agreement and whether the application of that law supports a finding that the tribunal has jurisdiction. In *BCY v BCZ*, the court was confronted with an application under Section 10(3) of the IAA following an arbitrator's determination (in the form of a 'First Partial Award') that a valid arbitration agreement had come into existence. The arbitrator had relied on *Sulamérica Cia Nacional de Seguros SA and others v Enesa Engenharia SA* for the proposition that if parties had not identified an express choice of law governing their arbitration agreement, a rebuttable presumption arose that their implied choice of law was the governing law of the main contract.[70] On that basis, it was concluded that New York law governed the agreement, and that on the application of such law, the arbitration agreement was valid. Steven Chong J (as he then was) undertook a detailed analysis of his own regarding *Sulamérica*, rather than relying on the arbitrator's reasoning.[71] While reaching the same conclusion as the arbitrator with regard to the governing law of the arbitration agreement, the court held that a valid

---

[68] *BNA v BNB (SGCA)* (n 62) [80].

[69] *BQP v BQQ* (n 15) [129].

[70] *Sulamérica Cia Nacional de Seguros SA and others v Enesa Engenharia SA and others* [2013] 1 WLR 102.

[71] *BCY v BCZ* [2017] 3 SLR 357; [2016] SGHC 249 at [42]–[46].

G. IMPLICATIONS ON THE COURT'S POWER TO MAKE AN AWARD OR ORDER   121

arbitration agreement had not come into existence, thus declaring that the arbitrator lacked jurisdiction to hear the claims.

In *BNA v BNB*, the court was faced with a rather curious scenario.[72] A dispute arose out of a Takeout Agreement, which provided that 'such disputes shall be finally submitted to the Singapore International Arbitration Centre (SIAC) for arbitration in Shanghai, which will be conducted in accordance with its Arbitration Rules'.[73] A three-member tribunal had decided by majority that it had jurisdiction over a dispute, ruling that the arbitration agreement was seated in Singapore and governed by Singapore law.[74] The plaintiff thus applied under Section 10(3) of the IAA for a declaration that the tribunal lacked jurisdiction. Vinodh Coomaraswamy J undertook a *de novo* determination of the issue, noting that 'an application under s 10(3) of the Act is neither an application to set aside the tribunal's majority decision on jurisdiction nor an appeal against that decision'.[75] Applying the three-stage test for identifying the governing law of the arbitration agreement as laid out in *BCY v BCZ*, Coomaraswamy J dismissed the application, holding that Singapore law governed the arbitration agreement, and that Singapore was the seat.[76] This was however overturned on appeal; with the Court of Appeal holding that the ordinary meaning of 'arbitration in Shanghai' was that Shanghai was the seat of the arbitration.[77] Consequently, the appeal was allowed 'to the extent that Singapore was not the seat', as the Court of Appeal considered that 'it was only proper and logical that we express no view as to jurisdiction once we had determined that Singapore was not the seat'.[78]

9.32

G. Implications on the Court's Power to Make an Award or Order of Costs (Sections 10(7) and 10(8) of the IAA)

Under Section 10(7) of the IAA, the court or arbitral tribunal may make an award or order of costs of the proceedings against any party, including for the costs of the arbitration proceeding. This power is particularly useful in cases where the court rules the tribunal in fact did not have jurisdiction over the dispute or the parties, thereby terminating the arbitration proceedings.[79]

9.33

Unfortunately, a similar power has not been added in respect of Article 34 of the Model Law. Accordingly, where an arbitral tribunal issues a positive decision on jurisdiction,

9.34

---

[72] *BNA v BNB* [2019] SGHC 142 (hereafter *BNA v BNB* (SGHC)); *BNA v BNB* (*SGCA*) (n 62).
[73] *BNA v BNB* (SGHC) (n 72) [3].
[74] Ibid, [8].
[75] Ibid, [10].
[76] Ibid, [118]–[119].
[77] *BNA v BNB* (*SGCA*) (n 62) [65].
[78] Ibid, [96]–[97].
[79] R. Merkin and J. Hjalmarsson, *Singapore Arbitration Legislation Annotated* (2nd edn, Routledge 2016) 54.
  In proposing the amendment to Section 10 of the IAA to empower the courts to make cost orders relating to the arbitral proceedings.

and the court has set aside that decision, the court has no power to re-allocate the costs of the arbitral proceedings.[80]

9.35 The different regimes under Section 10(7) of the IAA and Article 34 of the Model therefore presents a discrepancy in the court's powers, giving the successful party, whose jurisdictional objections are upheld by the court, a better right if the tribunal issued its decision as a preliminary ruling than as an arbitral award. Unfortunately, because a court's power to interfere with the arbitral process and the award is controlled by statute, Parliament needs to resolve this discrepancy. The court has no inherent power to do otherwise, and the very fact Parliament enacted Section 10(7) of the IAA confirms this. This very lacuna was noted in *CBX v CBA*. In that case, the Singapore Court of Appeal had already partially set aside the merits award for excess of jurisdiction and held that, since the costs award was ancillary to and depended upon the validity of the merits award, the costs award too had to be set aside. The Court of Appeal expressed some regret that there did not appear to be a sensible method of addressing costs in such situations and noted that this was a potential area for law reform.[81]

H. Stay of Arbitration under Section 10(9)(a) of the IAA

9.36 Under Section 10(9)(a) of the IAA, an application made pursuant to Article 16(3) of the Model Law will not operate as a stay of the arbitral proceedings or of execution of any award or order made in the arbitral proceedings unless the High Court orders otherwise. This raises the question of when a stay of arbitration will be granted by the Court.

9.37 The applicable test was established by the High Court in *BLY v BLZ*.[82] The court will grant a stay where there are 'special circumstances' to do so, given the specific facts of the particular case.[83] This is because the statutory discretion must not be so easily exercised as to render the default position meaningless, and the phrase 'special circumstances' is wide enough to include the conduct of the other party,[84] or the conduct of the tribunal.[85] However, 'special circumstances' is also narrow enough that it does not cover several situations. Firstly, it does not cover so-called prejudice or detriment derived from wasted time and costs of what could be a potentially useless arbitration. This is because it is a usual and attendant by-product or consequence of a tribunal's decision to continue with the arbitral proceedings and hence cannot, in and of itself, justify a stay. Secondly, it does not cover potential prejudice or detriment stemming

---

[80] It remains an open question if evidence of pre-contractual negotiations should be admissible. See *BNA v BNB (SGCA)* (n 62) [81]; *BQP v BQQ* (n 15) [125]–[126].

[81] *CBX and anor v CBZ and ors* [2022] 1 SLR 47; [2021] SGCA(I) 3 [81], [85].

[82] *BLY v BLZ* [2017] 4 SLR 410; [2017] SGHC 59 [8], [14]–[18] (hereafter *BLY v BLZ*).

[83] Ibid, [13].

[84] Ibid, [14].

[85] Ibid, [20].

H. STAY OF ARBITRATION UNDER SECTION 10(9)(A) OF THE IAA

from the rendering of an arbitral award if the pending application for curial review has yet to be heard or concluded. Thirdly, it does not cover inconvenience and uncertainty associated with the need to set aside the award or resist the enforcement of the award using the court's adverse ruling on jurisdiction. Lastly, the choice of the party seeking a review of the tribunal's jurisdictional ruling of whether it ought to participate in the arbitration proceedings, also does not amount to a special circumstance.

This should be contrasted with an earlier decision, *AYY v AYZ*,[86] where the Assistant Registrar applied an 'irreparable prejudice' test. The High Court in *BLY*[87] clarified that irreparable prejudice is merely the consequence of special circumstances that exist in a particular case. Moreover, the irreparable prejudice test is flawed in that it is both over-inclusive and under-inclusive. It is over-inclusive 'if a tribunal directs parties to disclose confidential documents in furtherance of arbitral proceedings' because 'such disclosure cannot be undone or compensated by a costs order in the event that the tribunal was wrong in finding that it has jurisdiction'.[88] It can be under-inclusive where a stay of proceedings may be warranted despite the parties having not yet suffered any harm or prejudice. This could be because a hearing on the merits is slated to take place far later than the scheduled hearing for the review application under Section 10(3) of the IAA. Under the irreparable test, it is difficult to justify denying a stay if nothing much is going on in the arbitral proceeding.[89]

9.38

The High Court in *BLY*[90] also rejected a 'balance of convenience' test which it held was inconsistent with the manner in which the statutory discretion to stay arbitral proceedings pending curial review of a tribunal's ruling on jurisdiction should be exercised. Arbitral proceedings should only be stayed where the default position creates ill-effects that may lead to injustice and unfairness. Accordingly, the discretion must be exercised judiciously and with reference to all the circumstances of the case.[91]

9.39

Three criticisms have been levelled against the *BLY*[92] case: first, the court's reasons in *BLY* for preferring the special circumstances test are unfounded; second, the court had raised concerns which arguably point towards an outcome-based test instead; and third, the court's concerns are more adequately addressed by an outcome-based test which adopts a higher threshold than the prejudice test.[93]

9.40

---

[86] [2015] SGHCR 22 [3].

[87] *BLY v BLZ* (n 82) [18].

[88] Ibid, [19].

[89] Ibid, [20].

[90] Ibid, [8].

[91] Ibid.

[92] *BLY v BLZ* (n 82).

[93] V. Hoi Seng Leong, 'Examining the "special circumstances" test in *BLY v BLZ* [2017] SGHC 59: when should jurisdictional challenges result in stays of the arbitral proceedings?' (*Singapore Law* Blog, 21 April 2017) <http://www.singaporelawblog.sg/blog/article/184> accessed 25 December 2020, 2 (hereafter Leong, 'Examining the "special circumstances" test'). By contrast, there is no equivalent of Section 10(9) of the IAA under the English Arbitration Act 1996. Section 32(1) of the English Arbitration Act provides that a party may apply to court for a determination of the substantive jurisdiction of the tribunal. Unlike the IAA, Section 32(4) of the English Arbitration Act provides that '*unless otherwise agreed by the parties*, the arbitral tribunal may continue the arbitral proceedings and make an award while an application to the court under this section is pending'.

9.41 Respectfully, these criticisms are predicated on an overly narrow understanding of the special circumstances test. For example, it is not true that the special circumstances test looks *only* at the process and *not* the outcome.[94] The court did *not* state that it was impermissible to consider the outcome of denying a stay and had, in fact, left this open. Consider the example provided by the court of a tribunal directing parties to disclose confidential documents in furtherance of arbitral proceedings. The court recognised that such disclosure, strictly speaking, cannot be undone or compensated by a costs order in the event that the tribunal was wrong in finding that it has jurisdiction, that is that it would result in prejudice should the stay be denied. The court, however, stated that this is to be expected in the usual course of arbitral proceedings and thus does not amount to special circumstances. Yet, the court did not foreclose the possibility where in a proper case the documents are of such a sensitive nature that the disclosure of such documents might constitute a special circumstance.[95] In so holding, the court could be said to be departing from its very own test.[96] However, the better view is that whatever prejudice is alleged to be relevant to the court's consideration must meet the threshold of being a special or exceptional circumstance. This is consistent with the court's view that it 'is given the statutory discretion to stay arbitral proceedings pending curial review of a tribunal's ruling on jurisdiction *in circumstances where the default position creates ill-effects that may lead to injustice and unfairness*.'[97]

9.42 Accordingly, the fact that the court distinguished irreparable prejudice as 'the consequence or outcome that arises given the existence of some special circumstances in the case'[98] should not be taken to mean that it cannot look at prejudice, but rather the court simply saying that that would usually be the case. In exceptional cases, prejudice could be considered as either constituting in itself the special circumstance, or it is a basis on which to infer the existence of special circumstances. This explains why the court stated that 'prejudice or detriment derived from wasted time and costs of what could be a potentially useless arbitration ... cannot, *in and of itself*, justify a stay'.[99] This is the opposite of excluding it entirely from consideration.

I. Order 48 Rules of Court

Definitions of this Order (O. 48, r. 1)

1. In this Order, unless the context or subject matter otherwise indicates or requires —

    "Act" means the International Arbitration Act, and any reference to a section is a reference to a section in the Act;

---

[94] Ibid, 2.
[95] *BLY v BLZ* (n 82) [19].
[96] Leong, 'Examining the "special circumstances" test' (n 93) 5.
[97] *BLY v BLZ* (n 82) [8].
[98] Ibid, [8].
[99] Ibid, [15].

I. ORDER 48 RULES OF COURT   125

"arbitral tribunal" has the meaning given by Part II of the Act;

"award" has the meaning given by Part II of the Act;

"foreign award" has the meaning given by Part III of the Act;

"Model Law" means the UNCITRAL Model Law on International Commercial Arbitration set out in the First Schedule to the Act and as modified by the Act.

Matters for Judge in person (O. 48, r. 2)

2.—(1) Every application to a Judge —

    (a) to decide on the challenge of an arbitrator under Article 13(3) of the Model Law;

    (b) to decide on the termination of the mandate of an arbitrator under Article 14(1) of the Model Law;

    (c) to appeal against the ruling of the arbitral tribunal under section 10 or Article 16(3) of the Model Law; or

    (d) to set aside an award under section 24 or Article 34(2) of the Model Law, must be made by originating application.

(2) An application under paragraph (1)(*a*), (*b*) or (*c*) must be made within 30 days after the date of receipt by the applicant (who is referred to in the originating application and in this Order as the claimant) of the arbitral tribunal's decision or ruling.

(3) An application under paragraph (1)(*d*) may not be made more than 3 months after the later of the following dates:

    (a) the date on which the claimant received the award;

    (b) if a request is made under Article 33 of the Model Law, the date on which that request is disposed of by the arbitral tribunal.

(4) The affidavit in support must —

    (a) state the grounds in support of the application;

    (b) have exhibited to it a copy of the arbitration agreement or any record of the content of the arbitration agreement, the award and any other document relied on by the claimant;

    (c) set out any evidence relied on by the claimant; and

    (d) be served with the originating application.

(5) Within 14 days after being served with the originating application, the defendant, if the defendant wishes to oppose the application, must file an affidavit stating the grounds on which the defendant opposes the application.

(6) An application for permission to appeal against a decision of the Court under section 10 must be made within 14 days after the decision of the Court.

(7) For the purpose of this Rule, the date of receipt of any decision, ruling, award or corrected award is to be determined in accordance with Article 3 of the Model Law.

Matters for Judge or Registrar (O. 48, r. 3)

3. —(1) Every application or request to the Court —

(a) to hear an application in open court under section 22;

(b) for permission to enforce interim orders or directions of an arbitral tribunal under section 12(6);

(c) for interim orders or directions under section 12A;

(d) to reinstate discontinued proceedings under section 6(4);

(e) for permission to enforce an award under section 18 or 19; or

(f) for permission to enforce a foreign award under section 29, must be made to a Judge or the Registrar.

(2) Any application to which this Rule applies must, where an action is pending, be made by summons in the action, and in any other case by originating application.

(3) Where the case is one of urgency or an application under section 18, 19 or 29 for permission to enforce an award or foreign award, such application may be made without notice on such terms as the Court thinks fit.

Service out of Singapore of originating process (O. 48, r. 4)

4.—(1) Service out of Singapore of the originating application or of any order made on such originating application under this Order is permissible with the permission of the Court whether or not the arbitration was held or the award was made within Singapore.

(2) An application for the grant of permission under this Rule must be supported by an affidavit stating the ground on which the application is made and showing in what place or country the person to be served is, or probably may be found; and no such permission is to be granted unless it is made sufficiently to appear to the Court that the case is a proper one for service out of Singapore under this Rule.

(3) Order 8, Rules 2, 3, 7 and 8 apply in relation to any such originating application or order as is referred to in paragraph (1).

Enforcement of interim orders or directions (O. 48, r. 5)

5.—(1) An application for permission to enforce an order or direction given by an arbitral tribunal must be supported by an affidavit —

(a) exhibiting a copy of the arbitration agreement or any record of the content of the arbitration agreement and the original order or direction made by the arbitral tribunal sought to be enforced; and

(b) stating the provisions in the Act or the applicable rules adopted in the arbitration on which the applicant relies.

(2) Where the order sought to be enforced is in the nature of an interim injunction under section 12(1)(e) or (f), permission may be granted only if the applicant undertakes to abide by any order the Court or the arbitral tribunal may make as to damages.

Enforcement of awards and foreign awards (O. 48, r. 6)

6.—(1) An application for permission to enforce an award may be made without notice and must be supported by an affidavit —

(a) exhibiting the arbitration agreement or any record of the content of the arbitration agreement and the duly authenticated original award or, in either case, a duly certified copy of the arbitration agreement or record and a duly certified copy of the award and, where the award, agreement or record is in a language other than English, a translation of it in the English language, duly certified in English as a correct translation by a sworn translator or by an official or by a diplomatic or consular agent of the country in which the award was made;

(b) stating the name and the usual or last known place of residence or business of the applicant (called in this Rule the creditor) and the person against whom it is sought to enforce the award (called in this Rule the debtor) respectively; and

(c) as the case may require, stating either that the award has not been complied with or the extent to which it has not been complied with at the date of the application.

(2) An application for permission to enforce a foreign award may be made without notice and must be supported by an affidavit —

(a) exhibiting the arbitration agreement and the duly authenticated original award or, in either case, a duly certified copy of the arbitration agreement or award and, where the award or agreement is in a language other than English, a translation of it in the English language, duly certified in English as a correct translation by a sworn translator or by an official or by a diplomatic or consular agent of the country in which the award was made;

(b) stating the name and the usual or last known place of residence or business of the applicant (called in this Rule the creditor) and the person against whom it is sought to enforce the award (called in this Rule the debtor) respectively; and

(c) as the case may require, stating either that the award has not been complied with or the extent to which it has not been complied with at the date of the application.

(3) An order giving permission must be drawn up by or on behalf of the creditor and must be served on the debtor by delivering a copy to the debtor personally or by sending a copy to the debtor at the debtor's usual or last known place of residence or business or in such other manner as the Court may direct.

(4) Service of the order out of Singapore is permissible without permission, and Order 8, Rules 2, 3, 7 and 8 apply in relation to such an order.

(5) Within 14 days after service of the order or, if the order is to be served out of Singapore, within such other period as the Court may fix, the debtor may apply to set aside the order, and the award must not be enforced until

128 APPEALS FROM JURISDICTIONAL RULINGS AND ORDER 48

after the expiration of that period or, if the debtor applies within that period to set aside the order, until after the application is finally disposed of.

(6) The copy of that order served on the debtor must state the effect of paragraph (5).

(7) In relation to a body corporate, this Rule has effect as if for any reference to the place of residence or business of the creditor or the debtor there were substituted a reference to the registered or principal address of the body corporate; so, however, that nothing in this Rule affects any enactment which provides for the manner in which a document may be served on a body corporate.

Order to attend court and order to produce documents (O. 48, r. 7)

7. Order 15, Rule 4 applies in relation to the issue of an order to attend court and order to produce documents under section 13 as it applies in relation to proceedings in the Court.

Taking of evidence (O. 48, r. 8)

8. Order 9, Rule 24 applies in relation to the taking of evidence for arbitral proceedings under Article 27 of the Model Law as it applies for the purpose of proceedings in the Court.

9.43 Order 48 of the Rules of Court[100] provides for the procedure by which parties in an arbitration can seek recourse to the courts in matters related to the IAA. As noted in *ABC v XYZ Co Ltd*,[101] this is needed because Article 34 of the Model Law does not provide the relevant procedure.[102] This section addresses the more pertinent rules in Order 48 that are applicable to court applications under the IAA.

1. Rule 2

9.44 Order 48, Rule 2(1) provides that every application to decide on the challenge of an arbitrator or the termination of the mandate of an arbitrator, or to decide against the ruling of the arbitral tribunal, or to set aside an award, must be made by an originating application. Rules 2(3) and 2(4) governs the relevant time bars for such applications. In particular, Rule 2(4) shares the same time limit found in Article 34(3). Rule 2(4) then provides for the content of the affidavit in support of the application. It is well-established that the three-month time period within which to commence a set-aside challenge in court operates as a time-bar, and the court has no discretion or power to extend it.[103]

---

[100] Order 48 of the Rules of Court 2021 recently replaced, with some largely linguistic differences, the former Order 69A of the Rules of Court 2014.

[101] *ABC v XYZ Co Ltd* [2003] 3 SLR(R) 546; [2003] SGHC 107 (hereafter *ABC v XYZ*).

[102] Ibid, [4].

[103] *BXS v BXT* [2019] 4 SLR 390; [2019] SGHC(I) 10 [41].

I. ORDER 48 RULES OF COURT   129

The court in *ABC v XYZ* has explained why '[i]t is not an accident that Order 69A [now   **9.45**
Order 48] specifies that an application to set aside an award should be made by an
originating motion.'[104] An originating motion (now called an originating application) is required because it is one of the originating processes provided for by the Rules when a party
with a cause of action wishes to initiate proceedings to obtain a remedy against another
party. Unlike an appeal, an originating motion is not a process designed to impugn a pre-
existing judicial decision. Also, the remedy sought, that is, the setting aside of an arbitral
award, does not equate the application to an appeal. It is not a process by which facts already established by the tribunal are reassessed.[105] An application to set aside may require
new facts that were not considered by the arbitral tribunal to be established by the applicant, namely, such facts as are necessary to satisfy the enumerated grounds for set-aside.
This is the raison d'être of Rule 2(4), which requires the originating motion to be supported
by an affidavit that contains supporting evidence. While the foregoing analysis relates to
Rule 2(1)(d), it should be applicable to all applications made under Rule 2(1).

Rule 2(4) indicates that, as a default, an application under Rule 2(1)(d) to set aside an   **9.46**
award is to be resolved by way of affidavit evidence, and does not envisage a *de novo*
hearing of all the evidence in every such application as the default rule.[106] Doing otherwise would, in effect, turn every challenge into a complete rehearing that had happened
before the arbitral tribunal.[107]

At the same time, there is no absolute rule excluding the admission of fresh evidence.   **9.47**
Obvious examples might include new evidence that the award was obtained by fraud
or corruption. The court has the discretion to rule on its admissibility or attach the appropriate weight to such evidence, and/or to make an adverse costs order against the
applicant.[108] But where evidence should have been led before the tribunal, that fresh
evidence would only be admitted if (i) the party seeking to admit the evidence demonstrated sufficiently strong reasons why the evidence was not adduced at the arbitration
hearing, (ii) the evidence if admitted would probably have an important influence on
the result of the case though it need not be decisive, and (iii) the evidence had to be apparently credible though it need not be incontrovertible.[109]

---

[104] *ABC v XYZ* (n 101) [19].
[105] Ibid.
[106] *AQZ v ARA* (n 46) [39]–[60].
[107] Ibid, [49].
[108] *Jiangsu Overseas Group Co Ltd v Concord Energy Pte Ltd* [2016] 4 SLR 1336; [2016] SGHC 153 [53] (hereafter
Jiangsu Overseas v Concord Energy).
[109] This is the test articulated in *Ladd v Marshall* [1954] 1 WLR 1489, 1491 (Lord Denning); see, *Government
of Laos v Sanum Investments* (n 52) [43]–[44]. Note, however, this was said in the context of fresh evidence being
adduced before the Court of Appeal, after the High Court proceedings. In the High Court, the judge applied a
slightly laxer test found in *Lassiter Ann Masters v To Keng Lam* [2004] 2 SLR(R) 392 [26] applicable to, for example,
registrar's appeals to the High Court. The Court of Appeal did not directly address this as parties were agreed that
the relevant test for admission of the fresh evidence before the Court of Appeal was the *Ladd v Marshall* test. It is
suggested that the stricter test should apply as the standard of scrutiny by courts over awards is even stricter than
an appellate court reviewing a lower court's judgment. Curial review of awards, where permitted, is not generally
by way of appeal (save where permitted by statute, such as in relation to questions of law in domestic cases or in
relation to Section 10 of the IAA for jurisdictional issues). It is also not the function of the court to re-write awards.
Parties should be obliged to put forward their evidence before the tribunal.

130 APPEALS FROM JURISDICTIONAL RULINGS AND ORDER 48

9.48 Oral evidence and cross-examination are also not allowed by default. Witnesses who have already been heard by the tribunal will only be called when necessary. As the court in *AQZ v ARA*[110] notes, pursuant to former Order 28, Rule 4(3) (now Order 15 Rule 7(6)), the court may allow oral evidence and/or cross-examination when it considers (i) that there is or may be a dispute as to fact; and (ii) that to do so would secure the 'just, expeditious and economical' disposal of the application. Accordingly, the mere presence of factual disputes as to whether a party had made the relevant arbitration agreement is, by itself, not a sufficient reason to allow oral evidence and cross-examination.[111] Indeed, the decision of *Jiangsu Overseas Group Co Ltd v Concord Energy Pte Ltd*[112] underscores the court's reluctance to allow cross-examination in applications under Order 48.[113] This is because findings of facts by the tribunal are 'generally indisputable', and there is usually 'a substantial body of objective evidence including the exchange of correspondence between the parties to assist the court to determine this factual inquiry'. Accordingly, '[t]he objective evidence speaks for itself'.

2. Rule 3

9.49 Order 48, Rule 3(1) provides that certain applications or requests to the court must be made to a Judge or the Registrar.

9.50 Rule 3(2) provides that any application to which Rule 3 applies must, where an action is pending, be made by summons in the action, and in any other case by originating application.[114]

9.51 Rule 3(3) provides that urgent applications or applications made under Sections 18, 19, or 29 of the IAA for leave to enforce an award or foreign award may be made *ex parte* on terms as the court thinks fit. The case of *WSG Nimbus Pte Ltd v Board of Control for Cricket in Sri Lanka*[115] has provided some guidance as to what is 'urgent'. In *Nimbus*,[116] the plaintiffs made, *inter alia*, an *ex parte* application under Rule 3(3) for a prohibitive injunction to restrain the defendant from entering into a fresh contract covering the same subject matter with any third party. The court was satisfied that the plaintiffs' application was sufficiently urgent because 'the defendants had refused to confirm that they would not deal with the rights the subject of the [Master Rights Agreement]'.[117]

---

[110] *AQZ v ARA* (n 46) [4].
[111] Ibid, [55].
[112] *Jiangsu Overseas v Concord Energy* (n 108).
[113] Ibid, [43].
[114] *Beijing Sinozonto Mining Investment Co Ltd v Goldenray Consortium (Singapore) Pte Ltd* [2014] 1 SLR 814 [49].
[115] *WSG Nimbus Pte Ltd v Board of Control for Cricket in Sri Lanka* [2002] 1 SLR(R) 1088; [2002] SGHC 104 [66]–[70].
[116] Ibid, [5].
[117] Ibid, [70].

3. Rule 4

Order 48, Rule 4 governs service out of the jurisdiction of originating summons or **9.52** of any order made on such originating summons commenced under the IAA.[118] The court will grant leave to do so notwithstanding whether the arbitration was held or the award was made within the jurisdiction if it sufficiently appears to the court that the case is a *proper one* for service out of the jurisdiction.[119] The burden is on the plaintiff to prove this,[120] and the evidence required is stipulated in Rule 4(2). The application must be supported by an affidavit stating the ground on which the application is made, and showing the place or country where the person to be served is in or probably may be found. The applicant must show that the case is a proper one for service out of jurisdiction.[121]

In *Swift-Fortune Ltd v Magnifica Marine SA*,[122] the Court of Appeal referred to *PT* **9.53** *Garuda Indonesia v Birgen Air*,[123] and held that the relevant test would be similar to that for service out of jurisdiction application to all other forms of action.[124] The applicant has to show that there are merits in the case, and that Singapore courts are a *forum conveniens* for the consideration of the material issue.[125]

The test of a proper case is 'almost identical' to that in Order 8 Rule 2 (formerly Order **9.54** 11, Rule 2).[126] Under the former edition of the Rules of Court, Order 11 Rule 1 set out a number of specific circumstances in which the court may grant service out of jurisdiction. The new 2021 edition of the Rules of Court simplifies all this, merely requiring a showing of 'why the Court has jurisdiction or is the appropriate court to hear the action', where the defendant may be found, and whether the validity of the originating process needs to be extended.

This change has an incidental benefit to applications under the IAA. The previous edi- **9.55** tion of the Rules of Court presented slight technical issues because Order 69A, Rule 4 of that edition was formulated by reference to old Order 11 (now Order 8), which did not have an express provision for service out of jurisdiction where the only connection between the dispute and Singapore is that Singapore is the seat. The courts therefore had to reason that they did have jurisdiction by reference to the proposition that a selection of a seat is equivalent to an exclusive jurisdiction clause (since the supervisory court follows the choice of seat).[127] The broader formulation in the current Order 8 Rule 1

---

[118] *Front Carriers Ltd v Atlantic & Orient Shipping Corp* [2006] 3 SLR(R) 854 [38].
[119] Ibid, [38].
[120] Ibid, [38].
[121] Ibid, [29].
[122] *Swift-Fortune Ltd v Magnifica Marine SA* [2006] 2 SLR(R) 323; [2006] SGHC 36 [29] (hereafter *Swift-Fortune v Magnifica*).
[123] *PT Garuda Indonesia v Birgen Air* [2002] 1 SLR(R) 401 [32] and [34].
[124] *Swift-Fortune v Magnifica Marine* [2007] 1 SLR(R) 629 [11].
[125] Ibid, [60]. This point was not contested on appeal in *Swift-Fortune Ltd v Magnifica Marine SA* [2007] 1 SLR(R) 629; [2006] SGCA 42.
[126] See *PT Garuda Indonesia v Birgen Air* [2002] SGCA 12 [16].
[127] *Hilton International Manage (Maldives) Pvt Ltd v Sun Travels & Tours Pvt Ltd* [2018] SGHC 56 [29]–[30].

4. Rule 5 and 6

9.56 Order 48, Rules 5 and 6 govern the enforcement of interim orders, directions, awards and foreign awards. Rule 5 itself is relatively straightforward and requires an application exhibiting a copy of the arbitration agreement and any applicable rules, as well as the original order or direction sought to be enforced. For enforcement of injunctions under Section 12(1)(e) or (f) of the IAA, the applicant must give an undertaking to abide by any order of the court of tribunal to make good any damages. Rule 5 contemplates that the application must be brought *inter partes*.

9.57 Rule 6(1) and 6(2) provides that applications for leave to enforce an award or a foreign award may be made *ex parte* and prescribes the required evidence. In this regard, both provisions share common requirements. First, there has to be evidence of the arbitration agreement and the award. Secondly, the name and address of the applicant and the person whom it is sought to enforce the award must be provided. Thirdly, the applicant has to state either that the award has not been complied with or the extent to which it has not been complied with.

9.58 The requirement to show 'evidence of the arbitration agreement' is a low threshold at the *ex parte* stage. This was established in *Aloe Vera of America, Inc v Asianic Food (S) Pte Ltd*,[128] where the court characterised the first step of the enforcement process as a mechanistic one which does not require judicial investigation by the court of the jurisdiction in which enforcement is sought.[129] This approach was followed in *Strandore Invest A/S v Soh Kim Wat*.[130] The High Court in *Strandore* elaborated that:

> All the applicant seeking enforcement has to do is to produce the arbitration agreement, prove that the defendant was mentioned in the arbitration agreement exhibited by the applicant, and that an Arbitral Tribunal had made a finding that the defendant was a party to that agreement and that the Arbitral Tribunal had made an award against him, exhibiting the duly authenticated original award or a duly certified copy thereof. It does not require a judicial investigation by the court enforcing the award under the IAA, the examination that the court must make of the documents under O 69A r 6 RSC [now Order 48] is a formalistic and not substantive one.[131]

9.59 At this first *ex parte* stage, even if there were pending applications to set aside the award, this would not be a ground to refuse permission to enforce,[132] and the question of

---

[128] *Aloe Vera of America, Inc v Asianic Food (S) Pte Ltd* [2006] 3 SLR(R) 174; [2006] SGHC 78.
[129] Ibid, [42].
[130] *Strandore Invest A/S v Soh Kim Wat* [2010] SGHC 151 [22].
[131] Ibid, [22].
[132] *CKR v CKT* [2021] SGHCR 4 [30].

whether to adjourn the enforcement proceedings is a matter to be considered at the second *inter partes* stage of the enforcement proceedings.[133]

Service of an order giving permission is required under Rule 6(3), and service is the **9.60** event which triggers the running of time of 14 days from which the award debtor may apply to set aside the order under Rule 6(5).[134] It is important to note that valid service is needed. In this regard, the mere taking away of an *unopened* envelope containing the orders without evidence of notice does not constitute valid service.[135] This is because the party whom it is sought to enforce the award against is not notified that it is the 'debtor' for the purposes of Rule 6(1), and this denies the award debtor the opportunity to participate in or oppose the proceedings.[136]

The *ex parte* order giving permission is not immediately enforceable, and the foreign **9.61** award cannot be enforced until the applicable period of time has expired. If the award debtor does not contest the matter, judgment may be entered against the award debtor after expiry of the applicable time limit.

However, if the award debtor applies to set aside the *ex parte* order giving permission **9.62** within the time stipulated in the order, the foreign award may not be enforced until such application is finally resolved.[137] This then leads to a second *inter partes* stage, where the award debtor resists enforcement based on the grounds set out in the IAA, and the award debtor will have to prove the grounds on a balance of probabilities.[138] If the court rejects the challenge against the award, judgment on the foreign award can then be entered.[139]

Rule 6(4) provides that service of the order out of the jurisdiction is permissible without **9.63** permission and Order 8 Rules 2, 3, 7 and 8 shall apply in relation to such an order. In this regard, the court in *Josias Van Zyl v Kingdom of Lesotho* has clarified that in relation to awards to be served on States, the procedure prescribed in Section 14 of the State Immunity Act 1979 applies notwithstanding the silence in the Rules of Court.[140]

---

[133] Ibid, [36].
[134] *Josias Van Zyl v Kingdom of Lesotho* [2017] 4 SLR 849; [2017] SGHC 104 [25] (hereafter *Josias Van v Lesotho*).
[135] *Astro Nusantara International BV v PT Ayunda Prima Mitra* [2013] 1 SLR 636; [2012] SGHC 212 [55]–[60]. This case was overruled on appeal but not on this issue.
[136] *Josias Van v Lesotho* (n 134) [25].
[137] *Man Diesel Turbo SE v IM Skaugen Marine Services Pte Ltd* [2019] 4 SLR 537 [34].
[138] *Galsworthy Ltd of the Republic of Liberia v Glory Wealth Shipping Pte Ltd* [2011] 1 SLR 727 [11].
[139] *Man Diesel Turbo SE v IM Skaugen Marine Services Pte Ltd* [2019] 4 SLR 537 [35].
[140] *Josias Van v Lesotho* (n 134) [49]. It should be borne in mind that the enforcement of International Centre for Settlement of Investment Dispute awards and the service requirements in relation thereto are subject to a different regime spelt out in the Arbitration (International Investment Disputes) Act 1968.

10

Arbitrability

A. The Applicable Test	10.04	E. Claims Involving Section 216 of	
B. Choice of Law on Arbitrability	10.07	the Companies Act	10.17
C. Non-arbitrable Matters	10.11	F. Where Relief from Court	
D. Insolvency and Arbitration	10.13	is Required	10.20

<u>IAA, Section 11</u>

(1) Any dispute which the parties have agreed to submit to arbitration under an arbitration agreement may be determined by arbitration unless it is contrary to public policy to do so.

(2) The fact that any written law confers jurisdiction in respect of any matter on any court of law but does not refer to the determination of that matter by arbitration does not, of itself, indicate that a dispute about that matter is not capable of determination by arbitration.

10.01 Section 11 of the International Arbitration Act (IAA) relates to the arbitrability of disputes.[1] The UNCITRAL Model Law and the New York Convention both refer to arbitrability, by providing that their scope is limited to disputes that are 'capable of settlement by arbitration'. The IAA does not define 'arbitrability', a concept which is instead explained in case law.[2] Nevertheless, it is clear from the plain wording of Section 11 that a dispute is non-arbitrable where it is of such a nature that resolving it by arbitration is contrary to public policy.[3] Section 11(1) defines arbitrable disputes broadly, by stating that matters are presumed to be arbitrable unless they are 'contrary to public policy'.[4] Section 11(2) further clarifies that a dispute is not considered non-arbitrable simply because legislation confers jurisdiction on the courts without any reference to arbitration.[5]

10.02 As arbitrability has to do with prohibitions against the arbitration of particular categories of disputes based on public policy, determining whether a dispute is

---

[1] International Arbitration Act (Cap. 143A, 2020 Rev. Ed.), Section 11 (hereafter IAA).

[2] *Tomolugen Holdings Ltd v Silica Investors Ltd* [2016] 1 SLR 373; [2015] SGCA 57 [75] (hereafter *Tomolugen Holdings v Silica Investors*); *Larsen Oil and Gas Pte Ltd v Petroprod Ltd (in official liquidation in the Cayman Islands and in compulsory liquidation in Singapore)* [2011] 3 SLR 414; [2011] SGCA 21 [24] (hereafter *Larsen Oil v Petroprod*).

[3] *Tomolugen Holdings v Silica Investors* (n 2) [75].

[4] IAA (n 1), Section 11(1).

[5] Ibid, Section 11(2).

arbitrable is not always straightforward. The reader is directed elsewhere for a discussion on comparative approaches to the subject, which may vary because each state's determination of the scope of arbitrable disputes reflects particular political, social, and economic policy priorities that may change over time.[6]

The question of arbitrability can affect an award or proceeding in several ways. First, an award could be refused enforcement or set aside under the IAA.[7] Second, the court may refuse a stay of court proceedings in favour of arbitration on the basis that the arbitration agreement is 'null and void' or 'inoperative' or 'incapable of being performed' under Section 6(2) of the IAA.[8] Third, arbitrability can be relevant to the question of whether Singapore courts will grant an anti-suit injunction in favour of arbitration.[9] Fourth, non-arbitrability can be relied upon for a jurisdictional challenge before an arbitral tribunal on the basis that the arbitration agreement in respect of a particular category of disputes is unenforceable and against public policy.

10.03

A. The Applicable Test

In *Tomolugen Holdings*, the Court of Appeal laid out the analytical framework on the arbitrability of disputes. The general rule is that a dispute is presumed to be arbitrable so long as it falls within the scope of an arbitration clause.[10] This presumption can then be rebutted in two ways.

10.04

First, to the extent that the dispute involves the application of legislation, the Singapore courts may examine the text of a particular law and its legislative history to determine if Parliament had intended to preclude a particular type of dispute from being arbitrated. For example, in *Larsen Oil v Petroprod*[11] the Court of Appeal examined the statutory provisions in the insolvency regime and concluded that the objectives of the

10.05

---

[6] N. Blackaby, A. Redfern, and M. Hunter, *Redfern and Hunter on International Arbitration* (6th edn, Oxford University Press 2015)74, 112 ('Each state decides which matters may or may not be resolved by arbitration in accordance with its own political, social, and economic policy... Whether or not a particular type of dispute is "arbitrable" under a given law is, in essence, a matter of public policy for that law to determine. Public policy varies from one country to the next, and indeed changes over time.'); G.B. Born, *International Arbitration: Law and Practice* (3rd edn, Kluwer 2021) 97 ('The types of disputes that are nonarbitrable differ from nation to nation. In general, disputes or claims are deemed "nonarbitrable" because of their public importance or a perceived need for judicial protections.') (hereafter Born, *International Arbitration*); S. Vorburger, *International Arbitration and Cross-Border Insolvency: Comparative Perspectives* (Kluwer Law International 2014) 99. See generally, J. Ellis, 'A Comparative Law Approach: Enforceability of Arbitration Agreements in American Insolvency Proceedings' (2018) 92 American Bankruptcy Law Journal 141.

[7] United Nations Commission on International Trade Law (UNCITRAL), UN Doc A/40/17 Annex 1 (entered into force 21 June 1985) Article 34(2)(b)(i) (hereafter Model Law; IAA (n 1), Section 31(4)(a).

[8] *Tomolugen Holdings v Silica Investors* (n 2) [73]. The Court of Appeal noted the English position seeming to prefer the 'inoperative' limb, but thought that all three limbs were capable of being invoked where the dispute was subject matter non-arbitrable.

[9] See e.g. *Westbridge Ventures II Investment Holdings v Anupam Mittal* [2021] SGHC 244 [7] (hereafter *Westbridge Ventures v Anupam Mittal (HC)*); *Anupam Mittal v Westbridge Ventures II Investment Holdings* [2023] SGCA 1 (hereafter *Westbridge Ventures v Anupam Mittal (CA)*).

[10] *Tomolugen Holdings v Silica Investors* (n 2) [3]. The determination of whether a dispute falls within the scope of an arbitration clause is discussed elsewhere. See Chapter 7.

[11] *Larsen Oil v Petroprod* (n 2) [45].

136 ARBITRABILITY

regime—to recoup losses for the benefit of the company's creditors, including losses caused by misfeasance of the company's former directors—may be compromised if those very same directors could restrict the avenues by which the company's creditors could enforce their statutory remedies, including possible claims against the former management who were not be parties to any arbitration agreement.[12] On that basis, the Court of Appeal held that the presumption of arbitrability was rebutted because public policy considerations underlying the insolvency regime overrode the freedom of the company's pre-insolvency management to choose the forum where such disputes could be heard.[13]

10.06 Second, the presumption can be rebutted by showing that it would be contrary to the specific public policy considerations relevant to the dispute if the dispute were to be arbitrated.[14] One example is where an arbitration dispute may lead to the winding up of one entity. Even where shareholders are entitled to commence arbitration proceedings to determine issues of shareholding,[15] potentially leading to the dissolution of a company, the insolvency process has been held to be one 'in which the greater public beyond the parties to the dispute have an interest'.[16]

B. Choice of Law on Arbitrability

10.07 The law applicable to arbitrability will depend on when the question of arbitrability arises. Where arbitrability is relied upon for a setting aside or refusal of enforcement, Article V(2)(a) of the New York Convention and Article 34(2)(b)(i) of the Model Law provide that the national court concerned will apply its own law, the *lex fori*, to decide such issues. Consequently, Article 34(2)(b)(i) of the Model Law, read with Section 3 of the IAA, provides for the application of Singapore law on arbitrability in setting aside proceedings before Singapore courts. Similarly, Section 31(4)(a) provides for the application of Singapore law where refusal of enforcement is sought on non-arbitrability grounds in Singapore.

10.08 At the pre-award stage, however, the relevant IAA provisions and the Model Law do not expressly provide for the law applicable to arbitrability. The Court of Appeal has held that it is the law governing the arbitration agreement that applies to the question of arbitrability. Where that law is a foreign law (i.e. not Singapore law), and that law prohibits the subject matter of the dispute to be arbitrated, the Singapore court will not allow the arbitration to proceed because it would be contrary to (foreign) public policy. However, if the foreign law allows the dispute to be arbitrated but Singapore law (as the law of the seat) considers the dispute not to be arbitrable, then the arbitration would not also proceed.[17]

---

[12] Ibid. The Court also noted the need to avoid different findings by different adjudicators as being in the wider public interest.

[13] *Larsen Oil v Petroprod* (n 2) [46].

[14] *Tomolugen Holdings v Silica Investors* (n 2) [76], affirming *Larsen Oil v Petroprod* (n 2) [44].

[15] Ibid, para 79, citing with approval *A Best Floor Sanding Pty Ltd v Skyer Australia Pty Ltd* [1999] VSC 170.

[16] *Tomolugen Holdings v Silica Investors* (n 2) [83].

[17] *Westbridge Ventures v Anupam Mittal (CA)* (n 9) [55].

It is not entirely clear to the authors why there ought to be a difference in approach between the pre-award and post-award stages as this creates different outcomes purely based on whether the challenge is brought, and in turn, purely based on whether the tribunal issues a preliminary ruling or not. The question of whether a claim is arbitrable should, in principle, yield the same result regardless of the stage of proceedings since it goes to the jurisdiction of the tribunal to determine the issue. The decision may have the effect of tribunals wishing to preserve their jurisdiction refrain from ruling on jurisdiction until the final award. Further, parties choose a neutral or 'safe' seat precisely to ensure that their arbitration agreements will be upheld. If issues concerning the validity and scope of arbitration agreements start becoming subject to the law of the contract even where it would invalidate the parties' choice to arbitrate, much of the 'pro-arbitration' jurisprudence that have been developed in 'safe seat' jurisdictions like Singapore will be gradually undermined. The relevance of the governing law of the contract to issues of jurisdiction has played out in the context of determining the governing law of the arbitration agreement where there is no express choice.[18]

10.09

The position with respect to the applicable law may be different in other contexts—for example in the case of applications under Section 6 of the IAA where Singapore is not the seat of the arbitration. In those circumstances, there may be a prior question of whether Section 11(1) of the IAA even applies in the first place.[19]

10.10

C. Non-arbitrable Matters

In general, the submission of certain categories of disputes to arbitration may be held to be contrary to public policy where (i) it affects third parties,[20] or (ii) has broader public interest elements.[21] Fundamentally, the source of an arbitral tribunal's power is contractual, and thus a tribunal can only make binding orders involving the contracting parties, and the resolution of issues that go beyond the parties *inter se* may be inappropriate.

10.11

Accordingly, the following issues are generally accepted to be non-arbitrable: citizenship or legitimacy of marriage, grants of statutory licenses, winding-up of companies, bankruptcies of debtors, and administration of estates.[22] However, it must be

10.12

---

[18] See Chapter 5.

[19] See e.g. G. Born, *International Commercial Arbitration* (3rd edn, Kluwer Law International 2021) 640–57; B. Hanotiau, 'The Law Applicable to Arbitrability' (2014) 26 Singapore Academy of Law Journal 874, para 16.

[20] *Tomolugen Holdings v Silica Investors* (n 2) [81], citing with approval *In re Cybernaut Growth Fund LP* Cause No FSD 73 of 2013 (23 July 2013) [7].

[21] See, Conseil d'État, Legal Opinion (Avis) of 6 March 1986, No. 339710; J.D.M. Lew, L.A. Mistelis, and S.M. Kröll, *Comparative International Commercial Arbitration* (Kluwer Law International 2003) 733–7. See also *Aloe Vera of America, Inc v Asianic Food (S) Pte Ltd* [2006] 2 SLR(R) 174, where the Singapore High Court rejected the argument that a foreign award should not be enforced because the issue of whether a person was the later ego of a company was not arbitrable. At [72], 'Whether a person is the alter ego of a company is an issue which does not have a public interest element. It normally arises in a commercial transaction in which one party is trying to make an individual responsible for the obligations of a corporation. In my judgment, such an issue can in an appropriate case be decided by arbitration.'

[22] *Larsen Oil v Petroprod* (n 2) [29] citing *Review of Arbitration Laws, LRRD No. 3/2001*, Section 2.37.17. Note that the issue of the arbitrability of disputes concerning intellectual property rights must now be read in light of Part 2A, IAA (n 1), which statutorily provides that 'intellectual property disputes' (including the enforceability,

138 ARBITRABILITY

emphasised that the question of arbitrability is specific to the dispute in question, and requires consideration of the extent to which public interest or third-party elements are really central to the dispute. As discussed below, the Singapore Court of Appeal has made clear in *Tomolugen Holdings* that the mere unavailability of a remedy in arbitration, and the consequential need to seek such relief in court subsequently, does not itself render a dispute non-arbitrable. Rather, the 'essential criterion of non-arbitrability is whether the subject matter of the dispute is of such a nature as to make it contrary to public policy for that dispute to be resolved by arbitration'.[23]

D. Insolvency and Arbitration

10.13 Particular care should be taken in relation to disputes involving an insolvent company. In *Larsen Oil v Petroprod Ltd*, the Court of Appeal drew an important distinction between disputes that arise upon the onset of insolvency due to the operation of the statutory insolvency regime and disputes that involve an insolvent company that stem from pre-insolvency rights and obligations.[24] The former category of disputes is non-arbitrable, and this gives effect to the insolvency regime's objective of protecting third-party creditors: statutory provisions are in place to assist creditors in recouping losses, including those caused by the misfeasance and/or malfeasance of the company's former management.[25] This rule applies even if the parties had expressly included the dispute at hand within the scope of the arbitration agreement. Hence, disputes regarding the winding up of an insolvent company are non-arbitrable,[26] as are applications made pursuant to Section 131(1) of the Companies Act to seek the avoidance of a charge on the basis of non-registration.[27]

10.14 In contrast, where a dispute stems from an insolvent company's pre-insolvency rights and obligations, such dispute is arbitrable so long as creditors are not prejudiced.[28] For instance, where the arbitration agreement only concerns the resolution of prior private disputes between the company and another party, the pool of assets available to all creditors at the time of the company's liquidation will not be affected. In such a scenario, allowing a creditor to arbitrate his claim against the insolvent company will not undermine the insolvency regime's policy aims. Accordingly, such a dispute is likely to be arbitrable.

---

infringement, subsistence, validity, ownership, scope, duration or any other aspect of an intellectual property right) as defined in Section 26A, are capable of settlement by arbitration between the parties to that dispute. Significantly, pursuant to Section 26B(3), such disputes are not non-arbitrable simply because Singapore law or any law does not specifically provide that such disputes may be arbitrable.

[23] *Tomolugen Holdings v Silica Investors* (n 2) [75], [96]–[103].
[24] *Larsen Oil v Petroprod* (n 2) [45]–[51].
[25] Ibid, [45].
[26] *Tomolugen Holdings v Silica Investors* (n 2) [78] and [84].
[27] *Duncan, Cameron Lindsay v Diablo Fortune Inc* [2018] 4 SLR 240; [2017] SGHC 172 [14]–[21].
[28] *Larsen Oil v Petroprod* (n 2) [48]–[51].

In *AnAn (SGCA) (Merits)*, the Court of Appeal recently affirmed the distinction be- **10.15** tween pre-insolvency rights and obligations and those that arise only upon the onset of insolvency due to the operation of the insolvency regime.[29] The key issue on appeal was whether the triable issue standard or the *prima facie* standard applied to a dispute subject to an arbitration agreement that is raised by debtor to resist a winding-up application filed on the basis of an unsatisfied debt. As discussed elsewhere, the Court of Appeal held that the *prima facie* standard of review would apply to give effect to the principle of party autonomy.[30]

In a related case, *AnAn Group (SGCA) (Costs)*, the Court of Appeal further clari- **10.16** fied that not every dispute arising from winding up proceedings would necessarily be non-arbitrable.[31] Indeed, the Court held that insofar as the relief sought in arbitration is '*not* one that the court is only empowered to make under "statutory provisions of the insolvency regime"', such as the powers to order judicial management, winding up, or the appointment of a liquidator, then such a dispute would be *prima facie* arbitrable.[32] The issue on appeal was whether the Court had the power to make a creditor liable for a liquidator's fees (as the winding-up application had been set aside in its entirety) or whether that question should be determined in arbitration. In that context, the Court of Appeal had to determine whether a claim for liquidator's fees was arbitrable, which turned on whether such a claim should be characterised as a claim pursuant to the court's power to award costs arising from a setting aside order, which was non-arbitrable, or a claim for contractual damages arising from a breach of the arbitration agreement, which was arbitrable.[33] Ultimately, the Court of Appeal found that the dispute over the liquidator's fees could be arbitrable but did not oust the Court's separate jurisdiction to adjudicate on costs arising from a setting aside order.[34]

E. Claims Involving Section 216 of the Companies Act

Section 216 of the Companies Act allows members of a company to seek relief from **10.17** the Singapore courts if they consider that the affairs of the company are conducted in a manner oppressive to them, or if an act that is threatened or carried out unfairly discriminates or is prejudicial to them.[35] Relevantly, the types of relief a court may order under Section 216 include share buyouts or a dissolution of the company.

---

[29] *AnAn Group (Singapore) Pte Ltd v VTB Bank (Public Joint Stock Co)* [2020] 1 SLR 1158 (hereafter *AnAn v VTB Bank* (SGCA) (Merits)).
[30] Ibid, [75]–[82]. See Chapter 7.
[31] *AnAn Group (Singapore) Pte Ltd v VTB Bank (Public Joint Stock Company)* [2022] 1 SLR 771; [2021] SGCA 112 [47] (hereafter *AnAn* (SGCA) (Costs)).
[32] Ibid, [48].
[33] Ibid, [50].
[34] *AnAn Group v VTB Bank* (SGCA) (Merits) (n 29) [54].
[35] Companies Act (Cap 50, 2006 Rev. Ed.), Section 216(1) (hereafter Companies Act).

140   ARBITRABILITY

10.18   The Court of Appeal in *Tomolugen Holdings* held that Section 216 claims do not *per se* engage public policy considerations and are thus *generally* arbitrable.[36] Having regard to the legislative history and statutory purpose of Section 216, the Court reasoned that Section 216 was not introduced to protect or further any public interest.[37] Indeed, because Section 216 is concerned with 'protecting the commercial expectations of the parties to such an association', the use of an arbitral tribunal to resolve such a private *inter se* dispute seems eminently suitable.[38] Moreover, an application for relief under this provision almost always arises in the context of a solvent company,[39] and thus it is difficult to see how creditors would be prejudiced by such a claim.[40]

10.19   It has been suggested that in some circumstances, a successful Section 216 claim can affect the interests of third parties in a significant manner.[41] An example might include an order to vary or cancel any transaction or resolution under Section 216(2)(a) of the Companies Act[42] as one that would affect third parties, for example the parties to the transaction and creditors that facilitated the transaction. Indeed, this precise point was addressed in *L Capital Jones Ltd v Maniach Pte Ltd*, where the Court of Appeal clarified that while there was nothing intrinsically non-arbitrable about Section 216 claims, a *particular* dispute involving Section 216 can bear other features that raise public policy considerations against arbitrability.[43]

F. Where Relief from Court is Required

10.20   Even where a claim does not engage public policy considerations, such as the protection of creditors or the protection of public interest elements,[44] a dispute may be held to be non-arbitrable where an arbitral tribunal is unable to award the relief sought.[45] The Court of Appeal in *Tomolugen Holdings* was, however, of the firm view that a dispute is not rendered non-arbitrable simply on this ground.[46] This is because the matter can first be resolved by an arbitral tribunal, and the parties can thereafter apply to the court for the grant of specific relief that is beyond the power of the arbitral tribunal to

---

[36]   *Tomolugen Holdings v Silica Investors* (n 2) [84].
[37]   Ibid, [84]–[88]; see also *Ho Yew Kong v Sakae Holdings Ltd* [2018] SGCA 33 [120] (hereafter *Ho Yew Kong v Sakae Holdings*), where the Court of Appeal held that the injury that the plaintiff sought to vindicate under Section 216 must be distinct from, and not merely incidental to, the injury which the company suffered, that is a personal wrong and not a corporate wrong. This analysis reinforces the view that Section 216 claims generally concern a vindication of private rights.
[38]   *Tomolugen Holdings v Silica Investors* (n 2) [88].
[39]   Ibid.
[40]   *Tomolugen Holdings v Silica Investors* (n 2) [84], [88].
[41]   B. Yeo and F. Chew, 'The Arbitration and Litigation of Minority Shareholder Disputes: Tomolugen Holdings Ltd v Silica Investors Ltd [2016] 1 SLR 373' (2016) 28 Singapore Academy of Law Journal 382, para 17 (hereafter Yeo and Chew, 'The Arbitration and Litigation of Minority Shareholder Disputes').
[42]   Companies Act (n 35), Section 216(2)(a).
[43]   *L Capital Jones Ltd v Maniach Pte Ltd* [2017] 1 SLR 312; [2017] SGCA 3 [26].
[44]   *Tomolugen Holdings v Silica Investors* (n 2) [84], [88].
[45]   Ibid, [104].
[46]   Ibid, [98], [103].

F. WHERE RELIEF FROM COURT IS REQUIRED   141

award.[47] Thus, in *Tomolugen Holdings*, the Court of Appeal held that the factual dispute as to whether minority oppression had occurred may be arbitrated and, if necessary, winding up relief could be sought thereafter from a court.[48]

The above approach of the Singapore courts seeks to strike a balance between two con-   **10.21** cerns: (i) the need to uphold party autonomy, and (ii) the jurisdictional limitations on the powers that are conferred on an arbitral tribunal.[49] In *Tomolugen Holdings*, the Court of Appeal explained that in its attempt to balance the two considerations, it would be prepared to accept 'some, perhaps even substantial, inconvenience' and procedural complexity.[50] The Court of Appeal reasoned that such complexity could be mitigated because the parties to the arbitration would be bound by the arbitral tribunal's findings, even though the Court openly acknowledged the fact that the entire dispute will have to be resolved before two different *fora*.[51]

In Section 216 claims, there are two possible outcomes relevant to the present discus-   **10.22** sion. The first is a buy-out. There appears to be no indication that such a relief is not within the power of an arbitral tribunal to order, so long as the relevant shareholders are party to the arbitration agreement. The second is winding up, either as the primary relief or if a buy-out becomes unfeasible. It is unclear if it would be the place of an arbitral tribunal to propose or suggest the relief of winding up, but it may invariably have to, whether expressly or impliedly, as part of its mandate of resolving the dispute between the parties. Concern has been expressed that the court may be seen as 'rubber stamping' the tribunal's proposal or order.[52] But of course the court can always refuse to grant a winding up order or make it subject to terms.

Does this mean that the tribunal's award is not 'final and binding'? [53] The Court of   **10.23** Appeal in *Tomolugen Holdings* did not seem to think this would be the case. It would certainly be final and binding in relation to the issues it has determined, and the orders, if any, that it has the power to make. There is no reason why the award is not final and binding in respect of those issues. As for any proposal or order by the arbitral tribunal that relates to winding up, it may be possible to regard that as final and binding on the parties *inter se*, but subject to any final orders by the courts in respect of its final and binding effect *erga omnes*.

Finally, it has been suggested that this approach effectively means that parties in such   **10.24** cases agree, at the time of formation, to have their dispute heard by an arbitration tribunal first, subject to subsequent court proceedings to resolve the issue of remedies.[54] This further raises the question whether rational businessmen do in fact intend such an

---

47 Ibid, [100].
48 Ibid, [105]–[106].
49 Ibid, [103].
50 Ibid, [104].
51 Ibid, [105].
52 Yeo and Chew 'The Arbitration and Litigation of Minority Shareholder Disputes' (n 41), para 43.
53 Ibid, para 45.
54 Ibid, para 46.

outcome.[55] It is true that the general approach of the courts is not to construe an agreement in a way that compels a multiplicity of fora where possible, on the theory that commercial parties are taken to intend a 'one-stop' forum.[56] However, the better view is that the Court of Appeal's approach does not imply that parties intended a multiplicity of fora. It is simply attempting to give effect to the intention to arbitrate as much as possible. Similarly, the court's intervention at the final stages of the arbitration should be viewed as being in aid of the arbitral process, and is ultimately in support of the parties' choice of arbitration. The alternative would be to hold that all such disputes are not arbitrable at all. That would be more inconsistent with the parties' agreement and intention.

---

[55] Ibid.
[56] *Fiona Trust & Holding Corp and ors v Privalov and ors* [2008] 1 Lloyd's Rep 254, 258.

11

Powers of the Arbitral Tribunal

A. Legislative History of Section 12	11.03	G. Section 12(3)—Power to Adopt an Inquisitorial Process	11.22
B. Section 12(1)—Powers of an Arbitral Tribunal	11.05	H. Section 12(4)—Limitation on the Power to Award Security for Costs	11.24
C. Section 12(1)(a)—Security for Costs	11.07	I. Section 12(5)—Scope of Relief and Governing Law	11.28
D. Section 12(1)(b) and (c)— Discovery of Documents and Interrogatories	11.13	J. Section 12(5)(a)—Any Remedy or Relief in Civil Proceedings	11.33
E. Sections 12(1)(d)—Preservation, Interim Custody, or Sale of Property	11.15	K. Section 12(5)(b)—Interest	11.38
F. Section 12(1)(g)—Security for Claim	11.16	L. Section 12(6)—Enforceability of Orders and Directions with Leave of Court	11.40

<u>IAA, Section 12</u>

(1) Without prejudice to the powers set out in any other provision of this Act and in the Model Law, an arbitral tribunal has powers to make orders or give directions to any party for—

   (a) security for costs;

   (b) discovery of documents and discovery of facts;

   (c) giving of evidence by affidavit;

   (d) the preservation, interim custody or sale of any property which is or forms part of the subject matter of the dispute;

   (e) samples to be taken from, or any observation to be made of or experiment conducted upon, any property which is or forms part of the subject matter of the dispute;

   (f) the preservation and interim custody of any evidence for the purposes of the proceedings;

   (g) securing the amount in dispute;

   (h) ensuring that any award which may be made in the arbitral proceedings is not rendered ineffectual by the dissipation of assets by a party;

   (i) an interim injunction or any other interim measure; and

   (j) enforcing any obligation of confidentiality—

      (i) that parties to an arbitration agreement have agreed in writing, whether in the arbitration agreement or in any other document;

      (ii) under any written law or rule of law; or

144 POWERS OF THE ARBITRAL TRIBUNAL

   (iii) under the rules of arbitration (including the rules of arbitration of an institution or organisation) agreed to or adopted by the parties.

 (2) Unless the parties to an arbitration agreement have (whether in the arbitration agreement or in any other document in writing) agreed to the contrary, an arbitral tribunal has power to administer oaths or take affirmations of the parties and witnesses.

 (3) Unless the parties to an arbitration agreement have (whether in the arbitration agreement or in any other document in writing) agreed to the contrary, an arbitral tribunal has power to adopt, if the arbitral tribunal thinks fit, inquisitorial processes.

 (4) The power of the arbitral tribunal to order a claimant to provide security for costs as mentioned in subsection (1)(a) must not be exercised by reason only that the claimant is—

  (a) an individual ordinarily resident outside Singapore; or

  (b) a corporation or association incorporated or formed under the law of a country outside Singapore, or whose central management and control is exercised outside Singapore.

 (5) Without prejudice to the application of Article 28 of the Model Law, an arbitral tribunal, in deciding the dispute that is the subject of the arbitral proceedings—

  (a) may award any remedy or relief that could have been ordered by the General Division of the High Court if the dispute had been the subject of civil proceedings in the General Division of the High Court;

  (b) may award simple or compound interest on the whole or any part of any sum in accordance with section 20(1).

 (6) All orders or directions made or given by an arbitral tribunal in the course of an arbitration are, by permission of the General Division of the High Court, enforceable in the same manner as if they were orders made by a court and, where permission is so given, judgment may be entered in terms of the order or direction.

11.01 Section 12 concerns the powers of an arbitral tribunal.[1] While a number of provisions deal with general aspects of a tribunal's powers, the majority of provisions touch on the tribunal's powers in relation to procedure and interim measures.

11.02 During the arbitral life cycle, parties may require orders for evidence to be preserved or orders to compel witnesses to attend a hearing. They may also require injunctive relief to restrain a party from dealing with property or assets. This may be particularly important where irreparable harm may occur due to steps being taken by the other party or simply by the passage of time which will elapse during the arbitral process.[2] Section

---

[1] As explained in Chapter 4, this includes an emergency arbitrator. Although these sections should be read in tandem with Article 17 of the Model Law, amendments to the Model Law in 2006 were not reflected in the International Arbitration Act (IAA).

[2] As per Gary Born, 'Classic examples include dissipation of assets, destruction of evidence, loss of market value of property, disruption of a joint venture's operations, destruction of an ongoing business, disclosure or misuse of intellectual property and interference with customer relations'; see G. B. Born, *International Commercial Arbitration* (3rd edn, Kluwer Law International 2021) 2604 (hereafter Born, *International Commercial Arbitration*).

B. SECTION 12(1)—POWERS OF AN ARBITRAL TRIBUNAL   145

12 sets forth the express powers of arbitral tribunals to fashion the necessary orders for a fair and efficient process.

A. Legislative History of Section 12

In 1993, a Subcommittee of the Law Reform Committee on Review of Arbitration Laws **11.03** (Subcommittee) conducted a survey of the laws relating to arbitration in Singapore. In its report, the Subcommittee highlighted that the then Arbitration Act gave limited powers to arbitrators, and this was a cause for concern because, unlike a court, there was no clear authority for the proposition that an arbitrator had inherent procedural powers at common law, independently of statute.[3] To enable the proper functioning of international arbitrations in Singapore, the Subcommittee took the view that arbitral powers given by statute had to be 'substantially increased'.[4] In this regard, it considered that the express powers contained in Article 17 of the Model Law should be expanded.[5] Such powers should be concurrently exercisable by a tribunal and a court, and the parties would have the liberty to choose the forum in which it wishes to make such an application.[6]

These recommendations translated into the original Section 12 of the IAA, which has **11.04** since undergone a number of amendments, including: (i) the introduction of powers to order collection and testing of samples and preservation of evidence;[7] (ii) the introduction of guidelines concerning an order of security for costs;[8] and (iii) following the *Swift-Fortune Ltd v Magnifica Marine SA*[9] judgment, the deletion of then Section 12(7), and, most significantly, the insertion of Section 12A, which now separately and comprehensively governs the powers of the Singapore court to issue interim relief in aid of arbitration.[10]

B. Section 12(1)—Powers of an Arbitral Tribunal

Section 12(1) sets out ten categories of powers an arbitral tribunal has, most of which **11.05** deal with matters of procedure and interim measures. These are expressly without prejudice to any provision of the Act or the Model Law.

---

[3] Law Reform Committee, *Report on Review of Arbitration Laws* (Singapore Academy of Law 1993) 30 (hereafter 'LRC Report').

[4] Ibid, 31.

[5] Ibid.

[6] Ibid.

[7] International Arbitration (Amendment) Act, 2001 (Act No. 38 of 2001) (hereafter IAA 2001).

[8] Ibid.

[9] *Swift-Fortune Ltd v Magnifica Marine SA* [2006] SGCA 42. This decision is discussed in further detail in the Chapter 12.

[10] International Arbitration (Amendment) Act 2009, (Act No. 26 of 2009). See generally Chapter 13.

146   POWERS OF THE ARBITRAL TRIBUNAL

11.06   The ambit of Section 12 is wide. Section 12(1)(i) provides a catch-all, permitting an arbitral tribunal to grant '*any* other interim measure'.[11] As may be expected, Section 12 does not prescribe a legal test for the grant of relief, which would depend on the applicable law.[12]

C. Section 12(1)(a)—Security for Costs

11.07   Section 12(1)(a) allows a tribunal to make orders for security for costs. Section 12(1)(a) should be read with Section 12(4), which provides that foreign domicile or residence cannot be the sole basis for granting a security for cost application.

11.08   Considerations concerning when security for costs may be appropriate arose in *Zhong Da Chemical Development Co Ltd v Lanco Industries Pte Ltd*.[13] Strictly speaking, however, the application was not one under Section 12; it was a security for costs application made in the context of setting aside proceedings. Nonetheless, some of Prakash J's (as she then was) observations in that case may be relevant to a Singapore seated tribunal applying Singapore law to the question of security for costs.

11.09   Zhong Da was a company incorporated in China and Lanco was a company incorporated in India. A disagreement arose from a sale agreement between the parties, giving rise to arbitration proceedings. After the arbitral award was issued, Zhong Da applied to court to set aside the award under Section 24, on the basis that such award was obtained fraudulently. Lanco denied the allegation and applied for security for costs under Order 23 of the Singapore Rules of Court.

11.10   Prakash J first touched on the two requirements to an Order 23 security for costs application. First, the defendant must show that the plaintiff is ordinarily a resident out of jurisdiction.[14] Where the plaintiff is a corporation, the plaintiff is a resident in the jurisdiction where its central management and command takes place.[15] Second, the court will then consider all the circumstances to determine whether it is just that security should be ordered. There is no presumption in favour of, or against a grant of security for costs. No objective criteria can be laid down as to the weight any particular factor may be accorded. Where the court is of the view that the circumstances

---

[11] Some doubt was expressed by Chan J in his dissenting judgment in *PT Perusahaan Gas Negara v CRW Joint Operation* [2015] 4 SLR 364 (hereafter *PT Perusahaan v CRW*). He considered that the Act did not grant tribunals the power to order interim payment, as such a power was, unlike the UK Arbitration Act 1996, not provided for in Section 12(1): *PT Perusahaan v CRW* [220], [221], [222], [223].

[12] On the law that should apply, see e.g. Born, *International Commercial Arbitration* (n 2) 2644–49; A. Henderson, 'Lex Arbitri, Procedural Law and the Seat of Arbitration' (2014) 26 Singapore Academy of Law Journal 886; M. Hwang, 'The Applicable Standards For the Granting of Interim Injunctions in International Commercial Arbitrations Seated in Singapore' (2021) 1 Singapore Arbitration Journal 30.

[13] *Zhong Da Chemical Development Co Ltd v Lanco Industries Pte Ltd* [2009] 3 SLR(R) 1017 (hereafter *Zhong Da v Lanco*).

[14] Ibid, [9]. See also *Wishing Star Ltd v Jurong Town Corp* [2004] 1 SLR(R) 1.

[15] *Zhong Da v Lanco* (n 13) [9].

D. SECTION 12(1)(B) AND (C)—DISCOVERY OF DOCUMENTS AND FACTS   147

are evenly balanced, it would ordinarily be just to order security against a foreign plaintiff.[16]

Prakash J then went on to consider the factors in ordering security for costs under Section 12(4) of the IAA, which she considered would be somewhat different from the standards under the Rules of Court. In her view, in agreeing to a foreign arbitral forum, it is presumed that the defendant should have been mindful, and must be taken to have agreed, that any action to set aside the arbitral award would take place in the courts of the seat, and not the courts of the jurisdiction where the claimant is resident.[17] In her view therefore, the claimant should not be penalised for being ordinarily a resident out of the jurisdiction.[18] Unlike an application made under the Rules of Court, an application for security for costs under the IAA should ordinarily be dismissed when circumstances are evenly balanced.[19] Security was ultimately granted in this case, but for reasons independent of Zhong Da's domicile.[20]   **11.11**

Interestingly, this decision raises the question on the standards a tribunal should apply when considering a security for costs application. On one view, transnational standards should be applied.[21] If such an approach were to be adopted, the trend appears to be that foreign nationality or incorporation are not, by themselves, sufficient grounds for ordering security. A claimant's financial circumstances and whether there has been a material change of circumstances since the parties concluded their agreement (as opposed to looking merely at the claimant's financial condition at the time of the application) appear to be more material.[22] Prakash J's comment on the immateriality of foreign domicile, and the text of Section 12(4), appears to accommodate the application of such a transnational approach.   **11.12**

D. Section 12(1)(b) and (c)—Discovery of Documents and Interrogatories

Sections 12(1)(b) and (c), which concern the discovery of documents, interrogatories, and the giving of evidence by affidavit, are relatively straightforward provisions that do no more than confirm the tribunal's powers with respect to these procedural matters.   **11.13**

It should be noted that the process by which evidence is taken in arbitration is normally a matter the parties decide on, in consultation with the tribunal. In this regard, it is not uncommon for parties to select the International Bar Association (IBA) Rules on the   **11.14**

---

[16] Ibid, [10].
[17] Ibid, [13].
[18] Ibid.
[19] Ibid.
[20] Ibid, [15]–[23].
[21] See e.g. A. Henderson, 'Security for Costs in Arbitration in Singapore' (2011) 7(1) Asian International Arbitration Journal </IBT<54, 68 (hereafter Henderson, 'Security for Costs in Arbitration in Singapore').
[22] Ibid, 54, 73.

148   POWERS OF THE ARBITRAL TRIBUNAL

Taking of Evidence in International Arbitration,[23] either expressly in their agreement to arbitrate, or *ad hoc* upon the commencement of arbitration proceedings. Where the IBA Rules apply, the manner in which a party will discharge its disclosure obligations will be governed by those rules. In 2019, an independent group of practitioners published the Rules on the Efficient Conduct of Proceedings in International Arbitration (Prague Rules)[24] as an alternative to the IBA Rules, which they perceived underrepresented the civil law's inquisitorial approach to proceedings and evidence. The Prague Rules focus less on the need for documentary disclosure and place more of the fact-finding responsibility on the adjudicator.[25] Regardless of the system of evidentiary rules used, tribunals must be mindful of due process concerns and ensure that parties have had their cases heard.[26]

E. Sections 12(1)(d)—Preservation, Interim Custody, or Sale of Property

11.15   Section 12(1)(d) provides for 'the preservation, interim custody or sale of any property which is or forms part of the subject-matter of the dispute'. Section 12(1)(d) was discussed in *Five Ocean Corp v Cingler Ship Pte Ltd*.[27] The question before the court was whether, under Section 12A(4) read with Section 12(1)(d), the court could preserve the right to detain possession of the cargo as 'property', through an order for sale of that cargo in the circumstances where the cargo was perishable and diminishing in value. The court held that the right to detain cargo until payment was made was a form of 'chose in action' and therefore qualified as an 'asset' under Sections 12 and 12A.[28] Given the perishable nature of the goods in this case, the 'right to detain possession could be effectively preserved through an order for sale'.[29]

F. Section 12(1)(g)—Security for Claim

11.16   In its review of arbitration laws in Singapore in 1993, the Subcommittee considered the power to issue an order relating to security for a claim in its review of arbitration laws in

---

[23] International Bar Association, IBA Rules on the Taking of Evidence in International Arbitration (IBA Council, 29 May 2010).

[24] Rules on the Efficient Conduct of Proceedings in International Arbitration 2019 (hereafter Prague Rules).

[25] Ibid, Article 3, 'The arbitral tribunal is entitled and encouraged to take a proactive role in establishing the facts of the case which it considers relevant for the resolution of the dispute' and Article 4, 'Generally, the arbitral tribunal and the parties are encouraged to avoid any form of document production, including e-discovery'. See also N. Peter, 'The Prague Rules as Choice Architecture' (2019)13(2) Revista Română de Arbitraj 80.

[26] See e.g. Model Law, Article 18, 'The parties shall be treated with equality and each party shall be given a full opportunity of presenting his case', K.D. Beale and N. Goh, 'Due Process Challenges in Asia: An Emerging High Bar' (2017) 13(1) Asia International Arbitration Journal 1.

[27] *Five Ocean Corp v Cingler Ship Pte Ltd* [2015] SGHC 311 (hereafter *Five Ocean Corp v Cingler Ship Pte Ltd*).

[28] Ibid, [46].

[29] Ibid, [55].

F. SECTION 12(1)(G)—SECURITY FOR CLAIM   149

Singapore and noted that this was not contained in the Model Law.[30] The Subcommittee considered that the power to provide security for claims should also be available to tribunal adjudication over international disputes.[31]

To date, there has been little discussion by the Singapore courts regarding Section 12(1)(g).[32]   **11.17**
Only two cases have touched on section 12(1)(g), and even then, only briefly.[33]

However, at least one Singapore-seated arbitral tribunal has applied Section 12(1)(g). It   **11.18**
did so to secure part of the amount in dispute by ordering the respondent to place the money in a solicitors-controlled money trust account maintained by its solicitors for the purpose of providing assurance to the claimant of partial recovery, if the claimant was ultimately successful.[34] After the arbitral award was issued, the respondent entered voluntary administration, leaving the claimant with little recourse other than to pursue the trust money.[35] The administrators of the respondent objected to the claimant's claim on the trust money by arguing that the company might not be able to trade following the payment, which would lead to the respondent's winding up. Following that, the administrators also argued that there might be a liquidator's claim on the trust amount and the interests of other creditors to consider.[36]

The matter eventually came before the Supreme Court of Western Australia in *Dalian*   **11.19**
Huarui Heavy Industry International Company Ltd v Clyde & Co Australia (a firm).[37]
Kenneth Martin J held that, from the day the tribunal made the order for the money to be paid into a solicitor's trust, those funds were no longer property of the respondent. The respondent's solicitors were the trustees and the claimant's interest in the solicitors-controlled trust matured from a contingent equitable interest to be an absolute and unqualified beneficial entitlement in equity to receive the trust money.[38]

In his judgment, Kenneth Martin J considered the three reasons stated in the tribunal's   **11.20**
procedural order for its decision to exercise its power under Section 12(1)(g):[39] first, the tribunal expected to make an award in the near future, and that there would be irreparable harm to the claimant if the award could not be enforced because assets were not available;[40] second, the tribunal noted that the respondent had received funds from another arbitration, and it was likely that these funds would be dissipated;[41] and third,

---

[30] LRC Report (n 3) 43, 44.

[31] Ibid, 49.

[32] S. Menon and D. Brock (eds), *Arbitration in Singapore: A Practical Guide* (Sweet and Maxwell 2014) 11.092 (hereafter Menon and Brock, *Arbitration in Singapore: A Practical Guide*).

[33] *H&C S Holdings Pte Ltd v Mount Eastern Holdings Resources Co* [2015] SGHC 323; *Front Carriers Ltd v Atlantic & Orient Shipping Corp* [2006] SGHC 127.

[34] See *Dalian Huarui Heavy Industry International Company Ltd v Clyde & Co Australia (a firm)* [2020] WASC 132 [119], [120], [123], [139] (hereafter *Dalian Huarui Heavy Industry International Company Ltd v Clyde & Co Australia*).

[35] Ibid, [18].

[36] Ibid, [46].

[37] *Dalian Huarui Heavy Industry International Company Ltd v Clyde & Co Australia* (n 34).

[38] Ibid, [187], [188], [259].

[39] Ibid, [123].

[40] Ibid.

[41] Ibid.

150 POWERS OF THE ARBITRAL TRIBUNAL

while there were some other funds subject to a freezing order, it was not certain that the claimant would be entitled to receive them as the purpose of the freezing order was to secure sums for another arbitration.[42]

11.21 One commentator has suggested that tribunals should be cautious when exercising their powers to order security for the amount in dispute.[43] This is because it may put the claimant in a better position than if he had obtained relief of a more transitory or exceptional nature such as a freezing injunction.[44]

G. Section 12(3)—Power to Adopt an Inquisitorial Process

11.22 Section 12(3) provides that, subject to the parties' agreement, a tribunal has the power to adopt inquisitorial processes as it thinks fit. Section 12(3) was referred to in passing in *JVL Agro Industries v Agritrade International Pte Ltd*,[45] which concerned an application to set aside an award pursuant to Section 24(b) of the IAA and Article 18 of the Model Law. On the facts, Vinodh Coomaraswamy J agreed with the applicant that the tribunal had made its decision on a point of law which neither party had advanced or relied on in argument.[46] Coomaraswamy J observed that 'the mere fact that the Act consider[ed] it necessary expressly to empower a tribunal to proceed inquisitorially show that the starting point—at least in Singapore—is adversarial'.[47] The adversarial nature of the system meant that it was up to the parties, and not the adjudicator, to select the issues to be resolved.[48] A tribunal which decided an issue that neither party has argued ran the risk not only of breaching the rules of natural justice but of acting without jurisdiction.[49]

11.23 While it is likely to be the case that parties from common law jurisdictions or are represented by counsel familiar with the adversarial process would be familiar with the approach outlined in *JVL Agro*, it should be noted that there exist alternatives to the perceived rigidity of the adversarial approach. For instance, the Prague Rules,[50] discussed above, allow for arbitrators to take a more active role in the arbitral process, such as by expressing their preliminary views on issues, requesting evidence from parties or appointing experts.[51] The adoption of such rules may be preferred in cases where

---

[42] Ibid.

[43] Menon and Brock, *Arbitration in Singapore: A Practical Guide* (n 32), 11.092.

[44] Menon and Brock, *Arbitration in Singapore: A Practical Guide* (n 32).

[45] *JVL Agro Industries v Agritrade International Pte Ltd* [2016] 4 SLR 768 (hereafter *JVL Agro Industries v Agritrade International Pte Ltd*).

[46] Ibid, [185], [186], [187].

[47] Ibid, [169].

[48] Ibid, [170], [171], [172].

[49] Ibid, [174].

[50] Prague Rules (n 24).

[51] Ibid, Articles 2 and 3.

H. Section 12(4)—Limitation on the Power to Award Security for Costs

Section 12(4) should be read with Section 12(1)(a), which confirms a tribunal's power **11.24** to award security for costs. Section 12(4) states that the arbitral tribunal cannot order a claimant to provide security for costs solely by reason that the claimant is a resident, incorporated, or managed outside Singapore.

Under the Singapore Rules of Court, a defendant to an action or other proceeding may **11.25** make a security for cost application to court when the plaintiff is ordinarily a resident out of the jurisdiction.[52] The risk here is that if the plaintiff has no assets within the juris- diction, he can easily avoid paying the defendant's cost should the defendant succeed.[53] The defendant must prove that the plaintiff is ordinarily and not merely temporarily a resident. The words 'ordinary resident' are construed literally so it is sufficient if the for- eign jurisdiction is their normal and habitual residence even though the plaintiff may not be domiciled there and has a permanent home elsewhere.[54] However, being ordin- arily resident out of the jurisdiction is not a sufficient ground for ordering security, and the court must then move on to consider all factors before determining that it should exercise its discretion to make such an order.[55] Factors to consider include whether a de- fendant who is likely to incur considerable cost in defending a suit in respect of which he can show some merit,[56] negotiations for settlement, and payment into court.

In the context of international arbitration, it is common for the claimant not to be an in- **11.26** dividual resident in Singapore or a corporate entity incorporated in Singapore. Section 12(4) reflects this by providing guidance to arbitral tribunals as to how a Section 12(1) (a) power should be exercised. Neither the fact that an individual is ordinarily resident outside Singapore nor a corporation or association being incorporated, formed, or cen- trally managed or controlled outside Singapore should be determinative in ordering security for costs.[57]

These considerations were also appreciated by Prakash J in *Zhong Da Chemical* **11.27** *Development Co Ltd v Lanco Industries Pte Ltd* [2009] 3 SLR(R) 1017, discussed above.[58]

---

[52] Singapore Rules of Court Order 9, Rule 12(a).
[53] See e.g. Singapore Civil Procedure, Vol. 1, Commentary to Order 23 Rule 1(1) (Sweet & Maxwell 2020) (here- after Singapore Civil Procedure).
[54] *Jurong Town Corp v Wishing Star Ltd* [2004] 2 SLR(R) 427.
[55] Singapore Civil Procedure (n 53); *Sembawang Engineering Pte Ltd v Priser Asia Engineering Pte Ltd* [1992] 2 SLR(R) 358; *Amar Hoseen Mohammed Revai v Singapore Airlines* [1994] 3 SLR(R) 290 [60].
[56] *Thune v London Properties Ltd* [1990] 1 All ER 972.
[57] IAA, Section 12(4)(a) and 12(4)(b).
[58] *Zhong Da v Lanco* (n 13) [13]. See Chapter 11 section C.

152   POWERS OF THE ARBITRAL TRIBUNAL

I. Section 12(5)—Scope of Relief and Governing Law

11.28 Moving away from the arbitral procedure, Section 12(5) deals with the ultimate relief that arbitral tribunals can give. Section 12(5) is subject to one overarching caveat, which is that the latitude of the tribunal's powers to grant relief is '[w]ithout prejudice to the application of Article 28 of the Model Law'.

11.29 Article 28 of the Model Law provides that an arbitral tribunal 'shall decide the dispute in accordance with such rules of law as are chosen by the parties as applicable to the substance of the dispute'. This, in short, requires that relief be given in accordance with the applicable governing law.

11.30 In the event that the governing law is unclear or contested, an arbitral tribunal would have to decide based on conflict of law rules, consistent with Article 28(2) of the Model Law. Which conflict of laws rules apply to determine the substantive governing law of a dispute is a topic which goes beyond this commentary. Suffice to say, it is not a settled question. Some of the older decisions take the view that the conflict of laws rules at the seat apply.[59] This approach is analogous to that under cross-border litigation where the 'choice of law' rules at the forum, that is, the *lex fori*, apply. Others have however questioned why the conflict of laws rules of the seat should apply in international arbitration, given that, unlike court litigation there is no concept of a *lex fori* in international arbitration, and there is no reason to impose strictures on a tribunal to have to apply the forum's or seat's conflict rules.[60] One commentary suggests that a forum's conflict of laws rules is intended to delimit and regulate the scope of a state's legislative competence. However, this purpose is not advanced by requiring an international tribunal, which is not an organ of the state, to apply *national* conflict of laws rules.

11.31 In light of the foregoing divergence of views, while the law of the seat (as analogue for the *lex fori*) may be used to determine the law governing the substance of the dispute, this is by no means an automatic choice. Ultimately, a tribunal should have the latitude to select the 'conflict of laws rules which it considers applicable'.[61]

11.32 Articles 28(3) and 28(4) of the Model Law provide some guidance on the other rules potentially applicable to the dispute, including the tribunal deciding on an *ex aequo et bono* basis or based on usages of the trade applicable to the transaction. The latter is not uncommon in disputes in selected industry sections such as shipping or oil and

---

[59] *Austrian franchisor v South African franchisee*, Final Award, ICC Case No. 5460, 1987 in A.J. van den Berg (ed), *Yearbook Commercial Arbitration 1988*, Vol. XIII (Kluwer Law International 1988) 104–9, [1], [4] ('The place of this arbitration is London, and on any question of choice of law I must therefore apply the relevant rules of the private international law of England'); *Seller v Buyer*, Partial Award, in A.J. van den Berg (ed), *Yearbook Commercial Arbitration 1997*, Vol. XXII (Kluwer Law International 1997) Arb. 35; see more generally Born, *International Commercial Arbitration* (n 2) 2844–70.

[60] N. Blackaby et al., *Redfern and Hunter on International Arbitration* (6th edn, Oxford University Press 2015) 155–228, para 3.211 et seq.

[61] UNCITRAL Arbitration Rules Article 33.

J. Section 12(5)(a)—Any Remedy or Relief in Civil Proceedings

Section 12(5)(a) provides that a tribunal may award any remedy or relief which could **11.33** have been ordered by the High Court if the dispute was subject to civil proceedings in Court. As the Singapore courts have held, this is a 'wide remedial power'.[62]

However, Section 12(5)(a) is not without its limitations. For instance, a tribunal may be **11.34** limited in its ability to deal with matters of public policy or issue orders against third parties, which the Singapore Court could do.[63]

In *Silica Investors v Tomolugen Holding Ltd and ors*,[64] the court considered whether **11.35** some of the coercive powers of the High Court were encompassed by Section 12(5)(a). The court took guidance from discussions in a 1991 Report on Section 12 of the New Zealand Arbitration Act of 1996 which stated that the comparable provision '[fell] short of completely assimilating the powers of an arbitral tribunal to those of the High Court ... Obviously, the power to grant a remedy or relief does not include the High Court's coercive powers.'[65] The High Court in *Silica Investors* ultimately held that Section 12(5) of the IAA did not empower tribunals to grant all statute-based remedies available to the High Court but had a more limited purpose.[66] The Court of Appeal agreed with this general proposition although it qualified that such a limit to a tribunal's power did not necessarily mean a dispute (such as a shareholders' dispute) was non-arbitrable.[67]

Similarly, in *Maniach Pte Ltd v L Capital Jones Ltd and another*,[68] in determining a mi- **11.36** nority oppression claim, the court considered whether a tribunal could exercise the statutory power to order a buy-out on terms provided for under Section 216(2)(d) of the Companies Act. The court held that this power was not conferred on to the tribunal by Section 12(5)(a) and observed that it was 'as much uniquely a judge's power as the power to order a company to be wound up'[69] under the Companies Act. The court rejected the argument that in cases where all shareholders were parties to the arbitration agreement, the tribunal would have the power of a judge under Section 216(2)(f) of the Companies Act to alleviate oppression by ordering a majority shareholder to buy out

---

[62] See *Tomolugen Holdings Ltd and another v Silica Investors Ltd and other* [2015] SGCA 57 [97] (hereafter *Tomolugen Holdings*) where the judgment states 'the IAA confers wide remedial powers on arbitral tribunals'.
[63] Ibid, [97]; see also *BTY v BUA and other matters* [2018] SGHC 213 [106].
[64] *Silica Investors v Tomolugen Holding Ltd and ors* [2014] 3 SLR 815 (hereafter *Silica Investors*).
[65] Ibid, [106] (citing the Report on Section 12 of the New Zealand Arbitration Act of 1996, (1991)), [258].
[66] Ibid, [111].
[67] *Tomolugen Holdings* (n 62) [97], [98].
[68] *Maniach Pte Ltd v L Capital Jones Ltd and another*, [2016] SGHC 65 (hereafter *Maniach Pte Ltd*).
[69] Ibid, [164].

154 POWERS OF THE ARBITRAL TRIBUNAL

an oppressed minority shareholder on terms.[70] Basing its reasoning on *Silica Investors v Tomolugen*, the court held the power to order a buy-out on terms to be exclusively within the coercive powers of the court as it 'compels the subject of the order to acquire property on terms other than of its own choosing'.[71] Consequently, it held that such power could not be exercised by an arbitral tribunal and fell outside the scope of Section 12(5) of the IAA.

11.37 The court in *Tan Poh Leng Stanley v Tang Boon Jek Jeffrey*[72] had to address the question of whether a tribunal could recall or reverse a final award delivered by it. The High Court held that even though Section 12(5)(a) enabled the arbitrator to 'award any remedy or relief which could be ordered by the High Court if the dispute had been subject of civil proceedings in that court', such powers were limited to procedural powers which could 'only be exercised during the arbitration before the arbitrator becomes functus officio'.[73] Accordingly, there was nothing in Section 12 which empowered the arbitrator to recall or reverse a final award delivered by it.

K. Section 12(5)(b)—Interest

11.38 Section 12(5)(b) additionally provides for the power to award either 'simple or compound interest on the whole or part of the sum'. This is to be done in accordance with Section 20(1) which deals directly with the issue of interest on awards. The power to award compound interest is specifically made part of the framework under both Section 12 and Section 20 of the IAA. The power to award compound interest has also been recognised and upheld by Singapore courts.[74]

11.39 In *CBX and anor v CBZ and ors*,[75] the plaintiff alleged (amongst other things) that the tribunal had exceeded its jurisdiction in awarding compound interest of 15% in certain partial awards. The High Court found that the tribunal, which applied Thai law, did so within the realm of its powers.[76] The High Court also dismissed arguments that the award of compound interest should be set aside for being contrary to Thai or Singapore public policy or otherwise illegal.[77] On appeal, the Court of Appeal did not strictly have to consider the compound interest issue because it set aside the partial awards as the order for payments in those awards were made in excess of jurisdiction. Nonetheless, the Court of Appeal noted that the agreement between the Thai law experts that the contractual provision for compound interest was illegal and unenforceable under Thai law, as well as the agreement between the parties on the issue, restricted the scope of

---

[70] Ibid, [164].
[71] Ibid, [165], [166].
[72] *Tan Poh Leng Stanley v Tang Boon Jek Jeffrey*, [2000] SGHC 260 (hereafter *Tan Poh Leng Stanley*).
[73] Ibid.
[74] See *The Oriental Insurance Co Ltd v Reliance National Asia Re Pte Ltd.* [2008] SGHC 236.
[75] *CBX and anor v CBZ and ors* [2020] 5 SLR 184, [2020] SGHC(I) 17 (hereafter *CBX and anor v CBZ and ors*).
[76] Ibid, [47]–[49].
[77] Ibid, [51]–[69].

L. Section 12(6)—Enforceability of Orders and Directions with Leave of Court

In *PT Pukuafu Indah and others v Newmont Indonesia Ltd and another*,[79] the arbitral tribunal issued an interim anti-suit injunction under Section 12(1)(i) IAA.[80] This resulted in the defendants applying under Section 12(6) for leave of court to enforce the interim order, and the plaintiffs in turn applying to set aside the interim order.[81] In dismissing the defendant's application, Lee Seiu Kin J traced the legislative history of Section 12(6).

11.40

Lee J noted that Article 17 of the Model Law provided arbitral tribunals with the power to award interim measures, but was silent on the status and enforceability of such awards.[82] In its 1993 report, the Subcommittee of the Law Reform Committee on Review of Arbitration Laws considered that 'there [was] a lacuna in the Model Law which the Committee feels should be filled'.[83] It explained that such orders were important to expedite proceeding,[84] and suggested that such orders be given the status of awards in order to be enforceable.[85] However, when Parliament amended the IAA in 2012, rather than broadening the definition of an 'award' to allow the court to set aside interim orders, it filled the lacuna with an enforcement mechanism.[86]

11.41

Lee Seiu Kin J pointed out that national courts and arbitration statutes in various jurisdictions had differing approaches to the status of an interim order.[87] Some characterised an interim order as an award, which then gave rise to the question of whether they may be enforced or set aside.[88] In Singapore, however, Parliament opted for minimal curial intervention as the means of balancing fairness and efficiency. Further, interim orders possessed a temporary character as they may be modified or terminated during the course of the arbitration process; this made them distinct from awards which were final.[89] Viewed holistically, therefore, the IAA allows the court to grant interim relief under Section 12A in specific circumstances and to enforce interim orders made by tribunals under Section 12(6). However, the IAA did not give the court the power to

11.42

---

[78] *CBX and anor v CBZ and ors* [2021] SGCA (1) 3 [86]–[95].

[79] *PT Pukuafu Indah and others v Newmont Indonesia Ltd and another* [2012] SGHC 187 (hereafter *PT Pukuafu Indah*).

[80] Ibid, [1], [2], [3].

[81] Ibid, [1], [2], [3].

[82] Ibid, [21].

[83] LRC Report (n 3) 34.

[84] Ibid, .

[85] Ibid, .

[86] *PT Pukuafu Indah* (n 79) [21].

[87] Ibid, [25].

[88] Ibid.

[89] Ibid, [26].

156   POWERS OF THE ARBITRAL TRIBUNAL

set aside or review interim measures ordered by arbitral tribunals.[90] This approach reduces the risk of delay and prevents tactical attempts to obstruct the arbitration process by bringing challenges on interim orders.[91] The better remedy for an unsatisfied party would be to have recourse to the arbitral tribunal, not the courts.[92]

11.43   Lee J further observed that, while an order made under Section 12 cannot be set aside, the leave of the High Court is required to enforce a tribunal's interim order as an order of the court under Section 12(6).[93] Thus, although he did not express a conclusive view, Lee J suggested that there was a possibility that refusing leave could provide some measure of residual protection to parties dissatisfied with an interim order. For completeness, he noted that under Order 69A Rule 5(2) of the Rules of Court 2014 (which is now Order 48 Rule 5(2) of the Rules of Court 2021), leave is only to be given where the applicant undertakes to abide by any order that the court or arbitral tribunal may make as to damages.[94]

---

[90] Ibid, [25], [26].
[91] Ibid.
[92] Ibid, [26].
[93] Ibid, [27].
[94] Ibid; Singapore Rules of Court Order 48 Rule 5(2) ('Where the order sought to be enforced is in the nature of an interim injunction under section 12(1)(e) or (f), permission may be granted only if the applicant undertakes to abide by any order the Court or the arbitral tribunal may make as to damages.').

12

Court Powers in Aid of Arbitration

A. Section 12A—Court-ordered Interim Measures	12.01	G. Section 12A(4)—Urgency ... 12.33
B. Legislative Background to Section 12A	12.04	H. Section 12A(4)—Rights and Assets ... 12.37
C. Section 12A(1)	12.07	I. Section 12A(5) ... 12.44
		J. Section 12A(6) ... 12.46
D. Section 12A(2)—Scope of the Powers of a Court to Grant Interim Relief	12.08	K. Section 12A(7) ... 12.57
		L. Section 13—Summoning of Witnesses by Subpoena ... 12.58
E. Section 12A(2)—Anti-suit Injunctions	12.09	M. Subpoenas and Civil Procedure ... 12.62
1. R1 International Pte Ltd v Lonstroff AG	12.10	N. Principles Governing Subpoena Applications ... 12.63
		1. Section 13(1)–(2) ... 12.63
2. Hilton International v Sun Travels	12.16	2. Section 13(3) ... 12.71
3. Permanent Injunctions—The Source of the Power	12.22	3. Section 13(4) ... 12.72
		O. Subpoenas in Aid of Foreign-seated Arbitrations ... 12.73
F. Section 12A(3)	12.30	

<u>IAA, Section 12A</u>

(1) This section is to apply in relation to an arbitration—

    (a) to which this Part applies; and

    (b) irrespective of whether the place of arbitration is in the territory of Singapore.

(2) Subject to subsections (3) to (6), for the purpose of and in relation to an arbitration referred to in subsection (1), the General Division of the High Court has the same power of making an order in respect of any of the matters set out in section 12(1)(*c*) to (*j*) as it has for the purpose of and in relation to an action or a matter in the court.

(3) The General Division of the High Court may refuse to make an order under subsection (2) if, in the opinion of the General Division of the High Court, the fact that the place of arbitration is outside Singapore or likely to be outside Singapore when it is designated or determined makes it inappropriate to make the order.

(4) If the case is one of urgency, the General Division of the High Court may, on the application of a party or proposed party to the arbitral proceedings, make such orders under subsection (2) as the General Division of the High Court thinks necessary for the purpose of preserving evidence or assets.

(5) If the case is not one of urgency, the General Division of the High Court is to make an order under subsection (2) only on the application of a party to the arbitral

158   COURT POWERS IN AID OF ARBITRATION

proceedings (upon notice to the other parties and to the arbitral tribunal) made with the permission of the arbitral tribunal or the agreement in writing of the other parties.

(6) In every case, the General Division of the High Court is to make an order under subsection (2) only if or to the extent that the arbitral tribunal, and any arbitral or other institution or person vested by the parties with power in that regard, has no power or is unable for the time being to act effectively.

(7) An order made by the General Division of the High Court under subsection (2) ceases to have effect in whole or in part (as the case may be) if the arbitral tribunal, or any such arbitral or other institution or person having power to act in relation to the subject matter of the order, makes an order which expressly relates to the whole or part of the order under subsection (2).

<u>IAA, Section 13</u>

(1) Any party to an arbitration agreement may request for the issue of an order to attend or an order to produce documents.

(2) If the witness is in Singapore, the General Division of the High Court may order that—

(a) an order to attend be issued to compel the witness to attend before an arbitral tribunal and give evidence; or.

(b) an order to produce documents be issued to compel the witness to attend before an arbitral tribunal and produce specified documents.

(3) The General Division of the High Court may also issue an order under section 38 of the Prisons Act 1933 to bring up a prisoner for examination before an arbitral tribunal.

(4) A person must not be compelled under an order mentioned in subsection (1) to (2) (a) or (b) to produce any document which the person could not be compelled to produce on the trial of an action.

A. Section 12A—Court-ordered Interim Measures

12.01   The previous chapter addressed Section 12, which concerned the powers of a tribunal during the arbitral process, including its powers to grant interim measures. This chapter deals with the court's complementary powers to issue interim relief in aid of arbitration.[1] For a variety of reasons, parties to an arbitration agreement may also wish to seek interim measures from a local court. A party may consider that rights arising from an agreement is at risk of imminent and irreversible harm which cannot be addressed by the tribunal either because one has not been fully constituted or because third parties, who may not bound be by the tribunal's decisions, are involved. Section 12A, which

---

[1] Note though the Court's policy of minimal curial intervention. See e.g. *PT Pukuafu Indah and others v Newmont Indonesia Ltd and another* [2012] SGHC 187 [23], [24], [25].

B. LEGISLATIVE BACKGROUND TO SECTION 12A 159

was introduced as part of the 2009 Amendment to the International Arbitration Act (hereafter the 2009 Amendment), empowers the Singapore courts to grant certain interim measures to a party to an arbitration. Section 12A is consistent with Article 17J of the UNCITRAL Model Law on International Commercial Arbitration. Parts of Section 12A are also modelled after Section 44 of the English Arbitration Act.[2]

Sections 12A(1)–(3) set out the scope of the court's powers. The Act provides that a court is able to grant interim relief in respect of arbitrations to which Part II applies, that is, proceedings which qualify as 'international arbitrations' under Section 5, even if Singapore is not the seat of the arbitration.[3] As explained in further detail below, the court retains a discretion to refuse relief where the fact that the place of arbitration is outside of Singapore makes relief 'inappropriate'.[4] Second, a court is able to issue the same orders a tribunal may under Section 12(1)(c)–(i). Sections 12A(4)–(6) impose the relevant criteria for granting relief. In general terms, these include where the interim relief from the court is urgently needed, is consented to, or where the tribunal is unable to act. Section 12A(7) makes any court order subject to the arbitral tribunal, thereby giving primacy to the tribunal's decision making powers.

12.02

Section 12A does not alter the test that may be applicable to obtain a certain type of relief.[5] For instance, an application for a freezing injunction may require evidence of the risk of dissipation,[6] amongst other factors. Likewise, in the case of a prohibitory injunction, the applicant may need to fulfil the *American Cyanamide* test. In this context, Section 12A merely acts as a gateway provision permitting a party to an arbitration to seek relief from the Singapore court.

12.03

B. Legislative Background to Section 12A

Section 12A was introduced by the 2009 Amendment largely as a response to the Court of Appeal's decision in *Swift-Fortune*. Swift-Fortune had initially obtained a Mareva injunction but this was set aside by Prakash J in the High Court, whose decision was appealed against.[7] Prakash J set aside the injunction on the basis that the old Section 12(7) (now 12A(2)) of the IAA was intended to apply only to arbitrations that were seated in Singapore. As it turned out, after Prakash J's decision in *Swift-Fortune* but before the appeal in that case was heard, the High Court decided the case of *Front Carriers Ltd v Atlantic & Orient Shipping Corp*, where Ang J took a different view from Prakash J on

12.04

---

[2] *Five Ocean Corp v Cingler Ship Pte Ltd* [2015] SGHC 311 [40] (hereafter *Five Ocean Corp v Cingler Ship Pte Ltd*).
[3] IAA Section 12A(1).
[4] Ibid, Section 12A(3).
[5] See e.g. M. Hwang, 'The Applicable Standards for the Granting of Interim Injunctions in International Commercial Arbitrations Seated in Singapore' (2021) 1 Singapore Arbitration Journal 30.
[6] See e.g. *Solvadis Commodity GmbH v Affert Resources Pte Ltd* [2013] SGHC 217; See also *Dukkar SA v Thailand Integrated Services Pte Ltd* [2015] SGHC 234.
[7] *Swift-Fortune Ltd v Magnifica Marine SA* [2006] SGCA 42, [1] (hereafter *Swift-Fortune*).

160   COURT POWERS IN AID OF ARBITRATION

the Court's power to grant an interim order in aid of foreign arbitrations.[8] Ang J noted that under Section 4(10) of the Civil Law Act, the Court had such a power where it had personal jurisdiction over the defendant, and where 'there [was] a recognisable and justiciable right between the parties'[9] under Singapore law.[10]

12.05   In the *Swift-Fortune* appeal, the Court of Appeal therefore had to consider the scope of the powers of a Singapore Court to grant interim relief in respect of a foreign seated arbitration under the IAA.[11] After a careful review, the Court of Appeal concluded that the IAA did not empower the Singapore Court to grant interim injunctions for foreign-seated arbitrations.[12]

12.06   At the time, the unavailability of interim relief under the IAA for foreign-seated arbitration attracted some criticism on policy grounds.[13] In response to the issue, Parliament introduced new powers for court-ordered interim measures in support of foreign arbitrations via the 2009 Amendment Act.[14] It is worth noting that the Court's powers under the 2009 Amendment are limited to interim measures in support of arbitration[15] and 'do not extend to procedural or evidential matters dealing with the actual conduct of the arbitration itself—like discovery, interrogatories, or security for costs [as] these procedural matters should generally fall within the province of the arbitral tribunal and must be decided by the tribunal itself'.[16] Along with this, Section 12A(3) was inserted as a safeguard: it gives the Court a discretion to refuse to grant relief because it may be inappropriate to do so as the seat of arbitration is elsewhere.[17]

C. Section 12A(1)

12.07   Following the 2009 Amendment, Section 12A(1) now expressly empowers the High Court to grant interim relief in aid of an arbitration to which Part II of the Act applies,

---

[8] *Front Carriers Ltd v Atlantic & Orient Shipping Corp* [2006] 3 SLR(R) 854 [24] (hereafter *Front Carriers Ltd*).

[9] Ibid.

[10] A justiciable right refers to whether the subject matter of the dispute can be subject to the review of the Court; see L.S. Chan, 'Injunctions in Aid of Foreign Arbitration: The Singapore Experience' (2007) 3 Asian International Arbitration Journal 2, 144 (hereafter Chan 'Injunctions').

[11] The Court of Appeal was silent on whether such a power existed under Section 4(10) of the Civil Law Act. See *Swift-Fortune* (n 7) [93] et seq.

[12] Ibid, [40]–[58].

[13] R. Wong, 'Interim Relief in Aid of International Commercial Arbitration: A Critique on the International Arbitration Act' (2012) 24 Singapore Academy of Law Journal 522 (hereafter Wong, 'Interim Relief in Aid of International Commercial Arbitration'); J. Ho, 'Decoding Singapore's International Arbitration Act, Section 12(7), (2008) 24 Arbitration International 4, 609–14; see also for example Chan 'Injunctions' (n 10) 158, discussing the availability of granting Mareva relief irrespective of the arbitral seat in England and Wales. However, this power is limited, so as to not usurp the arbitral process. See e.g. *Company 1 v Company 2* [2017] EWHC 2319 (QB); *Petrochemical Logistics Ltd & Axel Krueger v PSB Alpha AG & Konstantinos Ghertsos* [2020] EWHC 975 (Comm).

[14] Explanatory Statement to the Arbitration Bill.

[15] Parliament Sitting on 19 October 2009, second reading of the International Arbitration (Amendment) Bill, Minister for Law, 3 [7] (hereafter Amendment Bill Second Reading).

[16] Ibid; see also *Equinox Offshore Accommodation Ltd v Richshore Marine Supplies Pte Ltd* [2010] SGHC 122.

[17] This is similar to Civil Judgments and Jurisdictions Act Section 25; see also Wong, 'Interim Relief in Aid of International Commercial Arbitration' (n 13) 499 [75]; *ETI Euro Telecom International NV v Republic of Bolivia* [2008] EWCA Civ 880; [2008] 2 Lloyd's Rep. 421 [78].

D. Section 12A(2)—Scope of the Powers of a Court to Grant Interim Relief

Section 12A(2) reflects the High Court's ability to grant the types of orders specified in Section 12(1)(c)–(j).[18] This provision clarifies that the scope of court-ordered relief generally mirrors that of a tribunal, with the exception of some aspects of procedure such as security for costs and the discovery of documents, which fall outside of the scope of the court's powers.

12.08

E. Section 12A(2)—Anti-suit Injunctions

Of the types of relief sought in the Singapore Court, anti-suit injunctions have attracted a fair amount of judicial treatment. In the context of Section 12A(2), the question arises as to whether the Court has the power to grant permanent and interim anti-suit injunctions, and this has given rise to a number of important decisions.

12.09

1. *R1 International Pte Ltd v Lonstroff AG*

R1 International Pte Ltd v Lonstroff AG[19] concerned an application for a permanent anti-suit injunction. R1 was a Singapore company operating in the business of wholesale trading and brokering of rubber. It conducted business with Lonstroff, a Swiss company, through its authorised agent R1 Europe GmbH. Lonstroff was a company operating in the processing of natural rubber and plastics.[20] R1 and Lonstroff contracted for R1 to supply rubber to Lonstroff via R1 Europe, through five orders. The dispute arose in relation to the second order, where Lonstroff complained about the smell of rubber supplied and alleged a breach of contract.[21] As a result, Lonstroff commenced litigation proceedings against R1 International in Switzerland. In turn, R1 requested the Singapore Commodity Exchange (SICOM) to 'set up an arbitration tribunal to resolve the dispute'.[22] However, SICOM stated that such request would only be considered

12.10

---

[18] Subparagraph (j) was added by way of the International Arbitration (Amendment) Act No. 32 of 2020, which extends the powers under Section 12A(2) to enforcing confidentiality obligations.

[19] *R1 International Pte Ltd v Lonstroff AG* [2014] 3 SLR 166 (hereafter *R1 International v Lonstroff*).

[20] Ibid, [5]–[6].

[21] Ibid, [15].

[22] Ibid, [16].

162 COURT POWERS IN AID OF ARBITRATION

when the proceedings before the Swiss courts were suspended and if the parties agreed to refer the dispute to SICOM.

12.11 Following this, R1 filed proceedings in the Singapore courts to obtain an anti-suit injunction preventing Lonstroff from continuing legal proceedings in Switzerland.[23] R1 was granted an interim injunction and Lonstroff applied for the decision to be reversed. On appeal, R1 then applied to make anti-suit relief permanent.

12.12 The first question for the Court concerned whether a separate contract note, containing the arbitration clause relied on, was incorporated into the main contract.[24] R1 failed at this hurdle, and the question of the appropriateness of a permanent anti-suit injunction was not strictly in issue.[25] Nonetheless, the High Court took the opportunity to consider: (i) whether it had the power to grant a permanent anti-suit injunction and, if so, what the source of power was; and (ii) if such power was available, how should it be exercised.[26]

12.13 R1 argued that Sections 12A(2) and 12A(4) should be read together with Sections 12(1) (c)–(i), which did not confine the court to just granting Anton Piller orders or Mareva injunctions. In its view, as long as it was necessary for the preservation of evidence or assets, the court had the power to grant injunctions, including permanent anti-suit injunctions.[27]

12.14 Prakash J accepted that Section 12A(2) read with Section 12(1)(i) of the IAA permitted interim injunctions in aid of both domestic and foreign international arbitration since such relief is generally given in aid of arbitration proceedings where a tribunal will eventually 'give ... orders that permanently resolve the dispute'.[28] However, she went on to hold that Section 12(1)(i) did not extend to permanent anti-suit injunctions in relation to arbitration proceedings. Instead, in her view, the source of the court's power in respect of permanent relief emanated from Section 4(10) of the Civil Law Act (CLA). While Section 4(10) of the CLA is normally used by local courts to grant permanent anti-suit injunction in aid of local proceedings, Prakash J considered that there was no reason why this power could not be exercised to make permanent anti-suit injunctions in aid of domestic international arbitration proceedings where the courts already had the power pursuant to Section 12A(2), read with Section 12(1)(i) of the IAA, to grant interim anti-suit injunctions.[29] Clear words would be required if the IAA was to abrogate Section 4(10) CLA.[30]

---

[23] Ibid, [17].

[24] Prakash J found that R1 did not establish that the arbitration agreement was incorporated by previous course of dealing or trade practice. This issue was later dealt with by the Court of Appeal in *R1 International Pte Ltd v Lonstroff AG* [2015] 1 SLR 521, where the court found that the relevant arbitration agreement, found in a contract note, was indeed incorporated into the main contract.

[25] *R1 International v Lonstroff)* (n 19) [34]–[36].

[26] Ibid, [18].

[27] The court also relied on Principle 3 found in paragraph 15 of the UNCITRAL Report on the work of its thirty-third session which supported the availability of provisional and protective measures in respect of domestic and foreign international arbitrations in general (hereafter UNCITRAL Report).

[28] Ibid, 42.

[29] Ibid, 43.

[30] Ibid, 44.

E. SECTION 12A(2)—ANTI-SUIT INJUNCTIONS   163

Prakash J referred to the UK Supreme Court decision of *AES Ust-Kamenogorsk*   **12.15**
Hydropower Plant LLP v Ust-Kamenogorsk Hydropower Plant JSC,[31] which considered a similar issue involving the equivalent English provisions. The question before the Supreme Court was whether Section 44 of the Arbitration Act 1996 qualified
the general power of the English High Court to grant injunctions under Section 37 of
the Senior Courts Act 1981. The Supreme Court held that, since the Arbitration Act
1996 did not apply where proceedings have not started, any injunction must be granted
under Section 37 of the Senior Courts Act 1981. The court's power to grant an interim
injunction under Section 44 of the Arbitration Act 1996 was not intended to exclude,
limit, or qualify the court's general power under Section 37 of the Senior Courts Act
1981 to act outside the scope of the Arbitration Act 1996.[32] Given that the language
in Section 37 of the Senior Courts Act was very similar to that of Section 10(4) CLA,
Prakash J reasoned that the IAA did not limit the scope and breath of the court's powers
under Section 4(10) CLA.[33]

2. *Hilton International v Sun Travels*

In contrast, the Court of Appeal in *Swift-Fortune Ltd v Magnifica Marine SA*[34] and the   **12.16**
High Court in *Hilton International Manage (Maldives) Pvt Ltd v Sun Travels & Tours
Pvt Ltd*[35] both observed that the court's power to grant *interim* injunctions is derived
from Section 4(10) CLA, while the power to grant *permanent* injunctions is derived
from Section 18(2) of the Supreme Court of Judicature Act (SCJA), read together with
paragraph 14 of the First Schedule to the SCJA.

In *Hilton International Manage (Maldives) Pvt Ltd v Sun Travels & Tours Pvt Ltd*,[36] the   **12.17**
dispute arose out of a management agreement. During the course of the agreement
the parties encountered various differences. Shortly after it purported to terminate the
contract in 2013, Hilton commenced an International Chamber of Commerce (ICC)
arbitration seated in Singapore and then applied for a permanent injunction seeking
to restrain the defendant from instituting or continuing proceedings in a foreign court,
'in breach of the arbitration agreement'.[37] A Partial Award was rendered in favour of
Hilton on 27 May 2015, followed by a Final Award on 17 August 2015, also in its favour.

Sun Travels & Tours commenced proceedings in the Maldivian courts in parallel with   **12.18**
the arbitration, and successfully obtained a judgement in a civil action on 9 March

---

[31] *AES Ust-Kamenogorsk Hydropower Plant LLP v Ust-Kamenogorsk Hydropower Plant JSC* [2013] 1 WLR 1889
(hereafter *AES Ust-Kamenogorsk Hydropower Plant LLP*).
[32] Ibid, [48].
[33] *R1 International v Lonstroff* (n 19).
[34] *Swift-Fortune* (n 7) [64].
[35] *Hilton International Manage (Maldives) Pvt Ltd v Sun Travels & Tours Pvt Ltd* [2018] SGHC 56 [38]–[43]
(hereafter *Hilton International Manage (Maldives) Pvt Ltd*).
[36] Ibid.
[37] Ibid, [1].

164 COURT POWERS IN AID OF ARBITRATION

2017. Hilton appealed against the Maldivian judgment, which contradicted the outcome of the arbitration. Subsequently, Hilton applied to the Singapore High Court on 24 July 2017 seeking a permanent anti-suit injunction restraining Sun Travel & Tours from commencing or proceeding with any action against it in the Maldivian courts, in relation to disputes that were subject to the arbitration agreement.[38] It also sought declarations that the arbitral awards were final and binding, and that the claim brought in the Maldivian courts were in breach of the arbitration agreements. The High Court issued: (i) a permanent anti-suit injunction; (ii) a declaration that the arbitral awards were final, valid, and binding on the parties; and (iii) a declaration that the Maldivian action in respect of disputes to have arisen out of or in connection with the agreement to be in breach of the arbitration agreement contained in the main agreement.

12.19 On the source of the court's power to issue a permanent anti-suit injunction, the High Court considered that it was not bound by *R1 International* where the Court observed, in *obiter*, that the source of its power to issue permanent anti-suit injunctions emanated from Section 4(10) of the CLA.[39] In contrast, the High Court in *Hilton* adopted the observations of the Court of Appeal in *Swift-Fortune*—which were also in *obiter*—that Section 4(10) CLA only gave the power to grant interlocutory injunctions instead of a permanent injunction, and that the court's power to grant a permanent anti-suit injunction instead stemmed from Section 18(2) of the SCJA, read with paragraph 14 of the First Schedule to the SCJA.[40]

12.20 On appeal, the Court of Appeal upheld the declaratory reliefs but discharged the anti-suit injunction on the basis that the injunction sought was in fact an anti-enforcement injunction which was sought too late in the day.[41] The Court of Appeal stressed that, unlike typical anti-suit injunctions, urgency was particularly critical in anti-enforcement injunctions. During the period of any delay, a foreign court may have expanded a vast amount of judicial time and cost on the enforcement action.[42] Further, an anti-enforcement injunction after the issuance of a court judgment would be likely to be an indirect interference with the execution of the judgment in the jurisdiction where the judgment was given, and where the judgment can be expected to be obeyed.[43] Accordingly, it was only in exceptional circumstances such as fraud where a court may, notwithstanding delay, grant an anti-enforcement injunction.

12.21 Of note, the Court of Appeal did not discuss the source of power for permanent anti-suit injunctions. It did, however, discuss the source of its power to grant declaratory relief. It explained that Section 18 of the SCJA, read with paragraph 14 of the First Schedule to the SCJA, gave the Court wide powers to grant all types of reliefs and remedies available

---

[38] Ibid, [1], [2], [20].

[39] Ibid, [1], [39], [40], [41].

[40] Ibid, [40]–[43].

[41] *Sun Travels & Tours Pvt Ltd v Hilton International Manage (Maldives) Pvt Ltd* [2019] 1 SLR 732 (hereafter *Sun Travels & Tours Pvt Ltd*).

[42] Ibid, [78] and [114(b)].

[43] Ibid, [89], [97], [114(c)].

at law or equity.[44] This power to grant declaratory relief was not unfettered and had to be exercised consistently with other express legislation. This is consistent with Article 5 of the Model Law which provided that 'in matters governed by [the Model Law], no court shall intervene except where so provided in the Model Law'.[45] Hence, in situations that are expressly regulated by the IAA, courts should only intervene where so provided in the IAA. The purpose was not to promote hostility towards judicial intervention, but to satisfy the need for certainty as to when judicial intervention would be permissible.[46] On the facts, the Court of Appeal found that there is nothing in the IAA or Model Law preventing it from granting declaratory relief, and therefore upheld the High Court's declaratory reliefs.[47]

3. Permanent Injunctions—The Source of the Power

As the Court of Appeal in *Hilton* did not resolve the question of the source of the power to grant a permanent injunction, it may be helpful to consider the history behind both the CLA and SCJA provisions. **12.22**

The historical origins of Section 4(10) of the CLA and the English equivalent, Section 37(1) of the Senior Courts Act 1981, can be traced back to the Supreme Court of Judicature Act 1873. Section 25(8) of this Act provides that **12.23**

> a mandamus or an injunction may be granted or a receiver appointed by an interlocutory Order of the Court in all cases in which it shall appear to the Court to be just or convenient that such Order should be made; and any such Order may be made either unconditionally or upon such terms and conditions as the Court shall think just: and if an injunction is *asked, either before, or at, or after the hearing of any cause or matter, to prevent any threatened or apprehended waste or trespass, such injunction may be granted,* if the Court shall think fit, whether the person against whom such injunction is sought is or is not in possession under any claim of title or otherwise, or (if out of possession) does or does not claim a right to do the act sought to be restrained under any colour of title; and whether the estates claimed by both or by either of the parties are legal or equitable.

A plain reading of the phrases 'injunction' and 'asked, either before, or at, or after the hearing of any cause or matter, to prevent any threatened or apprehended waste or trespass, such injunction may be granted' suggests that the power conferred on the High Court is wide enough to cover both interim and permanent injunctions.[48] **12.24**

---

[44] Ibid, [133].

[45] Ibid, [134].

[46] Ibid, [134] (citing *LW Infrastructure Pte Ltd v Lim Chin San Contractors Pte Ltd* [2013] 1 SLR 125 at [36]).

[47] Ibid, [135].

[48] Supreme Court of Judicature Act 1873, Section 23 ('The jurisdiction by this Act transferred to the said High Court of Justice and the said Court of Appeal respectively shall be exercised (so far as regards procedure and practice) in the manner provided by this Act, or by such Rules and Orders of Court as may be made pursuant to this Act; and where no special provision is contained in this Act or in any such Rules or Orders of Court with reference

166 COURT POWERS IN AID OF ARBITRATION

12.25 This view is supported by the UK Supreme Court in *AES Ust-Kamenogorsk Hydropower Plant LLP v Ust-Kamenogorsk Hydropower Plant JSC*[49] where it held that Section 37(1) of the Senior Courts Act 1981 gave the High Court the 'jurisdiction to grant an injunction (whether interlocutory or final) in all cases in which it appears to the court just and convenient to do so'.[50] For completeness, Section 37(1) of the Senior Courts Act 1981 provides that 'the High Court may by order (whether interlocutory or final) grant an injunction or appoint a receiver in all cases in which it appears to the court to be just and convenient to do so'.

12.26 Section 4(10) CLA is phrased in similar terms as Section 25(8) Judicature Act 1873 and was enacted in Singapore through the Civil Law Ordinance 1878.[51] Section 4(10) CLA provides that:

> a Mandatory Order or an injunction may be granted or a receiver appointed by an interlocutory order of the court, either unconditionally or upon such terms and conditions as the court thinks just, in all cases in which it appears to the court to be just or convenient that such order should be made.

12.27 Accordingly, it is reasonable to conclude that Section 4(10) of the CLA confers the same scope of powers to the Singapore High Court that its predecessor, Section 25(8) of the Supreme Court of Judicature Act 1873, conferred on the English High Court. With respect, the Singapore High Court's decision in *RI International* therefore appears to be more consistent with the text and legislative history of Section 4(10) CLA.

12.28 Contrast this with the relevant SCJA provisions. Section 18(2) of the SCJA first provides that 'the High Court shall have the powers set out in the First Schedule'. Turning to the First Schedule, paragraph 14 states that the High Court has the 'power to grant all reliefs and remedies at law and in equity, including damages in addition to, or in substitution for, an injunction or specific performance'. This provision was recently discussed in *Turf Club Auto Emporium Pte Ltd v Yeo Boong Hua*[52] and *I-Admin (Singapore) Pte Ltd v Hong Ying Ting and others*,[53] both of which dealt with the court's power to award damages in lieu of specific performance or injunctions.[54]

12.29 The words used in Section 18(2) of the SCJA and paragraph 14 of its First Schedule are *in pari materia* to Section 50 of the UK Senior Courts Act 1981, which provides that 'where

---

thereto, it shall be exercised as nearly as may be in the same manner as the same might have been exercised by the respective Courts from which such jurisdiction shall have been transferred, or by any of such Courts.').

[49] *AES Ust-Kamenogorsk Hydropower Plant LLP* (n 31).

[50] Ibid, [27] (citing the Court of Appeal in *West Tankers* [2007] 1 Lloyd's Rep 391).

[51] G.W. Bartholomew, 'The Singapore Statute Book' (1984) 26 Malaya Law Review 1, 12; P. Mahy and I. Ramsey, 'Legal Transplants and Adaptation in a Colonial Setting: Company Law in British Malaya' (2014) Singapore Journal of Legal Studies 123, 130–1.

[52] *Turf Club Auto Emporium Pte Ltd v Yeo Boong Hua* [2018] 2 SLR 655 (hereafter *Turf Club*).

[53] *I-Admin (Singapore) Pte Ltd v Hong Ying Ting and others* [2020] 1 SLR 1130 (hereafter *I-Admin (Singapore) Pte Ltd*).

[54] Ibid, [77]; *Turf Club* (n 52) [141] and [286].

the Court of Appeal or the High Court has jurisdiction to entertain an application for an injunction or specific performance, it may award damages in addition to, or in substitution for, an injunction or specific performance.[55] While it may be possible to ground the Court's powers to grant injunction relief, including permanent injunctive relief in aid of arbitration, in Section 18 of the SCJA, that provision appears to be focused on the power of the court to award damages in lieu of an injunction.

F. Section 12A(3)

12.30 Section 12A(3) should be read in tandem with Section 12A(1). In effect, while the Court now has the power to grant interim relief, including in aid of foreign arbitrations, it may decline doing so if the judge concludes, in his or her discretion, that it would be inappropriate to do so.[56]

12.31 A public consultation was conducted before the 2009 Amendment was introduced.[57] In response to the proposed Section 12A(3), practitioners commented that the use of 'inappropriate' may be too ambiguous a test. It was instead proposed that for the Court to grant relief in aid of foreign-seated arbitrations, the following criteria be met: (i) that the order will not offend the principle of comity; (ii) the High Court must have personal jurisdiction over the respondent; and (iii) the applicant must have a justiciable cause of action against the respondent under Singapore law. In response, the Ministry of Law considered that no amendments were necessary as there was sufficient case law to guide the Court in its exercise of discretion. Of interest, however, was its position on the proposed justiciability requirement. It explained that Section 12A(3) was intended to 'create a provision ... wider than the House of Lords' decision in *Channel Tunnel* [1993] AC 334' where it was held that injunctive relief could only be given if the cause of action was justiciable under English law.[58]

12.32 Section 12A(3) may be compared with Section 44 read with Section 2(3) of the English Arbitration Act 1996, which also carries the 'inappropriate' proviso.[59] *Malhotra v Malhotra* is an example of when it may be inappropriate to grant relief in support of a foreign-seated arbitration.[60] There, the applicant sought an anti-suit injunction to

---

[55] See also *Lawrence and another v Fen Tigers Ltd and others* [2014] AC 822 [101].

[56] One reason it may be inappropriate is because the seat of the arbitration is the most suitable court to issue relief: see *Econet Wireless Ltd v Vee Networks Ltd* [2006] 2 Lloyd's Rep 428 [19].

[57] International Arbitration (Amendment Bill), Ministry of Law's Responses to Public Feedback Received, <https://www.mlaw.gov.sg/files/linkclick1e3a.pdf> accessed 22 June 2022 (hereafter *Ministry of Law's Responses to Public Feedback*).

[58] Ibid, 4.

[59] Conceptually, Section 12A(3) of the IAA and Section 44 of the UK Arbitration Act 1996 are similar to Section 25(2) of the English Civil Judgments and Jurisdiction Act 1982, under which the English Court would refrain from injunctive relief in aid of foreign proceedings if such relief was not 'expedient'. See e.g. *ETI Euro Telecom International NV v Republic of Bolivia* [2008] EWCA Civ 880; [2008] 2 Lloyd's Rep. 421 [78]. The Court of Appeal granted the freezing order under Section 25 of the Civil Jurisdiction and Judgments Act 1982 as the English proceedings were not related to any substantive proceedings in New York.

[60] *Malhotra v Malhotra* [2012] EWHC 3020 (Comm) (Walker J).

168 COURT POWERS IN AID OF ARBITRATION

restrain Indian proceedings, allegedly in breach of an arbitration agreement stipulating Switzerland as the seat. As the only nexus to England was the substantive governing law, Walker J considered that it was inappropriate for relief to be granted by the English Courts as the Indian Courts would be better suited to manage the process. In all cases, there should at least be some connection to Singapore[61] or possibly, some form of exceptional necessity for the Singapore Courts to act.[62]

G. Section 12A(4)—Urgency

12.33 Section 12A(4)–(6) sets out the criteria for the grant of court-ordered interim relief. Section 12A(4) first states that such relief can be granted if the case is one of urgency. Where those criteria are satisfied, orders which are 'necessary for the purpose of preserving evidence or assets' may be made.

12.34 The urgency criterion was discussed at length in *Five Ocean Corp v Cingler Ship*, where the High Court exercised its power under Section 12A to grant an interim injunction to enjoin the sale of cargo. The relevant facts are as follows: Five Ocean Corp time-chartered a vessel from its shipowner for a one-time trip from Indonesia to India. Shortly after, Five Ocean Corp voyage-chartered the vessel to Cingler Ship, which then voyage-chartered the vessel to a third party. The head voyage charter between Five Ocean Corp and Cingler Ship contained a clause stipulating that the owner would have a lien over the cargo, as well as all other amounts due. Subsequently, Cingler Ship failed to pay freight to Five Ocean Corp. Therefore, Five Ocean Corp and the shipowner gave 'notice of lien and the exercise of lien over the cargo to the interested parties and the vessel remained in international waters to give effect to the exercise of the lien'. The cargo deteriorated, and both the vessel and the crew were at risk. Therefore, and pursuant to the dispute resolution clause in the contract, Five Ocean Corp filed a notice of arbitration but did not obtain a response from Cingler. Five Ocean Corp then made an application to the Singapore courts to enjoin the sale of the cargo under Section 12A(4).[63]

12.35 On the issue of urgency, the applicant cited the following factors: (i) the crew had been on board the vessel for four months and were falling ill; (ii) there was a lack of fresh food, water, and medical supplies; (iii) overheating of the cargo had been detected; and (iv) the monsoon season at the Bay of Bengal was exacerbating the already dire situation.[64] In these circumstances, Belinda Ang J concluded that the order for sale was

---

[61] See also *Mobil Cerro Negro Ltd v Petroleos de Venezuela SA* [2008] 1 Lloyd's Rep 684; *Recydia Atik Yonetimi Yenilenebilir Enerji Uretimi Nakliye Ve Lojisk Ik Hizmetleri San Ve Ticaret AZ v Collins-Thomas* [2018] EWHC 2506 (Comm); *U&M Mining Zambia Ltd v Konkola Copper Mines plc* [2013] 2 Lloyd's Rep 218.

[62] See e.g. *Motorola Credit Corporation v Uzan* [2003] EWCA Civ 752; *Republic of Haiti v Duvalier* [1989] 2 WLR 261; *Credit Suisse Fides Trust SA v Cuoghi* [1998] QB 818.

[63] *Five Ocean Corp v Cingler Ship Pte Ltd* (n 2).

[64] Ibid, [56].

H. SECTION 12A(4)—RIGHTS AND ASSETS 169

'necessary' to preserve Five Ocean Corp's right to detain possession of the cargo, and noted that there were no reasonable alternatives.[65] Ang J then provided the following reasons: (i) on the condition of the cargo, there was a risk that the value would diminish over time; and (ii) there was 'no end in sight to stop this impasse that arose from a confluence of matters'.[66] The elements of urgency under Section 12A(4) IAA were deemed to be satisfied.

The question of urgency may also need to be assessed in the context of the availability **12.36** of emergency arbitrations under the applicable rules. This is discussed further below in the commentary to Section 12A(6).

H. Section 12A(4)—Rights and Assets

The final part of Section 12A(4) states that the High Court or Judge may make such **12.37** orders necessary for the purpose of 'preserving evidence or assets'. Although this particular phrase is unique, it broadly mirrors the matters covered by Section 12(1)(c)–(i).

The meaning of the word 'asset' was discussed in *Maldives Airports Co. v GMR Male* **12.38** *International Airport.* There, *Maldives Airports Co.* appealed against a decision by the High Court to grant an interim injunction, which restrained the appellants, Maldives Airports, and the Republic of the Maldives from, *inter alia*, directly or indirectly interfering with the performance by Maldives Airport Co. of its obligations under the Concession Agreement.[67]

In its arguments to retain the injunction, Maldives Airport Co. asserted that it was ne- **12.39** cessary for 'the purpose of preserving evidence or assets' and that Section 12A(4) must be construed widely to include its 'contractual right' to operate the airport.[68] It relied on the English Court of Appeal decision *Cetelem SA v Roust Holdings Ltd*, [2005] 1 WLR 3555 (hereinafter *Cetelem*)[69] to support its position. In *Cetelem*, the English Court had granted a freezing injunction which restrained Roust Holdings Ltd from disposing (or otherwise dealing) with its assets, which included shares. As regards the term 'assets', Clarke LJ (as he then was) accepted that it included choses in action,[70] which may not be physical or tangible assets. On that basis, Clarke LJ reasoned that there was no reason not to include a contractual right as an 'asset' within Section 44(3) of the Arbitration Act 1996.

---

[65] Ang J relied on *Maldives Airports Co. Ltd and another v GMR Male International Airport Pte Ltd* [2013] 2 SLR 449, [44] (hereafter *Maldives Airports*).

[66] *Five Ocean Corp v Cingler Ship Pte Ltd.* (n 2) [63].

[67] *Maldives Airports* (n 65) [8]

[68] Ibid, [36].

[69] *Cetelem SA v Roust Holdings Ltd* [2005] 1 WLR 3555 (hereafter *Cetelem*).

[70] Ibid, [37]. In general, a chose in action is a personal right which can only be claimed or enforced by action and not by taking physical possession. A chose in action is an asset which cannot be physically held. See e.g. *Torkington v Magee* [1902] 2 KB 427.

170   COURT POWERS IN AID OF ARBITRATION

12.40   Notably, *Cetelem* was relied on by the Ministry of Law when formulating the International Arbitration (Amendment) Bill, which introduced Section 12A into the IAA. In a press release, the Ministry highlighted that a wide definition of assets should be used.[71] The same explanation was given by the Minister of Law during a debate on the Bill[72] and was included in the Explanatory Statement to the Bill.

12.41   Unsurprisingly, the Court of Appeal[73] noted that 'extrinsic evidence indicative of Parliament's intention vis-a-vis the scope of the term "assets" strongly suggests that the holding in *Cetelem* was intended to govern the proper interpretation of Section 12A(4) of the IAA [and] Section 12A(4) of the IAA encompasses rights under a contract'. The Court of Appeal explained, however, that the inclusion of choses in action 'must be confined to such contractual rights as lend themselves to being preserved'. If a party faced with an alleged breach is not entitled to preserve its right to have the contract performed, 'the primary obligation to perform the contract gives way to a secondary obligation to pay damages'.[74] As the contractual right to operate the airport was not a right which could be preserved, the appeal was allowed and the injunction discharged.

12.42   In *Five Ocean Corp v Cingler Ship*,[75] Five Ocean Corp applied for an injunction to enjoin the sale of cargo.[76] Cingler Ship did not oppose the application. In relation to Section 12A(4), the question before the Court was whether '[Five Ocean Corp's] right to detain possession [was] an "asset" within the meaning of section 12A(4)?'[77] In reaching its conclusion, the court relied upon *Maldives Airports*.[78] Five Ocean Corp had argued that its contractual right to a lien over the cargo in question fell within the definition of assets in Section 12A(4) as its lien was 'in the nature of security and may be defined as a right to retain possession of goods or documents belonging to another until all claims against that other are satisfied'.[79] The High Court agreed, holding that because Five Ocean Corp had a right to detain the cargo, this qualified as an 'asset' within the meaning of Section 12A(4) of the IAA.[80]

12.43   In the same case, the Court was asked to consider if the right to detain possession of the cargo could be preserved through an order for sale of the cargo.[81] Ang J noted that 'at first glance, an order for the sale of the Cargo appears inconsistent with the concept

---

[71] According to the press release, the Ministry of Law 'did not consider it necessary to delete the suggested words. Instead [they] clarified in the Explanatory Statement to the Bill that a wide meaning of the term "assets" be adopted to include choses in action and rights under a contract (as decided by the English Court of Appeal in *Cetelem*). According to the Explanatory Statement to the Arbitration Bill 2009, it is intended that a wide meaning of the term "assets" be adopted to include choses in action and rights under a contract.' 10.

[72] Singapore Parliamentary Debates, Official Report, Eleventh Parliament dated 19 October 2009, vol 86, col 1628.

[73] *Maldives Airports* (n 65).

[74] Ibid, [39].

[75] *Five Ocean Corp v Cingler Ship Pte Ltd.* (n 2).

[76] Pursuant to IAA Sections 12A(4) and 12(1)(d).

[77] *Five Ocean Corp v Cingler Ship Pte Ltd.* (n 2).

[78] Ibid, [42].

[79] Ibid, [44].

[80] Ibid, [46].

[81] Ibid, [47].

of a right to detain which typically does not give rise to a right to sell unless expressly provided for in the contract'.[82] She then concluded that Five Ocean Corp's right to detain possession could be 'effectively preserved through an order of sale'[83] as the asset it was seeking to preserve was the value of the cargo and not the cargo itself.[84] Ang J relied on *Castleton Commodities*[85] where Waksman J accepted that the claimant was entitled to the proceeds of sale, and ultimately granted the order for sums to be paid out to the claimant.[86]

I. Section 12A(5)

Section 12A(5) serves as an exception to Section 12A(4). Even though an application **12.44** may not be urgent, a court may still grant interim relief in two circumstances, namely where: (i) the party has given notice to the other parties and the arbitral tribunal; and (ii) where the arbitral tribunal has given permission to proceed, or the parties have given their consent.[87]

Section 12A(5) mirrors Section 44(4) of the English Arbitration Act, and some **12.45** recent English cases may therefore be instructive. In *VTB Commodities Trading DAC v JSC Antipinsky Refinery*, VTB applied to continue an injunction granted in April 2019 against JSC Antipinsky on a 'without notice' basis. In order for the Court to have jurisdiction over VTB's application, VTB required permission from the Tribunal and by virtue of its Agreement with JSC Antipinsky, to make a Continuation Application for the injunction under Section 44(4). However, VTB did not obtain the Tribunal's permission, and it did not rely upon its agreement with JSC Antipinsky. Therefore, the Court found that it did not have jurisdiction to act on VTB's injunction application, as it did not meet the requirements of Section 44(4).[88] The importance of meeting the conditions of Section 44(4) was reiterated in *A and B v C, D and E*. In this case, the Court of Appeal held, in passing, that 'if the thresholds or gateways are satisfied, as they were in this case, there is nothing in any of the subsections relied upon which restricts the power of the Court' to make an order it deems necessary.[89]

---

[82] Ibid.

[83] Ibid, [55].

[84] Ibid, [48], citing *Cetelem* (n 69), [65].

[85] Ibid, [49] (quoting Waksman J in *Castleton Commodities*, at [9]).

[86] Ibid, [50]. See also *The Stelios B*, and *Emilia Shipping Inc v State Enterprise for Pulp and Paper Industries* [1991] 1 SLR(R) 411. Here Chan J recognised that although a lien did not confer a right of sale, the court had the power to order the sale of the cargo pursuant to Order 29 Rule 4 of the Rules of the Supreme Court 1970, which provided for the sale of moveable property the subject matter of an action 'which is of a perishable nature or likely to deteriorate if kept or which for any other good reason is desirable to sell forth with'.

[87] International Arbitration Act 2009 Amendment Section 12A(5); see also *H&C S Holdings Pte Ltd v Mount Eastern Holdings Resources Co. Limited* [2015] SGHC 323 where the provision is mentioned in passing.

[88] *VTB Commodities Trading DAC v JSC Antipinsky Refinery* [2020] EWHC 72 (Comm), [39].

[89] *A and B v C, D and E* [2020] EWCA Civ 409, [36].

172   COURT POWERS IN AID OF ARBITRATION

J. Section 12A(6)

12.46 A court may grant interim relief 'only if or to the extent' that a tribunal or institution vested with the relevant power 'has no power or is unable for the time being to act effectively'. As Section 12A(6) is in *pari materia* with Section 44(5) of the UK's Arbitration Act 1996, English case law may be relevant.[90]

12.47 In *Starlight Shipping Co & Anor v Tai Ping Insurance Co Ltd, Hubei Branch & Anor*,[91] the claimant owners and managers sought an anti-suit injunction to restrain the defendant cargo insurers from continuing proceedings in the Wuhan maritime court, which had been brought in breach of an arbitration clause. In parallel, the claimants and defendants had appointed their arbitrator under London Maritime Arbitrators Association (LMAA) terms, but the third arbitrator had not been appointed. Notably, LMAA terms vested sufficient power in the two already appointed arbitrators to make a final award restraining the pursuit of Chinese proceedings, but did not give the power to arbitrators to issue interim injunctions.

12.48 Cooke J considered that the arbitrators were unable for the time being to act effectively under Section 44(5) as they would have to appoint a third arbitrator in order to obviate any potential stalemate which may arise should the two already appointed arbitrators disagree. There was also evidence that one of the two appointed arbitrators would not be able to hear any application within that month, and would not be able to produce a final award on the subject within the relevant time scale. Considering that the injunction was 'plainly necessary to preserve the owners' right to arbitrate the dispute with the cargo owners and insurers', Cooke J issued an anti-suit injunction 'to cover the position up to such time when the arbitration tribunal can itself determine this matter and make a final award in relation to the restraining orders sought'.[92]

12.49 Likewise, in *Pacific Maritime (Asia) Ltd v Holystone Overseas Ltd*, a freezing injunction was previously ordered, restraining the defendant from removing from England and Wales, disposing, dealing with, or diminishing the value of any of its assets or its vessel. The defendant then applied to vary the freezing injunction as an arbitral tribunal was now constituted and should decide the appropriate relief. The arbitral tribunal also had the power to make an order for the detention of the vessel, which would provide the same relief as a freezing order.[93] Nevertheless, Clarke J considered that the arbitral tribunal lacked the power to act effectively in relation to the preservation of assets, because any such order would not bind third parties or be buttressed by sufficient

---

[90] Relevant English case law includes *Gerald Metals SA v Trustees of the Timis Trust & others* [2016] EWHC 2327, and *Seele Middle East Fze v Drake & Scull Int Sa Co* [2013] EWHC 4350 (TCC). However, the court will not attempt to second guess what order the tribunal might make when it is able to act: *Permasteelisa Japan KK v Bouyguesstroi* [2007] EWHC 3508; *Sabmiller Africa BV v Tanzania Breweries Ltd* [2009] EWHC 2140.

[91] *Starlight Shipping Co & Anor v Tai Ping Insurance Co Ltd, Hubei Branch & Anor* [2007] EWHC 1893 (Comm) (hereafter *Starlight Shipping Co & Anor*).

[92] Ibid, [27].

[93] *Pacific Maritime (Asia) Ltd v Holystone Overseas Ltd* [2007] EWHC 2319 (Comm), [25], (hereafter *Pacific Maritime (Asia) Ltd*).

sanctions.[94] With the freezing injunction issued by the court in place, third parties, such as harbour authorities, would be unlikely to assist with removing the vessel if it is aware that there was a court issued injunction.[95]

In *Seele Middle East Fze v Drake & Scull Int Sa Co*,[96] the TCC granted an interim in- **12.50** junction under Section 44 of the English Arbitration Act 1996. The dispute arose out of a construction project, where the defendant asked the claimant (the subcontractor) to provide a schedule demonstrating how it would remedy its breach of contract. The defendant then prevented the subcontractor from returning back on site until the schedule was completed. The contract provided for arbitration under the ICC rules to be seated in London. The subcontractor then applied to the Technology and Construction Court (TCC) for an interim injunction allowing it to access the site and remove its documents, in order to prepare the schedule. Here, Ramsey J (as he then was) held that the requirement of urgency under Section 44(3) was satisfied because the subcontractor needed the documents to prepare the schedule, or face termination. On Section 44(5), although the ICC arbitration was commenced, it was not subject to the changes in those rules allowing an emergency arbitrator to deal with applications. There was therefore no tribunal in a position to act effectively.[97]

On the other hand, in *Ikon International (HK) Holdings Public Company Limited v Ikon* **12.51** *Finance Limited and Ors*, urgent court relief was rejected. In *Ikon*, the dispute arose from a joint venture agreement that contained an arbitration agreement. The claimant commenced London Court of International Arbitration (LCIA) arbitration and then sought an injunction from the English High Court to prohibit the defendants from procuring or soliciting customers who are primarily resident in or trading from China, including Hong Kong, Taiwan, and Macau, pursuant to Section 44 of the English Arbitration Act 1996.[98] Smith J considered that no evidence was put before him to explain why the Tribunal could not act effectively to grant interim relief. He noted that the application for an injunction in respect of Chinese customers was based on information obtained earlier, and had a prompt application been made to the tribunal, there was no reason to think that it would not have been dealt with timeously.[99]

In *NCC International AB v Alliance Concrete Singapore Pte Ltd*,[100] the Singapore **12.52** Court of Appeal denied issuing interim relief as there was no urgency or special circumstances which warranted it, and instead directed parties to the arbitral tribunal which was already constituted. While this decision was rendered before Section 12(7) was replaced by Section 12A, the court's reasoning remains applicable. The Court

---

[94] Ibid, [80].

[95] Ibid.

[96] *Seele Middle East Fze v Drake & Scull Int Sa Co* [2014] EWHC 435 (TCC) (hereafter *Seele Middle East Fze*).

[97] Ibid.

[98] *Ikon International (HK) Holdings Public Company Limited v Ikon Finance Limited and ors.* [2015] EWHC 3088 (Comm), [5], [14], (hereafter *Ikon International (HK) Holdings Public Company Limited*).

[99] Ibid, [16].

[100] *NCC International AB v Alliance Concrete Singapore Pte Ltd* [2008] 2 SLR(R) 565 (hereafter *NCC International AB*).

174 COURT POWERS IN AID OF ARBITRATION

of Appeal acknowledged that while a court had concurrent jurisdiction with an arbitral tribunal to order interim relief, a court will 'nevertheless scrupulously avoid usurping the function of the tribunal in exercising such jurisdiction and will only order interim relief where this will aid, promote and support arbitration proceedings'.[101] It observed that parties should not be allowed to bypass seeking interim relief from an arbitral tribunal merely because curial assistance is available.[102] Rather, help from court should be sought only when relief from the tribunal is inappropriate, ineffective, or incapable of securing the particular relief sought.[103] Such examples include those where third parties over whom the arbitral tribunal has no jurisdiction are involved, where matters are very urgent or where the court's coercive powers of enforcement are required.[104]

12.53 In *Gerald Metals SA v Trustees of the Timis Trust & others* [2016] EWHC 2327, a dispute concerning a contract of guarantee was referred to LCIA arbitration. The claimant also applied for the appointment of an emergency arbitrator, and wanted to seek interim relief, which included an order preventing the respondent from disposing of its assets. In response, the respondent undertook not to dispose any assets unless they were at full market value, and confirmed that it would give the claimant seven days' notice for disposing any asset worth more than £250,000. The LCIA rejected the application for an emergency arbitrator, following which the claimant applied to the High Court for an injunction under Section 44 of the English Arbitration Act 1996. Relief was ultimately declined. In relation to Section 44(5) of the English Arbitration Act 1996, the English High Court noted that the court could not intervene because there was an arbitral institution that could 'act effectively' within the meaning of Section 44(5).

12.54 Ultimately, as seen from the above cases, everything will depend on the facts of the case. However, it remains an open question whether the 'urgency' requirement will be more difficult to meet given the proliferation of emergency arbitrator provisions in the various institutional rules.[105]

12.55 For completeness, it should be noted that the constitution of a tribunal does not necessarily preclude an application to Court for interim relief.[106] Some contracts expressly provide that this may be permitted, even though arbitral proceedings are ongoing. More critically, the wording of Section 44 of the English Arbitration Act 1996 and Section 12A of the IAA makes it clear that a party remains free to approach a competent

---

[101] Ibid, [41].
[102] Ibid, [40].
[103] Ibid.
[104] Ibid, [41].
[105] See e.g., ICC Arbitration Rules (2021) Appendix V; SIAC Rules (2016) Schedule 1; LCIA Rules (2020) Article 9B.
[106] R. Kent and A. Hollis, 'Concurrent Jurisdiction of Arbitral Tribunals and National Courts to Issue Interim Measures in International Arbitration' in D. Ziyaeva (ed), *Interim and Emergency Relief in International Arbitration* (JurisNet 2015) 87, (hereafter Kent and Hollis, 'Concurrent Jurisdiction of Arbitral Tribunals and National Courts to issue Interim Measures in International Arbitration').

L. SECTION 13—SUMMONING OF WITNESSES BY SUBPOENA   175

court to obtain interim relief,[107] subject to the criteria set out in Section 12A(4)-(6). This is consistent with the spirit of the Model Law.[108]

Where a third party needs to be bound by an order for interim relief (e.g. a bank when restraining a call on a performance bond), it may be necessary to seek relief from the Court even if as between the parties to the arbitration agreement, an emergency arbitrator would have been able to deal with the issue.   **12.56**

K. Section 12A(7)

There has been no reported decision discussing Section 12A(7). It should be noted that although similar, the wording of Section 12A(7) does not track the language of Section 44(6) of the English Arbitration Act 1996. According to a statement by the Ministry of Law,[109] the intent of this provision is to give primacy to the arbitral tribunal, to the extent that any decision or order the tribunal makes is one it has the power to make.   **12.57**

L. Section 13—Summoning of Witnesses by Subpoena

Section 13 deals with the summoning of witnesses by subpoena to testify or produce documents.   **12.58**

Prior to an amendment in 2001, Section 13 of the IAA was identical to Section 14 of the 1987 version of the domestic Arbitration Act. It provided that any party to an arbitration agreement could take out a subpoena for a witness to testify or produce documents, subject to the Court's power to grant or set aside such subpoenas. In March 2002, the current domestic Arbitration Act 2001 came into force,[110] and Section 14 of the older Act was replaced by a new Section 30.   **12.59**

To ensure the subpoena provisions in the domestic Arbitration Act and IAA remained consistent, minor changes to Section 13 of the IAA were introduced through the International Arbitration (Amendment) Act 2001. This ensured that Section 13 of the IAA mirrored the new Section 30 of the domestic Arbitration Act. Some additional minor amendments were made to Section 13 in 2006 and 2012.[111]   **12.60**

---

[107] Ibid, 87, 90, 94 and 97.

[108] Article 17J was added in the 2006 revisions to the UNCITRAL Model Law. Paragraph 30 of the Explanatory Note to the 2006 revisions explained that the purpose of Article 17J was 'to put it beyond any doubt that the existence of an arbitration agreement does not infringe on the powers of the competent court to issue interim measures and that the party to such an arbitration agreement is free to approach the court with a request to order interim measures'.

[109] Ministry of Law's Responses to Public Feedback (n 57) 6.

[110] Singapore Parliamentary Debates, Official Report dated 5 October 2001, Title: International Arbitration (Amendment) Bill, vol 73, col 2221.

[111] The 2006 Amendment replaced the phrase of 'a writ of subpoena *ad testificandum* or a writ of subpoena *duces tecum*' to 'a subpoena to testify or a subpoena to produce documents': Schedule 5, Statutes (Miscellaneous Amendments) (No. 2) Act 2005. The 2012 Amendment substituted the word 'court' for 'High Court or a Judge thereof': see International Arbitration (Amendment) Act 2012 Section 6.

176 COURT POWERS IN AID OF ARBITRATION

12.61 Section 13 should be seen as complementary to Section 12A. Its purpose is to make available to parties to arbitration proceedings the same processes as are available to parties to litigation to compel the attendance of witnesses or the production of documents.[112]

M. Subpoenas and Civil Procedure

12.62 An application for a subpoena pursuant to Section 13 must be made under Order 48 of the Rules of Court 2021, which apply to civil proceedings in connection with the IAA. The specific provision is Order 48 Rule 7, which in turn provides that the general rules governing subpoenas under Order 15 Rule 4 of the Rules of Court 2021, will apply.

N. Principles Governing Subpoena Applications

1. Section 13(1)–(2)

12.63 Section 13(1) provides that any party to an arbitration agreement may take out a subpoena against a witness to testify or produce documents.[113] In addition, Section 13(2) expressly empowers the Court to order that a subpoena be issued to compel the attendance of a witness before an arbitral tribunal or to produce documents.

12.64 In *The Lao People's Democratic Republic v Sanum Investments Ltd & Anor* (hereafter *Lao PDR v Sanum Investments*),[114] Quentin Loh J examined the factors that a Judge should consider when deciding whether to grant an application for the issuance of a subpoena to produce documents. In that case, which involved arbitrations under two bilateral investment treaties, the claimants alleged that an audit conducted by Ernst & Young Singapore was improperly conducted.[115] The parties agreed at a procedural conference that documents relating to the audit exercise should be requested from Ernst & Young Singapore.[116] Following the refusal by Ernst & Young Singapore to release the relevant documents, the respondent State applied for a subpoena to compel the production of the said documents.[117]

12.65 Drawing from a range of English and Singaporean authorities, Loh J held that the Court must carefully balance the interests of justice in the individual case against a possible invasion of confidentiality,[118] such that the documents sought are 'relevant,

---

[112] Explanatory Statement, Arbitration Bill (No. 37/2001).
[113] IAA, Section 13(1).
[114] *The Lao People's Democratic Republic v Sanum Investments Ltd and another and another matter* [2013] 4 SLR 947, [2013] SGHC 183.
[115] Ibid, [6]–[8].
[116] Ibid, [10].
[117] Ibid, [11].
[118] Ibid, [22].

N. PRINCIPLES GOVERNING SUBPOENA APPLICATIONS   177

material, and necessary for the fair disposal of the matter'.[119] In addition, the subpoena must be sufficiently precise, and it must not amount to 'an attempt to obtain discovery against a third party'.[120] In the event, Loh J found that the documents were highly relevant and material to the issues raised in the two arbitration, and therefore granted the application.[121]

In *ALC v ALF*,[122] a decision relating to Section 30 of the domestic Arbitration Act, is also instructive. As mentioned above, Section 30 is very similar to Section 13 of the IAA.   **12.66**

In *ALC v ALF*, the plaintiff and the defendant were parties to an arbitration arising out of a construction contract which stipulated that the domestic Arbitration Act would apply.[123] In the course of two procedural hearings, it was decided under Procedural Order No. 1 (hereafter Procedural Order) that the 1999 IBA Rules on the Taking of Evidence would apply. The Procedural Order also provided that either party could submit a Request to Produce Documents to the Arbitrator, if it was dissatisfied with the disclosure of documents by the other party.[124]   **12.67**

As it turned out, the defendant was dissatisfied with the plaintiff's disclosure and wrote to the arbitrator, questioning the adequacy of the disclosure and requesting that the plaintiff produce sworn statements from one of its employees. This request was rejected, and the defendant subsequently applied to the Singapore High Court for the issuance of a subpoena against the same witness to give evidence on matters relating to the adequacy of the plaintiff's disclosure.[125] The plaintiff applied to set aside the subpoena on the grounds of abuse of process.   **12.68**

The court first acknowledged that there were no local authorities dealing with subpoenas issued in support of arbitration proceedings.[126] Traditionally, subpoenas of a witness in civil proceedings are objected on the basis that they are insufficiently precise that they constitute an abuse of process.[127] Further, the threshold for setting aside a subpoena is high and not an easily surmountable one.[128]   **12.69**

Nonetheless, the Court in *ALC v ALF* took the view that the interplay of considerations operated differently in the context of a subpoena being issued for a witness to testify before an arbitral tribunal.[129] Examining the Procedural Order and the IBA Rules, the Assistant Registrar found that it had been contractually agreed that if either party wished to adduce evidence from a person who will not appear voluntarily, they would   **12.70**

---

[119] Ibid, [24].
[120] Ibid, [23]. Affirmed in *BVU v BVX* [2019] SGHC 69, [103].
[121] Ibid, [22].
[122] *ALC v ALF* [2010] SGHC 231 (hereafter *ALC v ALF*).
[123] Ibid, [15].
[124] Ibid, [6].
[125] Ibid, [9].
[126] Ibid, [1].
[127] Ibid, [18].
[128] Ibid, [20].
[129] Ibid, [22].

178 COURT POWERS IN AID OF ARBITRATION

have to submit a request to the arbitrator, and the arbitrator shall decide on this request based on its own discretion.[130] Accordingly, the respect for party autonomy in arbitration meant that the Court should recognise the arbitrator as the master of procedure, and exercise minimal judicial interference.[131] On the facts, while the defendant had written to the arbitrator to question the adequacy of disclosure, the arbitrator had rejected its request for the witness to produce a sworn statement. Furthermore, the arbitrator was not informed of the defendant's intention to apply to Court for a subpoena. Accordingly, the court found that the defendant had effectively 'usurp[ed]' the arbitrator's control of the arbitral process which constituted an abuse of the court's process.[132]

2. Section 13(3)

12.71 Section 13(3) states that the High Court or a Judge has the power to issue an order pursuant to Section 38 of the Prisons Act (Cap. 247) to bring up a prisoner for examination before an arbitral tribunal. This ensures that the processes available to parties in litigation are available for parties in arbitration. The process for this is set out at Order 15 Rule 4(10) to 4(12) of the Rules of Court 2021.

3. Section 13(4)

12.72 Section 13(4) serves as an exception to Sections 13(1)–(3), and states that no witness can be compelled to produce any document which he cannot be compelled to produce on the trial of an action.

O. Subpoenas in Aid of Foreign-seated Arbitrations

12.73 Section 13 is silent on whether a subpoena can be issued in aid of a foreign-seated arbitration. An unreported High Court decision has held that the court had no power to issue a subpoena in support of a foreign arbitration. However, no reasons have been published and no appeal was brought. It is therefore necessary to consider the question as a matter of principle.

12.74 First, there is no obvious impediment to Section 13 applying to foreign-seated arbitrations. Section 13 is contained in Part II of the IAA, the application of which is governed by Section 5. Sections 5(1) and (2) in turn defines an 'international arbitration' by

---

[130] Ibid, [29].
[131] Ibid, [37], [38], [39], and [40].
[132] Ibid, [49].

O. SUBPOENAS IN AID OF FOREIGN-SEATED ARBITRATIONS

criteria other than the seat of arbitration; whether Part II applies to an arbitration is determined more by the cross-border nature of the transaction and parties than the seat.

In addition, even though subpoenas are governed by Section 13 (and not Section 12A), **12.75** it could be argued that they are in substance similar to the types of interim relief permitted under Section 12A which are permitted in aid of foreign-seated arbitration. This is consistent with the Singapore Government's[133] and courts'[134] pro-arbitration approach. It is also supported by leading commentators. As noted by a leading commentator: 'If carefully applied, in order to assist and not undermine the arbitral process, judicial assistance in evidence-taking should be no different from court-ordered provisional relief in aid of arbitrations—including foreign arbitrations.'[135]

Finally, a number of courts in other jurisdictions have granted orders concerning evidence taking in aid of arbitration.[136] Interpreting Section 13 as applying to foreign-seated arbitrations would be compatible with this trend. **12.76**

However, the legislative history of Sections 12, 12A, and 13 may be more open-ended. **12.77** As a starting point, there is no record of Parliament's specific intention when it enacted Section 13 as to whether it applied to foreign-seated arbitrations. The closest is the Ministry of Law's response to feedback received from a public consultation for the International Arbitration (Amendment) Bill 2009. As discussed earlier in this chapter, this round of legislative amendment included a proposed amendment to reverse the conclusion of the Court of Appeal in *Swift-Fortune* that Section 12(7) of the IAA did not permit court-ordered interim relief in aid of foreign-seated arbitrations. During the public consultation, it was asked whether the 'giving of evidence' under Section 12(1)(c), which would now be included within powers applicable to foreign-seated arbitrations, included the taking of evidence of witnesses.[137] The Ministry of Law's response was that the court's power to secure the attendance of a witness was governed by Section 13 of the IAA, and 'the amendments are not intended to compel the attendance of witness ... this power is provided for under section 13 of the IAA.' Whether this was an implied acceptance that Section 13 of the IAA could apply to foreign arbitrations is unclear.

As against this position, it could also be argued that Section 13 is an expression of **12.78** Article 27 of the Model Law, which, by virtue of Article 1(2) of the Model Law, applies only if the place of arbitration is in Singapore.[138] However, the drafting history of the

---

[133] See Singapore Parliamentary Debates, Official Report (19 October 2009) vol 86, Second Reading of the International Arbitration (Amendment) Bill 2009 and Singapore Parliamentary Debates, Official Report (5 October 2020) vol 95, Second Reading of the International Arbitration (Amendment) Bill 2020.

[134] See *Tjong Very Sumito and others v Antig Investments Pte Ltd* [2009] 4 SLR(R) 732 at [28] where the court recognised the 'unequivocal judicial policy of facilitating and promoting arbitration', cited with approval in *International Research Corp PLC v Lufthansa Systems Asia Pacific Pte Ltd and another* [2013] SGCA 55 (at [27]) and *Larsen Oil and Gas Pte Ltd v Petroprod Ltd (in official liquidation in the Cayman Islands and in compulsory liquidation in Singapore)* [2011] SGCA 21 (at [19]).

[135] G. Born, *International Commercial Arbitration* (3rd edn, Kluwer International 2021) para 16.03[B].

[136] See e.g. *Transfield Philippines, Inc. v Luzon Hydro Corporation* [2002] VSC 215; *Dalian Deepwater Developer Ltd v Dybdahl* [2015] NZHC 151.

[137] Ministry of Law's Responses to Public Feedback (n 57).

[138] T. Cooke, *International Arbitration in Singapore* (Sweet & Maxwell 2018) 91.

180 COURT POWERS IN AID OF ARBITRATION

Model Law does not suggest that the topic of subpoenas was specifically discussed, and in any event, the Model Law is to be read 'subject to' the IAA.

12.79 The key to this puzzle may be to discern whether, by the introduction of Section 12A, Parliament was doing so because it believed the Court of Appeal in *Swift-Fortune* was wrong and that the Singapore courts did have the power to support foreign arbitrations, or whether it agreed with the Court of Appeal that the courts did not then have the power to do so, and that such power needed to have a statutory basis. Indeed, the debate over interim relief (specifically injunctions) in the *Swift-Fortune* case was in part over whether Section 4(10) of the Civil Law Act could be a basis for interim relief in support of foreign arbitrations because the Court of Appeal did not appear to consider that the IAA conferred independent powers. Unfortunately, the Parliamentary debates are again unclear as to whether it was reversing the decision or the effect of *Swift-Fortune*.

12.80 Ultimately, what is interesting is that the previous Section 12 was, on its face, applicable to 'an arbitration to which Part II applies'. The Court of Appeal in *Swift-Fortune* acknowledged that this meant it was capable of applying to all international arbitrations, but ultimately concluded that such an interpretation could cause issues of comity. On this basis, it could be argued that the subpoena power was once capable of applying to all arbitrations and that issues of comity are perhaps overstated. The trend in relation to interim measures has been in the opposite direction in the 15 years or so since where the court's powers are used to support and not intervene in arbitration proceedings whether seated in Singapore or elsewhere.

13

Disapplication of the Model Law and the IAA, the Application of Rules of Arbitration, and Conciliation

A. Section 15—Law of Arbitration Other than Model Law	13.01	3. Section 16(4)—Anti-Delay	13.17
		4. Sections 17(1)—(2)—Arbitrator Able to Act as Conciliator	13.18
B. Section 15A—Application of Rules of Arbitration	13.05	5. Section 17(2)—Confidentiality	13.19
		6. Section 17(3)—Disclosure of Information	13.20
C. Sections 16 and 17—Conciliation	13.10		
1. Sections 16(1)–(2)—Appointment of Conciliator	13.14	7. Section 17(4)—No Objection to Arbitral Process	13.21
2. Section 16(3)—Protection of Conciliator	13.15		

A. Section 15—Law of Arbitration Other than Model Law

<u>IAA, Section 15</u>

(1) If the parties to an arbitration agreement (whether made before or after 1st November 2001) have expressly agreed either—

(a) that the Model Law or this Part shall not apply to the arbitration; or

(b) that the Arbitration Act 2001 or the repealed Arbitration Act (Cap. 10, 1985 Revised Edition) is to apply to the arbitration,

then, both the Model Law and this Part do not apply to that arbitration but the Arbitration Act 2001 or the repealed Arbitration Act (Cap. 10, 1985 Revised Edition) (if applicable) applies to that arbitration.

(2) To avoid doubt, a provision in an arbitration agreement referring to or adopting any rules of arbitration is not of itself sufficient to exclude the application of the Model Law or this Part to the arbitration concerned.

Section 15 of the International Arbitration Act (IAA) addresses the situation where **13.01** parties expressly agree to disapply the Model Law. Arbitration is founded on party autonomy, and just as the parties are able to decide on their forum of choice, adjudicators,

182   DISAPPLICATION OF THE MODEL LAW AND THE IAA

and procedural rules, they are also able to select the applicable law of their choice, within certain limits.

13.02   As a general matter, due to its cross-border nature, international arbitration tends to attract the application of various sets of rules and laws. For example, a Chinese manufacturer and a German buyer of goods may agree to English governing law, International Chamber of Commerce (ICC) arbitration, the International Bar Association (IBA) Rules on the Taking of Evidence, and a Singapore seat. In this example, English law governs their contractual rights, the ICC rules govern the procedural aspects of the arbitration save that the IBA Rules on the Taking of Evidence supplement specific aspects concerning evidence, and Singapore law, as *lex arbitri*, provides the legal framework for the entire arbitration, interim relief, and enforcement, amongst other aspects. More complexity ensues if one asks which law of attorney–client privilege applies, or if there are mandatory rules of the jurisdiction of business which apply. The reader is directed elsewhere for a detailed discussion on the applicable laws and the conflict of laws in international arbitration.[1] For present purposes, Section 15 deals with the *lex arbitri*—the local arbitration law which applies by virtue of Singapore being the seat. Section 15 addresses the disapplication of the Model Law or Part II of the IAA as the *lex arbitri* of a Singapore-seated arbitration.

13.03   Section 15 states that if the parties decide to (i) disapply the Model Law of Part II of the IAA, or (ii) apply the domestic Arbitration Act, then by default, the domestic Arbitration Act applies. As explained in Chapter 1 of this commentary, the domestic Arbitration Act is largely similar to the IAA but provides broader scope for curial supervision. A brief overview of the legislative changes to Section 15 is also discussed in Chapter 1 of this commentary.

13.04   It should be noted that the Model Law is recognised as the standard bearer for international commercial arbitration. At the time of writing, it has been adopted as a framework for international commercial arbitration in 117 jurisdictions and 84 States.[2] The cross-border nature of international commercial arbitration is likely to result in parties being more comfortable and preferring to opt for the application of the Model Law than against it. In light of this, Section 15(2) provides that the parties' selection of other 'rules of arbitration', without more, is not sufficient to be deemed to exclude the application of the Model Law of Part II of the IAA.

---

[1] See generally, C. Croff, 'The Applicable Law in an International Commercial Arbitration: Is It Still a Conflict of Laws Problem' (1982) 16 International Law 613; S. Luttrell, 'An Introduction to Conflict of Laws in International Commercial Arbitration' (2011) 14 International Trade & Business Law Review 404; N. Blackaby et al., *Redfern and Hunter on International Commercial Arbitration* (6th edn, Oxford University Press 2015) Chapter 3.

[2] Accounting for States, principalities, or territories in Australia, Canada, the People's Republic of China, the United Arab Emirates, the United Kingdom (although England and Wales notably do not adopt the Model Law), and the United States of America. See 'Status: UNCITRAL Model Law on International Commercial Arbitration (1985), with amendments as adopted in 2006' (*UNCITRAL*) <https://uncitral.un.org/en/texts/arbitration/model law/commercial_arbitration/status> accessed 12 December 2020.

B. Section 15A—Application of Rules of Arbitration

<u>IAA, Section 15A</u>

(1) To avoid doubt, it is declared that a provision of rules of arbitration agreed to or adopted by the parties, whether before or after the commencement of the arbitration, applies and is given effect to the extent that the provision is not inconsistent with a provision of the Model Law or this Part from which the parties cannot derogate.

(2) Without prejudice to subsection (1), subsections (3) to (6) apply for the purposes of determining whether a provision of rules of arbitration is inconsistent with the Model Law or this Part.

(3) A provision of rules of arbitration is not inconsistent with the Model Law or this Part merely because it provides for a matter on which the Model Law and this Part is silent.

(4) Rules of arbitration are not inconsistent with the Model Law or this Part merely because the rules are silent on a matter covered by any provision of the Model Law or this Part.

(5) A provision of rules of arbitration is not inconsistent with the Model Law or this Part merely because it provides for a matter which is covered by a provision of the Model Law or this Part which allows the parties to make their own arrangements by agreement but which applies in the absence of such agreement.

(6) The parties may make the arrangements referred to in subsection (5) by agreeing to the application or adoption of rules of arbitration or by providing any other means by which a matter may be decided.

(7) In this section and section 15, "rules of arbitration" means the rules of arbitration agreed to or adopted by the parties including the rules of arbitration of an institution or organisation.

13.05 Section 15A of the IAA clarifies the interplay between the various rules which may apply to an arbitration, as agreed to or adopted by the parties, and the Model Law and Part II of the IAA. Section 15A was introduced by way of Section 3 of the International Arbitration (Amendment) Act 2002 (No. 28 of 2002).

13.06 For purposes of this section, the phrase 'rules of arbitration' is defined in Section 15A(7) as the rules of arbitration agreed to or adopted by the parties including the rules of arbitration of an institution or organisation. In practice, this covers the rules of institutions such as the Hong Kong International Arbitration Centre (HKIAC), the ICC, the London Court of International Arbitration (LCIA), and the Singapore International Arbitration Centre (SIAC). It also encompasses rules of industry bodies.[3] It is likely to include protocols such as the IBA Rules on the Taking of Evidence,[4] as well as other rules concerning expert evidence,[5] cybersecurity,[6] and video-conferencing.[7]

---

[3] For example, the 2017 Terms of the London Maritime Arbitrators Association.

[4] IBA Rules on the Taking of Evidence in International Arbitration (2010).

[5] See e.g. Chartered Institute of Arbitrators (CIArb) Protocol for the Use of Party-Appointed Expert Witnesses in International Arbitration.

[6] See e.g. the International Council for Commercial Arbitration's (ICCA) draft protocol on cybersecurity, <https://cdn.arbitration-icca.org/s3fs-public/document/media_document/ICCA-reports-no-6-icca-nyc-bar-cpr-protocol-cybersecurity-international-arbitration-2022-edition.pdf> accessed 12 April 2023.

[7] SIAC Secretariat, *Taking Your Arbitration Remote* (August 2020).

184 DISAPPLICATION OF THE MODEL LAW AND THE IAA

13.07   Section 15A provides a canon for resolving rule conflicts. In the first instance, Section 15A(1) states that a provision of rules of arbitration selected by the parties 'shall apply ... to the extent [it is] not inconsistent' with a provision of the Model Law or Part II of the IAA 'from which the parties cannot derogate'. Thus, the parties' chosen arbitration rules will apply and be given effect insofar as they are not inconsistent with a provision in IAA Part II or the Model Law that is mandatory and non-derogable.

13.08   Sections 15A(3)–(6) then explain when a rule might be inconsistent with the Model Law or Part II. Section 15A(3) provides that a rule of arbitration is not inconsistent merely because the Model Law or Part II is silent on the point it addresses. Conversely, Section 15A(4) clarifies that rules of arbitration are not inconsistent merely because they are silent on aspects covered by the Model Law or Part II. Section 15A(5) states that a rule of arbitration is not inconsistent with the Model Law or Part II even if it covers a topic that is also covered by the Model Law or Part II which allows the parties to make their own arrangements but nonetheless provides a default. Some examples include aspects such as the nomination of arbitrators (Sections 9 and 9A), splitting of awards (Section 19A) or interest (Section 20). Section 15A(6) complements subsection (5) by putting beyond doubt the ability of parties to make their own arrangements.

13.09   As evident from the waterfall of provisions, Section 15A ultimately seeks to uphold party autonomy. The provisions in Section 15A attempt to make it clear that parties to an arbitration in Singapore are free to adopt the arbitration rules of their choice to govern their arbitration, and that their choice of arbitration rules will be respected by Singapore law and be given the fullest effect possible.[8]

C. Sections 16 and 17—Conciliation

<u>IAA, Section 16</u>

(1) Where an agreement provides for the appointment of a conciliator by a person who is not one of the parties and that person refuses to make the appointment or does not make it within the time specified in the agreement or, if no time is so specified, within a reasonable time of being requested by any party to the agreement to make the appointment, the president of the Court of Arbitration of the Singapore International Arbitration Centre may, on the application of any party to the agreement, appoint a conciliator who is to have the like powers to act in the conciliation proceedings as if he or she had been appointed in accordance with the terms of the agreement.

(2) The Chief Justice may, if he or she thinks fit, by notification in the Gazette, appoint any other person to exercise the powers of the president of the Court of Arbitration of the Singapore International Arbitration Centre under subsection (1).

---

[8] Singapore Parliamentary Debates, Official Report (1 October 2002) vol 75, cols 1107–1109, quoted in *Insigma Technology Co Ltd v Alstom Technology Ltd* [2009] SGCA 24, [42].

C. SECTIONS 16 AND 17—CONCILIATION   185

(3) Where an arbitration agreement provides for the appointment of a conciliator and further provides that the person so appointed is to act as an arbitrator in the event of the conciliation proceedings failing to produce a settlement acceptable to the parties—

(a) no objection is to be taken to the appointment of that person as an arbitrator, or to that person's conduct of the arbitral proceedings, solely on the ground that that person had acted previously as a conciliator in connection with some or all of the matters referred to arbitration; and

(b) if that person declines to act as an arbitrator, any other person appointed as an arbitrator is not required first to act as a conciliator unless a contrary intention appears in the arbitration agreement.

(4) Unless a contrary intention appears therein, an agreement which provides for the appointment of a conciliator is deemed to contain a provision that in the event of the conciliation proceedings failing to produce a settlement acceptable to the parties within 4 months, or any longer period that the parties may agree to, of the date of the appointment of the conciliator or, where the conciliator is appointed by name in the agreement, of the date of receipt by the conciliator of written notification of the existence of a dispute, the conciliation proceedings are to thereupon terminate.

(5) For the purposes of this section and section 17—

(a) any reference to 'conciliator' includes a reference to any person who acts as a mediator;

(b) any reference to 'conciliation proceedings' includes a reference to mediation proceedings.

<u>IAA, Section 17</u>

(1) If all parties to any arbitral proceedings consent in writing and for so long as no party has withdrawn the party's written consent, an arbitrator or umpire may act as a conciliator.

(2) An arbitrator or umpire acting as conciliator—

(a) may communicate with the parties to the arbitral proceedings collectively or separately; and

(b) must treat information obtained by him or her from a party to the arbitral proceedings as confidential, unless that party otherwise agrees or unless subsection (3) applies.

(3) Where confidential information is obtained by an arbitrator or umpire from a party to the arbitral proceedings during conciliation proceedings and those proceedings terminate without the parties reaching agreement in settlement of their dispute, the arbitrator or umpire must before resuming the arbitral proceedings disclose to all other parties to the arbitral proceedings as much of that information as he or she considers material to the arbitral proceedings.

(4) No objection is to be taken to the conduct of arbitral proceedings by a person solely on the ground that that person had acted previously as a conciliator in accordance with this section.

186 DISAPPLICATION OF THE MODEL LAW AND THE IAA

13.10 Sections 16 and 17[9] are the only provisions of the IAA which deal with conciliation.[10] Conciliation is an alternative dispute resolution (ADR) process where the disputing parties typically seek to reach an agreed resolution with the help of an independent third-party conciliator to find a tailored solution and where possible, reconcile relationships.[11] While the process appears more similar to mediation than arbitration, it differs from the former in that the conciliator tends to play a direct and central role in the actual resolution of a dispute, especially where he or she is appointed due to specialist knowledge. Mediators, by contrast, do not normally propose a resolution to the dispute. Similar to mediation, the process is intended to be non-adversarial and non-binding unless the parties agree to a settlement. Under Section 16(5) of the IAA, conciliation is defined to include mediation.

13.11 Notwithstanding its limited mention in the IAA, conciliation remains a connected and important form of ADR to arbitration. Its importance is recognised in the preamble to the IAA,[12] as well as the Sub-Committee on Review of Arbitration Laws' report, which hailed its advantages of flexibility, lack of complexity, and relative cost-effectiveness. The Sub-Committee also highlighted the increasing use of ADR procedures in other jurisdictions[13] and the cultural receptiveness to conciliation by Asian parties.[14] Consistent with the Singapore Government's approach to alternative dispute resolution, mediation was included within the ambit of this section by an amendment in 2001.[15]

13.12 In respect of Sections 16 and 17, and especially Sections 16(3) and 17, the Sub-Committee relied heavily on the Hong Kong Law Reform Commission's (HKLRC) recommended improvements to the conciliation section[16] of the United Nations Commission on International Trade Law (UNCITRAL) Model Law. Under the then prevailing law in Hong Kong, an arbitrator who saw one party alone for the purpose of attempting to reach a settlement was likely to be considered as acting in breach of rules of natural justice, making his award susceptible to being set aside.[17] The HKLRC found

---

[9] Neither of these provisions of the IAA have been interpreted by Singapore courts.

[10] Section 18 of the IAA provides for awards by consent, i.e. when the arbitral award records the terms of settlement between the parties. The same section also calls for treatment of these awards as awards on an arbitration agreement, capable of being enforced.

[11] See generally P. Sander, 'UNCITRAL's Model Law on International Commercial Conciliation' (2007) 23 Arbitration International 105; J.H. Salminen, 'The Different Meanings of International Commercial Conciliation' (2011) 1 Nordic Journal of Commercial Law 1; K. Rooney, 'Conciliation and Mediation of International Commercial Disputes in Asia and UNCITRAL's Working Group on the International Enforcement of Settlement Agreements' (2016) 18 Asian Dispute Review 195; L.C. Reif, 'Conciliation As a Mechanism for the Resolution of International Economic and Business Disputes' (1990–1991) 14 Fordham International Law Journal 578 (hereafter Reif, 'Conciliation As a Mechanism for the Resolution of International Economic and Business Disputes').

[12] In its Preamble, the IAA is defined as '[a]n Act to make provision for the conduct of ... conciliation proceedings'.

[13] Sub-Committee on Review of Arbitration Laws, *Report on Review of Arbitration Laws* (1993) para 77. See also para 83(c).

[14] Ibid, para 78.

[15] Section 13, International Arbitration (Amendment) Act, 2001 (No. 38 of 2001).

[16] The Law Reform Commission of Hong Kong, *Report on The Adoption of the UNCITRAL Model Law of Arbitration (Topic 17).* paras 4.32–4.35 (hereafter *Report on the Adoption of the UNCITRAL Model Law of Arbitration (Topic 17)*.

[17] Ibid, para 4.34.

that position to be too restrictive given the potentially helpful role played by conciliation during the arbitral process.

Accordingly, the HKLRC recommended a provision to allow both court intervention **13.13** in the appointment of a conciliator, and a conciliator to act as arbitrator on parties' agreement. The HKLRC also proposed an anti-delay procedure, and allowed a conciliator to see parties separately or together. As for the information received by the conciliator from parties, the recommendation called for confidentiality during the conciliation, and should an arbitration commence thereafter, the arbitrator was required to disclose material information given to him during the conciliation process. These safeguards in respect of confidential information and the ability to see parties individually were intended to provide a statutory framework within which an arbitrator could conduct conciliation fairly and effectively, if and for as long as the parties want, without misconduct, and without impairing his or her capacity to make an award thereafter.[18] The language of these proposed provisions was laid out at pages 61–2 and 98–9 of the HKLRC's Report. The Sub-Committee's recommendations (which were adopted *in toto* in the IAA) are identical to the HKLRC's proposal, save for procedural differences.

1. Sections 16(1)–(2)—Appointment of Conciliator

Section 16(1) of the IAA[19] provides that if there is a refusal or an unreasonable delay **13.14** by one party in the appointment of a conciliator, the other party to the agreement may apply to the President of the Court of Arbitration of the Singapore International Arbitration Centre for appointment. Section 16(2) of the IAA allows the Chief Justice to exercise discretion to delegate the appointment powers of the President of the Court of Arbitration of the Singapore International Arbitration Centre to any other person. To date, no such additional delegation has been made.

2. Section 16(3)—Protection of Conciliator

In certain situations, it may be more efficient for the person acting as a conciliator to go **13.15** on to act as an arbitrator, or for an appointed arbitrator to commence the proceedings with some form of conciliation. Section 16(3)(a) of the IAA[20] protects the appointment of the conciliator as an arbitrator. It prohibits either party from taking objection to the appointment of a conciliator as arbitrator, or her or his conduct of the arbitration proceedings solely on the ground that they had acted previously as a conciliator or mediator in either the same or a connected matter.

---

[18] Ibid, para 4.35.
[19] See Ibid, Section 2A(1) 61.
[20] See Ibid, Section 2A(2)(a) 61.

188 DISAPPLICATION OF THE MODEL LAW AND THE IAA

13.16 Section 16(3)(b)[21] explains that if a conciliator declines to act as arbitrator, no other person appointed as an arbitrator shall be required to act first as a conciliator unless the arbitration agreement provides otherwise.

3. Section 16(4)—Anti-Delay

13.17 Section 16(4) of the IAA[22] provides a time limit for the conciliation process. Unless otherwise agreed by the parties, the IAA provides for default termination of conciliation proceedings should they fail to result in a settlement acceptable to the parties within four months.

4. Sections 17(1)—(2)—Arbitrator Able to Act as Conciliator

13.18 Section 17[23] concerns the situation where, after an unsuccessful conciliation or mediation process, a conciliator or mediator could still act as arbitrator in connection with some or all of the matters referred to arbitration. Section 17(1)[24] provides that the parties must expressly consent to such a situation.[25]

5. Section 17(2)—Confidentiality

13.19 Confidentiality is central to the communications and information obtained by the conciliator. Section 17(2)[26] expressly permits conciliators to communicate with the parties either separately or together, as long the information received by her or him is treated as confidential. The parties are allowed to waive confidentiality.

6. Section 17(3)—Disclosure of Information

13.20 Section 17(3) deals with the situation where a conciliator subsequently acts as arbitrator,[27] and requires the arbitrator to disclose confidential information obtained during his or her role as conciliator, where such information is considered to be material to the arbitral proceedings. The rationale for requiring a conciliator-arbitrator to disclose confidential information is to address the potential problem of

---

[21] See Ibid, Section 2A(2)(b) 61.
[22] See Ibid, Section 2A(3) 61.
[23] See Ibid, Section 2B 98.
[24] See Ibid, Section 2B(1) 98.
[25] See also Section 16(3)(a), IAA.
[26] See Section 2B(2), *Report on the Adoption of the UNCITRAL Model Law of Arbitration (Topic 17)* (n 16) 98.
[27] See Ibid, Section 2B(3) 98.

C. SECTIONS 16 AND 17—CONCILIATION 189

a conciliator-arbitrator[28] relying on unproven allegations and other confidential information divulged during caucusing.[29] Disclosure of such information and material therefore aims to put both parties on a level playing field by creating information symmetry.[30] This is in line with the general standard set by the IBA Guidelines on Conflicts of Interest.[31] It is also similar to the conciliation provision in the Hong Kong Ordinance,[32] which seeks to provide a statutory safeguard where an arbitrator can conciliate without breaching the rules of natural justice,[33] whilst respecting party autonomy.[34]

7. Section 17(4)—No Objection to Arbitral Process

Section 17(4) [35] prohibits a party from objecting to the conduct of arbitral proceedings on the sole basis that the arbitrator has previously acted as conciliator in accordance with Section 17.   **13.21**

---

[28] See e.g. ICSID Rules of Procedure for Arbitration Proceedings (amended 10 April 2006), Rule 1(4).

[29] See generally B.A. Pappas, 'Med-Arb and the Legalization of Alternative Dispute Resolution' (2015) 20 Harvard Negotiation Law Review 157, 180; M. Hwang, 'The Role of Arbitrators as Settlement Facilitators: Commentary' in A.J. Van Den Berg (ed), *ICCA Congress Series No 12* (Kluwer Law International 2005) 573.

[30] G. Weixia, 'The Delicate Art of Med-Arb' (2014) 31 UCLA Pacific Basin Law Journal 97, 117.

[31] IBA Guidelines on Conflicts of Interest in International Arbitration (2014), General Standard 3(a), 3(d).

[32] Hong Kong Arbitration Ordinance (Cap. 69, 2011), Section 33(4)(b).

[33] *Report on the Adoption of the UNCITRAL Model Law of Arbitration (Topic 17)* (n 16) para 4.35.

[34] Reif, 'Conciliation as a Mechanism for the Resolution of International Economic and Business Disputes' (n 11) 585.

[35] See Section 2B(4), *Report on the Adoption of the UNCITRAL Model Law of Arbitration (Topic 17)* (n 16) 98–9.

14

Awards and Interest on Awards

A.	Section 18 of the IAA and Article 30 of the Model Law—Award by Consent	14.01	C.	Section 19A of the IAA—Awards Made on Different Issues	14.16
	1. Consequences of Issuing an Award by Consent	14.08	D.	Section 19B—Award is 'Final and Binding'	14.26
	2. Use of Awards by Consent in Conjunction with Mediation	14.10	E.	Section 19B—Finality Does Not Preclude Challenge	14.30
B.	Section 19 of the IAA—Enforcement of Awards	14.11	F.	Section 19C—Authentication of Awards and Arbitration Agreements	14.34
	1. Scope of Application	14.11	G.	Section 20—Interest on Awards	14.36
	2. Enforcement of Domestic International Arbitration Awards	14.13		1. The Tribunal's Broad Discretion to Award Pre-Award Interest	14.38
	3. Grounds to Resist Enforcement of Domestic International Arbitration Awards	14.14		2. Post-Award Interest Rate under Section 20	14.43

A. Section 18 of the IAA and Article 30 of the Model Law— Award by Consent

<u>IAA, Section 18</u>

If the parties to an arbitration agreement reach agreement in settlement of their dispute and the arbitral tribunal has recorded the terms of settlement in the form of an arbitral award on agreed terms in accordance with Article 30 of the Model Law, the award—

(a) is to be treated as an award on an arbitration agreement; and

(b) may, by permission of the General Division of the High Court, be enforced in the same manner as a judgment or an order to the same effect, and where permission is so given, judgment may be entered in terms of the award.

<u>Model Law, Article 30</u>

(1) If, during arbitral proceedings, the parties settle the dispute, the arbitral tribunal shall terminate the proceedings and, if requested by the parties and not objected to by the arbitral tribunal, record the settlement in the form of an arbitral award on agreed terms.

(2) An award on agreed terms shall be made in accordance with the provisions of Article 31 and shall state that it is an award. Such an award has the same status and effect as any other award on the merits of the case.

A. SECTION 18 OF THE IAA AND ARTICLE 30 OF THE MODEL LAW   191

Section 18 of the IAA and Article 30 of the Model Law concern the settlement of arbi-   **14.01**
tration disputes and consent awards. When parties agree to settle their dispute, they may
decide to record their settlement in the form of a consent award, although they are not required to do so. Parties may choose to do so for their settlement agreements to acquire 'the
legal force of an award'[1] and enjoy greater enforceability under the New York Convention
and national arbitration laws.[2] Parties may also choose to record their settlement as a consent award so as to add certainty and formality to their settlement agreement.[3] There are
also reasons why parties may prefer not to have a consent award. They may, for example,
wish to avoid disclosure of the terms of their settlement to the arbitrators and the potential
loss of confidentiality more generally. As Section 18 of the International Arbitration Act
(IAA) refers to and is premised on Article 30 of the Model Law, we discuss the latter provision first.

Article 30 deals with settlement and the making of consent awards. It makes clear that   **14.02**
the settlement of the parties' dispute results in a requirement by the tribunal to terminate
proceedings but it does not expressly require the tribunal to issue a consent award. It also
stipulates that an arbitral tribunal can only make a consent award at the request of the parties, and not of its own accord. Although Article 30 does not expressly provide for a requirement that all the parties must agree to a consent award, this appears to be implied.
The drafters' intent was that all parties must agree to have the settlement converted into
a consent award, regardless of which party the request for a consent award comes from.[4]

As Article 30 provides, an arbitral tribunal has discretion to refuse to record a settle-   **14.03**
ment and may object to the issuance of a consent award. This reflects the drafters' intent that arbitrators should 'normally accede to a request by the parties to enter the
settlement in an award', but that 'they should not be compelled to do so in all circumstances'.[5] As noted by several commentators, the drafters envisaged that arbitral
tribunals may refuse to make a consent award where there is evidence of fraud, corruption, illegality, violation of applicable mandatory laws, or grossly unfair settlement
terms.[6]

---

[1] United Nations Commission on International Trade Law (UNCITRAL) Report of the Secretary General,
'Preliminary Draft Set of Arbitration Rules for Optional Use in Ad Hoc Arbitration Relating to International Trade
(UNCITRAL Arbitration Rules)' (1973) UN Doc. A/CN.9/97 (1973) 178.

[2] G. Born, *International Commercial Arbitration* (3rd edn, Kluwer Law International 2021) 3270 (hereafter
Born, *International Commercial Arbitration*); G. Marchisio, *The Notion of Award in International Commercial
Arbitration: A Comparative Analysis of French Law, English Law, and the UNCITRAL Model Law* (Kluwer Law
International 2017) 119 (hereafter Marchisio, *The Notion of Award*).

[3] Born, *International Commercial Arbitration* (n 2) 3270–1.

[4] An earlier proposal providing that only one party could unilaterally make a request was not accepted
by the UNCITRAL. H.M. Holtzmann et al. *A Guide to the 2006 Amendments to the UNCITRAL Model Law on
International Commercial Arbitration: Legislative History and Commentary* (Kluwer Law International 2015) 822–
3 (hereafter Holtzmann et al., *A Guide to the 2006 Amendments to the UNCITRAL Model Law*).

[5] Ibid, 824, 827.

[6] M. Polkinghorne and P. Satija, *Article 30: Settlement*, in I. Bantekas et al. (eds), *UNCITRAL Model Law on
International Commercial Arbitration* (Cambridge University Press 2020) 772, 779 ('During the discussions for the
finalisation of the text, the Working Group noted that the discretion may be exercised in a negative fashion in cases
where public order was implicated, there was suspected fraud, unfair settlement terms, violation of antitrust laws,
furtherance of a conspiracy or where the award would be contrary to the mandatory applicable law provisions');

192 AWARDS AND INTEREST ON AWARDS

14.04 Section 18 expands upon Article 30(2) of the Model Law[7] and removes any doubt that consent awards are subject to recognition and enforcement in the same manner as other arbitral awards under the IAA. The corollary of this is that consent awards may be set aside, just like any other arbitral award.[8]

14.05 Consent awards also give rise to a separate cause of action, namely a common law 'action on the award' to enforce the implied promise to honour the award.[9] Where no consent award has been made, no such separate cause of action is available. Instead, as a general matter, a settlement agreement is enforced by bringing an action for breach of contract.[10]

14.06 In terms of formal requirements, both Section 18(a) of the IAA and Article 30(1) of the Model Law simply require that a consent award record the settlement on agreed terms.[11] Article 30(2) of the Model Law imports the generally applicable formal requirements of Article 31 of the Model Law, including that '[t]he award shall be made in writing and shall be signed by the arbitrator or arbitrator,' and that '[t]he award shall state its date and the place of arbitration'. Article 31(2) of the Model Law clarifies that there is no need for a consent award under Article 30(1) to state the reasons upon which it is based.[12]

14.07 The Singapore legal framework on consent awards is largely similar to that in other Commonwealth jurisdictions such as England and Hong Kong. Like the IAA, Section 51(2) of the English Arbitration Act 1996 provides for the recording of 'settlement[s] in the form of an agreed award' if 'so requested by the parties and not objected to by the tribunal'.[13] Section 51(3) provides that the 'agreed award shall state that it is an award of the tribunal and shall have the same status and effect as any other award on the merits of the case'.[14] The Hong Kong Arbitration Ordinance also incorporates Articles 30 and 31 of the Model Law,[15] but Section 66(2) of the Arbitration Ordinance allows a settlement agreement to be treated as an arbitral award even where parties do not request a

---

Born, *International Commercial Arbitration* (n 2) 3273 ('Consistent with this analysis, the drafting history of the Model Law indicates that an arbitral tribunal could appropriately refuse to make a consent award in cases of fraud, illegality or gross unfairness').

[7] S. Menon et al. (eds), *Arbitration in Singapore: A Practical Guide* (2nd edn, Sweet & Maxwell Singapore 2014) [13.033].

[8] Born, *International Commercial Arbitration* (n 2) 3275.

[9] *A v B (Rev 1)* [2020] EWHC 2790 (Comm); [2021] 1 Lloyd's Rep. 281 [30] (hereafter *A v B*). *See Xiamen Xinjingdi Group Co Ltd v Eton Properties Limited and Others* [2020] HKCFA 32 for a recent decision of the Hong Kong Court of Final Appeal on whether, in a common law action on an award, the enforcing court has the power to grant relief wider than that in the award.

[10] A.H. Ali et al., *The International Arbitration Rulebook: A Guide to Arbitral Regimes* (Kluwer Law International 2019) 690.

[11] Born, *International Commercial Arbitration* (n 2) 3279.

[12] Article 31(2) provides that '[t]he award shall state the reasons upon which it is based, unless the parties have agreed that no reasons are to be given or the award is an award on agreed terms under Article 30'.

[13] See also A. Connerty, 'ADR as a "Filter" Mechanism: The Use of ADR in the Context of International Disputes' (2013) 79(2) Arbitration: The International Journal of Arbitration, Mediation and Dispute Management 120, 127.

[14] English Arbitration Act 1996, Section 51(3).

[15] Hong Kong Arbitration Ordinance, Sections 66(1) and 67(1).

A. SECTION 18 OF THE IAA AND ARTICLE 30 OF THE MODEL LAW   193

consent award recording the agreed terms. In Hong Kong, therefore, there is no need to record settlement agreements as consent awards for such agreements to enjoy the benefits of enforcement as an award. Although this approach has the benefit of facilitating the enforcing of settlement agreements, it reduces the role played by an arbitral tribunal in scrutinising a settlement agreement and deciding whether it should be recorded and thereby enforced as a consent award.

1. Consequences of Issuing an Award by Consent

Singapore courts have recognised that a tribunal is *functus officio* after making an award, in respect of the issues addressed in the award, save for the exceptions under Articles 33 and 34(4) of the Model Law (correction and interpretation of an award, additional awards, and remission).[16] As discussed further below in this chapter, the *functus officio* doctrine means that after issuing an award, a tribunal no longer has jurisdiction over the issues finally determined in that award.[17] The Singapore courts have however, not yet examined the *functus officio* doctrine in the context of consent awards.[18]   **14.08**

English authorities may be of persuasive guidance in the absence of Singapore precedent. In *A v B*, the English High Court held that, after a consent award on the agreed terms of the settlement had been issued, the arbitral tribunal was *functus officio*. This meant that any issues to do with the implementation of the consent award, including the determination of any issues of fact (e.g., the determination of whether particular conditions for payment in the settlement award are met), would be left to the English courts.[19] In the case of a partial settlement, however, an arbitral tribunal would retain jurisdiction with regard to any unresolved matters.[20]   **14.09**

2. Use of Awards by Consent in Conjunction with Mediation

Consent awards may also be utilised for mediated settlements, where the parties include an arb-med-arb clause or a med-arb clause as part of the dispute resolution clause.[21]   **14.10**

---

[16] *Soh Beng Tee & Co Pte Ltd v Fairmount Development Pte Ltd* [2007] 3 SLR(R) 86 [27]; *AKN and another v ALC and others and other appeals* [2016] 1 SLR 966 [18], [50], [51]; *Kingdom of Lesotho v Swissbourgh Diamond Mines (Pty) Ltd and others* [2019] 3 SLR 12 [345].

[17] *PT First Media TBK (formerly known as PT Broadband Multimedia TBK) v Astro Nusantara International BV and others and another appeal* [2014] 1 SLR 372 [105], [208] (hereafter *PT First Media*). See the discussion relating to Section 19A below.

[18] The scope and meaning of the *functus officio* doctrine have been subject to debate. See e.g. Born, *International Commercial Arbitration* (n 2) 3370–81; N. Blackaby et al. , *Redfern and Hunter on International Arbitration* (6th edn, Kluwer Law International 2015) 507–8.

[19] *A v B* (n 9) [24], [33].

[20] Marchisio, *The Notion of Award* (n 2) 122.

[21] For instance, parties may include the model language of an arb-med-arb clause proposed by the SIAC and the Singapore International Mediation Centre (SIMC) for a tiered dispute resolution mechanism administered by both organisations. See SIAC, 'The Singapore Arb-Med-Arb Clause' <https://www.siac.org.sg/model-clauses/the-singapore-arb-med-arb-clause>, accessed 30 March 2022.

194   AWARDS AND INTEREST ON AWARDS

Under med-arb, the disputing parties commence with mediation, and then proceed to arbitration where they have reached a settlement, in order for that settlement to be recorded as a consent award. Under arb-med-arb, the disputing parties commence an arbitration with the intention of suspending it in favour of mediation. If the mediation results in a settlement, the arbitration process is resumed for a consent award to be recorded; otherwise, the arbitration process resumes for the purposes of the tribunal's adjudication of the dispute.[22]

B. Section 19 of the IAA—Enforcement of Awards

1. Scope of Application

IAA, Section 19

An award on an arbitration agreement may, by permission of the General Division of the High Court, be enforced in the same manner as a judgment or an order to the same effect and, where permission is so given, judgment may be entered in terms of the award.

14.11 Section 19 is found in Part II of the IAA and applies only to so-called domestic international arbitration awards. Such an award is an award that is rendered in an arbitration seated in Singapore but relates to an arbitration that is international in nature, as defined under Section 5 of the IAA. Section 19 does not apply to a 'foreign award', which is defined in Section 27 of the IAA as 'an arbitral award made in pursuance of an arbitration agreement in the territory of a Convention country other than Singapore'.[23] The enforcement of foreign awards is subject to the New York Convention and addressed at Sections 27–33 of the IAA.

14.12 The origins of Section 19 of the IAA can be traced to Section 26 of the 1950 English Arbitration Act (the 1950 Act), the direct forebear of Section 20 of the Singapore Arbitration Act 1953, on which Section 19 of the IAA was based.[24] In *PT First Media TBK v Astro Nusantara International BV* (hereafter *PT First Media*), the Singapore Court of Appeal considered a number of English cases concerning the interpretation of Section 26 of the 1950 Act to be persuasive in interpreting Section 19 of the IAA, albeit that these cases were decided before the New York Convention had come into existence.[25]

---

[22] N.Y. Morris-Sharma, 'Chapter III: The Courts, The Changing Landscape of Arbitration: UNCITRAL's Work On The Enforcement Of Conciliated Settlement Agreements' in C. Klausegger et al. (eds), *Austrian Yearbook on International Arbitration 2018* (Manz'sche Verlags- und Universitätsbuchhandlung 2018) 135.

[23] International Arbitration Act, Section 27(1).

[24] *PT First Media* (n 17) [34] *et seq.*

[25] Ibid, [34]–[43].

2. Enforcement of Domestic International Arbitration Awards

Section 19 provides that domestic international arbitration awards may be enforced in the same manner as a judgment or order to the same effect. Application for leave to enforce a domestic international award may be made *ex parte* under Order 48, Rule 6 of the Rules of Court 2021.[26] The application must be supported by an affidavit exhibiting the arbitration agreement and the duly authenticated original award. After obtaining leave to enforce the award, the order granting leave must be served on the award debtor, and the award debtor has to take steps to challenge the enforcement order within 14 days of service.[27]

14.13

3. Grounds to Resist Enforcement of Domestic International Arbitration Awards

Section 19 does not contain any express provisions regarding the power or the grounds to resist enforcement of domestic international arbitration awards. In *PT First Media*, the Singapore Court of Appeal held that Singapore courts had the power to refuse enforcement under Section 19, and that power was to be exercised 'in a manner which is compatible with the overarching philosophy of the Model Law on the enforcement of awards'.[28]

14.14

The Court of Appeal also held that the grounds for resisting enforcement of a foreign award under Article 36(1) of the Model Law are equally applicable to resisting enforcement of a domestic international award under Section 19 of the IAA.[29] The Court of Appeal reasoned that this was aligned with the grounds for refusing enforcement under the New York Convention and would be 'the most efficacious method of giving full effect to the Model Law philosophy', by de-emphasising the role of the seat and maintaining the award debtors' 'choice of remedies' (i.e. the choice between active and passive remedies[30]).[31]

14.15

C. Section 19A of the IAA—Awards Made on Different Issues

IAA, Section 19A

(1) Unless otherwise agreed by the parties, the arbitral tribunal may make more than one award at different points in time during the arbitral proceedings on different aspects of the matters to be determined.

---

[26] See Chapter 9.
[27] W. Lin and M.W.Y. Chong, 'Enforcement of Arbitral Awards in Singapore—Pitfalls and Strategies' (2019) 1 Singapore Arbitration Law and Practice [5]–[6].
[28] *PT First Media* (n 17) [50].
[29] Ibid, [84], [85], and [99]; *CDI v CDJ* [2020] 5 SLR 484 [5].
[30] See Chapter 16.
[31] *PT First Media* (n 17) [84].

196 AWARDS AND INTEREST ON AWARDS

    (2) The arbitral tribunal may, in particular, make an award relating to—

        (a) an issue affecting the whole claim; or

        (b) a part only of the claim, counterclaim or cross-claim, which is submitted to it for decision.

    (3) If the arbitral tribunal makes an award under this section, it must specify in its award, the issue, or claim or part of a claim, which is the subject-matter of the award.'

14.16 Sections 19A and 19B were introduced as part of the 2001 amendments to the IAA.[32] They were, in part, a legislative response to the Singapore Court of Appeal decision in *Tang Boon Jek Jeffrey v Tan Poh Leng Stanley* [2001] 2 SLR(R) 273, whereby the court held that an arbitral tribunal is only *functus officio* after it renders a final award and may alter and reconsider earlier partial or interim awards that it had rendered.[33] That position is now superseded by Sections 19A and 19B, which together make clear that, once issued, an award—whether an interim, partial, or final award—is final and conclusive as to the merits of the issue or claim determined under that award. Such an award could thereafter only be altered in the limited circumstances provided for in Articles 33 and 34(4) of the Model Law.[34]

14.17 Section 19A was modelled after Section 47 of the 1996 English Arbitration Act. As noted by the Departmental Advisory Committee on Arbitration Law, Section 47 was intended to clarify rather than expand the powers that arbitral tribunals already had, and to emphasise the flexibility that arbitral tribunals have to select issues for early determination or decide different issues in different awards, depending on the circumstances of the case.[35] English courts have recognised the power of arbitral tribunals to make more than one award pursuant to this section.[36] Section 71 of the Hong Kong Arbitration Ordinance is also similarly worded, and the Hong Kong courts have also recognised the same power.[37]

14.18 Section 19A therefore clarifies that a tribunal may make more than one award at different points in time, each of which is final and binding. This is consistent with Section 2(2) of the IAA, which defines an 'award' as 'a decision of the arbitral tribunal on the substance of the dispute and includes any interim, interlocutory or partial award but excludes any order or direction made under section 12 [of the IAA]'.[38]

14.19 In *PT Perusahaan Gas Negara (Persero) TBK v CRW Joint Operations* (hereafter *Persero*), the Singapore Court of Appeal held that, under Section 19A, an arbitral tribunal may

---

[32] Ibid, [137], [140].

[33] *Tang Boon Jek Jeffrey v Tan Poh Leng Stanley* [2001] 2 SLR(R) 273 [32]–[40]; *PT Asuransi Jasa Indonesia (Persero) v Dexia Bank SA* [2007] 1 SLR(R) 597 [69].

[34] *PT First Media* (n 17) [140].

[35] Departmental Advisory Committee on Arbitration Law, *1996 Report on the Arbitration Bill* (February 1996) paras 226–233 (hereafter DAC Report 1996).

[36] *Lorand Shipping Limited v Davof Trading (Africa) B.V., MV 'Ocean Glory'* [2014] EWHC 3521 (Comm), [2015] 2 All ER (Comm) 940 [18].

[37] *W v P* [2016] HKCFI 316 [6].

[38] See generally Chapters 4 and 14.

C. SECTION 19A OF THE IAA—AWARDS MADE ON DIFFERENT ISSUES 197

make partial and interim awards, both of which are capable of enforcement and susceptible to being set aside.[39] As the majority noted in its judgment:

> A typical dispute can be divided along topical lines. Section 19A of the IAA permits
> a tribunal to issue a series of interim or partial awards on each of these topics. Each
> award in that series is both final and binding on its subject-matter... If the parties have
> agreed that their dispute can be divided in that manner, into two temporal aspects, s
> 19A of the IAA allows the tribunal to give full effect to the parties' agreement and de-
> cide each temporal aspect separately and by separate awards, each of which is final,
> binding and enforceable on its subject matter.[40]

The IAA does not define 'partial' or 'interim' awards. Despite the fact that the two **14.20**
terms are sometimes used interchangeably to refer to awards that are not the ultimate
award made in an arbitration that disposes of all remaining claims—what is usually
called a 'final award'—the Court of Appeal in *Persero* considered that they refer to distinct categories of awards. The Court defined a 'partial award' as an award that 'finally
disposes of part of but not all of the parties' claim in an arbitration',[41] and an 'interim
award' as one that does not dispose finally of a particular claim but instead decides a
preliminary issue relevant to the disposing of such claim (e.g., choice of law, or construction of a contractual provision).[42] The meaning of the term 'interim award' is not
free from controversy,[43] and some commentators have opined that, given that such
awards 'do not dispose, finally or otherwise, of any claim for relief' by definition, they
are not proper 'awards' and therefore 'should be subject neither to annulment nor recognition and enforcement'.[44]

In *Persero*, the Court of Appeal further distinguished partial and interim awards **14.21**
from 'provisional' awards, which include a tribunal's orders or directions for interim
measures made pursuant to Section 12 of the IAA. The Court held that such decisions were not properly regarded as 'award[s]' for the purposes of the IAA because
they do not finally dispose of an issue or claim in the arbitration.[45] Although this is
consistent with the views of some commentators and the approach taken in some
other jurisdictions,[46] it does not appear to be a universally accepted position. Other
commentators and decisions have reasoned that awards of interim or provisional

---

[39] *PT Perusahaan Gas Negara (Persero) TBK v CRW Joint Operation* [2015] 4 SLR 364 [48] (hereafter *Persero*).
See also Born, *International Commercial Arbitration* (n 2) 3263.
[40] *Persero* (n 39) [165].
[41] Ibid, [46]. See also Born, *International Commercial Arbitration* (n 2) 3263.
[42] Ibid, [47].
[43] See e.g. DAC Report 1996 (n 35), [233] ('we have been careful to avoid use of the term 'interim award',
which has become a confusing term, and in its most common use, arguably a misnomer'); Born, *International
Commercial Arbitration* (n 2) 3268–70.
[44] Ibid.
[45] *Persero* (n 39) [50].
[46] D.A.R. Williams QC, 'Interim Measures' in M.C. Pryles and M.J. Moser (eds), *The Asian Leading Arbitrators'
Guide to International Arbitration* (JurisNet LLC 2007) 225, 244. This is, for example, the approach taken in
Switzerland. See Judgment of 13 April 2010, DFT 136 III 200.

198   AWARDS AND INTEREST ON AWARDS

relief should be enforced as 'awards' because they finally dispose of a request for relief.[47]

14.22   The *Persero* case also illustrates the complexities and pitfalls inherent in labelling awards as 'partial', 'interim', or 'provisional'. In that case, the arbitral tribunal issued, by a majority and at the claimant's request, an interim award to enforce the decision of a Dispute Adjudication Board (DAB) requiring payment to the claimant of a certain sum, pending the resolution of the parties' underlying dispute. The interim award stated that it would only be 'final up to a certain point in time', and that '[would] not and [could not] be altered until the arbitration hearing'.[48] When the claimant sought to enforce the interim award, the respondent argued that it was merely provisional and 'subject to future variation', and therefore did not finally resolve the issue in dispute between the parties.[49]

14.23   The Court of Appeal came to a split decision on whether the award issued by the arbitral tribunal was in fact an interim award under the IAA, or whether it was instead a provisional award that was not enforceable as an award under the IAA. The majority held that it was an interim award because it was a final determination of whether the respondent had an immediate and enforceable contractual obligation to comply with the DAB decision, even though the financial effects and consequences of the interim award were provisional and subject to modification.[50] In a dissenting opinion, Senior Judge Chan Sek Keong held that the interim award was instead a provisional award because it was subject to alteration or revision, and was binding only until the final adjudication of the parties' underlying dispute.[51]

14.24   In the authors' view, the position adopted by the majority in *Persero* is to be preferred because it focuses on whether the award finally disposes of an issue or claim, and what that issue or claim is, rather than the temporal characteristics of the award.[52] Determining whether a decision rendered by an arbitral tribunal is an 'award' capable of enforcement as such under the IAA should ultimately be a matter of substance, not form.

14.25   In summary, adopting the views of the majority in *Persero*, the position in Singapore is that whether an award is an 'award' under the IAA capable of enforcement depends on whether it finally disposes of an issue or claim in dispute. In this respect, under Singapore law, a provisional award is not an 'award' under the IAA, an interim award

---

[47] See Born, *International Commercial Arbitration* (n 2) 2698–704, 3268–70; K. C. Lye, C. T. Yeo, and W. Miller, 'Legal Status of the Emergency Arbitrator under the SIAC 2010 Rules: Neither Fish nor Fowl?' (2011) 23 Singapore Academy of Law Journal 93 [31] (suggesting that orders on interim relief issued by a tribunal could potentially be enforced as awards under Section 19).

[48] *Persero* (n 39) [143].

[49] Ibid, [26], [90].

[50] Ibid, [100].

[51] Ibid, [192]–[232].

[52] See also K.T.J. Hua, 'Case Note: Interim Enforcement of an Adjudication Decision' (2016) 28 Singapore Academy of Law Journal 354 [56]–[57].

that finally disposes of an issue in dispute is an 'award under the IAA, and a partial award that finally disposes of some but not all of the parties' claims is an 'award' under the IAA.

D. Section 19B—Award is 'Final and Binding'

IAA, Section 19B

(1) An award made by the arbitral tribunal pursuant to an arbitration agreement is final and binding on the parties and on any persons claiming through or under them and may be relied upon by any of the parties by way of defence, set-off or otherwise in any proceedings in any court of competent jurisdiction.

(2) Except as provided in Articles 33 and 34(4) of the Model Law, upon an award being made, including an award made in accordance with section 19A, the arbitral tribunal must not vary, amend, correct, review, add to or revoke the award.

(3) For the purposes of subsection (2), an award is made when it has been signed and delivered in accordance with Article 31 of the Model Law.

(4) This section does not affect the right of a person to challenge the award by any available arbitral process of appeal or review or in accordance with the provisions of this Act and the Model Law.

Section 19B addresses the consequences of classifying a decision of an arbitral tribunal **14.26** as an 'award'. As the Court of Appeal held in *PT First Media*, the intent of Section 19B was to clarify that all awards—whether they are interim, partial, or final—would reflect the 'principle of finality'.[53] In the Court's words:

> What this meant was that an award, once issued, was to be final and conclusive as to the merits of the subject-matter determined under that award; and it could thereafter only be altered in the limited circumstances provided for in Arts 33 and 34(4) of the Model Law. This is nothing more than another way of saying that the issues determined under the award are *res judicata*.[54]

In *Persero*, the Court of Appeal held that the effect of Section 19B was to render the **14.27** interim award issued by the arbitral tribunal 'final and binding' as regards 'the particular issue determined in the award'.[55] The Court of Appeal also noted that the effect of Section 19B was to reflect the 'accepted position that the issues decided ... were *res judicata*' and 'not ... amenable to revision by the arbitral tribunal'.[56]

---

[53] *PT First Media* (n 17) [137]–[140]. See also *Parliamentary Debates Singapore: Official Report*, vol 73, col 2221 (5 October 2001) (Assoc. Prof. Ho Peng Kee (Minister of State for Law)) on the International Arbitration (Amendment) Bill.

[54] *PT First Media* (n 17) [140].

[55] *Persero* (n 39) [100], [126], [205]. On this issue, the majority and the dissenting judge were of the same view.

[56] Ibid, [105].

200 AWARDS AND INTEREST ON AWARDS

14.28 In other words, a partial or interim award gives rise to *res judicata* and therefore has preclusive effects. This means a partial or interim award may give rise to issue or claim estoppel but only in respect of the issues or claims finally resolved in the award. In addition, as Section 19B(2) clarifies, the tribunal is *functus officio* in respect of those issues or claims resolved in the award,[57] meaning it does not have the jurisdiction to vary, amend, correct, review, add to, or revoke its decisions on those issues or claims. The corollary of this is that issues or claims not decided in the award are not *res judicata*, and the arbitral tribunal is not *functus officio* in respect of those issues.[58]

A relevant aspect of whether a tribunal is *functus officio* or not, is if an award issued is final. In its recent judgment,[59] the High Court addressed factors which are helpful in determining whether an award is final or not. The Court, while relying on principles set out in an English High Court decision,[60] considered the following factors: whether the award includes a decision on quantum, whether the award fully resolves the disputes between the parties, whether the award contains an express reservation of jurisdiction, and whether the award has attributes of a final award.[61] In determining the last factor, the Court considered the title of the award (i.e. "Final Award") relevant, and the fact that the award included an order on costs.[62]

14.29 As distinct from partial or interim awards, a procedural order issued by an arbitral tribunal is not subject to the principle of finality, meaning that an arbitral tribunal is not *functus officio* in respect of the matters determined in the order and the order does not give rise to any issue estoppel or *res judicata*.[63] Consequently, an arbitral tribunal is not precluded from reconsidering any of its decisions in its procedural orders.[64]

E. Section 19B—Finality Does Not Preclude Challenge

14.30 Section 19B(4) provides that the other sub-provisions in Section 19B do not affect the right of a party 'to challenge the award by any available arbitral process of appeal or review or in accordance with the provisions of this Act and the Model Law'. In *PT First Media*, the Court of Appeal held that Section 19B(4) confirms that while the issues determined under the award are *res judicata*, that does not mean that the award becomes 'unimpeachable'.[65]

14.31 The reference to 'any available arbitral process of appeal or review' includes, obviously, any statutorily-provided avenues for challenge under the law of the seat to which

---

[57] *PT First Media* (n 17) [105], [208].
[58] Ibid, [105], [207].
[59] *York International Pte Ltd v Voltas Ltd* [2022] SGHC 153.
[60] *ZCCM Investment Holdings Plc v Kansanshi Holdings Plc and another* [2019] EWHC 1285 (Comm).
[61] *York International Pte Ltd v Voltas Ltd* [2022] SGHC 153, [54]-[85].
[62] Ibid, [77]-[85].
[63] *Republic of India v Vedanta Resources plc* [2020] SGHC 208 [41] (hereafter *Vedanta Resources*).
[64] Ibid, [42]-[43] (discussing the decision of Rix LJ in *Charles M Willie & Co (Shipping) Ltd v Ocean Laser Shipping Ltd ('The Smaro')* [1999] CLC 301).
[65] *PT First Media* (n 17) [142].

parties have subjected the dispute. Commentators have also suggested that parties may have recourse to any built-in mechanisms for appeal to an appellate arbitral tribunal if provided by the parties' agreement or the parties' agreed arbitration rules.[66] Courts in other jurisdictions have upheld arbitration agreements incorporating such appeals procedures, including, for instance, an agreement to a procedure for the reconsideration of that award by another arbitral tribunal.[67]

14.32 Section 19B of the IAA is worded very similarly to Section 58 of the English Arbitration Act, with one difference. Section 58 provides that an award is final and binding both on the parties and on any persons claiming through or under them, '[u]nless otherwise agreed by the parties'. However, this difference in wording is not likely to be material. In *Berkeley Burke SIPP Administration LLP v Wayne Charlton and Financial Ombudsman Service Ltd*, the English High Court clarified that 'unless otherwise agreed' was meant to cover situations where the arbitration agreement envisaged an appeal process involving an 'appellate arbitration panel'.[68]

14.33 Singapore courts have not yet considered whether, where the parties have agreed to a two-tiered arbitration agreement involving an appellate arbitral tribunal, a first-tier arbitral award issued remains final and binding if the appeal process is invoked. However, Section 19 provides that an award on an arbitration agreement is to be 'enforced in the same manner as a judgment', and a number of Singapore decisions have held, in the context of foreign judgments, that a judgment that may be subject to appeal to a court of higher jurisdiction is nonetheless to be considered as being 'final and conclusive' for the purpose of enforcement.[69] By analogy, it is arguable that a first-tier arbitral award should be considered final and binding while it is subject to a pending appeal. It falls on the party appealing the award to seek a stay of enforcement.

F. Section 19C—Authentication of Awards and Arbitration Agreements

IAA, Section 19C

(1) For the purposes of the enforcement of an award in any Convention country, the Minister may by order appoint such persons holding office in such arbitral institution or other organisation as the Minister may specify in the order, to authenticate any award or arbitration agreement or to certify copies thereof.

---

[66] L.S. Chan SC, *Singapore Law on Arbitral Awards* (Academy Publishing 2011) [4.12] (hereafter Chan, *Singapore Law on Arbitral Awards*).

[67] See e.g. *PEC Limited v Asia Golden Rice Co Ltd* [2012] EWHC 846 (Comm), [2013] 1 Lloyd's Rep. 82; *A v B (Arbitration: Security)* [2010] EWHC 3302 (Comm), [2011] 2 All ER (Comm) 935; *Centrotrade Minerals and Metals Inc v Hindustan Copper Ltd.* (2017) 2 SCC 228 [27].

[68] *Berkeley Burke SIPP Administration LLP v Wayne Charlton and Financial Ombudsman Service Ltd* [2017] EWHC 2396 (Comm), [2018] 1 Lloyd's Rep. 337 [17].

[69] *Equatorial Marine Fuel Management Services Pte Ltd v The 'Bunga Melati 5'* [2010] SGHC 193 [109]; *The 'Vasiliy Golovnin'* [2007] 4 SLR 277 [40], [42].

202 AWARDS AND INTEREST ON AWARDS

    (2) Any person appointed under subsection (1)—

        (a) must comply with any condition imposed by the Minister; and

        (b) must not, without the written consent of the parties, directly or indirectly disclose any matter, including the identity of any party to the award or arbitration agreement, to any third party.

    (3) An award or arbitration agreement or a copy thereof duly authenticated or certified by a person appointed under subsection (1) is deemed to have been authenticated or certified by a competent authority in Singapore for the purposes of enforcement in any Convention country.

    (4) For the avoidance of doubt, nothing in this section —

        (a) prevents any person from authenticating any award or arbitration agreement or certifying copies thereof in any other manner or method or by any other person, institution or organisation; or

        (b) affects the right of a person to challenge or appeal against any award by any available arbitral process of appeal or review, or in accordance with the provisions of this Act and the Model Law.

    (5) In this section, 'Convention country' has the meaning given by section 27(1).

14.34   Section 19C of the IAA empowers the Minister for Law to appoint any person holding office in an arbitral institution or other organisation to authenticate any award or arbitration agreement or to certify copies thereof for the purposes of the enforcement of an award in a country which is a Contracting State to the New York Convention, without any dispute as to the award's authenticity.[70] Pursuant to this provision, the Minister for Law has appointed the Registrar and Deputy Registrar of the Singapore International Arbitration Centre (SIAC), the Chief Executive and Deputy Chief Executive of Maxwell Chambers, as well as the Registrar and the Chairman of the Singapore Chamber of Maritime Arbitration, as persons to authenticate any award or arbitration agreement or to certify copies thereof under the IAA.[71]

14.35   Section 19C provides one option by which parties can seek to authenticate awards and arbitration agreements, or to certify copies thereof and is by no means mandatory.[72] For the avoidance of doubt, Section 19C(4)(a) provides that nothing in the section will prevent any person from authenticating any award or arbitration agreement or certifying copies thereof in any other manner or method or by any other person, institution, or organisation.[73]

---

[70] *Parliamentary Debates Singapore: Official Report*, vol 86, col 1626 (19 October 2009) (Mr K Shanmugam (Minister for Law)) on the International Arbitration (Amendment) Bill (hereafter International Arbitration (Amendment) Bill 2009 Second Reading). See also Chan, *Singapore Law on Arbitral Awards* (n 66) [5.98].

[71] International Arbitration (Appointed Persons under Section 19C) Order 2009 (GN No. S 651/2009); International Arbitration (Appointed Persons under Section 19C) Order 2010 (GN No S 738/2010).

[72] International Arbitration (Amendment) Bill 2009 Second Reading (n 70).

[73] Ibid.

G. Section 20—Interest on Awards

<u>IAA, Section 20</u>

(1) Subject to subsection (3), unless otherwise agreed by the parties, an arbitral tribunal may, in the arbitral proceedings before it, award simple or compound interest from such date, at such rate and with such rest as the arbitral tribunal considers appropriate, for any period ending not later than the date of payment on the whole or any part of—
   (a) any sum which is awarded by the arbitral tribunal in the arbitral proceedings;
   (b) any sum which is in issue in the arbitral proceedings but is paid before the date of the award; or
   (c) costs awarded or ordered by the arbitral tribunal in the arbitral proceedings.

(2) Nothing in subsection (1) affects any other power of an arbitral tribunal to award interest.

(3) Where an award directs a sum to be paid, that sum, unless the award otherwise directs, carries interest as from the date of the award and at the same rate as a judgment debt.

The UNCITRAL Model Law is silent on the issue of interest. Section 20 of the IAA therefore fills that gap and addresses the arbitral tribunal's power to award interest. Prior to the International Arbitration (Amendment) Act 2012, Section 20 of the IAA provided only that, '[w]here an award directs a sum to be paid, that sum shall, unless the award otherwise directs, carry interest as from the date of the award and at the same rate as a judgment debt'. Section 20 was then expanded by the International Arbitration (Amendment) Act 2012 to cover both pre-award and post-award interest. **14.36**

Both the English Arbitration Act 1996 and the Hong Kong Arbitration Ordinance contain similar provisions in relation to the awarding of interest.[74] Both statutes, however, also clarify that interest may also be awarded in respect of an amount payable in consequence of a declaratory award.[75] Notwithstanding the absence of such express language in Section 20 of the IAA, the phrase 'any sum which is awarded by the arbitral tribunal in the arbitral proceedings' in Section 20(1)(a) is arguably broad enough to encompass any sums awarded in a declaratory award. **14.37**

1. The Tribunal's Broad Discretion to Award Pre-Award Interest

Section 20 of the IAA has been described as 'particularly permissive' on interest.[76] In *BRQ v BRS*, the Singapore High Court held that the granting of pre-award interest is a **14.38**

---

[74] English Arbitration Act 1996, Section 49; Hong Kong Arbitration Ordinance, Sections 79–80.

[75] Ibid, Section 49(5) ('References in this section to an amount awarded by the tribunal include an amount payable in consequence of a declaratory award by the tribunal.'); Hong Kong Arbitration Ordinance, Section 79(3) ('A reference in subsection (1)(a) to money awarded by the tribunal includes an amount payable in consequence of a declaratory award by the tribunal').

[76] M. Secomb, *Interest in International Arbitration* (Oxford University Press 2019) [3.426] (hereafter Secomb, *Interest in International Arbitration*).

204 AWARDS AND INTEREST ON AWARDS

matter entirely within the discretion of arbitral tribunals because Section 20(1) specifies that interest may be awarded 'from such date, at such rate and with such rest as the arbitral tribunal considers appropriate'.[77] In exercising this discretion, the arbitral tribunal is not bound by the parties' submissions on interest. Accordingly the Court held that an arbitral tribunal may decide as it 'considers appropriate', without needing to give reasons, what date interest should run from, and what the interest rate should be, even in the absence of submissions by the parties.[78]

14.39 The law governing the award of interest is a vexed issue, with some approaches treating interest as a substantive issue to be determined by the law applicable to the substance of a dispute, and others treating interest as a procedural issue to be governed by the law of the arbitral seat.[79] One sensible approach is to distinguish between the authority to grant interest, which is better regarded as governed by the law of the arbitral seat, and the standards governing the award of interest (e.g. the interest rate and whether interest runs on a simple or compound basis), for which there is little consensus on the law that applies.[80]

14.40 Such a distinction has been recognised by the Singapore International Commercial Court. Thus, for arbitral tribunals seated in Singapore, even though a different substantive law may govern the type of interest that may be granted, Section 20(1) of the IAA determines the scope of the tribunal's power to award interest. This has the consequence of limiting the avenues for challenging an award based on a tribunal's decisions with respect to interest.

14.41 In *CBX v CBZ*, the Singapore International Commercial Court had to consider whether an arbitral tribunal exceeded its jurisdiction by awarding compound interest, when Thai law, the applicable substantive law, did not permit the award of compound interest under a sale and purchase agreement.[81] Reyes IJ held that, because Singapore was the seat of the arbitration, Section 20 of the IAA applied and conferred on the tribunal the power to 'award simple or compound interest from such date, at such rate and with such rest as [it] considers appropriate'.[82] Although Reyes IJ held that the arbitral tribunal reached a conclusion that was wrong as a matter of Thai law, he reasoned that the parties to an arbitration had accepted the risk of such an erroneous application of Thai law, and therefore the arbitral tribunal's error could not be characterised as an excess of jurisdiction.[83]

---

[77] *BRQ v BRS* [2019] SGHC 260 [161], [163] (hereafter *BRQ v BRS*).

[78] Ibid, [163].

[79] Born, *International Commercial Arbitration* (n 2) 3360–3; Secomb, *Interest in International Arbitration* (n 3) [2.187]–[2.190].

[80] Born, *International Commercial Arbitration* (n 2) 3360–3. Some commentators suggest a uniform approach that neither applies a national law nor selects a reasonable rate, but instead focuses on any agreement between the parties on the rate of interest, the loss incurred by the loss of use of money, and a default commonly used commercial rate. See Secomb, *Interest in International Arbitration* (n 76) [3.264]–[3.474].

[81] *CBX v CBZ* [2020] SGHC(I) 17 [47] (hereafter *CBX v CBZ*).

[82] Ibid, [47].

[83] Ibid, [49].

G. SECTION 20—INTEREST ON AWARDS   205

Notwithstanding the relatively broad discretion granted to arbitral tribunals on interest, **14.42** it is important for arbitral tribunals seated in Singapore to be clear about when they will address interest in their awards. In circumstances where a final award is made without including interest, an arbitral tribunal cannot make an additional award to address issues of interest unless it has expressly reserved the power to award interest in a separate award, because the arbitrators are *functus officio* in respect of the issues or claims decided in the final award.[84]

2. Post-Award Interest Rate under Section 20

Section 20(3) provides that sums directed to be paid in an award 'shall, unless the award **14.43** otherwise directs, carry interest as from the date of the award and at the same rate as a judgment debt'. This provides for a default rate of interest, which runs at the rate for judgment debt,[85] which is 5.33%.[86] This is only a default provision, meaning that an arbitral tribunal can determine the applicable rate for post-award interest up to the date of payment.

---

[84] *L W Infrastructure Pte Ltd v Lim Chin San Contractors Pte Ltd and another appeal* [2012] SGCA 57.
[85] Chan, *Singapore Law on Arbitral Awards* (n 66) [3.57].
[86] Supreme Court Practice Directions (last updated 31 August 2021), 77(11).

15

Assessment of Costs and Proceedings Otherwise Than in Open Court

A.	Section 21—Assessment of Costs	15.01	C.	Section 23—Restrictions on
B.	Section 22—Proceedings to			Reporting of Proceedings
	Be Heard in Private	15.05		Otherwise than in Open Court	15.07

A. Section 21—Assessment of Costs

IAA, Section 21

(1) Any costs directed by an award to be paid are, unless the award otherwise directs, assessable by the Registrar of the Singapore International Arbitration Centre (called in this section the Registrar).

(2) Unless the fees of the arbitral tribunal have been fixed by a written agreement or such agreement has provided for determination of the fees by a person or an institution agreed to by the parties, any party to the arbitration may require that the fees be assessed by the Registrar.

(3) A certificate signed by the Registrar on the amount of costs or fees assessed forms part of the award of the arbitral tribunal.

(4) The Chief Justice may, if he or she thinks fit, by notification in the *Gazette*, appoint any other person to exercise the powers of the Registrar under this section.

15.01 Although the IAA does not expressly provide for an arbitral tribunal's powers to award costs, this power has never been doubted as a matter of Singapore law. This is plain from Section 12(5)(a) of the IAA as well, which empowers tribunals to award any relief or remedy that the High Court may award in civil proceedings. Awarding costs is one such power.

15.02 In an indirect way, Section 21 confirms the power of an arbitral tribunal to award costs. It addresses the assessment[1] of costs and provides that an award for costs would be taxable by the Registrar of the Singapore International Arbitration Centre unless the

---

[1] The word 'taxation', present in the older version of the IAA, was replaced with the word 'assessment' by way of Courts (Civil and Criminal Justice) Reform Act No. 24 of 2021.

award otherwise directs. Respectfully, this appears to be a slightly odd way of phrasing the rule. But presumably, an award in which the tribunal has fixed the costs to be paid would not then need to be taxed again by the Registrar.

The same principle applies to the fees of the tribunal.[2] They may be fixed by the Registrar unless they have been fixed by written agreement, or where there is an agreement for such fees to be fixed by a particular person or the institution agreed by the parties. In most cases, if a party has selected an institution, the institution's rules will include a provision for the administrative and tribunal fees to be determined by the institution. **15.03**

To ensure the enforceability of such determinations of costs, it is provided that a certificate signed by the Registrar of the SIAC exercising Section 21 powers shall form part of the award of the arbitral tribunal.[3] **15.04**

B. Section 22—Proceedings to Be Heard in Private

IAA, Section 22

(1) Subject to subsection (2), proceedings under this Act in any court are to be heard in private.

(2) Proceedings under this Act in any court are to be heard in open court if the court, on its own motion or upon the application of any person (including a person who is not a party to the proceedings), so orders.

Section 22 of the IAA provides that proceedings under the IAA 'are to be heard in private' although a court, on its own motion, or the application by a person (including a non-party), could order proceedings to be heard in open court.[4] **15.05**

Anecdotally, the practice has been mixed. It is not uncommon for applications to set aside or resist enforcement of an award to be heard in open court, while by contrast, applications for interim measures from the court under Section 12A of the IAA tend to be in chambers and therefore *in camera*. It is suggested that if parties desire confidentiality of awards challenged in court, they should apply for the proceedings to be heard in camera, and also to apply for the court to exercise its powers under Section 23 (discussed below). **15.06**

---

[2] International Arbitration Act 1994, Section 21(2) (hereafter IAA).
[3] Ibid, Section 21(3).
[4] Section 22 was amended to make clearer that the default would be for hearings under the IAA to be in private. The amendment was introduced by Courts (Civil and Criminal Justice) Reform Amendment Act No. 25 of 2021.

208 ASSESSMENT OF COSTS AND PROCEEDINGS

C. Section 23—Restrictions on Reporting of Proceedings Otherwise than in Open Court

<u>IAA, Section 23</u>

(1) This section applies to proceedings under this Act in any court heard in private.

(2) A court hearing any proceedings to which this section applies is, on the application of any party to the proceedings, to give directions as to whether any and, if so, what information relating to the proceedings may be published.

(3) A court is not to give a direction under subsection (2) permitting information to be published unless—

   (a) all parties to the proceedings agree that the information may be published; or

   (b) the court is satisfied that the information, if published in accordance with such directions as it may give, would not reveal any matter, including the identity of any party to the proceedings, that any party to the proceedings reasonably wishes to remain confidential.

(4) Despite subsection (3), where a court gives grounds of decision for a judgment in respect of proceedings to which this section applies and considers that judgment to be of major legal interest, the court is to direct that reports of the judgment may be published in law reports and professional publications but, if any party to the proceedings reasonably wishes to conceal any matter, including the fact that the party was such a party, the court is to—

   (a) give directions as to the action that is to be taken to conceal that matter in those reports; and

   (b) if it considers that a report published in accordance with directions given under paragraph (a) would be likely to reveal that matter, direct that no report may be published until after the end of any period, not exceeding 10 years, that it considers appropriate.

15.07 To the extent a hearing is heard in camera, the court shall, on the application of any party to the proceedings, give directions as to whether and if so what information relating to the proceedings may be published.[5] A court is prohibited from permitting information to be published unless all parties consent, or if the directions are sufficient to ensure that the information published will not reveal any matter, including the identity of any party to the proceedings, that any party to the proceedings reasonably wishes to remain confidential.[6]

15.08 Equally, directions may be given in respect of grounds of decision for a judgment to be issued by the court. Where the court considers the judgment to be of 'major legal interest', the court shall direct that reports of the judgment may be published in law reports and professional publications but if a party reasonably wishes to conceal any

---

[5] Ibid, Section 23(1) read with Section 23(2).
[6] Ibid, Section 23(3).

C. SECTION 23—RESTRICTIONS ON REPORTING 209

matter including the party's identity, the court shall give directions to conceal those matters, or if that does not suffice, direct that no report shall be published until the end of such period it considers appropriate. Such period however cannot exceed 10 years.[7]

These provisions ultimately strike a balance between a party's desire for confidentiality in arbitral processes and the generally open nature of court proceedings. **15.09**

It should not be assumed that these concerns apply equally to both parties. The Court may well grant a request to anonymise one party's identity but not another where the latter is not able to justify its request and had in fact taken a contrary position earlier in the proceedings.[8] **15.10**

---

[7] Ibid, Section 23(4).
[8] *CES v International Air Transport Association* [2020] 4 SLR 44.

16

Setting Aside an Award

A. Introduction and Overview	16.01	11. Power to Suspend an Award Pending Setting Aside	16.68
B. Scope of Setting Aside Action and other Cross-Cutting Issues	16.08	12. Correction and Interpretation of the Award; Additional Award	16.71
1. Only 'Awards' May be Set Aside	16.08	13. Costs Issues	16.81
2. Not an Action to Resist Enforcement	16.09	C. Grounds for Setting Aside	16.86
3. Not Judicial Review of a Ruling on Jurisdiction	16.13	1. Article 34(2)(a)(i): Incapacity of a Party or Invalidity of the Arbitration Agreement	16.89
4. Relationship between Setting Aside and an Article 13 Challenge of an Arbitrator	16.16	2. Article 34(2)(a)(ii): Lack of Proper Notice of Appointment or Unable to Present Case	16.128
5. Article 34(1) Model Law—Exclusive Recourse	16.18	3. Article 34(2)(a)(iii): Excess of Authority or Jurisdiction	16.184
6. Article 34(1) Model Law—Not an Appeal	16.22	4. Article 34(2)(a)(iv): Non-Compliance with Agreement of the Parties or the Model Law	16.220
7. Agreements to Limit or Waive Grounds for Setting Aside; Implied Waiver of Grounds for Setting Aside	16.29	5. Article 34(2)(b)(i): Subject-Matter Not Capable of Settlement by Arbitration	16.269
8. Article 34(2) Model Law—Residual Discretion and Prejudice	16.40	6. Article 34(2)(b)(ii): Conflict with the Public Policy of Singapore	16.273
9. Article 34(3) Model Law—Application to be Made within Three Months	16.42	7. Section 24(a): Fraud or Corruption	16.311
10. Article 34(4) Model Law Remission in lieu of Setting Aside	16.50	8. Section 24(b): Breach of the Rules of Natural Justice	16.326

IAA, Section 24

Despite Article 34(1) of the Model Law, the General Division of the High Court may, in addition to the grounds set out in Article 34(2) of the Model Law, set aside the award of the arbitral tribunal if—

(a) the making of the award was induced or affected by fraud or corruption; or

(b) a breach of the rules of natural justice occurred in connection with the making of the award by which the rights of any party have been prejudiced.

Model Law, Article 34

(1) Recourse to a court against an arbitral award may be made only by an application for setting aside in accordance with paragraphs (2) and (3) of this Article.

(2) An arbitral award may be set aside by the court specified in Article 6 only if:
   (a) the party making the application furnishes proof that:
      (i) a party to the arbitration agreement referred to in Article 7 was under some incapacity; or the said agreement is not valid under the law to which the

parties have subjected it or, failing any indication thereon, under the law of this State; or

    (ii) the party making the application was not given proper notice of the appointment of an arbitrator or of the arbitral proceedings or was otherwise unable to present his case; or

    (iii) the award deals with a dispute not contemplated by or not falling within the terms of the submission to arbitration, or contains decisions on matters beyond the scope of the submission to arbitration, provided that, if the decisions on matters submitted to arbitration can be separated from those not so submitted, only that part of the award which contains decisions on matters not submitted to arbitration may be set aside; or

    (iv) the composition of the arbitral tribunal or the arbitral procedure was not in accordance with the agreement of the parties, unless such agreement was in conflict with a provision of this Law from which the parties cannot derogate, or, failing such agreement, was not in accordance with this Law; or

(b) the court finds that:

    (i) the subject-matter of the dispute is not capable of settlement by arbitration under the law of this State; or

    (ii) the award is in conflict with the public policy of this State.

(3) An application for setting aside may not be made after three months have elapsed from the date on which the party making that application had received the award or, if a request had been made under Article 33, from the date on which that request had been disposed of by the arbitral tribunal.

(4) The court, when asked to set aside an award, may, where appropriate and so requested by a party, suspend the setting aside proceedings for a period of time determined by it in order to give the arbitral tribunal an opportunity to resume the arbitral proceedings or to take such other action as in the arbitral tribunal's opinion will eliminate the grounds for setting aside.

A. Introduction and Overview

This chapter examines the setting aside of arbitral awards under Section 24 of the International Arbitration Act (IAA) and Article 34 of the Model Law. **16.01**

Setting aside—also termed 'annulment'—is a means of challenging arbitral awards before courts at the seat of arbitration.[1] As Article 34(1) of the Model Law makes clear, for international arbitrations seated in Singapore, setting aside is the 'exclusive' recourse **16.02**

---

[1] Only awards made in Singapore can be set aside by Singapore courts pursuant to Article 34 of the Model Law or Section 24 of the IAA. See Model Law, Article 1(2). The corollary to this is that Singapore courts cannot set aside awards that are not made in Singapore. This is consistent with the special role preserved for the seat in Article V(1)(e) of the New York Convention.

212 SETTING ASIDE AN AWARD

for parties dissatisfied with an arbitral award.[2] In other words, unless the parties have otherwise agreed,[3] no other action exists for a dissatisfied party to actively challenge an international arbitration award under the IAA or the Model Law.[4] However, a dissatisfied party also has available the passive remedy of resisting enforcement of the award under Sections 19 or 31 of the IAA.

16.03 A setting aside application is not an appeal on the substantive merits.[5] The limited grounds for setting aside an award are instead focused on the jurisdiction of the arbitral tribunal, the conduct of the arbitration, compliance with the parties' agreed procedures, basic rules of due process, subject matter arbitrability, and the public policy of the seat.[6] This gives effect to the IAA's policy of minimal curial intervention, which proscribes undue judicial interference in the arbitral process in favour of the finality of the dispute resolution mechanism chosen by the parties, while permitting judicial control for serious procedural irregularities or violations of due process.[7]

16.04 Prior to the adoption of the Model Law, arbitration legislation in Singapore was modelled after the English Arbitration Act 1950 and provided only for the setting aside of awards for arbitrator 'misconduct', although errors of fact and law were considered to be 'misconduct',[8] and parties could apply to declare an award non-binding for lack of jurisdiction.[9] Since the enactment of the IAA in 1994, which implemented the Model Law in Singapore, the statutory framework for the setting

---

[2] In contrast, domestic arbitration awards are subject to appeal on questions of law under Section 49 of the domestic Arbitration Act. See Arbitration Act 2001 (2020 Rev. Ed.), Section 49 (hereafter 'domestic Arbitration Act').

[3] For example, parties may agree to an arbitral appeal mechanism. See also Report of the United Nations Commission on International Trade Law (UNCITRAL) Secretary-General, 'International Commercial Arbitration: Analytical Commentary on Draft Text of a Model Law on International Commercial Arbitration' (1985) UN Doc. A/CN.9/264 71 (hereafter Analytical Commentary on the Model Law) ('Finally, article 34(l) would not exclude recourse to a second arbitral tribunal, where such appeal within the arbitration system is envisaged (as, e.g., in certain commodity trades).').

[4] There is no basis for a Singapore court to intervene in an international arbitration except as provided in the IAA and the Model Law. See Model Law, Article 5 ('In matters governed by this Law, no court shall intervene except where so provided in this Law.').

[5] Indeed, in the context of the IAA, Singapore courts have cautioned against the abuse of setting aside applications by parties seeking to obtain a backdoor appeal on the substantive merits of an arbitral tribunal's decision, recognising the need to guard against a 'natural inclination' to be drawn to arguments regarding the substantive merits of the underlying dispute in deciding a setting aside application. See *BLC and others v BLB and another* [2014] 4 SLR 79 [53] (hereafter *BLC (SGCA)*).

[6] See also N. Blackaby et al., *Redfern & Hunter on International Arbitration* (6th edn, Oxford University Press 2015) (hereafter Blackaby et al., *Redfern & Hunter*) [10.04].

[7] *CRW Joint Operation v PT Perusahaan Gas Negara (Persero) TBK* [2011] 4 SLR 305 [25]–[26] (hereafter *CRW v Persero (I) (SGCA)*).

[8] See domestic Arbitration Act (n 2), Section 17(2) ('Where an arbitrator or umpire has misconducted himself or the proceedings, or an arbitration or award has been improperly procured, the court may set aside the award.'). See M. Hwang SC and S. Zihua, 'Egregious Errors and Public Policy: Are the Singapore Courts too Arbitration Friendly?' in T.M. Yeo et al. (eds), *SAL Conference 2011: Developments in Singapore Law between 2006 and 2010—Trends and Perspectives* (Academy Publishing 2011) [6].

[9] Prior to 1994, a party may apply for a declaration under Order 69 Rule 3 of the Rules of Court that an award made by an arbitrator is not binding on the ground that it was made without jurisdiction. *See* G.G.J. Yuh, 'The Law of Recognition and Enforcement of Arbitration Awards in Singapore' (1993) 14 Singapore Law Review 220, 228.

A. INTRODUCTION AND OVERVIEW   213

aside of international arbitration awards is set forth in Article 34 of the Model Law and Section 24 of the IAA.

Consistent with the drafters' intentions of harmonising the grounds for judicial re-   **16.05**
course against arbitral awards, Article 34 of the Model Law sets forth limited grounds for setting aside that intentionally mirror the grounds for refusing enforcement of an award under the New York Convention.[10] As a consequence, as reflected in the jurisprudence of Singapore courts,[11] decisions on resisting enforcement of an award are relevant and persuasive authority for setting aside actions under Article 34 of the Model Law and Section 24 of the IAA, and *vice versa*.

Section 24 of the IAA was introduced together with the IAA in 1994 and supple-   **16.06**
ments Article 34 of the Model Law with additional limited grounds for setting aside an award. Section 24(a) was based on a recommendation by the Singapore Law Reform Committee to include an adaptation of Section 36(3) of the then Draft New Zealand Arbitration Act as 'a further safeguard' for awards obtained by corruption, fraud or the partiality of the arbitrators.[12] There did not appear to be discussion, however, in the Singapore Law Reform Committee's report or the preparatory materials for the International Arbitration Bill 1994 regarding the inclusion of references to 'rules of natural justice'. Besides Singapore, only Australia, Fiji, and New Zealand have arbitration statutes that include references to breaches of 'the rules of natural justice' as a ground for setting aside. [13]

The remaining sections of this chapter elaborate on the scope of the provisions on set-   **16.07**
ting aside in Article 34 of the Model Law and Section 24 of the IAA, cross-cutting issues that apply to setting aside applications before the Singapore courts, and the grounds available to parties for setting aside an award.

---

[10] Report of the Secretary-General, 'Possible Features of a Model Law on International Commercial Arbitration' (1981) UN Doc. A/CN.9/207 [110].

[11] *AJU v AJT* [2011] SGCA 41; [2011] 4 SLR 739 [34]–[38] (hereafter *AJU v AJT*) (on public policy); *Jiangsu Overseas Group Co Ltd v Concord Energy Pte Ltd* [2016] 4 SLR 1336 [46]–[47] (hereafter *Jiangsu Overseas Group*) (no valid arbitration agreement under Article 34(2)(a)(i) and Article 36(1)(a)(i) Model Law); *Vitol Asia Pte Ltd v Machlogic Singapore Pte Ltd* [2021] 4 SLR 464 [121] (hereafter *Vitol Asia*) (inability to present case under Article 34(2)(a)(ii) and Article 36(1)(a)(ii) Model Law); *Bloomberry Resorts and Hotels Inc and another v Global Gaming Philippines LLC and another* [2020] SGHC 113 [74] (hereafter *Bloomberry (Final Award) (SGHC)*) (breach of natural justice and Article 18 equal opportunity to be heard under Section 24(b) and Article 34(2)(a)(ii) IAA and Article 36(1)(a)(ii) Model Law); *Sanum Investments Ltd v ST Group Co Ltd and others* [2020] 3 SLR 225 [113]–[114] (hereafter *Sanum v ST (SGHC)*) (incorrect number of arbitrators—Article 34(2)(a)(iv) and Article 36(1)(a)(iv) Model Law).

[12] Law Reform Committee, Singapore Academy of Law, *Report on Review of Arbitration Laws* (August 1993) [23].

[13] Unlike Section 24 of the IAA, those statutes expressly link any such breaches to the question of whether the arbitral award is contrary to public policy. See New Zealand Arbitration Act 1996, Section 34(6); Australia International Arbitration Act 1974 (Cth), Section 19; Fiji International Arbitration Act 2017, Section 55(1). See also J. Lim, 'Chapter 17: Country Report: Singapore' in F. Ferrari et al. (eds), *Due Process as a Limit to Discretion in International Commercial Arbitration* (Kluwer Law International 2020) 358 (hereafter Lim, 'Country Report (Singapore)'). In *CPU v CPX* [2022] SGHC(I) 11 [55], Sir Bernard Eder IJ observed that Section 24(b) of the IAA was focused on events that occurred in connection with the actual making of the award such as procedural decisions.

214 SETTING ASIDE AN AWARD

B. Scope of Setting Aside Action and other Cross-Cutting Issues

1. Only 'Awards' May be Set Aside

16.08 Setting aside is available only against an 'award' as defined in Section 2(1) of the IAA. An 'award' under the IAA includes interim, partial, or interlocutory awards.[14] Other decisions rendered by an arbitral tribunal that do not qualify as 'awards', such as procedural orders or directions, cannot be set aside.

2. Not an Action to Resist Enforcement

16.09 An action to set aside an award is distinct from an action to resist enforcement under Sections 19 or 29 of the IAA. They are remedies of a different nature. As noted by the Analytical Commentary on the Model Law, a setting aside application is the 'only means for actively attacking the award' by initiating proceedings at the seat for judicial review.[15] This is different from a party's 'right to defend himself against the award' by requesting refusal of recognition or enforcement in proceedings initiated by another party.[16]

16.10 This distinction was affirmed by the Singapore Court of Appeal in *Astro (SGCA)*.[17] Following an examination of the *travaux preparatoires* of the Model Law, the Court of Appeal held that an award debtor had a 'choice of remedies' between the active remedy of setting aside the award and the passive remedy of resisting enforcement of the award.[18] Finding that this 'choice of remedies' is at 'the heart' of the Model Law architecture, the Court of Appeal held that an award debtor may resist enforcement of an award even if it had not applied to set aside the award and the time limits for setting aside had expired.[19]

16.11 Different consequences also flow from a successful setting aside application and a successful application to resist enforcement. The immediate effect of a setting aside is that the award ceases to have legal effect, at least in the arbitral seat, and no longer has *res judicata* effect on the parties, any of whom may start a fresh arbitration to the extent the arbitration agreement survives the setting aside action, and any arbitration claims remain admissible.[20] In contrast, a successful application to resist enforcement will not generally result in the award losing its *res judicata* effect.[21]

---

[14] See generally Chapters 4 and 14.

[15] Analytical Commentary on the Model Law (n 3) 71.

[16] Ibid.

[17] *PT First Media TBK (formerly known as PT Broadband Multimedia TBK) v Astro Nusantara International BV and others and another appeal* [2014] 1 SLR 372 (hereafter *Astro (SGCA)*).

[18] Ibid, [65]–[71]. See Chapter 14 section C.

[19] Ibid, [75]–[77].

[20] *AKN and another v ALC and others and other appeals* [2016] 1 SLR 966 [52]–[54] (hereafter *AKN v ALC (II)*).

[21] There may be exceptions in circumstances where a refusal to enforce an arbitral award by courts at the arbitral seat is the functional equivalent of a setting aside. For example, this may be the case where an award is refused enforcement because the arbitral seat was designated wrongly and contrary to the parties' agreement. See e.g. *ST Group v Sanum Investments Limited* [2020] 1 SLR 1 (hereafter *Sanum v ST (SGCA)*).

B. SCOPE OF SETTING ASIDE ACTION AND OTHER CROSS-CUTTING ISSUES   215

An arbitral award that has been set aside at the seat may also be refused enforcement   **16.12**
in other jurisdictions pursuant to Article V(1)(e) of the New York Convention.[22] The
Singapore Court of Appeal has referred to this as the *erga omnes* effect of a successful
setting aside application.[23] In contrast, a successful application to resist enforcement does not give rise to a separate ground for refusal of enforcement, although the
Singapore High Court has observed that it may be possible for a decision on enforcement to give rise to issue estoppel with respect to other enforcement proceedings in
other jurisdictions.[24] However, Singapore courts have rejected the application of issue
estoppel in the context of setting aside applications before the arbitral seat that call for a
de novo review of the arbitral award.[25]

3. Not Judicial Review of a Ruling on Jurisdiction

An application to set aside an award under Article 34 of the Model Law or Section 24 of   **16.13**
the IAA is also distinct from an application for judicial review of a ruling of jurisdiction
under Article 16(3) of the Model Law, read with Section 10 of the IAA. As explained
in Chapter 10, an application for judicial review under Article 16(3) of the Model Law
can only be invoked against a decision which deals purely with the jurisdiction of the
tribunal.[26] If the decision deals even marginally with the substance of the dispute, it
cannot be reviewed under Article 16(3) of the Model Law and the only recourse available against the decision is through a setting aside application.[27]

As discussed in Chapter 10, there are several differences between a setting aside action   **16.14**
and an appeal from a jurisdictional ruling that may inform a choice between these remedies. First, the grounds for challenge are different.[28] Second, an appeal from a jurisdictional ruling has to be brought within 30 days, whereas a setting aside application has
to be brought within three months.[29] Finally, in an appeal from a jurisdictional ruling,
the court is empowered to make an award or order of costs, but the court has no such
power when it sets aside an award.[30]

A party that elects not to challenge a tribunal's preliminary ruling on its jurisdiction under   **16.15**
Article 16(3) of the Model Law is precluded from initiating setting aside proceedings

---

[22] See New York Convention, Article V(1)(e) ('The award has not yet become binding on the parties, or has
been set aside or suspended by a competent authority of the country in which, or under the law of which, that
award was made.'). See G. Born, *International Commercial Arbitration* (3rd edn, Kluwer Law International 2021)
3270 (hereafter Born, *International Commercial Arbitration*) 1677–8 ('Article V(1)(e) permits non-recognition of
awards in virtually any case where they have been annulled in the arbitral seat, without expressly imposing international limits on the permissible grounds for such annulment.'). See Chapter 18.
[23] *Astro (SGCA)* (n 17) [65]–[71].
[24] *BAZ v BBA* [2020] 5 SLR 266 [43], [50] (hereafter *BAZ (SGHC)*). See Chapter 9.
[25] Ibid, [44]–[52].
[26] *AQZ v ARA* [2015] 2 SLR 972 [65], [69] (hereafter *AQZ v ARA*).
[27] Ibid, [69].
[28] See Chapter 9.
[29] See Chapter 9.
[30] See Chapter 9.

216 SETTING ASIDE AN AWARD

under Article 34 on grounds that could have been raised earlier. In *Astro (SGCA)*,[31] the Singapore Court of Appeal considered this question, albeit *obiter dicta*. The Court of Appeal observed that, in light of the policy of certainty and finality under the Model Law, it would be surprising for a party to retain the right to bring an application to set aside an award under Article 34 on a ground which it could have raised via the active remedy in Article 16(3) before the supervising court at an earlier stage.[32] This was subsequently affirmed by Quentin Loh J (as he then was) in *Rakna Arakshaka (SGHC)*, however, this too was *obiter dicta* given that Loh J ultimately held that a failure to challenge under Article 16(3) would have no preclusive effect in a case where a party does not participate in arbitration proceedings at all.[33] The Court of Appeal in that case was of the same view.

4. Relationship between Setting Aside and an Article 13 Challenge of an Arbitrator

16.16 Article 13(3) of the Model Law provides for the right to challenge an arbitrator before courts at the arbitral seat. This is also different from a setting aside application: Article 13 is directed at an arbitrator, whereas Article 34 is directed at the award. The two remedies are, however, interrelated. In *Astro (SGCA)*, the Singapore Court of Appeal observed *obiter dicta* that it would be surprising for a party to retain the right to bring an application to set aside an award under Article 34 on a ground where it did not bring a challenge it could have brought under Article 13(3) at an earlier stage.[34]

16.17 An unresolved question is whether, in circumstances where an arbitrator has rendered awards before an Article 13 challenge has been fully heard, a successful challenge to the arbitrator would have the consequential effect of setting aside any award or awards issued by that arbitrator. In *PT Central Investindo*, Belinda Ang J considered this question, but her observations were *obiter dicta* because she had found no apparent bias on the part of the arbitrator. Considering the silence in Article 13(3), and in light of the principle of limited judicial intervention under Article 5, Ang J's view was that Singapore courts had no consequential powers to annul the award on the ground that a challenged arbitrator had been successfully removed, and a separate application to set aside an award had to be filed.[35] Nonetheless, Ang J observed that an arbitrator's apparent bias or partiality would be a ground for setting aside under Article 34(2)(a)(iv).[36] As a practical matter, if they wish to preserve the right to set aside such awards, parties should ensure that they bring a separate setting aside application within the three month time period.

---

[31] *Astro (SGCA)* (n 17) [100]–[123].
[32] Ibid, [130].
[33] *Rakna Arakshaka Lanka Ltd v Avant Garde Maritime Services (Private) Limited* [2019] 4 SLR 995 [71]–[77] (hereafter *Rakna Arakshaka (SGHC)*).
[34] *Astro (SGCA)* (n 17) [130].
[35] *PT Central Investindo v Franciscus Wongso and others and another matter* [2014] 4 SLR 978 [123]–[128] (hereafter *PT Central Investindo*).
[36] Ibid, [133]–[134].

B. SCOPE OF SETTING ASIDE ACTION AND OTHER CROSS-CUTTING ISSUES   217

5. Article 34(1) Model Law—Exclusive Recourse

The word 'only' indicates that the grounds for setting aside under Article 34 of the Model **16.18**
Law were intended to be exhaustive. During the drafting of the Model Law, the United
Nations Commission on International Trade Law (UNCITRAL) Secretariat proposed
at the outset that the Model Law should incorporate the New York Convention grounds
for refusing recognition and enforcement of an award as grounds for setting aside, and
that these grounds should constitute the exclusive means for judicial recourse against
the award.

This principle was accepted very early on by the UNCITRAL Working Group and not **16.19**
significantly questioned thereafter. This eventually found expression in Article 34(1)
and is also mentioned in the heading of Article 34.[37] As noted in the Working Group's
Report:

> That solution would facilitate international commercial arbitration by enhancing
> predictability and expeditiousness and would go a long way towards establishing a
> harmonized system of limited recourse against awards and their enforcement. It
> was [further] stated in support that the reasons set forth in article V of the New York
> Convention provided sufficient safeguards, and that some of the grounds suggested as
> additions to the list were likely to fall under the public policy reason.[38]

Although Section 24 of the IAA contains two additional grounds for setting aside an **16.20**
arbitral award, the Singapore Court of Appeal has confirmed that this does not alter
the fact that the setting aside grounds listed in the IAA and the Model Law constitute
an exclusive means of recourse against an award before Singapore courts.[39] The principle of exclusive recourse in Article 34 of the Model Law and Section 24 of the IAA is
consistent with, and gives effect to, the Singapore courts' philosophy of minimal curial
intervention.[40]

In contrast to Article 34(1) of the Model Law, the word 'only' does not appear in Section **16.21**
48 of the domestic Arbitration Act, the equivalent provision applicable to the setting
aside of domestic arbitration awards, although the grounds for setting aside listed in
Section 48 are the same as those in Article 34 of the Model Law and Section 24 of the
IAA. In theory, this may mean that Section 48 of the domestic Arbitration Act permits setting aside a domestic arbitration award on grounds additional to those listed

---

[37] H.M. Holtzmann and J. Neuhaus, 'Model Law, Chapter VII, Article 34 [Application for setting aside as exclusive recourse against arbitral award]' in H.M. Holtzmann and J. Neuhaus, *A Guide to the UNCITRAL Model Law
on International Commercial Arbitration: Legislative History and Commentary* (Kluwer Law International 1989)
911–12 (hereafter Holtzmann and Neuhaus, *Guide to the UNCITRAL Model Law*).

[38] Ibid, 912–13.

[39] See e.g. *Astro (SGCA)* (n 17) [79].

[40] *PT Asuransi Jasa Indonesia (Persero) v Dexia Bank SA* [2007] 1 SLR(R) 597 [57] (hereafter *PT Asuransi
(SGCA)*); *Soh Beng Tee & Co Pte Ltd v Fairmount Development Pte Ltd* [2007] SGCA 28; [2007] 3 SLR(R) 86 [65]
(hereafter *Soh Beng Tee (SGCA)*).

218   SETTING ASIDE AN AWARD

in Section 48, although Singapore courts have not yet considered this question or the ambit of any such additional grounds for setting aside.[41]

6. Article 34(1) Model Law—Not an Appeal

16.22   Another key distinction between the IAA and the domestic Arbitration Act is that the latter allows an appeal from arbitral awards on questions of law,[42] whereas the former does not permit any appeals on questions of law. In *PT Asuransi (SGCA)*, the Singapore Court of Appeal held that any errors or law or fact are 'final and binding on the parties and may not be appealed against or set aside'.[43] Thus, an error of law, *without more*, is unlikely to be sufficient for an award to be set aside under the IAA. In that case, the Court of Appeal specifically rejected the argument that the public policy provision in Article 34 of the Model Law would permit awards to be set aside for errors of law or fact.[44] The Court of Appeal reaffirmed this principle in *Prometheus Marine (SGCA)*, holding that an error of law, 'however irrational', cannot be a ground for setting aside an award.[45]

16.23   Singapore courts are reluctant to permit a setting aside application to be used as an avenue for appealing errors of law or fact made by the arbitrators. As the Singapore Court of Appeal held in *BLC (SGCA)* in the context of a challenge based on Section 24(b) of the IAA, Singapore courts will be wary of attempts by parties disgruntled with an award to obtain what is effectively an appeal on the substantive merits through a setting aside application.[46]

16.24   Thus, the Court of Appeal held in *BLC (SGCA)* that, even in circumstances where an arbitrator had misunderstood the arguments presented to him and made erroneous assumptions, this would not be a breach of natural justice even if it amounted to a 'serious error of law and/or fact'. In *AKN v ALC (I)*, the Court of Appeal affirmed this view, noting that the courts have to bear in mind that 'there is no right of appeal from arbitral awards' and that the grounds for curial intervention are 'narrowly circumscribed'.[47]

---

[41] Some commentators have doubted whether Section 48 of the domestic Arbitration Act in fact contemplates a broader discretion for Singapore courts to set aside a domestic arbitration award. See C.T. Tan and T. Cooke, 'Challenge of Arbitral Awards' in S. Menon and D. Brock (eds), *Arbitration in Singapore: A Practical Guide* (Sweet & Maxwell 2014) 466 (hereafter Tan and Cooke, 'Challenge of Arbitral Awards').

[42] Domestic arbitration awards are subject to appeal on questions of law under Section 49 of the domestic Arbitration Act. Singapore courts have held that an 'error of law' is not the same as a 'question of law', and the former does not give rise to a right of appeal. See *Northern Elevator Manufacturing Sdn Bhd v United Engineers (Singapore) Pte Ltd* [2004] 2 SLR(R) 494 [18]–[19].

[43] *PT Asuransi (SGCA)* (n 40) [57].

[44] Ibid, [57]. The Singapore Court of Appeal declined to follow the approach of the Supreme Court of India in *Oil & Natural Gas Corporation Ltd v SAW Pipes Ltd* AIR 2003 SC 2629.

[45] *Prometheus Marine Pte Ltd v King, Ann Rita and another appeal* [2018] 1 SLR 1 [57] (hereafter *Prometheus Marine (SGCA)*).

[46] *BLC (SGCA)* (n 5) [53].

[47] *AKN and another v ALC and others and other appeals* [2015] SGCA 18; [2015] 3 SLR 488 [38]–[39] (hereafter *AKN v ALC (I)*).

B. SCOPE OF SETTING ASIDE ACTION AND OTHER CROSS-CUTTING ISSUES   219

This restrictive approach to curial intervention has been extended to procedural orders   **16.25**
as well.[48] In *Republic of India v Vedanta Resources plc*,[49] the Singapore Court of Appeal
denied the applicant's request for declaratory relief on the basis it was an abuse of process and would amount to a 'backdoor appeal' on an arbitral tribunal's procedural order
with regard to cross-disclosure of evidence.[50]

A few jurisdictions permit appeals on questions of law from an international arbitra-   **16.26**
tion award. For example, Section 69 of the English Arbitration Act 1996 provides that,
unless parties otherwise agree, a party to arbitral proceedings may appeal to English
courts on a question of law arising from an arbitral award. Such a right of appeal can
only be invoked with the agreement of all the other parties to the proceedings or with
the leave of the English courts.[51] Other jurisdictions provide for an opt-in right of
appeal.[52]

In 2019, the Ministry of Law announced a public consultation on proposed amendments   **16.27**
to the IAA that included a proposal permitting appeals to the Singapore High Court
on questions of law, provided that parties have agreed to opt in to such a mechanism.[53]
Various commentators have opined on the merits of such a proposed amendment, with
some arguing that it would permit the development of commercial law jurisprudence.[54]
Other commentators have signalled the need for caution, in light of the competing interests in efficiency and the finality of awards.[55] Following the public consultation, the
subsequent amendments to the IAA came into effect on 1 December 2020 without any
amendments regarding appeals on questions of law. At the time of publication, these
proposals were still being studied and evaluated by the Ministry of Law.[56]

---

[48] *Republic of India v Vedanta Resources plc* [2021] 2 SLR 354 (hereafter *Republic of India v Vedanta Resources plc*).
[49] Ibid.
[50] Ibid, [2], [34].
[51] English Arbitration Act 1996, Section 69(2). The conditions under which the Court may grant leave are strictly circumscribed. Leave will only be granted if the court is satisfied that the determination of the question of law will substantially affect the rights of one or more of the parties, the question is one which the arbitral tribunal was asked to determine, the decision of the tribunal on that question was obviously wrong or (for a question of general public importance) open to serious doubt, and it is just and proper in all the circumstances for the court to determine that question. See English Arbitration Act 1996, Section 69(3).
[52] See e.g. Hong Kong Arbitration Ordinance, Section 99 and Schedule 2, Section 5; New Zealand Arbitration Act 1996, Schedule 2, Section 5.
[53] See Ministry of Law, 'Public Consultation on International Arbitration Act' (Ministry of Law, 26 June 2019) <https://www.mlaw.gov.sg/news/public-consultations/public-consultation-on-international-arbitration-act> accessed 4 April 2022, [11]–[12] (hereafter Ministry of Law Public Consultation).
[54] See e.g. Singapore Academy of Law, Law Reform Committee, *Report on the Right of Appeal against International Arbitration Awards on Questions of Law* (Singapore Academy of Law, February 2020) [2.13]–[2.40]; G. Goh, 'Curial Review on Questions of Law: A Desirable Move for Singapore' (Law Gazette, February 2020) <https://lawgazette.com.sg/feature/curial-review-on-questions-of-law/> accessed 4 April 2022.
[55] See e.g. L.Y. Tan and C. Sim, 'Appeals on Questions of Law in International Arbitration—A Comparative Perspective from New York' [2020] Singapore Arbitration Law and Practice 18 [20]–[22]; Herbert Smith Freehills, 'Singapore Arbitration Update: A Potential Change for 'Opt-In' Appeals for Errors of Law and Court Confirmation of the Correct Standard to Be Met to Restrain Winding Up Proceedings Where a Claim Is Subject to Arbitration' (Herbert Smith Freehills, 9 May 2019) <https://hsfnotes.com/arbitration/2019/05/09/singapore-arbitration-upd ate-a-potential-change-for-opt-in-appeals-for-errors-of-law-and-court-confirmation-of-the-correct-standard-to-be-met-to-restrain-winding-up-proceedings-where-a-claim-is-s/> accessed 4 April 2022.
[56] *Parliamentary Debates Singapore: Official Report*, vol 95 (5 October 2020) (Mr Edwin Tong Chun Fai (Second Minister for Law)) on the International Arbitration (Amendment) Bill.

220   SETTING ASIDE AN AWARD

16.28   In the authors' respectful view, the concerns surrounding a proposed right of an opt-in appeal may have more to do with perception rather than substance. In principle, considerations of finality and efficiency need not trump party autonomy. Where parties have specifically agreed on an appeal mechanism, there is no risk of undermining parties' expectations of finality. Where such agreement exists, there is little or no basis to deny parties their desire for greater control by national courts at the seat. It is, however, important to ensure that the ambit of any potential appeal is clearly and carefully circumscribed to avoid unnecessary disputes about scope and adding to the complexity and costs of arbitral proceedings.

7. Agreements to Limit or Waive Grounds for Setting Aside; Implied Waiver of Grounds for Setting Aside

16.29   Parties may wish to waive or limit their ability to set aside awards for a variety of reasons. For example, they may wish to enhance the finality of arbitral decision-making and reduce the risks and costs of having to deal with unmeritorious annulment applications. They may also wish to avoid 'double control' of an award, that is, judicial review at both the seat and the place of enforcement, as well as the risk of conflicting decisions between courts at the seat and courts at the place of enforcement.

16.30   The provisions of the Model Law and the IAA are silent on whether the grounds for setting aside are mandatory or waivable.[57] Singapore courts have not specifically addressed whether they will recognise or give effect to agreements to waive, or otherwise limit, the scope of review of awards under Article 34 of the Model Law and Section 24 of the IAA.

16.31   In *John Holland*, the Singapore High Court held that the parties' choice of the International Chamber of Commerce (ICC) Rules had the effect of excluding the application of the Model Law entirely (but not the IAA).[58] As a consequence, the High Court held that only the grounds for setting aside in Section 24 of the IAA applied, but not the grounds for setting aside in Article 34 of the Model Law.[59] This decision was legislatively overruled by Section 15(2) of the IAA, which clarifies that a provision in an arbitration agreement referring to or adopting any rules of arbitration shall not of itself be sufficient to exclude the application of the Model Law or the IAA to the arbitration. In light of these developments, it is not clear whether *John Holland* remains good authority for the proposition that parties can contract out of the grounds for setting aside under the Model Law or the IAA.

---

[57] The principle of party autonomy is only given effect to the extent it does not conflict with provisions of the IAA or the Model Law that are expressly or impliedly of mandatory application. See e.g. A. Henderson, 'Lex Arbitri, Procedural Law and the Seat of Arbitration' (2014) 26 Singapore Academy of Law Journal 86, [33].

[58] *John Holland Pty Ltd (formerly known as John Holland Construction & Engineering Pty Ltd) v Toyo Engineering Corp (Japan)* [2001] 1 SLR(R) 443 [14] (hereafter *John Holland*).

[59] Ibid, [16]–[18].

B. SCOPE OF SETTING ASIDE ACTION AND OTHER CROSS-CUTTING ISSUES   221

In a more limited context, Singapore courts have found that parties can impliedly waive   **16.32**
objections based on breaches of due process if they fail to promptly raise such objections.[60] In *Kempinski Hotels (SGCA)*,[61] having already found there was no breach of
due process, the Singapore Court of Appeal noted *obiter dicta* that any such breach was
waived because the challenging party proceeded with the arbitration without promptly
stating any objection. In the context of an enforcement application, the Singapore
Court of Appeal also appeared to accept that jurisdictional objections relating to the existence of an arbitration agreement could be waived in principle, so long as such waiver
was communicated in clear and equivocal terms.[62]

This is consistent with Article 4 of the Model Law, which provides that parties are   **16.33**
deemed to have waived their right to object if they know of any non-compliance with
any 'provision of this [Model Law] from which the parties may derogate' and do not
object in a timely manner. The commentary by the UNCITRAL Secretariat states
that Article 4 only covers waiver of non-compliance with a 'non-mandatory' provision of the Model Law and not intended to cover 'fundamental procedural defects'.[63]
This begs the question of which of the provisions of Article 34 of the Model Law and
Section 24 of the IAA are mandatory, which has not been conclusively resolved by
Singapore courts.

Very few jurisdictions have express provisions in arbitration legislation that address the   **16.34**
issue of wavier of setting aside grounds.[64] For example, France provides in its arbitration legislation that the parties may, at any time, expressly waive their right to bring a
setting aside action;[65] however, France only permits a full wavier of judicial review and
not partial or '*a la carte*' waivers.[66]

In a number of Model Law jurisdictions, absent express statutory guidance, courts   **16.35**
have permitted waiver or limitation of setting aside actions to varying extents. For example, Ontario courts have held that Article 34 of the Model Law is non-mandatory
and therefore judicial review on Article 34 grounds can be excluded by agreement of
the parties, 'so long as their agreement does not conflict with any mandatory provision of the Model Law', which includes provisions such as Article 18 of the Model Law

---

[60] See Lim, 'Country Report (Singapore)' (n 13) 371.

[61] *PT Prima International Development v Kempinski Hotels SA and other appeals* [2012] 4 SLR 98 [63] (hereafter *Kempinski Hotels (SGCA)*).

[62] *Astro (SGCA)* (n 17) [199]–[202].

[63] Analytical Commentary on the Model Law (n 3) 17.

[64] Some jurisdictions, such as Belgium, Sweden, and Switzerland, have legislation that expressly provides for the enforceability of agreements to limit or waive judicial review of awards, provided none of the parties is a na-tional or domicile of the arbitral seat. See Belgian Judicial Code, Article 1718; Swedish Arbitration Act, Section 51; Swiss Private International Law Act, Article 192(1). Other jurisdictions, such as Egypt, Italy, and Portugal, ex-pressly provide in their arbitration legislation that agreements to limit or waive the parties' right to seek annulment of the award are not enforceable. See Italian Code of Civil Procedure, Article 829(1); Portuguese Law on Voluntary Arbitration 2011, Article 46(5); Egyptian Arbitration Law, Article 54(1).

[65] French Civil Procedure Code, Article 1522.

[66] M. Scherer, 'The Fate of Parties' Agreements on Judicial Review of Awards: A Comparative and Normative Analysis of Party-Autonomy at the Post-Award Stage' (2016) 32 Arbitration International 437, 443 (hereafter Scherer, 'The Fate of Parties' Agreements on Judicial Review').

222 SETTING ASIDE AN AWARD

(addressing the equality of parties and the parties' right to present their cases).[67] New Zealand courts have reached the opposite conclusion, holding that parties cannot derogate by agreement from Article 34 of the Model Law.[68] In Germany, waiver is possible for the four setting aside grounds under Article 34(2)(a) of the Model Law but not for the two setting aside grounds under Article 34(2)(b) of the Model Law, because the latter grounds are deemed to be in the public interest and therefore non-waivable.[69]

16.36 As part of the 2019 public consultation, the Singapore Ministry of Law proposed amendments to the IAA to allow parties to agree to waive or limit the grounds for setting aside under the Model Law and the IAA.[70] Specifically, the Ministry of Law proposed that parties should have the option—only after the award has been rendered—to limit or waive by agreement, the annulment grounds set forth in Section 24(b) of the IAA and Article 34(2)(a), but may not limit or waive by agreement, the annulment grounds in Section 24(a) and Article 34(2)(b).[71] Commentators have expressed support for such a proposal, although there are different views on how it should be implemented.[72]

16.37 In the authors' view, there is much to recommend the proposed amendment to the IAA by the Ministry of Law. It would clarify the existing uncertainty regarding the enforceability of agreements to waiver or limit grounds for setting aside. It also takes a balanced position that weighs party autonomy against concerns about the need for judicial control of awards at the seat to protect against extreme misconduct by arbitrators, including fraud, corruption, or arbitrariness. The waiver of the right to set aside an award does not mean that judicial control over an award is excluded entirely—courts at the place of enforcement are still able to review the award in recognition and enforcement proceedings. Accordingly, where commercial parties have agreed to limit or waive judicial review of an arbitral award at the seat so that the arbitrator's decision enjoys a greater degree of finality, this bargain should be upheld.

16.38 If the proposed amendment were adopted, there are good reasons for permitting *ex ante* waiver (i.e. before a dispute has even arisen) and dispensing with the requirement in the Ministry of Law's proposal that waiver can only be made 'after the award has been rendered'. Given that any agreement on wavier would be a central element of the

---

[67] *Noble China Inc v Lei Kat Cheong*, (1998) 42 OR (3d) 69 (Ontario Superior Court) (hereafter *Noble China*). See also *Popack v Lipszyc* 2015 ONSC 3460 (Ontario Superior Court) [47]–[52] (affirming the approach in *Noble China* and noting that the 'proper approach is to consider to what extent the Arbitration Agreement seeks to exclude Article 34, and if it does, to what extent it is effective in doing so given the specific matters at issue.'). Although the Uniform Law Conference of Canada published a Uniform Arbitration Act in 2016 that provides that parties may not contract out of court review of arbitral decisions, these provisions have not been adopted or implemented in Ontario. See Ontario International Commercial Arbitration Act 2017.

[68] *Methanex Motunui Ltd v Spellman* [2004] NZCA 418; [2004] 3 NZLR 454.

[69] Scherer, 'The Fate of Parties' Agreements on Judicial Review' (n 66) 444.

[70] See Ministry of Law Public Consultation (n 53) [16].

[71] Ibid, [16].

[72] See W. Tan, 'Allowing the Exclusion of Set-Aside Proceedings: An Innovative Means of Enhancing Singapore's Position as an Arbitration Hub' (2019) 15(2) Asian International Arbitration Journal 87; I. Ng, 'A closer look at proposed amendments to the International Arbitration Act: How far should parties be allowed to contract out of the grounds for annulling an award?' (Singapore Law Blog, 20 August 2019) <https://singaporelawblog.sg/blog/article/239> accessed 4 April 2022.

B. SCOPE OF SETTING ASIDE ACTION AND OTHER CROSS-CUTTING ISSUES   223

parties' agreement to arbitrate, there is little basis in principle to distinguish between *ex ante* waiver and waiver after an award has been rendered. Practically speaking, the freedom to waive the right to set aside an award after it has been rendered is of more limited utility—parties are unlikely to agree after an award has been rendered.

In addition, if agreements to waive or limit setting aside actions before Singapore courts were permitted, such agreements should be strictly construed and any waiver or limitation must be clear, unequivocal, and specific.[73] Many arbitration rules include provisions that state that an award is 'final and binding' and that the parties waive their rights to 'any form of appeal, review or recourse' to any court with respect to such an award in so far as such wavier may be validly made.[74] It is a matter of construction in each case whether the parties' agreement to such arbitration rules constitutes an agreement to waive or limit setting aside actions. In a slightly different context, the Singapore High Court has held that agreement to the 1998 version of the ICC Rules, whose Article 28(6) provided for waiver of all 'recourse' against an award, was sufficient to exclude the right of appeal under Section 49 of the domestic Arbitration Act.[75] Notwithstanding that authority, however, the better view is probably that the mere assent to arbitration rules that incorporate such broad but generic provisions cannot be sufficient to constitute wavier or limitation of the parties' important rights of recourse against the award at the seat, without further convincing evidence that the parties truly intended to make such waiver or limitation.[76] Indeed, practical reality bears this out: many setting aside cases involve arbitrations under the ICC Rules or SIAC Rules, both of which contain generic waiver provisions, without the issue of waiver of setting aside having come before the Singapore courts.

16.39

8. Article 34(2) Model Law—Residual Discretion and Prejudice

The use of the word 'may', rather than 'shall', in Article 34(2) of the Model Law suggests an element of discretion, and Singapore courts have held that they have a residual discretion, once a ground for setting aside has been made out, to decide whether to set aside the award.[77] This discretion is also recognised in other Model Law jurisdictions,

16.40

---

[73] See Born, *International Commercial Arbitration* (n 22) 3668–71.

[74] See e.g. SIAC Rules 2016, Rule 32.11; ICC Arbitration Rules 2021, Article 35.6. See also C. Bratic, 'The Parties Hereby Waive All Recourse … But Not That One: Why Parties Adopt Exclusion Agreements and Why Courts Hesitate to Enforce Them' (2018) 12 Dispute Resolution International 105, 106 (hereafter Bratic, 'Exclusion Agreements').

[75] *Daimler South East Asia Pte Ltd v Front Row Investment Holdings (Singapore) Pte Ltd* [2012] 4 SLR 837 [18]. Section 49 of the domestic Arbitration Act provides for a statutory right of appeal on a question of law against the arbitral award. Section 49(2) of the domestic Arbitration Act provides that such right of appeal may be excluded by agreement: 'Notwithstanding subsection (1), the parties may agree to exclude the jurisdiction of the Court under this section and an agreement to dispense with reasons for the arbitral tribunal's award shall be treated as an agreement to exclude the jurisdiction of the Court under this section.'

[76] This is consistent with the approach taken in a number of jurisdictions, including France and Switzerland. See Born, *International Commercial Arbitration* (n 22) 3668–71; Bratic, 'Exclusion Agreements' (n 74) 114–16.

[77] *CRW v Persero (I) (SGCA)* (n 7) [97]. See also Born, *International Commercial Arbitration* (n 22) 3435–6 ('It is equally clear that the grounds specified in Article 34(2) of the Model Law are permissive and discretionary, not mandatory. That is, a court in the arbitral seat may annul an award if one or more of the Article 34(2) grounds are satisfied, but the court is not mandatorily required by the Model Law to annul the award, even where one of these grounds applies.').

224 SETTING ASIDE AN AWARD

including Hong Kong, New Zealand, and Australia.[78] In *CRW v Persero (I) (SGCA)*, the Court of Appeal held that its residual discretion will only be exercised in very few cases, and only where 'no prejudice had been sustained by the aggrieved party'.[79]

16.41 Subsequent High Court cases have clarified that the absence of prejudice is not a sufficient condition for the Singapore courts to exercise their residual discretion to refuse to set aside an award. In *Triulzi*,[80] in the context of an application under Article 34(2)(a)(ii), Belinda Ang J noted that prejudice was only one factor relevant to the exercise of the discretion, rather than a legal requirement for a setting aside, meaning that there may be instances in which the Singapore courts will nonetheless set aside an award despite the absence of prejudice. In the circumstances, Ang J held that the exercise of the courts' residual discretion to refuse to set aside an award depends on the facts of the particular case at hand, taking into account any prejudice suffered by the award debtor as well as the seriousness of the breach.[81] This fact-specific approach was later affirmed by Steven Chong J (as he then was) in *Coal & Oil*.[82] In the context of a setting aside application under Article 34(2)(a)(iv) of the Model Law, Chong J opined that Singapore courts should not set aside an award for a breach 'of an arid, technical or trifling nature', and should only set aside an award if there has been a 'material breach of procedure' that is 'serious enough', which would often but not always require proof of prejudice.[83]

9. Article 34(3) Model Law—Application to be Made within Three Months

16.42 Under Article 34(3) of the Model Law, an application for setting aside must be made within three months from the receipt of the award or from the date on which a request under Article 33 had been disposed of by the arbitral tribunal.[84]

16.43 The three-month time bar is strict and the Singapore courts have repeatedly held they do not have the power to extend the three months.[85] Although Article 34(3) uses the words 'may not', Singapore courts have held that these words should be interpreted as meaning 'cannot', in light of the clear legislative intention to limit the time during which an award may be challenged and the absence of any provision for the extension

---

[78] *Triulzi Cesare SRL v Xinyi Group (Glass) Co Ltd* [2015] 1 SLR 114 [61]–[62] (hereafter *Triulzi*).

[79] *CRW v Persero (I) (SGCA)* (n 7) [97], [100].

[80] *Triulzi* (n 78) [64], (citing *Grand Pacific Holdings Ltd v Pacific China Holdings Ltd (in liq) (No 1)* [2012] 4 HKLRD 1).

[81] Ibid, [65].

[82] *Coal & Oil Co LLC v GHCL Ltd* [2015] 3 SLR 154 [51] (hereafter *Coal & Oil*).

[83] Ibid, [51].

[84] Commentators note that this is intended to provide a fairly short period of time for the making of a setting aside application. Holtzmann and Neuhaus, *Guide to the UNCITRAL Model Law* (n 37) 919.

[85] *ABC v XYZ Co Ltd* [2003] 3 SLR(R) 546 [9] (hereafter *ABC v XYZ*); *Astro Nusantara International BV and others v PT Ayunda Prima Mitra and others* [2013] 1 SLR 636 [97]; *PT Pukuafu Indah and others v Newmont Indonesia Ltd and another* [2012] 4 SLR 1157 [30] (hereafter *PT Pukuafu*).

B. SCOPE OF SETTING ASIDE ACTION AND OTHER CROSS-CUTTING ISSUES 225

of time.[86] In *PT Pukuafu*, Lee Seiu Kin J further noted that this reading of Article 34(3) is consistent with Order 69A Rule 2(4) of the Rules of Court (now Order 48 Rule 2(3)), which provides that an application to set aside an award under Article 34 of the Model Law and Section 24 of the IAA 'shall be made within 3 months'.[87]

Section 24 of the IAA does not expressly refer to a three-month time bar. The question **16.44** therefore arises as to whether applications for setting aside under Section 24 of the IAA are subject to the three-month time bar under Article 34(3) of the Model Law.

In *Bloomberry (Partial Award) (SGCA)*, the Court of Appeal affirmed the decision of **16.45** the court below to apply the three-month time bar to Section 24 of the IAA,[88] for the following reasons. First, the Court of Appeal held that the legislative materials suggested that Section 24 did not form 'a separate regime' but instead provided additional setting aside grounds as a 'subset of the public policy ground in Art 34(2)(b)(ii)', and therefore it would be absurd to subject Section 24 to more permissive procedural requirements.[89] Second, the Court found that its reading was consistent with Order 69A Rule 2(1) of the Rules of Court (now Order 48 Rule 2(3)) provided that an application to set aside an award under Section 24 or Article 34(2) 'may not be made more than three months after' the receipt of the award.[90] Third, the Court of Appeal held that Model Law jurisdictions (e.g. Malaysia, New Zealand, Ireland, and Italy) that have disapplied the Article 34(3) time limit in the case of fraud have done so by specific legislation.[91] Finally, the Court of Appeal rejected the argument that applying the three-month time bar to fraud would cause unjust results.[92]

The clarification in *Bloomberry* is welcome as the question had hitherto been **16.46** considered in High Court decisions, but not conclusively settled by the Court of Appeal.[93] While the Court of Appeal itself in *Bloomberry* considered its own decision on the time-bar issue to be strictly *obiter*,[94] given the thoroughness of the Court of Appeal's reasoning, this decision is likely to be considered highly persuasive for future cases.

It has been held that the 'application' to be filed within three months under Article **16.47** 34(3) refers to the originating summons, and there is nothing in the Rules of Court which requires an affidavit to be filed at the same time as the originating summons.[95]

---

[86] Ibid, [30].

[87] Ibid.

[88] *Bloomberry Resorts and Hotels Inc and another v Global Gaming Philippines LLC and another* [2021] 1 SLR 1045 [91] (hereafter *Bloomberry (Partial Award) (SGCA)*).

[89] Ibid, [91]–[95].

[90] Ibid, [95].

[91] Ibid, [96].

[92] Ibid, [97].

[93] *Astro Nusantara International BV and others v PT Ayunda Prima Mitra and others* [2016] 2 SLR 737 [120]; *Bloomberry Resorts and Hotels Inc and another v Global Gaming Philippines LLC and another* [2021] 3 SLR 725 [39] (hereafter *Bloomberry (Partial Award) (SGHC)*).

[94] *Bloomberry (Partial Award) (SGCA)* (n 88) [73].

[95] *BZW and another v BZV* [2022] SGCA 1 [45]–[47] (hereafter *BZV (SGCA)*).

226 SETTING ASIDE AN AWARD

A brief statement of the grounds for setting aside is all that an applicant needs to state in the originating summons.[96]

16.48 If a party files an application to set aside an award within the three-month period, can it add fresh grounds outside that time period by way of amendment? In *ABC v XYZ*, Prakash J (as she then was) considered this issue in some detail and observed that it was not addressed by Article 34 of the Model Law.[97] Taking reference from Order 69A Rule 2(1) (now Order 48 Rule 2(3)), which provides that applications to set aside awards are to be made by originating summons, Prakash J held that an amendment would be allowed only if the new grounds proposed to be added 'arise out of the same facts or substantially the same facts' as the grounds specified originally.[98]

16.49 Article 34(3) provides that the three-month time bar begins running 'from the date on which the party making that application had received the award or, if a request had been made under Article 33, from the date on which that request had been disposed of by the arbitral tribunal'. In *BRS v BRQ*, the Court of Appeal held that an Article 33 request did not have to be granted by the tribunal for an extension of three-month period to be effective, as the extension would operate even if the request were denied.[99] However, a request that was an Article 33 request in form but not substance would not be sufficient to extend time.[100] In making such a determination, the Singapore courts are not fettered by the arbitral tribunal's views on whether a request was a properly an Article 33 request.[101] The High Court in *CNA v CNB* further clarified that, so long as *one party* makes a proper Article 33 request, time will be extended for *all parties* under Article 34(3).[102]

10. Article 34(4) Model Law Remission in lieu of Setting Aside

16.50 The remedy under Article 34(4) is also known as 'remission'. There were initial doubts at the UNCITRAL Working Group about its inclusion in the Model Law because remission was not a remedy known to all legal systems.[103] Ultimately, despite the divergent views within the Working Group, the remedy of remission was included as a mechanism for curing remediable defects without having to set aside the award.[104]

16.51 Although remission was stated in an earlier draft of Article 34(4) to apply '[i]f the trial court sets aside the award', this language was not adopted in the final version of Article 34(4), which instead provides that remission is an alternative to, rather than consequence

---

[96] Ibid, [48].
[97] *ABC v XYZ* (n 85) [11].
[98] Ibid, [12]–[20].
[99] *BRS v BRQ and another and another appeal* [2021] 1 SLR 390 [66] (hereafter *BRS v BRQ*).
[100] Ibid, [66], [72].
[101] Ibid, [73]–[81]; *CNA v CNB and another and another matter* [2021] SGHC 192 [39] (hereafter *CNA v CNB*).
[102] Ibid, [64]–[68].
[103] Holtzmann and Neuhaus, *Guide to the UNCITRAL Model Law* (n 37) 920.
[104] Ibid, 920.

B. SCOPE OF SETTING ASIDE ACTION AND OTHER CROSS-CUTTING ISSUES 227

of, setting aside.[105] During the drafting process for Article 34(4), the UNCITRAL Working Group declined to accept an earlier proposal for the courts at the seat to give instructions to the arbitral tribunal on the matters to be considered upon a remission.[106] This was subsequently revised to make clear that remission would be ordered to give the arbitral tribunal an opportunity to 'resume the arbitral proceedings or to take such other action as in the arbitral tribunal's opinion will eliminate the grounds for setting aside'.

(a) Limits on Remission

It has been held that Singapore courts have no power under Article 34(4) to remit matters back to an arbitral tribunal *after* an award has been set aside.[107] In *AKN v ALC (II)*, the Singapore Court of Appeal reasoned that this was based on the plain wording of Article 34(4), read in light of the purpose of remission in Article 34(4) as an alternative to setting aside.[108] The Singapore Court of Appeal also distinguished the judgment of the Singapore High Court in *Kempinski Hotels (SGHC)*, where the High Court remitted certain matters to the arbitral tribunal after setting aside an award, on the basis that the parties in that case had agreed that the arbitrator was not *functus officio*.[109]

16.52

Under Article 34(4), remission is only available if requested by a party, and the effect of remission is to confer jurisdiction to consider the matters remitted on the same tribunal that had made the award.[110] Without remission, the tribunal would have been *functus officio* in respect of the matters determined, having already rendered a final and binding award and thereby having exhausted its mandate.[111] This is supported by the text of Article 32(3) of the Model Law.[112]

16.53

Singapore courts also do not have the power under Article 34(4) to remit matters determined in an award to a new or different tribunal. In *BLC (SGCA)*, the Singapore Court of Appeal confirmed that Article 34(4) did not permit the remission of the award to a new tribunal.[113] Although the Singapore High Court in *Front Row* set aside part of an award and then ordered that the relevant issues 'be tried afresh by a newly appointed

16.54

---

[105] Ibid.
[106] Ibid, 921. This earlier proposal read as follows: 'The Court, when asked to set aside an award, may also order, where appropriate [and if so requested by a party], that the arbitral proceedings be continued. Depending upon the [reason for setting aside] [procedural defect found by the Court], this order may specify the matters to be considered by the arbitral tribunal and may contain other instructions concerning the composition of the arbitral tribunal or the conduct of the proceedings.' UNCITRAL (17th Session) 'Report of the Working Group on International Contract Practices on the Work of its Sixth Session' (22 September 1983) UN Doc. A/CN.9/245 [154]–[155] ('Under another view, the provision should be deleted since remission was not known in all legal systems and, in particular, the idea of orders or instructions to an arbitral tribunal was not acceptable. Under yet another view, the option of remission should be retained, without the giving of orders or instructions as envisaged in the second sentence'). These passages were referred to by the Singapore Court of Appeal in *AKN v ALC (II)* (n 20).
[107] *AKN v ALC (II)* (n 20)[34].
[108] Ibid, [17]–[34].
[109] Ibid, [36]. The Court of Appeal held that to the extent that *Kempinski Hotels (SGHC)* is understood as standing for the proposition that remission may be ordered after setting aside, then it is incorrect and should be regarded as overruled. See Ibid, [38].
[110] *BSM v BSN and another matter* [2019] SGHC 185 [23]; *AKN v ALC (II)* (n 20) [17]–[19]; *CKH v CKG and another matter* [2022] 2 SLR 1 [6]-[8] (hereafter *CKG v CKH (SGCA)*).
[111] *AKN v ALC (II)* (n 20), [17]–[19].
[112] See e.g. Ibid, [19]–[20]; *BLC (SGCA)* (n 5) [119].
[113] Ibid, [119].

228 SETTING ASIDE AN AWARD

arbitrator',[114] the Singapore Court of Appeal subsequently confirmed that this was not remission, but instead a consequential order to the parties to commence a fresh arbitration following a successful setting aside.[115]

16.55 In *CBP (SGCA)*,[116] the Singapore Court of Appeal had to consider whether it could exercise the power to remit under Article 34(4) as an appellate court when remission had not been considered by the Singapore High Court, and after the High Court had already set aside the award. The Court of Appeal held that it did not have the power to remit because the reference to 'court' in Article 34(4) does not include the Court of Appeal, which is not being 'asked to set aside an award'.[117] The Court of Appeal also reasoned that this interpretation is consistent with the purpose of Article 34(4) and the principle that the Singapore courts cannot remit an award after it had been set aside.[118] In other words, the Court of Appeal's function is limited to affirming or reversing the High Court's decision on whether to remit, but only if remission had been applied for and a decision had been made on remission by the High Court.[119]

16.56 Article 34(4) does not require Singapore courts to conduct an analysis of the appropriateness of remission in every case as a precondition to the exercise of its power to set aside an award. This can be contrasted with Section 68(3) of the English Arbitration Act 1996, which provides that an English court 'shall not exercise its power to set aside or to declare an award to be of no effect, in whole or in part, unless it is satisfied that it would be inappropriate to remit the matters to the tribunal for reconsideration'.[120] Section 68(3) applies where a party alleges and establishes a 'serious irregularity' in accordance with Section 68(2),[121] and it requires English courts to satisfy themselves that remission would be inappropriate before setting aside an award, whether in whole or in part.

(b) Circumstances Justifying Remission

16.57 Article 34(4) expressly provides that remission may be ordered 'where appropriate'. Although the term 'where appropriate' may seem vague, this appears to have been a deliberate choice of words. The UNCITRAL Secretariat suggested that the meaning of the term 'where appropriate' was self-evident, noting that it was not possible to describe in detail the 'great variety of cases where remission would either be appropriate or inappropriate'.[122]

16.58 Singapore courts have adopted a similarly broad formulation of the circumstances that justify remission. In *AKN v ALC (II)*, the Singapore Court of Appeal held that, in order

---

[114] *Front Row Investment Holdings (Singapore) Pte Ltd v Daimler South East Asia Pte Ltd* [2010] SGHC 80 (hereafter *Front Row*).
[115] *AKN v ALC (II)* (n 20) [35].
[116] *CBS v CBP* [2021] 1 SLR 935 (hereafter *CBP (SGCA)*).
[117] Ibid, [102]–[103].
[118] Ibid, [104]–[106].
[119] Ibid, [108], [111].
[120] English Arbitration Act 1996, Section 68(3).
[121] It does not apply to jurisdictional challenges under Section 67 of the English Arbitration Act 1996.
[122] Holtzmann and Neuhaus, *Guide to the UNCITRAL Model Law* (n 37) 920–1.

B. SCOPE OF SETTING ASIDE ACTION AND OTHER CROSS-CUTTING ISSUES 229

to exercise its power to remit under Article 34(4), a court had to be satisfied that the circumstances of the case warrant a remission in order to give the same tribunal an opportunity to take steps as may be required to eliminate the grounds for setting aside.[123]

In *Tan Poh Leng*, GP Selvam J declined to apply Article 34(4) and remit the award to the arbitrator in circumstances where he had set aside the award for lack of jurisdiction, because Article 33(4) 'can be invoked only when there are irregularities in the award and not when the award is a nullity'.[124] In that case, the arbitrator had held a further hearing and made an additional award after issuing a final award dismissing the parties' claims and counterclaims. Selvam J held that the additional award was issued after the arbitrator was *functus officio* and therefore outside of the arbitrator's mandate or jurisdiction.[125]   **16.59**

Although Selvam J did not refer to the setting aside grounds in Article 34 of the Model Law, the reasoning in *Tan Poh Leng* suggests that remission is likely to be inapposite in cases where an award is set aside for lack or excess of jurisdiction under Article 34(2)(a)(i) or Article 34(2)(a)(iii) of the Model Law. This is principled and accords with the purpose of the remission mechanism in Article 34(4): remission is inappropriate because such jurisdictional defects are not remediable by remission to the same tribunal.   **16.60**

There are few reported cases in which Singapore courts have ordered remission. In *JVL Agro*, Vinodh Coomaraswamy J decided not to set aside an award in the context of an alleged breach of natural justice, and instead suspended the setting aside proceedings for six months to remit the award to the arbitral tribunal.[126] Coomaraswamy J noted that the purpose of remission was for the arbitral tribunal to consider whether and to what extent it was necessary or desirable to receive further evidence or submissions on three specific issues on which the plaintiff complained the tribunal had not afforded it a reasonable opportunity to be heard.[127] After hearing further submissions from the parties, the arbitral tribunal found that it was neither necessary nor desirable to receive further evidence or submissions, and Coomaraswamy J subsequently set aside the award.[128]   **16.61**

In *CKG v CKH (SICC)*,[129] Cooke IJ also ordered remission on the basis that, although the tribunal failed to decide a set-off, if that was rectified, it would have consequential impact on other parts of the award including costs. It was thought preferable that the same tribunal, more familiar with the overall dispute, should determine the issue that it had failed to decide. Cooke IJ also remarked that even though the tribunal had rejected   **16.62**

---

[123] *AKN v ALC (II)* (n 20) [25].
[124] *Tan Poh Leng Stanley v Tang Boon Jek Jeffrey* [2000] 3 SLR(R) 847 [36] (hereafter *Tan Poh Leng*).
[125] Ibid, [32].
[126] *JVL Agro Industries Ltd v Agritrade International Pte Ltd* [2016] 4 SLR 768 [1] (hereafter *JVL Agro*).
[127] Ibid, [1].
[128] Ibid, [1]–[3].
[129] *CKG v CKH* 5 SLR 84; [2021] SGHC(I) 5 (hereafter *CKG v CKH (SICC)*). The appeal against Cooke IJ's decision was dismissed: *CKG v CKH (SGCA)* (n 110).

230 SETTING ASIDE AN AWARD

an earlier application for an additional award, he did not consider that the only outcome possible was an affirmation of that same decision.[130]

16.63 In *CAJ v CAI*, the Court of Appeal observed that on the occasions when awards were remitted to the tribunal, it was to consider fresh evidence or submissions to deal with a point which was already before the tribunal, that is, the point had already been pleaded or arose from existing pleadings.[131] In that case, however, the Court of Appeal had found that the tribunal had acted in excess of jurisdiction as well as in breach of natural justice by adjudicating on an unpleaded defence where such a defence was raised at the eleventh hour. In the circumstances, remission was inappropriate because the only way for the tribunal to adjudicate properly on the unpleaded defence was by way of an application to amend the defence, but it would be manifestly unfair to allow such an amendment at the stage of a setting aside application.[132]

(c) Circumstances where Remission is Inappropriate

16.64 Singapore courts have generally held that remission is not appropriate in a number of situations: first, where the tribunal is biased or there is no 'genuine opportunity' that the plaintiff will receive a different result;[133] second, where the tribunal's breaches are so interwoven into the reasoning of the award that remission would require the tribunal to reconsider the case *de novo*;[134] and third, where remission will be 'wholly disproportionate' because court remedies are more appropriate.[135]

16.65 The second and third situations have received only scant judicial treatment. The first situation flows from the basic principles set out above—since remission is only permitted to the same tribunal and not a new tribunal, it follows that if the defect lies within the tribunal itself, then remission would not 'cure' any such defects. There is, however, no consensus on the precise standard required for remission to be refused. In *Kempinski Hotels (SGHC)*,[136] Prakash J (as she then was) found that there was no apparent bias on the part of the tribunal,[137] and held that remission of the award to the same arbitrator was permissible, so long as he/she had not been 'disqualified'.[138] It was perhaps notable that the case was 'complicated', and therefore it would be more efficient to remit the case to the same arbitrator.[139]

16.66 The Court of Appeal had the opportunity to consider this question in *BZV (SGCA)*.[140] The Court of Appeal held that the test is whether a reasonable person would no longer

---

[130] Ibid, [69]–[70].
[131] *CAJ and another v CAI and another appeal* [2021] SGCA 102 [70] (hereafter *CAJ v CAI*).
[132] Ibid, [71].
[133] *BZV v BZW and another* [2021] SGHC 60 [223]–[224] (hereafter *BZV (SGHC)*); *Kempinski Hotels SA v PT Prima International Development* [2011] 4 SLR 633 [116]–[117] (hereafter *Kempinski Hotels (SGHC)*).
[134] *BZV (SGHC)* (n 133) [222].
[135] *CEB v CEC and another matter* [2020] 4 SLR 183 [64] (hereafter *CEB v CEC*).
[136] *Kempinski Hotels (SGHC)* (n 133).
[137] Ibid, [76].
[138] Ibid, [116].
[139] Ibid, [117].
[140] *BZV (SGCA)* (n 95).

B. SCOPE OF SETTING ASIDE ACTION AND OTHER CROSS-CUTTING ISSUES 231

have confidence in the tribunal's ability to come to a fair and balanced conclusion.[141] Referring to both Singapore law and English law authority, the Court of Appeal summarised the factors which the court will typically take into consideration: (i) the principle of limited curial intervention militates against the exercise of remission; (ii) the court should consider whether the breach is in respect of a single isolated or stand-alone point; (iii) the court should take into account whether the arbitrators are unfit to continue the hearing; and (iv) the court should consider whether there is a real risk, judged objectively, that the tribunal may subconsciously be tempted to achieve the same result as before.

The Court of Appeal's approach in *BZV (SGCA)* aligns Singapore's approach on this issue with that taken by English courts. In *Raytheon Systems*,[142] the English High Court had to consider the effect of arbitrator irregularities on the appropriateness of remission, and formulated the relevant test as whether a fair minded and informed observer will wonder if the arbitrator will act impartially and 'deliver justice'.[143] The facts that go into this inquiry of 'appropriateness' are broad and wide-ranging,[144] and can include pragmatic considerations such as cost, time, and justice. It should be noted, however, that Section 68(3) of the English Arbitration Act 1996 differs from Article 34(4) of the Model Law and mandates remission unless it is inappropriate, in which case the award will be set aside instead. It is not clear, however, if this necessarily dictates a different approach with respect to the interpretation of Article 34(4).

16.67

11. Power to Suspend an Award Pending Setting Aside

Singapore courts have not yet had to determine whether they have the power to suspend the enforcement of an award in other jurisdictions pending the determination of a setting aside application. Neither the Model Law nor the IAA expressly provide for the Court to have such a power. However, Article V(1)(e) of the New York Convention contemplates that an award may be 'suspended ... by a competent authority' at the arbitral seat, which presupposes a power of suspension belonging to supervisory courts of the arbitral seat.[145] Article V(1)(e) of the New York Convention is not only expressly incorporated by the Second Schedule of the IAA as part of Singapore law, it is also reflected in Section 31(2)(f) of the IAA.[146]

16.68

---

[141] Ibid, [65]–[67].

[142] *The Secretary of State for the Home Department v Raytheon Systems Ltd* [2015] EWHC 311 (TCC) (hereafter *Raytheon Systems*).

[143] Ibid, [20], [23(a)].

[144] Ibid, [4]; *Sinclair Roche & Temperley, Jeff Morgan, Stuart Beadnall, Michael Stockwood, Struan Robertson v Siân Heard, Siân Fellows* [2004] 7 WLUK 669 [46].

[145] Commentators have noted that in order for an award to be 'suspended by a competent authority', there needs to be a determination by supervisory courts at the seat, and the mere fact of a setting aside application made before courts of the seat would not be sufficient to suspend the award. See N. Darwazeh, 'Article V(1)(e)' in H.H. Kronke et al. (eds), *Recognition and Enforcement of Foreign Arbitral Awards: A Global Commentary on the New York Convention* (Kluwer Law International 2010) 341–2.

[146] See also IAA, Section 31(5); Model Law, Article 36(1)(a)(v).

232 SETTING ASIDE AN AWARD

16.69 English courts have held that they have the authority to suspend the enforcement of an award pending a setting aside. In *Apis AS v Fantazia*, the Commercial Court held that Article V of the New York Convention and Section 103.2(f) of the English Arbitration Act 1996 presupposed that English courts have the power to suspend an award made in England, and that such power existed under the English court's inherent jurisdiction.[147]

16.70 This analysis should be persuasive in Singapore, given that Section 103.2(f) is essentially identical to Section 31(2)(f) of the IAA. Although the drafting history of the Model Law is inconclusive, given that the UNCITRAL Secretariat's proposal for a request for suspension was not discussed or adopted,[148] the existence of a power to suspend the enforcement of an award that is derived from the Singapore courts' inherent jurisdiction is compatible with the provisions of the Model Law. This is confirmed by authorities from Model Law jurisdictions such as the Netherlands.[149]

12. Correction and Interpretation of the Award; Additional Award

16.71 Article 33 of the Model Law provides for three post-award remedies apart from those already discussed. These are correction of the award, interpretation of the award, and a request for an additional award. A request for correction or interpretation of award, or request for an additional award, must be made within thirty days of receipt of the award unless otherwise agreed by the parties.[150] Article 33(2) also provides that a tribunal may correct an award of its own motion within 30 days of the date of the award

16.72 Where a correction or interpretation of the award is requested, and if the tribunal considers the request justified, the tribunal is required to make the correction or give the interpretation within thirty days of receipt of the request. Where an additional award is requested and considered justified, the tribunal is required to make the additional award 'within sixty days'.[151] These timelines for the making of the correction, interpretation, or additional award may be modified at the discretion of the tribunal 'if necessary'.[152]

(a) Correction

16.73 Correction will only be justified if the error in question is an '[error] in computation, any clerical or typographical errors or any errors of similar nature'. Such errors include mistakes arising out of miscalculations, use of wrong data in calculations,

---

[147] *Apis AS v Fantazia Kereskedelmi KFT* [2001] 1 All E.R. (Comm) 348 Com Ct 1999/1252.

[148] The drafting history of the Article 36 of the Model Law suggests that the Working Group never discussed or considered the Secretariat's proposal that an express provision be enacted to permit a request for suspension under Articles 33(1)(a) and (b) of the Model Law and 'in conjunction with an application for setting aside under article 34'. See Holtzmann and Neuhaus, *Guide to the UNCITRAL Model Law* (n 37) 944.

[149] See *Russian Federation v Everest Estate LLC et al.*, Gerechtshof, The Hague, Case No. 2019200.250.714-01, 11 June 2019.

[150] Model Law, Article 33(1) and Article 33(3).

[151] Ibid, Article 33(1) and Article 33(3).

[152] Ibid, Article 33(4).

B. SCOPE OF SETTING ASIDE ACTION AND OTHER CROSS-CUTTING ISSUES   233

omission of data in calculations, clerical or typographical errors made in the course of typing or drafting the award, errors of expression, spelling mistakes, or errors in references. [153]

The power of the arbitrator to correct the award, however, is 'not intended to permit the tribunal to re-visit issues canvassed and decided or to re-consider any part of the decisions consciously made'.[154] Outside of the type of errors that Article 33 of the Model Law addresses—that is, 'clerical or typographical errors'—the tribunal has no power to reconsider or make a reversal of the substantive award even if it is perceived to be in error, whether in law or in fact.[155] Even if a tribunal, on the face of the award, quite clearly misunderstood or overlooked some critical provision of the parties' agreement or some essential piece of evidence, the remedy is not generally a correction of the award under Article 33 but rather an application to set aside the award or the relevant portion of the award.[156]   **16.74**

In *CNA v CNB*, Ang Cheng Hock J appeared to expand the scope of mistakes falling within Article 33(1)(a) as also including 'errors in the nature of inadvertent acts or omissions by the arbitral tribunal, which if corrected, do not affect the substance of what the tribunal intended to decide'. He then went on to find that this included the situation where 'a party had conveyed to the tribunal that it was abandoning its claim for a specific relief in the course of the closing submissions, but the tribunal had not noted this in the award, and then proceeded to grant that relief mistakenly'.[157] This appears to expand the scope of Article 33(1)(a) materially beyond an 'error in computation' or a 'clerical or typographical error'; in fact, this may arguably amount to what has typically been termed an error of law.[158]   **16.75**

(b) Interpretation

During the deliberations on the Model Law, participants considered that a party should not have the right to request for an interpretation of the award unless parties had expressly agreed that a party may have such a right. The reason for this was because it may 'encourage an unseemly race between the winning party to request an interpretation, if he perceived any grounds in the text of the award for his opponent seeking to annul   **16.76**

---

[153] *Econ Piling Pte Ltd and another (both formerly trading as Econ-NCC Joint Venture) v Shanghai Tunnel Engineering Co Ltd* [2011] 1 SLR 246 [116] (hereafter *Econ Piling*); *CNA v CNB* (n 101) [59].
[154] *Econ Piling* (n 153) [116].
[155] *Tan Poh Leng* (n 124) [17]–[29]; *BRS v BRQ* (n 99) [73]–[74]; *CNA v CNB* (n 101) [52]; *Tay Eng Chuan v United Overseas Insurance Ltd* [2009] 4 SLR(R) 1043 [16]–[19].
[156] *CNA v CNB* (n 101) [52].
[157] Ibid, [61].
[158] *Prestige Marine Services Pte Ltd v Marubeni International Petroleum (S) Pte Ltd* [2012] 1 SLR 917 [39]: 'Errors of law include misinterpretation of a statute or any other legal document or a rule of common law; asking oneself and answering the wrong question, taking irrelevant considerations into account or failing to take relevant considerations into account when purporting to apply the law to the facts; admitting inadmissible evidence or rejecting admissible and relevant evidence; exercising a discretion on the basis of incorrect legal principles; giving reasons which disclose faulty reasoning or which are inadequate to fulfil an express duty to give reasons; and misdirecting oneself as to the burden of proof.'

234 SETTING ASIDE AN AWARD

it, and the losing party to bring an action for recourse'.[159] As a result, the provision was amended to provide that the right to request for an interpretation would only be allowed 'if so agreed by the parties'.[160] Since most of the major arbitration rules provide for a right to request for interpretation,[161] such an agreement will be found if the parties agree to arbitrate under such rules.

16.77 It has been suggested by commentators that in order for a party to succeed on a request for interpretation under Article 33(1)(b), a party needs to demonstrate that the award is ambiguous and requires clarification for its effective execution.[162] The High Court appeared to have endorsed this test in *CNA v CNB*, where it held that the interpretation request in question was not validly, and suggested that the test was whether the award in question was 'ambiguous ... such that it could have caused genuine confusion'.[163]

(c) Additional award

16.78 A request for an additional award would only be available if it is in respect of 'claims presented in the arbitral proceedings but omitted from the award'. This provision can only be invoked if the arbitrator omitted to make a determination on a claim which had been presented to it, that is, where the tribunal acted *infra petita* and did not entirely fulfil its mandate.[164]

16.79 The case of *L W Infrastructure* is instructive. In that case, the Court of Appeal set aside an additional award that had been issued in breach of natural justice. The Court of Appeal held that when a request for an additional award is made, the tribunal must hear the parties on two separate questions: first, whether the requirements of Article 33(3) were met, which is a 'jurisdictional' question; second, if the requirements of Article 33(3) were met, whether the substantive additional award sought ought to be granted, and if so, to what extent.[165]

16.80 When will a claim be considered as having been 'omitted from the award' for the purposes of Article 33(3)? In *L W Infrastructure*, the Court of Appeal cited a leading commentator for the view that the mere fact that an arbitral tribunal has not expressly addressed a particular claim does not automatically require issuance of an additional award; a tribunal may be taken to have impliedly rejected claims as to which it does not

---

[159] UNCITRAL, 'Summary Records of the United Nations Commission on International Trade Law for meetings devoted to the preparation of the UNCITRAL Model Law on International Commercial Arbitration: 329th Meeting' (18 June 1985) UN Doc. A/CN.9/246, annex; A/CN.9/263 and Add. 1-2, A/CN.9/264) 495.

[160] Model Law, Article 33(1)(b).

[161] SIAC Rules 2016, Rule 33; ICC Arbitration Rules 2021, Article 36; HKIAC Administered Arbitration Rules 2018, Article 39. Interestingly, the LCIA Arbitration Rules 2020 do not provide for a right of interpretation, suggesting that parties who arbitrate under the LCIA Arbitration Rules 2020 may have to separately agree.

[162] Born, *International Commercial Arbitration* (n 22) 3401.

[163] *CNA v CNB* (n 101) [43], [50].

[164] *BLC (SGCA)* (n 5) [107].

[165] *L W Infrastructure Pte Ltd v Lim Chin San Contractors Pte Ltd and another appeal* [2013] 1 SLR 125 [58]–[74] (hereafter *L W Infrastructure*).

B. SCOPE OF SETTING ASIDE ACTION AND OTHER CROSS-CUTTING ISSUES   235

grant relief.[166] However, the Court of Appeal left that question open, and rightly so, as it is the tribunal and not the court that is to decide whether a claim has been 'omitted from the award'.

13. Costs Issues

Setting aside applications raise interesting issues to do with costs. The first is whether **16.81** a subsequent costs award may or ought to be set aside in the event that a prior merits award has been set aside. The second is the award of costs for a setting aside application before the Singapore courts.

In *CBX v CBZ (SGCA)*, the Singapore Court of Appeal had to consider the novel ques- **16.82** tion of whether to set aside a costs award as a consequential order to the Court's partial set aside of the merits award. After considering the relevant authorities,[167] the Court of Appeal held that where a later order is ancillary to and depends upon the validity and premises of a prior order, the legislature cannot have intended that the later order should survive the setting aside of the former.[168] Thus, if an entire merits award had been set aside for excess of jurisdiction or breach of natural justice, the costs award should similarly be set aside.[169] As for where the merits award had only been *partially* set aside, the test of whether a costs order can survive is one of materiality and judgment.[170] As costs awards are usually ancillary to and reflective of the outcome of the substantive issues, the likelihood that they can survive any significant change in the substantive outcome is therefore greatly diminished, and justice will commonly require their setting aside.[171] Taking into account the fact that the portion of the merits award which was set aside was 'clearly a significant matter in the Tribunal's mind when it made its Costs Award',[172] the Court of Appeal decided to set aside the entirety of the costs award as well.[173]

If the court decides that the costs award ought to be set aside, what then is the proper **16.83** mechanism for costs to be re-adjudicated? The Court of Appeal noted that under the IAA and the Model Law, it had no power to remit to the same tribunal after setting aside.[174] In *AKN v ALC (I)* itself, although the award had been set aside and the original tribunal had been determined by the Court of Appeal to be *functus officio*, the arbitration agreement still remained in force and thus the Court of Appeal in *AKN v ALC (I)*

---

[166] Ibid, [87], citing G. Born, *International Commercial Arbitration* (2nd edn, Kluwer Law International 2009) 2542.
[167] *CBX and another v CBZ and others* [2022] 1 SLR 47 [68]–[70] (hereafter *CBX v CBZ (SGCA)*).
[168] Ibid, [73].
[169] Ibid, [71].
[170] Ibid, [74].
[171] Ibid, [75].
[172] Ibid, [72].
[173] Ibid, [80].
[174] Ibid, [78]–[79].

236   SETTING ASIDE AN AWARD

made a limited declaration to the effect that outstanding claims and defences remained as yet undetermined, which were capable of being addressed separately and severally by a new tribunal.[175] However, no such declaration was sought in *CBX v CBZ (SGCA)*. The Court of Appeal found that it could do no more than to determine that the whole of the costs award was set aside, and left parties to 'advise themselves and to agree or decide how to proceed'.[176] It expressed its regret that some sensible method of addressing the issues of costs may not exist in such situations,[177] noting that a costs award ought typically to be made by the tribunal charged with the substantive award,[178] and that this was a potential area of law reform.[179] As a practical matter, parties seeking clarity on cost consequences following a setting aside should therefore seek relevant declarations on costs.

(a) Principles Governing Award of Costs in Setting Aside Applications

16.84   The winning party in a setting aside application is typically entitled to costs on a standard basis, and Singapore courts will be slow to award costs on an indemnity basis. In *CDM v CDP*, the Court of Appeal noted Hong Kong authority in support of the position that a party unsuccessful in an application to set aside an arbitral award ought to be ordered to pay costs on an indemnity basis.[180] However, the Singapore Court of Appeal declined to follow the Hong Kong position.

16.85   The Court of Appeal reaffirmed that the imposition of costs on an indemnity basis was dependent on there being exceptional circumstances to warrant a departure from the usual course of awarding costs on a standard basis.[181] Whether indemnity costs should be ordered turns on a highly fact-specific assessment of the totality of the facts and circumstances, and the court may find that such exceptional circumstances arise where the action was brought in bad faith, as a means of oppression or for other improper purposes; where the action was speculative, hypothetical, or clearly without basis; where a party's conduct in the course of proceedings was dishonest, abusive, or improper; or where the action amounted to wasteful or duplicative litigation or was otherwise an abuse of process.[182] In *Asiana Airlines*, the Singapore High Court confirmed that a special case for ordering indemnity costs might exist where so provided by the parties' contractual agreement, but in ordering such costs, the court would not be enforcing the contract but taking it into account in the exercise of its own discretion.[183]

---

[175] Ibid, [79].
[176] Ibid, [80].
[177] Ibid, [81].
[178] Ibid, [81]–[85].
[179] Ibid, [85].
[180] *CDM and another v CDP* [2021] 2 SLR 235 [49] (hereafter *CDM v CDP*).
[181] Ibid, [52]–[55].
[182] Ibid, [56]–[57]; *BTN and another v BTP and another* [2021] 4 SLR 603 [15].
[183] *Asiana Airlines, Inc v Gate Gourmet Korea Co, Ltd* [2022] 4 SLR 158.

C. Grounds for Setting Aside

There are six grounds for setting aside an award under Article 34 of the Model Law **16.86** and two further grounds under Section 24 of the IAA. One distinction between the grounds for setting aside in Articles 34(2)(a) and 34(2)(b) of the Model Law is that the former grounds are to be invoked only by the party making the application,[184] whereas the latter grounds may be invoked by Singapore courts on their own motion, that is, *sua sponte* or *ex officio*.[185] The *travaux preparatoires* makes clear that this was by design, primarily to reflect a similar distinction drawn between the grounds for refusal of enforcement under Articles V(1) and V(2) of the New York Convention.[186] Although Singapore courts have affirmed this distinction in principle,[187] to the best of the authors' knowledge there has not yet been a reported decision where a Singapore court invoked the grounds under Article 34(2)(b) on its own motion, without such grounds being raised by a party, to set aside the award.

Consistent with the express terms of Article 34(2)(a) of the Model Law, Singapore **16.87** courts have held that the applicant making the setting aside application bears the burden of proof of establishing the relevant grounds for setting aside.[188] As commentators have noted, placing the burden of proof on the applicant underscores the presumptive validity and finality of an arbitral award.[189] Singapore courts have similarly affirmed that the burden of proof remains on the applicant with respect to Article 34(2)(b) grounds for setting aside.[190] It is accepted that the difference in wording does not justify the application of different burdens of proof.[191] While Section 24 of the IAA

---

[184] Article 34(2)(a) requires 'the party making the application to furnish proof' that one of the grounds in Article 34(2)(a) applies.

[185] Article 34(2)(b) only provides that an award may be set aside 'if the court finds' that one of the grounds in Article 34(2)(b) are established. The grounds for setting aside in Article 34(2)(b) may be invoked by the Singapore courts because they engage the public policy of the seat. See Holtzmann and Neuhaus, *Guide to the UNCITRAL Model Law* (n 37) 974 (Mr Loefmarck (Sweden): 'It was disturbing that the question of whether an award was in conflict with public policy could be settled by a court only if the parties so requested. A court located in the country where enforcement was sought ought to be able to take a decision of its own motion, and not only at the request of a party.').

[186] Born, *International Commercial Arbitration* (n 22) 3436. See also Holtzmann and Neuhaus, *Guide to the UNCITRAL Model Law* (n 37) 975, comment of Sir Michael Mustill (United Kingdom): 'the Working Group's discussion had produced a sharp distinction in the text between sub-paragraph (a), which was to be invoked only if the party making the application furnished proof, and sub-paragraph (b), under which the court could take up a matter on its own motion'.

[187] *Beijing Sinozonto Mining Investment Co Ltd v Goldenray Consortium (Singapore) Pte Ltd* [2014] 1 SLR 814 [58] (hereafter *Beijing Sinozonto*); *Westbridge Ventures II Investment Holdings v Anupam Mittal* [2021] SGHC 244 [43].

[188] *PT Perusahaan Gas Negara (Persero) TBK v CRW Joint Operation* [2015] 4 SLR 364 [33] (hereafter *CRW v Persero (II) (SGCA)*); *Dongwoo Mann + Hummel Co Ltd v Mann + Hummel GmbH* [2008] 3 SLR(R) 871 [74] (hereafter *Dongwoo*).

[189] Born, *International Commercial Arbitration* (n 22) 3436, 3451.

[190] *Beijing Sinozonto* (n 187) [58]; *CDI v CDJ* [2020] 5 SLR 484 [31] (hereafter *CDI v CDJ*).

[191] See Born, *International Commercial Arbitration* (n 22) 3436–7 ('[I]t would be wrong to conclude that the burden of proof allocations noted above are inapplicable to Article 34(2)(b)'s public policy and nonarbitrability exceptions. On the contrary, many public policy and nonarbitrability rules are designed in part for the protection of particular parties, and it is entirely appropriate to conclude that the party seeking to annul an award bears the ultimate burden of demonstrating that one of these exceptions applies.').

238   SETTING ASIDE AN AWARD

does not refer to the burden of proof, Singapore courts have also held that the burden of proof lies with the applicant.[192]

16.88   While the Singapore courts have stated that the standard of proof for a challenge to an award is on the balance of probabilities,[193] they have also affirmed on numerous occasions that a 'high threshold' has to be met before a court will set aside the award. For instance, the Court of Appeal has stated that the threshold for a finding of breach of natural justice is a 'high one', and it is only in 'exceptional cases' that a court will find that threshold crossed.[194] Where it is argued that the award ought to be set aside for being *infra petita*, the court would only draw an inference that the tribunal had failed to consider an issue if such an inference was 'clear and virtually inescapable'.[195] Where fraud is concerned, a 'convincing case' must be strong and the claimant would have to produce evidence that is 'cogent and strong'.[196] Where it is alleged that the award is said to contravene public policy because it was secured by fraudulent or unconscionable means, a 'high standard of proof' applies.[197]

1. Article 34(2)(a)(i): Incapacity of a Party or Invalidity of the Arbitration Agreement

16.89   Article 34(2)(a)(i) mirrors Article V(1)(a) of the New York Convention[198] and both provisions provide for annulment of the award on the basis of the incapacity of one of the parties, or the invalidity of the agreement. These grounds for annulling an award are rooted in the fundamental importance of consent to international arbitration—without such consent, there is no basis for an international arbitration award.[199]

(a) Incapacity of a Party

16.90   Article 34(2)(a)(i) provides that the 'incapacity' of 'a party to the arbitration agreement' is a ground for setting aside an award. In contrast to Article V(1)(a) of the New York Convention, which provides that an award may be refused enforcement based on the incapacity of the parties to the arbitration agreement 'under the law applicable to them', Article 34(2)(a)(i) is silent on the law governing the incapacity of a party for the purposes of a setting aside application. The words 'under the law

---

[192] *Swiss Singapore Overseas Enterprises Pte Ltd v Exim Rajathi India Pvt Ltd* [2010] 1 SLR 573 [64] (hereafter *Swiss Singapore*); *Dongwoo* (n 188) [74].

[193] *CDI v CDJ* (n 190) [31(b)].

[194] *China Machine New Energy Corp v Jaguar Energy Guatemala LLC and another* [2020] 1 SLR 695 [87] (hereafter *China Machine (SGCA)*).

[195] *AKN v ALC (I)* (n 47) [46].

[196] *BVU v BVX* [2019] SGHC 69 [46] (hereafter *BVU v BVX*), citing *Swiss Singapore* (n 192) [64].

[197] Ibid, [46], citing *Dongwoo* (n 188) [147].

[198] Article V(1)(a) of the New York Convention: 'The parties to the agreement referred to in article II were, under the law applicable to them, under some incapacity, or the said agreement is not valid under the law to which the parties have subjected it or, failing any indication thereon, under the law of the country where the award was made.'

[199] Born, *International Commercial Arbitration* (n 22) 3449–50.

C. GROUNDS FOR SETTING ASIDE   239

applicable to them' were criticised in the UNCITRAL Working Group as being 'too simplistic and not accepted in all legal systems', and the decision was eventually made to leave those words out altogether because they were 'either incomplete or misleading'.[200] The UNCITRAL Commission Report clarified, however, that the removal of those words was not intended to signal any 'substantive discrepancy' between the Model Law provision and the corresponding provision in the New York Convention.[201]

The capacity of a party to enter into an arbitration agreement falls to be determined by ordinary principles of contract law. However, the question of capacity can be governed by a number of possible laws: the law of a natural person's nationality or domicile, the law of the place of incorporation of a corporate person, the law of the place of residence of a party, the law of the contract, or the law governing the arbitration agreement.[202] Choice-of-law rules dealing with capacity largely differ across jurisdictions; for example, in many civil law systems, capacity of corporations is governed by the law of the seat of the corporation in question, whilst in common law jurisdictions the law of the place of incorporation ordinarily applies to issues of capacity.[203]   **16.91**

Cases relying on this ground have been few and far between. There was a passing reference to incapacity as a ground for setting aside in *Jiangsu Overseas Group Co Ltd v Concord Energy Pte Ltd (Jiangsu Overseas Group)*.[204] The High Court judgment appeared to assume that the relevant question for the purposes of Article 34(2)(a)(i) is whether a party is under an incapacity at the time of entry into the arbitration agreement, rather than the time of commencement of arbitration proceedings. However, Steven Chong J (as he then was) did not eventually rule on this question because the argument on 'incapacity' was not pursued during the setting aside hearing.[205] Chong J nonetheless noted *obiter dicta* that the award debtor would still be bound by the contracts under Singapore law even in circumstances where the award debtor's agent acted outside his scope of authority, unless the award creditor had notice of the agent's lack of authority.[206] Although the contract in that case was governed by Singapore law, the award debtor was a company incorporated in the People's Republic of China. Given that there were no submissions on choice of law before the court, it is not clear what was the basis for the assumption that Singapore law would apply, in particular whether this was because of the application of an implicit choice-of-law rule or the absence of specific evidence on Chinese law.   **16.92**

---

[200] Holtzmann and Neuhaus, *Guide to the UNCITRAL Model Law* (n 37) 916.

[201] UNCITRAL (18th Session) 'Report of the United Nations Commission on International Trade Law on the work of its eighteenth session' (June 1985) UN Doc A/40/17 [321] (hereafter *UNCITRAL 18th Session Report*).

[202] Blackaby et al., *Redfern & Hunter* (n 6) [2.34]–[2.37]; Born, *International Commercial Arbitration* (n 22) 3469–70.

[203] Ibid.

[204] *Jiangsu Overseas Group* (n 11) [67].

[205] Ibid, [67].

[206] Ibid, [68].

240 SETTING ASIDE AN AWARD

16.93 In *CPU and others v CPX*,[207] it was alleged that certain of the parties to the contracts containing the arbitration agreement lacked capacity. It was held that there was insufficient evidence to establish the alleged incapacity, but of significance was the Court's observation that the issue should be determined *de novo* as it affected the jurisdiction of the tribunal.[208] Indirectly, the Court has also held that if the effect of an award was to enforce an agreement on minors, or to hold minors liable for the wrongdoing of their principals or guardians, this would violate the public policy of Singapore.[209]

(b) Lack of Jurisdiction and *De Novo* Review

16.94 Article 34(2)(a)(i) provides that the invalidity of the arbitration agreement is a ground for setting aside an award. In setting aside applications, Singapore courts undertake a *de novo* hearing of arguments relating to the jurisdiction of the arbitral tribunal.[210] This is consistent with the *de novo* review of a tribunal's jurisdiction in Section 10 of the IAA or Article 16(3) of the Model Law appeal from a tribunal's jurisdictional ruling, which is further discussed in Chapter 9. The below section discusses the applicable principles in a setting aside application, although these do not materially differ from much of the principles are the same.

16.95 In *Astro (SGCA)*, the Singapore Court of Appeal endorsed the principle of *de novo* judicial review resoundingly, adopting the position of the UK Supreme Court in *Dallah v Pakistan* that an arbitral tribunal's own view of jurisdiction had no legal or evidential value before a court that has to determine that same question.[211] However, a *de novo* review does not mean that a Singapore court should disregard all that had transpired before the arbitral tribunal; instead, it simply means that the court should consider the correctness of the tribunal's decision on jurisdiction without any fetter on its fact-finding abilities.[212]

16.96 What evidence are parties permitted to introduce in a *de novo* review of jurisdiction before the Singapore courts? In *AQZ v ARA*, Judith Prakash J (as she then was) held *obiter dicta* that nothing in Order 69A Rule 2(4A)(c) of the Rules of Court (now Order 48 Rule 2(4)(c)) restricts parties from adducing new material that was not before the arbitrator.[213] The court may even order deponents to appear and be cross-examined.[214] However, Prakash J agreed with the caution sounded by the English court in *Electrosteel Castings*[215] that parties should not 'seek two evidential bites of the cherry' in relation to the jurisdiction of the arbitrators, including because evidence introduced late in the

---

[207] [2022] SGHC(I) 11.
[208] Ibid, [77].
[209] *BAZ (SGHC)* (n 24) [180]-[187].
[210] *Astro (SGCA)* (n 17) [163].
[211] Ibid, [162]–[163]. See also *Dallah Real Estate and Tourism Holding Co v Ministry of Religious Affairs of the Government of Pakistan* [2010] UKSC 46; [2011] 1 AC 763 [30] (hereafter *Dallah v Pakistan*).
[212] *AQZ v ARA* (n 26) [57]–[58].
[213] Ibid, [59].
[214] Ibid, [59].
[215] *Electrosteel Castings Ltd v Scan-Trans Shipping & Chartering Sdn Bhd* [2002] EWHC 1993 (Comm); [2003] 1 Lloyd's Rep 190 [23] (hereafter *Electrosteel Castings*).

C. GROUNDS FOR SETTING ASIDE   241

day may be viewed with scepticism and because of the broad powers of the courts to address any issues of abuse through costs orders.

The award debtor in *AQZ v ARA* had initially made the submission that a *de novo* **16.97**
hearing meant that a Singapore court was 'required' to carry out a *de novo* rehearing
of the jurisdictional questions.[216] Although this submission was subsequently withdrawn,[217] Prakash J (as she then was) rejected it nonetheless, noting that Order 69A
Rule 2 (now Order 48 Rule 2) does not envisage a default *de novo* rehearing in every
case, and instead contemplates that setting aside applications would be resolved by affidavit evidence.[218]

These *obiter* observations were developed further in *Jiangsu Overseas Group*, where **16.98**
Steven Chong J (as he then was) dismissed an application by the applicant to be heard
partly on oral evidence, with cross-examination of witnesses.[219] Chong J endorsed
Prakash J's views that the mere existence of factual disputes is not sufficient to justify allowing oral evidence and cross-examination, and that additional reasons were
required.[220] Chong J also held that the fact that Jiangsu did not participate in the arbitration or the arbitration hearing was not a sufficiently good reason to permit oral
evidence and cross-examination in setting aside proceedings.[221]

Chong J did not have to decide in *Jiangsu Overseas Group* on the conditions under which **16.99**
fresh evidence should be admitted in setting aside proceedings because the award creditor did not object to the admissibility of the new evidence adduced. Nonetheless, he
noted that the court has discretion to rule on the admissibility and/or weight of any
new evidence sought to be adduced, as well as to make any adverse costs orders.[222]
Chong J did, however, point out that there were two different approaches to the admissibility of new evidence set forth in two decisions of the Singapore High Court.

The first is that taken in *Lao v Sanum (SGHC)*,[223] which was strictly a case under Section **16.100**
10 of the IAA, where the court applied a modified test for admissibility based on *Ladd
v Marshall* principles. Under that test, a court would admit fresh evidence only if (i) the
party seeking to admit the evidence demonstrated sufficiently strong reasons why the
evidence was not adduced at the arbitration hearing; (ii) the evidence, if admitted,

---

[216] *AQZ v ARA* (n 26) [38].
[217] Ibid, [39].
[218] Ibid, [52]. Prakash J also noted that the court should bear in mind the fact that the parties would already have conducted an examination of witnesses once fully before the arbitral tribunal, and thereby the mere existence of substantial disputes of fact alone would not justify allowing oral evidence and/or cross-examination. See *AQZ v ARA* (n 26) [54]–[55].
[219] *Jiangsu Overseas Group* (n 11) [41]–[42].
[220] Ibid, [43].
[221] Ibid, [43].
[222] Ibid, [53].
[223] *Government of the Lao People's Democratic Republic v Sanum Investments Ltd* [2015] 2 SLR 322 [43]–[44] (hereafter *Lao v Sanum (SGHC)*). On appeal, the Court of Appeal noted that, although the modified *Ladd v Marshall* test is helpful, where the substantive dispute engages questions of public international law, the court must consider questions of admissibility and weight within the framework of any other applicable principles of inter-national law: *Sanum Investments Ltd v Government of the Lao People's Democratic Republic* [2016] 5 SLR 536 [103] (hereafter *Lao v Sanum (SGCA)*).

242 SETTING ASIDE AN AWARD

would probably have an important, though not necessarily decisive, influence on the result of the case; and (iii) the evidence is apparently credible, though it need not be incontrovertible.[224]

16.101 The other approach was laid out in the *obiter* observations of Prakash J in *AQZ v ARA*, that the parties are free to introduce new evidence, subject to the court's ability to determine the weight to be given to the evidence and issue adverse costs orders.[225] The High Court appeared to take a similar approach in *obiter* comments in *Vitol Asia*.[226] This latter approach is more closely aligned with the approach under English law with respect to setting aside applications involving jurisdictional questions under Section 67 of the English Arbitration Act 1996.[227] In the authors' view, it is preferable and strikes the best balance between the nature of a *de novo* hearing on jurisdiction and the need for judicial control and to prevent abuse of setting aside proceedings.[228]

16.102 The *Central Trading* case illustrates how these principles are applied under English law. In that case, Males J held that the starting point is that a party is entitled to adduce evidence that was not before the arbitrators, and the English courts will not normally exclude evidence which is relevant and admissible, even if it may cause prejudice to the other side.[229] Males J further held that, given that a Section 67 challenge is a 'full judicial determination on evidence', the parties may decide what evidence they wish to rely on and are not limited to whatever evidence was before the arbitrators.[230] That said, the parties' right to adduce evidence is not entirely unconstrained under English law—it is subject to control by the courts, who have discretion to decide on the weight that should be accorded to the evidence and, in appropriate cases, exclude evidence.[231] Thus, for example, an English court may refuse to allow a party to produce documents selectively that would prejudice the other party or to allow evidence that does not comply with the Court's own rules, which ensures that evidence is presented in a fair manner.[232]

16.103 On the facts, Males J noted that the new evidence sought to be admitted was an attempt to plug the gaps in the award debtor's case, after a deliberate failure to comply with their order for disclosure.[233] Further, the award debtor also sought to admit a letter from two individuals, who did not provide witness statements compliant with CPR 32

---

[224] Ibid, [44]. Note, however, that in this case, the parties agreed that the modified *Ladd v Marshall* test should apply and only disagreed about whether it was met on the facts. See Ibid, [23].

[225] *AQZ v ARA* (n 26) [59].

[226] *Vitol Asia* (n 11) [41]–[43]. The Judge noted that it was not necessary to constrain the general discretion to receive evidence to deter tactical abuse. The Judge also noted that the *Ladd v Marshall* test should be confined to situations like *Lao v Sanum* where a party makes a second attempt to adduce evidence on the same issue against the same party (as was the case with the jurisdictional issue in *Lao v Sanum*).

[227] *Central Trading & Exports Limited v Fioralba Shipping Company* [2014] EWHC 2397 (Comm) (hereafter *Central Trading*).

[228] See also D. Chan, 'The Scope of "De Novo" Review of an Arbitral Tribunal's Jurisdiction' (Law Gazette, November 2015) <https://v1.lawgazette.com.sg/2015-11/1428.htm> accessed 4 April 2022.

[229] *Central Trading* (n 227) [29].

[230] Ibid, [30].

[231] Ibid, [32].

[232] Ibid.

[233] Ibid, [41], [45].

C. GROUNDS FOR SETTING ASIDE   243

of the English Civil Procedure Rules and would expose the makers of the statement to contempt proceedings for knowingly false statements.[234] It was also not apparent to the court that the two individuals had personal knowledge of the matters addressed in the letter.[235] In these circumstances, Males J refused to admit the new evidence.

Singapore courts have held that *de novo* review of jurisdictional questions applies equally in applications involving investor-state arbitration awards. In *Lesotho v Swissbourgh (SGHC)*, Kannan Ramesh J held that it was settled law and undisputed that the court must apply a *de novo* standard of review in assessing jurisdictional objections in a setting aside application, 'even in relation to an investor-state arbitration invoking principles of public international law'.[236] Ramesh J further noted that, while a Singapore court will consider what the arbitral tribunal has said and may even find it persuasive, as a matter of principle it is not bound to accept the arbitral tribunal's findings on jurisdiction.[237]   **16.104**

De novo review is, however, limited only to jurisdictional issues and does not extend to issues of admissibility. The distinction between jurisdiction and admissibility was considered in *BAZ (SGCA)*,[238] where it was contended that Singapore courts were entitled to undertake a *de novo* review of whether the respondent's claim for fraud was time-barred. The award debtors submitted that questions of limitation should go towards jurisdiction, given that the governing law of the substantive agreement (Indian law) treated limitation as jurisdictional.[239] The award creditor argued instead that the law of the seat (Singapore law) should apply, and that the issue of limitation did not go towards the tribunal's jurisdiction.[240] The Court of Appeal held that these issues fell within decision-making prerogative of the seat court,[241] noting that the choice of Singapore as the seat included the choice of Singapore law to govern the classification question, which was independent of the parties' choice as to the governing law of the agreement.[242]   **16.105**

The Court of Appeal then held that issues of time bar which arise from statutory limitation periods go towards admissibility, not jurisdiction, with the consequent effect that Singapore courts are not entitled to review the issue *de novo*.[243] The Court of Appeal held that the 'tribunal versus claim' test underpinned by a consent-based analysis should apply for purposes of distinguishing whether an issue goes towards jurisdiction or admissibility.[244] The 'tribunal versus claim' test asks whether the objection is targeted   **16.106**

---

[234] Ibid, [45].
[235] Ibid, [44].
[236] *Kingdom of Lesotho v Swissbourgh Diamond Mines (Pty) Ltd and others* [2019] 3 SLR 12 [87] (hereafter *Lesotho v Swissbourgh (SGHC)*).
[237] Ibid, [87].
[238] *BBA and others v BAZ and another appeal* [2020] 2 SLR 453 (hereafter *BAZ (SGCA)*).
[239] Ibid, [62].
[240] Ibid, [63].
[241] Ibid, [65].
[242] Ibid, [66].
[243] Ibid, [73], [82].
[244] Ibid, [76].

244 SETTING ASIDE AN AWARD

at the tribunal (in the sense that the claim should not be arbitrated due to a defect in or omission to consent to arbitration), or at the claim (in that the claim itself is defective and should not be raised at all).[245] Arguments as to existence, scope, and validity of the arbitration agreement are regarded as jurisdictional, as they related to whether jurisdiction was properly founded on party consent.[246] Conversely, admissibility relates to the 'nature of the claim, or to particular circumstances connected with it'.[247] Applying the 'tribunal versus claim' test, a plea of statutory time bar goes towards admissibility as it attacks the claim, that is, it is an argument that the claim is defective, rather than an argument that the time-barred claim falls outside the scope of consent to arbitration.[248] The Court of Appeal noted that a plea of statutory time bar may go towards jurisdiction if the arbitration agreement expressly provided that the tribunal may not hear such a claim.[249]

16.107 There are other issues that will go towards admissibility, rather than jurisdiction, applying the 'tribunal versus claim' test in *BAZ (SGCA)*. For example, it is arguable that issues such as compliance with pre-arbitration requirements in a multi-tier arbitration clause are admissibility issues.

(c) Choice of Law for the Arbitration Agreement

16.108 Article 34(2)(a)(i) provides that the validity of the arbitration agreement is to be determined by 'the law to which the parties have subjected it or, failing any indication thereon, under the law of [Singapore]'. This mirrors the choice-of-law provision in Article V(1)(a) of the New York Convention.

16.109 During the drafting of Article 34(2)(a)(i), a proposal was made to delete the choice-of-law provision on the basis that the seat of arbitration was not necessarily connected with the subject matter of the dispute, and that a default rule providing for the applicability of the law of the seat would be inconsistent with the trend towards applying the law of the main contract to the arbitration agreement.[250] However, the choice-of-law provision was ultimately retained because it recognised party autonomy and the default rule, selecting the law of the seat, provided parties with a degree of certainty.[251]

16.110 In *Jiangsu Overseas Group*, Steven Chong J (as he then was) held that the choice-of-law provision in Article 34(2)(a)(i) consisted of two limbs: first, the application of the parties' express or implied choice of law governing the arbitration agreement; and second, if no express or implied choice can be found, then the application of the law of the seat

---

[245] Ibid, [77].
[246] Ibid, [78].
[247] Ibid, [79].
[248] Ibid, [80].
[249] Ibid, [80]–[81].
[250] Holtzmann and Neuhaus, *Guide to the UNCITRAL Model Law* (n 37) 999, [283].
[251] Ibid, 1000, [284].

as a default rule.[252] This analysis was later affirmed by the Court of Appeal in *BNA v BNB*.[253] Chapter 5 discusses in greater detail the relevant choice-of-law analysis under these two limbs.

(d) Burden of Proof of Foreign Law

In the event that the law governing the arbitration agreement is determined to be a foreign law and not Singapore law, the burden of proof lies with the award debtor to establish that the arbitration agreement is invalid under that foreign law.[254] Therefore, where a setting aside application is heard by the High Court, an applicant must adduce proof of foreign law, which is an issue of fact that must be proved either by directly adducing sources of foreign law as evidence of that law or by adducing the opinion of an expert in that foreign law.[255] Any such opinion should be independent and objective, and it should meet the requirements for expert evidence in Order 40A Rules 2 and 3 of the Rules of Court.

16.111

Where the setting aside application is heard by the Singapore International Commercial Court (SICC), a party may apply to the SICC to make an order under Order 110 Rule 25(1) to allow any question of foreign law to be determined on the basis of submissions instead of proof. Before making such an order, the Court must be satisfied that each party is or will be represented by counsel with the adequate qualifications,[256] and the order would specify the person(s) who may make submissions on the relevant questions of foreign law on behalf of each party.[257]

16.112

Failing to prove foreign law to show that the agreement is invalid under the relevant foreign law can be fatal to a setting aside application. In *Aloe Vera*, in the context of a refusal of enforcement under Section 31(b) of the IAA, the award debtor submitted an affidavit filed by its attorney in Arizona, which was held not to constitute 'independent expert evidence' on the law of Arizona.[258] In the circumstances, there was no evidentiary basis for a finding that the arbitration agreement was invalid under the law of Arizona.[259] Similarly, in *DSK v Ultrapolis*, another case concerning Section 31(2)(b) of the IAA, the award debtor sought to argue that the arbitration agreement was invalid under Danish law but did not adduce any independent expert evidence apart from an affidavit by the lawyer who had represented the award debtor in the

16.113

---

[252] *Jiangsu Overseas Group* (n 11) [55].

[253] *BNA v BNB and another* [2020] 1 SLR 456 [54] (hereafter *BNA v BNB*).

[254] *Aloe Vera of America, Inc v Asianic Food (S) Pte Ltd and another* [2006] 3 SLR(R) 174 [61] (hereafter *Aloe Vera*).

[255] See *Pacific Recreation Pte Ltd v S Y Technology Inc and another appeal* [2008] 2 SLR(R) 491 [54].

[256] Order 3 Rule 1 of the Singapore International Commercial Court Rules 2021 ("the SICC Rules") prescribes that the SICC must be satisfied that the party is or will be represented by an advocate and solicitor, a person admitted under section 15 of the Legal Profession Act, a registered foreign lawyer (either full registration foreign lawyers or restricted registration foreign lawyers) or a registered law expert who is suitable and competent to submit on the relevant questions of foreign law.

[257] Order 3 Rule 1(1)(d) of the SICC Rules.

[258] *Aloe Vera* (n 254) [63].

[259] Ibid.

246   SETTING ASIDE AN AWARD

arbitration.[260] Belinda Ang J preferred the opinion of an independent expert on Danish law proffered by the award creditor, and held that the arbitration agreement was valid under Danish law.[261]

(e) Invalidity of the Arbitration Agreement

16.114   Article 34(2)(a)(i) of the Model Law provides that an award may be set aside if an award debtor can furnish proof that the arbitration agreement is 'not valid'. It is well-established that this ground for setting aside encompasses both issues of formal and substantive validity—in other words, it deals with questions regarding compliance with formality requirements as well as the existence of consent to arbitration.[262]

16.115   The requirements for formal validity of arbitration agreements are set forth in Section 2A of the IAA and Article 7 of the Model Law, which are addressed in Chapter 5. Applying those requirements, Prakash J (as she then was) held in *AQZ v ARA* that the writing requirement was satisfied where one party had recorded the arbitration agreement in writing, and it did not matter that the written version was neither signed nor confirmed by all the parties involved.[263] Similarly, in *BXH v BXI (SGHC)*, Vinodh Coomaraswamy J held that the writing requirement was satisfied for an implied contract alleged to have been formed by virtue of the parties' conduct after the expiry of a distributor agreement, because the arbitration agreement was recorded in the expired distributor agreement.[264]

16.116   With respect to issues of substantive validity, an applicant needs to establish the substantive invalidity of the arbitration agreement and not just the substantive invalidity of the main contract in which the arbitration agreement is contained. This is a consequence of the separability presumption, which is the presumption that arbitration agreements are separable from the underlying contract in which they are found or associated.[265] Thus, for example, Singapore courts have applied the separability presumption in the context of allegations of fraud and corruption that may vitiate the main contract: an applicant would need to establish that those allegations vitiate the arbitration agreement itself, and not just the main contract.[266]

16.117   Singapore courts have also held that arbitration agreements survive the expiry of the main contract, although whether this is so depends in each case on an analysis of the parties' objective intentions. In *BXH v BXI (SGHC)*, the respondent relied on the

---

[260] *Denmark Skibstekniske Konsulenter A/S I Likvidation (formerly known as Knud E Hansen A/S) v Ultrapolis 3000 Investments Ltd (formerly known as Ultrapolis 3000 Theme Park Investments Ltd)* [2010] 3 SLR 661 [44] (hereafter *DSK v Ultrapolis*).

[261] Ibid, [45].

[262] See e.g. *AQZ v ARA* (n 26) [121]. See also Born, *International Commercial Arbitration* (n 22) 3449–63; see Tan and Cooke, 'Challenge of Arbitral Awards' (n 41) [15.022].

[263] *AQZ v ARA* (n 26) [119]–[120].

[264] *BXH v BXI* [2020] 3 SLR 1368 [88]–[102] (hereafter *BXH v BXI (SGHC)*).

[265] See Model Law, Article 16(1). See also Born, *International Commercial Arbitration* (n 22) 3452–62; Chapter 3 this volume.

[266] See e.g. *Vitol Asia* (n 11). Although this was a case concerning enforcement of a domestic international arbitration award under Section 19 of the IAA, the principles set forth by Vinodh Coomaraswamy J are equally applicable to setting aside applications under Article 34(2)(a)(i) of the Model Law.

C. GROUNDS FOR SETTING ASIDE 247

separability presumption to argue that the arbitration agreement survived the expiry of the distributor agreement.[267] Vinodh Coomaraswamy J endorsed the principle of separability, quoting Lord Hoffmann's judgment in *Fiona Trust*, holding that the invalidity of a contract does not necessarily entail the invalidity of an arbitration agreement that is part of that contract.[268] However, noting that separability does not insulate the arbitration agreement from the main contract for all purposes, Coomaraswamy J held that the relevant question was whether it was the parties' intention, ascertained objectively, that the arbitration agreement should survive the expiry of the distributor agreement.[269]

On the facts, Coomaraswamy J held that the arbitration agreement survived the distributor agreement. He held that there was a general presumption that the parties intended for a dispute resolution clause to survive the termination of the main contract, so that the clause can fulfil its purpose of governing the resolution of disputes arising from that contract.[270] He also noted that no circumstances suggested a departure from this presumption, and in fact the parties had also expressly agreed in the distributor agreement that the arbitration agreement would survive expiry of the distributor agreement.[271] In any event, Coomaraswamy J held that the parties' continued course of dealing after the expiry of the distributor agreement gave rise to an implied contract or estopped the award debtor from denying that it was bound by the arbitration agreement.[272] **16.118**

Another issue that arose in *BXH v BXI (SGHC)* was whether an arbitration agreement is valid if the main contract that it is contained in also contains a jurisdiction clause provided for the jurisdiction of 'any legal action' to be a Singapore court. The award debtor argued that this gave rise to an 'irreconcilable inconsistency'. Coomaraswamy J disagreed, holding that where the parties have evinced a clear intention to submit their disputes to arbitration, the court should give effect to this intention as far as possible, and the proper approach therefore was to construe the arbitration agreement and jurisdiction clause in such a way as to give effect to both.[273] Accordingly, Coomaraswamy J held, adopting the reasoning in the judgment of Steyn J in *Paul Smith Ltd v H&S International Holding Inc* [1991] 2 Lloyd's Rep 127, that the parties intended to resolve substantive disputes in arbitration, pursuant to the arbitration agreement, and intended for the Singapore courts to resolve disputes in exercise of their supervisory jurisdiction, pursuant to the jurisdiction clause.[274] This was affirmed on appeal by the Singapore Court of Appeal, which held that in such cases 'a generous and harmonious interpretation should be given to the purportedly conflicting clauses such as to give effect to the parties' true intention'.[275] **16.119**

---

[267] *BXH v BXI (SGHC)* (n 264) [46], [69].
[268] Ibid, [82].
[269] Ibid, [83].
[270] Ibid, [84].
[271] Ibid, [87].
[272] Ibid, [88]–[110].
[273] Ibid, [234].
[274] Ibid, [243]–[244].
[275] *BXH v BXI* [2020] 1 SLR 1043; [2020] SGCA 28 [60] (hereafter *BXH v BXI (SGCA)*).

248   SETTING ASIDE AN AWARD

(f) Non-Existence of the Arbitration Agreement

16.120   Article 34(2)(a)(i) of the Model Law is also applicable where an award debtor alleges that no arbitration agreement exists or that it is not a party to an arbitration agreement. As the Singapore Court of Appeal held in *Astro (SGCA)*, the existence of an arbitration agreement is an issue concerning the material validity of a contract.[276] Thus, in the context of a refusal of enforcement, the Court of Appeal held that issues to do with the existence of an arbitration agreement (or lack thereof) fell within the equivalent of Article 34(2)(a)(i) rather than the equivalent of Article 34(2)(a)(iii) of the Model Law, which deals with the scope of an arbitration agreement rather than its existence.[277] In reaching this conclusion, the Court of Appeal cited the opinion of Lord Collins JSC in *Dallah v Pakistan*, as well as the leading English law treatise on conflict of laws.

16.121   Singapore courts have affirmed these views in the context of a setting aside application under Article 34(2)(a)(i) of the Model Law.[278] In *Jiangsu Overseas Group*, the applicant sought to set aside the award on the basis that it had never signed the contracts containing the arbitration agreement.[279] There, the Singapore High Court considered the principles applicable to the formation of contracts under Singapore law, which considers whether the parties have reached an agreement on all material terms based on the objective intentions of the parties.[280] Applying these principles, the High Court held that the conduct of the parties showed that they had concluded the relevant contracts and therefore a valid arbitration agreement was formed, noting that the non-signing was not itself a bar to the formation of the contracts.[281]

16.122   A similar argument was attempted in *AQZ v ARA*, where the award debtor argued that there was no valid arbitration agreement because the main contract was never concluded between the parties. However, on the evidence, Prakash J (as she then was) declined to set aside the award and held that a valid and binding contract had been concluded based on the conduct of the parties, who agreed on the main terms and intended for these terms to be binding on both of them, despite the absence of any formal signed document.[282]

16.123   In *BXH v BXI (SGCA)*, the Court of Appeal had to grapple with whether a dispute relating to the right to arbitrate following an assignment of the underlying contract was a dispute pertaining to the existence or scope of the arbitration agreement.[283] The applicant in that case had based its application on Article 34(2)(a)(i) and not Article 34(2)(a)(iii) of the Model Law. At first instance, the High Court held that this was a dispute relating to the scope of an arbitration agreement because there was no question that

---

[276] *Astro (SGCA)* (n 17) [156]–[158].
[277] Ibid, [152]–[156].
[278] *BXH v BXI (SGCA)* (n 275) [79], [90]–[91]; *Jiangsu Overseas Group* (n 11) [46].
[279] Ibid, [47].
[280] Ibid, [76]–[77].
[281] Ibid, [79]–[93].
[282] *AQZ v ARA* (n 26) [92].
[283] *BXH v BXI (SGCA)* (n 275) [3], [76].

the award debtor and award creditor were parties to an implied contract in relation to unassigned related rights.[284] The Court of Appeal disagreed and held that this was a dispute to do with the existence of the right to arbitrate in relation to the assigned rights because an arbitration agreement does not have a purpose or life independent of the substantive obligations it is attached to.[285]

In the context of investor–state arbitration, Singapore courts have held that the question of whether a State has consented to arbitration can be dealt with under either Article 34(2)(a)(i) or Article 34(2)(a)(iii) of the Model Law. In *Lesotho v Swissbourgh (SGCA)*, the Singapore Court of Appeal observed that, when a state enters into an investment treaty that provides for the submission of disputes to arbitration, it makes a unilateral offer to arbitrate, which an investor accepts by initiating arbitration proceedings in accordance with those terms.[286] Thus, if an investor argues that a dispute falls outside the scope of the arbitration clause in an investment treaty, it is an allegation that the arbitration agreement has not been perfected and therefore there is no arbitration agreement at all (Article 34(2)(a)(i)) and/or that the dispute falls outside the scope of submission to arbitration (Article 34(2)(a)(iii)).[287] **16.124**

As a practical matter, it may not always be easy to delineate the line between a dispute regarding the existence of the arbitration agreement and a dispute regarding the scope of that agreement. In the circumstances, award debtors may wish to consider whether to preserve an element of flexibility with respect to the grounds pleaded for a setting aside application. **16.125**

Arguments concerning the proper parties to the arbitration and arbitration agreement also implicate issues to do with the existence of an arbitration agreement with those parties, and therefore fall within Article 34(2)(a)(i) of the Model Law. As explained by the Singapore Court of Appeal in *Astro (SGCA)*, the question of the arbitral tribunal's jurisdiction over the sixth to eighth respondents in that case was an issue of whether a valid arbitration agreement was formed between the claimant and those respondents.[288] In that case, the arbitration agreement between the claimant and those respondents was alleged to have been created by the joinder procedure under the 2007 SIAC Rules.[289] Following an extensive comparative analysis of international arbitration rules and related commentary, the Court of Appeal held that Rule 24(b) of the 2007 SIAC Rules did not confer on the arbitral tribunal the power to join third parties who were not parties to the arbitration agreement, and therefore the arbitral tribunal did not have jurisdiction over the sixth to eighth respondents.[290] Although this was a **16.126**

---

[284] *BXH v BXI (SGHC)* (n 264) [140]–[141].
[285] *BXH v BXI (SGCA)* (n 275) [83].
[286] *Swissbourgh Diamond Mines (Pty) Ltd and others v Kingdom of Lesotho* [2019] 1 SLR 263 [75]–[78] (hereafter *Lesotho v Swissbourgh (SGCA)*).
[287] Ibid, [79].
[288] *Astro (SGCA)* (n 17) [158].
[289] Ibid.
[290] Ibid, [165]–[198].

250   SETTING ASIDE AN AWARD

case concerning enforcement of an award under Section 19 of the IAA,[291] the analytical framework set out by the Court of Appeal is likely to be applicable to setting aside applications under Article 34(2)(a)(i) of the Model Law that involve similar issues.

16.127   As explained in Chapter 5, Section 2A(6) of the IAA provides that if one party asserts the existence of an arbitration agreement and the opposing party does not deny the assertion in circumstances where the assertion calls for a reply, there is deemed to be an effective arbitration agreement between the parties. In the context of an Article 34(2)(a)(i) setting aside application, the respondent in *Vitol Asia* argued that it was immaterial whether the words 'Singapore law shall be applied' in the contract constituted an arbitration agreement, as a valid and effective arbitration agreement was deemed to exist by virtue of Section 2A(6) of the IAA.[292] Coomaraswamy J accepted this argument, finding that a valid arbitration agreement was deemed to exist because the applicant asserted the existence of an arbitration agreement twice, and the respondent merely denied that a contract existed between the parties but failed specifically to deny the existence of an arbitration agreement.[293]

2. Article 34(2)(a)(ii): Lack of Proper Notice of Appointment or Unable to Present Case

16.128   Article 34(2)(a)(ii) of the Model Law closely mirrors the wording of Article V(1)(b) of the New York Convention. There is only one superficial difference, in that Article 34(2)(a)(ii) refers to the 'appointment of an arbitrator' instead of 'appointment of the arbitrator'. This was intended to clarify that, in arbitral proceedings with more than one arbitrator, failure to give proper notice of any one of the arbitrators would be a ground for setting aside an award.[294]

16.129   The first limb of Article 34(2)(a)(ii) provides that, where a party is not provided adequate or timely notice of arbitrator appointments or important steps in the arbitral proceedings, such as hearings, this will be a basis for setting aside an award. Based on a review of reported decisions, Singapore courts have not yet had to consider a setting aside application based on a failure to give 'proper notice of the appointment of an arbitrator or of the arbitral proceedings'.

16.130   Commentators have noted that 'proper notice' does not refer to the type and form of notice (or service) required in national court proceedings, but instead notice that is appropriate in light of the parties' contract, the provisions of their arbitration agreement, and any applicable arbitration rules.[295] It bears noting that most arbitration rules have

---

[291] See Chapter 14.
[292] *Vitol Asia* (n 11) [48]–[50].
[293] Ibid, [53]–[55].
[294] Holtzmann and Neuhaus, *Guide to the UNCITRAL Model Law* (n 37) 1000.
[295] Born, *International Commercial Arbitration* (n 22) 3504–6.

broadly drafted notice provisions which cater to a variety of modes of communication and these may be treated as deeming notice to have occurred upon delivery in accordance with such provisions.[296]

16.131 The second limb of Article 34(2)(a)(ii) provides that a party's inability to present its case is a basis for setting aside an award. This will be the focus of the remaining discussion on Article 34(2)(a)(ii).

16.132 It is often suggested that there is no real distinction between Article 34(2)(a)(ii) of the Model Law and Section 24(b) of the IAA, which provides for the breach of the rules of natural justice as a ground for setting aside an award.[297] Thus, it is commonplace for parties to rely on both grounds for setting aside in Article 34(2)(a)(ii) and Section 24(b) based on the same set of facts, and also for Singapore courts to then treat both as involving a single inquiry as to whether the award debtor was denied a reasonable opportunity to be heard.[298] Much of the discussion in this section therefore applies equally to setting aside applications under Section 24(b) of the IAA. It may also apply to setting aside applications under Article 34(2)(a)(iv) of the Model Law on the ground that the composition of the arbitral tribunal or the arbitral procedure is not in accordance with the agreement of the parties or the provisions of the Model Law and the IAA.

16.133 However, the authors would suggest that in cases where the arbitrator's bias does not infringe on parties' right to be heard, the more appropriate ground for setting aside the award is arguably Section 24(b) of the IAA rather than Article 34(2)(a)(ii), given that the right to be heard is a distinct principle of natural justice from the right to an unbiased tribunal. Although there are no direct judicial pronouncements on this issue, this has been implicit in a number of reported decisions, which have tended to consider issues of bias under Section 24(b) and Article 34(2)(a)(iv).[299] In any case, it appears that Singapore courts will also resolve arbitrator bias issues under Article 34(2)(a)(iv) on the basis that the composition of the arbitral tribunal is not in accordance with the provisions of the Model Law.[300]

(a) Due Process and the Parties' Right to Present their Case

16.134 The setting aside of an award in circumstances where a party is 'unable to present his case' reflects that due process, or procedural fairness, is foundational to the integrity and legitimacy of the arbitral process.[301] Article 34(2)(a)(ii) should be understood in

---

[296] See SIAC Rules 2016, Rule 2.1; ICC Arbitration Rules 2021, Article 3; HKIAC Administered Arbitration Rules 2018, Article 3; LCIA Rules 2020, Article 4.3.

[297] *Triulzi* (n 78) [123], citing *ADG and another v ADI and another matter* [2014] 3 SLR 481; [2014] SGHC 73 [118] (hereafter *ADG v ADI*).

[298] Ibid, [123]–[124].

[299] *BYL and another v BYN* [2020] 4 SLR 1 [45], [50] (hereafter *BYL v BYN*).

[300] *PT Central Investindo* (n 35) [133]–[134].

[301] L. Reed, 'Ab(use) of Due Process: Sword vs Shield' (2017) 33 Arbitration International 361, 366 (hereafter Reed, 'Ab(use) of Due Process'); M. Scherer, 'Violation of Due Process, Article V(1)(b)' in R. Wolff (ed), *New York Convention on the Recognition and Enforcement of Foreign Arbitral Awards, A Commentary* (Hart Publishing 2013) 280.

252 SETTING ASIDE AN AWARD

light of the due process guarantees in Article 18 of the Model Law, which provides that the parties 'shall be treated with equality and each party shall be given a full opportunity of presenting his case'.

16.135 As also discussed elsewhere in this chapter, Article 18 sets out mandatory minimum standards of treatment. The reference to equality of treatment does not require identical treatment and equal treatment depends upon a consideration of the parties' respective positions, claims, and evidence, as well as the arbitral process as a whole.[302] Similarly, the reference to a 'full' opportunity has been interpreted to mean a party's '*reasonable* opportunity to present its case'.[303]

16.136 Because the due process guarantees in Articles 18 and 34(2)(a)(ii) of the Model Law are framed in broad terms, there is a legitimate concern that due process protections can be abused by parties seeking to gain a procedural advantage in an arbitration, which leads to arbitrators being overly conservative in an effort to avoid post-award challenges.[304] Thus, in deciding challenges under Article 34(2)(a)(ii) and Section 24(b), the Singapore courts apply a four-step test. The applicant must establish (i) which rule of natural justice was breached; (ii) how it was breached; (iii) in what way the breach was connected to the making of the award; and (iv) how the breach did or could prejudice a party's rights.[305]

(b) High Threshold for Challenge

16.137 It is not difficult for a party to dress up its grievances with the substantive outcome of an arbitration as defects in due process or violations of the right to present its case—for example, a party may cast disagreements about the substantive merits as a failure to permit additional submissions, or a failure to consider fully or address an argument or evidence in reasoning. Unsurprisingly, due process violations are among the most frequently invoked grounds for challenging arbitral awards before Singapore courts.

16.138 Singapore courts are keenly aware of this and the concern to avoid such challenges turning into backdoor appeals on the merits.[306] Thus, Singapore courts have emphasised that the threshold for a successful challenge is high and limited only to egregious cases where the error is 'clear on the face of the record', and that cases which succeed 'are few and far between'.[307] Indeed, Singapore courts have reasoned that, by construing the power to set aside arbitral awards too widely for breaches of due process, they would 'fail to support

---

[302] *Triulzi* (n 78) [112].

[303] *JVL Agro* (n 126) [145]; *ADG v ADI* (n 297) [104].

[304] Reed, 'Ab(use) of Due Process' (n 301) 361–77; M. Polkinghorne and B. Ainsley Gill, 'Due Process Paranoia: Need We Be Cruel to Be Kind?' (2017) 34(6) Journal of International Arbitration 935–46; K.P. Berger and J.O. Jensen, 'Due Process Paranoia and the Procedural Judgment Rule: A Safe Harbour for Procedural Management Decisions by International Arbitrators' (2016) 32(3) Arbitration International 415, 416; B. Cremades, 'The Use and Abuse of "Due Process" in International Arbitration' (2016 Chartered Institute of Arbitrators' Alexander Lecture, 17 November 2016). See generally, Born, *International Commercial Arbitration* (n 22) 2308–50.

[305] *Soh Beng Tee (SGCA)* (n 40) [29]; *L W Infrastructure* (n 165) [48]; *China Machine (SGCA)* (n 194) [86].

[306] *AKN v ALC (I)* (n 47) [39].

[307] See *Coal & Oil* (n 82) [2].

C. GROUNDS FOR SETTING ASIDE   253

arbitration as a useful efficient alternative dispute resolution process' and that '[r]efusing to set aside an award on arid and technical challenges' is also a facet of procedural fairness and due process.[308]

The Singapore Court of Appeal's decision in *AKN v ALC (I)* illustrates the application of this high threshold in practice. In that case, the Court of Appeal partially allowed a set of three appeals against a Singapore High Court decision to set aside an award—although the Court of Appeal set aside the award, it reversed three of the five grounds the High Court had relied upon for the set-aside.[309] Among other things, the Court of Appeal did not agree with the High Court's view that very poor or erroneous reasoning, even an internal contradiction in the award or a clear misunderstanding of the parties' arguments, could amount to a basis for a due process challenge.[310] Referring to its prior judgment in *BLC (SGCA)*,[311] the Court of Appeal observed that Singapore courts are 'not required to carry out a hypercritical or excessively syntactical analysis of what the arbitrator has written' nor should it approach an arbitral award with a 'meticulous legal eye endeavouring to pick holes, inconsistencies and faults … with the objective of upsetting or frustrating the process of arbitration.'[312]   **16.139**

(c) Deference to Arbitral Tribunal's Broad Case Management Powers

In deciding whether there has been a violation of a party's right to present its case that would justify a setting aside, the Singapore courts pay significant deference to arbitral tribunals' broad case management powers. Thus, in *Triulzi*, the Singapore High Court held that parties are entitled to no more than a 'reasonable opportunity to present one's case', which is to be balanced against other competing factors that a tribunal may have regard to, such as their duty to conduct the arbitration expeditiously and cost-effectively.[313] In the High Court's view, in light of these considerations, the supervisory role of curial courts should be exercised with a 'light hand' in any challenge to an arbitrator's procedural decisions based on due process.[314] Other considerations that may need to be weighed in the balance include confidentiality protections belonging to a third party to the arbitration.[315]   **16.140**

Consistent with this light touch approach, Singapore courts are slow to intervene where the breach of due process is said to have arisen from a procedural or case management decision of the tribunal.[316] As an exemplar of this approach, the Court of Appeal in *China Machine (SGCA)* held that, in deciding whether a party had been afforded a reasonably full opportunity to present its case, Singapore courts should consider whether   **16.141**

---

[308] *ADG v ADI* (n 297) [98]–[99].
[309] *AKN v ALC (I)* (n 47) [30]–[35].
[310] Ibid, [30]–[35].
[311] *BLC (SGCA)* (n 5) [86].
[312] *AKN v ALC (I)* (n 47) [59].
[313] *Triulzi* (n 78) [131].
[314] Ibid, [132].
[315] *Dongwoo* (n 188) [141].
[316] *ADG v ADI* (n 297) [114].

16.142 The judicial deference to the tribunal's broad case management powers can be seen as part of the broader principle identified in *China Machine (SGCA)*, that what due process or natural justice demands in each case turns on a construction of the agreement to arbitrate.[318] Thus, Singapore courts are likely to accord significant weight to specific language in the parties' arbitration clause when calibrating the balance between the arbitrators' case management powers and the parties' due process guarantees. For example, where the parties have agreed to a degree of expedition, they will not be entitled to the same reasonable opportunity of presenting their case in a full-length arbitration.[319]

16.143 However, an arbitral tribunal's broad case management powers are not without limits. Singapore courts have affirmed that, although arbitral tribunals are masters of their own procedure, their broad procedural powers cannot override the substantive rights of parties and are limited by the fundamental rules of natural justice.[320] This was considered in *CBP (SGHC)*,[321] where the arbitrator had insisted that Rule 33.1(c) of the Singapore Chamber of Maritime Arbitration (SCMA) rules granted broad case management powers that permitted him or her to 'gate' witnesses, that is, prevent parties from calling witnesses.[322] The arbitrator did not permit any of the plaintiff's witnesses to testify, and consequently the plaintiff applied to set aside the award under Section 24(b) of the IAA.[323]

16.144 Belinda Ang J found the SCMA rules did not expressly grant the arbitrator witness gating powers,[324] and that although the arbitrator has broad case management powers to 'ensure the just, expeditious, economical and final determination of the dispute',[325] such powers have to be exercised subject to the fundamental rules of natural justice.[326] Ang J further noted that the core purpose of witness-gating is to prevent 'unnecessary delay', and therefore it can only be exercised if the witnesses' evidence is 'plainly irrelevant or repetitive'.[327] This was affirmed on appeal, whereby the Singapore Court of Appeal found that the fundamental rules of natural justice 'must not be sacrificed in the name of efficacy'.[328] How the balance is to be struck would depend on the circumstances of each case.[329]

---

[317] *China Machine (SGCA)* (n 194) [103].

[318] Ibid, [143]. See also *China Machine New Energy Corp v Jaguar Energy Guatemala LLC and another* [2018] SGHC 101 [118(a)] (hereafter *China Machine (SGHC)*).

[319] Ibid, [125]–[127].

[320] *CBP v CBS* [2020] SGHC 23 [73] (hereafter *CBP (SGHC)*).

[321] Ibid, [73].

[322] Ibid, [33]–[35].

[323] Ibid, [48].

[324] Ibid, [68].

[325] Ibid, [71].

[326] Ibid, [76].

[327] Ibid, [77].

[328] *CBP (SGCA)* (n 116)[68].

[329] Ibid.

C. GROUNDS FOR SETTING ASIDE   255

(d) Requirements of Causal Nexus and Prejudice

To successfully set aside an award based on a violation of a party's right to present its **16.145** case, the applicant has to demonstrate that the violation of that due process right affected the making of award. In other words, the applicant has to establish that there is a 'causal nexus' between the breach and the award, and that the party was prejudiced by such denial of due process.[330] The requirements of causal nexus and prejudice are expressly provided for under Section 24(b) of the IAA, which provides that a breach of the rules of natural justice needs to have 'occurred in connection with the making of the award' and that the rights of any party must be 'prejudiced'. However, Article 34(2)(a) (ii) of the Model Law does not contain similar language.

Nonetheless, Singapore courts have applied the requirements of causal nexus and prejudice **16.146** in relation to both grounds of challenge, in relation to an alleged breach of a party's right to be heard, on the basis that the two provisions are 'co-extensive in scope and result'.[331] Although the cases do not discuss the textual differences between Section 24 of the IAA and Article 34(2)(a)(ii) of the Model Law, it is possible to explain the decisions on Article 34(2) (a)(ii) on the basis of the court's residual discretion not to enforce an arbitral award even if the grounds for setting aside are satisfied—for example, where there is no prejudice.[332]

The requirement of a causal nexus involves an inquiry as to whether the breach in- **16.147** fluenced or affected the ultimate decision by the arbitrators.[333] Thus, the Singapore High Court have held that the requirement is not satisfied where the issue affected by the breach found 'no place in the [t]ribunal's reasoning'.[334] Singapore courts have also held that it is not satisfied where the findings affected by the breach were 'subsidiary' or 'merely *obiter*', rather than part of arbitrators' main holding.[335]

(e) Factual Scenarios: Denial of Opportunity to Make Written Submissions or Adduce Evidence

Singapore courts have considered alleged violations of the right to be heard in a wide **16.148** range of factual circumstances. In general, each decision has been reached on its own facts, with multiple factors of varying weight often considered cumulatively. This and the next few sections outline a number of possible factual scenarios in which parties have attempted to set aside or refuse enforcement of an award based on the denial of an opportunity to be heard.

The first scenario relates to alleged denials of an opportunity to make written submis- **16.149** sions or adduce evidence on particular issues. Such challenges do not often succeed.

---

[330] *Soh Beng Tee (SGCA)* (n 40) [86], [91]; *Triulzi* (n 78) [126]; *John Holland* (n 58) [18].
[331] *ADG v ADI* (n 297) [118], [127]–[151].
[332] *CRW v Persero (I) (SGCA)* (n 7) [100].
[333] *Soh Beng Tee (SGCA)* (n 40) [77], [81].
[334] *ADG v ADI* (n 297) [130], [139].
[335] *Soh Beng Tee (SGCA)* (n 40) [75], [77].

256 SETTING ASIDE AN AWARD

16.150 For example, in *Sanum Investments Ltd v Lao PDR*, the Singapore High Court rejected a challenged based on the argument that the application of collateral estoppel principles under New York law precluded the award debtors from being heard on the merits of their claims.[336]

16.151 However, a small handful of challenges have succeeded where arbitral tribunals did not permit parties to put in submissions or evidence at all on issues central to the tribunal's award. For example, in *CRW v Persero (I) (SGCA)*, the arbitral tribunal reached a final award after an initial hearing to determine only some preliminary issues, without giving the parties the opportunity to put in any relevant submissions and evidence on issues other than the preliminary issues.[337] The Singapore Court of Appeal held that this was 'an affront to the principle that each party must have a reasonable opportunity to present its case', and caused prejudice to the award debtor who was unable to properly defend its position on why the sums awarded were excessive.[338]

16.152 In *AKN v ALC (I)*, the arbitral tribunal raised the possibility of assessing damages using a 'loss of chance' analysis on the *final* day of a 20-day hearing—even though the claimant had proceeded on the basis it was claiming loss of profits throughout the arbitration.[339] The arbitral tribunal then made a finding that the claimant lost a 55% chance of making enhanced profits, without any submissions having been made or expert evidence adduced by either party on the quantum of the chance lost.[340] The Court of Appeal held that this violated the parties' right to present their case and set aside the portions of the award relating to the 'loss of chance' claim.[341]

16.153 In *CAJ v CAI*, the Court of Appeal held that an arbitral tribunal had breached natural justice by relying on an extension-of-time defence that was raised for the first time in post-hearing closing submissions, observing that this was a 'completely new defence' that was 'factually and conceptually distinct' from other defences that had been put forward prior to that.[342] Notably, the Court of Appeal affirmed the High Court's finding that the opportunity given by the arbitrators to put in legal submissions on the newly raised defence could not 'constitute a reasonable opportunity to present one's case' because it did not remedy the absence of any opportunity to present evidence and respond 'in a fulsome manner' to the new defence.[343] In the context of an emergency arbitration, Chua Lee Ming J reached a similar result, finding that an emergency arbitrator breached natural justice by granting injunctive relief based on a new case presented only in post-hearing submissions, and only as an alternative case.[344]

---

[336] *Sanum Investments Ltd and another v Government of Lao People's Democratic Republic and others and another matter* [2022] SGHC(I) 9 [35]–[43].

[337] *CRW v Persero (I) (SGCA)* (n 7) [89]–[94].

[338] Ibid, [94]–[96].

[339] *AKN v ALC (I)* (n 47) [69], [75].

[340] Ibid, [76].

[341] Ibid, [79]–[80].

[342] *CAJ v CAI* (n 131) [54].

[343] Ibid, [58], [116].

[344] *CVG v CVH* [2022] SGHC 249 [54]–[55].

In *Sai Wan Shipping Ltd*,[345] Philip Jeyaretnam J had to consider whether an arbitrator **16.154** breached natural justice by issuing a peremptory order that the respondent serve its defence submissions by a specified timing, with the stipulation that non-compliance would bar the respondent from advancing any defence or counterclaim or adducing any evidence. Jeyaretnam J found that the arbitrator breached natural justice by failing to give the respondent any opportunity to provide input on the time needed to serve its defence submissions on whether there had been a default, whether there had been sufficient cause for the default, or whether the peremptory order should have been issued.[346]

Apart from these rare cases, Singapore courts will generally defer to the tribunal's assess- **16.155** ment of whether further submissions are necessary. For example, in *AUF v AUG*, the arbitral tribunal denied a party leave to respond to a 'new case' by the other party, which led to a challenge based on a denial of the opportunity to respond. The High Court rejected the challenge on the basis that the arbitral tribunal had made a case management decision that further submissions were unnecessary, noting that the challenging party did in fact have an opportunity to respond in the proceeding.[347]

(f) Factual Scenarios: Extensions of Timelines and Exclusion of New/Late Evidence

Attempts to challenge decisions by tribunals to set timelines for the submission of evidence **16.156** or to exclude evidence are invariably unsuccessful. Instead, Singapore courts have affirmed that the power to set timelines and enforce them falls within the tribunal's broad case management powers.

In *China Machine (SGHC)*, the award debtor alleged that the arbitral tribunal treated **16.157** the parties unequally by excluding the award debtor's expert report. Kannan Ramesh J rejected the inequality argument on the basis that the different circumstances surrounding the reports justified the differential treatment; the excluded report was submitted very late, barely a week before the main hearing, whereas the admitted report was submitted three weeks earlier without objection.[348] The award debtor also argued that the tribunal did not permit it a reasonable opportunity to present its case by 'unreasonably [insisting] that [it] adhere to existing procedural timelines', rejecting several requests for extension of time and granting shorter extensions than requested.[349] Ramesh J also rejected this, noting that the challenging party had agreed to adhere to the timelines and confirmed it would be able to meet them.[350] These views were later affirmed by the Singapore Court of Appeal.[351]

Similarly, in *Triulzi*, the challenging party alleged that a 10-day extension to file an ex- **16.158** pert report was too short and therefore violated its right to present its case, as did the

---

[345] *Sai Wan Shipping Ltd v Landmark Line Co, Ltd* [2022] SGHC 8 (hereafter *Sai Wan Shipping*).
[346] Ibid, [45], [57], [64], [69].
[347] *AUF v AUG and other matters* [2016] 1 SLR 859 [62(c)], [114]–[117] (hereafter *AUF v AUG*).
[348] *China Machine (SGHC)* (n 381) [189].
[349] Ibid, [184], [189].
[350] Ibid, [190].
[351] *China Machine (SGCA)* (n 194) [156].

258   SETTING ASIDE AN AWARD

tribunal's refusal to admit the late expert report filed on the last day of the hearing and in breach of the extended timeline.[352] The Singapore High Court held that the tribunal's conduct was 'not capable of criticism whatsoever' in the circumstances of the case and that the tribunal had made its procedural decisions fairly and in consideration of the points raised by the parties.[353]

16.159   In *CMJ v CML*,[354] Simon Thorley IJ declined to find a breach of natural justice in circumstances where the tribunal had refused to admit new evidence. He noted that, in such cases involving a late application to adduce evidence, a tribunal is often placed in an 'invidious position' of either refusing to admit the evidence, which could be unfair to the adducing party, or allowing the evidence, which may lead to an injustice to the other party, and accommodating both parties may jeopardise the hearing date.[355] Thorley IJ eventually found that the tribunal had exercised its discretion in a way that was fair to both parties, taking into account the proximity of the hearing.[356]

(g) Factual Scenarios: Oral Hearings and Cross-Examination

16.160   Attempts to challenge awards in Singapore courts based on a denial of a right to an oral hearing or cross-examination are also frequently unsuccessful, particularly if such a hearing was not requested or in the reasonable contemplation of the parties.

16.161   In *PT Asuransi (SGHC)*, the challenging party argued that it was denied the opportunity to make oral submissions at a hearing scheduled after the filing of written submissions but was never held before the tribunal issued its award.[357] The High Court, with which the Court of Appeal agreed, held that there was no merit in this argument given that the parties never filed their written submissions by the appointed date in the procedural timetable meaning the 'intended hearing could not go on'; thus, when further directions were subsequently given, there was no direction for an oral hearing thereafter.[358] In rejecting the challenge, the Court also noted that neither party requested an oral hearing.[359]

16.162   A similar complaint was rejected in *Philippines v Philippine International Air Terminals*.[360] The High Court noted that a hearing is not required under Article 20(2) of the ICC Rules or Article 24(1) of the Model Law unless the parties call for it or the tribunal so decides of its own motion.[361] The Singapore Court of Appeal reached a similar

---

[352] *Triulzi* (n 78) [119].
[353] Ibid, [136]–[141].
[354] *CMJ and another v CML and another* [2022] 3 SLR 319 (hereafter *CMJ v CML*).
[355] Ibid, [63]–[64].
[356] Ibid, [62], [65].
[357] *PT Asuransi Jasa Indonesia (Persero) v Dexia Bank SA* [2006] 1 SLR(R) 197 [51] (hereafter *PT Asuransi (SGHC)*).
[358] Ibid, [51]–[52].
[359] Ibid, [52].
[360] *Government of the Republic of the Philippines v Philippine International Air Terminals Co, Inc* [2007] 1 SLR(R) 278 [33] (hereafter *Philippines v Philippine International Air Terminals*).
[361] Ibid, [33].

C. GROUNDS FOR SETTING ASIDE   259

result in *Kempinski Hotels (SGCA)*, rejecting the challenging party's arguments that it had been deprived of the opportunity to cross-examine the other side's expert witness because there was no indication that it had requested such cross-examination and, in any event, no objection had been made at the time and was therefore waived.[362]

(h) Factual Scenarios: Document Production Orders

Parties may also allege a violation of the right to be heard in relation to document production orders by the arbitral tribunal. These issues may arise where one party alleges some commercial or technical sensitivity that warrants non-disclosure to one or more parties or their legal representatives, resulting in information disclosure that is asymmetrical.   **16.163**

In *Dongwoo*, the tribunal ruled on the applicant's document requests and ordered production of certain technical documents, but was invited by the respondent to reconsider because the requested information was confidential and proprietary.[363] Subsequently, the respondent sent the technical documents to the tribunal, but not the applicant, and both parties made further applications in respect of production.[364] The tribunal then dismissed both the applicant's request for further production of documents and the respondent's request for modification of the tribunal's original ruling, reserving to the applicant the right to argue that adverse inferences should be drawn.[365]   **16.164**

Chan Seng Onn J rejected the argument that the tribunal had denied the applicant a fair opportunity to be heard by examining various documents that were not extended to the applicant and failing to direct that such documents be provided to it.[366] Chan J held that the applicant had obtained a decision in its favour on document production and therefore suffered no prejudice,[367] noting also that the applicant had been given an opportunity to present extensive arguments on whether an adverse inference could be drawn.[368] Chan J thus was 'not minded to interfere' with the arbitral tribunal's exercise of its procedural discretion with respect to document production issues.[369]   **16.165**

Another asymmetrical document production order was considered by the Singapore High Court in *China Machine (SGHC)*.[370] There, the tribunal put in place an 'attorneys eyes only' document production regime (AEO Regime) to address allegations by one party that the information requested contained sensitive information which could be misused against it.[371] Documents subject to the AEO Regime would be first disclosed   **16.166**

---

[362] *Kempinski Hotels (SGCA)* (n 61) [63], [67].
[363] *Dongwoo* (n 188) [27]–[28].
[364] Ibid, [28]–[34].
[365] Ibid, [35].
[366] Ibid, [51].
[367] Ibid, [64].
[368] Ibid, [68]–[69].
[369] Ibid, [73]–[87].
[370] *China Machine (SGHC)* (n 318).
[371] Ibid, [55]–[56].

260 SETTING ASIDE AN AWARD

only to external counsel, and then to specified employees of the challenging party upon application to the tribunal.

16.167 Rejecting the challenging party's argument that the AEO Regime was inappropriate, indiscriminate, and unjustified, Kannan Ramesh J considered the reference to expedition in the parties' arbitration agreement and the fact that the order made by the tribunal was consistent with the broad powers conferred on it under Article 20(7) of the applicable 1998 ICC Rules.[372] Ramesh J also rejected arguments that the challenging party was denied an opportunity to present its case because its counsel and experts could not effectively analyse certain documents due to the AEO Regime, holding that any such denial of opportunity was self-inflicted because the award debtor had never applied under the terms of the AEO Regime for its employees to access the relevant material or applied to the Tribunal to modify the AEO Regime in respect of redactions that it complained of.[373] For these reasons, the court held that the challenging party suffered no prejudice that would justify setting aside the award.[374]

16.168 The challenging party also argued that the AEO Regime did not treat the parties equally because it allowed the award creditor to withhold or redact large volumes of documents while placing a disproportionate burden on the award debtor.[375] Ramesh J rejected this argument, noting its earlier holding that the tribunal had the power to impose the AEO Regime and the fact that the tribunal was concerned with safeguarding both parties' interests in making the order.[376] On appeal, the Court of Appeal agreed with Ramesh J, finding that parties' right to a 'full opportunity' to be heard is impliedly limited by considerations of reasonableness and fairness.[377] Furthermore, the challenging party could not be permitted to challenge the award based on alleged material breaches of natural justice that it did not raise before the arbitral tribunal during the arbitration proceedings.[378] The Court of Appeal held that there must be 'fair intimation' to the arbitral tribunal about the alleged irregularity so that both the arbitral tribunal and the non-complaining party would have the opportunity to consider the position.[379]

(i) Factual Scenarios: Other Procedural Directions

16.169 Besides the procedural decisions discussed above, dissatisfied parties may also seek to challenge numerous other procedural decisions that an arbitral tribunal has to make over the lifecycle of an arbitration. Attempts to challenge such decisions based on a right to present one's case have largely been unsuccessful before Singapore courts, which often give tribunals a wide margin of appreciation in making such decisions.

---

[372] Ibid, [121]–[133].
[373] Ibid, [163]–[166].
[374] Ibid, [167]–[169].
[375] Ibid, [183].
[376] Ibid, [187]–[188].
[377] *China Machine (SGCA)* (n 194) [97].
[378] Ibid, [166]–[168].
[379] Ibid, [170].

C. GROUNDS FOR SETTING ASIDE   261

In *ADG v ADI* the challenging party alleged that the arbitral tribunal acted unilaterally, **16.170**
unfairly, and unreasonably in declaring the SIAC arbitral proceedings closed and giving
them only three business days to comment; it also complained that the tribunal subsequently refused to reopen proceedings and allow additional evidence.[380] The High
Court dismissed the challenge, holding that there was nothing unreasonable or unfair about setting a 'perfectly reasonable deadline' which was 'imposed to be observed
and carries consequences if it is not'.[381] Similarly, in *Coal & Oil*, Steven Chong J (as he
then was) rejected the argument by the award debtor that the tribunal should have invited submissions on whether it should close proceedings before it decided to issue its
award.[382] In doing so, he distinguished between the right to be heard on issues which
affected the determination of the parties' dispute and the right to be heard on procedural decisions by the tribunal.[383] Chong J appeared to be of the view that the parties did
not have 'a right to be heard before the Tribunal makes a decision on whether it ought to
declare the proceedings closed before releasing the award'.[384]

Other types of procedural decisions that could be challenged include lists of issues or **16.171**
terms of reference drawn up at the start of the arbitration. In *BLC (SGCA)*, the challenging party alleged that the arbitrator had failed to consider its proposed list of issues
and simply adopted the other party's list of issues.[385] The Court of Appeal disagreed
with the challenging party's account of the facts based on a closer scrutiny of the parties' lists and the tribunal's list of issues, holding that the arbitrator had read and carefully considered both lists of issues before coming to his decision and that the tribunal's
list featured issues from both parties.[386] Even if this were not the case, there should be
no basis in principle for a successful challenge based simply on the adoption of one
side's list of issues, so long as the arbitral tribunal has given due consideration to lists
from all parties.

Arbitral tribunals sometimes proceed with an arbitration despite the non-participation **16.172**
of one of the parties; indeed, some arbitration rules expressly provide for the tribunal's
entitlement to do so.[387] Where a party has notice of the arbitration but chooses not
to participate, Singapore courts have shown some willingness to entertain challenges
based on a denial of an opportunity to be heard.

In *Rakna Arakshaka (SGHC)*, the challenging party did not respond or participate at **16.173**
all in the arbitration as it had taken the position that the tribunal had no jurisdiction.
Nevertheless, it sought to challenge the award on the basis that it was not sent certain

---

[380] *ADG v ADI* (n 297) [119].
[381] Ibid, [121].
[382] *Coal & Oil* (n 82) [68]–[70].
[383] Ibid, [70].
[384] Ibid, [70].
[385] *BLC (SGCA)* (n 5) [90].
[386] Ibid, [91]–[92].
[387] See SIAC Rules 2016, Rule 24.3; LCIA Arbitration Rules 2020, Article 15.8; HKIAC Administered Arbitration
Rules 2018, Article 26; ICC Arbitration Rules 2021, Article 6(8).

262   SETTING ASIDE AN AWARD

correspondence or documents—in particular, the notes of evidence for the substantive hearing.[388] The High Court held that it had 'little hesitation' in saying that the ground for challenge had 'no merit whatsoever' because the challenging party had chosen not to participate in the arbitration despite having ample opportunity to do so.[389] The court also rejected the argument that the non-participating party suffered any prejudice as a result of not being sent certain correspondence or documents.[390] On appeal, while the natural justice challenge was not pursued, the Court of Appeal noted in the context of its findings on the preclusive effects of a failure to mount an Article 16(3) challenge that there was no duty to participate in proceedings.[391] It remains to be seen whether the absence of a duty to participate will have any bearing on natural justice challenges based on the non-participation of a party, and much will depend on the circumstance of each case.

16.174   Arguments based on a party's inability to present its case are also often attempted to seek to delay or postpone hearing dates that have already been fixed. In *Triulzi*, Belinda Ang J considered the argument that the tribunal's decision to refuse an application to vacate hearing dates denied the challenging party an opportunity to present expert evidence.[392] Ang J dismissed this challenge, noting that the hearing dates had been fixed for over a year and that the tribunal was not informed by the challenging party of the alleged issues concerning the availability of the experts it intended to engage.[393] Ang J further observed that the right of each party to be heard does not mean that the Tribunal must 'sacrifice all efficiency in order to accommodate unreasonable procedural demands by a party'.[394]

(j) Factual Scenarios: Failure to Give Reasons

16.175   Article 31(2) of the Model Law provides that an award shall state the reasons upon which it was based, unless parties have agreed otherwise. In certain cases, parties might claim that the arbitral award should be set aside because of deficient reasoning or a complete absence of any reasoning. Singapore courts have found that an arbitral tribunal is generally bound to give reasons for its decisions.[395] In *TMM Division*, the High Court set forth the following principles concerning the scope of an arbitrator's duty to give reasons: (i) the standard of explanation required in every case must correspond to the requirements of the case; (ii) in very clear cases there may be no need to give reasons; and (iii) there may be no need to give reasons for decisions or findings which do not bear directly on the substance or affect the final resolution of the parties'

---

[388] *Rakna Arakshaka (SGHC)* (n 33) (reversed on appeal on other grounds) [33].
[389] Ibid, [76].
[390] Ibid, [78]–[79].
[391] *Rakna Arakshaka Lanka Ltd v Avant Garde Maritime Services (Pte) Ltd* [2019] 2 SLR 131 (hereafter *Rakna Arakshaka (SGCA)*) [77].
[392] *Triulzi* (n 78) [142]–[143].
[393] Ibid, [140], [144]–[150].
[394] Ibid, [151].
[395] *TMM Division Maritima SA de CV v Pacific Richfield Marine Pte Ltd* [2013] 4 SLR 972 [102] (hereafter *TMM Division*); *AUF v AUG* (n 347) [78]; *CEF and another v CEH* [2021] SGHC 114 [183] (hereafter *CEF v CEH*).

C. GROUNDS FOR SETTING ASIDE   263

rights.[396] The Court specifically noted that there was no requirement for an arbitral tribunal to touch on 'each and every point in dispute', holding that the crucial question is whether the contents of the arbitral award taken as a whole inform the parties of the bases on which the arbitral tribunal reached its decision on the material or essential issues.[397]

In rare cases, extremely deficient reasoning might indicate a breach of natural justice and could lead to a setting aside. In *BZV (SGCA)*, the Court of Appeal agreed with the High Court's decision to set aside the award on the basis that the tribunal had adopted a chain of reasoning that had no nexus with the parties' submissions, which indicated that the tribunal had failed to apply its mind at all to the essential issues arising from the parties' arguments.[398] The Court of Appeal also found that the tribunal was 'manifestly incoherent' in its decision, and that this breached the fair hearing principle.[399] In most other cases, however, Singapore courts will reject arguments based on deficient reasoning.   **16.176**

For example, in *Asiana Airlines*, the High Court rejected an application to set aside an award based on a complaint that the arbitral tribunal had failed to give any or proper consideration to the expert report of a Korean law expert and failed to address aspects of that expert report in its reasoning.[400]   **16.177**

In general, the Singapore courts have held that a chain of reasoning would be open to an arbitral tribunal: (a) if it arises from the party's express pleadings; (b) if it is raised by reasonable implication by a party's pleadings; (c) if it does not feature in a party's pleadings but is in some other way brought to the opposing party's actual notice; or (d) if the links in the chain flow reasonably from the arguments actually advanced by either party or are related to those arguments.[401] The overall inquiry is not intended to be overly technical but aimed at determining whether or not a reasonable party to the arbitration could have foreseen the tribunal's chain of reasoning.[402]   **16.178**

Relatedly, can an award be set aside for breaches of natural justice where material findings are made without any evidential basis at all? In England and in Australia, the 'no evidence' rule holds that an award can be attacked on the basis that there is no evidence at all to support its material findings.[403] However, several High Court decisions have taken the view that the 'no evidence' rule does not form part of Singapore law, on the   **16.179**

---

[396] Ibid, [104].
[397] Ibid, [104]–[105].
[398] *BZV (SGCA)* (n 95) [61].
[399] Ibid, [56].
[400] *Asiana Airlines, Inc v Gate Gourmet Korea Co, Ltd* [2022] 4 SLR 158, [91]–[93].
[401] *BZV (SGCA)* (n 95) [60(b)]; *JVL Agro* (n 126) [149]–[162].
[402] *JVL Agro* (n 126) [149]–[162].
[403] *R v Deputy Industrial Injuries Commissioner, ex parte Moore* [1965] 1 QB 456, 488; *TCL Air Conditioner (Zhongshan) Co Ltd v Castel Electronics Pty Ltd* [2014] FCAFC 83; and *Emerald Grain Australia Pty Ltd v Agrocorp International Pte Ltd* [2014] FCA 414.

264 SETTING ASIDE AN AWARD

basis that it is inconsistent with Singapore's adoption of the Model Law and the strong policy of minimal curial intervention.[404]

(k) Factual Scenarios: Surprising Decisions

16.180 Where a tribunal departs from the parties' submissions before it in making a decision, a challenge based on the denial of an opportunity to address the tribunal's reasoning may be upheld where a party can show objectively that 'a reasonable litigant in his shoes could not have foreseen the possibility of reasoning of the type revealed in the award'.[405] In determining whether a party was given an opportunity to address a point in submissions, Singapore courts are likely to look at substance over form, considering the totality of the correspondence, evidence and written submissions.

16.181 In *Kempinski Hotels (SGHC)*, the Singapore High Court had set aside a tribunal's third and fourth awards because the tribunal had made a decision on the basis of a new factual development which had not been pleaded by the parties and arose only after the tribunal's second award.[406] However, the Singapore Court of Appeal disagreed, holding that the challenging party had 'ample notice' of the case it had to meet based on extensive correspondence, written submissions, and even expert evidence on the issue, and had therefore been given 'ample opportunity to address' the issue.[407]

16.182 In a somewhat unusual context, a breach of natural justice may arise where a tribunal first dismisses an application to amend pleadings to introduce a new issue but then subsequently re-introduces the same issue on its own accord at a late stage. In *Phoenixfin v Convexity*,[408] the appellants sought to amend their pleadings to include an issue regarding a penalty clause after the pleadings and the agreed list of issues had been filed.[409] This application to amend pleadings was dismissed.[410] The tribunal subsequently unilaterally reintroduced the issue at an oral reply hearing *after* the evidentiary hearing had taken place and after closing submissions were filed.[411] The Court of Appeal found that the tribunal's reintroduction of the penalty clause issue at a late stage, without allowing parties to amend their pleadings or to lead evidence on the issue, constituted a breach of natural justice.[412] This was particularly so given that the penalty issue was an issue of mixed fact and law, and thus the award debtor had not been granted an opportunity to know what the evidentiary basis for the decision on the penalty clause issue was, nor was it granted an opportunity to respond to that evidence.[413] Importantly, the Court of Appeal also found that the tribunal's subsequent attempts to allow further

---

[404] See *AUF v AUG* (n 347) [76]; *CEF v CEH* (n 395) [152].

[405] *Soh Beng Tee (SGCA)* (n 40) [65(d)]; *JVL Agro* (n 126) [160]; *CIM v CIN* [2021] 4 SLR 1176 [41]–[42] (hereafter *CIM v CIN*).

[406] *Kempinski Hotels (SGCA)* (n 61) [25]–[26].

[407] Ibid, [51].

[408] *Phoenixfin Pte Ltd and others v Convexity Ltd* [2022] SGCA 17 (hereafter *Phoenixfin v Convexity*).

[409] Ibid, [42].

[410] Ibid, [41]–[48].

[411] Ibid, [47].

[412] Ibid, [47], [54]–[68].

[413] Ibid, [68].

written submissions and evidence from the award debtor after the hearing were insufficient to remedy the breach, because it effectively reversed the burden of proof.[414]

(l) Factual Scenarios: Remote Hearings

While there has yet to be a Singapore case concerning an alleged breach of the right to be heard in the conduct of remote hearings, this may become inevitable as such hearings become more commonplace. In the authors' respectful submission, absent exceptional circumstances, challenges to remote hearings are not likely to succeed. As a starting point, as discussed elsewhere, the right to a full opportunity to be heard under Article 18 of the Model Law is not absolute and limited by the considerations of reasonableness and fairness,[415] and balanced against the need for efficiency.[416] In these circumstances, absent any agreement by the parties on the mode of hearing, the mere decision to hold a remote hearing is not likely to constitute a breach of the right to be heard so long as each party is given a reasonable opportunity to present its case before the arbitral tribunal.   **16.183**

3. Article 34(2)(a)(iii): Excess of Authority or Jurisdiction

Article 34(2)(a)(iii) reflects the basic principle that, even when constituted pursuant to a valid arbitration agreement, an arbitral tribunal lacks jurisdiction to decide issues not referred to it for determination by the parties.[417] In other words, the disputes that the parties submit to arbitration will delimit the scope of an arbitral tribunal's jurisdiction,[418] and an arbitral tribunal's award may be set aside to the extent it exceeds the scope of that delimited jurisdiction.   **16.184**

Singapore courts have held that the 'excess of jurisdiction' ground of setting aside covers both: (i) circumstances where an arbitral tribunal improperly decided matters that had not been submitted to it; and (ii) circumstances where an arbitral tribunal failed to decide matters that had been submitted to it.[419] These are discussed in greater detail in the subsections below.   **16.185**

Article 34(2)(a)(iii) refers to the possibility of a partial set-aside and requires courts to consider the extent to which the parts made in excess of an arbitral tribunal's jurisdiction are severable from other parts of the award. Specifically, Article 34(2)(a)(iii) provides that 'if the decisions on matters submitted to arbitration can be separated from those not so submitted, only that part of the award which contains decisions on matters not submitted to arbitration may be set aside'. Consistent with this provision, where   **16.186**

---

[414] Ibid, [65]–[68].
[415] *China Machine (SGCA)* (n 194) [97].
[416] Ibid, [95].
[417] *Kempinski Hotels (SGCA)* (n 61) [31]–[32]; *CRW v Persero (I) (SGCA)* (n 7) [31]; *PT Asuransi (SGCA)* (n 40) [37].
[418] Ibid, [32].
[419] *CRW v Persero (I) (SGCA)* (n 7) [31].

266 SETTING ASIDE AN AWARD

a tribunal's decisions on matters in excess of its jurisdiction are severable from other parts of the award, Singapore courts have only set aside the parts of the award made in excess of the tribunal's jurisdiction.[420] Conversely, where other findings in the award were linked to and flowed from the parts of the award made in excess of the tribunal's jurisdiction, all of the linked findings in addition to the part of the award made in excess of the arbitral tribunal's jurisdiction would be set aside.[421]

(a) Decisions on Matters Outside the Scope of Submission to Arbitration

16.187 Singapore courts generally adopt a two-stage inquiry in deciding setting aside applications under Article 34(2)(a)(iii), considering:[422]

- first, what matters were within the scope of submission to the arbitral tribunal; and
- second, whether the arbitral award involved such matters, or whether it involved 'a new difference outside the scope of the submission to arbitration and accordingly irrelevant to the issues requiring determination'.

16.188 The courts will determine these issues *de novo*.[423] To determine the scope of submission to arbitration, Singapore courts will have regard to multiple sources, not limited to the parties' pleadings, including any agreed list of issues, opening statements, evidence adduced, and any closing submissions.[424] As the Court of Appeal noted in *Prometheus Marine (SGCA)*, although the pleadings in arbitral proceedings can provide a reference point for determining the scope of an arbitral tribunal's jurisdiction, they are by no means conclusive, and the Singapore courts will take a 'practical view' of the 'substance of the dispute being referred to arbitration' regardless of how the issues were termed or labelled.[425]

16.189 Singapore courts take a broad view of what comprises the parties' pleadings for the purposes of determining the scope of submission to arbitration. In *CDM v CDP*, the Court of Appeal rejected the suggestion by the award debtor that the parties' pleadings were confined to just the Statement of Claim and Notice of Arbitration. Instead, the Court of Appeal considered that the relevant pleadings comprised all of the parties' written submissions in the arbitration, including the Statement of Defence and Counterclaim, the Reply and Defence to the Counterclaim, and the Rejoinder to the Reply and Defence to the Counterclaim.[426] Consequently, although the Notice of Arbitration and Statement of Claim made no mention of the issue of approval for a certain second launch, the Court of Appeal held that this point was put in issue before the arbitrators based on the

---

[420] See e.g. *BLB and another v BLC and others* [2013] 4 SLR 1169 [102] (hereafter *BLC (SGHC)*).
[421] *GD Midea Air Conditioning Equipment Co Ltd v Tornado Consumer Goods Ltd and another matter* [2018] 4 SLR 271 [72]–[76] (hereafter *GD Midea*).
[422] *CDM v CDP* (n 180) [17]; *CRW v Persero (I) (SGCA)* (n 7) [30]; *PT Asuransi (SGCA)* (n 40) [40], [44]; *CBX v CBZ (SGCA)* (n 167) [11].
[423] Ibid, [11]; *AKN v ALC (I)* (n 47) [112]; *Dallah v Pakistan* (n 211).
[424] *CDM v CDP* (n 180) [18].
[425] *Prometheus Marine (SGCA)* (n 45) [58]–[60]. See also *CEF v CEH* (n 395) [87]–[90] which made a similar point regarding the Terms of Reference under the ICC Rules.
[426] *CDM v CDP* (n 180) [20]–[24].

C. GROUNDS FOR SETTING ASIDE   267

totality of the pleadings, as well as the agreed list of issues, the parties' opening statements, witness testimony, and the parties' closing submissions.[427]

Any new fact or change in the law arising after the submission to arbitration, which is **16.190** ancillary to the dispute submitted for arbitration and known to all the parties to the arbitration, is part of that dispute and need not be specifically pleaded to fall within the scope of the arbitral tribunal's jurisdiction.[428] In *Kempinski Hotels (SGHC)*, following the issuance of a second award by the sole arbitrator, the arbitration defendant learned of a new management venture involving the arbitration claimant and wrote to the arbitrator to seek clarification on a finding in the second award that the parties' hotel management contract was still capable of being performed. After inviting submissions from the parties, the sole arbitrator held in a third award that the arbitration claimant could no longer perform its obligations from the commencement date of the new management venture and therefore was not entitled to damages from that date. The High Court set aside the third award on the basis that the parties were not free to raise material and unpleaded points without having first applied to amend their pleadings, which circumscribes the scope of an arbitrator's jurisdiction.[429] The Court of Appeal disagreed, holding instead that the new management venture was a new fact arising in the course of arbitration that affected the arbitration claimant's right to the remedies claimed, and the legal effect of that new fact was therefore well within the arbitrator's jurisdiction.[430] Where a new fact or change in the law has occurred, the Singapore courts are more likely to find that it falls within the scope of the tribunal's jurisdiction if sufficient notice was given to the other parties to the arbitration, and the other parties were given an opportunity to address the new fact or development.[431]

Where an issue has not been specifically pleaded but can be subsumed within a more **16.191** general issue raised in the parties' submissions, a decision on that issue does not exceed the tribunal's jurisdiction. In *AKN v ALC (I)*, the arbitration claimants made a generic prayer for 'damages' and the parties proceeded throughout the arbitral proceedings on the basis that the damages claim was one for actual loss of profits.[432] The arbitral tribunal subsequently re-characterised the claim *sua sponte* as one for loss of an opportunity to earn profits and made its award on that basis. The High Court set aside the award on several grounds, including because the finding on loss of opportunity exceeded the tribunal's jurisdiction. The Singapore Court of Appeal disagreed in respect of excess of jurisdiction, holding that the generic claim for damages was broad enough to encompass a claim for loss of opportunity; however, the award was set aside on the basis that the parties did not have an opportunity to address the point.[433]

---

[427] Ibid, [21]–[24].
[428] *Kempinski Hotels (SGCA)* (n 61) [47]–[48]. See also *CEF v CEH* (n 395) [92].
[429] *Kempinski Hotels (SGHC)* (n 133) [54]-[64].
[430] *Kempinski Hotels (SGCA)* (n 61) [47]–[48].
[431] Ibid, [61]; *CIM v CIN* (n 405) [44].
[432] *AKN v ALC (I)* (n 47) [69].
[433] Ibid, [74].

268 SETTING ASIDE AN AWARD

16.192 Singapore courts have also held that an arbitral tribunal may determine ancillary issues necessary for the determination of issues expressly submitted to arbitration. In *TMM Division*, the High Court held that the issue of whether a contractual clause was a condition of the contract was in fact put in issue by the parties' submissions in the arbitration, but in any event it also reasoned that it would have been open to the sole arbitrator to determine the issue as an ancillary issue to the issue it was asked to determine in the parties' agreed list of issues, namely whether a breach of that clause amounted to a repudiatory breach.[434]

16.193 This reasoning was subsequently considered but not applied in *GD Midea*, a rare case in which the High Court set aside an award for an excess of jurisdiction. The arbitral tribunal exceeded its jurisdiction by basing its decision on a breach of Clause 4.2 of the relevant contract, even though that breach was not mentioned in any of the submissions in the arbitration or the agreed list of issues.[435] The award creditor had argued, relying on *TMM Division*, that the arbitral tribunal had the jurisdiction to determine whether Clause 4.2 was breached as part of its jurisdiction over the issues that were indisputably submitted to arbitration, namely whether the arbitration claimant was in breach of its sales targets and whether the arbitration defendant was entitled to terminate.[436] The High Court rejected this argument, holding that that the arbitral tribunal's finding on Clause 4.2 was not 'necessary' for the determination of those issues.[437] The High Court declined to follow Hong Kong authority holding that the words 'decisions on matters beyond the scope of submission to arbitration' in Article 34(2)(a)(iii) should be construed narrowly to include only decisions that were 'clearly unrelated to or not reasonably required' for the determination of disputes subject to arbitration.[438]

16.194 It may be queried whether the decision in *GD Midea* is consistent with the approach taken by the Court of Appeal in *AKN v ALC (I)*, given that the question of whether Clause 4.2 had been breached was arguably subsumed within the broader, generic question of whether the arbitration defendant was entitled to terminate the contract.[439] Applying the Court of Appeal's approach in *AKN v ALC (I)*, the Clause 4.2 issue could be said to have fallen within the scope of the arbitral tribunal's jurisdiction. However, the unique facts in *GD Midea* were that the award creditor had not relied on Clause 4.2 as a basis for termination, and both parties appeared to have a common understanding of Clause 4.2. Given that the issue of whether Clause 4.2 had been breached was not before the tribunal, the High Court ruled that the tribunal's finding of breach was in excess of jurisdiction. In any case, as Chua J held, the arbitral tribunal's surprise finding on Clause 4.2 was in breach of the rules of natural justice, and the award could have

---

[434] *TMM Division* (n 395) [57], [67]–[69].
[435] *GD Midea* (n 421) [43].
[436] Ibid, [55].
[437] Ibid, [57].
[438] Ibid, [58]–[59].
[439] *AKN v ALC (I)* (n 47) was not cited or referred to in the High Court judgment.

been set aside on that ground alone. This decision was upheld on appeal although the Court of Appeal did not issue separate grounds.

In general, an error of law or fact, no matter how manifest, is not sufficient to consti- **16.195** tute an excess of jurisdiction such as to warrant setting aside an arbitral award under Article 34(2)(a)(iii) of the Model Law.[440] Following English authority, Singapore courts have affirmed the distinction between the 'erroneous exercise by an arbitral tribunal of an available power vested in it (which would amount to no more than a mere error of law)' and the 'purported exercise by the arbitral tribunal of a power which it did not possess'.[441] An error, however gross, in the exercise of the arbitral tribunal's available powers does not take the arbitral tribunal outside its jurisdiction.[442]

Applying these principles, Judith Prakash J (as she then was) in *Sui Southern Gas* de- **16.196** clined to set aside an award on the basis that the tribunal's decision was based on a 'perverse and irrational construction' of the relevant contract and in 'manifest disregard' of the principles of English law, holding that neither of these contentions has any effect on the scope of the submission to arbitration, which clearly involved the matters decided by the arbitral tribunal in its award.[443] In *Sobati General Trading*, Tay Yong Kwang J also dismissed an application for setting aside that was based on the argument that the arbitral tribunal's failure to apply Indonesian law, the law governing the disputed contract, exceeded the scope of its jurisdiction.[444] Similarly, in the context of an enforcement proceeding, Chua Lee Ming J in *Quanzhou Sanhong* held that an error by an arbitral tribunal in respect of the governing law of the contract would not cause the tribunal to exceed its jurisdiction.[445] However, an arbitral tribunal exceeds its jurisdiction where it grants relief not requested by the parties or bases its award on claims or defences that have not been made by the parties, although whether this alone is sufficient for the award to be set aside will depend on the circumstances of each case.

The *CIZ v CJA* case highlights the difficulties in determining when a claim, defence, or **16.197** request for relief falls within the scope of submission to arbitration. In *CIZ v CJA*,[446] the High Court had originally set aside an award that had dismissed all the arbitration claimant's claims on its pleaded case, but nonetheless found for that party on an argument that was nowhere to be found in the Notice of Arbitration, pleadings, or submissions.[447] On appeal, the Court of Appeal reversed the decision, finding that the court ought not to 'apply an unduly narrow view of what the issues were', but rather ought

---

[440] *CRW v Persero (I) (SGCA)* (n 7) [31], [33]; *AKN v ALC (I)* (n 47) [73]; *Sui Southern Gas Co Ltd v Habibullah Coastal Power Co (Pte) Ltd* [2010] 3 SLR 1 [37] (hereafter *Sui Southern Gas*); *Quanzhou Sanhong Trading Limited Liability Co Ltd v ADM Asia-Pacific Trading Pte Ltd* [2017] SGHC 199 [11] (hereafter *Quanzhou Sanhong*).

[441] *AKN v ALC (I) (SGCA)* (n 47) [73]; *CRW v Persero (I) (SGCA)* (n 7) [33].

[442] *AKN v ALC (I)* (n 47) [73]; *CRW v Persero (I) (SGCA)* (n 7) [33].

[443] *Sui Southern Gas* (n 440) [35]–[41].

[444] *Sobati General Trading LLC v PT Multistrada Arahsarana* [2010] 1 SLR 1065 [29] (hereafter *Sobati General Trading*).

[445] *Quanzhou Sanhong* (n 440) [13]–[19].

[446] *CIZ v CJA* [2021] SGHC 178 (hereafter *CIZ v CJA (SGHC)*).

[447] Ibid, [69], [63].

270   SETTING ASIDE AN AWARD

to 'have regard to the totality of what was presented to the tribunal whether by way of evidence, submissions, pleadings or otherwise and consider whether, in the light of all that, these points were live'.[448] The Court of Appeal found that, while the arbitral tribunal had found for the arbitration claimant on a contractual interpretation argument that went further than that advanced by the claimant, these findings were premised on points that were in fact raised by the parties and involved issues that were 'clearly canvassed before' the tribunal.[449] It was also significant that the reasoning adopted by the tribunal did not involve fact-sensitive issues on which further evidence would have to be led.[450]

16.198   In some circumstances, however, an arbitral tribunal can exceed its jurisdiction by basing its decision on a belated claim or defence that was not properly pleaded. In *CAJ v CAI*, the Court of Appeal affirmed a decision by the lower court to set aside an award because it relied on a contractual extension of time defence that was raised for the first time in post-hearing submissions. The Court of Appeal observed that the extension of time defence (and the fulfilment of the conditions for its invocation) ought to be have been pleaded.[451] And given the fact-sensitive nature of the defence,[452] the Court held that the correct procedure would have been for the tribunal to invite the appellants to amend the defence, invite submissions from the parties, and to consider whether there needed to be consequential amendments to the respondent's pleadings, specific discovery, leave to adduce fresh evidence, and recalling witnesses for cross-examination.[453] The Court of Appeal therefore found that the tribunal had both exceeded its jurisdiction and breached the rules of natural justice.[454]

16.199   The principles in *CAJ v CAI* are likely to apply only to specific instances where the claim or defence raised at a late stage has a material impact on the outcome of the arbitration *and* is highly fact-sensitive.[455] It is not clear that the considerations animating the Court of Appeal's decision would apply to a purely legal defence or claim that is raised at a late stage or a claim or defence whose factual basis has already been addressed in the pleadings and evidence.

16.200   The Court of Appeal in *CKG v CKH (SGCA)* has since confirmed that '[w]hether a matter falls or has become within the scope of the agreed reference depends ultimately

---

[448]   *CJA v CIZ* [2022] 2 SLR 557 [38] (hereafter *CIZ v CJA (SGCA)*).
[449]   Ibid, [57]-[60].
[450]   Ibid, [61].
[451]   *CAJ v CAI* (n 131) [31].
[452]   Ibid, [29].
[453]   Ibid, [40].
[454]   Ibid, [52], [62]. The Court also considered the effect of Article 23(4) of the applicable ICC Rules, which precludes new 'claims' after the Terms of Reference, and whether it extends to a prohibition of new defences. The Court noted *obiter dicta* that Article 23(4) did not prohibit new defences after the Terms of Reference: Ibid, [39].
[455]   For example, in *CAJ v CAI* (n 131) itself, the Court of Appeal noted that the raising of the extension of time defence in and of itself would have required evidence and submissions to be led on as many as four other different sub-issues, i.e. (i) the grounds giving rise to the extension of time; (ii) whether there was critical delay as a result of such grounds; (iii) what a fair and reasonable period of extension of time would be; and (iv) whether any such delay had been mitigated by the appellants.

upon what the parties, viewing the whole position and the course of events objectively and fairly, may be taken to have accepted between themselves and before the Tribunal'.[456] The question of what matters are within the scope of the parties' submission to arbitration is answerable by reference to five sources: the parties' pleadings, the agreed list of issues, opening statements, evidence adduced, and closing submissions at the arbitration.[457] Moreover, the way in which an arbitration develops may lead to a widening of its scope explicitly by an amendment of the pleadings or by the consent of the parties, but equally this may also arise implicitly in circumstances where the point in issue is clearly raised and there is an adequate opportunity to address it.[458]

Where the ICC Rules are applicable, they provide that, unless authorised by the tribunal, no new claims can be made outside the Terms of Reference established by the tribunal. Do these Terms of Reference impose jurisdictional limitations? In *CBX v CBZ (SGCA)*, the Court of Appeal partially set aside an award that determined a claim in respect of certain 'Remaining Amounts' that had not been identified in the Terms of Reference.[459] The Court reasoned that the tribunal never clearly identified or ruled on its exercise of jurisdiction over that claim, and by failing to make any ruling on whether the new claims could be admitted, the tribunal therefore exceeded its jurisdiction and breached the rules of natural justice.[460] The Court therefore set aside the parts of the award relating to the 'Remaining Amounts', including the tribunal's related findings on compound interest.[461]

16.201

With respect, given that the ICC Rules expressly empower an arbitral tribunal to determine whether to admit new claims, it is not clear that the alleged defect in the award in *CBX v CBZ (SGCA)* should have been characterised as jurisdictional. The better view is that the award was not in excess of jurisdiction but rather breached natural justice because the parties were denied the opportunity to address the question of whether the new claim should have been let in. This is more consistent with the principle that an error in the exercise of the arbitral tribunal's powers, however gross, does not take the arbitral tribunal outside its jurisdiction.[462]

16.202

(b) Decisions Outside the Scope of the Arbitration Agreement

Awards may also be set aside under Article 34(2)(a)(iii) of the Model Law where an arbitral tribunal decides issues that are not within the scope of the parties' arbitration agreement. This was affirmed in *Lesotho v Swissbourgh (SGCA)* by the Court of Appeal, which held that there was no reason why the term 'submission to arbitration' in Article 34(2)(a)(iii) should be limited solely to the submissions made by the parties

16.203

---

[456] *CKG v CKH (SGCA)* (n 110) [16].
[457] Ibid.
[458] Ibid, [17]; *see also Asiana Airlines, Inc v Gate Gourmet Korea Co, Ltd* [2022] 4 SLR 158 [17].
[459] *CBX v CBZ (SGCA)* (n 166) [45]–[46].
[460] Ibid, [53]–[56], [63].
[461] Ibid, [56]–[57], [93]–[94].
[462] Ibid.

272   SETTING ASIDE AN AWARD

in particular arbitral proceedings, and as excluding the matters submitted to arbitration by the parties' arbitration agreement.[463] Thus, the Court of Appeal held that the Kingdom of Lesotho's jurisdictional objections—that the disputes determined by the arbitral tribunal fell outside the scope of its consent to arbitration under the arbitration agreement contained in the applicable treaty—fell within both Articles 34(2)(a)(i) and 34(2)(a)(iii).[464]

16.204   Although made in the context of the setting aside of an investment treaty award, the Court of Appeal's comments on Article 34(2)(a)(iii) are of more general application. Indeed, the Court of Appeal endorsed academic commentary that stated that a decision on issues that are not within the scope of the parties' arbitration agreement is one of the 'paradigmatic examples of an excess of authority'.[465]

16.205   Singapore courts are not likely to find that an arbitral tribunal has decided issues outside the scope of the parties' arbitration agreement merely because the award refers to other contracts. In *JVL Agro*, the award debtor argued that the arbitral tribunal exceed its jurisdiction by making findings on a collateral contract, which was a distinct contractual arrangement from the disputed contracts, and thereby dealt with a dispute that did not fall within the terms of the submission to arbitration.[466] The High Court rejected this argument, noting that the tribunal's only finding was that a certain price-averaging arrangement amounted to a collateral contract, which was a component of the arbitral tribunal's decision on whether obligations under the disputed contracts were due.[467] Similarly, in *AMZ v AXX*, the award debtor argued that the arbitral tribunal exceeded its jurisdiction by deciding two issues arising in respect of a buy-back contract, a different contract to the disputed contract, and those issues were not within the ambit of the arbitration agreement.[468] The High Court rejected this argument, holding that the arbitral tribunal had merely relied on the existence of the different contract to decide issues that were submitted to arbitration under the disputed contract, and that the arbitral tribunal had not determined any issues arising in respect of the buy-back contract.[469]

16.206   Where parties have signed an agreement to settle their disputes that is operative upon execution, there is no longer a dispute before the arbitral tribunal to decide upon after the signing of the agreement, meaning that any subsequent continuance of arbitral proceedings and the issuance of an award would fall outside the scope of the submission to arbitration. In *Rakna Arakshaka (SGCA)*, the Singapore Court of Appeal held that, from the time it takes effect, a valid settlement agreement (i) puts an end to proceedings; (ii) precludes the parties from taking any further steps in the action, except where

---

[463]   *Lesotho v Swissbourgh (SGCA)* (n 286) [71]–[72].
[464]   Ibid, [80]–[81].
[465]   Ibid, [71]–[72]; see also Born, *International Commercial Arbitration* (n 22) 3584–5.
[466]   *JVL Agro* (n 126) [222].
[467]   Ibid, [223]–[225].
[468]   *AMZ v AXX* [2016] 1 SLR 549 [165] (hereafter *AMZ v AXX*).
[469]   Ibid, [166]–[173].

C. GROUNDS FOR SETTING ASIDE 273

provided for in the settlement agreement; and (iii) supersedes the original cause of action altogether.[470] The logical consequence of this is that any claims regarding breach or repudiation of the settlement agreement are disputes arising out of the settlement agreement, and not disputes that fell within the scope of the original submission to arbitration.[471]

(c) Failure to Decide Matters That Had Been Submitted to It

Article 34(2)(a)(iii) of the Model Law not only permits the setting aside of decisions by arbitral tribunals that fall outside the parties' submission to arbitration, but also permits the setting aside of an award for an arbitral tribunal's failure to decide matters submitted to it by the parties. This ground for setting aside of awards *infra petita*[472] is not expressly referred to in Article 34 of the Model Law or the IAA. **16.207**

However, Singapore courts have consistently held that an arbitral tribunal's failure to decide matters that had been submitted to it amounts to an excess of jurisdiction that falls within Article 34(2)(a)(iii).[473] Singapore courts have also analysed awards *infra petita* based on a potential breach of the rules of natural justice, which would justify setting aside an award under Article 34(2)(a)(ii) of the Model Law or Section 24(b) of the IAA.[474] **16.208**

In *CRW v Persero (I) (SGCA)*, the Court of Appeal held that not every failure by an arbitral tribunal to deal with every issue raised by the parties would render its award liable to be set aside. That would depend ultimately on the importance of the issue in question and whether the failure to deal with the issue caused the parties real prejudice.[475] In that case, the Court of Appeal held that the arbitral tribunal was required under sub-clause 20.6 of the relevant contract to decide the parties' dispute by way of a rehearing from an Adjudicator's decision, and the arbitral tribunal's failure entirely to assess the merits of the dispute before endorsing the Adjudicator's decision as 'final' amounted to an excess of jurisdiction.[476] **16.209**

Consistent with the approach in *CRW v Persero (I) (SGCA)*, Chan Seng Onn J held in *TMM Division* that an arbitral tribunal is only required to ensure that all essential issues are dealt with in its award, noting that the courts should be slow to intervene, **16.210**

---

[470] *Rakna Arakshaka (SGCA)* (n 391) [95].
[471] Ibid, [83]–[96].
[472] In other words, failing to decide a material issue that was within the scope of submission.
[473] *CRW v Persero (I) (SGCA)* (n 7) [31]. See also Born, *International Commercial Arbitration* (n 22) 3582–3. Some Model Law jurisdictions, such as France, do not permit annulment for failure to consider issues submitted to the tribunal. Some commentators argue that Article 34(2)(a)(iii) of the Model Law and Article V(1)(c) of the New York Convention do not contemplate any option for parties to set aside an award *infra petita* or refuse its enforcement based on a failure to decide issues. See e.g. A.J. van den Berg, 'The New York Convention of 1958: An Overview' in E. Gaillard and D. Di Pietro (eds), *Enforcement of Arbitration Agreements and International Arbitral Awards: The New York Convention in Practice* (Cameron May 2008) 16; C. Borris and R. Hennecke, 'Article V' in R. Wolff (ed), *New York Convention—An Article-by-Article Commentary* (Bloomsbury Publishing 2012) 326.
[474] *CKG v CKH* (n 129) [61]; *BLC (SGHC)* (n 420) [70]–[93].
[475] *CRW v Persero (I) (SGCA)* (n 7) [32].
[476] Ibid, [82]–[86].

274   SETTING ASIDE AN AWARD

according a wide degree of latitude to the arbitral tribunal in deciding what issues are essential.[477] Chan J also held that an arbitral tribunal need not expressly deal with an issue in its award and may instead resolve it implicitly; thus, where the outcome of certain issues flows from the tribunal's conclusion on a logically prior issue, the tribunal need not consider the merits to do with the former set of issues.[478]

16.211   The threshold for a successful challenge is high. Singapore courts will only draw an inference that the tribunal has failed to consider an issue where such an inference was 'clear and virtually inescapable'.[479] *BLC (SGHC)* illustrates this. The High Court partially set aside an award where the arbitral tribunal omitted to deal with the award debtor's counterclaim.[480] Noting that the arbitral tribunal had failed to exercise the authority granted to it by the parties, the High Court set aside the part of the award that dealt with issues that were the subject of the counterclaim and remitted the counterclaim to a new arbitral tribunal for determination.[481] The Court of Appeal reversed, holding that the arbitral tribunal had implicitly determined the counterclaim in finding that the arbitration defendants were in breach of contract, which meant that the arbitration defendants would not be entitled to the amounts counterclaimed.[482] The Court of Appeal cautioned against approaching an award 'with a meticulous legal eye endeavouring to pick holes, inconsistencies and faults in awards, with the objective of upsetting or frustrating the process of arbitration', and noted instead that the court should read the award in a 'reasonable and commercial way, expecting, as is usually the case, that there will be no substantial fault that can be found with it'.[483] Another example is *CKG v CKH (SICC)*,[484] where the SICC held that the mere fact the tribunal had disposed of a claim in the dispositive section of the award was sufficient. This was despite the fact that in rejecting an application for an additional award, the tribunal could not identify where it had addressed the issue in any other part of the award and in fact identified passages that did not deal with the issue.

16.212   In cases involving awards *infra petita*, what is the significance of Article 33(3) of the Model Law, which provides that, unless otherwise agreed, a party may request the arbitral tribunal to make an additional award as to 'claims presented in the arbitral proceedings but omitted from the award'? In *BLC (SGHC)*, the High Court noted that, although it had partially set aside the arbitral tribunal's award, the case before the High Court was 'the type of case that Article 33(3) of the Model Law would have been intended to provide redress for'.[485] The High Court appeared to assume that parties were not required to first seek redress under Article 33(3) as a prerequisite to a setting aside

---

[477] *TMM Division* (n 395) [74].
[478] Ibid, [77].
[479] *AKN v ALC (I)* (n 47) [46].
[480] *BLC (SGHC)* (n 420) [85].
[481] Ibid, [94]–[99], [101]–[103].
[482] *BLC (SGCA)* (n 5) [85]–[98].
[483] Ibid, [86]. See also *AKN v ALC (I)* (n 47) [46].
[484] [2021] SGHC(I) 5 at [62]–[64]
[485] *BLC (SGHC)* (n 420) [103].

application, and instead noted the hope that parties in future would first attempt to avail themselves of any opportunities for redress from the tribunal itself before seeking recourse from the courts.[486]

Given its decision, the Court of Appeal in *BLB (SGCA)* did not have to decide the question of whether Article 33(3) was a prerequisite to a setting aside application. However, the Court of Appeal did note that, while a party is not obliged to invoke Article 33(3) before commencing a setting aside application, such a party takes the risk that the court would not exercise its discretion to set aside the award or invoke its powers of remission under Article 34 of the Model Law.[487] In *CEB v CEC*, Simon Thorley IJ cited these *obiter* comments with approval and held that a party's failure to request for an additional award was a factor that the court was entitled to take into account in deciding whether to exercise its discretion to not set aside the award. Thorley IJ did not set aside the relevant awards, noting that the plaintiff had no good reason not to seek an additional award, which weighed the balance heavily in favour of minimal curial intervention.[488]

16.213

In practice, where there has been a failure to decide an issue, parties will be well-advised to seek an additional award under Article 33(3) or be prepared to provide reasons why they did not do so in seeking a setting aside. In contrast to the position in Singapore, arbitration statutes in England and the Netherlands expressly provide that a setting aside applicant has to first exhaust any available recourse before the arbitral tribunal, including an application for an additional award.[489]

16.214

(d) Requirement to Show Prejudice

There is ostensibly conflicting Singapore authority on whether an award debtor is required to show that actual or real prejudice has been suffered to prevail in a setting aside application under Article 34(2)(a)(iii) of the Model Law. In *CRW v Persero (I) (SGCA)*, the Singapore Court of Appeal held that the court must be satisfied that there has been real or actual prejudice suffered by the parties to the dispute in order to set aside the award.[490] This was later cited by the Singapore Court of Appeal in *AKN v ALC (I)*, which framed the principle in broader terms and found that '[i]n order to set aside an arbitral award on the grounds of excess of jurisdiction, the court must further be satisfied that the aggrieved party has suffered actual or real prejudice'.[491] In *AMZ v AXX*, the Singapore High Court also found, citing *CRW v Persero (I) (SGCA)*, that the requirement to show prejudice applies when a party seeks to set

16.215

---

[486] Ibid, [103].

[487] *BLC (SGCA)* (n 5) [103]–[117].

[488] *CEB v CEC* (n 135) [61]–[64].

[489] See English Arbitration Act 1996, Section 70(2)(b); Netherlands Arbitration Act, Article 1065(6). See also P. Tan and J. Ahmad, 'The UNCITRAL Model Law and Awards *infra petita*' (2014) 31(3) Journal of International Arbitration 413, 420–1.

[490] *CRW v Persero (I) (SGCA)* (n 7) [32]–[33], [85].

[491] *AKN v ALC (I)* (n 47) [72].

276 SETTING ASIDE AN AWARD

aside an award under Article 34(2)(a)(iii).[492] The High Court also made a similar finding in *TMM Division*[493] and *BTN v BTP (II) (SGHC)*.[494]

16.216 However, in *GD Midea*, the Singapore High Court held that in cases involving an excess of jurisdiction under Article 34(2)(a)(iii), apart from cases involving an arbitral tribunal that had failed to address matters submitted to it, there is no requirement on a setting aside applicant to show real or actual prejudice before the award may be set aside.[495] This is consistent with the views of academic commentary, which considers that the Singapore Court of Appeal's finding on prejudice in *CRW v Persero (I) (SGCA)* was limited only to awards *infra petita*.[496] This is arguably at odds with the Singapore courts' endorsement of the requirement to show prejudice in excess of jurisdiction cases more generally in other cases. However, in those cases, the courts ultimately held that there was no excess of jurisdiction, so the courts' findings on the requirement of prejudice were, strictly speaking, *obiter dicta*.

16.217 The Court of Appeal in *CBX v CBZ (SGCA)* has since attempted to reconcile the conflicting authorities on this issue. In that case, the Court of Appeal stated that 'once an order is shown to have been made in excess of an arbitrator's jurisdiction, there is no further logical or legal requirement, on an application to set the order aside, to show prejudice', citing *GD Midea* with approval.[497] The Court of Appeal then distinguished *CRW v Persero (I) (SGCA)* on the basis that *CRW v Persero (I) (SGCA)* was limited only to awards *infra petita*.[498]

16.218 In the authors' view, the approach in *CBX v CBZ (SGCA)* is correct in principle. As discussed elsewhere, the failure of an arbitral tribunal to address matters submitted to it can also justify the setting aside of an award under Article 34(2)(a)(ii) of the Model Law and Section 24(b) of the IAA, and for those setting aside grounds, the Singapore courts have consistently imposed a requirement on the setting aside applicant to show prejudice.

16.219 However, in all other cases involving an excess of jurisdiction, the fact that an arbitral tribunal has decided on matters in respect of which it does not have jurisdiction should, without more, be sufficient to satisfy the requirements of Article 34(2)(a)(iii), at least in respect of those decisions for which the arbitral tribunal is without jurisdiction. This is, of course, subject to the Singapore courts' residual discretion to decline to set aside the award under Article 34(2) where there is no prejudice or where the breach is not sufficiently serious, or where a party had by subsequent conduct precluded itself from

---

[492] *AMZ v AXX* (n 468) [104].

[493] *TMM Division* (n 395) [53].

[494] *BTN and another v BTP and another and other matters* [2021] SGHC 271 [99] (hereafter *BTN v BTP (II) (SGHC)*).

[495] *GD Midea* (n 421) [60].

[496] See Tan and Cooke, 'Challenge of Arbitral Awards' (n 41) [15.048].

[497] *CBX v CBZ (SGCA)* (n 167) [11].

[498] Ibid, [11].

C. GROUNDS FOR SETTING ASIDE   277

relying on or waived the excess of jurisdiction.[499] In general, immaterial excesses of authority that do not cause actual prejudice to the parties are unlikely to warrant the setting aside of an award.[500]

4. Article 34(2)(a)(iv): Non-Compliance with Agreement of the Parties or the Model Law

Article 34(2)(a)(iv) gives effect to the parties' autonomy to agree on the composition of **16.220** the arbitral tribunal or the procedure that applies to their arbitration proceedings.[501] This is a foundational aspect of the international arbitration process and is reflected in multiple provisions of the Model Law and the IAA.[502]

The parties' autonomy to agree on procedural issues is generally unfettered, subject **16.221** only to mandatory provisions in the IAA and the Model Law that the parties may not derogate from. One example of such a mandatory provision is Article 18 of the Model Law which prescribes the minimum procedural requirements of equality of treatment and natural justice that all arbitral tribunals must abide by.[503] Thus, Article 34(2)(a)(iv) provides that any agreement of the parties on the composition of the arbitral tribunal or the arbitral procedure was not absolute, and would not be applied where 'in conflict with a provision of this Law from which the parties cannot derogate'—a phrase not found in Article V(1)(b) of the New York Convention, on which Article 34(2)(a)(iv) was based. The addition of this phrase in Article 34(2)(a)(iv) was intended to make clear that any agreement of the parties would be subject to mandatory provisions in the Model Law, which would prevail over any contrary term in the parties' agreement.[504]

In the absence of any agreement on arbitral procedure between parties, Article 19(2) of **16.222** the Model Law gives the arbitral tribunal broad procedural powers to conduct the arbitration in the manner it considers appropriate, including the power to determine the applicable rules of evidence on admissibility, relevance, materiality, and weight of any evidence.[505] However, any such powers are still subject to mandatory provisions of the Model Law and the IAA. Article 34(2)(a)(iv) provides that an award may be set aside if it is not 'in accordance with [the IAA]', for example, where the award is in violation of the mandatory procedural requirements set forth in Article 18 of the Model Law.[506]

Article 34(2)(a)(iv) provides that an award may be set aside in two broad categories of **16.223** circumstances: (i) the composition of the arbitral tribunal was not in accordance with

---

[499] *CBX v CBZ (SGCA)* (n 167) [11].
[500] *Kempinski Hotels (SGCA)* (n 61) [51]. See also e.g. Born, *International Commercial Arbitration* (n 22) 3597–8.
[501] *Triulzi* (n 78) [46].
[502] See e.g. Model Law, Article 19; IAA, Section 15A(1).
[503] *Triulzi* (n 78) [46].
[504] See Holtzmann and Neuhaus, *Guide to the UNCITRAL Model Law* (n 37) 917.
[505] *Triulzi* (n 78) [47].
[506] Ibid, [50].

278   SETTING ASIDE AN AWARD

the agreement of the parties or the Model Law, or (ii) the arbitral procedure was not in accordance with the agreement of the parties or the Model Law. The sub-sections below separately consider each of these categories, before then addressing issues of waiver and whether there is a requirement of prejudice.

(a) Composition of the Arbitral Tribunal Not in Accordance with the Parties' Agreement or the Model Law

16.224   The right to select the arbitrators is an important feature of the arbitral process and one of the principal reasons why parties agree to arbitrate their disputes. Article 34(2)(a) (iv) reflects the parties' autonomy to impose, by agreement, requirements or restrictions on the composition of the arbitral tribunal. For example, the parties may, in their arbitration agreement or in a separate submission agreement after a dispute has arisen, stipulate criteria that governs the selection or qualification of the arbitrators.[507] Indeed, the possibility of agreement by the parties on qualifications of their arbitrators is expressly contemplated by Articles 11(5) and 12(2) of the Model Law.

16.225   One common example of a qualification that parties may agree upon is a requirement that any sole or presiding arbitrator not have the same nationality as that of the parties; this requirement is found in many leading institutional arbitration rules, including the ICC Arbitration Rules.[508] Other examples include requirements to do with language proficiency, legal training, and particular work experiences or professional backgrounds.[509]

16.226   If the parties have reached any agreement on criteria for the composition of the arbitral tribunal, a breach of such agreement can justify the setting aside of the award. For example, if the parties' arbitration agreement specifies that an arbitral tribunal must have certain characteristics or must meet a particular description, an award by an arbitral tribunal that does not have those characteristics or meet that description may be liable to be set aside.[510]

16.227   Singapore courts are likely to give effect to the parties' agreement on the composition of the arbitral tribunal even if it involves the hybrid application of more than one set of institutional arbitration rules. In the context of the review of an arbitral tribunal's decision on jurisdiction pursuant to Article 16(3) of the Model Law, Prakash J (as she then was) held in the *Insigma* case that the constitution by the SIAC of an arbitral tribunal under the ICC Rules, pursuant to an arbitration clause providing for 'arbitration before the Singapore International Arbitration Centre in accordance with the Rules of Arbitration of the International Chamber of Commerce', was done in accordance with

---

[507] See Born, *International Commercial Arbitration* (n 22) 1882–8.
[508] See ICC Arbitration Rules 2021, Article 13(5).
[509] See Born, *International Commercial Arbitration* (n 22) 1882–8.
[510] See *DSK v Ultrapolis* (n 260) [46]–[49] (accepting, in principle, an award could be set aside if the parties agreed that the Danish Engineers' Association should have decided the dispute and the arbitral tribunal was not the Danish Engineers' Association, although no such agreement was established on the facts).

C. GROUNDS FOR SETTING ASIDE   279

the agreement of the parties.[511] Similar reasoning is likely to apply in the context of a setting aside application under Article 34(2)(a)(iv).

If the number of arbitrators deciding the dispute deviates from the stipulated number of arbitrators in the parties' arbitration agreement, that can also form a basis for setting aside the arbitrators' award. This results from a straightforward application of the plain language of Article 34(2)(a)(iv).   **16.228**

In some cases, although the parties' arbitration agreement specifies that their dispute is to be heard by three arbitrators, the parties may also agree to the application of arbitration rules that permit an arbitral institution to appoint a different number of arbitrators under certain specified conditions. For example, many arbitration rules, including the SIAC Rules and the ICC Rules, contain an expedited procedure and expressly state that, where the expedited procedure applies, the arbitral institution would appoint a sole arbitrator by default. In these circumstances, the Singapore courts have repeatedly affirmed that they would take a commercially sensible interpretation of the parties' chosen arbitration rules as according discretion to the arbitral institution to appoint a sole arbitrator where the expedited procedure applies, and have consistently held that the appointment of a sole arbitrator in those circumstances is consistent with the parties' agreement.[512]   **16.229**

The approach of the Singapore courts can be contrasted with the approach of the Shanghai No. 1 Intermediate People's Court in the *Noble Resources* case.[513] In that case, the Shanghai No. 1 Intermediate People's Court refused enforcement of an award rendered by a sole arbitrator pursuant to the SIAC expedited procedure because the appointment of a sole arbitrator was not in accordance with the parties' arbitration agreement, which expressly provided for three arbitrators. However, that case was decided under the SIAC Rules 2013 on the basis that the parties' arbitration agreement did not specify that the arbitration rules would prevail over contrary provisions in the parties' arbitration clause. It is not clear whether other enforcing courts would take a different approach under the SIAC Rules 2016, which includes a new Rule 5.3 that provides that SIAC may appoint a sole arbitrator even where the parties' arbitration agreement contains a contrary stipulation.   **16.230**

What about the situation whereby an arbitration clause makes no express stipulation regarding the number of arbitrators, but the parties have chosen arbitration rules that provide for a default number of arbitrators? In *Sanum v ST (SGCA)*, the Singapore Court of Appeal held that an SIAC award issued by three arbitrators was not in accordance with Rule 6.1 of the parties' agreed SIAC Rules 2013, which provided for one   **16.231**

---

[511] *Insigma Technology Co Ltd v Alstom Technology Ltd* [2009] 1 SLR(R) 23 [42]–[43] (hereafter *Insigma*) (upheld on appeal: *Insigma Technology Co Ltd v Alstom Technology Ltd* [2009] 3 SLR(R) 936 [37]–[40]).

[512] *AQZ v ARA* (n 26) [132]–[137]; *BXS v BXT* [2019] 5 SLR 48 [10]–[17].

[513] *Noble Resources International Pte Ltd v Shanghai Xintai International Trade Co Ltd* (2016) Hu 01 Xie Wai Ren No. 1 (hereafter *Noble Resources*).

280   SETTING ASIDE AN AWARD

arbitrator by default, but that case involved very special facts and its holding should not be of more general application to other cases.[514]

16.232   In that case, even though the Master Agreement under which the disputes arose did not contain any provisions on the number of arbitrators, the SIAC had appointed three arbitrators assertedly in reliance of arbitration clauses in certain related contracts that expressly provided for the appointment of three arbitrators, but the Court of Appeal held (disagreeing with the arbitral tribunal) that the parties' dispute did not arise from those related contracts. Although Rule 6.1 of the SIAC Rules 2013 provided for one arbitrator to be appointed by default, it also granted discretion to the SIAC Registrar to appoint three arbitrators, giving due regard to the complexity, the quantum involved or other relevant circumstance of the dispute.[515] However, the Court of Appeal held that the Registrar did not in fact exercise discretion under Rule 6.1 when it appointed the three arbitrators, because it expressly—and erroneously, in the Court of Appeal's view—placed reliance on the arbitration clauses of related contracts. On this basis, the Court of Appeal held that the composition of the arbitral tribunal was not in accordance with the parties' agreement.[516]

16.233   With respect, the Court of Appeal's conclusion that the SIAC Registrar did not exercise discretion in appointing three arbitrators is open to doubt. In all cases under the SIAC Rules 2013, unless the parties have otherwise agreed, the SIAC Registrar exercises discretion under Rule 6.1 in determining the number of arbitrators to appoint, and Rule 6.1 permits the SIAC Registrar a broad discretion to consider all 'relevant circumstances of the dispute' in making that determination, and such relevant circumstances may include the consideration of related contracts. As the Court of Appeal expressly acknowledged in its judgment, the parties' arbitration agreement was 'completely silent on the composition of the arbitral tribunal',[517] and therefore the decision made by the SIAC Registrar regarding the number of arbitrators must have been one made in exercise of the discretion under Rule 6.1 of the SIAC Rules 2013. Given that the appointment of three arbitrators was made pursuant to the SIAC Registrar's discretion under Rule 6.1, and given the silence of the parties' arbitration agreement on the number of arbitrators, it is difficult to see how the award debtor could have met its burden of establishing that the composition of the arbitral tribunal in that case was not in accordance with the parties' agreement.

16.234   In any event, the holding in the *Sanum v ST (SGCA)* case should be consigned to the particular facts of the case, which involved a difference of opinion between the arbitrators and the Singapore courts on whether the dispute arose out of a Master Agreement and certain related contracts or whether the dispute arose solely out of the Master Agreement. In general, where the parties make no express stipulation regarding the number of arbitrators in the arbitration agreement, the appointment of three arbitrators

---

[514] *Sanum v ST (SGCA)* (n 21) [88]–[89].
[515] Rule 6.1 of the SIAC Rules 2013 is materially similar to Rule 9.1 of the SIAC Rules 2016.
[516] *Sanum v ST (SGCA)* (n 21) [89].
[517] Ibid, [88].

C. GROUNDS FOR SETTING ASIDE   281

by an arbitral institution, even though the arbitration rules provide for a different default number of arbitrators, cannot be sufficient to warrant the setting aside of an award, in circumstances where the decision on the number of arbitrators is made in exercise of discretion expressly provided for in those arbitration rules.

The lack of independence or impartiality of an arbitrator can also form a basis to set **16.235** aside an arbitral tribunal's decision under Article 34(2)(a)(iv).[518] As the Singapore High Court held in *PT Central Investindo*, the requirement of independence and impartiality is implied under Article 12(2) of the Model Law and a breach of such a requirement would mean that the composition of the arbitral tribunal is 'not in accordance with this Law' under Article 34(2)(a)(iv).[519] The requirement of independence and impartiality is also found in most leading arbitration rules, and a breach of that requirement would therefore also justify setting aside an award on the basis that the composition of the arbitral tribunal is 'not in accordance with the agreement of the parties'.[520] Where an arbitrator has been removed under Article 13(3) of the Model Law on the basis of justifiable doubts as to his or her independence or impartiality, the court's removal order itself will generally be a sufficient basis to set aside the arbitral award, and the grounds for removal of an arbitrator would generally be sufficiently serious to warrant setting aside without any need separately to show prejudice.[521]

The removal of arbitrators under Article 13(3) of the Model Law may also occur prior to **16.236** any award being issued. Article 13(2) of the Model Law provides a default time period of 15 days from being aware of the circumstances giving rise to a potential challenge to issue that challenge to the arbitrator, which may prompt a voluntary withdrawal by the arbitrator, or consent by the other party, or require a determination by the tribunal itself. Where parties have agreed to arbitration rules regulating the challenge of arbitrators, those will apply by virtue of Article 13(1) of the Model Law.

There have only been two reported decisions in Singapore addressing the removal of **16.237** arbitrators, both successful. Where a tribunal has prejudged an issue without hearing both sides on the issue, the tribunal 'must be removed'.[522] English case law has articulated the test as being whether the way the tribunal had conducted themselves such that the parties can no longer have confidence in them.[523] In another case, the court also removed an arbitrator on the basis that, in addition to evidence of prejudgment, [524] his sarcastic and hostile language reasonably caused the complaining party to lose confidence in the arbitrator's impartiality.[525]

---

[518] This may also be a basis to set aside the award under Section 24(b) of the IAA.
[519] *PT Central Investindo* (n 35) [52], [129]–[134].
[520] Ibid, [52].
[521] Ibid, [143]–[145].
[522] *Koh Bros Building and Civil Engineering Contractor Pte Ltd v Scotts Development (Saraca) Pte Ltd* [2002] 2 SLR(R) 1063 [47] (hereafter *Koh Bros*).
[523] Ibid, [33].
[524] *Turner (East Asia) Pte Ltd v Builders Federal (Hong Kong) Ltd & Anor (No 2)* [1988] 1 SLR(R) 483 [83] (hereafter *Turner*).
[525] Ibid, [87].

282   SETTING ASIDE AN AWARD

(b) Arbitral Procedure Not in Accordance with the Parties' Agreement or the Model Law

16.238   In order to set aside an award under Article 34(2)(a)(iv) on the basis that the arbitral procedure was not in accordance with the parties' agreement, an applicant needs to establish that there was an agreement between the parties on a particular arbitral procedure and that the arbitral tribunal failed to adhere to that agreed procedure.[526] The agreement in question has to be an agreement on procedural and not substantive issues.[527]

16.239   Any such agreement can be found in the parties' arbitration clause or in any subsequent agreement by the parties in the course of arbitral proceedings. Singapore courts have also confirmed that the parties' agreement can include implied terms such as a duty to cooperate in good faith in arbitral proceedings, although whether such a duty is implied will depend ultimately on the law governing the arbitration agreement.[528] In *China Machine (SGHC)*, the Singapore High Court noted *obiter dicta* that a duty of good faith will be implied into most, if not all, arbitration agreements, although whether this is the case would depend ultimately on the law governing the arbitration agreement.[529] The High Court also doubted whether the bad faith use of guerrilla tactics—which it found insufficient evidence of, on the facts of the case—would itself be sufficient to warrant the setting aside of an award in circumstances where such tactics do not render an award in breach of public policy and do not involve fraud or corruption afflicting the award.[530]

16.240   In *CEF v CEH*,[531] the High Court had the opportunity to consider whether the arbitral procedure agreed by the parties or prescribed by the Model Law requires the award to be workable or enforceable. In that case, the challenging party argued that an order made by the Tribunal to transfer title of a plant was 'not legally or factually possible' and therefore 'unenforceable'.[532] The challenging party argued that it was an implied term in law in all arbitration agreements, or alternatively required by the governing arbitration rules (ICC Rules) or the Model Law, that an award must be enforceable.[533] Coomaraswamy J disagreed, holding that while it was 'desirable' that an award should be enforceable, a tribunal does not have a contractual or statutory duty to do so, let alone that a breach of this alleged duty renders an award liable to be set aside under Article 34(2)(a)(iv) of the Model Law.[534] Coomaraswamy J also found that the arbitral

---

[526]   See e.g. *AMZ v AXX* (n 468) [102]. Note that High Court's holding that the failure to adhere to the parties' agreed procedure must be casually related to the tribunal's decision is no longer good law given the Singapore Court of Appeal's subsequent findings regarding the requirement of establishing prejudice in attempts to resist enforcement under Article V(1)(d) of the New York Convention.

[527]   *PT Perusasahaan Gas Negara (Persero) TBK v CRW Joint Operation* [2010] 4 SLR 672 [39] (hereafter *CRW v Persero (I) (SGHC)*); *CEF v CEH* (n 395) [39].

[528]   *China Machine (SGHC)* (n 318) [196]–[199], not subject to appeal in *China Machine (SGCA)* (n 194).

[529]   *China Machine (SGHC)* (n 318) [196]–[199].

[530]   Ibid, [213].

[531]   *CEF v CEH* (n 395).

[532]   Ibid, [30].

[533]   Ibid, [45]–[56].

[534]   Ibid, [57].

C. GROUNDS FOR SETTING ASIDE   283

procedure agreed by the parties or prescribed by the Act does not require an award to be 'workable', and held that an award was not liable to be set aside merely because it was 'unworkable'.[535] This was affirmed on appeal.[536]

Not just any breach of agreed procedure, however, would warrant the setting aside of an award. Singapore courts have consistently affirmed that, to justify the exercise of the court's discretion to set aside an award, the breach of procedure complained of cannot be 'of an arid, technical or trifling nature' and needs to be a material breach of procedure.[537] As discussed further below, an applicant will often, although not invariably, need to prove actual prejudice, unless the breach is sufficiently serious to independently warrant setting aside the award.[538]   **16.241**

Attempts to challenge an award for a breach of the parties' agreed procedure often do not succeed, particularly where the challenge involves evidential or case management decisions in respect of which arbitral tribunals enjoy broad discretion. For example, in *Luzon Hydro Corp*, the setting aside applicant argued that the tribunal-appointed expert played a greater role in the preparation of the award than the parties had agreed, by not only performing purely administrative tasks but also being actively involved in analysing the evidence.[539] Judith Prakash J (as she then was) dismissed the challenge, holding that there was no evidence that the expert had gone beyond the bounds of his terms of engagement.[540] Prakash J also noted that the Singapore court would not unduly cast aspersions on what the tribunal said in its award about the role of the expert, observing that there would have to be 'strong and unambiguous evidence of irregularity' in the conduct of the arbitration for any challenge to succeed, and that the court would not permit speculative challenges amounting to backdoor appeals on the merits.[541] In similar vein, Vinodh Coomaraswamy J in *AMZ v AXX* dismissed a challenge based on the argument that an arbitral tribunal deviated from the parties' agreed procedure by preferring the evidence of one party's witness in the absence of corroborating evidence and thereby failing to accord equal weight to the evidence of both party's witnesses, noting that this was just 'part of the ordinary procedure by which a finder of fact makes findings of fact'.[542]   **16.242**

In *Triulzi*, Belinda Ang J dismissed the argument that the arbitral tribunal had deviated from the parties' agreed arbitral procedure by admitting an expert report filed by the award creditor, allegedly in violation of an agreement by the parties to dispense with expert evidence.[543] After reviewing the correspondence in the arbitration and the   **16.243**

---

[535] Ibid, [60].
[536] *CEF v CEH* [2022] SGCA 54 [34]-[42].
[537] *Coal & Oil* (n 82) [51]. See also *Triulzi* (n 78) [52].
[538] *Sanum v ST (SGCA)* (n 21) [93]–[104].
[539] *Luzon Hydro Corp v Transfield Philippines Inc* [2004] 4 SLR(R) 705 [14] (hereafter *Luzon Hydro Corp*).
[540] Ibid, [17]–[20].
[541] Ibid, [17]–[20].
[542] *AMZ v AXX* (n 468) [157]–[158].
[543] *Triulzi* (n 78).

284   SETTING ASIDE AN AWARD

arbitral tribunal's directions, Ang J held that there was no such agreement between the parties to dispense with expert evidence.[544]

16.244   Ang J also went on to articulate two principles of broader application. First, Article 34(2)(a)(iv) is not engaged if any non-observance of an agreed procedure is due to an applicant's own doing.[545] In *Triulzi*, Ang J took into consideration the fact that the failure by the applicant to file any expert evidence in the arbitration was entirely the applicant's own doing.[546] Second, Article 34(2)(a)(iv) is not engaged if the challenge is against an arbitral tribunal's procedural orders or directions, which 'fall within the exclusive domain of the arbitral tribunal'.[547] This principle applies with particular force in circumstances where the parties agree to international arbitration rules that expressly accord broad discretion and case management powers on arbitral tribunals to conduct the arbitration procedure, including the ICC Rules and the SIAC Rules.[548]

16.245   Singapore courts have accorded similar deference to determinations by arbitral tribunals regarding the substantive governing law of the dispute. In *Quarella*, Judith Prakash J (as she then was) dismissed the argument that an arbitral tribunal's application of Italian law rather than the CISG to the merits of the dispute breached the parties' agreed procedure in Article 17 of the ICC Rules 2004, which provide that the parties shall be free to agree upon the rules of law to be applied by the arbitral tribunal to the merits of the dispute.[549] Prakash J reasoned that the arbitral tribunal did in fact respect the parties' choice of law clause by interpreting and applying it, as was evident from the arbitral tribunal's reasoning, and thereby acted in accordance with Article 17 of the ICC Rules 2004.[550] In Prakash J's view, the applicant's contention was simply that the arbitral tribunal had applied the choice of law clause wrongly, and such an invitation to review the merits of the award did not engage Article 34(2)(a)(iv).[551] The judgment in the *Quarella* case does, however, implicitly leave open the possibility that an arbitral tribunal's complete failure to even consider or apply the parties' choice of law clause may justify a setting aside application under Article 34(2)(a)(iv).

16.246   As discussed elsewhere in this commentary,[552] the reference to arbitration rules in the parties' arbitration agreement is sufficient to incorporate the provisions of such rules into the parties' agreement. If an arbitral tribunal acts contrary to the terms in the parties' chosen arbitration rules, this can form the basis for a setting aside application under Article 34(2)(a)(iv). For example, if the arbitration rules expressly provide for a time limit for the issuance of an award by an arbitral tribunal, the failure to make the award within that time limit may form a basis for the setting aside of the arbitral

---

[544] Ibid, [88].
[545] Ibid, [51].
[546] Ibid, [106].
[547] Ibid, [52].
[548] ICC Arbitration Rules 2021, Article 22; SIAC Rules 2016, Rule 19.
[549] *Quarella SpA v Scelta Marble Australia Pty Ltd* [2012] 4 SLR 1057 [32]–[40] (hereafter *Quarella*).
[550] Ibid, [37]–[39].
[551] Ibid, [26]–[27], [40].
[552] See Chapter 13.

tribunal's award,[553] although this would depend in each case on the construction of the particular arbitration rules.

In determining whether there has been a breach of a provision in the parties' chosen arbitration rules, Singapore courts are likely to undertake a detailed exercise in construing the relevant provision, examining the drafting history and purpose of the provision in question, as well as the practical commercial implications of the interpretations offered by the parties.[554] In each case, Singapore courts are also likely to take into account the broad powers of case management that are granted to arbitral tribunals under most arbitration rules and be slow to interpret arbitration rules as limiting a tribunal's freedom of action in the absence of express provision. **16.247**

For example, in *Coal & Oil*, the Singapore High Court rejected the applicant's argument that Rule 27.1 of the 2007 SIAC Rules imposed a duty on the arbitral tribunal to declare the arbitral proceedings closed.[555] In doing so, the High Court examined the drafting history of Rule 27.1 and observed that the 2007 version was unique in providing that the arbitral tribunal 'may declare the hearings closed' while also imposing a timeline for the release of the award from the date of closure, noting that the equivalent provision in 1991 and 1997 versions of the SIAC Rules provided for a power to declare hearings closed without imposing any timeline, while the equivalent provision in the 2010 and 2013 versions of the SIAC Rules imposed a timeline but also a duty to declare proceedings closed.[556] On the basis of this drafting history, the High Court concluded that it could not accept the applicant's construction of Rule 27.1 of the SIAC Rules 2007 as imposing an unqualified obligation to declare proceedings closed, as that would be even stricter than the 2010 and 2013 versions of the SIAC Rules, that only imposed such a duty if, after consulting with the parties, the arbitral tribunal was satisfied that the parties did not have further evidence or submissions to present.[557] The High Court further reasoned that imposing such an unqualified obligation on the arbitral tribunal to declare proceedings closed would be impractical and inconsistent with the function of a closure declaration as a case management tool, particularly in light of the broad case management powers granted to an arbitral tribunal under the SIAC Rules.[558] **16.248**

Whether the arbitration procedure complies with the parties' chosen arbitration rules may depend on the version of the arbitration rules that apply in the particular dispute. Arbitration rules are frequently updated to reflect recent developments and international best practice; as a result, the arbitration rules in force at the time arbitration is commenced may contain different procedural provisions from the arbitration rules **16.249**

---

[553] See e.g. *Coal & Oil* (n 82) [54]–[59] (holding that breaches of agreed time limits for the issuance of the award can be a basis for setting aside an award but noting that the 2007 SIAC Rules did not contain any express time limits for making of awards).

[554] Ibid, [31]–[39].

[555] Ibid, [23]–[38].

[556] Ibid, [24]–[30].

[557] Ibid, [32].

[558] Ibid, [33]–[38].

286 SETTING ASIDE AN AWARD

in force at the time the parties entered into their arbitration agreement. These new procedural provisions can be significant updates, and may include, for example, including entirely new fast-track procedures or mechanisms for obtaining emergency interim relief that are not available under older versions of the arbitration rules.

16.250 As discussed elsewhere, Singapore courts apply the presumption that a reference to arbitration rules in an arbitration clause refers to rules that are applicable at the date of commencement of the arbitration, and not at the date of the contract, provided that the rules contain mainly procedural provisions.[559] Thus, in *AQZ v ARA*, the Singapore High Court rejected the applicant's argument that the arbitration conducted under the SIAC expedited procedure under Rule 5 of the SIAC Rules 2010 was not in accordance with the parties' agreement, even though the rules in force when the parties concluded their contract were the SIAC Rules 2007, which did not contain any provisions on an expedited procedure.[560] The High Court applied the presumption that the parties' intention was to refer to the rules in force at the time the arbitration was commenced, that is, the SIAC Rules 2010.[561]

16.251 The designation of an arbitral seat that is contrary to the agreement of the parties can also form a basis for setting aside an award on the ground that the arbitral procedure was not in accordance with the parties' agreement. In *Sanum v ST (SGCA)*, the Singapore Court of Appeal held that the arbitral tribunal's designation of Singapore as the arbitral seat was contrary to the parties' arbitration agreement, because the stipulation for arbitration 'using an internationally recognized ... arbitration company in Macau, SAR PRC' was an express choice of Macau as the seat of the arbitration.[562] This holding is consistent with other Singapore case law on the interpretation of arbitration agreements.[563]

16.252 There is, however, room to query whether the Singapore Court of Appeal should have deferred to the arbitral tribunal's interpretation of the arbitration agreement in circumstances where the governing law was Lao law and the arbitral tribunal, not the Court of Appeal, had heard the expert evidence proffered by the parties on Lao law.[564] This consideration is particularly pertinent where the Court of Appeal had itself acknowledged that the reference to 'internationally recognized ... arbitration company in Macau, SAR PRC' in the parties' arbitration agreement was at best 'ambiguous', and that this was common ground amongst the parties to the arbitration.[565]

16.253 In the absence of any breach of agreed arbitral procedure, Article 34(2)(a)(iv) is also engaged when the arbitral procedure is not in accordance with the Model Law or the IAA.

---

[559] See Chapter 2.
[560] *AQZ v ARA* (n 26) [123]–[125].
[561] Ibid, [123]–[125].
[562] *Sanum v ST (SGCA)* (n 21) [76]–[85].
[563] See e.g. *BNA v BNB* (n 253) [65].
[564] See *Sanum v ST (SGHC)* (n 11) [31]–[37].
[565] *Sanum v ST (SGCA)* (n 21) [79].

C. GROUNDS FOR SETTING ASIDE   287

As discussed above, Article 19(2) of the Model Law grants an arbitral tribunal broad powers to conduct the arbitration in such manner as it considers appropriate, including the power to determine the admissibility, relevance, materiality, and weight of any evidence, and such powers are subject only to mandatory provisions of the Model Law and Part II of the IAA.[566]

Therefore, an application to set aside an award can be made on the basis that the arbitral **16.254** procedure is not in accordance with the Model Law or the IAA when the arbitral procedure violates mandatory provisions of the Model Law and the IAA.[567] In particular, Singapore courts have recognised that a breach of the minimum procedural requirements in Article 18 of the Model Law would warrant the setting aside of an arbitral award under Article 34(2)(a)(iv).[568]

Article 18 sets forth two mandatory procedural requirements: first, that '[t]he parties **16.255** shall be treated with equality'; and second, that 'each party shall be given a full opportunity of presenting his case'. The terms 'equality' and 'full opportunity' were modelled after Article 15 of the UNCITRAL Arbitration Rules 1976, and the delegates to the UNCITRAL Working Group considered that these terms were so well understood across legal systems that detailed definitions were unnecessary and might 'limit the flexible and broad approach needed to ensure fairness' in a wide variety of circumstances.[569] Singapore courts have provided helpful guidance on how the mandatory procedural requirements in Article 18 of the Model Law will be applied in the context of setting aside and enforcement cases.

In *Triulzi*, the Singapore High Court clarified that the term 'equality' in Article 18 is **16.256** to be 'interpreted reasonably' and does not require identical treatment of the parties, in the sense of the parties having an exactly equal amount of time or an equal number of pleadings or speeches.[570] The High Court noted that an arbitral tribunal can determine the amount of time to be afforded to the parties as part of the discretionary exercise of its case management powers and may take into account factors such as the conduct of the parties, the stage of the proceedings, and considerations of urgency and efficiency.[571] Ultimately, the High Court noted that the requirement to accord equality needed to be considered together with, as well as balanced against, the requirement to accord each party a full opportunity to present its case.[572] Applying these principles, the High Court held that the award debtor was not treated unequally for the sole reason that the award creditor was the only party armed with expert evidence at the hearing,

---

[566] See *Triulzi* (n 78) [47].

[567] Article 34(2)(a)(iv) refers to 'this Law', which may be interpreted as either a reference to the Model Law to the exclusion of the IAA or a reference to both the Model Law and the IAA. Although Singapore courts have not yet considered an application on the basis that the arbitral procedure is not in accordance with the IAA, the better view is that the reference to 'this Law' refers to both the Model Law and the IAA.

[568] *Triulzi* (n 78) [50]; *China Machine (SGHC)* (n 318) [185].

[569] See Holtzmann and Neuhaus, *Guide to the UNCITRAL Model Law* (n 37) 551. See also *Triulzi* (n 78) [109].

[570] Ibid, [111]–[112].

[571] Ibid, [114]–[115].

[572] Ibid, [112].

288 SETTING ASIDE AN AWARD

because the arbitral tribunal had ensured that both parties had the opportunity to submit expert evidence and the award debtor could not complain of its own failure to make use of such opportunity.[573]

16.257 With respect to the requirement of providing each party with a 'full opportunity' of presenting its case in Article 18, any alleged breach of this requirement will overlap substantially with the grounds for setting aside an award under Article 34(2)(a)(ii) of the Model Law and Section 24(b) of the IAA. As explained above, Singapore courts have also held that the reference to a party's 'full opportunity' to present its case in Article 18 confers 'no more and no less … than a right to have a *reasonable* opportunity to present its case'.[574] The approach of the Singapore courts to determining whether or not a party has been afforded a reasonable opportunity to present its case is discussed in greater detail in the sections on Article 34(2)(a)(ii) of the Model Law and Section 24(b) of the IAA.

16.258 If an arbitral tribunal acts beyond the powers circumscribed by the Model Law and the IAA, and in the absence of any specific agreement between the parties on the issue, the resulting award may be set aside under Article 34(2)(a)(iv) of the Model Law on the basis that it is contrary to the Model Law and IAA. For example, Singapore courts have held that an award that is issued when a tribunal is *functus officio* can be set aside or refused enforcement on the basis that the award is contrary to the provisions of the Model Law and IAA.[575]

16.259 Singapore courts have also dismissed the argument that the making of a default award, in the event that one of the parties fails to participate in the arbitration, constitutes an arbitral procedure that was not in accordance with the agreement of the parties or an arbitral procedure that is not in accordance with the Model Law and the IAA.[576] In particular, such an argument is likely to fail where the parties' agreed arbitration rules provide for the power of the arbitral tribunal to proceed with the hearing and make an award in the event that one of the parties fails to appear or participate.[577]

(c) Waiver of Procedural Irregularities

16.260 Article 4 of the Model Law provides that where, any party knows that any requirement under the parties' arbitration agreement or any provision of the Model Law has not been complied with, and yet fails to object without undue delay, that party shall be deemed to have waived its right to object to the procedural irregularity. Most, if not virtually all, arbitration rules also similarly provide for waiver of the right to object to a failure to comply with any provision of the rules where either party has failed to object.[578]

---

[573] Ibid, [116].
[574] *JVL Agro* (n 126) [145]; *ADG v ADI* (n 297) [104].
[575] *L W Infrastructure* (n 165) [41]; *DSK v Ultrapolis* (n 260) [50]–[52].
[576] See *Re An Arbitration Between Hainan Machinery Import and Export Corp and Donald & McArthy Pte Ltd, Re* [1995] 3 SLR(R) 354 [19]–[27] (hereafter *Hainan Machinery*).
[577] Ibid, [24], [27].
[578] See e.g. ICC Arbitration Rules 2021, Article 40; SIAC Rules 2016, Rule 41.1.

C. GROUNDS FOR SETTING ASIDE   289

These principles on waiver were applied by the Singapore High Court in the context   **16.261**
of an Article 34(2)(a)(iv) setting aside application in *Triulzi*.[579] Citing Article 39 of the
ICC Rules 2012, which provides that a party would be deemed to have waived its right
to object to any failure to comply with any procedural rules if it proceeds in the arbitration without raising such objection, Belinda Ang J held that a party should not be
allowed to withhold any arguments that it could have made before an arbitral tribunal
and then later make them in a setting aside application.[580] Applying these principles,
Ang J held that the setting aside applicant was precluded from making the argument
that the arbitral tribunal's direction on the 'Filing of Witness Statements' constituted
an agreement to dispense with expert evidence when read with the IBA Rules on the
Taking of Evidence, because the applicant had failed to raise this argument before the
arbitral tribunal.[581]

These principles have also been applied in the context of respondents that have failed   **16.262**
entirely to participate in arbitral proceedings. In *Hainan Machinery*, which concerned
the enforcement of an arbitral award under Section 31(2)(e) of the IAA, the Singapore
High Court observed *obiter dicta* that the non-participation of certain respondents in
arbitral proceedings, in circumstances where they had been given every opportunity to
present their case, meant that they had 'very little right to criticise the way in which the
arbitration had been conducted'.[582]

More recent Court of Appeal authority calls into question whether the failure to par-   **16.263**
ticipate in arbitral proceedings would preclude a party from raising complaints at the
post-award stage about the arbitral procedure being inconsistent with the parties'
agreement or being inconsistent with the Model Law and the IAA. In *Rakna Arakshaka
(SGCA)* the Singapore Court of Appeal held that the non-participation of a respondent
in arbitral proceedings does not necessarily preclude that party from raising objections to jurisdiction before Singapore courts in post-award proceedings, relying in part
on the proposition that there was no duty to participate in proceedings.[583] Citing its
previous decision, the Singapore Court of Appeal in *Sanum v ST (SGCA)* held that a
non-participating respondent was not precluded from raising its objections to the seat
and composition of the arbitral tribunal in enforcement proceedings before Singapore
courts.[584] The Court of Appeal also reasoned that Article 4 of the Model Law was inapplicable because the non-participating respondent had not 'proceeded with the
arbitration'.[585]

Finally, although not strictly a waiver issue, the Court of Appeal in *China Machine*   **16.264**
(SGCA) held that a party intending to complain that there had been a fatal failure in

---

[579] *Triulzi* (n 78).
[580] Ibid, [92]–[94].
[581] Ibid, [95]–[97].
[582] *Hainan Machinery* (n 576) [25].
[583] See *Rakna Arakshaka (SGCA)* (n 391) [73]–[76].
[584] *Sanum v ST (SGCA)* (n 21) [92].
[585] Ibid, [92].

290   SETTING ASIDE AN AWARD

the arbitral process must give 'fair intimation' to the tribunal that it intends to take that point at the appropriate juncture.[586] The Court of Appeal elaborated that this would 'ordinarily require that the complaining party, at the very least, seek to suspend the proceedings until the breach has been satisfactorily remedied (if indeed the breach is capable of remedy) so that the tribunal and the non-complaining party has the opportunity to consider the position'.[587] A mere reservation of one's position until the award is issued is insufficient.

16.265   In *CAJ v CAI*,[588] the Court of Appeal had the opportunity to revisit its remarks on 'hedging' in *China Machine (SGCA)*. *CAJ v CAI* concerned a situation where an unpleaded defence had been raised at the eleventh hour in closing submissions, and the respondent had opposed the raising of this new defence. The Court of Appeal found that this was sufficient to amount to an unequivocal and fair intimidation to the tribunal of the respondent's objections to the unpleaded defence, and not an attempt to hedge its position.[589] The Court of Appeal further went on to hold that the facts of *China Machine (SGCA)* ought to be distinguished from that in *CAJ v CAI*, and that it was not necessary for the respondent in *CAJ v CAI* to have specifically intimidated to the tribunal that it intended to commence setting aside proceedings if its objections were ignored. *China Machine (SGCA)* was a case in which there had been a 'fatal failure in the process of the arbitration' at an early stage of the arbitration, and it was only fair for the complaining party to raise its objections rather than keeping silent and proceeding with the arbitration.[590] In contrast, in *CAJ v CAI*, at the time when the arbitration was declared closed, there was no indication by the tribunal that it would allow the unpleaded defence, and the respondent was only made aware of this when the award itself was delivered. It would have been premature for the respondent to alert the tribunal of any potential challenge to its decision prior to the award.[591]

16.266   Although it is correct that a party who seeks to challenge an award on the basis of a breach of natural justice having occurred during the process should have at least raised the objection at the material time, requiring parties to signal their dissatisfaction to the tribunal and even to seek to suspend the proceedings until the breach can be remedied raises an interesting question as to the interaction between setting aside and the challenge procedure under Article 13 of the Model Law. If a tribunal has indeed acted in a way that a party deems to be a fatal failure in the arbitral process, presumably that party will have lost confidence in the tribunal as well. This would be sufficient to raise a challenge under Article 13 of the Model Law. If the challenge is then not raised within the time prescribed under Article 13 or the applicable rules,

---

[586] *China Machine (SGCA)* (n 194) [170].
[587] Ibid, [170].
[588] *CAJ v CAI* (n 131).
[589] Ibid, [65]–[66].
[590] Ibid, [67].
[591] Ibid, [68].

C. GROUNDS FOR SETTING ASIDE 291

would that preclude a setting-aside challenge on the same grounds? If the answer is in the affirmative, that would put a heavy burden on parties to decide either to issue an Article 13 challenge immediately, or else lose a potential setting-aside ground. It may also result in unnecessary or disruptive challenges in circumstances where a party may now know if any potential alleged breaches would be material to the outcome in the award.

(d) Prejudice

There is apparently conflicting authority on whether a party who seeks to set aside an award under Article 34(2)(a)(iv) of the Model Law is required to show that the procedural irregularity complained of has caused real prejudice. In *AMZ v AXX*, the High Court held that a setting aside applicant under Article 34(2)(a)(iv) must prove that it has suffered actual or real prejudice by reason of the procedural irregularity, meaning that the arbitral tribunal could reasonably have arrived at a different result if not for the procedural irregularity.[592] However, in *Triulzi*, the Singapore High Court held that prejudice is only a factor relevant to the exercise of the court's discretion to decline to set aside an award, rather than a legal requirement for an application under Article 34(2)(a)(iv) of the Model Law.[593] On this basis, the High Court held that a setting aside application would not necessarily be dismissed where there is no evidence of prejudice, so long as it can be shown that the procedural irregularity is sufficiently material or serious.[594] In *Lao Holdings NV,* the applicant accepted that, if the admission of additional evidence in that case were a breach of the agreed arbitral procedure, the award could only be set aside if prejudice could be shown.[595] This was presumably because the breach in question was not sufficiently serious to constitute, of itself, a basis for setting aside the award.

16.267

In the context of an enforcement proceeding on the basis of the grounds in Article 36(1)(a)(iv) of the Model Law, the Singapore Court of Appeal in *Sanum v ST (SGCA)* endorsed the latter approach, holding that it was not necessary for a party who is resisting enforcement of an award arising out of a wrongly seated arbitration to demonstrate actual prejudice.[596] The Court of Appeal noted that the choice of the seat was of vital importance to parties, entailing a choice of both the procedural law of the arbitration and the forum for remedies to do with the arbitral proceedings and award, and that therefore an award that ensues from a wrongly seated arbitration should not be recognised and enforced without the need to show actual prejudice.[597]

16.268

---

[592] *AMZ v AXX* (n 468) [103].
[593] *Triulzi* (n 78) [64].
[594] Ibid, [66].
[595] *Lao Holdings NV v Government of the Lao People's Democratic Republic and another matter* [2021] 5 SLR 228; [2021] SGHC(I) 10 [201].
[596] *Sanum v ST (SGCA)* (n 21) [103].
[597] Ibid, [96]–[103].

5. Article 34(2)(b)(i): Subject-Matter Not Capable of Settlement by Arbitration

16.269 Article 34(2)(b)(i) provides that an award may be set aside when the subject matter of the dispute is not arbitrable under Singapore law.[598] The approach of Singapore courts to the subject matter arbitrability of disputes is discussed in greater detail in Chapter 10.

16.270 The law that should govern arbitrability at the setting aside stage was the subject of extensive debate during the drafting of the Model Law. There was a proposal to delete Art 34(2)(b)(i) altogether, which received considerable support, based on the view that the law of the seat should not necessarily govern the question of arbitrability. Some suggested that this question should be governed instead by the law applicable to the substance of the dispute on that issue. There was also a concern that, unlike in the context of recognition and enforcement, application of the law of the seat in a setting aside would give that law 'global effect'.[599] Another suggestion was to delete the reference to 'the law of this State' and thus to leave open the question as to which was the law applicable to arbitrability.[600]

16.271 The Working Group decided to leave the decision up to the Commission, which eventually decided to retain the current wording of Art 34(2)(b)(i). This appears to have been motivated by the desire for consistency with the New York Convention and the need to provide certainty on the law governing arbitrability.[601]

16.272 Non-arbitrability as a ground of setting aside has rarely been invoked before Singapore courts. In *Twarit v GPE*, Roger Giles IJ noted that the applicants had not properly raised non-arbitrability as a ground for setting aside in their originating summons but dismissed it nonetheless as a meritless basis for challenge. Specifically, Giles IJ rejected the argument that the underlying transaction was illegal under Indian law and was therefore non-arbitrable.[602] He noted that the presumption of arbitrability, which was not displaced by the applicants' bald assertions that the legality or otherwise of the transaction would have an impact on unidentified regulators and third-party stakeholders.[603] In the context of an attempt to resist enforcement, in *Aloe Vera*, Judith Prakash J (as she then was) rejected the argument that the issue of whether a person was the alter ego of a company was not arbitrable, reasoning that this was a commercial issue and not one with a wider public interest element.[604]

---

[598] Article 34(2)(b)(i) refers to 'the law of this State'. Read with Section 3(2) of the IAA, arbitrability in a setting aside application is governed by Singapore law.

[599] Holtzmann and Neuhaus, *Guide to the UNCITRAL Model Law* (n 37) 918.

[600] Ibid, 950.

[601] Ibid, 973–7; *UNCITRAL 18th Session Report* (n 201) [291].

[602] *Twarit Consultancy Services Pte Ltd and another v GPE (India) Ltd and others* [2022] 3 SLR 211 [76]–[79].

[603] Ibid, [85]–[93].

[604] *Aloe Vera* (n 254) [72].

6. Article 34(2)(b)(ii): Conflict with the Public Policy of Singapore

Article 34(2)(b)(i) provides that an award may be set aside where it is in conflict with the public policy of Singapore.[605] This is sometimes considered together with the overlapping setting aside grounds in Sections 24(a) and 24(b) of the IAA, which also relate to public policy.[606]

16.273

Even though 'public policy' is not defined in the IAA or the Model Law, it is generally understood to be a narrow ground for setting aside. During the drafting of the Model Law, it was understood that the 'public policy' ground was not to be equated with domestic public policy, and instead was narrowly confined to fundamental notions and principles of justice.[607] Thus, the Commission Report for the Model Law reflects that the term 'public policy' was intended to cover 'fundamental principles of law and justice in substantive as well as procedural respects', including 'corruption, bribery or fraud and similar serious cases' as a ground for setting aside.[608]

16.274

In *PT Asuransi (SGCA)*, the Singapore Court of Appeal held that the scope of the public policy ground for challenging an award is narrow.[609] It should only operate in instances where the upholding of an arbitral award would 'shock the conscience', is 'clearly injurious to the public good', 'wholly offensive to the ordinary reasonable and fully informed member of the public', or 'where it violates the forum's most basic notion of morality and justice'.[610] This is said to reflect a high threshold, as Singapore courts will rarely intervene on such grounds in commercial disputes.[611]

16.275

The threshold for challenge on public policy grounds is equally high in setting aside and enforcement cases. In *AJU v AJT*, the Court of Appeal rejected the argument that the enforcement regime was concerned with 'international public policy' whereas the setting aside regime was concerned with a wider concept of public policy.[612] Accordingly, the case law on the enforcement regime is relevant to setting aside cases, and *vice versa*.[613] However, it is not settled whether the concept of 'public policy' under the domestic Arbitration Act is wider than under the IAA. The applicant in *BNX v BOE* argued that it was, but the High Court declined to decide the issue as it had already found that there had been no breach of public policy.[614]

16.276

---

[605] Article 34(2)(b)(ii) refers to 'the law of this State'. Read with Section 3(2) of the IAA, arbitrability in a setting aside application is governed by Singapore law.

[606] See e.g. *Swiss Singapore* (n 192) [24]; *PT Asuransi (SGCA)* (n 40) [59].

[607] *UNCITRAL 18th Session Report* (n 201) [296]–[297].

[608] Holtzmann and Neuhaus, *Guide to the UNCITRAL Model Law* (n 37) 914. This statement of the interpretation of public policy has been endorsed in Singapore: see *PT Asuransi (SGCA)* (n 40) [59].

[609] Ibid, [59].

[610] Ibid, [59].

[611] *CEB v CEC* (n 135) [50].

[612] *AJU v AJT* (n 11) [37].

[613] Ibid, [38].

[614] *BNX v BOE* [2017] SGHC 289 [97] (hereafter *BNX v BOE*).

294 SETTING ASIDE AN AWARD

(a) Legal Framework and Standard of Review

16.277 To set aside an award on the ground that it is contrary to public policy, a challenging party must first identify the public policy that the award allegedly breaches and then show which part of the award conflicts with that public policy.[615] Vague assertions that an award is 'perverse' and 'irrational' will not be sufficient to establish a breach of public policy.[616]

16.278 There are competing public policies at play in any such challenge under the public policy ground. This involves a balancing exercise between the policy of enforcing arbitral awards and minimal curial intervention, on the one hand, and the alleged public policy that the award purported violates.[617] In general, the balance is in favour of enforcing arbitral awards, and the balance only tilts in the favour of the countervailing public policy where violation of that policy would 'shock the conscience' or be contrary to the 'forum's most basic notion of morality and justice', which would involve a consideration of the subject nature of that policy, the degree of violation of that public policy, and the consequences of the violation.[618]

16.279 Singapore courts have thus held that not every breach of law will justify setting aside an award on the ground of public policy.[619] Similarly, errors of law or fact in an arbitral decision are final and binding on parties and do not *per se* engage the public policy of Singapore.[620] Such findings of law or fact cannot be reopened 'except where there is fraud, breach of natural justice or some other vitiating factor'.[621] This is true even for 'egregious' errors of law.[622]

16.280 There are, however, some exceptions. One is where an arbitral tribunal makes an error of law as to what the public policy of Singapore is. As the Court of Appeal held in *AJU v AJT*, Singapore courts 'cannot abrogate its judicial power to the Tribunal to decide what the public policy of Singapore is'.[623] Another exception is where there is 'palpable and indisputable illegality', in which case Singapore courts would intervene as a matter of Singapore public policy, because not to do so would be to ignore or condone obvious criminality.[624] The scope of these exceptions is subject to some debate and they are discussed in greater detail below in relation to illegality allegations.

---

[615] *VV and another v VW* [2008] 2 SLR(R) 929 [17] (hereafter *VV v VW*); *BNX v BOE* (n 614) [95]; *CDI v CDJ* (n 190) [22], [24].

[616] *Sui Southern Gas* (n 440) [47]–[48].

[617] *BAZ (SGHC)* (n 24) [159].

[618] Ibid, [159].

[619] *PT Asuransi (SGCA)* (n 40) [54]–[55].

[620] Ibid, [57].

[621] *AJU v AJT* (n 11) [65]; *Bloomberry Resorts and Hotels Inc v Global Gaming Philippines LLC* [2021] 2 SLR 1279 [162] (hereafter *Bloomberry (Final Award) (SGCA)*).

[622] *BAZ (SGCA)* (n 238) [102].

[623] *AJU v AJT* (n 11) [62].

[624] Ibid, [67]; *CBX and another v CBZ and others* [2020] 5 SLR 184 [67] (hereafter *CBX v CBZ (SICC)*).

C. GROUNDS FOR SETTING ASIDE   295

(b) Scenarios Where Public Policy Challenges Have Failed and Succeeded

Given the high threshold for a successful challenge, the public policy ground has been **16.281** described as 'the last refuge of the desperate'.[625] It is often pleaded but rarely succeeds. This subsection considers some scenarios where Singapore courts have rejected challenges based on the public policy ground.

In *Prometheus Marine (SGHC)*, the High Court refused to set aside a challenge based **16.282** on the arbitrator's failure to state whether the domestic Arbitration Act or the IAA applied as the *lex arbitri*. The Court held that the failure to specify the relevant statute was not an error, much less a breach of public policy.[626] This was affirmed on appeal.[627]

Issues arising from an arbitral tribunal's evidentiary determinations are unlikely to re- **16.283** sult in a successful public policy challenge. In *BNX v BOE*, the High Court rejected the argument that the tribunal's alleged admission of and reliance on hearsay evidence was contrary to public policy. The Court noted that the hearsay rule is subject to exceptions, and in fact Singapore courts routinely act on hearsay evidence in dealing with finality parties' rights and obligations in chambers, for example on a summary judgment application. There is therefore nothing in the public policy of Singapore which requires a tribunal to exclude hearsay evidence in finally determining a party's rights and obligations in a civil claim.[628] In any event, the High Court held that the arbitral tribunal neither admitted nor relied on hearsay evidence.[629]

Procedural breaches in an arbitration are also unlikely to result in a successful chal- **16.284** lenge based on public policy. As the High Court held in *Coal & Oil*, breaches of the parties' agreed procedure only affect the conduct of the arbitration *inter se* and do not have wider public policy implications.[630] The Court therefore rejected the argument that a 19-month delay in issuing an award constituted a violation of public policy.[631] In similar vein, in *VV v VW*, the High Court rejected the argument that an arbitrator's costs award offended the principle of proportionality and was thereby inconsistent with the public policy of Singapore. The Court held that it was not part of the public policy of Singapore to ensure that the costs incurred by parties to private out-of-court litigation are assessed on the basis of any particular principle.[632]

Singapore courts have also rejected public policy challenges involving attempts to effect- **16.285** ively reopen an arbitral tribunal's decision on the merits. In *BTN v BTP (I) (SGHC)*, the High Court rejected the argument that the relevant award breached public policy because

---

[625] *Coal & Oil* (n 82) [61].
[626] *Prometheus Marine Pte Ltd, v Ann Rita King and other matters* [2017] SGHC 36 [99]–[107] (hereafter *Prometheus Marine (SGHC)*).
[627] *Prometheus Marine Pte Ltd v King, Ann Rita and another appeal* [2017] SGCA 61, [44]–[50].
[628] *BNX v BOE* (n 614) [100].
[629] Ibid, [101].
[630] *Coal & Oil* (n 82) [62].
[631] Ibid, [63].
[632] *VV v VW* (n 615) [28]–[31].

296   SETTING ASIDE AN AWARD

the award debtors were prevented from having the merits of their cases ventilated before any forum by the tribunal's decision to accord preclusive effect to a prior decision of the Malaysian Industrial Court. The Court held that, in according preclusive effect to the prior decision, the tribunal had properly applied the applicable law to determine the legal issues submitted for its consideration, with the award debtors given a full opportunity to present their case on those issues.[633] This was affirmed by the Court of Appeal, which also observed that the tribunal's decision on the *res judicata* effect of a prior decision pertained to admissibility, and therefore any errors were not reviewable by Singapore courts.[634]

16.286   In *BAZ (SGHC)* and the subsequent appeal therefrom, the High Court and Court of Appeal (respectively) rejected the argument that the arbitral tribunal's finding on joint and several liability was contrary to public policy because it ignored the fundamental principle that a shareholder's rights and liabilities in a company are limited to the size of its shareholding.[635] Similarly, in *Bloomberry (Final Award) (SGHC)*, the High Court rejected the argument that the grant of damages to one party was contrary to the public policy of Singapore because that entity was a sham entity incorporated to evade Philippines taxes, noting that the arbitral tribunal had already rejected the sham entity argument.[636] The High Court also rejected the argument that the grant of a pre-tax 'gross-up' figure for damages would violate Philippine tax laws, noting that compliance with Philippines tax laws had been addressed by the tribunal.[637] The Court of Appeal also dismissed this argument as a 'non-starter'.[638]

16.287   In *BYL v BYN*, the issue was whether it was against Singapore public policy for an arbitral tribunal to render an award which provided for alternative orders for payment and the contingency that, in the event the award was declared unenforceable, different parts of the dispositive would be distinct and severable. Anselmo Reyes IJ rejected the argument that such an award was 'circular', 'contingent', and 'unworkable', holding that the pragmatic way in which the tribunal had handled the issues did not result in an award that was against Singapore public policy.[639]

16.288   The public policy ground of challenge has been successful, however, in rare cases where the high threshold was met. To take one straightforward example, in *BAZ (SGHC)*, the High Court partially set aside an award against certain minors. The Court reasoned that it would violate Singapore's most basic notions of justice to enforce an award against minors without capacity to enter into binding contracts.[640] The Court also treated the part of the award that pertains to the minors as severable from the rest of the award, and only set aside the award as against the minors.[641]

---

[633]   *BTN and another v BTP and another* [2020] 5 SLR 1250 [115]–[117] (hereafter *BTN v BTP (I) (SGHC)*).
[634]   *BTN and another v BTP and another* [2021] 1 SLR 276 [71]–[73] (hereafter *BTN v BTP (I) (SGCA)*).
[635]   *BAZ (SGHC)* (n 24) [164]–[168]; *BAZ (SGCA)* (n 238) [99]–[100].
[636]   *Bloomberry (Final Award) (SGHC)* (n 11) [86]–[87].
[637]   Ibid, [89].
[638]   *Bloomberry (Final Award) (SGCA)* (n 621) [163]–[164].
[639]   *BYL v BYN* (n 299) [36]–[45].
[640]   *BAZ (SGHC)* (n 24) [180]–[187].
[641]   Ibid, [187].

C. GROUNDS FOR SETTING ASIDE   297

(c) Illegality of the Underlying Contract or Contracts

Allegations of illegality frequently arise in public policy challenges. These cases invariably involve considerations to do with the standard of review of an arbitral tribunal's findings on any such illegality, balancing the policy in favour of the finality of arbitral awards against the policy of preventing serious instances of illegality.   **16.289**

In the leading case of *AJU v AJT*, the issue was whether an interim award that enforced a settlement agreement obliging one party to discontinue criminal proceedings in exchange for terminating arbitration proceedings should be set aside on public policy grounds. The High Court set aside the award, accepting the applicant's argument that the arrangement was illegal both under the governing law of the agreement, Singapore law, and the law of the place of performance, Thai law, as its purpose was to 'to stifle prosecution of non-compoundable offences'.[642] However, the Court of Appeal reversed and held that the High Court Judge was not entitled to reject the arbitral tribunal's findings on illegality and substitute his own findings for them.[643]   **16.290**

In its judgment, the Court of Appeal affirmed the principle that findings of law or fact cannot generally be reopened 'except where there is fraud, breach of natural justice or some other vitiating factor'.[644] Nonetheless, the Court of Appeal drew a distinction between findings of fact and law, noting that the application of the public policy objection in Article 34(2)(b)(ii) of the Model Law should be limited to findings of law to the exclusion of findings of fact.[645] The Court of Appeal characterised the arbitral tribunal's decision on illegality as a factual finding as to the parties' intentions and therefore held that such a factual finding could not engage the public policy of Singapore.[646] The Court of Appeal added the gloss that, where Singapore law is applicable (as it was in the case), Singapore courts can review and decide for itself whether a contract is illegal under Singapore law.[647] Seen in the light of the judgment as a whole, this gloss should be read as referring to the ability of Singapore courts to review questions of Singapore law (rather than fact) relating to alleged illegality under Singapore law.   **16.291**

The Court of Appeal also weighed in on two approaches taken by English courts at the time to the standard of review of a tribunal's findings on illegality. On the one hand, there was the approach taken by Colman J and the majority of the English Court of Appeal in the *Westacre* case,[648] a case concerning bribery allegations that had been dismissed by an ICC tribunal. Under this approach, if the arbitration agreement conferred jurisdiction to determine whether the underlying contract was illegal, then   **16.292**

---

[642] *AJT v AJU* [2010] 4 SLR 649 [33].
[643] *AJU v AJT* (n 11) [65].
[644] Ibid, [65]; *Bloomberry (Final Award) (SGCA)* (n 621) [162].
[645] *AJU v AJT* (n 11) [63]–[69].
[646] Ibid, [63],[70].
[647] Ibid, [62].
[648] The English High Court decision by Colman J is at *Westacre Investments Inc v Jugoimport-SPDR Holding Co Ltd and others* [1999] QB 740 (hereafter *Westacre (EWHC)*); the English Court of Appeal decision is at *Westacre Investments Inc. v Jugoimport-SPDR Holding Co. Ltd. and Others* [2000] QB 288 (hereafter *Westacre (EWCA)*).

298   SETTING ASIDE AN AWARD

prima facie the award would be enforced unless an allegation could be made 'on the basis of facts not placed before the arbitrators' that the contract was indeed illegal, in which case the courts would consider whether the policy against enforcement of illegal *contracts* outweighed the countervailing public policy in support of the finality of *awards*.[649] Applying this approach, the majority of the Court of Appeal declined to reopen the ICC tribunal's findings on bribery and held that the public policy of sustaining awards outweighed the public policy in discouraging international commercial corruption.[650]

16.293   The other approach was the one taken in the *Soleimany* case, whereby the English Court of Appeal held that public policy would not allow the enforcement of an illegal contract, and the interposition of the award did not isolate the arbitration claimant's claim from the illegality that gave rise to it.[651] That case involved a contract for the smuggling of carpets out of Iran, and the Court of Appeal noted that the illegality under the law of the place of performance was plain on the face of the underlying contract, observing that it was not reopening the finding of fact by the tribunal that there was a common intention to commit an illegal act.[652] However, Waller LJ observed *obiter* that, in other cases where tribunals have not found any illegality or not made any such finding, courts should inquire further to some extent 'if there is *prima facie* evidence from one side that the award is based on an illegal contract'.[653] In this respect, he disagreed with the *Westacre* position that the courts may inquire into the illegality issues only where the relevant facts were not put before the arbitrator.[654] Waller LJ took a similar position in his dissent when the *Westacre* case came up for appeal.[655]

16.294   The Singapore Court of Appeal preferred to follow the first approach taken by the majority of the Court of Appeal in the *Westacre* case, holding that this approach was more consistent with the legislative policy of the IAA, which is to give primacy to the autonomy of arbitral proceedings and uphold the finality of arbitral awards.[656] This is consistent with two recent judgments by the UK Supreme Court and the Privy Council, both of which preferred the approach of the majority of the Court of Appeal in the *Westacre* case over the approach in the *Soleimany* case.[657]

16.295   The approach adopted in *AJU v AJT* does not mean that illegality, however serious, cannot justify the setting aside of an award. Indeed, the Court of Appeal accepted that, in the case of 'palpable and indisputable illegality', an award could be found to be inconsistent with the public policy of Singapore, just that this threshold was not satisfied on

---

[649] *Westacre (EWHC)* (n 648) 767G–768A; *Westacre (EWCA)* (n 648) 316D–317D.
[650] *Westacre (EWHC)* (n 648) 772G–H; *Westacre (EWCA)* (n 648) 316D–317D.
[651] *Soleimany v Soleimany* [1999] QB 785 800A–C (hereafter *Soleimany*).
[652] Ibid, 797B.
[653] Ibid, 800D–H.
[654] Ibid, 800B–C.
[655] *Westacre (EWCA)* (n 648) 314D–314C.
[656] *AJU v AJT* (n 11) [60].
[657] *Betamax Ltd v State Trading Corporation (Mauritius)* [2021] UKPC 14 [51] (hereafter *Betamax*); *RBRG Trading (UK) Ltd v Sinocore International Co Ltd* [2018] EWCA Civ 838 [25(2)].

C. GROUNDS FOR SETTING ASIDE   299

the facts of the case.[658] The *Soleimany* case is one example of the sort of circumstances that would amount to 'palpable and indisputable illegality', given that the tribunal had acknowledged the underlying illegality of the transaction in its award.

These principles were applied in *Rakna Arakshaka (SGHC)*, where the award debtor **16.296** sought to argue that the relevant agreements were procured by bribery and corruption, and therefore it would be against public policy to enforce the award. The High Court noted that the allegations were based on pending corruption trials in the Sri Lankan courts but declined to make any findings based on that fact, given the presumption of innocence under Sri Lankan law.[659] As for the argument that a clause in the master agreement required the performance of an act that would be illegal under the law of the place of performance, Sri Lankan law, the tribunal had considered that issue and found 'no sign of illegality or even in the slightest', which the High Court found to be a finding of fact that was binding on a supervisory court.[660] The Court of Appeal affirmed this analysis.[661]

To what extent can Singapore courts review findings of foreign law in a public policy **16.297** challenge? In *CBX v CBZ (SICC)*, Reyes IJ held that where a tribunal wrongly concludes that a contract is not illegal under foreign law, even though this was an error of law, 'it may be appropriate for the Singapore court to intervene as a matter of Singapore public policy, because not to do so would be to ignore or condone obvious criminality'.[662] Anselmo Reyes IJ further clarified that the term 'palpable and indisputable illegality' describes contracts involving 'conduct of an obvious criminal nature', such as contracts that would require parties to contravene the criminal law of some countries (e.g. smuggling or bribery).[663] On that basis, Reyes IJ rejected the argument that an arbitral tribunal's award of compound interest was contrary to Singapore public policy because it contravened Thai mandatory law, despite the fact that the parties' Thai law experts had allegedly agreed that the award of compound interest contravened Thai law.[664]

Other judgments have taken a different approach, proceeding on the basis that findings **16.298** of foreign law are findings of fact under Singapore law. In *Gokul Patnaik*, Sir Vivian Ramsey IJ declined to reopen the arbitral tribunal's finding that the relevant share purchase agreement was not illegal under Indian law, which involved findings of fact as to the nature of the transactions and whether they included an assured return.[665]

---

[658] *AJU v AJT* (n 11) [64]. This was a proposition that was accepted under both the *Westacre* and *Soleimany* approaches. See Ibid, [49].

[659] *Rakna Arakshaka (SGHC)* (n 33) [89]. The High Court also rejected the argument that an adjournment was justified because counsel was not able to give any indication as to when proceedings would be likely to be concluded, and an indefinite adjournment was inappropriate.

[660] Ibid, [92].

[661] *Rakna Arakshaka (SGCA)* (n 391) [100]. The Court also observed that it was 'telling' that the award debtors still continued to perform the master agreement, and this cast doubt on whether they could seriously take the position that the performance of the master agreement was illegal.

[662] *CBX v CBZ (SICC)* (n 624) [43], [66]–[67].

[663] Ibid, [57]–[58].

[664] Ibid, [43], [51]–[53].

[665] *Gokul Patnaik v Nine Rivers Capital Ltd* [2021] 3 SLR 22 [182]–[187] (hereafter *Gokul Patnaik*).

300   SETTING ASIDE AN AWARD

However, Ramsey IJ went on to hold that, even if the findings were to be characterised as findings of Indian law, Singapore courts could not review them because findings of foreign law they were findings of fact, unless there was fraud, breach of natural justice, or some other vitiating factor.[666] Ramsey IJ took a similar approach in *CHY v CIA*, where he affirmed the principle that a finding of foreign law is a finding of fact for a Singapore court. On that basis, he found that the arbitral tribunal's findings on the legality of the contract under Indian law could not be reopened under the public policy challenge.[667]

16.299   As for the standard of review for Singapore law findings, the Court of Appeal had observed in *AJU v AJT* that Singapore courts cannot abrogate judicial power on what the public policy of Singapore is and should have the power to decide for themselves whether a contract is illegal under Singapore law.[668] This may appear to suggest that a Singapore court is not bound by findings of law by an arbitral tribunal on whether a contract is illegal under Singapore law. Indeed, this approach was applied by the High Court in *BNX v BOE*, although the Court in that case ultimately rejected the argument that the share purchase agreement in that contract was illegal because it involved the sale of a business that is prohibited under the Urban Redevelopment Authority's use restriction.[669]

16.300   The recent decision by the Privy Council in *Betamax* may cast some doubt on the width of the proposition in *AJU v AJT* that Singapore courts may review illegality findings under Singapore law. In *Betamax*, the Privy Council held that, under a Mauritian statutory provision identical to Article 34(2)(b)(ii) of the Model Law, courts may not review all questions of law and fact, absent specified vitiating factors.[670] On that view, a court's task is therefore to determine whether, 'on the findings of law and fact made in the award, there is any conflict between the award and public policy'.[671] It was said that this accorded with the outcome of prior English decisions and *AJU v AJT*; *Soleimany* was the only case where the award was refused enforcement on public policy grounds, and that was because the illegality was manifest from the award and so there was no need to review findings of fact or law by the tribunal.[672]

16.301   While endorsing most of the Singapore Court of Appeal's decision in *AJU v AJT*, the Privy Council further noted that the portion on the reviewability of illegality findings under Singapore law was 'not easy to reconcile' with other parts of the judgment. The Privy Council thus held that any proposition that the courts had the power to reopen findings in an award on the legality of an agreement under Singapore law 'went further than was necessary for the decision'.[673] The Committee did note, however,

---

[666] Ibid, [188]–[189].
[667] *CHY and another v CIA* [2022] SGHC(I) 3 [43], [50]–[51] (hereafter *CHY v CIA*).
[668] *AJU v AJT* (n 11) [62].
[669] *BNX v BOE* (n 614) [105]–[110].
[670] *Betamax* (n 657) [48].
[671] Ibid, [49].
[672] Ibid, [50]–[51].
[673] Ibid, [39].

that there might be 'exceptional cases' where a court under Article 34(2)(b)(ii) might be entitled to review an arbitral tribunal's decision on legality, but declined to set forth any concrete examples or circumstances that may qualify as such exceptional cases.[674]

In *CHY v CIA*, Ramsey IJ noted the observations of the Privy Council in *Betamax* but declined to decide on its implications for the reviewability of tribunals' findings on illegality under Singapore law, given that it was not necessary for decision in that case.[675] Therefore, as of the time of writing, Singapore courts have not had occasion to fully consider the impact of the decision of the Privy Council in *Betamax*.

16.302

With respect, the approach in *Betamax* should be preferred to *AJU v AJT* as regards the issue of whether a Singapore court may review and reopen errors in a tribunal's findings on the legality or otherwise of an underlying contract. On this view, a tribunal's findings on illegality, including findings of Singapore law, should only be reviewed in 'exceptional cases', and not as a matter of course.

16.303

It is important to bear in mind that Singapore courts are not being asked to give effect to the underlying *contract* but to give effect to the *award*. Thus, in the context the Model Law and the New York Convention, the prevailing presumption should be that the policy in support of the finality of *awards* should generally outweigh the policy against enforcement of illegal *contracts*.[676] The policy in support of the finality of the awards provides the relevant constraint on the Singapore courts' ability to review a tribunal's findings of Singapore law, just as it does in other contexts (except for jurisdictional questions).

16.304

Moreover, this approach avoids the situation whereby Singapore courts take a different approach to errors of law depending on whether it is Singapore law or foreign law that applies. It is not clear why there should be a difference, bearing in mind the policy objectives of the New York Convention and the Model Law and the uniform approach therein to awards derived from international arbitration proceedings, regardless of the applicable law.

16.305

As for what might constitute an 'exceptional case' that would justify closer scrutiny of a tribunal's findings on illegality under Singapore law, this has not been elucidated by case law. In principle, the relevant inquiry should be (i) whether upholding an award that contains such an error would itself be a violation of the public policy of Singapore, and (ii) whether this outweighs the policy in support of the finality of awards. Possible factors that may weigh in the balance include the egregiousness of the error of law, the importance of the countervailing public policy in question, and the materiality of the error of law to the tribunal's decision in its award.

16.306

---

[674] Ibid, [52].
[675] *CHY v CIA* (n 667) [40].
[676] See e.g. *AJU v AJT* (n 11) [43]; *Westacre (EWHC)* (n 648) 767G–768A; *Westacre (EWCA)* (n 648) 316D–317D.

302 SETTING ASIDE AN AWARD

(d) Fraud or Corruption

16.307 Where the making of an award was induced or affected by fraud or corruption, Section 24(a) provides that an award may be set aside. Although such issues may also form the basis for challenge under the public policy ground in Article 34(2)(b)(ii), they are separately discussed in greater detail below.

16.308 As for allegations that the underlying contracts—as distinct from the award—have been induced by fraud or corruption, such allegations can be dealt with under the framework discussed above in relation to illegality allegations. Thus, for example, in *Rakna Arakshaka (SGHC)*, the High Court rejected the argument that the relevant agreements were procured by bribery and corruption, noting that the arbitral tribunal had already found that there was 'no sign of illegality or even in the slightest', which was a finding of fact that the Court could not reopen.[677] This was affirmed on appeal.[678]

16.309 In *Vitol Asia*, Vinodh Coomaraswamy J had to consider whether allegations that there was fraud and corruption in the formation of the underlying contract could be raised for the first time at the post-award stage. Coomaraswamy J expressed some discomfort at having to make findings of fact on such serious allegations based on affidavit evidence alone.[679] Nonetheless, he noted that, even taking the award debtor's case at its highest and assuming that the contract was in fact procured by fraud and corruption, this would not be sufficient to refuse enforcement of the award. Coomaraswamy J noted in particular that the award debtor had the opportunity to place the issue before the arbitral tribunal, but did not, which attracted the application of the extended doctrine of *res judicata* and precluded the raising of the issue as a ground for refusing enforcement of the award.[680]

(e) Breaches of Natural Justice

16.310 There have also been statements *obiter dicta* that a breach of the rules of natural justice,[681] including the lack of impartiality or independence on the part of an arbitrator,[682] would render an award contrary to Singapore public policy. However, in *CDI v CDJ*, the High Court noted that not every award made in breach of natural justice would, *ipso facto*, be contrary to the public policy of Singapore.[683] Although this issue has not yet been fully resolved by Singapore courts, it stands to reason that, in order to set aside an award for breaches of natural justice pursuant to Article 34(2)(b)(ii) of the Model Law, requirements set forth in the jurisprudence under Article 34(2)(a)(ii) of the Model Law and Section 24(b) of the IAA must also be met.

---

[677] *Rakna Arakshaka (SGHC)* (n 33) [89], [92].
[678] *Rakna Arakshaka (SGCA)* (n 391) [100]. The Court also observed that it was 'telling' that the award debtors still continued to perform the master agreement, and this cast doubt on whether they could seriously take the position that the performance of the master agreement was illegal.
[679] *Vitol Asia* (n 11) [167]–[168].
[680] Ibid, [178]–[187].
[681] *AJU v AJT* (n 11) [66].
[682] *PT Central Investindo* (n 35) [52], [132] and [135]; *Beijing Sinozonto* (n 187) [41].
[683] *CDI v CDJ* (n 190) [26].

7. Section 24(a): Fraud or Corruption

Section 24(a) provides that an award may be set aside if it 'was induced or affected by fraud or corruption'. As explained above, this overlaps with the ground for setting aside an award based on inconsistency with the public policy of Singapore, where issues of fraud and corruption are also relevant. The scope of Section 24(a) is narrower: as the Court of Appeal made clear in *Rakna Arakshaka (SGCA)*, allegations of fraud or corruption relating to the underlying contract do not fall within the scope of Section 24(a).[684]

16.311

The threshold for establishing fraud or corruption is a high one and involves 'a showing of bad faith during the arbitration proceedings, such as bribery, undisclosed bias of the arbitrator, or wilful destruction or withholding of evidence'.[685] To succeed in setting aside an award for fraud, an award debtor will need to produce cogent and convincing evidence of fraud or corruption.[686] Although it has been said that the standard of proof is high,[687] Singapore courts have clarified that this does not require something other than proof on a balance of probabilities; instead, the seriousness of the allegation of 'dishonesty' means that it is inherently more unlikely and therefore more cogent evidence is needed to establish it.[688] In addition, where new evidence is introduced to demonstrate fraud, the award debtor will also need to show why it was not available or could not have been obtained with reasonable diligence during the arbitration.[689]

16.312

Proof of conduct that amounts to fraud or corruption is not sufficient for a setting aside. An award debtor needs to additionally show a causative link between the fraudulent or corrupt conduct and the making of the award.[690]

16.313

As to the exact degree of causation that needs to be established, the Singapore Court of Appeal has held in *Bloomberry (Partial Award) (SGCA)* that the words 'induced or affected' are to be understood more broadly than simply 'induced', and Section 24(a) therefore requires the showing of 'a connection' between the alleged fraud or corruption and the making of the award, such that that the fraud or corruption is not merely 'peripheral'.[691] It is not clear whether this suggests a more relaxed degree of causation than several High Court decisions that have seemingly provided for a stricter causative link, namely that any fraud must have 'substantially impacted' the making of an award.[692] In *Swiss Singapore*, the High Court elaborated on the 'substantial impact' standard by reference to the standard under English law for setting aside a judgment on

16.314

---

[684] *Rakna Arakshaka (SGCA)* (n 391) [98].
[685] *Beijing Sinozonto* (n 187) [41].
[686] Ibid, [69]; *Swiss Singapore* (n 192) [64].
[687] *Dongwoo* (n 188) [147].
[688] *BVU v BVX* (n 196) [46]; *Beijing Sinozonto* (n 187) [48], [63]–[69].
[689] *Bloomberry (Partial Award) (SGHC)* (n 93) [107]; *BVU v BVX* (n 196) [106].
[690] *Bloomberry (Partial Award) (SGHC)* (n 93) [105]–[108]; Ibid, [47].
[691] *Bloomberry (Partial Award) (SGCA)* (n 88) [41]–[42].
[692] *CLX v CLY and another and another matter* [2022] SGHC 17 [84] (hereafter *CLX v CLY*); *Bloomberry (Partial Award) (SGHC)* (n 93) [110]; *Swiss Singapore* (n 192) [29].

304 SETTING ASIDE AN AWARD

the ground that it was obtained by fraud. To do so, a challenging party has to show that there has to be evidence newly discovered after the trial that could not have been produced at the trial, and which was so material that its production would 'probably have affected the result' and so strong that it 'could reasonably be expected to be decisive at a re-hearing'.[693]

16.315 Singapore courts have not yet addressed the current status of the 'substantial impact' standard after the Court of Appeal's decision in *Bloomberry*.[694] In the authors' respectful submission, it was unlikely to have been the Court of Appeal's intention to overrule the 'substantial impact' standard, at least in the context of procedural fraud in the form of perjury or the concealment of material information, and in any event the relaxation of the causative link was not necessary for the Court's *ratio* in that case.[695] In addition, the 'substantial impact' test is more consistent with the principle of minimal curial intervention and better gives effect to the policy in favour of finality of arbitral awards.

16.316 The term 'fraud' in Section 24(a) has been held to encompass procedural fraud (i.e. fraud on the arbitration procedure), including where a party commits perjury, conceals material information, or suppresses evidence that would have a substantial effect on the making of the award.[696] Other forms of fraud may also be relied upon as grounds for challenge,[697] although most of the reported cases in Singapore thus far have focused more on procedural fraud.

16.317 The issue of perjury arose in *Swiss Singapore*, where the High Court held that a setting aside applicant must prove that its new evidence could not have been discovered or produced despite reasonable diligence in the arbitration, and that new evidence must be decisive in that it would have prompted the arbitrator to have ruled in favour of the applicant instead of the other party.[698] Applying these principles, the High Court disagreed with the applicant's contention that the respondent's witness had made a false statement under oath with the deliberate intention of misleading the applicant and the arbitrator, noting that the documents in the arbitration supported the witness's testimony, and the new information produced by the applicant did not have any relevance to the arbitrator's findings on liability or quantum.[699]

---

[693] Ibid, [29] (citing *DDT Trucks of North America Ltd and ors v DDT Holdings Ltd* [2007] EWHC 1542 (Comm), [2007] 2 Lloyd's Rep 213 and *Westacre (EWCA)* (n 648)).

[694] In *CLX v CLY*, the High Court applied the 'substantial impact' standard without consideration of whether it was consistent with the Court of Appeal's findings on the meaning of 'induced or affected' under Section 24(a) of the IAA. See *CLX v CLY* (n 692) [84].

[695] *Bloomberry (Partial Award) (SGHC)* (n 93) [41] (defining 'procedural fraud' as 'when a party commits perjury, conceals material information and/or suppresses evidence that would have substantial effect on the making of the award').

[696] Ibid, [41].

[697] For example, in *Bloomberry*, the appellants unsuccessfully argued that the respondents' concealment of the fraudulent actions of their principals constituted fraud that led to the making of the award. See Ibid, [37].

[698] *Swiss Singapore* (n 192) [30].

[699] Ibid, [62]–[84].

C. GROUNDS FOR SETTING ASIDE   305

In the case of the non-disclosure or suppression of material information, Singapore **16.318** courts have established three requirements for such conduct to warrant the setting aside of the award.[700] First, it must be shown that the concealment is deliberate, as opposed to innocent or negligent, and aimed at deceiving the tribunal. Second, the concealment must be causative, in the sense of having substantially impacted the making of the award. Third, there must be no good reason for the disclosure.

These principles were first applied in *Dongwoo*, where the High Court held that the **16.319** award creditor had honestly believed that it had a good reason not to disclose the relevant documents because they were covered by a confidentiality agreement.[701] For that reason, the intentional non-disclosure could not amount to reprehensible or unconscionable conduct that would shock the conscience and warrant the setting aside of the award.[702]

Similarly, in *BVU v BVX*, the High Court dismissed the argument that the award **16.320** creditor's decisions not to call a witness and not to disclose certain internal documents were aimed at deceiving the tribunal.[703] In particular, the Court noted that there was no obligation to call the witness or disclosure those internal documents, as neither was the subject of an order by the tribunal.[704] In these circumstances, the Court held that there was no deliberate concealment of witness evidence or documents in order to deceive the tribunal.[705] In any event, there was no causative link between the alleged concealment and the award.[706]

In *Bloomberry (Partial Award) (SGCA)*, the Court of Appeal had to consider arguments **16.321** relating both to perjury and concealment of material information that addressed issues of broader relevance to arbitrations involving parallel regulatory investigations. Notably, the Court of Appeal rejected the argument that a party had a general obligation to disclose information inimical to his interests even where irrelevant to the subject matter of the arbitration, particularly in the context of commercial contracts in which each party is fully able to negotiate terms to protect its own interests.[707] Thus, there was no obligation on the award creditor to disclose the existence of US Department of Justice (DOJ) and US Securities and Exchange Commission (SEC) investigations into Las Vegas Sands, a non-party to the arbitration that was the former employer of certain principals at the award creditor.[708]

---

[700] *CLX v CLY* (n 692); *BVU v BVX* (n 196) [47]; *Dongwoo* (n 188) [132]–[134].
[701] Ibid, [141]–[142].
[702] Ibid, [143]–[144].
[703] *BVU v BVX* (n 196) [59]–[60].
[704] Ibid, [61]. The Court also observed that the award debtor had in fact made an application to the tribunal to order the appearance of certain of the award creditor's witnesses, which was rejected by the tribunal. See *BVU v BVX* (n 196) [62]–[69].
[705] Ibid, [71]–[72].
[706] Ibid, [76]–[95].
[707] *Bloomberry (Partial Award) (SGCA)* (n 88) [43]–[44].
[708] Ibid, [43]–[44], [55].

306 SETTING ASIDE AN AWARD

16.322 In the context of the award debtor's argument that the award creditor and his lawyers gave false information in certain 2012 statements to mislead the arbitral tribunal, the Court of Appeal had to consider whether certain findings by the SEC and DOJ resulting from their investigations. The Court of Appeal agreed with the High Court Judge that those findings were not findings of a court of law or an independent factfinder, and that they therefore did not establish to the required degree of proof that the award creditor's principals were implicated in the bribery of certain Chinese government officials and state-owned entities while they were previously employed by Las Vegas Sands.[709] The Court of Appeal also agreed with the Judge's determination that the findings by the SEC and DOJ were only in respect of certain accounting provisions of the US Foreign Corrupt Practices Act, and not its anti-bribery provisions.[710]

16.323 Importantly, in dismissing the perjury allegations, the Court of Appeal noted that none of the findings by the SEC and DOJ concerned conduct by the principals in relation to the subject matter of the arbitration.[711] The Court of Appeal further noted that the 2012 statements were not statements made in the course of the arbitration proceedings, and that in any event there was no evidence of dishonesty or fraud by the lawyers in preparing them.[712]

16.324 With respect to the alleged concealment of documents in the arbitration, the award debtor had sought to rely on the non-production of documents from a personal email account in response to the tribunal's document disclosure orders. The Court of Appeal agreed with the High Court Judge that this did not amount to procedural fraud as there was no evidence that the decision not to produce was made dishonestly, particularly given the number of emails that had in fact been produced and the explanations given by the lawyers for the non-disclosure.[713]

16.325 There are fewer cases involving allegations that the award has been induced or affected by corruption. In *Beijing Sinozonto*, the award debtor argued that the award should be refused enforcement because the award creditor, through its representatives or intermediaries, had 'an improper arrangement with the Tribunal to get the Tribunal to issue an award' that supported the award creditor's claims.[714] The High Court held that this was a very serious and improbable allegation for which there was no cogent evidence at all, noting that the award debtor's case based on certain emails by the award creditor's

---

[709] Ibid, [52]–[53], [55]–[57].
[710] Ibid, [58].
[711] Ibid, [61].
[712] Ibid, [64]–[66].
[713] Ibid, [71]. The lawyers in question explained that most of the relevant information would have already been captured in the data that were in fact collected, that the communications with other Chinese speakers on the personal email account were almost exclusively have been in Chinese and could not have been searched using English search terms, and that the collection and translation of additional documents would have been time-consuming and expensive. The Court of Appeal noted that it was not relevant whether or not the decision not to produce was correct; what the explanation demonstrated is that any failure to disclose was, at most, negligent, and not aimed at deceiving the tribunal.
[714] *Beijing Sinozonto* (n 187) [22], [59].

C. GROUNDS FOR SETTING ASIDE   307

lawyers 'did not even get off the ground'.[715] There have been no reported instances of successful challenges under Section 24(a) on the basis of corruption that has induced or affected an award.

8. Section 24(b): Breach of the Rules of Natural Justice

Section 24(b) provides that an award may be set aside if a breach of the rules of natural justice occurred in connection with the making of the award by which the rights of any parties have been prejudiced. As explained above, there is substantial overlap between Article 34(2)(a)(ii) of the Model Law and Section 24(b) of the IAA, and many cases treat these setting aside grounds interchangeably, particularly with respect to violations of a party's right to be heard and present its case. These cases are discussed above in greater detail, and many of the principles and requirements discussed in relation to Article 34(2)(a)(ii) also apply to setting aside applications under Section 24(b) of the IAA.   **16.326**

The right to a neutral and unbiased decision-maker is a distinct rule of natural justice from a party's right to be heard and present its case.[716] Thus, notwithstanding the potential overlap with Article 34(2)(a)(ii), most cases have dealt with alleged bias of arbitrators under Section 24(b) (as well as under Article 34(2)(a)(iv)). This section therefore discusses in some detail the rules that apply to setting aside application on the ground of bias.   **16.327**

Bias can take the form of actual bias, imputed bias, or apparent bias.[717] Imputed bias arises where an arbitrator is said to be acting in his own cause, for example, where he has a pecuniary or proprietary interest in the case.[718] The bias is said to be imputed because it is irrelevant whether or not the arbitrator was in fact actually biased, because of the principle that justice must not only be done, it must be seen to be done. The importance of the appearance of justice also undergirds the doctrine of apparent bias, which under Singapore law, is determined based on a 'reasonable suspicion' test.[719] The test is whether a fair-minded, reasonable person with knowledge of the relevant facts would have a reasonable suspicion or apprehension that the arbitral tribunal was biased.[720]   **16.328**

These principles were applied in *PT Central Investindo*, where Belinda Ang J dismissed the argument that the award should be set aside for the apparent bias of the arbitrator, which was based on *inter alia* on the arbitrator's issuance of directions apparently without hearing one party, threats to draw adverse inferences against that party,   **16.329**

---

[715] Ibid, [71]–[92].
[716] *China Machine (SGCA)* (n 194) [1]; *Coal & Oil* (n 82) [67].
[717] *PT Central Investindo* (n 35) [15].
[718] Ibid, [15].
[719] Ibid, [15].
[720] *TMM Division* (n 395) [123] (citing *Re Shankar Alan s/o Anant Kulkarni* [2007] 1 SLR(R) 85 [91]; *Kempinski Hotels (SGHC)* (n 133) [66]).

308 SETTING ASIDE AN AWARD

and costs orders made against that party.[721] Ang J held that the arbitrator's procedural directions, including the power to draw adverse inferences, fell within his broad case-management discretion, and did not evince any partiality on the arbitrator's part.[722] Ang J further held that undue delay, of itself, would not suggest any form of partiality or bias.[723]

16.330 In *TMM Division*, Chan Seng Onn J also rejected the argument that 'egregious errors of law and fact' by the arbitrator invited the reasonable suspicion that he was biased.[724] Chan J held that even if the arbitrator had 'utterly misapplied the law or misunderstood the facts', that would not suffice even as *prima facie* evidence of apparent bias.[725]

16.331 Similarly, in *Kempinski Hotels (SGHC)*, Prakash J (as she then was) rejected the argument that the arbitrator had improperly 'entered the fray' and impermissibly taken on an adversarial role, based on allegations that the arbitrator had requested further information from the award debtor and requested submissions on possible adverse inferences.[726] Prakash J also dismissed the argument that the arbitrator had closed his mind on matters of Indonesian law by drawing conclusions on those matters without expert evidence being adduced, noting that the arbitrator had reached his conclusions on the basis of submissions and evidence.[727]

16.332 Recently, in *CFJ v CFL,* a three-member court of the SICC rejected a challenge to an award based on the apparent bias of the presiding arbitrator, applying the reasonable suspicion test as elaborated on and restated in *BOI v BOJ*.[728] In particular, the SICC rejected a challenge to the presiding arbitrator on the basis that he was appointed to a panel of experts (with no adjudicatory functions) constituted by the highest court of a state and one of the parties to the arbitration was a state-owned entity owned by that state.[729] The SICC also held that the non-disclosure of this fact by the presiding arbitrator did not give rise to any justifiable doubts about his impartiality or independence.[730]

16.333 This decision highlights the dangers of an increasingly commonplace facet of modern life in the arbitration community, whereby arbitrators are called upon to serve upon multiple boards, committees, panels, and even courts. The multiplicity of these affiliations may be acceptable to those in the arbitration community, but there is a sense that, in some cases, the fair-minded, reasonable arbitration litigant might not be willing to accept these associations, particularly where one party to an arbitration is a state or state-owned entity, and certain affiliations with a particular state may give rise to certain reasonable connotations. Each case will of course vary on its facts, but in very

---

[721] *PT Central Investindo* (n 35) [89]–[97].
[722] Ibid, [69]–[80].
[723] Ibid, [68].
[724] *TMM Division* (n 395) [124].
[725] Ibid, [124].
[726] *Kempinski Hotels (SGHC)* (n 133) [69]–[75].
[727] Ibid, [77]–[82].
[728] [2018] 2 SLR 1156; See also *CFJ v CFL* [2023] SGHC(I) 1 [54].
[729] Ibid [55]–[73].
[730] Ibid [74]–[75].

C. GROUNDS FOR SETTING ASIDE   309

hard-fought cases, the smallest indications of apparent bias might reasonably cause one party to feel unjustly treated, and this may also raise fair questions about the legitimacy of international arbitration as a system for the fair adjudication of international disputes.

If it is successfully demonstrated that *one* of the arbitrators in a *three*-member tribunal was indeed biased, would that be sufficient to set aside an award, or must an award debtor demonstrate that the bias affected the decision-making of the entire tribunal? In *AMZ v AXX*, the High Court dismissed the argument that the award creditor's nominee arbitrator prejudged the claims and improperly entered into the fray by conducting an inquisitorial cross-examination and issuing a dissenting opinion on a preliminary issue of jurisdiction.[731] The Court noted that there was 'absolutely no basis' on the facts for an allegation of apparent bias against the nominee arbitrator and 'even less basis for an allegation that the apparent bias alleged against him somehow influenced the remaining two arbitrators'.[732] In the authors' respectful submission, this should not be interpreted as a requirement that an award debtor must also demonstrate that any bias on the part of one member of a three-member tribunal affected the other arbitrators. The High Court does not appear to have intended any such requirement.[733] Most contemporary national arbitration statutes and institutional rules requires *all three* arbitrators in a tribunal to be impartial and independent.[734] Thus, one arbitrator's lack of independence and impartiality is a sufficiently serious breach of this requirement and denies the parties' their right to an unbiased tribunal (consisting of three arbitrators). **16.334**

---

[731] *AMZ v AXX* (n 468) [176].

[732] Ibid.

[733] The High Court appears to have been responding to a point raised by the award debtor in its submissions, rather than formulating a rule of general application. See Ibid, [174].

[734] Born, *International Commercial Arbitration* (n 22) 3280. See Model Law, Article 12; Swiss Federal Act on Private International Law, Article 180; and the English Arbitration Act 1996, Section 24(1)(a).

17

Immunities of Arbitrators, Appointing Authorities and Arbitral Institutions

A. Section 25—Immunity of Arbitrators   17.01

B. Section 25A—Immunity of Appointing Authorities and Arbitral Institutions   17.08

A. Section 25—Immunity of Arbitrators

<u>IAA, Section 25</u>

An arbitrator shall not be liable for—

(a) negligence in respect of anything done or omitted to be done in the capacity of arbitrator; and

(b) any mistake in law, fact or procedure made in the course of arbitral proceedings or in the making of an arbitral award.

17.01 The UNCITRAL Model Law does not address the liability or immunity of arbitrators. Thus, in 1993, the Singapore Academy of Law Sub-Committee of the Law Reform Committee on Review of Arbitration Laws recommended the inclusion of an express statutory provision on arbitrator immunity in the IAA.[1] This was subsequently introduced as Section 25 of the IAA.

17.02 Section 25(a) essentially codifies the English common law principle that arbitrators are, by analogy to judges, immune from liability for negligence.[2] When proposed in 1993, the text of the provision was modelled after Clause 11 of the then New Zealand Draft Arbitration Act, and it is identical to Section 13 of the New Zealand Arbitration Act 1996.[3] The policy rationale for the conferral of immunity on arbitrators is to preserve their independence and impartiality by reducing exposure to litigation concerning

---

[1] Singapore Academy of Law Sub-Committee on Review of Arbitration Laws, *Report on Review of Arbitration Laws*, August 1993, 58. See New Zealand Arbitration Act 1996, Section 13.

[2] *Sutcliffe v Thackrah* [1974] AC 727 ('Those employed to perform duties of a judicial character are not liable to their employers for negligence. This rule has been applied to arbitrators for a very long time.'); *Arenson v Casson Beckman Rutley & Co.* [1977] AC 405.

[3] Ibid.

A. SECTION 25—IMMUNITY OF ARBITRATORS 311

their discharge of adjudicative functions, as well as 'to encourage and build up a core of competent professionals in dispute resolution.'[4]

Section 25(b) further provides that any mistakes in law, fact, or procedure in the course of arbitral proceedings, or in the course of the making of an award, cannot found any claim against an arbitrator.[5] This means that, even absent any proof of negligence, findings made by arbitrators in their award—however wrong on issues of law, fact, or procedure—cannot be used as a basis for claims against the arbitrator. This rule is presumably intended to avoid a situation whereby claims are made against arbitrators as a form of collateral recourse against the award, and is consistent with the well-established principle that substantive errors, even manifest errors of law, are not a sufficient basis to set aside or refuse enforcement of an award.[6] **17.03**

The scope of arbitrator immunity is limited to the circumstances enumerated in Sections 25(a) and 25(b). Immunity under Section 25 therefore does not extend to cases where an arbitrator has willfully misconducted himself[7] or cases of gross negligence.[8] In addition, because immunity in Section 25(a) applies only to acts or omissions done in the capacity of an arbitrator, it might be argued that a total failure to act removes a putative arbitrator from the protection of Section 25.[9] **17.04**

There is no case law interpreting the scope of Section 25 of the IAA and caution should perhaps be exercised when relying on case law based on different statutory provisions in other jurisdictions.[10] Although the vast majority of modern arbitration statutes provide arbitrators with expansive immunities from civil claims based on the performance of their duties as an arbitrator, there is no uniform approach to arbitrator immunity internationally, and different arbitration statutes define the scope of arbitrator immunity differently.[11] For example, under the English Arbitration Act 1996, an arbitrator is not liable for any act or omission done in the 'discharge or purported discharge of his functions as arbitrator' unless it is shown that such act or omission was 'in bad faith'.[12] The same immunity is also extended to any employee or agent of an arbitrator.[13] The Hong Kong Arbitration Ordinance takes a materially similar approach, although it refers to **17.05**

---

[4] See Singapore Academy of Law Sub-Committee on Review of Arbitration Laws, *Report on Review of Arbitration Laws*, August 1993, para 58. See New Zealand Arbitration Act 1996, Section 13. See also G. Born, *International Commercial Arbitration*, International Commercial Arbitration (3rd edn, Kluwer Law International 2021) 2178–9.

[5] Singapore Academy of Law Sub-Committee on Review of Arbitration Laws, *Report on Review of Arbitration Laws*, August 1993, para 58.

[6] See Born, *International Commercial Arbitration* (n 4) 2179. See Chapter 16.

[7] Singapore Academy of Law Sub-Committee on Review of Arbitration Laws, *Report on Review of Arbitration Laws*, August 1993, para 58.

[8] S Franck 'The Liability of International Arbitrators: A Comparative Analysis and Proposal for Qualified Immunity' New York Law School Journal of International and Comparative Law 1, 36

[9] See e.g. R. Merkin and J. Hjalmarsson, *Singapore Arbitration Legislation: Annotated* (2nd edn, Informa Law 2016) 109.

[10] c.f. Merkin (n 9) 109.

[11] See e.g. Born, *International Commercial Arbitration* (n 4) 2180–3; Franck (n 8) 1

[12] English Arbitration Act, Section 29(1).

[13] Ibid, Section 29(2).

312 ARBITRATORS, APPOINTING AUTHORITIES AND ARBITRAL INSTITUTIONS

'dishonesty' instead of 'bad faith.'[14] The same immunity extends to '[a]n employee or agent of an arbitral tribunal.'[15] Unlike Section 25 of the IAA, these provisions extend immunity to all intentional conduct and also gross negligence, so long as there is no dishonesty involved, as well as persons working for an arbitral tribunal, including tribunal secretaries and other administrative personnel.

17.06   Arbitration rules, which are incorporated as part of the parties' arbitration agreement, can also contractually address and supplement the scope of arbitrator immunity.[16] Arbitration rules typically contain broad provisions on the immunity of arbitrators. According to commentary, Article II of the New York Convention mandates giving such provisions full effect because they form part of the arbitration agreement.[17]

17.07   Thus, for example, Article 41 of the ICC Rules provides for a very broad limitation of liability, stating that the arbitrators 'shall not be liable to any person for any act or omission in connection with the arbitration, except to the extent such limitation of liability is prohibited by applicable law.'[18] Rule 38(1) of the SIAC Rules contains a similarly broad formulation and provides that an arbitrator 'shall not be liable to any person for any negligence, act or omission in connection with any arbitration administered by SIAC in accordance with [the SIAC Rules]'.[19] Rule 38(2) goes further and states that 'any person appointed by the Tribunal, including any administrative secretary and any expert' shall be under no obligation to make any statement in connection with any arbitration administered by the SIAC in accordance with the SIAC Rules, and that such persons cannot be compelled to act as a witness in any related legal proceedings.[20]

B. Section 25A—Immunity of Appointing Authorities and Arbitral Institutions

<u>IAA, Section 25A</u>

(1) The appointing authority, or an arbitral or other institution or person designated or requested by the parties to appoint or nominate an arbitrator, shall not be liable for anything done or omitted in the discharge or purported discharge of that function unless the act or omission is shown to have been in bad faith.

(2) The appointing authority, or an arbitral or other institution or person by whom an arbitrator is appointed or nominated, shall not be liable, by reason only of having appointed or nominated the arbitrator, for anything done or omitted by the arbitrator,

---

[14] Hong Kong Arbitration Ordinance, Article 104.
[15] Ibid, Article 104(2).
[16] Some commentators note that this is more properly termed a contractual exclusion or limitation of liability. See e.g. E. Gaillard and J. Savage (eds), *Fouchard Gaillard Goldman on International Commercial Arbitration*, para 1077.
[17] Born, *International Commercial Arbitration* (n 4) 2176, 2185.
[18] ICC Rules, Article 41.
[19] SIAC Rules, Rule 38(1).
[20] Ibid, Rule 38(2).

the arbitrator's employees or agents in the discharge or purported discharge of the arbitrator's functions as arbitrator.

(3) This section applies to an employee or agent of the appointing authority or of an arbitral or other institution or person as it applies to the appointing authority, institution or person.

Section 25A is modelled after Section 74 of the English Arbitration Act 1996.[21] As noted by the UK Departmental Advisory Committee's 1996 Report on Section 74 of the English Arbitration Act 1996, the policy rationale for granting a degree of immunity to arbitral institutions and appointing authorities is that, absent such immunity, there is a 'real risk' that matters submitted to arbitration would be re-opened by claims against such entities.[22] This is complementary to the rationale for granting arbitrator immunity under Section 25 of the IAA. **17.08**

Section 25A(1) restricts the scope of any immunity from liability to anything done or omitted in the 'discharge or purported discharge' of an arbitral institution or appointing authority's functions in respect of appointing or nominating arbitrators. It does not, by its terms, extend to any other acts done by an arbitral institution or appointing authority that do not relate to the appointment or nomination of arbitrators. Section 25A(2) provides for immunity of the arbitral institution or appointing authority for any acts or omissions by the arbitrators in the exercise of their functions solely by reason of the arbitral institution or appointing authority's role in the appointment or nomination. Again, this does not exclude liability for acts done by the arbitral institution or appointing authority that go beyond the appointment or nomination of arbitrators. Section 25A(3) extends the immunities in Sections 25A(1) and 25A(2) to an employee or agent of the arbitral institution or appointing authority. **17.09**

Unlike other arbitration statutes, Section 25A does not appear to stipulate for a broad scope of immunity for all administrative acts and functions performed by arbitral institutions.[23] For example, Article 105(1) of the Hong Kong Arbitration Ordinance provides that any person that 'exercises or performs any other function of an administrative nature in connection with' arbitral proceedings can only be liable in law for any act or omission in the exercise or purported exercise of such functions 'only if it is proved that the act was done or omitted to be done dishonestly'.[24] **17.10**

Arbitration rules can also contractually address and supplement the scope of the immunity of arbitral institutions and appointing authorities. For example, Article 41 of the ICC Rules provides for a very broad limitation of liability, stating that: **17.11**

> the [ICC] Court and its members, ICC and its employees, and the ICC National Committees and Groups and their employees and representatives shall not be liable

---

[21] Attorney-General's Chambers Law Reform and Revision Division, Review of Arbitration Laws, para 2.11.4
[22] 'The 1996 DAC Report on the English Arbitration Bill: The Last Part' (1999) 15(4) Arbitration International 413, para 300.
[23] Born, *International Commercial Arbitration* (n 4) 2185.
[24] Hong Kong Arbitration Ordinance, Article 105(1).

to any person for any act or omission in connection with the arbitration, except to the extent such limitation of liability is prohibited by applicable law.[25]

Rule 38(1) of the SIAC Rules provides that 'the President, members of the Court, and any directors, officers and employees of SIAC ... shall not be liable to any person for any negligence, act or omission in connection with any arbitration administered by SIAC in accordance with these Rules'.[26] This formulation leaves open the possibility that actions or omissions that are not in accordance with the SIAC Rules would not fall within the scope of Rule 38(1).

---

[25] ICC Rules, Article 41.
[26] SIAC Rules, Rule 38(1).

18

Recognition and Enforcement of Foreign Awards

A. Introduction	18.01	1. Section 31(2)(f)—Awards Not Yet Binding, Set Aside, or Suspended	18.19
B. Sections 27 and 28—Scope and Interpretation of Part III	18.03	2. Section 31(3)—Partial Non-Recognition of a Foreign Award	18.29
C. Sections 29 and 30—Procedure for Enforcement of Foreign Awards	18.09	3. Section 31(5)—Adjournment of Enforcement Proceedings	18.31
D. Section 31—Refusal of Enforcement	18.14	E. Enforcement of Awards under Other Provisions of Law	18.37

A. Introduction

The process for recognition and enforcement of international arbitration awards in Singapore is bifurcated, with the regime that applies depending upon the nationality of the award.[1] This bifurcation results from the application of the New York Convention, which Singapore ratified on 19 November 1986. This chapter examines the recognition and enforcement of foreign awards under Part III of the International Arbitration Act (IAA), which governs international arbitration awards made outside of Singapore and in another New York Convention State signatory, otherwise known as 'foreign awards'. A separate provision, Section 19, applies to the enforcement of international arbitration awards made in Singapore.   **18.01**

Among other things, this chapter will discuss the grounds for resisting enforcement of a foreign award. Although an action to set aside an award is distinct from an action to resist enforcement of an award, there will inevitably be overlap in any discussion of the grounds for setting aside and the grounds for resisting enforcement, which are very similar because the drafters of the Model Law drew heavily upon the grounds for resisting enforcement in Article V of the New York Convention.[2] Readers are therefore encouraged to read the discussion of the grounds for resisting enforcement in this chapter in conjunction with Chapter 16 for a more comprehensive picture.   **18.02**

---

[1] The nationality of the award is determined by reference to the seat that is stated in the award. Article 31 of the Model Law provides that an award 'shall state its date and the place of arbitration' and that the award 'shall be deemed to have been made at that place'.

[2] See Chapter 16.

316 RECOGNITION AND ENFORCEMENT OF FOREIGN AWARDS

B. Sections 27 and 28—Scope and Interpretation of Part III

IAA, Section 27

(1) In this Part, unless the context otherwise requires—

'agreement in writing' includes an agreement contained in an exchange of letters, telegrams, telefacsimile or in a communication by teleprinter;

'arbitral award' has the meaning given by the Convention, but also includes an order or a direction made or given by an arbitral tribunal in the course of an arbitration in respect of any of the matters set out in section 12(1)(c) to (j);

'arbitration agreement' means an agreement in writing of the kind referred to in paragraph 1 of Article II of the Convention;

'Convention' means the Convention on the Recognition and Enforcement of Foreign Arbitral Awards adopted in 1958 by the United Nations Conference on International Commercial Arbitration at its twenty-fourth meeting, the English text of which is set out in the Second Schedule;

'Convention country' means a country (other than Singapore) that is a Contracting State within the meaning of the Convention;

'court' means the General Division of the High Court in Singapore;

'foreign award' means an arbitral award made pursuant to an arbitration agreement in the territory of a Convention country other than Singapore.

(2) In this Part, where the context so admits, 'enforcement', in relation to a foreign award, includes the recognition of the award as binding for any purpose, and 'enforce' and 'enforced' have corresponding meanings.

(3) For the purposes of this Part, a body corporate is taken to be habitually resident in a country if it is incorporated or has its principal place of business in that country.

IAA, Section 28

(1) This Part applies to arbitration agreements made before 27 January 1995 as it applies to arbitration agreements made on or after that date.

(2) This Part does not apply to foreign awards made before 19 November 1986.

18.03 The definitions in Section 27(1) were introduced with the Arbitration (Foreign Awards) Bill 1986,[3] the instrument of accession that gave effect to the New York Convention in Singapore. The definitions of 'agreement in writing', 'arbitral award', and 'arbitration agreement' thus mirror the equivalent definitions in Articles I(2), II(1), and II(2) of the New York Convention. The definition of an 'arbitration agreement' has been superseded

---

[3] Arbitration (Foreign Awards) Act 1986 and Arbitration (Foreign Awards) Bill No. 16/1986.

B. SECTIONS 27 AND 28—SCOPE AND INTERPRETATION OF PART III   317

by the enactment of Section 2A, which defines the term 'arbitration agreement' in the IAA (including Part III).[4]

Sections 27 and 28 demarcate the scope of Part III of the IAA in three important ways.   **18.04**

First, Section 27(a) defines 'foreign award' to mean an arbitral award made 'in the territory of a Convention country other than Singapore'. This reflects the reciprocity reservation made by Singapore when acceding to the New York Convention, namely that Singapore would only apply the New York Convention to the recognition and enforcement of awards of another Contracting State, which is one of the permitted reservations under Article I(3) of the New York Convention. The reservation circumscribes the scope of Part III of the IAA. However, this may not be much of a practical limitation given the widespread ratification of the New York Convention, which, at the time of the publication of this commentary, has 170 Contracting Parties.   **18.05**

Second, Sections 28(1) and 28(2) define the temporal scope of the provisions of Part III. Section 28(1) provides that Part III applies to arbitration agreements made before 27 January 1995 in the same way that it applies to arbitration agreements made on or after that day. 27 January 1995 is the day that the IAA came into force, and Section 28(1) therefore extends the application of Part III of the IAA to all arbitration agreements made before the IAA came into force. Section 28(2) provides that Part III does not apply to foreign awards made before 19 November 1986. This simply reflects that the New York Convention was ratified by, and thereby came into force for Singapore on 19 November 1986, and the provisions of Part III cannot apply to awards made before the date of ratification.   **18.06**

Third, Section 27(1) includes a modified definition of an 'arbitral award'. The Arbitration (Foreign Awards) Bill 1986 originally defined an 'arbitral award' as having the meaning given by the New York Convention. However, as a result of a 2012 amendment,[5] the definition in Section 27(1) now expressly includes 'an order or a direction made or given by an arbitral tribunal in the course of an arbitration in respect of any of the matters set out in Section 12(1)(c) to (j)' of the IAA. This stands in contrast to Section 2(1) of the IAA, which excludes 'any order or direction made under section 12' from the definition of 'award' for the purposes of Part II. Section 27(1) therefore is intended to ensure that any orders in respect of Section 12(1)(c) to (j) of the IAA may be enforced in a similar manner to 'awards' under Part II of the IAA, even though such decisions would not otherwise be considered as 'awards' for other parts of the IAA.   **18.07**

In *CVG v CVH*, the Singapore High Court confirmed that foreign emergency awards were also 'arbitral awards' within the meaning of Section 27(1) of the IAA. In that case, the party challenging enforcement of the award contended that the definition of an 'arbitral award' in Section 27(1) of the IAA excluded awards made by emergency   **18.08**

---

[4] IAA, Section 2A(1) ('In this Act, "arbitration agreement" means ...').
[5] International Arbitration (Amendment) Bill on 9 April 2012.

318   RECOGNITION AND ENFORCEMENT OF FOREIGN AWARDS

arbitrators and therefore could not be enforced.[6] Justice Chua Lee Ming disagreed, finding that on a purposive interpretation, the term 'arbitral award' in Section 27(1) includes awards by emergency arbitrators.[7] He observed that this was supported by the 2012 amendments to the definition of an "arbitral tribunal" in Section 2 and the definition of an "arbitral award" in Section 27, which 'speak to an intention to make the IAA applicable to all awards, including foreign interim awards by emergency arbitrators'.[8]

C. Sections 29 and 30—Procedure for Enforcement of Foreign Awards

<u>IAA, Section 29</u>

(1) Subject to this Part, a foreign award may be enforced in a court either by action or in the same manner as an award of an arbitrator made in Singapore is enforceable under section 19.

(2) Any foreign award which is enforceable under subsection (1) must be recognised as binding for all purposes upon the persons between whom it was made and may accordingly be relied upon by any of those parties by way of defence, set-off or otherwise in any legal proceedings in Singapore.

<u>IAA, Section 30</u>

(1) In any proceedings in which a person seeks to enforce a foreign award by virtue of this Part, the person must produce to the court—
   (a) the duly authenticated original award or a duly certified copy thereof;
   (b) the original arbitration agreement under which the award purports to have been made, or a duly certified copy thereof; and
   (c) where the award or agreement is in a foreign language, a translation of it in the English language, duly certified in English as a correct translation by a sworn translator or by an official or by a diplomatic or consular agent of the country in which the award was made.

(2) A document produced to a court in accordance with this section is, upon mere production, to be received by the court as prima facie evidence of the matters to which it relates.

18.09   Section 29 addresses recognition and enforcement, which are distinct but related concepts.[9] Recognition happens automatically, without an award creditor needing to take any action. As Section 29(2) provides, recognition simply means that the award is to be

---

[6] *CVG v CVH* [2022] SGHC 249 ('*CVG*') at [27].
[7] Ibid, [28].
[8] Ibid, [31]–[32].
[9] See *Astro Nusantara International BV v PT Ayunda Prima Mitra* [2013] 1 SLR 636 at [14]. *See also Kingdom of Spain v Infrastructure Services Luxembourg S.A.R.L. and anor* [2021] FCAFC 3 at [26].

C. SECTIONS 29 AND 30—PROCEDURE FOR ENFORCEMENT   319

treated as binding and may 'be relied upon ... by way of defence, set-off or otherwise in any legal proceedings'. Enforcement of an award goes a step further and refers to the process by which the award creditor seeks the assistance of courts to ensure compliance with the award. Section 29(1) provides that an award creditor may enforce a foreign award either 'by action' or in the same manner as under Section 19.

As discussed elsewhere in this commentary, Section 19 provides that awards may be enforced in the same manner as a judgment or order to the same effect. In summary, Section 19 provides for a two-stage process that first starts with an *ex parte* application for leave to enforce, supported by an affidavit that satisfies the requirements set out in Section 30(1) of the IAA and Order 48, Rule 6 of the Rules of Court.[10] After leave is granted to enforce, the order must then be served on the award debtor, which leads to the second *inter partes* stage, whereby recognition and enforcement may be refused only if the award debtor applies to set aside the order granting leave on any of the exhaustive grounds under Sections 31(2) and 31(4) of the IAA.[11]   **18.10**

The term 'by action' in Section 29(1) refers to enforcement by a common law action on the award. This is a common law remedy that operates to enforce the parties' implied promise to honour an arbitration award. Singapore courts have not had occasion to consider the specific contours of the common law action in a reported case.   **18.11**

In Hong Kong, the courts have had to consider the novel question of whether, in a common law action on the award, an enforcing court has the power to grant relief that is different from, and wider than, that provided for in an award. The Hong Kong Court of Final Appeal rejected the argument that the statutory regime for enforcement of awards restricted the common law action to one that only provided for mechanistic enforcement.[12] The Court of Final Appeal also held that an action for breach of the implied promise to perform the award was not subject to the arbitration agreement,[13] and rejected the argument that the common law enforcement was bounded by the scope of the award.[14] Therefore, the Court of Final Appeal affirmed the decisions of the lower courts, which had granted damages and equitable compensation as an alternative remedy to the remedy of specific performance ordered in the award.   **18.12**

Difficult questions might arise in an enforcement action if a party to an arbitration (and award) is misnamed or if the original party to the arbitration (and award) ceases to exist. In a recent decision, the Court of Appeal considered if an award is enforceable against a party in a 'misnomer' situation.[15] In *National Oilwell*, the original party to the contract (Hydralift) had merged with another entity (NOV Norway), which had assumed all   **18.13**

---

[10] See Chapter 9.

[11] *CKR v CKT* [2021] SGHCR 4 at [23]–[28].

[12] *Xiamen Xinjingdi Group Co Ltd v Eton Properties Limited and Others* [2020] HKCFA 32 at [90]–[97].

[13] Ibid, [99]–[108].

[14] Ibid, [127]–[143].

[15] *National Oilwell Varco Norway AS (formerly known as Hydralift AS) v Keppel FELS Ltd (formerly known as Far East Levingston Shipbuilding Ltd)* [2022] 2 SLR 115 ("*National Oilwell*").

320 RECOGNITION AND ENFORCEMENT OF FOREIGN AWARDS

the rights and liabilities of Hydralift. The counterparty to the contract, KFELS, commenced arbitration against Hydralift; however, by then, Hydralift had ceased to exist
as a separate entity and NOV Norway appeared in the arbitration, defended against
KFELS's claims, and succeeded in its counterclaims, without disclosing that Hydralift
had ceased to exist. The award was made in favour of Hydralift, which NOV Norway
then sought to enforce against KFELS. The Court of Appeal held that NOV Norway
was entitled to enforce the award against KFELS under Section 19 of the IAA.[16] In a
'misnomer' situation where an actual party to the arbitration had been described or referred to by an incorrect name, the enforcing court could deviate from the name used
in the dispositive terms of an award and instead enforce the award in favour of the
correct party even if it was not named as such in the award.[17] The test of whether there
was a misnomer was whether the name stated in the award, seen objectively against the
relevant factual and legal background, was nothing more than the incorrect name of
the legal person the award was in fact and in law to be enforced in favour of or against.[18]

D. Section 31—Refusal of Enforcement

<u>IAA, Section 31</u>

(1) In any proceedings in which the enforcement of a foreign award is sought by virtue
of this Part, the party against whom the enforcement is sought may request that the
enforcement be refused, and the enforcement in any of the cases mentioned in subsections (2) and (4) may be refused but not otherwise.

(2) A court so requested may refuse enforcement of a foreign award if the person against
whom enforcement is sought proves to the satisfaction of the court that—

(a) a party to the arbitration agreement pursuant to which the award was made
was, under the law applicable to the party, under some incapacity at the time
when the agreement was made;

(b) the arbitration agreement is not valid under the law to which the parties have
subjected it or, in the absence of any indication in that respect, under the law
of the country where the award was made;

(c) the party was not given proper notice of the appointment of the arbitrator or
of the arbitration proceedings or was otherwise unable to present the party's
case in the arbitration proceedings;

(d) subject to subsection (3), the award deals with a difference not contemplated by, or not falling within the terms of, the submission to arbitration
or contains a decision on the matter beyond the scope of the submission to
arbitration;

---

[16] Ibid, [76].
[17] Ibid, [79].
[18] Ibid, [104].

D. SECTION 31—REFUSAL OF ENFORCEMENT   321

(e) the composition of the arbitral authority or the arbitral procedure was not in accordance with the agreement of the parties or, failing such agreement, was not in accordance with the law of the country where the arbitration took place; or

(f) the award has not yet become binding on the parties to the arbitral award or has been set aside or suspended by a competent authority of the country in which, or under the law of which, the award was made.

(3) When a foreign award referred to in subsection (2)(d) contains decisions on matters not submitted to arbitration but those decisions can be separated from decisions on matters submitted to arbitration, the award may be enforced to the extent that it contains decisions on matters so submitted.

(4) In any proceedings in which the enforcement of a foreign award is sought by virtue of this Part, the court may refuse to enforce the award if it finds that—

(a) the subject matter of the difference between the parties to the award is not capable of settlement by arbitration under the law of Singapore; or

(b) enforcement of the award would be contrary to the public policy of Singapore.

(5) Where, in any proceedings in which the enforcement of a foreign award is sought by virtue of this Part, the court is satisfied that an application for the setting aside or for the suspension of the award has been made to a competent authority of the country in which, or under the law of which, the award was made, the court may—

(a) if the court considers it proper to do so, adjourn the proceedings or (as the case may be) so much of the proceedings as relates to the award; and

(b) on the application of the party seeking to enforce the award, order the other party to give suitable security.

Section 31 sets forth the grounds for refusing enforcement of a foreign award under Part III of the IAA. Section 31(1) expressly states that the grounds in Section 31 are the only grounds on which a foreign award may be refused enforcement. Arguably, Sections 31(1)–(5) also provide Singapore courts with the discretion whether to refuse enforcement even if one of the grounds in Section 31 is not established. This is clear from the repeated use of the word 'may'. However, this proposition remains untested. **18.14**

An action to resist enforcement of an award is distinct from an action to set aside an award. The latter is the only means of actively attacking the award at the seat of arbitration under the Model Law and the IAA, while the former flows from an award debtor's right to defend itself against an award by requesting refusal of recognition or enforcement in proceedings initiated by the award creditor.[19] **18.15**

Under Singapore law, an award debtor has a 'choice of remedies', meaning that it may choose between the active remedy of setting aside the award and the passive remedy **18.16**

---

[19] Analytical Commentary on Draft Text of a Model Law on International Commercial Arbitration (A/CN.9/264, 25 March 1985) 71.

322 RECOGNITION AND ENFORCEMENT OF FOREIGN AWARDS

of resisting enforcement of the award.[20] Thus, for example, an award debtor may resist enforcement of an award even if it had not applied to set aside the award and the time limits for setting aside had expired.[21] A party may also apply to resist enforcement of an award even after an unsuccessful attempt to set aside an award, subject to the application of any issue estoppel that may be recognised by the enforcement court.[22]

18.17 The main grounds for refusing enforcement of a foreign award in Sections 31(2) and 31(4) are substantially similar to the grounds for setting aside under Article 34 of the Model Law. Thus, as the jurisprudence reflects, decisions in Singapore on setting aside actions under Article 34 of the Model Law and Section 24 of the IAA are persuasive authority on the grounds for resisting enforcement of an award under Section 31 of the IAA, and *vice versa*.[23]

18.18 A more detailed examination of the grounds that apply to both setting aside and refusal of enforcement can be found in Chapter 16 and is not repeated here. This discussion below focuses instead on the ground for refusing enforcement of a foreign award under Section 31(2)(f) of the IAA, which has no equivalent or analogue in Article 34 of the Model Law and Section 24 of the IAA, before addressing the partial non-enforcement of foreign awards under Section 31(3) of the IAA and the adjournment of enforcement proceedings under Section 31(5) of the IAA.

1. Section 31(2)(f)—Awards Not Yet Binding, Set Aside, or Suspended

18.19 Section 31(2)(f) of the IAA provides that Singapore courts may refuse the enforcement of a foreign award if 'the award has not yet become binding on the parties to the arbitral award or has been set aside or suspended by a competent authority of the country in which, or under the law of which, the award was made'. This ground for refusal of enforcement has not been relied upon by a party in a reported case in Singapore. However, Section 31(2)(f) is based on Article V(1)(e) of the New York Convention, which has been the subject of considerable attention by commentators and courts in other jurisdictions, particularly with respect to the consequences of annulment and the legal status of annulled awards.

---

[20] *PT First Media TBK (formerly known as PT Broadband Multimedia TBK) v Nusantara International BV and others and another appeal* [2013] SGCA 57; [2014] 1 SLR 372 (hereafter *PT First Media*) [65]–[71].

[21] Ibid, [75]–[77].

[22] Ibid, [75].

[23] *AJU v AJT* [2011] SGCA 41; [2011] 4 SLR 739 [34]–[38] (on public policy); *Jiangsu Overseas Group Co Ltd v Concord Energy Pte Ltd* [2016] SGHC 153; [2016] 4 SLR 1336 [46]–[47] (no valid arbitration agreement under Article 34(2)(a)(i) and Article 36(1)(a)(i) Model Law); *Vitol Asia Pte Ltd v Machlogic Singapore Pte Ltd* [2020] SGHC 209 at [121] (inability to present case under Article 34(2)(a)(ii) and Article 36(1)(a)(ii)); *Bloomberry Resorts and Hotels Inc and another v Global Gaming Philippines LLC and another* [2020] SGHC 113 [74] (breach of natural justice and Article 18 and equal opportunity to be heard under Section 24(b) and Article 34(2)(a)(ii) Model Law and Article 36(1)(a)(ii) Model Law); *Sanum Investments Ltd v ST Group Co Ltd and others* [2018] SGHC 141; [2020] 3 SLR 225 [113]–[114] (incorrect number of arbitrators—Article 34(2)(a)(iv) and Article 36(1)(a)(iv)).

D. SECTION 31—REFUSAL OF ENFORCEMENT   323

With respect to awards that have been set aside, the Singapore Court of Appeal has **18.20** expressed 'serious doubt' *obiter dicta* as to whether an award that has been set aside in a foreign seat may nonetheless be enforced in Singapore.[24] While acknowledging that the express wording of Article V(1)(e) of the New York Convention contemplates the possibility of enforcing an annulled award, the Court of Appeal reasoned that the con-templated *erga omnes* effect of a successful application to set aside an award 'would gen-erally lead to the conclusion that there is simply no award to enforce'.[25] Although these remarks were made in the context of a Singapore-seated award rather than a foreign award falling under Part III of the IAA, they purport to apply more generally to the no-tion of enforcing awards that have been annulled at the seat. In any event, the Court of Appeal made clear that the issue was not directly engaged in the instant appeal and that its remarks should only be treated as 'tentative thoughts' on the subject.[26]

As the enforceability of annulled awards is not settled by authority in Singapore, it bears **18.21** noting that courts and commentators have reached divergent views on this controver-sial issue. There are also varying positions in terms of the standards and criteria that would apply for the enforcement of an annulled award.

On one view, annulled awards may be recognised with little deference to the decision **18.22** of the setting aside court. For example, the long-standing position in France is that an award which has been annulled in the arbitral seat may nonetheless be recognised.[27] Thus, in the *Hilmarton* line of cases, the French courts recognised an award made in Switzerland, which had been annulled by Swiss courts. The French courts relied upon Article VII of the New York Convention, which provides that an interested party is not deprived of any right it may have to avail itself of an arbitral award in the manner and to the extent allowed by the law of the country where such award is sought to be relied upon, and relied upon more liberal recognition standards in Article 1502 of the French Code of Civil Procedure.[28] The same analysis was adopted in subsequent cases, with the

---

[24] *PT First Media* (n 20) [76].

[25] Ibid, [77].

[26] Ibid, [77].

[27] See e.g. Fouchard, 'La Portée Internationale de l'Annulation de la Sentence Arbitrale dans son Pays d'Origine' (1997) Rev. Arb. 329; E. Gaillard, 'Enforcement of Awards Set Aside in the Country of Origin: The French Experience' in A. van den Berg (ed), *Improving the Efficiency of Arbitration Agreements and Awards: 40 Years of Application of the New York Convention* (1999) 505, 512; Gharavi, 'Enforcing Set Aside Arbitral Awards: France's Controversial Steps Beyond the New York Convention' (1996) 6 Journal of Transnational Law and Policy 93; Poudret, 'Quelle Solution pour en Finir avec l'Affaire Hilmarton?—Réponse à Philippe Fouchard' (1998) Rev. Arb. 7.

[28] See e.g. *Judgment of 10 June 1997, Omnium de Traitement et de Valorisation v Hilmarton*, 1997 Rev. Arb. 376 (French Cour de Cassation Civ. 1), Note, Fouchard (annulled award may be recognised) (1997); *Judgment of 23 March 1994, Omnium de Traitement et de Valorisation*, 1994 Rev. Arb. 327 (French Cour de Cassation Civ. 1), Note, Jarrosson ('The lower court's decision correctly held that, applying Article VII of the 1958 [New York Convention], [the award-creditor] could rely upon the French law on international arbitration concerning the recognition and enforcement of international arbitration awards rendered abroad, and especially upon Article V of the 1958 Convention among the grounds for refusal of recognition and enforcement. Lastly, the award rendered in Switzerland is an international award which is not integrated in the legal system of that State, so that it remains in existence even if set aside and its recognition in France is not contrary to international public policy.'). See also *Judgment of 29 June 2007, PT Putrabali Adyamulia v Rena Holding*, 2007 Rev. Arb. 507 (French Cour de Cassation Civ. 1).

324 RECOGNITION AND ENFORCEMENT OF FOREIGN AWARDS

French courts also reasoning that the award is an international award that is 'not integrated in the legal order' of the seat such that 'its existence remains established despite its being annulled'.[29]

18.23 On another view, awards that have been annulled may be enforced but only in limited circumstances. For example, Dutch courts have recognised and enforced annulled awards, but only where the foreign annulment decision violates Dutch public policy.[30] In *Yukos Capital v Rosneft*, a Dutch appellate court recognised an award that had been annulled at the seat of the arbitration in Russia because the annulment proceedings did not comply with due process.[31] The court reasoned that the foreign annulment decision did not comply with principles of due process and therefore violated Dutch public policy.[32]

18.24 English courts adopt a similar position. In *Yukos Capital v Rosneft Oil*, several awards that had been annulled in Russia were enforced by the English courts, which held that the awards were annulled by a 'partial and dependent judicial system'.[33] In *Malicorp v Egypt*, the English High court held that an Egyptian award that had been annulled could only be enforced if the annulment decision offended 'basic principles of honesty, natural justice and domestic concepts of public policy'.[34] On the facts, the award was not enforced because there was insufficient evidence to find that the annulment decisions in Egypt were tainted by pro-government bias.[35]

18.25 Apart from court decisions, there has also been much academic commentary on the status and enforceability of annulled awards. Some commentators argue that an annulled award may only be recognised if the annulment was based upon the arbitral seat's 'local standards' rather than a faithful application of the setting aside grounds that mirror Article V of the New York Convention.[36] On this analysis, an annulment may

---

[29] See e.g. *Judgment of 14 January 1997*, 1997 Rev. Arb. 395 (Paris Cour d'Appel); *Judgment of 29 June 2007, PT Putrabali Adyamulia v Rena Holding*, 2007 Rev. Arb. 507 (French Cour de Cassation Civ. 1); *Judgment of 19 February 2013, République Démocratique Populaire du Lao v Thai Lao Lignite Co.*, Case No. 12/09983 (Paris Cour d'Appel) ('Considering that the setting aside of a foreign award by the Courts of the State in which the award has been rendered is not a ground for refusing recognition in France; there is thus no basis for revoking the order closing the proceedings to allow for the production of a judgment rendered in Kuala Lumpur, seat of the arbitration, setting aside the award'); *Judgment of 24 November 2011, Egyptian Gen. Petroleum Corp. v Nat'l Gas Co.*, 2012 Rev. Arb. 134 (Paris Cour d'Appel); *Judgment of 12 February 1993, Unichips Finanziara v Gesnouin*, 1993 Rev. Arb. 276 (Paris Cour d'Appel).

[30] *Judgment of 28 April 2009, Yukos Capital Sarl v OAO Rosneft*, XXXIV Y.B. Comm. Arb. 703 (Amsterdam Gerechtshof) (2009) (recognising award that had been set aside by Russian courts). See also *Judgment of 27 September 2016*, XLII Y.B. Comm. Arb. 461 (Amsterdam Gerechtshof) (2017) (annulment decisions rendered in country of origin may be disregarded in exceptional circumstances); *Judgment of 17 November 2017, Maximov v OJSC 'Novolipetsky Metallurgichesky Kombinat'*, XXXVII Y.B. Comm. Arb. 274 (Amsterdam Gerechtshof) (2012).

[31] *Judgment of 28 April 2009, Yukos Capital Sarl v OAO Rosneft*, XXXIV Y.B. Comm. Arb. 703 (Amsterdam Gerechtshof) (2009).

[32] *Judgment of 28 April 2009, Yukos Capital Sarl v OAO Rosneft*, XXXIV Y.B. Comm. Arb. 703 (Amsterdam Gerechtshof) (2009), para 5.

[33] *Yukos Capital v OJSC Rosneft Oil Co.* [2012] EWCA Civ 855.

[34] *Malicorp Ltd v Government of Arab Republic of Egypt* [2015] EWHC 361 (Comm), para 22 (English High Ct.).

[35] Ibid, para 26 (English High Ct.).

[36] J. Paulsson, 'Rediscovering the N.Y. Convention: Further Reflections on *Chromalloy*' (1997) 12(4) Mealey's International Arbitration Report 20; J. Paulsson, 'The Case for Disregarding LSAs (Local Standard Annulments) Under the New York Convention' (1996) 7 American Review of International Arbitration 99. See also E. Gaillard and J. Savage (eds), *Fouchard Gaillard Goldman on International Commercial Arbitration*, para 1687 (1999) ('If an

D. SECTION 31—REFUSAL OF ENFORCEMENT 325

be disregarded if it was based on impermissible substantive review of the award or idiosyncratic rules of subject matter non-arbitrability or public policy.[37] Other commentators argue that an award may never be recognised outside of the place of arbitration after it has been annulled because it ceases to exist thereafter,[38] or because the structure of the Convention dictates that annulment decisions by the seat of arbitration should have *erga omnes* effect.[39]

Singapore courts have not yet expressed a view on the meaning of the words 'not yet **18.26** become binding' in Section 31(2)(f). The drafting history of Article V(1)(e) indicates that it was intended to deny enforcement to awards that were 'still subject to an appeal with a suspensive effect'.[40] Consistent with what was envisaged by the drafters, it is generally accepted that if the parties' arbitration agreement provides for the review of an arbitral award by another arbitral tribunal or some other appellate authority, the contemplated possibility of that second-level review would prevent the first-level arbitral award from becoming binding and therefore be a basis for denying enforcement to that award.[41]

There is no uniform approach internationally concerning the effect of pending judi- **18.27** cial review at the seat and whether that renders an award 'not yet ... binding'. However, the better view is that an award does not cease to become 'binding' simply because it is subject to an action to annul or appeal in courts at the seat of arbitration.[42] To find otherwise appears to be inconsistent with the underlying objectives of the New York Convention and the elimination of the requirement for 'double exequatur' (a process under the Geneva Convention whereby a party seeking enforcement had to first confirm the award at the seat before seeking enforcement).[43]

---

award is set aside in its country of origin, it loses the benefit of the New York Convention'; '[t]he decision causing the award to lose the benefit of the Convention must be a genuine decision setting aside the award, and not simply a ruling overturning the award following the review of the merits of the dispute'); G. Born, *International Commercial Arbitration* (3rd edn, Kluwer Law International 2021) 3991.

[37] Ibid, 3889.

[38] A. van den Berg, 'Enforcement of Annulled Arbitral Awards?' (1998) 9(2) ICC Court Bulletin 15 ('The problem, however, is that after annulment, an arbitral award no longer exists under the applicable arbitration law (which is mostly the arbitration law of the place of arbitration). How can a court before which such an 'award' is presented declare it enforceable? *Ex nihilo nil fit*.').

[39] W.M. Reisman, *Systems of Control in International Adjudication and Arbitration* (1992) 114–15.

[40] United Nations Economic and Social Council, Summary Record of the Seventeenth Meeting of the United Nations Conference on International Commercial Arbitration, UN Doc. E/CONF.26/SR.17, 3 (1958) ('The Working Party agreed that an award should not be enforced if under the applicable arbitral rules it was still subject to an appeal which had a suspensive effect').

[41] See e.g. *Ministry of Defense & Support for the Armed Forces of Iran v Cubic Defense Sys., Inc.,* 665 F.3d 1091, 1100 (9th Cir. 2011). See also Born, *International Commercial Arbitration* (n 36) 3965–6.

[42] See e.g. *Dowans Holding SA v Tanzania Elec. Supply Co. Ltd* [2011] EWHC 1957 [12]–[27]; *IPCO (Nigeria) Ltd v Nigerian National Petroleum Corporation* [2005] EWHC 726 (Comm) [12]. Other authorities in other jurisdictions have taken a different approach, distinguishing between an appeal and an annulment action, finding that an award is not 'binding' if it is subject to an appeal. See Born, *International Commercial Arbitration* (n 36) 3963–5.

[43] Born, *International Commercial Arbitration* (n 36) 3965. See also *Dowans Holding SA v Tanzania Elec. Supply Co. Ltd* [2011] EWHC 1957 [18].

326 RECOGNITION AND ENFORCEMENT OF FOREIGN AWARDS

18.28 Singapore courts also have not yet weighed in on what would constitute a suspension for the purposes of refusing enforcement of a foreign award under Section 31(2)(f). In principle, the automatic suspension of enforcement of an award by operation of statutory provisions at the seat should not be a sufficient basis to refuse enforcement of a foreign award.[44] As noted by commentators, this would be inconsistent with the New York Convention's objectives and the elimination of the 'double exequatur' requirement.[45] Such an analysis would apply, for example, to provisions similar to the previous Article 1506 of the French Code of Civil Procedure (prior to 2011), which provided that the time period for seeking annulment 'suspends the execution of the arbitral award'.[46] The prevailing view appears to be that a formal suspension resulting from a court decision is required for a 'suspension' under Article V(1)(e) of the New York Convention.[47]

2. Section 31(3)—Partial Non-Recognition of a Foreign Award

18.29 It is apparent from Section 31(3) of the IAA that Singapore courts may 'sever' parts of an award that are subject to non-recognition, while recognising and enforcing other parts of the award. This is consistent with the New York Convention's aim of facilitating the enforcement of arbitral awards.[48]

18.30 Article V(1)(c) of the New York Convention in fact provides for partial non-recognition in the context of a specific ground for refusing enforcement (mirrored in Section 31(2)(c) of the IAA). However, as commentators have noted, partial recognition should apply, and has in fact been applied, more broadly to the other grounds for refusing enforcement in Article V of the New York Convention.[49]

3. Section 31(5)—Adjournment of Enforcement Proceedings

18.31 Section 31(5) of the IAA implements Article VI of the New York Convention and provides that a Singapore court may adjourn an application to enforce a foreign award, as well as order the grant of suitable security upon application by the award creditor, if it is satisfied that 'an application for the setting aside or for the suspension of the award

---

[44] UNCITRAL Secretariat Guide on the Convention on the Recognition and Enforcement of Foreign Arbitral Awards (New York, 1958) (2016 Edition) 222–223.

[45] Born, *International Commercial Arbitration* (n 36) 3966–7.

[46] See French New Code of Civil Procedure, Article 1506 ('The time limit for the procedure of Articles 1501, 1502, and 1504 [dealing with annulment actions] suspends the execution of the arbitral award. Institution of one of these procedures within the time limit has the same suspensive effect.'). The 2011 reform of French arbitration law deleted this provision and awards made in France are no longer suspended during the time period for annulment. See French Code of Civil Procedure, Article 1526.

[47] UNCITRAL Secretariat Guide on the Convention on the Recognition and Enforcement of Foreign Arbitral Awards (New York, 1958) (2016 Edition) 222–3 (citing Swiss Federal Tribunal, Switzerland, 21 March 2000, 5P.371/1999).

[48] Born, *International Commercial Arbitration* (n 36) 3748.

[49] Born, *International Commercial Arbitration* (n 36) 3748; UNCITRAL Secretariat Guide on the Convention on the Recognition and Enforcement of Foreign Arbitral Awards (New York, 1958) (2016 Edition) 181.

D. SECTION 31—REFUSAL OF ENFORCEMENT   327

has been made to a competent authority' of the seat of arbitration. Article VI of the New York Convention is intended to strike a balance between two competing concerns: the interest in promoting the enforceability of foreign arbitral awards and the need to preserve effective judicial oversight over awards by courts at the seat of arbitration.[50]

The wording of Section 31 is permissive. The word 'may' and the phrase 'if the court considers it proper to do so' indicate that Singapore courts enjoy a broad discretion in deciding whether or not to adjourn enforcement proceedings and, relatedly, whether to order security to be furnished with an adjournment.[51] Section 31(5)(a) also makes clear that the court may adjourn the enforcement proceedings in full or in part.   **18.32**

Both Section 31(5) of the IAA and Article VI of the New York Convention are silent on the test or standard to be applied to determine whether a proper case for adjournment exists. As Belinda Ang J held in *Man Diesel & Turbo SE v IM Skaugen Marine Services Pte Ltd*, Singapore courts take a 'multi-factorial approach' in the exercise of their discretion, and an enforcing court would have to 'weigh in the balance factors of the case in favour of or against adjournment'.[52]   **18.33**

The burden of justification falls upon the applicant for adjournment, who must establish that he is 'demonstrably pursuing a meritorious application' in the seat court.[53] The aim of this inquiry is to determine if the setting aside application is being pursued in good faith and to 'guard against attempts at frustrating or delaying the enforcement of a binding foreign award'.[54] At this stage, the court would not engage in a detailed assessment of the facts or the legal arguments for or against setting aside the award.[55] The court would also consider any resulting prejudice to either party and the likely consequences of an adjournment, particularly the likely length of delay.[56]   **18.34**

Ang J also noted the similarities between Section 31(5) of the IAA and Section 103(5) of the English Arbitration Act 1996 and therefore took guidance from English case law. Observing that English courts have often considered the issue of adjournment and provision of security together, Ang J cited two factors that Staughton J considered important to an application for security in *Soleh Boneh International Ltd and anor v Government of Republic of Uganda and National Housing Corporation*: (i) the strength of the argument that the award is invalid, and (ii) the ease or difficulty of enforcement of the award.[57] On the first factor, Staughton LJ stressed that the court is not asked to   **18.35**

---

[50] See e.g. UNCITRAL Secretariat Guide on the Convention on the Recognition and Enforcement of Foreign Arbitral Awards (New York, 1958) (2016 Edition) 264; *IPCO (Nigeria) Ltd v Nigerian National Petroleum Corporation* [2005] EWHC 726 (Comm) [14].

[51] See *Man Diesel & Turbo SE v IM Skaugen Marine Services Pte Ltd* [2019] 4 SLR 537; [2018] SGHC 132 [45] (hereafter *Man Diesel*); D. Joseph QC and D. Foxton QC, *Singapore International Arbitration: Law & Practice* (LexisNexis 2014) 493.

[52] See *Man Diesel* (n 51) [46].

[53] Ibid, [47].

[54] See Ibid, [47].

[55] See Ibid, [47].

[56] See Ibid, [47]–[49].

[57] *Soleh Boneh International Ltd and anor v Government of Republic of Uganda and National Housing Corporation* [1993] 2 Lloyd's Rep 208, 212.

328   RECOGNITION AND ENFORCEMENT OF FOREIGN AWARDS

decide the issue and 'must be careful to express no opinion on it'.[58] With respect to the
second factor, Staughton LJ stated that the court must consider whether enforcement
would be rendered more difficult, for example, by movement of assets or improvident
trading, if enforcement was delayed.[59] If that is likely to occur, then the case for security
is stronger.[60]

18.36   Ang J also stressed that, given the fluid nature of the analysis and the wide discretion
enjoyed by the courts, the adoption of a threshold test for Section 31(5) would be 'un-
satisfactory' or 'unhelpful'.[61] In Ang J's view, the approach of Singapore courts is to aim
to strike a balance between the competing interests and for the court to 'come down on
the side of an outcome that is most just or least unjust'.[62]

E. Enforcement of Awards under Other Provisions of Law

<u>IAA, Section 33</u>

(1) Nothing in this Part affects the right of any person to enforce an arbitral award otherwise than as is provided for in this Part.

(2) Despite section 3(5) of the Reciprocal Enforcement of Commonwealth Judgments
Act 1921, where a foreign award is both enforceable under this Part and registrable
as a judgment under that Act, proceedings to enforce the award under this Part may
be commenced without any disentitlement to recover any costs of the proceedings,
unless otherwise ordered by the court.

(3) Despite section 7 of the Reciprocal Enforcement of Foreign Judgments Act 1959,
proceedings to enforce a foreign award under this Part may be commenced where
the award is both enforceable under this Part and registrable as a judgment under
that Act.

18.37   Section 33(1) of the IAA preserves the right of an award creditor to seek alternative
means of enforcement other than under Part III of the IAA. This includes enforcement
of a foreign award under the provisions of the domestic Arbitration Act or by way of a
common law action on an award.

18.38   As Section 33(2) of the IAA indicates, one other alternative means to enforce a foreign award in Singapore is by way of the Reciprocal Enforcement of Commonwealth
Judgments Act 1921 (the RECJA). To be enforceable under the RECJA, therefore, an
award has to be for a 'sum of money payable', has to have become 'enforceable in the
same manner as a judgment given at the seat of the arbitration', and have been made in

---

[58] Ibid, 210.
[59] Ibid, 212.
[60] Ibid, 212.
[61] See *Man Diesel* (n 51) [62].
[62] See Ibid, [62].

E. ENFORCEMENT OF AWARDS UNDER OTHER PROVISIONS OF LAW   329

Hong Kong (on or before 30 June 1997), New Zealand, Sri Lanka, Malaysia, Windward Island, Pakistan, Brunei Darussalam, Papua New Guinea, and India (except the state of Jammu and Kashmir).[63] Section 3 of the RECJA further states that a foreign judgment (as defined under the RECJA) obtained in the superior courts in the United Kingdom of Great Britain and Northern Ireland would only be registered in Singapore 'if in all the circumstances of the case [the General Division of the Singapore High Court] thinks it is just and convenient that the judgment should be enforced in Singapore'.[64]

Another avenue to enforce a foreign award in Singapore may be through the Reciprocal Enforcement of Foreign Judgments Act 1959 (the REFJA). The definition of 'judgment' in Section 2(1) of the REFJA does not make any explicit reference to arbitral awards.[65] However, Section 33(3) of the IAA appears to suggest that a foreign award may be enforced under the REFJA. The REFJA currently only applies to Hong Kong (from 1 July 1997).   **18.39**

On 3 October 2019, the Reciprocal Enforcement of Foreign Judgments (Amendment) Act came into force and extended the scope of the REFJA to non-money judgments, lower court judgments, and interlocutory judgments.[66] The accompanying Reciprocal Enforcement of Commonwealth Judgments (Repeal) Act 2019 was gazetted on 1 October 2019 but has yet to come into effect as of the time of publication. The intended effect of the two statutory amendments is to consolidate the statutory regime for the reciprocal enforcement of foreign judgments; the countries in the Schedule of the RECJA are expected to be transitioned to the REFJA upon repeal of the RECJA, along with the deletion of Section 33(2) of the IAA.[67]   **18.40**

---

[63] Reciprocal Enforcement of Commonwealth Judgments Act 1921, Section 2(1), Schedule.
[64] Reciprocal Enforcement of Foreign Judgments Act 1959, Section 3.
[65] Ibid, Section 2(1).
[66] See Reciprocal Enforcement of Foreign Judgments (Amendment) Act 2019.
[67] See Reciprocal Enforcement of Commonwealth Judgments (Repeal) Act 2019.

Index

AA *see* Arbitration Act 1953
'act effectively' 12.53
ad hoc admission to proceedings 2.22,
    2.25–2.27
ad hoc arbitration
  agreement for 5.33, 11.14
  funding of 2.41
  procedure 2.05–2.06, 2.09–2.11
administration of justice
  reporting restrictions 15.07–15.10
  see also appeals; powers, rights and duties;
    proceedings
ADR *see* alternative dispute resolution
allocation of jurisdiction, seat of
    arbitration 6.12
alternative dispute resolution (ADR)
  adherence to procedures 3.05
  arbitration as form of 1.01
  arbitration in conjunction with 1.03
  forms of *see* arbitration; expert determination;
    mediation; negotiation
  multiplicity of fora for 1.35
  see also conciliation
anti-suit injunctions, courts' powers and
    duties 12.09–12.29
appeals
  court's power to make award or order of costs
    order 9.33–9.35
  court's power to rule on arbitral tribunal's
    jurisdiction, ambit of 9.23–9.24
  court's power to rule on arbitral tribunal's
    jurisdiction, nature of 9.12–9.22
  IAA and Model Law provisions
    compared 9.03–9.10
  jurisdictional rulings, from 9.01–9.02
  negative jurisdictional rulings 9.11
  Rules of Court as to 9.43–9.63
  setting aside is not an appeal under Model
    Law 16.22–16.28
  standard of review 9.25–9.32
  stay of arbitration 9.36–9.42
appointing authorities
  ad hoc arbitration 2.05
  'appointing authority', IAA definition of 4.05
  appointment of arbitrators 8.03
  designation of 1.30, 2.10

immunity of 17.08–17.11
arbitrability
  arbitral tribunal unable to award relief,
    when 10.20–10.24
  choice of law on 10.07–10.09
  Companies Act 2006 claims, and 10.16–10.18
  determination of 10.02
  effect on awards or proceedings 10.03
  insolvency and 10.12–10.15
  non-arbitrable matters 10.10–10.11
  provisions for 10.01
  relief given by court is required,
    when 10.20–10.24
  test for 10.04–10.06
arbitral institutions
  ability to 'act effectively', meaning of 12.53
  appointment of arbitrators, power
    for 16.229–16.234
  authentication of awards and arbitration
    agreements, power for 14.34
  case management by 2.06
  decisions of 2.18
  emergency arbitrator procedures 4.03
  hybrid arbitrations, and 7.68
  immunity of 17.08–17.11
  institutional arbitration rules, use
    of 2.07–2.08
  multi-party appointment of arbitrators,
    and 8.12
  seat of arbitration, decisions as to choice
    of 6.12
  UNCITRAL Arbitration Rules,
    and 2.09–2.11
arbitral tribunals
  arbitral institutions as 4.02
  competence to determine own
    jurisdiction 7.17
  duties of *see* arbitrators' powers and duties
  IAA definition of 4.02–4.04
  powers of *see* arbitrators' powers and duties
  unable to award relief 10.20–10.24
arbitration 7.68
  ADR in conjunction with 1.03
  (dis)advantages of commercial
    arbitration 1.08–1.011
  arbitrability *see* arbitrability

332 INDEX

arbitration (*cont.*)
  confidentiality 1.08
  emergency arbitrator procedures 4.03
  enforcement 1.10
  future of 1.36–1.40
  history of 1.12–1.14
  international institutions *see* arbitral
    institutions
  introduction to international arbitration in
    Singapore 1.01–1.02
  investor-State arbitration 1.42–1.43, 2.09,
    9.25, 16.104, 16.124
  legislation *see* Arbitration Act 1953;
    International Arbitration Act 1994; Model
    Law
  legislative framework for 1.12
  orders *see* orders
  other dispute resolution forums 3.01–3.13
  overview of 1.03–1.07
  place of arbitration *see* seat of arbitration
  preference for 1.04, 1.08
  pro-arbitration regime 1.36–1.40
  procedure *see* procedure
  proceedings heard in private 15.05–15.06
  stay of court proceedings in favour of *see* stay
    of proceedings
  subject- matter not capable of
    settlement 16.269–16.272
Arbitration (Foreign Awards) Act 1986,
    enactment of 1.14
Arbitration Act 1953 (AA)
  enactment of 1.12
  IAA distinguished from 1.19–1.20
  usability 1.13
arbitration agreements
  asymmetric clauses 5.22–5.24
  authentication of 14.34
  bills of lading 5.42–5.43
  construction of 5.13–5.17
  existence of 5.19–5.21, 5.30–5.35
  forms of 5.25
  IAA definition of 4.06, 5.01, 5.18–5.34
  incapable of being performed 7.65–7.68,
    7.75–7.77
  incorporation by reference 5.36–5.43
  inoperative 7.65–7.68, 7.73–7.74
  law governing 5.05–5.06, 9.30–9.31, 10.08,
    11.31, 14.39, 16.108–16.111, 16.239
  non-compliance with, setting aside
    for 16.220–16.268
  null and void 7.65–7.68, 7.71–7.72
  optional clauses 5.22–5.24
  setting aside of award because of invalid
    agreement 16.89–16.127

stay of court proceedings, and *see* stay of
    proceedings
  validity of 5.13–5.17
  in writing 5.26–5.29
arbitration awards
  arbitrability, and 10.03
  authentication of 14.34–14.35, 14.34
  'award', IAA definition of 4.07–4.08
  consent, by 14.01–14.10
  consequences of issuing award by
    consent 14.08–14.09
  court's power to make award, appeals as
    to 9.33–9.35
  different issues, made on 14.16–14.25
  domestic international arbitration
    awards 14.13
  enforcement of 14.11–14.15
  final and binding 14.26–14.29
  finality does not preclude
    challenge 14.30–14.33
  interest on 14.36–14.43
  post-award interest rate 14.43
  pre-award interest, discretion to
    award 14.38–14.42
  setting aside of *see* setting aside (of awards)
  see also New York Convention on the
    Recognition and Enforcement of Arbitral
    Awards 1958 (New York Convention)
Arbitration Ordinance 1809 1.12
arbitration rules
  ad hoc arbitration (UNCITRAL Arbitration
    Rules) 2.05–2.06, 2.09–2.11
  application of 13.05–13.09
  incorporation of 2.14–2.18
  institutional arbitration 2.05–2.08
  procedural aspects of 2.03–2.18
  SIAC Arbitration Rules 2.12–2.13
arbitrators
  able to act as conciliator 13.18
  appointment of, different
    numbers 16.229–16.234
  appointment of, in general 8.03–8.05
  appointment of, in multi-party
    arbitrations 8.06–8.13
  emergency arbitrator procedures 4.03
  immunities of 17.01–17.11
  immunity of appointing
    authorities 17.08–17.11
  liability of 17.01–17.07
  notice of appointment, lack of
    proper 16.128–16.183
  number of 8.01–8.02
  setting aside, and 16.16–16.17
  see also appointing authorities

INDEX 333

arbitrators' powers and duties
  discovery of documents 11.13–11.14
  enforceability of orders and directions with
    leave of court 11.40–11.43
  governing law, scope of 11.28–11.32
  inquisitorial process 11.22–11.23
  interest, award of 11.38–11.39
  interrogatories 11.13–11.14
  limitation on the power to award security for
    costs 11.24–11.27
  powers of arbitral tribunal 11.05–11.06
  preservation, interim custody, or sale of
    property 11.15
  relief, scope of 11.28–11.32
  remedies and reliefs in civil
    proceedings 11.33–11.37
  security for claim 11.16–11.21
  security for costs 11.07–11.12
  see also courts' powers and duties
assessment *see* costs assessments
authority, excess of (*ultra vires*), setting aside
  and 16.184–16.219
award *see* arbitration awards

bills of lading, incorporation by reference 5.43

case management
  arbitral institutions, by 2.06
  stay of proceedings 7.78–7.89
champerty 2.34–2.37
choice of forum *see* allocation of jurisdiction
choice of law
  arbitrability, as to 10.07–10.09
  arbitration agreement, as to *see* law governing
    arbitration agreements
  arbitrators' powers and duties as
    to 11.28–11.32
  capacity, as to 16.91–16.92
  privilege, as to 2.26
  seat of arbitration, decisions, as to 6.12
  the merits of the dispute, as to 16.245
civil procedure
  ad hoc admission to proceedings 2.22, 2.25–2.27
  anti-suit injunctions, courts' powers and
    duties 12.09–12.29
  arbitral procedure *see* procedure
  assessment *see* costs assessments
  case management 7.78–7.89
  champerty 2.34–2.37
  choice of forum *see* allocation of jurisdiction
  courts' powers and duties *see* courts' powers
    and duties
  discovery, arbitrators' powers and duties as
    to 11.13–11.14

orders *see* orders
privilege 2.34–2.37
relief *see* relief
remedies *see* remedies
remission 16.50–16.67
security for costs 11.07–11.12
setting aside *see* setting aside (of awards)
stay of court proceedings in favour of
  arbitration *see* stay of proceedings
subpoenas *see* subpoenas
Companies Act 2006, arbitrability
  and 10.16–10.18
conciliation
  appointment of conciliator 13.14
  arbitrator able to act as conciliator 13.18
  confidentiality 13.19
  disclosure of information 13.20
  mediation and 13.11
  no objection to arbitral process 13.21
  protection of conciliator 13.15–13.16
confidentiality 1.08, 1.31, 2.12, 2.57–2.65, 12.65,
  13.13, 13.19, 15.06–15.09, 16.319
conflict of interest, IBA Guidelines 2.45, 2.47
conflict of laws *see* choice of law
contracts
  bills of lading 5.43
  champerty 2.34–2.37
  incorporation by reference 5.36–5.43
corruption, setting aside because
  of 16.311–16.325
costs
  setting aside and 16.81–16.85
  assessment of 15.01–15.04
costs orders, appeals as to 9.33–9.35
counsel *see* representation
courts' powers and duties
  anti-suit injunctions 12.09–12.29
  grant of interim relief, as to 12.07–12.56
  interim measures, as to 12.01–12.03
  summoning of witnesses by
    subpoena 12.57–12.80
  see also arbitrators' powers and duties

definitions
  'act effectively' 12.53
  'appointing authority' 4.05
  'arbitral tribunal' 4.02–4.04
  'arbitration agreement' 4.06, 5.01
  'award' 4.07–4.08
  'incapable of being performed' [arbitration
    agreement] 7.75–7.77
  'inoperative' [arbitration
    agreement] 7.73–7.74
  'Model Law' 4.09

334 INDEX

definitions (*cont.*)
 'null and void' [arbitration agreement] 7.71–7.72
 'party' 4.10
 precedence of IAA definitions over Model
  Law 4.11
directions
 enforceability by arbitrators with leave of
  court 11.40–11.43
 see also orders
disclosure *see* discovery
discovery, arbitrators' powers and duties as
  to 11.13–11.14
discovery, conciliation and 13.20
discretion
 discretionary stay of proceedings 7.10,
  7.65–7.89
 pre-award interest, discretion to
  award 14.38–14.42
 residual discretion and prejudice under
  Model Law 16.40–16.41
dispute resolution
 expert determination 3.12–3.13
 mediation and negotiation 3.01–3.08
 Singapore International Commercial
  Court 3.09–3.11
 see also mediation; negotiation
documents, arbitrators' powers and duties as to
  discovery 11.13–11.14
due process 1.39, 11.14, 16.03, 16.32,
  16.134–16.183, 18.23
 inability to present case 16.128–16.183

emergency arbitrator procedures 4.03–4.04,
  12.54–12.56, 16.153, 18.08
enforcement
 application to arbitration 14.11–14.12
 arbitration awards 14.11–14.15, 18.01–18.40
 domestic international arbitration
  awards 14.13
 foreign awards *see* foreign awards
  (recognition and enforcement)
 grounds to resist enforcement 14.14–14.15
 post-award interest rate 14.43
 pre-award interest, discretion to
  award 14.38–14.42
 setting aside is not an action to resist
  enforcement 16.09–16.12
 see also New York Convention on the
  Recognition and Enforcement of Arbitral
  Awards 1958
ethics (professional) *see* representation
evidence, IBA Rules on the Taking of
  Evidence 2.48
expert determination 3.12–3.13

finality
 awards, of 1.10
 challenge is not precluded by 14.30–14.33
 final and binding awards 14.26–14.29
foreign awards (recognition and enforcement)
 adjournment of enforcement
  proceedings 18.31–18.36
 awards not yet binding 18.19–18.28
 bifurcated process for 18.01
 enforcement under other provisions of
  law 18.37–18.40
 grounds for resisting enforcement 18.02
 New York Convention, and 18.01–18.02
 Part III of IAA, under 18.01–18.34
 partial non-recognition of 18.29–18.30
 procedure for enforcement of 18.09–18.13
 refusal to enforce 18.14–18.18
 scope and interpretation of Part
  III 18.03–18.08
 set-aside awards 18.19–18.28
 suspended awards 18.19–18.28
foreign-seated arbitrations, witness subpoenas
  in aid of 12.73–12.80
fraud, setting aside because of 16.311–16.325

governing law *see* choice of law

IAA *see* International Arbitration Act 1994
IBA *see* International Bar Association
ICSID Convention 1.42
illegal contracts
 champerty 2.34–2.37
 maintenance 2.34–2.37
immunity (arbitrators') 17.01–17.11
'incapable of being performed' [arbitration
  agreement] 7.75–7.77
incorporation by reference
 arbitration agreements 5.36–5.43
 bills of lading 5.43
injunctions, anti-suit 12.09–12.29
'inoperative' [arbitration agreement] 7.73–7.74
insolvency, arbitrability and 10.12–10.15
interest
 arbitration awards, on 14.36–14.43
 arbitrators' powers and duties as to award
  of 11.38–11.39
 post-award interest rate 14.43
 pre-award interest, discretion to
  award 14.38–14.42
interim relief *see* courts' powers and duties
international arbitration *see* arbitration
International Arbitration Act 1994 (IAA)
 AA distinguished from 1.19–1.20
 amendments to 1.21–1.32

INDEX 335

definitions 4.01–4.11
history of 1.15–1.18
Model Law, and *see* Model Law
other arbitration-related
legislation 1.33–1.35
see also definitions
International Arbitration (Amendment) Act
2020 1.30–1.32
International Bar Association (IBA)
Guidelines on Conflicts of Interest 2.45
Guidelines on Party Representation 2.31
Rules on the Taking of Evidence 2.48
International Centre for Settlement of
Investment Disputes by Convention 1996
(ICSID Convention) 1.42
international treaties *see* treaties
interpretation
interpretation of award, and setting
aside 16.68–16.70
interpretation of Model Law via reference to
other UNCITRAL documents 6.05–6.07
interrogatories, arbitrators' powers and duties as
to 11.13–11.14
investor-State arbitration 1.43, 9.25

jurisdiction
appeals as to 9.01–9.63
choice of forum *see* allocation of jurisdiction
excess of, setting aside because
of 16.184–16.219
setting aside is not judicial review of ruling on
jurisdiction 16.13–16.15

lawyers *see* representation
legal advice and funding *see* costs assessments;
costs orders
Legal Profession Act 1966
disclosure of third-party funding
arrangements 2.44
party representation requirements 2.21–2.28
Legal Profession (Professional Conduct) Rules 2015
disclosure of third-party funding
arrangements 2.44
party representation requirements 2.27–2.30

maintenance 2.34–2.37
mediation
arbitrators acting as mediators 3.01
award by consent , conjoined with 14.10
Civil Law Act 1909 amendments 2.39, 2.42
conciliation and 13.11
process of 3.02–3.08
Singapore Convention on Mediation
2018 1.35, 3.03

Singapore International Mediation
Centre 3.06
third-party funding 2.33
Model Law
adoption of 1.13, 1.15–1.18
amendments to IAA provisions as to 1.21–1.32
applicability 1.19–1.20
counsel qualification requirements 2.19
definitions, precedence of IAA
definitions 4.11
disapplication of 13.01–13.04
force of law 6.01–6.04
IAA Part II applied to 6.08–6.16
IAA Part II definition of 4.09
interpretation via reference to other
UNCITRAL documents 6.05–6.07
New York Convention as model for 1.05
procedural latitude 2.03
setting aside, and *see* setting aside (of awards)
multilateral treaties *see* treaties

natural justice, setting aside because of breach
of 16.326–16.334
New York Convention on the Recognition and
Enforcement of Arbitral Awards 1958
(New York Convention)
accession to 1.14, 1.18
application of 1.06
counsel qualification requirements 2.19
entry into force 1.04
finality of awards 1.10
impact of 1.04–1.05
Model Law modelled on 1.05
previous multilateral treaties 1.04
privilege, retention of 2.48
ratification 1.04
signatories 1.04
universality of enforcement 1.10
see also foreign awards (recognition and
enforcement)
non-arbitrable matters 10.10–10.11
'null and void' [arbitration
agreement] 7.71–7.72

orders
enforceability by arbitrators with leave of
court 11.40–11.43
see also directions
overseas-seated arbitrations, witness subpoenas
in aid of 12.73–12.80

'party' 4.10, 7.04, 7.41–7.42
party representation *see* representation
PCA *see* Permanent Court of Arbitration

336 INDEX

Permanent Court of Arbitration (PCA) 2.10
place of arbitration *see* seat of arbitration
powers, rights and duties
  arbitrators, of *see* arbitrators' powers and
    duties
  jurisdiction *see* jurisdiction
prejudice, setting aside and 16.40–16.41
prima facie standard of review 7.08, 7.17–7.24,
    7.34, 10.15
privilege, third-party funding 2.48–2.51
procedure
  ad hoc arbitration 2.05–2.06, 2.09–2.11
  confidentiality 2.57–2.65
  counsel qualification requirements 2.19–2.20
  institutional arbitration 2.05–2.08
  international arbitration rules 2.03–2.04,
    2.14–2.18
  party representation requirements under
    Singapore law 2.21–2.25
  professional conduct rules 2.26–2.32
  regulation of counsel in international
    arbitration 2.19–2.20
  SIAC Arbitration Rules 2.12–2.13
  third-party funding 2.33–2.56
proceedings *see* arbitration
professional conduct, procedural rules as
    to 2.26–2.32
professional ethics *see* representation
professional representation *see* representation
property *see* real property
public policy, setting aside because of conflict
    with 16.273–16.310

real property, arbitrators' powers and duties as
    to 11.15
relief
  arbitrators' powers and duties as
    to 11.33–11.37
  interim relief, courts' powers and duties as
    to 12.01–12.56
  scope of, arbitrators' powers and duties as
    to 11.28–11.32
  see also remedies
remedies
  arbitrators' powers and duties as
    to 11.33–11.37
  see also relief
remission, setting aside and 16.50–16.67
representation
  ad hoc admission to proceedings 2.22,
    2.25–2.27
  counsel qualification requirements 2.19–2.20
  IBA Guidelines on Party Representation
    2013 2.31

Legal Profession Act 1966 *see* Legal Profession
    Act 1966
  professional conduct rules 2.26–2.32
  Professional Conduct Rules *see* Legal Profession
    (Professional Conduct) Rules 2015
  Singapore law requirements 2.21–2.25
reviews, *prima facie* standard of 7.17–7.24

seat of arbitration
  decisions as to choice of 6.12
  foreign-seated arbitrations, witness
    subpoenas in aid of 12.73–12.80
security for costs, arbitrators' powers and duties
    as to 11.07–11.12
setting aside (of awards)
  additional award 16.71–16.80
  agreements to limit or waive grounds for
    setting aside; implied waiver of grounds for
    setting aside 16.29–16.39
  application under Model Law to be made
    within three months 16.42–16.49
  breach of rules of natural
    justice 16.326–16.334
  challenge to arbitrator, and 16.16–16.17
  conflict with public policy 16.273–16.310
  correction of award 16.68–16.70
  corruption 16.311–16.325
  costs issues 16.81–16.85
  excess of authority or
    jurisdiction 16.184–16.219
  exclusive recourse under Model
    Law 16.18–16.21
  foreign awards 18.19–18.28
  fraud 16.311–16.325
  grounds for 16.86–16.88
  inability to present case 16.128–16.183
  incapacity of party or invalidity of arbitration
    agreement 16.89–16.127
  interpretation of award 16.68–16.70
  lack of proper notice of
    appointment 16.128–16.183
  non-compliance with agreement of parties or
    Model Law 16.220–16.268
  not an action to resist
    enforcement 16.09–16.12
  not an appeal under Model Law 16.22–16.28
  not judicial review of ruling on
    jurisdiction 16.13–16.15
  only 'awards' may be set aside 16.08
  overview of 16.01–16.07
  remission in lieu of setting aside under Model
    Law 16.50–16.67
  residual discretion and prejudice under
    Model Law 16.40–16.41

INDEX 337

subject-matter not capable of settlement by
  arbitration 16.269–16.272
suspension of award pending setting
  aside 16.68–16.70
SIA *see* Singapore Institute of Arbitrators
SIAC *see* Singapore International Arbitration
  Centre
SIMC *see* Singapore International Mediation
  Centre
Singapore Convention on Mediation 2018 1.35
Singapore Institute of Arbitrators (SIA),
  Guidelines on Party- Representative Ethics
  (SIArb Guidelines) 2.31
Singapore International Arbitration Centre
  (SIAC) Arbitration Rules 1990 & 2016
  disclosure of third-party funding
    arrangements 2.46–2.46
  litigation costs 2.54
  procedure 2.12–2.13
Singapore International Commercial Court
  (SICC)
  jurisdiction 1.41
  number of judges 1.41
  proceedings 3.09–3.11
Singapore International Mediation Centre
  (SIMC) 3.06
solicitors *see* representation
standard of review, *prima facie* 7.17–7.24
stay of proceedings
  arbitration agreement incapable of being
    performed 7.65–7.68
  burden of proof for 7.13–7.16
  case management stays 7.78–7.89
  discretionary stay 7.10, 7.65–7.68,
    7.65–7.89
  existence of valid arbitration agreement,
    determination of 7.28–7.39
  IAA provision for 7.01–7.10
  inoperative arbitration agreement 7.65–7.68
  mandatory nature of 7.11–7.12
  mandatory stay, conditions for 7.04–7.08,
    7.28–7.64
  nullity of arbitration agreement 7.65–7.68
  other remedies for breach of arbitration
    agreement 7.25–7.27
  particular procedural acts, determination as
    to whether step in proceedings 7.49–7.54

parties are only persons permitted to apply
  for 7.40–7.42
prima facie standard of review of existence of
  arbitration agreement 7.17–7.24
stay of arbitration, appeals as to 9.36–9.42
subject matter scope for granting
  of 7.55–7.64
timing of 7.09
timing of application for, general approach
  to 7.43–7.48
void arbitration agreement 7.65–7.68
waiver of rights to obtain 7.44
subpoenas
  civil procedure as to 12.61–12.62
  foreign-seated arbitrations, in aid
    of 12.73–12.80
  principles governing applications
    for 12.63–12.72
  summoning of witnesses by 12.57–12.60

third-party funding
  champerty 2.34–2.37
  Civil Law Act 1909 amendments of 2017 and
    2021 2.38–2.42
  definition of 2.33
  disclosure of arrangements 2.43–2.47
  litigation costs 2.52–2.56
  maintenance 2.34–2.37
  privilege, retention of 2.48–2.51
  regulatory framework 2.33

ultra vires, setting aside and 16.184–16.219
United Nations Commission on International
  Trade Law (UNCITRAL) Arbitration Rules
  1976 2.09–2.11
United Nations Commission on International
  Trade Law (UNCITRAL) Model Law on
  International Commercial Arbitration
  1985 (Model Law) *see* Model Law
United Nations Convention on International
  Settlement Agreements Resulting from
  Mediation 2018 (Singapore Convention on
  Mediation) 1.35

'void' *see* 'null and void'

witness summonses, subpoenas 12.57–12.80